MW01236229

DEFENCE POLICY OF NIGERIA: CAPABILITY AND CONTEXT

A READER

Celestine Oyom Bassey and
Charles Quarker Dokubo

authorHOUSE®

AuthorHouse™
1663 Liberty Drive
Bloomington, IN 47403
www.authorhouse.com
Phone: 1-800-839-8640

First published by AuthorHouse 1/18/2011

ISBN: 978-1-4567-3155-7 (e)
ISBN: 978-1-4567-3156-4 (sc)

Library of Congress Control Number: 2011900929

Printed in the United States of America

DEDICATION

To the gallant Officers and Men of the Nigerian Legion who laid down their lives so that peace may reign in Liberia and Sierra Leone.

PREFACE

This Reader was motivated by one primary consideration: to address the imperative need of the increasing population of students specializing in defense studies in the Nigerian Universities, and military academies for a current and comprehensive text of reference on the defence policy of Nigeria. This should not be surprising as any inquiry on the internet for reference materials on Nigeria Defence policy reveals a scandalously limited listings in this vital area of public policy. Beyond the efforts of some scholars and military professionals in the 1980s and 1990s (E. Ekoko and M. Vog (eds) Nigerian Defence policy Lagos: Malthouse, 1990 and Thomas Imobighe, Nigerian Defence and Security: Issues and options for policy. Kuru: NIPSS 1987) the Google listings only reflect some postgraduate projects (M.Sc) of the Nigeria Defence Academy, Kaduna. Systematic inquiry exhibiting the conceptual, theoretical and methodological sophistication and convention readily seen in the "West" and "East" are yet to have a major impact on defence policy analysis of Nigeria. It is as if the "golden age" of strategic thinking (involving the best and the brightest in North America, Europe and Asia) is still distant horizon from the Nigerian periphery.

The dearth of books on a range of issue-areas (structural as well as strategic) has been a constant source of embarrassment in a country endowed with intellectual resources in all spheres of military science and defence studies. This is testified to by brilliant reflections in monographs (such as those of National Defence College Commandants) and academic journals. These include among others, Rear admiral G. A. Shiyanbade, The Military in Democratic Nigeria: Institutionalizing Professionalism (2000), Rear Adm. G. A. Adedeji, Building A Learning Armed Forces: Option for the Nigerian Security in the 21st Century (2004), Rear Adm. A. A. M. Isa, Grouping the Nigeria armed Forces Organizations: the Imperative of strategic Leadership (2005) and the Rear Adm. G. J. Jonah, Maritime Dimension of Nigeria's National Security (2008).

Part of the problem resides in declining intellectual culture in Nigeria (as symbolized in the virtual absence of international bookshop of repute within her borders and partly in the forlorn and costly publishing enterprises which seldom yield profit incentives to authors. Another dimension of the problem relates to Professor Bolaji Akinyemi's observation (former Director General of the Nigerian Institute of International Affairs) concerning the atmosphere of secrecy surrounding the Defence Establishments in Nigeria which constitutes formidable hurdles to research:

> It is regrettable that ever since independence; there has been a tradition that there should be a veil of secrary surrounding the size of the armed forces, the kinds of the equipment they posses and perhaps the dispersal of this equipment. One must immediately concede that on the surface the reason for this veil of secrecy which is to hide from the enemy the disposition of the Nigerian security forces is indeed very plausible. But when we come to define the enemy, we in fact then discover that at least from the point of view of secrecy, we are defining the enemy

*in terms of Nigerians rather that in terms of non-Nigerians. There
is no branch of the Nigerian armed forces where there are no non-
Nigerians whether as technicians or officers or both. In effect, it is
Nigerians who are kept in the dark about the Nigeria security forces
rather than non-Nigerians. And herein lies the dilemma. Most of the
foreign policy elite in important countries of the world know more
about the Nigerian armed forces than Nigerians themselves know
(NJIA, 1982).*

This observation in many ways presages the thought provoking debate on external
auditing of the Nigerian Defence Establishment under the American Military
Assistance Programme and Foreign military sale program under the Administration
of President Olusegun Obansanjo. The principled opposition of the former chief
of Army Staff, General Malu and the former boss of the Center for Democratic
Studies (CDS), Professor Omo Omoruyi, to the audit exercise set the basis for public
discourse and sensitization. While the former was concern about the syndrome
of informal penetration, the later articulated forcefully the dangers of structural
subordination of the Nigerian military to the Pentagon. Both concerns no doubt
arose from the technological underdevelopment of Nigeria (especially in the critical
sphere of military-industrial complex) and will continue to hunt the Nigerian state
as a consequence of its peripherality and dependence.

This collection of essays essentially represents a systematic endeavour to analyse and
comprehend the defence policy of Nigeria in terms in its institutional dynamics
and strategic development. It proceeds from the general assumption that unlike the
era of the First Republic (1960-1966) when defence policy was largely viewed as
the unwanted step-child of factional interests, assumed by policy elites but neither
properly contemplated nor adequately understood, the period since the end of the civil
war in 1970 saw an irreversible dynamic towards acceptance of a realist philosophy in
Nigeria's defence community, which views military power as the "basis of diplomacy
and of all contractual obligations beyond the boundaries of the state".

Consequently, there has been in this period a magnified role conception and
organizational task expansion for the Nigerian military establishment in foreign
policy. However, despite the extensive and vigorous debate (in the media, academic
and official circles in this period) on the theory and practice of Nigeria military
statecraft, the defence policy problematique remains unresolved. This involves the
imperative necessity of making explicit judgment about the scope and direction
of defence policy commitments as well as the conditions for processing the ability
(structure, magnitude and institutional parameters of Nigeria's defence establishment)
to meet these functions and challenges.

This volume, therefore, endeavours to offer a structurally coherent explanation and
critique of this development within the broader context of global and African affairs.
It argues that the persistent problematique and multiple disorder in the "core complex"
of Nigeria's defence posture (in terms of significant disharmonies or disequilibrium
between the various component elements) owes its form and tragic dynamism not to

sheer oversight of defence planners or bureaucratic ineptitude and manipulation but to the "cumulation of choices and the interactions of processes framed by a technical – rational grammar of thought". These interactive processes gravitate around and are in turn rooted in the double antimony of class and function bearing on Nigeria's position in the international division of labour. In other words, Nigeria's defence problematique is fundamentally a resultant of its political economy and public policy: that even the decision a country such as Nigeria could take on defence (what weapons it buys abroad, for instance, how much and from whom) reflects not only elite preferences, but also pre-eminently related both to its development policy and its "earning of surpluses from the international economy".

Professor Celestine Oyom Bassey
Visiting Fulbright Scholar,
William Penn University,
Oskaloosa, Iowa State,
United States of America.

FOREWORD

Defence in the words of the British Air Vice Marshall, John Downey, is "probably the most intractable single branch of public policy of any kind, even in the complex world of today". This is not surprising, since in the celebrated words of Samuel Huntington, defence policy encompasses and transcends two spheres of activities: the world of domestic politics ("the world of interest and goals") and the world of international politics ("the world of balance of power, wars and alliances, the subtle and the brutal uses of force and diplomacy to influence the behaviour of other states"). Thus, the defence policy of any country is conditioned by two primary forces: "a functional imperative stemming from the threats to the country's security and societal imperative arising from the social forces, ideologies and institutions dominant within the society". The threat factor, as one of the editors rightly contend, constitutes a major dynamic in defence strategy and force planning. Defence policy decision inevitably hinges on the threat perception and the determination by relevant military planners as to whether the forces available are adequate to deal with it.

Any major decision in defence policy "influences and is influenced by both worlds". The defence policy of Nigeria, like other states in the global system, is, therefore, not only an extension of its core domestic values but it is also critically shaped by its strategic environment. Since national military systems and their employment are intended to achieve national policy objectives in the international arena, as this *Reader* argues, their usability and effectiveness is always conditional on particular circumstances. This observation notwithstanding, the military, as John Garnett explains, is "one of the many instruments in the orchestra of power which states use at an appropriate moment in the pursuit of their respective national interests". However, since the character of a nation's strategy is determined by its philosophy of war, the employment of its armed forces as instrument for the pursuit of foreign policy objectives is necessarily influenced by certain domestic and systemic factors.

This consideration has generated and conditioned debate on the structural as well as strategic dimensions of the Nigerian Armed Forces modernization programme since the end of the Civil War in 1970. Structural issues involved the debate from the 1970s through 1980s on force structure and force level, defence budget, personnel training, sources of arms and foreign military assistance programme, defence industries (DICON) and integrated logistical infrastructure for the armed forces. The strategic issues concern program and use decisions "concerning the deployment, commitment, and employment" of the Nigerian armed forces for internal pacification (Niger Delta) and peace support operations in the various flashpoints in the continent (notably Liberia and Sierra Leone). Taken together, these spheres of debate in the defence policy of Nigeria underscore the micro – and macro-competence of the Nigerian armed forces: that is, on the one hand, the ability to operate and support modern weapons, and on the other, the ability to organize and manage forces for military ends as was evident in the series of military exercises and manoeuvres, combat in the Lake Chad Basin, and peace support operations in Liberia and Sierra Leone.

It is my pleasure to write the foreword to this *Reader* as a symbol of scholarship and intellectual direction of the National Defence College during my tenure as the Deputy Commandant and Director of Studies of the College. Under the *able leadership* of Rear Admiral G. J. Jonah, the college engaged in transformative exercise that did not only affect the physical appearance of the College but also the system re-engineering and institutional rebranding in curriculum and intellectual productivity through the African Centre for Strategic Research and Studies. The Chapters in this book aptly articulates the profound efforts of a generation of Nigerian policy makers and military planners to evolve a professional military establishment to confront the multi-dimensional challenges in its strategic environment. The success of this effort in reflected, among others, in the high ratings of the Nigerian armed forces in peace support operations in the continent. This effort to transform and sustained the professionalism of the Nigerian Armed Forces is also registered in the submission of the Armed Forces Transformation Committee (under AVM O Faloyin) and its recommendation of programmed implementation of the necessary reforms and capacity building in the years ahead. I, therefore, applaud the efforts of both the editors and contributors to this volume and recommend the *Reader* to both practitioners and students of Nigeria's defence strategy.

Major General L. P. Ngubane
Former Deputy Commandant and Director of Studies,
National Defence College

ACKNOWLEDGEMENT

This *Reader* on the Defence Policy of Nigeria was ultimately made possible by the approval of my sabbatical position in the National Defence College by the Commandant, Rear Admiral A. A. M. Isa on the recommendation and support of his Deputy and Director of Studies, Major General K. A. Role. I, therefore, owe them immense gratitude for their foresight and dedication to the transformation of the African Centre for Strategic Research and Studies, National Defence College.

However, the proposal and eventual approval of this book as a contribution to the resurgence of research activities in the College was granted by the current Commandant, Rear Admiral G. Jonah on the recommendation of his amiable and intellectually engaging Deputy, Major-General L. P. Ngubane. He did not only welcome my observation in one of the Faculty Board (Steering Group) meetings about the prominence accorded National Defence Colleges the World over as a result of their publications (Books, Journal and Monographs), he took up the challenge as the Director of Studies to ensure the approval (by the Commandant) of this project and the reactivation of the Journal Series (Africa Peace Review and African Strategic Review), Monographs and Books series.

As a consequence the tenure of the current Commandant (Rear Admiral G. I. Jonah) has seen a step-level renaissance not just in the College infrastructural transformation but also in stimulating intellectual output through Journal, books, and monograph publications. At the personal level, the sabbatical period in the National Defence College was no doubt intellectually rewarding. I did not only complete editing a volume on Governance and Border Security in Africa (with the Director of Research and Policy Analysis at the Institute For Peace and Conflict Resolution, Abuja, Dr. Oshita Oshita), but also benefited from the necessary contacts, discussions, advise and support of a number of the Directing Staff of the College. I, therefore, owe the Commandant and his exceedingly hardworking team immense gratitude for creating the necessary environmental condition for the publication of this volume.

Finally, the publication of this volume was made possible by the Visiting Fulbright Scholar Fellowship of the United States Government to William Penn University, Iowa State, in the 2009/2010 academic year. The uninterrupted power supply and internet facilities of William Penn University made the task of editing and communicating with all the publishers (including University Press of America) that expressed interest in the manuscript. My unreserved gratitude, therefore, to the United States Government for the generous Fulbright Scholar Fellowship grant that provided the financial resources for my one year sojourn in the United States of America and ultimately funded this publication.

LIST OF CONTRIBUTORS

Abidoye, L. is a General and Commandant Nigerian Army College of Logistics (COMT NACOL), Lagos.

Abbo, H. is a Director in the State Security Service (SSS), Abuja, Nigeria.

Adekeye, G. T. is a retired Admiral and a former Chief of Naval Staff, Nigerian Navy.

Are, L. K. K. is a Director in the National Intelligence Agency of Nigeria.

Azazi, A. is a retired General and the former Chief of Defence Staff in the Administration of President Olusegun Obasanjo.

Bassey, C. is a Professor of Political Science at the University of Calabar and currently a Visiting Fulbright scholar at William Penn University, Iowa, United States. He was a Directing staff and Sabbatical Fellow at the National Defence College, Abuja.

Bonchuks, M. is a senior lecturer in the Department of History, University of Calabar.

Danbaba, B. G. is an Air Vice Marshall and the Air Officer Logistics Command, Ikeja, Lagos.

Dike, P. is currently the Chief of Defence Staff (CDS). He has held several command positions in the Nigeria Air Force including the Chief of Air staff (CAS) under the President Olusegun Obasanjo Administration.

Dokkubo, C. is an Associate Professor of International Relations and Strategic studies at the Nigerian Institute of International Affairs (NIIA), Lagos

Enahoro, D. O. is a retired General and the former Chief of policy and plans at Army Headquarters. He was also a former AG. Commandant of the National College, Abuja, Nigeria.

Garuba, C. is a retired General and the former Commandant of the Defence College, Abuja, Nigeria. He also commanded the United Nations Monitoring Mission in Angola (UNAVEM).

Ibrahim, O. S is an Admiral and the Chief of Training and Operations, Naval Headquarters, Abuja.

Jokotola, L. O. is a General and Commandant of Training, Doctrine and Command (TRADOC), Minna, Nigeria.

Mohammed, A. is a retired General and a former National Security Adviser under the Presidency of Olusegun Obasanjo.

Maitama, B. U. is in the office of the Permanent Secretary, Ministry of Defence, Abuja, Nigeria.

Nyong, M. is an Associate Professor of International Economics in the Department of Economics University of Calabar, Nigeria.

Ogaba, Oche is a Professor of International Relations and the Director of Research at the Nigerian Institute of International Affairs Lagos.

Okonkwo, F. O. is a retired General and former Commander of the African Union Force in Darfur, Sudan. He also Commanded ECOMIL, Liberia.

Olunloyo, V. O. S. is a Professor of Systems Engineering at the University of Lagos, Nigeria.

Osokogu, F. N. is a Major General and Chief of Logistics, Defence Headquarters, Abuja, Nigeria.

Penap, I. D. is the Chief of Training and Operations Defence Headquarters, Abuja, Nigeria.

Sanusi, H. U. was a Permanent Secretary in the Ministry of Defence, Abuja.

Saleh, M. S. is a General and the Chief of Operations, Nigeria Army.

Yoroms, G. is a Principal Research Fellow at the African center for strategic Research and Studies, National Defence College, Abuja.

Yusuf, J. is a retired General and the former Chief of Army Staff, Nigerian Army.

Yanga, W. G. is an Admiral and currently in the Naval Headquarters, Garki, Abuja.

Umaru, M. N. is a retired Air Vice – Marshall and the Former Air Officer Logistics Command. He also served as Commander Technical Training Group, Kaduna, and Commander Base Services Organization, Markurdi .

CONTENTS

INTRODUCTION

THE CHALLENGES OF MILITARY STATECRAFT IN NIGERIA

CELESTINE BASSEY

A foreign Policy Objective beyond a state's capacity inevitably establishes requirements that military planners cannot meet[1].

FRED GREENE

The defence policy of Nigeria has been a major subject of academic and policy debate since the First Republic. The reason for this controversy stems partly from the nature of the subject matter – the meaning and scope of defence policy and partly from the manifest disharmony arising from the policy responses of different administrations since independence[2]

Conventional approach to the analysis of defence policy of Nigferia has proceeded largely from considerations of the structural properties of Nigeria's security environment, threat assessment, and the adequacy of institutional peremeters developed to meet these challenges[3]. This volume, takes a slight departure from the conventional approach and focuses rather on the constellation of factors which give structure and content to Nigeria's defence policy posture. These have been labeled, respectively, as the structural and strategic components as well as the perceptual processes that underscore the formulation and implementation of defence policy. As one analyst has rightly noted, "the reality of any situation is what the decision-makers, as aware (or unaware) of geographic, historical, political, and technological considerations as they may be, perceive it to be, and while the actions resulting from their perceptions may prove to be disastrous, such an outcome is "due to the observable miscalculations of fallible men and not to the unknowable impact of inexorable forces"[4]

Such an exposition necessarily requires a preliminary contextual clarification of basic epistemological issues bearing on the meaning and nature of defence policy as it relates to the Nigerian state. This consideration will be followed by analysis of the domestic and external determinants of Nigeria's defence policy as well as the value parameters and attitudinal prisms of Nigeria's policy makers and planners which have conditioned their attitudes ad perceptions of the instrumentality of military power in Nigerian foreign policy since independence. The final section dwells on the impact of the civil-military conundrum as if structures and impact on strategic policy decisions of the Nigerian State.

It argues basically that while capitulation to military view point on matters of strategy ("relation of military force to national purposes") in a democratic order is constitutionally unsound and politically untenable, the relegation of military point of view may equally engender undesirable backlash and likely to prove counterproductive. What is, therefore, required is a dialogue between political and military minds, since, as Kissinger put it, "a separation of strategy and policy can be achieved only to the detriment of both."[5]. This can be maximized and sustained through an integrated, innovative and representative national security management regime which combines the functions of the National Defence Council and the National Security Councils. Such a novel institutional arrangement and design, it will be contended, will facilitate coordination and thereby ensure balance and coherence in strategic policy response to situational challenges.

CONTEXT

Reduced to fundamentals, the crux of defence policy is "the relation of force to national purposes"[6]. The latter involves basic values, the enhancement of which is often considered the high-priority goals of state' foreign policy. It follows, therefore, that as an instrument of foreign policy, defence policy is concerned with the provision, deployment, and use of military power to facilitate the protection and promotion of perceived national interests of the state in the international arena. Such "national interest" may concern 'core' values, which are near constant and few in number, involving the survival of society and its population, political sovereignty, and territorial independence. A second value dimension is context-sepcific "high-priority" values; these derive from ideological and/or material interests as defined by decision-makers at the time of a particular crisis (e.g. Nigeria's role in the struggle for liberation of Angola, Zimbabwe, and Namibia as an expression of its Pan-African ideals). Core values by contrast, are shared by changing regimes and decisions making groups, as well as by attentive and mass publics, of the state under inquiry. In this respect, it is instructive to compare the conception of Nigeria's national interests articulated by two radically different administration: the conservative administration of the First Republic under Prime Minister Tafawa Balewa and the dynamic, Afro-centre Mohammed Obasanjo military government[7].

Thus, to the extent that foreign policy objectives are outward-directed (that is, concerned with "acquiring something of value coveted by a foreign actor"), then there are virtually no values of concern to states that do not directly or indirectly impinge on considerations of military power calculus. Conversely, the sheer imperative of preserving physical security – territorial integrity – from external intrusions (such as foreign intervention in civil wars – e.g. Nigeria, 1966 – 1970, or South Africa's atrocious scorched earth policy in Angola) invariably entailed the expansion of national "power of resistance" as a counter to such a threat – real or perceived.

This complex interplay between objectives and military power underscores the commonplace assertion in the literature that defence policy should reflect the fundamental assumptions and objectives of foreign policy and, when necessary provide the means for their acatualisation. Conversely, foreign policy objectives should be reflections of and be limited by the ability of armed forces to give them a military underpinning. As an instrument of foreign policy, therefore, "defence policy is concerned with the protection and promotion of the States against perceived systemic threats, but also with the institutional structure by which governments make and implement their defence policies", as well as the "whole... domestic political process as it affects policy-making[8].

To be an effective policy instrument, defence planners must need ensure adequate symmetry and harmony among these structural sand strategic component of defence of policy and between the later and the operational environment in the present and like future conditions. In other words, whether national defence systems, (the military instrument) and their operational doctrine contribute to the achievement of policy goals, and the extent of any contribution, depend upon the nature of foreign and defence policy objectives as well as on the properties of the international/regional arena and the suitability of the military instrument and their use. In short, successful defence policy and performance – whether in the role of deterring, threatening or war making demands that capabilities, objectives and environment are properly reconciled. As historical antecedents have clearly highlighted, failure to integrate these divergent properties into the defence policy planning process may invite disaster at the operational level of warfare[9].

On this view, the defence policy paradigm encompasses certain "given". (i) a legal entity (the state) as a unit of analysis; (ii) an authoritative embodiment (the governments) responsible for allocation of values both within and between it and other governments; (iii) a "threat" system – the international arena; (iv) and military power as the kingpin of the interstate power structure [10]. In the light of these properties, for the defence planner the question "what is a state", for instance, ceases to be a first order question and becomes a locational and conceptional question (a "where' and "how" question). States are seen as "authority structures", or "gateways" mediating challenges, through "a national sovereignty which functions so as to "admit and domesticate certain forces, and to exclude other forces by strategies of rejection that entail legitimate violent sanctions"[11]. It is in domain of state sovereignty that the logic of war as politics finds its provenance.

Given this basic premise, the notion of security (from the standpoint of the disciplinary matrix of strategy) measure, in an objective sense "the absence of fear that such values will be attacked" [12]. Thus in some ways security can be defined or computed by the threats which challenges it. As a consequence, the defence policy of a state may be seen as "that set of decisions and external order congenial to its interests and values primarily (although not exclusively) through the use of force "However, conceptualisation and explication of the complex interplay between systemic threats, national interests, and institutional response has been a subject of animated debate in the academic and policy circles. This is so because the three main referents of this proposition concern realities that are, first, interdependent, second, highly complex, and third subject to change over time[13].

In the Nigerian defence community, this debate has been dominated by a "maximalist" and "minimalist" conceptions of Nigeria's defence policy posture. Perhaps the principal difference between these two schools of thought on the nature and dimensions of threats to the national interests of Nigeria (and the necessary policy response) resides, first, in the mode of thought and, second, in their prognosis for action[14]. The "maximalist" conception is preeminently expansive in thrust: it visualizes the threat to Nigeria's interests as primarily external in origin and military in character. The 'milimalist' perspective, on the other hand, sees the threat to the Nigerian State as preeminently internal and socio-economic in nature. It emphasis the grave limitations imposed on the Nigerian state by its structural and technological underdevelopment and, therefore, counsel tact and circumspection in the conduct of its external relations.

The 'maximalist' explication, which clearly saw Nigeria as primus inter pares (first among equals) in Africa and as such a prime target of foreign machinations (e.g. France and South Africa) argued for an activist approach to regional issues and strong defence system to meet these challenges. For example, the drastic alternation in the perceived threat to Nigeria's security – largely the function of traumatic civil war experiences and continental developments which shattered the naïve optimism of the immediate post – independence era of the early 1960s – engendered unprecedented commitment to the armed forces modernization and augmentation programme of the late 1970s and 1980s that touches upon all elements of Nigerian Military Power. These include its size and composition; quality and performances of equipment, logistical reach; capability of performing sustained, active operations; mobilizable resources and productive capacity; leadership and doctrine; communications and control; military intelligence and effectiveness; and manpower quality in terms of skill, training, physical stamina and morale. The operative criteria, as stipulated in official policy speeches were the need to meet the capabilities of potential adversaries and to economise resources[15].

This commitment to the quantitative and qualitative expansion of Nigeria's defence capabilities marked and was in turn sustained by the incorporation of West African and the continent at large, especially Southern Africa, into Nigeria's vision of systemic security. Thus, judging from policy statements and the direction of its defence policy planning, it may be valid to assert that in the three decades since the end of the civil war, the "territorial threshold" no longer constitutes the exclusive radius of security concern as was clearly the case in the case in the First Republic (1960-1966). On the contrary, unlike the prevailing attitude, perception and complacency which characterized the defence posture of the Balewa administration, the dominant "mind set" in Nigeria's government circle since the civil war has been well-expressed by a former Head of State, General Yakubu Gowon. That "the survival, security and independence of Nigeria cannot be assured as long as any part of Africa remains under colonial rule, or an apartheid regime[16].

As a consequence of these developments, the parameters of Nigeria's strategic environment was widely reconceptualised in terms of three concentric circles. First, is the territorial threshold. Second the "ring of countries" that surround Nigeria's boarder. Third, the West African bulge and the rest of the continent of Africa as this is affected and conditioned both by intra-regional and extra-regional (global) processes of intervention interaction. In concrete terms, this expansive and elemental reformulation of Nigeria's security environment elicited certain fundamental conclusions about the nature and direction of Nigeria's defence policy posture and strategy.[17]

The 'maximalist' (or realist, as some scholars would call it) perspective which has dominated and shaped our foreign and defence policy over the last three decade no doubt reflect the anxieties and the aspirations our policymakers since the civil war. However, there are essentially two major problems with this perspective in the light of our national experience in the past three decades. First, the Nigerian State is seen as a homogenous monolithic entity not as a differentiated arena dominated by competing social forces. Just as it is a well known fact that governments differ widely in their assumptions about the international system and perception of threat to national interests, it is also a demonstrable fact the groups within the same country (especially in plural or segmented societies such as Nigeria) may react differently to one and the same external challenges, as was the case over Liberia and Sierra Leone. Hence, it would be simplistic to thing of defence policy only as a singular national policy, for it can also be a class or clique policy, since the values pursued in the external environment depend on the interests of those who have political influence. This fact explains the policy divergences and perceptions between the status quo and pro-Western oriented elite in the Ministry of External Affairs and the radical fraction of the military which took control of government (after the Ouster the Gowon Administration) over the exclusive recognition of MPLA in Angola in 1975[18].

Second, defining threats to the national interests in Nigeria primarily in military terms conveys, as Richard Ullman observes, a profoundly false image of reality"[19]. On the one hand, it compels or induces Nigerian policy makers to concentrate on military threats and to ignore other and perhaps even more harmful dangers of socio-economic and political nature that promise to undermine the stability of many states in Africa. On the hand, it contributes to accelerated defence build-up that in the long-run compromised the "total security" of the country.

It is on basis of these considerations that citics of the maximalist assumptions and their validating "concentric circles" hypothesis that guides Nigeria's defence policy planning in that last couple of decades have argued that national security problems should be seen as political issues set in a wider context of social relations between societies.

Hence the call for an 'expanded agenda' of national defence policy implies for Nigeria is that conventional wisdom about threats to national interests represent what one analyst has termed the "symptomatic level of the question." National defence issues:

> *Must now be understood in wider and subtler terms crude employment of violence .... It requires the integration of military economic, and*

*political factors, not an approach that presumes the independence of
these factors in shaping the exterior behaviours of other states[20]"*

Within such a context, critical consideration will have to be given to a spectrum of factors (both military and non-military, internal and external) in the determination, formulation and implementation of defence policy of Nigeria. This necessarily involves addressing complex set of interrelated issues in policy formulation and planning: social and economic questions of mass poverty and immizerisation; the mode of national integration; effective bargaining strategies in North-South economic negotiations such as Lome convention; the prices and output policies of OPEC and other primary products; the development of regional economic co-operation, control of the activities of the major MNCS; and development policies aimed at building self-sufficiency within national economy.

What follows below is a general consideration of these policy determinants as they influence Nigeria's military statecraft – that is, the "production, maintenance, and employment of armed strength in support of the government's foreign policy"[21]. In analytical terms, consideration of the internal and external determinants of a state's use of military force is part of a broader systematic inquiry into its sources of foreign and security policy. As a consequence, these determinants are more often than not assumed in case studies of national foreign and defence policy, but seldom adequately analysed. Further, such an inquiry is also inescapably subject to the same gamut of strictures and problems that has so far bedeviled endeavours to develop universal theory of foreign policy behaviour [22].

These observations notwithstanding, the military, as John Garnett, explains, is "one of the many instrument in the orchestra of power which states use at an appropriate moment in the pursuit of their respective national interests"[23]. But since, as Rapoport aptly contends, "the nature of war is itself to a large extent determined by how man conceives of it, and the general character of a nation's strategy is, in turn, determined by its philosophy of war,[24]" the conscious exploitation of military power as a rational technique for the pursuit of foreign policy objectives is necessarily influenced by certain domestic and external factors which, although analytically distinct, cannot be completely understood in isolation from the other. Nigeria is not an exception in this regard.

DETERMINANTS

As alluded to above, in pursuit of defence policy objectives, national military power can be employed for threatening, deterring, war-fighting, or peacekeeping. It can be employed coercively in order to either influence the behaviour of opponents or alter or preserve the status quo. Ideally, the frequency and intensity of states' applications of military power in pursuit of one or a combination of these objectives are functions of either capability and intentions – viewed within the general context of foreign and domestic political objectives ad constraints.

However, in specific circumstances, the military response provoked by external stimulus is invariably conditioned by a set of antecedent factors/determinants that predispose a society or regime towards a military reaction. In contemporary parlance of strategy, it is these factors that constitute the political and cultural component in the military potential of states. These domestic antecedent factors may be categorized according to the way in which they are produced as either direct or indirect. They may also be classified according to the way they function as either long-term or short-term. They may further be codified according to the way in which they expedite the use of force as either anticipatory or reactive. Four such antecedent factors with relevance to the Nigerian experience are considered here in brief.

The first involves certain psycho-cultural dynamics which predisposes a society towards the use of force externally (as well as internally). This 'attitude complex', which more or less favours a military response to international situations of conflict, has been evident in the old martial ethic (warrior and Jihad traditions) associated with the diverse ethic groups in Nigeria, especially with the dominant Hausa-Fulani[25]. The latter were the 'fighting tribes' from which the British recruited the bulk of the infantry for the Nigerian Regiment of the Royal West African Frontier Force (RWAFF). The extent to which relevant impacts of historical experience may have dissipated this old martial ethic among the Nigerian population (as Ali Mazrui has contended) is highly debatable. If anything, the events of the civil war and the unprecedented tantrum of the Nigerian public following the killing of five Nigerian soldiers on routine border patrol by Camerounian gendarmes, are clearly indicative of the population's underlying propensity to mobilize and use military strength in conflict situations[26]. Such a disposition toward the use of force is not alien to Nigeria's social ethic; it parallels in many ways the 'cult of violence and of aggression' which several writers have associated with the American way of life[27]'

The second antecedent factor is public disposition to support the foreign and defence policy of government. "To accept it as authoritative ad hence binding," simply because it is seen as the prerogative of the government. For example, in Nigeria the public's attitude toward the acquisition and use of military force had been largely benign until the mid-1970s, as this "issue-area' was considered the legitimate domain of the government alone. However, increasing public awareness since the late 1970s-especially as a result of media coverage of the 'Gun or Gari' controversy-has engendered groundswell discontent about the direction of government policy concerning defence. Not surprisingly, therefore, support for the relatively horrendous (in terms of the federal budget) military expenditures under the Shagari administration tended to accrue from groups who expected to derive personal or corporate benefits. This generally holds true for the Nigerian military establishment, who benefit in terms of career interest, professional relevance, and social prestige. It also holds true for business interests that derive profit from logistics policy are to be found in the attentive publics (especially in academic and media circles) who consider the current military build-up an affront to egalitarian and social ideals.

The third antecedent factor involves differences in political systems frequently associated with the potential for generating and using military power in the literature. As Kenneth Waltz has incisively articulated in *Man, the State and War,* one of the most potent sources of theories about military conflict is the idea that a state's form of government influences its propensity to use force. Thus, Quincy Wright has argued that:

> *Absolutistic states with geographically and functionally centralized governments under autocratic leadership are likely to be most belligerent, whereas constitutional states with geographically and functionally federalized governments under democratic leadership are likely to be most peaceful*[28].

Seen the light of Wright's argumentation, it may be contended that certain legal and constitutional aspects-some explicit and some general – of Nigeria's presidential system and multi-state federalism, were quintessentially less supportive to the use of military power than the military regimes they superseded and preceded. The "War provisions" of the civilian constitution, for instance, expressly prohibits the President from declaring a state of war between Nigeria and another country 'except with the sanction of a resolution of each of the Houses of the National Assembly' (Article 5, 3a). Furthermore, in a move to deny a Nigerian President the maneuverability which several United States President have used to commit troops abroad without a formal declaration of war, the Constituent Assembly added Section 5 (3b) which stipulates: "except with the prior approval of the Senate no member of the Armed Forces of the Federation shall be deployed on combat duty outside the Federation[29]. Moreover, while the Nigerian President held most of the powers of initiative and was the Commander-in-Chief of the Armed Forces, the National Assembly retained financial veto through budgetary control (that is, appropriation and authorization of funds for military operations). In practice, however, such constitutional and legal restraints on the Executive – as the American experience amply demonstrates – were so easily circumvented; i.e., when the President's use of force was extremely unpopular. In Nigeria's limited experience with the presidential system, Shagari resisted near unanimity of the National Assembly for punitive military action against Cameroun in May 1981, in the teeth of popular pressure while sanctioning, two years later (June and July 1983), a limited military action against Chadian forces in the Lake Chad Basin without prior approval from the Legislature. Such dialectic of inaction and action simply underscores the relative importance of the personality variable and of perceptions in foreign and defence policy decision-making; it serves to confirm the observation of R.V. Denenberg that 'When threatened with external danger, the complex system of checks and balances reverts to a tribal dependence on the warrior chief[30].

In the military-strategic domain, the power of war and peace (irrespective of the political system) in the contemporary international order tends to rest in the 'unfettered hands' of government, and the 'man who holds the trigger inevitable gives the orders.' If in theory differences in political system per se impinge on the propensity to use force, historical records do not provide adequate comparable data to establish such an association conclusively.

The fourth, and final, domestic antecedent fact is the occasionally irresistible pressure of the military establishment itself. As several theorists of civil-military relations have noted, in essentially praetorian polity such as Nigeria, the Jingoistic attitude of the military is often a force with which to reckon by civilian policy makers in periods of interstate conflict[31]. This is, however, a double-edged sword, since external ventures without the support of the military can topple a government, while undue restraints in situations unyielding to pacific strategies could invite an adverse response from the military.

A balance sheet of the Nigerian military (in and out of government) is on the whole inconclusive. Gowon's administration (1966-1975) astutely resisted public pressures for military action against Equatorial Guinea – following the massacres of Nigerians on the island-as inconsistent with the precepts of the OAU. Similarly, Shagari successfully withstood the tempestuous reaction of the defence staff, favouring instead a diplomatic solution to the Nigerian-Cameroun border crisis (May 1981). Perhaps the administration's apprehension that such restraint may be interpreted by the military as inexcusable appeasement (with incalculable consequences for its survival elicited the subsequent decision in June 1983 to permit a military response against *Chadian forces in the Lake Chad Basin*).

From a decision-making perspective, however, these domestic determinants are not in themselves sufficient explanatory and predictive categories for the use of military force. If government behaviour in the international arena is a function both of perceptions of environmental situations and of predispositions brought to perceptions, then the significance of the various antecedent factors analysed above depends on developments within the strategic environment. These two determinants (internal and external) may either reinforce or conflict with each other, and policy-makers may also entertain more or less correct assumptions about the properties of such contingencies. Nevertheless, as Knorr has aptly noted, 'the stronger the preexisting attitude (antecedent factors) presses for a particular course of action, the more it will have its way even when environmental stimuli are week or confusing, or vice versa[32]"

In the Nigerian context, this means that the various domestic determinants are not in themselves sufficient to trigger a military reaction. Linkages between antecedent and situational conditions in its strategic environment have to be considered irreducible essentials in the calculus of such a reaction. Specifically, developments with Nigeria's strategic environment with bearing on its security have been primary situational determinants in its use or threat to resort to the military instrument in the post-independence era. These include, *inter alia:i)* The violation of territorial 'threshold' by armed forces of neighbouring states (in particular, Cameroun and Chad); ii) Acts of external aggression unacceptable to its policy makers (e.g. the attempt by foreign mercenaries to overthrow the government of neighbouring Republic of Benin); iii) The need for military stabilization through peace-keeping (Tanzania) or through peace-enforcement (as in the Congo and Liberia), both of which were considered essential to peace and security in Africa; and iv) Developments in Southern Africa in the late-1970s and 1980s (particularly in Angola, Mozambique and Zimbabwe), when the process of deconlonisation escalated with 'elemental fury'. In an impressive *volte face* from the attitude and perception of Prime Minster Belawa of the First Republic, two subsequent heads of Nigerian military governments (Gowon and Obasanjo) aggressively canvassed the OAU on the imperative of a Pan-African Force 'against the racist and imperialist' domination of African territories.

Accordingly, while rejecting the idea of a multi-purpose continent force, General Gowon argued at the Rabat Ministerial Conference of the OAU in 1972 for a specific functional Task Force to be deployed in Southern Africa. In a similar vein, head of the successor military government, General Obasanjo in his valedictory speech to the OAU, called for the establishment of a 'truly Pan-African Force', urging in the process that 'the problem can no longer be shelved and must be squarely faced[34]. As one Nigerian scholar has noted:

> *There were manifold reasons for Nigeria's spirited advocacy for the formation an African High Command, a shift in its declared foreign policy. For one Nigerian leader had come increasingly to perceive the continued existence of Portuguese colonial rule and white minority governments in Africa as a threat not only to Nigeria but to Africa. Portugal, South Africa and Rhodesia were alleged to have supported Nigerian secessionists during the civil war. Logic and the rhetoric of the Gowon and Obasanjo administrations on African Liberation dictated support for the creation of a force that might serve to eliminate these regimes.[35]*

These developments within Nigeria's strategic environment have, in diverse ways generated a greater appreciation of the relevance of the defence component in its foreign policy, and have accordingly been considered part of the external stimuli that provoke or threaten to provoke a military reaction on the part of its decision – makers. In the next and final section, a concise review of Nigeria's policy-makers attitude and perceptions about the instrumentality of military power in Nigerian foreign policy will be considered. The logic and relevance of such a review can be readily appreciated from the literature on political psychology about the dynamic of personality variables in policy-making. In a nutshell, this analytical perspective takes as its premise the incontestable fact that many of the decisions made in an official capacity are not merely products of bureaucratic, organizational, domestic, ad external imperatives and constraints, but also products of the individual's personality. In other words, policy derives both from the requirements of 'high office and from personal conviction and individual experience', the difference lying principally in degree or relative potency of the two variables. As one theorist of this field explains 'the individual, far from being a mechanism manipulated by forces such as the 'national interest' or 'power relationships', is a significant independent actor in the decision-making process. His perceptual screen, his emotions, his personality, and

his social background are all independent variables that may affect a nation's foreign behaviour[36].

While the variability in relative potency of personality factors in defence and foreign policy between the civilian and military governments of Nigeria cannot be denied, the personalized nature of foreign policy decision-making under Balewa, for example, has had a much impact (adverse) on the production and use of military power as it had in the military era (astronomical) – the latter based as it were on complete fusion of legislative and executive powers.

STRUCTURE OF DECISION

One of the pre-eminent features of the history Nigeria's foreign relations is the marked re-orientation from a period of conservatism and self-effacement to a more dynamic posture from 1960 to the present. The latter is characterized by an increasing acceptance of a 'realist' philosophy which views military power as 'one of the bases of diplomacy and of contractual obligations beyond the boundaries of the State'. As will be appreciated below, this development in Nigeria's foreign policy posture is not entirely haphazard; neither is it part of a syndromes of aggressive negritude' as some critics have contended (e.g. the tirade of a British Conservative MP following Nigeria's nationalization of BP shares at a height of the 'Rhodesian' Crisis).

On the contrary, the increasing acceptance of this essentially Clausewitzian precept as a 'value parameter' by Nigerian policy-makers derives from a complex set of rapidly evolving relationships between historical circumstances and present condition. It has been an end-result of domestic tumult as well as untoward developments in the African continent since the early 1960s (that is, a response to distinctive historical conjunctures of forces). Unprecedented levels of foreign intervention in the Nigerian Civil War (especially of France, Portugal, South Africa and defunct Rhodesia), the Portuguese invasion of Guinea, the radical changes of decision-makers, the search for greater intellectual functions in foreign policy, the remarkable increases in Nigeria's revenue, and the crisis in Southern Africa, have, in many ways generated a greater appreciation of the relevance of the military component in the foreign policy of Nigeria[37]. And with these changing parameters of strategic thinking in the policy-making circle have proceeded the parallel expansion of the military instrument through a military modernization and augmentation programme that touches upon all elements of military power.

As this development in the history of post-independence foreign policy of Nigeria also coincided with changing regimes and actors at the helm of power, a clear picture of this evolving posture may be appreciated from specific examination of individual Nigerian policy-maker's attitude and perception of the instrumentality of military power in statecraft. This examination may in turn be divided into two broad categories: the pre-civil war era (1960-1966) and the civil war and post civil war era (1966-2010). The former era corresponds to the administration of Alhaji Abubakar Tafawa Balewa; the latter era spans the period from 1970 to the present.

As has been implicit in the preceding analysis, 'attitudinal prisms and elite images' which condition foreign policy decisions are generally part of the psychological environment and are, therefore, subject to change over time with the sifting dynamics of the operational environment of a decision-maker. Furthermore, the relationship between attitudinal and perceptual variable, official policy and international behaviour of a government, is not always symmetrical 'States', as Nazil Choucri remind us, 'do not always behave in accordance with their declared policies, nor are their actions necessarily congruent with dominant attitudes and perceptions'[38].

Thus, while Balewa's conservatism and pacifist inclinations cannot be denied, it may, nevertheless, be a prejudgement to say whether given relevant changes in the operational environment, his perception of the relation of forces in the international system would not have altered dramatically and with it his attitudes towards the production and use of military power. However, this reservation about the durability of a conservative streak in Balewa's policy over time notwithstanding, it can be concluded from specific policy behaviour of the Balewa's government that his thinking about the role and utility of military power in international relations was at best naïve and at worst malign.

First, his commitment to maintain a largely ceremonial Army for internal and border duties was consistent with, and predicated upon, his virulently anti-'realist' ethos: that is, his avowed rejection of the view that power (as ultimately expressed in military capability) constitutes the basis of 'all contractual obligations beyond the boundaries of States'. As a consequence, by 1966 the Nigerian military ranked as one of the smallest (10,500) and under-equipped war machines in the continent. Such an attitude and policy toward the development, maintenance and use of military power as an instrument of policy by Balewa contrasted markedly with the perceptions of the high status and role of Nigeria in the post-independence Africa by a significant section of the government functionaries and informed public alike. That is, given Nigeria's geographical expanse, human endowment, and political pluralism (parliamentary and federal rule), its 'manifest destiny' is to exercise leadership on the continent. It may, nevertheless, be argued that while this widespread self-image and role-conception of Nigeria was not altogether unpopular with Balewa (as suggested by his responses to Nkrumah), his perception of the functionality of military power in the resolution of vital African issues hardly accorded with this dominant 'realist' precepts[39].

Second and related to the first, Balewa aversion to military power as an instrument of statecraft was clearly evident from his vehement opposition to Nkrumah's proposal of a continental defence system (an African High Command) to keep 'the imperialist invaders at bay". Most attempts to explain Balewa's stance on continental defence have shifted between the personality factor and his 'naïve and legalistic conception of international processes[40]'. In addition to these considerations, however, must be noted the underlying conflicting conceptions of international and regional order, two different views of historical processes, and two variant visions of the future between Balewa and the foremost advocate of Pan-African Force: Nkrumah. Furthermore,

domestic capability factors – the fragile political system and the serious limitations imposed by an essentially dependent and neo-colonial economy – may also have partly contributed to Balewa's cautionary inclination.

Nevertheless, since Nigerian's foreign and defence policy was largely formulated and rigidly controlled by the Prime Minister', his attitudinal and perceptual prism particularly his incurable dislike for all types and militancy has to be considered as a major factor in his administration's derogation of military power as an instruments of statecraft. In the final analysis, it was a policy marked by neglect rather than by conscious promotions of the military option, and an inclination towards quiet diplomacy rather than international or regional vigilantism. This period of uncertainty and self-effacement which characterized Nigeria's foreign policy posture came to an abrupt end at the beginning of 1966 with the assassination of Balewa in a military coup. However, as will be argued below, the policy approach of his protégé (Shehu Shagari) in the Second Republic, despite significant alteration in both domestic and external (regional and global) environments and the rhetoric of a Jihad against the 'evil of apartheid', was in some ways reminiscent of this initial post independence era[41].

The overt intervention of the Nigerian Military in politics injected into the national arena a corpus of decision-making elite whose Afro-centric activism and ideals underscored the unmistakable reorientation of Nigeria's post-independence foreign relations from the Balewa period of quiet diplomacy to the more dynamic and uncompromising posture of the military era, which later saw its climax in the subsequent Mohammed-Obasanjo administration. However, the different between the two eras centered less on substantive policy departures than on style and means; especially the greater appreciation of the military component in foreign policy by the Gowon administration. This became visible at several policy levels.

First, the unprecedented augmentation of the capability of the Nigerian military during and after the civil war (which may have resulted in part from the corporate interest of the Nigerian military establishment) reflects a general concern of the policy elite that (as a later Head of state put it) 'our dynamic foreign policy posture can only be credible if we have a well-equipped and disciplined defence force capable of defending our territorial integrity and national interests. As a consequence, the qualitative and quantitative expansion of the Nigerian military (especially Air Force and Navy) became a matter of great urgency after the Gowon era. For example, by 1975 the Nigerian Navy had grown from its 1967 level of 1,500 to 6,500 personnel and the Air Force from 1,000 to 7,500. In terms of operational requirements, both services acquired new frigates and long-range fighters, respectively. The NAF, which by early 1970 had thirty-three combat aircraft, expanded to about sixty by mid-1975[42]

Second, the shift in attitude of the new policy-elite towards the instrumentality of military power was also demonstrated by its aggressive commitment to revolutionary force as the only viable means of change in 'colonial Africa'. Unlike the ambivalence which characterized the Balewa era, the predominant 'mind set' of the successor

government was 'that the survival, security and independence of Nigeria cannot be assured as long as any part of Africa remains under colonial rule, or an apartheid regime[43]. Part of the reason for this position has been noted above: the intervention of the racist and imperialist states of South Africa, 'Rhodesia' and Portugal in the Nigerian Civil War, in a calculated attempt to balkanize the country. It was also due partly to the developments within the international system which convinced the new administration about the determination of the former imperial powers to preserve their economic and strategic dominance in Africa.[51]

This new direction in the security policy of Gowon's administration became unquestionably obvious in its radical departure from the policy guide of the Balewa government concerning a regional defence system in Africa. At the 1970 OAU summit, Gowon also castigated what he called 'the evils and the plots of forces of colonialism, racism and oppression to divide us', and ended with the assertion that 'we have no choice but to commit ourselves wholly to the struggle against racial oppression".

Accordingly, the Nigerian delegation presented at the 1972 Rabat Ministerial conference, a modified version of Nkrumah's proposal for a regional defence force – an African Task Force – to be deployed in Southern Africa to:

a. Assist African liberation movements based, and trained, in neighbouring African countries; and

b. Participate in the militant armed struggles for the total liberation of Southern Africa[44].

As previously noted, the reasons for such a departure from the Balewa era involved a combination of internal and external developments which has became obvious even to the most conservative circles in Nigeria. As Gowon declared.

> *The forces which impede the freedom and independence of Africa and which at the same time seek to undermine our achievements remain very formidable. They will never leave us alone to develop our natural and human resources to our advantage. They will forever want us to waste our time and energy in negative pursuits[45].*

This new inclination toward radical assertiveness in the Gowon administration was undoubtedly reinforced by the post-civil war economic prosperity which the oil boom engendered. The heightened basis of national economic power (in terms of international liquidity, as a result of the oil revenues) increased the confidence and means of the administration to pursue a new, active and effective policy within the continent and to influence the decisions of extra-regional powers. The finest hours' of this policy was the early Muhammed-Obasanjo era.

Although the militancy of the Muhammed-Obasanjo Government far outstripped the assertiveness of both its predecessor and successor, the tough rhetoric of this administration was not accompanied by any drastic or fundamental change in the

use of Nigeria's military as an instrument of policy compared, for instance, with Libyan vigilantism.

However, given the celebrated purposefulness of General Muhammed, it maybe hypothesized that such restraint on the part of the Nigerian leadership in this period was more a consequence of the limited 'striking power' of the Nigerian military rather than conscious policy choice. Such a limitation was not insurmountable, however, (given astronomical oil revenues) and, judging from the Angolan episode, it is not unthinkable that had the 'tough, inflexible, strong minded and aggressively intolerant' Muhammed survived, the Nigerian military would, perhaps, have been drawn into a defensive operations in Mozambique or Zambia at the height of the Rhodesian crisis in the late-1970s. As one analyst of this era has noted:

> *Muhammed held the view that there was no reason why Nigerian Soldiers should not go and fight in South Africa along-side the liberation forces, whatever the obstacles. From this incident it was obvious that Muhammed as Head of State would not hesistate to push Nigeria into a confrontation with South Africa if the situation were to arise.46.*

Indeed, the unprecedented commitment of this regime to a military solution in situations unyielding to pacific strategies was highlighted by the announcement of the Chief of Army Staff, T. Y. Danjuma, in 1977, that the government would be prepared to send troops to assist the freedom fighters in order to speed up the collapse of the 'albinocracies' in Southern Africa. However, since undoubtedly the new level of radicalism and militant assertiveness as well as the tacit encouragement of the radicals and left-wing elements in the country had General Muhammed as its prime mover, it was not entirely surprising that his premature death, coupled with the slump in oil revenues, renewed restraint and caution in Nigeria's defence and foreign policy posture. It was, perhaps, the latter realization that prompted Alaba Ogunsanwo's observation in his critique of the Muhammed – Obasanjo foreign policy performances, that:

> *Bold foreign policy positions and stances are hardly sustainable for a considerable period without domestic infrastructural underpinnings which form the solid foundation for such policies. Long-term pursuit of national interests is facilitated through the availability of policy options that decisions makers may resort to. They degree of maneuverability depends to a large extent on a country's dependence on the external environment for the life-sustaining resources that are needed....47.*

The creation, maintenance and use of armed forces on which Nigeria's foreign defence policy partly rest, requires a concomitant expansion in the primary foundation of its national military power: economic and technological resources. To recall the analysis in the second section above, economic strength constitutes the basis of two components of putative military power in Africa as elsewhere: mobilized or ready military forces and military potential (from which additional military capabilities can be derived). While, as Timothy Shaw noted, 'the ineluctable progress towards semi-peripheral capitalism' (towards a more industrialized economy dominated by an ever-changing balance of fractional forces among national, transactional and bureaucratic bourgeoisie or capital) has profoundly altered the economic basis of Nigeria's military power, persistent fluctuations in this essentially monocultural economy have imposed serious limits on the use and usability of force as an instrument of policy[48]. The realization of this paralyzing factor on Nigeria's foreign and security policy posture no doubt underlies the feverish debate about the viability of the industrialization strategy initiated under the Fourth National Development Plan.

A comparison of these two initial era (1966-1976) suggests and element of continuity as well as discontinuity. There has been an undeniable element of continuity in terms of fundamental policy objectives, as Ogunbadejo and Aluko among others have argued. However, in terms of policy means – the primary focus of this study – the era exhibit significant departures, if discontinuity, especially in terms of appreciation of the military component in foreign policy.

These differences in style and means, which is not unrelated to the fortuitous augmentation of national economic base as result of considerable oil revenue, is, nevertheless, to be seen more in terms of the incommensurable dissimilarity of personalities and 'mind-sets' of the leadership in the two periods. In this respect, there are sufficient grounds to hypothesize that a Balewa (or his successor in the Second Republic) in the helm of power in 1975-76 would have reacted differently to South Africa's incursion into Angola. However, although the military interregnum between the two civilian eras strengthened in many ways the defence underpinnings in Nigerian foreign policy, it will be contended below that the Shagari era did not necessarily represent a return to 1966 ante. This contention is supported by the unabated level of defence expenditures the revanchist posture toward unruly neighbours and the intensification of support for liberation movements in Southern Africa.

Despite the obvious differences in personality and foreign policy posture between the second civilian administration and it's military predescessor, the emergence of a 'gentle, patient and cool-headed' leadership in the person of Shehu Shagari in the Second Republic was not accompanied by a depreciation of the military component in Nigeria's foreign policy as was widely expected. Instead, in line with the NAN Manifesto, there was continued emphasis on an enhancement of the 'military underpinning' of Nigeria's foreign policy. This undiminished trend in policy posture under Shagari was succinctly represented by Aminu Tijjnani and David Williams .

> Inspite of the growing criticism of the deficiencies of military rule,
> there has been, since the soldiers handed over power, no sign of the
> expected civilian criticism of the high proportion of the Federal budget
> devoted to defence, still the highest single item in the 1981 budget.
> Nigerians seem to feel that they have a duty to match their political
> importance in Africa and the world with military strength.... More

money is being spent on equipment and training, and the President has promised that Nigeria's defence system will become "the best in Africa" and "comparable to the best in the world". A modernized and well-equipped force "can be expected to discharge creditably and positively the task of defending the largest Black nation on earth; and only such a force can give adequate credibility and expression to Nigeria's strong foreign policy posture." This is an attitude which "radicals" as much as "conservatives" agree[49].

Thus, unlike his conterpart and political superior in the First Republic, the military instrument was far from regarded as an anomaly by Shagari. Instead, the president's response to critical Situations (such as Nigeria-Cameroun border conflict of May 1981) was a judicious combination of 'carrot and stick' a threat of military reprisal if diplomacy failed to yield a mutually acceptable solution. However, unlike the Muhammed-Obasanjo era, the second civilian president will, perhaps be remembered for his 'low-key style of quiet diplomacy' reminiscent of the Balewa's republic. As one reviewer of the foreign policy performance of the Shagari administration has applied noted, 'some people greet the mention of Nigeria's foreign policy during the last four years with a derisive: What foreign policy? There is obviously some nostalgia behind this view, which glances backward in time to the 1975 struggle in the OAU over recognizing the MLPA and General Mutala Muhammed's position role. There was also the strong position the Obasanjo government took on the French and Balgian intervention in Shaba. Some consider these to be high pints from which the NPN has descended into uncertainty [50].

Much like its military predecessors, the fundamental policy orientation of the Second Republic continues to reflect a considerable appreciation of defence components in foreign policy. However, unlike the buoyant petrodollar era of the 1970s, a worsening balance-of-payment deficit coupled with mounting debt burden have combined to compel retrenchment of policy objectives in order to bring them into a proper relation with the means available for their implementation.

Thus, in a marked contrast to the confrontational policy posture toward South Africa in the late 1970s, the guarded pronouncement by the Defence Minister, General D. Bali, on his return from the "Front Line" States registered unmistakably the atrophied economic condition and constraint on defence policy planners[51]. This fact of liquidity may have necessitated adjustment in notwithstanding, while the factors of distance and defence posture towards targets of geographic distance, the forceful reaction of the Babangida regime to the expanding presence of South Africa on the Island of Bioko (Equatorial Guinea) and the Liberian operations suggest the persistence of such policy direction towards contiguous territories. That is, on the one hand, the strategic position of the Island of Bioko in Nigeria's "triangle of survival" (TOS) necessitates constant monitoring to prevent a deterioration in the geographic and military status quo in that territory as in other neighbouring countries. On the other hand, its membership of ECOWAS and as a signatory of the "Protocol Relating to mutual Assistance on Defence" of May 1981, Nigeria is commited to the milieu goals and security in the sub-region. Such a defence policy objective is seen by the Babangida regime as a "national interest of the highest order". Hence his contention that:

> *The ECOWAS region completes what has been termed the three concentric circles governing Nigerian foreign and defence policies....* *There is, therefore, no gainsaying the fact that when certain events occurs in this sub-region depending upon their intensity and magnitude, which are bound to affect Nigeria's politico-military and socio-economic environment, we should not stand by as a helpless and hapless spectators. We believe that if the event are such that have the potentials to threaten the stability, peace and security of the sub-region, Nigeria in collaboration others, in this sub-region, is duty bound to react or respond in appropriate manner necessary to either avert the disaster or to take adequate measures to ensure peace, tranquility and harmony*[52].

In this regard, the General has trenchantly noted that "it is the duty of this administration to protect our national interest and to ensure the existence of a credible deterrent force to sustain such interest[53]". As a consequence, the military regime of General Babangida initiated a period of costly and traumatic military intervention in Liberia and Sierra Leone (1990-2000). The ostensible reason for the intervention derived from the imperative need to end the fatricidal civil war through a sub-regional peace-support operation. However, in both Liberia and Sierra Leone, the operation quickly degenerated into tragic and protracted encounter with local insurgent factors that absorbed a phenomenal portion of Nigeria's oil revenue and considerably eroded the combat power of its military establishment. Daniel Bach has noted in an indicting review that:

> *By 1999..... the Nigerian military itself was in a state of decay, its professionalism eroded, corruption rife were equally how. In 2000, an American audit of the state of Nigerian armed forces reported that 75% of army equipment was "damaged or completely out of commission". Only ten out of the Navy's 52 vessels could be considered as seaworthy and perhaps five Alpha Jets of the Airforce could still fly out of a total of 90 combat aircrafts*[54].

Despite this costly strategic engagement, this period also saw initial effort under the General Babangida administration to sustain the armed forces modernization programme involving a range of structural components of the Nigerian military.

The regime's effort in this regard was directed toward, first, maintenance of 'existing hardware and improvement on mobility and communications of the armed forces in order to sustain an acceptable state of preparedness"[55]. Second, expansion of the critical underpinning of national military power: the local military industrial complex. The necessity for such an expansion was construed in terms of the imperative of 'military development":

> *The development of a Nigerian defence industry should not be dictated by threat to our National Security alone. In order to minimize the costs of military development, particularly our foreign exchange, we must embark on a radical programmed for developing our defence industrial base. This should be our cardinal and deliberate policy[56].*

In pursuit of this primary goal, a significant percentage of the capital budget on defence has been initially allocated the Defence Industries Corporation (DIC) which, the same source has noted, ' suffered greatly due to paucity of fund and of recognition, inspite of a number of government pronouncement on the need for Nigeria to be self-sufficient in arms production[57]. Seen in the context of the present state of neglect and irrelevance the Defence Industries Corporation has been reduced, President Babangida's observation (made while the Chief of Army Staff) is largely incomprehensible. From a policy standpoint, such a discrepancy between intention and manifest behaviour in office only suggest, as one scholar has aptly noted, that a distinction often exist between 'declaratory policy,' planned policy' and 'actual policy':

> *Sometimes these are the same: that is to say, the policy which the government declares it is going to follow is the same as that which it actually intends to follow and does in fact follow when the decisions are implemented. Very often, however, they do not coincide, either intentionally because of government policy, or because of the limitations, restrictions and changing circumstances outside government control. Very often the term used in a 'declaratory' sense refers to policy statements which have as their objective certain political or psychological effects. At the same time the government may have a 'planned policy' different from that which has been announced, which refers to the general guidelines which it believes should and will in reality govern its actions in various contingencies[58].*

The regime of General Sani Abacha (as a key player in the Babangida era) simply drove these prevalent tendencies in Nigeria's defence policy to their logical extremes with the expansion of war in Sierra Leone and military engagement in the Bakassi Pennisula. The operation on Bakassi was ostensibly to secure the "oil-rich" peninsula once and for all against the incursion of Cameround gendarmes. From the account of officers involved the operation was badly conducted without clear strategic objective. As a consequence, avoidable and unnecessary casualties were sustained until the "Green Tree" Agreement brought the tragic Saga to a dishonourable end for Nigeria. The cumulative and costly experience in force projection into regional domestic quagmire especially in Chad, Liberia, Sierra Leone and Somalia compelled a policy reconsideration on peace-support operations.

This became clear in the sustained policy of disengagement from Sierra Leone and the cautious response to the crisis in Cort d' Voire by the Obasanjo Administration. In the light of infrastructural decay (especially the generating capacity of the Nigerian Electric Power Authority which reached a disastrous proportion by 2009), and the enormity of social crisis of stagflation, and mass immiserisation, it is not surprising that the Nigerian Governments in the Fourth Republic (1999-2009) under Obasanjo and Yar'Adua have tended generally to retreat from ambitious and unilateral proactive peace-support operations. The current wisdom is to serve under the direction of the United Nations as currently the case in Sierra Leone and Darfur. In this context, the Nigerian Military gains from offset arrangement in weapons acquisition and maintenance, while its officers and men benefit from the professional experience of mission-task in an increasingly dangerous regional neigbourhood such as the Democratic Republic of Congo and Sudan. This policy disposition also explains the reticence of the Federal Government about participating in the AU peacekeeping operation in Somalia which has run into a stormy political sea as the coalition of Islamic resistance groups step up their assault on the capital, Mogadisu.

In overall terms, however, this brief review of the inclinations of successive Nigerian policy-makers towards military power as an instrument of policy is suggestive of fundamental differences of style and means rather than substantive departure in policy objectives. Unfortunately, space precludes a detailed comparison, evaluation and explanation of the complex mechanics (personality, organizational, socio-economic and political, and systemic variables) underlying these differences.

However, viewed in conjunction with the domestic and external determinants of the use of Nigeria's military as an instrument of foreign and defence policy discussed above, it should suffice in my judgement to elicit a tentative conclusion. Considered both in terms of the crucial distinction between a state's role conception (that is, its world view, or orientation, general policy commitments to and plans for action) and its role enactment (that is, it actual international behaviour), significant differences exist between periods, reflecting not only relevant changes in parameters (domestic and systemic) but also the personalized nature of leadership, combined with the relative degree of latitude in decision-making afforded the foreign and defence policy elite. In this regard, apart from the uncertainties and naïve slipshodness which characterized the formative years of the Balewa era, the role definition (as different from the role enactment) of the military instrument in Nigerian foreign policy has been remarkably consistent with the Clausewitzian or 'neorealist' tradition in international politics.

There has been among the policy elite wide-ranging perceptions of the military both as the basis of national security and as instrument of prevalence in situations unyielding to pacific strategies, as in the Lake Chad Basin in Summer 1983. Explicitly in the form of threats or implicitly through silent calculations, considerations of Nigerian military power have acted as counters in diplomatic bargaining (e.g. Nigeria-Cameroun confrontation over Bakassi in the 1980s and 1990s). Given the current reorganization and expansion of Nigeria's military capability it is to be expected that such a trend in strategic thinking among its decision-making elite will heighten rather then diminish, especially in relation to internal pacification (e.g. Niger Delta) and Peace-Support Operations in the continent.

In the current democratic dispensation, as was the case in First and Second Republic the danger of capricious confrontation between the Political class and the Military

Establishment over fundamental direction of strategic policy (as in the Nigeria Delta) is a constant source of apprehension.

CIVIL-MILITARY CONUNDRUM

The civil-military conundrum remain one of the most intractable issue-area in any consideration of the process of democratization in Nigeria. Although the fiction of political scholars has been military propounded by a generation of liberal strategic implications and dimension of the interlay between military institutions and societal political processes remain unresolved policy issue.

Partly this reflects the complexity of the problem itself, particularly the fact that the use and usability of military power in pursuit of national objectives takes place under various conditions and differ greatly in their character. Largely, however, because systematic inquiry into strategic phenomena exhibiting the conceptual, theoretical and methodological convention readily seen in other regional subsystems, are yet to have a major impact on security policy analysis concerning Africa.

Reduced to fundamentals, core-complex of the issue revolves around the fundamental policy question as to whether in any given conflict situation involving either the manifest use of power as a counter to diplomatic bargaining, is it the military may be in line with doctrine of "civilian view point that should prevail or, as it may be in line with doctrine of "civilian supremacy" in a democratic order, and as Clemenceau once trenchantly noted, would the express use of military force (war) be considered "much too serious a matter to be left to the generals".

As events during the Second Republic (The Nigeria Cameroun border crisis of May, 1981) Nigeria – Chad border crisis of April – June, 1983 and the Niger-Delta attest, such a dichotomy of outlook on potent policy question between the professional military and civilian elite, it strong enough and left unchecked, tends to produce tension and in an extreme case may push the military into open rebellion against the civilian authorities. As reported in Africa Confidential this was the case after the Nigeria-Chad border "fiasco", the political handling of which infuriated nearly all senior officers involved and may have expedited the overthrow of Shagari's administration[59].

Nigeria's resort to coercive violence to dislodge regiments of Chadian forces from the Island of Kinsara (April-June, 1983) was a timely reminder of the chequered and potentially explosive situation on its highly amorphous frontier. But unlike the May, 1981 incident, during functioned largely as a counter in diplomatic bargaining, the Shagari's administration unleashed its military forces on Chad.

However, Nigeria's response to this particular incident cannot be understood or judged in isolation from earlier provocations involving its Eastern and Western neighbours (Cameroun and Benin). Institutional (especially the military and legislature) and public (media, university students, trade unions and the masses) reactions to these unwarranted provocations" made it almost impossible for President Shagari to eschew the use of force in the Lake Chad basin incident. As the Africa Research Bulletin notes: Some newspapers have accused his government of once again being "spineless" in the face of "aggression particularly unwelcome comment during the run-up to Nigeria's elections in August.

Such an accusation was apparently directed against the strict operational limitation imposed on the generals in the conduct of the reprisal campaign against Habre's forces. As reported by Africa Confidential, following the 1983/84 coup in Nigeria, the political handling of the border battle with Chad infuriated nearly all senior officers involved and may have expedited the overthrow of Shagari's administration. It is not surprising that one of the ring-leaders in the coup-General Babangida – disclosed that the coup was first planned for July, 1983, that is just after the cessation of hostilities in the Lake Chad basin[60]. Similarly, the disposition of the current military establishment has been a major obstacle to the peaceful resolution of the Niger Delta Crisis.

The current dimension of the crisis is arguably a systemic resultant of intense "bureaucratic politics" with the military establishment pushing for a "final solution" in line with the decisive action against Biafran secession. This melodrama is played out in the official circles of Nigeria's Federal Government with the unmistakable paradigm shift of policy discourse from accommodation, empathy and negotiation which characterized the initial period after Sani Abacha's death to the language of criminality, gangsterism, social banditry, terrorism and force.

MEND and NDV leadership are now declared criminals and the 2009 Appropriation Bill of the Federal Government entrenches four hundred and fifty billion, naira for "security" in the Niger Delta while only sixty billion naira is allocated for infrastructure and social programs intervention through Niger Delta Development Commission. The implication is unmistakable: with less sympathy for the struggle against "domestic colonialism" in the Niger Delta, the dominant "groupthink" in the Yar'Adua Administration reflects the Columbian/Zairean solution – a crushing military response to the audacity of MEND and its affiliates. It is not surprising, therefore, in May 2009, the Nigerian state unleashed its armed forces, as Awhefeada put it:

> On the hapless and long exploited people of the Niger Delta. A most horrendous and fratricidal onslaught, the ongoing military blitzkrieg has been conceived to brutally subjugate, and if need be annihilate, a target group that has championed the Niger Delta struggle for a decade now--- so far thousands of innocent citizens have died, hundreds of thousands displaced; hunger and hardship now stalk the living --- the ongoing state orchestrated war will achieve noting [61].

It would be tempting to conclude that Yar' Adua action is a clear viewpoint which his predecessor (with the exception of the "Scorth earth" retaliation for the killing of police officers at Odi) has long resisted as futile. However, as Wole Soyinka has noted in his indicting piece, the "stubborn retention of the status quo, and its manifest rejection by components parts, is at the heart of the Delta crisis". President

Yar'Adua's "lackadaisical approach towards these contentious issues has become increasingly clarified as not one of governance indifference or lack of understanding, but complicity through inaction"[62]. It is not surprising, therefore, that surrounded by his military chiefs after that "horrendous and fratricidal onslaught", he dictated the terms of "amnesty". Militants must surrender arms in 60days"[63].

There is no doubt that the case for force is invariably predicated on the consideration that it is the primary responsibility of the armed forces of any country to defend its core and context specific values against external aggression and domestic insurrections. Thus, whether conceived in terms of its direct or indirect employment, the military has become in the modern era the legally sanctioned instrument of violence which states use in their relations with each other, and, where necessary, in an internal security role.

However, differences between the service chiefs and their political bosses in the National Defence and National Security Councils during the 1981 and 1983 border crises (as well as the prevailing crisis in Niger Delta) raises vital constitutional question bearing on the direction of national military statecraft. First, while from a purely military standpoint, the frustration of the officers regarding the conduct of both border crises can be understood, it has to be remembered that war as Clemenceau is reputed to have said, is "much too serious a matter to be left to the generals" it has been one the distinguishing traits of the military mind (the "groupthink" factor) in conflict situations that operational imperatives tend to dominate all other aspects of policy. In this respect, General, MacArthur's defiant comment in relation to the Korean Stalemate – that "in war there is no substitute for Victory" – touches a responsive chord in most, if not all, military establishment[64].

Nevertheless, if war is too deadly a business to be left to the Generals, it is also too technical to be left to the politicians. What is, therefore, required as Henry Kissinger has persuasively argued, is a "dialogue, between political and military minds." As he put it:

> .....a separation of strategy and policy can be achieved only to the detriment of both. It causes military policy to become identified with the most absolute applications of power and it tempts diplomacy into an over concern with finesse. Since the difficult problems of national policy are in the area where political, economic, psychological and military factors overlap, we should give up the fiction that there is such a thing as "purely military" advice[65].

There is substantive evidence to support the view of a lapse in "dialogue" between military and political elites during both the border crises of May, 1981 (with Cameroun) and April to June 1983 (with Chad). The reason was, perhaps, primarily organizational. As the Chief Executive and Commander-in-Chief of the Armed Forces, President Shagari had the Armed Forces" subject, of course, to the provision of Section 167 (4a) which empowered the National Assembly to amend the "powers exercisable by the President as Cammender-in-Chief of the Armed Forces". However, the President was required under section 131 of the constitution to seek advice from the National Defence Council "on matters relating to the defence of the sovereignty and the territorial integrity of Nigeria".

The National Defence Council consisted of the President (Chair), the Vice-President, the Defence Minster, Head of the Combined Armed Forces, and the Army and Navy. One significant omission was the Minister for External Affairs – Ishaya Audu. As was anticipated and forewarned by a number of foreign policy scholars, this omission was to create avoidable divergences in crisis management between the Ministry of External Affairs and the Defence Establishment. Commenting on the Exclusion of the Minister of External Affairs from the National Defence Council, Akindele, for example, wrote:

> If war is diplomacy by other means, as Clausewitz has correctly stated, it is rather difficult to understand why the Minister for External Affairs, charged with the statutory duty of assisting the President to formulate and implement foreign policy, has been excluded from membership of the Council[66].

It became fairly obvious from decision-making process during the two border incidents involving Cameroun (May, 1981) and Chad (April to June, 1983) analysed above, that it was the Ministry of External Affairs rather than the National Defence Council, which became the dominant bureaucratic agent in the resolution of the conflicts. As a consequence, the military establishment's perception and position on the changing operational environment tended to be ignored or relegated. Given the potentially volatile and unstable (praetorian) civil-military relations in Nigeria, it was to be expected, as was reported at the time that a "secret" meeting of senior officers, including Buhari, decided after the "border fiasco" that the army would not support Shagari politically[67].

Despite such lapses in co-operation among "political and military minds", what is, however, impressive about the entire border episode was the quickness and decisiveness with which the politician Shagari dictated the limit of what was acceptable to the Generals. Thus reminding them, in Clausewitz's words, that "the subordination of the political points of view to the military would be unreasonable, for policy has created the war, policy is the intelligent faculty, war only the instrument, and not the reverse[68].

For Clausewitz, as well as most contemporary strategists, policy direction and control of war are paramount, irrespective of one's attitude towards war's desirability. If policy creates war, the "political object" – the original motive for the war will thus determine both the military objectives to be reached and the amount of effort require. Thus a conception of international conflict resolution in terms of "military victory" versus "political victory" would be a contradiction in terms. As Clausewitz aptly notes: "there can be no question of purely military evaluation of a great strategic issue, or of a purely military scheme to solve it."[69]. When war is divorced from "political life in our thinking we are left with something pointless and devoid of sense[70].

Seen in this context, it is thus to be concluded that the Shagari administration's skillful combination of "stick and carrot" approach effectively contained the crises before it escalated into senseless conflagration with incalculable consequences for the policy of "good neighbourliness" which Nigeria had carefully cultivated and formalized in the ECOWAS treaty. If the barrier was broken, there was no way of knowing the consequences and future ramifications of invading Cameroun or Chad. Yet it is also to be granted that in any given conflict situation, the choice of means may depend not only on their availability to decision-makers, but also on their expected cost and efficacy. In this regard the extent to which different instruments of power are of unequal effectiveness also limits the substitution of one for the other.

The major problem with techniques of influence other than military is their historically – proven ineffectiveness. This is preeminently the case with the diplomatic instrument and with the various uses of national or collective economic power and propaganda to coerce or influence foreign governments. This is not to imply of course that diplomacy ends when "the shooting starts" or that military force is always a more reliable instrument of foreign policy whenever diplomacy fails to secure policy objectives. Furthermore, what strengthens the necessity for a mutually reinforcing relationship between the military and diplomatic means is not merely that war, as Ken Booth puts it, has become "a deadly business" but also that in so far as both means lie at the root of the "sovereign equality of a political community" their exercise by governments are necessarily inseparable. Henry Kissinger explain why:

> It is an illusion of posterity that past international settlement were brought about entirely by reasonableness and negotiating skill. In a society of "sovereign" states, a power can in the last resort vindicate its interpretation of justice and defend its "vital interests" only by the willingness to employ force. Even during the period of seemingly greatest harmony. It was understood that a negotiation which failed did not return matters to their starting points but might call other pressures into play. The motive force behind international settlements has always been a combination of the belief in the advantages of harmony and the fear of the consequences of proving obdurate. A renunciation of force, by eliminating the penalty for intransigence, will therefore place the international order at the mercy of its most ruthless or its most irresponsible member[72].

In the light of this consideration it may on the balance be argued that the decision to activate Nigeria's military power against Habre's forces does not represent a fundamental departure from its defence policy posture towards its neighbours. It signified rather a policy of measured response based on a compelling need for deterrence and restraint, if further armed infringements on its territory are to be effectively contained. Since such an option requires as sound military policy, the reflection of professional military view point in both the management of the crisis and conduct of war was imperative. In future contingences, this dialogue between political and military minds could be sustained through and innovative and representative national security management "regime" which combines the functions of the National Defence Council and the National Security Council of the defunct Second Republic. Such a novel institutional arrangement and design will facilitate co-ordination at the policy level and thereby ensure consensus and coherence in strategic policy response to situational challenges.

While the assertiveness of the Generals in the current Niger Delta Crisis has been less publicly combative, the consequence of their stand has been unmistakable: that the "seemingly unending violence in the Niger Delta area was being championed by a dangerous band of psychopathic, merciless mercenaries who exploit their sophistry to kill, rape, kidnap, destroy and extort money from anybody available"[73]. This affront to the security of the Nigerian State must, therefore, be met frontally and decisively as it did in response of Isaac Boro's rebellion, Maitasine uprising, Odi and Zaki Biam Crisis.

On this view, the failure of the armed forces to accomplish the operational objectives of Operation Restore Hope and Operation Flush Out ("arresting the deteriorating security situation in the region and to prevent spread of the crisis to other parts of the Niger Delta") has less to do with the difficult terrain of the Niger Delta and the determination and dexterity of youth militancy, but more to governmental equivocation at providing the necessary logistical resources to the Joint Task Force. It is, however, quiet pertinent to ask whether if all the above requirements for operational effectiveness were met, the military option alone can contain and stifle the current rebellion against the Nigerian state and multinational oil companies. The answer of course is categorically no. As Sunny Awhefeada trenchantly argues:

> The ongoing state orchestrated war will achieve nothing. It will further exacerbate the crisis. The Niger Delta fighters, be they revolutionaries, militants, or "criminals" as the state brands them, should be invited to peace talk. What is needed is neither force nor monologue. The resistance being put up by MEND is Justifiable. In all history every people, under such inhuman oppression ultimately took to arms to right wrongs. [74]

The May 2009 military offensive was calculated destroy the infrastructure that supports MEND and its affiliates in the Niger Delta and in the process weaken their power of resistance. The result was quite the opposite as MEND accepted neither the "carrot" of amnesty (and surrender arms within 60days) or tremble and bow to the vastly augmented military might of the Joint Task Force. Quite the contrary. They launched a devastating attack on the petroleum complexes – (depot, flow stations, pipelines etc) in the Delta region and, for the first time, extended their reach to Atlas ⌐ove in Lagos.

⌐SIS

⌐l inferences can be drawn from the contributions in this volume. First,
⌐l level, consideration of Nigerian military power as an instrument of

security and crisis – management is fundamentally hampered by two ambiguities and one unknown. These conceptual problems stem partly from the conditional nature of the instrumentality of military power as it applies to Nigeria in existing and likely future conditions, and partly from the general ambivalence and nebulous posture of the Nigerian state in regional and world politics.

Nevertheless, it has been the basic contention in the volume that for Nigeria, as is the case with most countries, the pivotal link between the military instrument and the imperatives of national security and crisis management is a direct consequence of the nature of contemporary international system as a "threat system"--- a competition of units in the kind of a "state of nature that knows no restraints other than those which the changing necessities of the game and the shallow conveniences of the players impose"[75]. In this respect, the development and expansion of national "power of resistance" has been widely viewed by the Nigerian policy-makers since the civil war era as the <u>Sine qua non </u>for preservation of basic values on which the country's survival as a socio-political entity rests. Similarly, in terms of crisis management, considerations of military power have acted as counters in diplomatic bargaining, so that in serious disputes, diplomacy became a 'trial of influence and strength, including military strength even though it is also a test of wits and skill[76], as was the case of Chad (1983) and Cameroun over Bakassi Peninsula.

In this regard, Nigerian Military power has featured severally (with a varying mix of diplomacy and economic sanctions) in the post-independence era as an instrument of security and crisis management. It has been employed coercively in order to influence the behaviour of opponents (Equatorial Guinea and Cameroun) or in order to alter or preserve the status quo, either by the sheer feat of attack or defence (e.g., against 'Biafra' and Chad) or through peacekeeping/peace-enforcement actions (the Congo and Tanzania in the early 1960s; Chad and Lebanon in the late 1970s and early 1980s; Liberia and Sierra Leone in the 1990s).

Second, and parallel to the first, at the level of defence decision-making and planning, there has been a definite and qualitative change in perceptions and attitudes among Nigeria's policy elite towards the use and usability of national military power as an instrument of policy. This marked re-orientation in 'value parameter' concerning force has arguably coincided with, indeed been expedited by, changing domestic capabilities, systemic challenges, and regimes: from the conservative and highly introspective period of Balewa (1960-1966) to a more dynamic and assertive era of Mohammed/Obasanjo (1975-1976) and Babangida-Abacha (Liberia and Sierra Leone. The later is characterized by an increasing acceptance and cultivation of a 'realist' philosophy which views military power as "but one of the many technique of statecraft, taking its place alongside diplomacy, economic sanctions, propaganda and so on".

This development, eminently symbolized by the Afrocentric activism of the Mohammed/Obasanjo administration (or even by the less tempestuous, albeit unprecedented revanchist posture toward unruly neighbours of the Babangida-Abacha governments), has been neither haphazard nor transient. On the contrary derives from a complex set of rapidly evolving relationships between recent historical circumstances and present conditions (both domestic and external). It has been an end-result of internal tumult as well as untoward events in the African continent since the early sixties. For instance, the unprecedented levels of foreign intervention (especially of France, Portugal, Spain, South Africa and the defunct Rhodesia) in the Nigerian civil war, contributed to dramatic alteration of threat perceptions (and definitions) held by Nigeria's policy-makers of their country's security. Nigeria's security (that is, the protection of its basic and 'context-specific' values) has since been inextricably linked to the elimination of colonialism in Southern Africa and to the containment of French influence in West Africa. In other words, judging from the direction of Nigeria's foreign and defence policy planning since the civil war, the domestic environment no longer constitutes the exclusive radius of security concern as was clearly the case in the First Republic.

Thus, unlike the prevailing attitudes, perception and complacency which characterized the security posture of the Balewa administration, the dominant 'mind set' in Nigerian government circles since the civil war has been that the survival, security and independence of Nigeria cannot be assured as long as Southern Africa remains under treacherous settler and colonial regimes sustained by powerful external interest and forces. As a consequence, it became integral to strategic thinking in Nigeria to view the country's boundaries in terms of three interrelated concentric circles.

Third, with this amplified redefinition of threat to security of Nigeria, coupled with the questionable claim of the country to be the dominant power in Black Africa came a magnified 'role-conception and 'organizational task expansion' for it's military establishment in foreign policy. Thus, unlike in the First Republic when the roles of the armed forces were conceived largely in terms of ceremonial and internal security duties (besides limited involvement in peace-keeping operations), the emerging pattern of Nigeria's military policy from the 1970s envisages active and vigorous involvement for the defence establishment in regional affairs[77]. Two policy statements by high ranking officials in the late 1970s and early 1980s attest to this trend. The first was the announcement in 1977 by then Chief of Army Staff, T. Y. Danjuma, that in order to speed up the collapse of the white regimes in South Africa, the government 'would be prepared to send troops to assist the freedom fighters. And the second was the reaction of Ishaya Audu, then Minister of External Affairs, to Washington's veto of the UN resolution condemning South Africa for its attack on Angola in September 1981:

> *There is definitely a feeling that Africa should participate in the defence of Angola. There is a feeling that if Cuba is in the position to help, then, Africa should be even more in a position to help......*
> *As far as Nigerian is concerned, if asked, Nigeria would look at it ...tively.*

...osition was later given expression in a series of peace-support ...) and response to Cameroun provocation in Bakassi Peninsula. ... of military power in Nigeria foreign and security policy has undergone a step-level change from the 'anti-militarist' proclivity of the Balewa era. For over a broad range of regional issues, the military instrument is now viewed as the ultima ratio: one of the bases of diplomacy and of contractual obligations beyond the boundaries of the state.

In this respect, the major preoccupations, indeed, the basic components of Nigerian defence policy and planning since the mid-1970s have been: a) armed forces modernization an augmentation that touches upon all elements of Nigerian military power with the aim of improving its efficiency, enhancing its conventional firepower and creating a regional mobility for the especial units (b) intensive materials and diplomatic support for the liberation movements, including, in the late 1970s, the deployment of the Nigerian Air Force Transport Command in Tanzania to provide logistical support to the Patriotic Front forces based in Zambia and Mozambique (c) actively coordinated operational planning between the ANC and the PAC through its military mission in Harare, and elements from both liberation movements and SWAPO also received advanced tactical training in the Nigerian Defence Academy, Kaduna; and pursuit of a strategy of collective defence through regional and /or continental coordination and cooperation, as expressed in peace support operations in the continent (ECOMOG and AU Force in Darfur).

Nigeria's principle objective in this regard has been to create, both at continental and regional levels, a 'collective security' mechanism that can provide 'African solutions to African conflicts' and thereby limit foreign penetration and control. However, the extremely low-degree of ideological consciousness in the AU-system as regards the real value of a regional defence mechanics, combined with the deepening dependence (military, economic, technological and political) of most African countries on the major industrial powers, has so far made the actualization of this strategy hopelessly limited despite the new AU Security architecture involving African standby force.

Nevertheless, since the failure of a collective ideological awareness regarding regional security is itself accentuated, above all, by dissonance in national ideologies of development, it is not altogether improbable that intensification of current contradictions in the global capitalist economy might engender increasing acceptance of strategies for collective self-reliance in economic as well as security related issues. To this extent, the AU Protocol Relating to the establishment of the peace and security council of the African Union (2001) and the inauguration of the ECOWAS protocol on Mutual Assistance on Defence may well strengthen the ideological (and political) bases of a collective strategy of providing "African solutions to African conflicts".

Finally, while three has undoubtedly been a fundamental re-orientation in both the role-conception and organizational task expansion for the military in Nigerian statecraft, the actual/potential use and usability (that is, policy operationalisation) of the Nigerian military instrument remains constrained by certain structural deficiencies in its domestic environment. These include a frail socio-economic and technological base, the limited striking power of its armed forces (a consequence of its nascent 'military-industrial complex) and its declining reserves of international liquidity (foreign exchange) resulting from global recession and OECD countervailing strategies against OPEC. Assuming the vitality of any threat of Nigeria's security interests, the latter factor – the state of Nigeria's foreign exchange reserves and balance of payments since 2008 has probably become a key influence on the actual employment of the Nigerian military as an instrument of national policy (either for warfighting or peacekeeping) beyond its immediate border.

As case studies of Libyan vigilantism in Africa and Iraqi activism in the Middle East suggest, the ability of a country to run a substantial import surplus on the strength of either large holdings of foreign currencies and gold, or borrowing power – permits it, for a time at least, to accelerate the buildup and use of military strength.

Nigeria's armed forces modernization programme (purportedly intended to make its defence system the best in Africa and comparable to the best the world") involving enormous capital expenditures on major weapons platforms (planes, tanks and naval vessels) was essentially predicated upon continued accumulation of foreign exchange earnings from oil production, estimated at 2.5 million barrels a day at $40 a barrel. There is no doubt that if such a huge spinoff from oil production had been sustained over time, Nigeria, like Libya or Iraq, would have significantly upgraded its conventional military capability, and with overriding confidence pursued a combative Afro-centric military policy.

Given the ramifications of Nigeria's diminished economic position ("the most significant development in Black Africa in the decade", as one analyst put it) grounds for optimistic forecasts about the future direction of Nigeria's military policy are necessarily diminished. In the immediate term, Nigeria is likely to continue to face formidable internal difficulties, and these problems will inescapably have an impact on its ability to function as a regional power. As Ogunsanwo has noted, 'bold foreign policy positions and stances are hardly sustainable for a considerable period without the domestic infrastructural underpinnings which form the solid foundation for such policies[79].

However, while intractable domestic problems may limit the choice of means available to Nigerian decision-makers, it is also be expected that, to the extent that they are of unequal effectiveness (thus limiting the substitution of one for the other), the role of military power in Nigerian policy will still expand, as regional conflict and domestic insurrection intensify.

This extrapolation of defence policy planning trends in the country is in accord with undiminished level of defence spending and the continued commitment of the government to build a viable 'military-industrial' base, while at the same time expediting deliveries of major weapons systems to the armed forces. Chuka Okadigbo, once noted: "People tend to think as a result of the glut in the world oil market, Nigerian will have to jettison its foreign policy. This is naïve. A temporary situation should not be considered a permanent situation"[80].

Indeed, as the great depression of the late 1920s and early 1930s engendered the Keynesian revolution in the Western capitalist economies, so the prevailing assumption in the country that Nigeria's economic problems are amenable over time to fundamental structural changes and comprehensive development strategies based on national 'self-reliance' is not altogether fatuous. 'Nigeria', as Pauline Baker once explained, still has reasonable options. With oil reserves of about 2.5 billion barrels, a large market potential, and a reputation as an under borrowed country whose political importance cannot ignored, Nigeria has the capacity to pull through this crisis just as it pulled through the civil war. What is less certain is the political impact that these conditions will have internally and the willingness of the general population to pay the price of recovery"[81].

Ultimately, of course, what is needed to sustain an effective strategic policy (independently or as part of a collective regional defence system) is the progressive development of a technological base of power by Nigeria. Such a self-reliant economic, industrial and financial base is the sine qua non of a strong military force, the inescapable prerequisite for Nigeria's emergence as an autonomous centre of power in the regional sub-system of Africa: the ultimate goals of its foreign and defence policies and plans.

REFERENCES

1. F. Greene, Dynamics of International Relations, New York: Holt Rinehart and Wisdom, 1966.
2. C. O. Bassey "Nigeria's Defence Policy in a future continental order" Nigerian Journal of International Affairs, 13, 2, 1987: 83-105.
3. See, among others, T. A. Imobighe, Nigerian Defence and Security. Kuru: NIPSS, 1987 and O. S. Kamanu "Nigeria : Reflections on the Defence Posture for the 1980s" Geneve – Afrique 16, 1977-78.
4. Claude, Sworrds Into Plowshares.
5. H. Kissinger, Nuclear Eeapons and Foreign Policy, New York: Harper and Row, 1957.
6. S. Huntington, The common Defence N. Y. Columbia University Press, 1966:1.
7. See B. Akinterinwa (ed): Nigeria's National Interests In a Globalising World. Ibadan: Bolytag Publishers, 2007 Vol5 1-3.
8. D. Murray and P. Vioti: (eds). The Defence Policy of Nations. Baltimore: The John Hopkins University Press, 1982:5-7.
9. K. Knorr, Power, Strategy and Security Princeton: Princeton University Press, 1983.
10. K. Booth Strategy and Ethnocentricism. N. Y. Holes and Mclver. 1979.
11. J. Lovell, "The Idiom of National Security" Journal of Political and Military Sociology 2, 1983:36.
12. Kolodzcerty, E. and Harkavy (eds). Security Policies of Developing Countries. Lexington: Lexington press, 1982.
13. See C. O. Bassey, "Nigeria's Defence Policy in a Future Continental Order "Nigerian Journal of International Affairs.

14. See M. Vogt and A. Ekoko eds. Defence Policy of Nigeria: Issues and problems. Lagos: Malthouse, 1990.
15. See C. O. Bassey, "Defence Planning and the Nigerian Armed Forces Modernization Process, 1970-1990: An Institutional Analysis" Armed Forces and Society, 1992/1993:253-277.
16. See B. Ate and B. Akinterinwa eds. Nigeria and its immediate Neighbours: Constraints and Prospects of Sub-Regional Security in the 1990s Lagos: Pumark, 1992.
17. See Report of the Armed Force Transformation Committee, Ministry of Defence April 2008.
18. See J. Garba, Diplomatic Soldering. Ibadan: Spectrum, 1987.
19. R. Ullman, "Redefining Security" International Security 8, 1983:129.
20. R. Barnett, The Root of War. Harmindsworth: Pengum.
21. C. O. Bassey, "Restraint Factor in Nigeria's Military Statecraft: Theory and Evidence" UNICAL Quarterly Vol. 1, No. 2 March 1996: 180-195.
22 J. Rosenau ed. In Search of Global Patterns N. Y. Free Press, 1976.
23. J. Garnett, "Strategic Studies and its Assumptions" in John Bayhs et. Al. Contemporary strategy N. Y. Holmes and Meiw, 1980.
24. A. Rapoport, "Introduction" to Clausewitz, On War. Harmondsworth: Pelican, 1978.
25. A. Mazrui, The Warrior Tradition in Modern Africa Leiden: Brill, 1977.
26. See C. O. Bassey "The Military Instrument and Strategic Policy in a Democratic Order: A Theoretical Reconsideration of some Unresolved Issues Concerning Nigeria" The Journal of Political Science, xiii, N 1, 2, 1990: 15-31.
27. R. Weighley, The American Way of War: A History of "United States Military Strategy and Policy. London: Collier MacMillan, 1973.
28. Q. Wright, A Study of War Chicago Press, 1964.
29. Constitution of the Federal Republic of Nigeria Abuja: Federal Ministry of Information, 1999.
30. R. V. Denenberg, Understanding American Politics: New York: Vintage, 1976.
31. See M. Janowitz, Military Institutions and Coercion in the Developing Nations Chicago: The University of Chicago Press, 1977.
32. K. Knorr, The Power of Nations: Basic Books, 1975
33. O. Fasehun, "Nigeria and the of an African High Command" Afrika spectrum 80, 3 (15 Jahrgang).
34. G. Ijewere, "Nigeria in International Relations" Review of International Affairs, 32, 738 (5 January, 1981), 26-80. Also see N. Chouri, "The Non-Alignment of Afro-Asian States: Policy, Perception and Behaviour" Canadian Journal of Political Science II, 1 (March 1969):14.
35. See O. Aluko, Nigerian Foreign Policy: London: 1983.
36. J. Derivera. The Psychological Dimension of foreign policy. Columbus: Merrill, 1968.
37. See C. O. Bassey, "African States and the Politics of Continental Defence" Nigerian Journal of International Affairs Vol. 19, No. 1 (1993) 48-71.

38 N. Chouri, "The Non-Alignment of Afro-Asian States: Policy, Perception and Behaviour" Canadian Journal of Political Science 11, 1 (March, 1969): 14

39. See G. Idang, Nigeria: Internal Politics and Foreign Policy. Ibadan: University of Ibadan Press, 1977.

40. Ibid:38.

41. A. Tijjani and D. William eds. Shehu Shagari: My vision of Nigeria. London: Frank Cass, 1981.

42. E. Ikwue, Chief of Airstaff, quoted in Daily Times, 21 March 1974.

43. Long Live Africa. Text of the Statement by Major General Yakubu Gowon at the Seventh OAU Assembly of Heads of State and Government, Addis Abacha, 1-4 September, 1970.

44. See the text of Gowon's address to the Agro-American Dialogue meeting in Lagos in March 1971, the Morning Post, 10 March 1971.

45. A. Sotunmbi, Nigeria's Recognition of the MPLA Government of Angola: A Case-Study in Decision making and implementation. Lagos: NIIA, 1981.

46. Ibid : 14.

47. A. Ogunsanwo, The Nigerian Military and Foreign Policy, 1975-1979 centre of International Studies, Princeton University, June 1980:75.

48. T. Shaw and A. Aluko eds: Nigerian Foreign Policy. London: Macmillan, 1983.

49. A. Tijjani and D. Williams (eds). Shehu Shagari: My vision of Nigeria.

50. See B. Akinterinwa ed; Nigeria's National Interests in a Globalising World. Ibadan: Bolytag Int. Publishers, 2007.

51. G. Copley "Ibrahim Babangida on Nigeria's Future" Defence and Foreign Affairs, February, 1987:15.

52. See A. Adebajo. Liberia's Civil War: Nigeria ECOMOG and Regional Security in West Africa. London: Lynne Rienner, 2002:20.

53. I. B. Babangida

54. See P. Williams, "From Non-Intervention to Non-Indifference: The Origins and Development of the African Unions Security Culture" African Affairs, 106/423, 2007:250.

55. C. O. Bassey, "Defence Planning and the Nigerian Armed Forces Modernization Process, 1970-1991, Armed Forces and Society, 19,2. 1993.

56. J. B. Adekanye, "Domestic Production of Arms and the Defence Industries Corporation of Nigeria" Current Research on Peace and Violence 4 (1983), 258-269.

57. Ibid:262

58. McGowan and Shapiro, The Comparative Study of Foreign Policy. NY. Free Press, 1967 . Also see J. Rosenau, el eds. World Politics. N. Y. Free Press, 1976:16.

59 Africa Confidential, 25, I January, 1984 P.I.

60. Africa Confidential 24, 12, June 8, 1983.

61. Suny Awhefeada. "The Guardian Newspaper" 29 May 2009.

62. Wole Soyinka,"

63. Nation

64. As qoted in B. Brodie, War and Politics London: MacMillan, 1973:103.
65. H. Kissinger, Nuclear Weapons and Foreign Policy. N. Y: Harper and Row, 1957:422.
66. R. Akindele "External Affairs and War Power Under the Draft Constitution" in Akinyemi ed. Foreign Policy and the Constitution. Lagos: NIIA Monograph Series
67. See African Research Bulletin, Vol. 20, 5, June 15, 1983.
68. Clausewitz On War edited and translated by M. Howard and P. Paret Princeton: Princeton University Press, 1976.
69. Ibid. pp 379-380
70. Ibid pp 605.
71. K. Booth. Strategy and Ethnocentricism, N. Y. Holmes and Mclver, 1979.
72. Kissinger, Nuclear Weapons and Foreign Policy p.4.
73. S. Dare, The News Magazine Vol. 11, No. 9. 14. September, 1998.
74. Awhefeada op. cit
75. S. Hoffmann, The State of War N. Y. Praeger, 1965:vii. Stanley Hoffmann, The State of War, (N. Y: Praeger 1965), p. vii.
76. Klaus Knorr, On the Uses of Military Power in the Nuclear Age, (Princeton: Princeton University Press, 1966), p.20.
77. See Aminu Tijjani and David Williams (eds), Shelu Shagari, (London: Frank Cass, 1981), Chapters 6 and 12, H. A. Hananiya, "Nigeria's Defence Policy Against South Africa", (SEC-1, 16); Falope Kola, "Regional Security for West Africa" (SEC-1, 16); and B. A. Idiagbon, "Strategies for Liberation of Southern Africa", all in National Institute Library, Kuru, November 1982. See also Pauline Baker, "A Giant Staggers: Nigeria as an emerging regional power" in Bruce Arlinghaus (ed.), African Security Issues, (Boulder: Westview, 1984), pp. 76-97.
78. West Africa, 3349, 5 October 1981, p. 2292. See also Shehu Shagari, "Nigeria's Foreign Policy", Nigeria Forum 2 12 (December 1982), p. 879.
79. Alaba Ogunsanwo, The Nigerian Military and Foreign Policy, 1975-1979, Research Monograph No. 45, Center of International Studies, Princeton University, June 1980, p. 73.
80. New York Times, 27 July, 1981.
81. Baker, "A Giant Staggers: Nigeria as an Emerging Regional Power", P. 89.

multi-form structures of threats to a broad spectrum of vital interests such as "organic survival of a given national population, protection".

Thus in contrast to the conventional at view, the nature and type of threats involved is the expanded concept of security in much more complex and hard to detect particularly due to dynamic causal links among four major dimensions of security; i.e., military, economic, ecological, and ethnic. As S. Dalby explains:

> The traditional approach presents many limitations when applied to developing countries... the complexity and multiple vulnerabilities of developing countries compel us to look at deeper structure and a broader spectrum of issue – nexus by which threat perceptions are perceived and security policies formulated and implemented. This is particularly true because there is no clear-cut distinction between national and regime security.[28]

Thus, the changing pattern of global ideological and regional security system relations has engendered fundamental ontological and epistemic reconstruction of the matrix of African security problematique in the conventional literature. The conventional paradigm of thought and analysis of defence – security nexus in Africa lacks historical contextualization. This metaphysical construction of security as stasis and partial exclusion entrenched benign neorealist assumption of the immutability of African Social order. A genealogical deconstruction of this rationalistic pretentions in the dominant epistemology on security discourse in Africa calls for, on the one hand, a demystification of latent assumptions and "thought forces" it enshrines. On the other hand, it requires a policy response which takes account of the changing character and structural deformities of the neocolonial state as the fundamental sources of insecurity in Africa.

This being the case "the most important task is to locate the complex relationships among these threat dimensions, instead of searching for an artificial priority ordering of the government's vital values". In the existing climate of economic collapse, mounting foreign debts and debt-servicing obligations, declining terms of trade, mass immiserisation, the intensification of class contradictions and conflict, the non-military dimension of security issues in Africa has been aptly described in reverse as "high politics". The immediate concern has centered on the dual issues of economic deprivation and protracted social conflict. Their overt structural expression is widely seeing in entropic syndrome leading to political disintegration and secessionist movements, triggering in turn intra-territorial threats to national security.[29]

Given the centrality of the state as defining characteristic of the socio-political process, the need to address significant structural and distributive problems is now considered the locus of security analysis and policy responses to the malignant social context of the African region. This is so because, primordial cleavages, as Gurr and Dalby have noted, do not "automatically lead to political disintegration and separatist movements and by implication a threat to national security". The State's role in terms of extractive and distributive capabilities is paramount and the question of "how to deal with political separatism and with related security dilemma is more of a political, social problem than one of the military strategic dimension".[30]

Nevertheless, the disruptive effects of revolutionary insurgency (as in Angola, Sierra Leone and the Democratic Republic of Congo), armed banditry (as in North East Zone of Nigeria) and the perceived need to deter external aggression (such as mercenary attack in Central African Republic and Irredentist movements in some parts of Africa) have all combined to heighten the need to maintain a professional military establishment in African countries. However, this calls for a balanced allocation of resources between the military and non-military sectors of the society, and among purposes of government. The persistent tendencies either to treat the defence component in the budgeting equation separately, something to be considered on merit without reference to other goals, unleashed an unprecedented groundswell of discontent and controversy about priorities in national planning and resource allocation in countries such as Nigeria in the 1980s and 1990s.

The magnitude of defence outlay in the Babangida – Abacha era (1985 -1998) became a key issue in the new pattern of fiscal politics in Nigeria as "the revolution of rising expectations" generated tremendous upsurge in demand for other social needs – education, health, agriculture, industry, communication. While the defence establishment still remains a vital instrument in the gamut of national security management regimes in Africa, there is an imperative need in responding to systematic changes to make explicit distinction between what is desirable and what is feasible in terms of accurate balancing of objectives and commitments within the overall context and projected capabilities. Policy objectives may be desirable but unrealistic because the military and non-military means of international prevalence available to African governments are insufficient to produce desired policy results; or, because employing the armed forces in certain ways is inappropriate in certain conditions to a particular policy goal, such as restoring normalcy in Chad or Liberia through peacekeeping. The reason for the latter is fairly obvious. Peacekeeping, as one analyst rightly argues, is "in the first place, likely to be rarely appropriate; the necessary satisfaction of numerous pre-conditions means that only very seldom will a peacekeeping force be both feasible and desirable".[31]

As the Congo, Cyprus, Lebanon and the Chadian examples have highlighted, peacekeeping in a domestic political quagmire is a trap for the overbold and the unwary. The existence of competing and mutually hostile armed factions (tied to the competitive intrusion of regional and extra-regional interests) invariably nullify the prospects of generating a consensus on which the success of peace-keeping operation is predicated. The possibility that the factions in such vortex of power struggle would simply utilize the presence of a peacekeeping force to augment their firepower in preparation for inevitable showdown has compelled even major powers to proceed with caution as was the case of NATO in Yugoslavia.

Nevertheless, for a number of reasons (organizational, doctrinal and the imponderables of warfare) it is far from easy to calculate the relevance of military means to the achievement of certain policy objectives. It is far from easy to foresee precisely because the "relevant realities and their interaction are complex", because the total problem was for purposes of decision –making, be 'decomposed into manageable parts', and because "the results of these analyses must be brought together and sensibly integrated for proper decision-making (Knorr and Morgernstern, 1968:333).

Nevertheless, in the emerging condition of 21st century (and in the light of the objective conditions in the region) a viable and sustainable defence policy for African States must be anchored on the harmonization of the various components elements of its defence policy-military power, policy objectives and international arena-if balance, order, stability, consensus, and habit is to replace the current uncertainties, conflict of choice, change and disorder. In other words, as an alternative to the current dysfunctions, a more realistic approach to defence policy planning in the changing dynamics of the operational environment is to integrate both national military capability and intentions, and to do so within a broad picture or frame work of a minimalist foreign and defence policy objectives and posture. This is so because defence policy is not only concerned with the calculated responses of states to perceive systemic threats, but also with "institutional structure by which government make and implement their defence policies," as well as with the "whole domestic political process as it affects policy-making" (Bobrow, 1965:9). It is in this regard that one may assert that the major focus of defence policy of African States in this century would be to confront squarely and resolve at the policy level the persistent problematique in military statecraft.

This involves the imperative necessity of making explicit judgment about the scope and direction of defence policy commitments as well as the conditions for possessing the ability (structure, magnitude and institutional parameters of defence establishment) to meet these functions and challenges. Although defence planners of a number of states in the region have in the past and present responded to situational challenges in their security environment with a mix of sophistication and foresight, significant disharmonies or disequlibrium, nevertheless, presently exist between the various elements of defence policy: capability, objectives, and environment. These disharmonies span two interrelated levels, corresponding to the most primary, "the most distinctive, the most fascinating and the most troublesome aspects" of defence policy. The first is essentially structural and involves in this case the operational readiness of their armed forces as a function of the materials decisions concerning acquisition of weapons and technology of war.

The second level defence policy problematique is preeminently strategic in nature: the discrepancy between the declare of policy goals of Nigeria and the operational ability of their armed forces to provide the means for their actualization. As Klaus Knorr (1979) has rightly noted, "foreign policy objectives must be retrenched in order to bring them into a proper relation with the means available for their implementation, or the conduct of foreign policy may suffer from lack of effective power[32]". A cursory examination of the relationship between defence and foreign policies of Nigeria reveals that in many respects the two related areas of policy have remained poles apart. This failure of Nigerian policy planners to coordinate foreign and defence policy in the past has meant that instead of an overall integrated course of action, a number of independent and often spasmodic lines of action were pursued. The consequence of this dearth of overall political direction and coordination of defence and foreign policy since the 1970s in the security policies has been in a state of flux as attempts have been made to meet changing situational challenges arising from regional as well as domestic circumstances.

Regarding the first problematique, under the conditions created by contemporary configurations in international power (dominated by NATO), the successful exploitation or utilization of military power as an instrument of policy by economically and militarily dependent states of Africa, resides in the extent to which procurement patterns, strategy, and force planning are brought into focus with overall policy objectives.

In other words, the selection of the correct direction in arms procurement and the adoption of soundly based decisions with respect to policy objectives constitute the crux of viable defence planning. What is clearly needed in the short-term is a "goal-oriented guidance" in defence planning. In this regard adherence to political reliability as the pre-eminent principle and decisional guide to arms acquisition. It is in this context that the deepening involvement of the United States of America in the reorganization and equipment of African Militaries (Military Profession Resources Initiatives, MPRI) has raised some concern and alarm in public circles.

Regarding the second problematique, a necessary distinction between what is desirable and what is possible in terms of commitment in the strategic environment, need to be made at the policy level. Since the military instrument is in the final analysis but "one of the many techniques of statecraft, taking its place alongside diplomacy, economic sanctions, and propaganda," the selection of the objectives which must be achieved by the armed forces to ensure that the foreign policy of the state has the necessary support becomes imperative. Obversely, the defence planning process must be directed toward achieving maximum military worth from a given volume of resource outlay in terms of the combat power and effectiveness of the African armed forces.

CONCLUSIONS

As a central component of national security management regime, defence policy specifies the "broad military objectives of a country and identify perceived threats" to the core and context-specific high priority values of the state. It is, therefore, but one of the vital issue areas of security policy, complementing efforts in public towards dealing with multiple challenges to health, economic, industrial and social welfare.

Priorities in national planning and resource allocation must, therefore, reflect this multiple balance in national security management. The persistent proclivities in African states either to treat each segment in the equation separately (despite the obvious interdependence of these budgetary components) or to assume that "one goal was of overriding importance and must have absolute priority over the others" can only result in sectoral underdevelopment of vital sectors of the society as it is presently the case of Nigeria.

Nevertheless, the prevalent civil disorder and violent discharges in the African region have necessitated the production and maintenance of professional defence establishment. There is, however, the imperative need in responding to systemic challenges to make explicit judgment between what is desirable and what is feasible in her direction of defence policy of Nigeria as the experience in Liberia and Sierra Leone arguably suggests.

REFERENCES

1. J. Downey, Management in the Armed Forces. London: McGraw-Hill, 1977:3.
2. J. Baylis (eds) British Defence Policy in a Changing World. London: Croom Helm, 1977:15.
3. B. Brodie, War and Politics . N. Y: Macmill an, 1973:345.
4. J. Baylis, op cit: 18
5. C. Vonclausewitz, On War edited and translated by Michael Howard and Peter Paret. Princeton: Princeton University Press, 1966:87.
6. Clausewitz Ibid: 605.
7. P. Garrigue, "Strategic Studies as Theory: An essay on their contribution Planning" Journal of Strategic Studies (1983): 254.
8. R. Osgood, NATO: The Entangling Alliance. Chicago: University of Chicago Press, 1962):5.
9. J. Baylis et al Contemporary Strategy. N. Y. Homes and Meir, 1980.
10. S. Huntington, The Common Defence N. Y: Columbia University Press, 1966:1.
11. K. Knorr on the Uses of Military Power in the Nuclear Age. Princeton: Princeton University Press, 1966).
12. F. Horton et. al. (eds) Comparative Defence Policy. Baltimore: John Hopkins University Press, 1982:6.
13. Downey: 13.
14. Huntington, Common Defence:4
15. Ibid:4
16. Ibid : 5
17. E. Luttwak, "The operational level of War" International Security Vol. 5 No. 3, Winter 1980/81:68.
18. C. Bassey "Ngieria's Defence Policy in a Future Continental Order" Nigerian Journal of International Affairs 13, 2, 1987:83-105.
19. C. Bassey, "Defence Planning and the Nigerian Armed Forces Modernization Process, 1970-1991: An Institutional Analysis Armed Forces and Society, 19, 2, 1993:256.
20. S. Huntington, Common Defense P : 4
21. J. Rosenau, The Scientific Study of Foreign Policy: 260.

22. K. Knorr, "Military Statecraft" in J. Rosenau et. al. World Politics N. Y: The Free Press, 1976:241.

23. S. Gberevbie, "Precision Guided Munitions and Modern Warfare: Issues and Prospects for Nigerian Air Force". National War College Dissertation, Abuja, 2001:47-48.

24. McGowan and Kegley, C, Threats, Weapons, and Foreign Policy. Beverly Hills: Sage, 1980.

25. K. Knorr et. al. Long Term Projections of Power. Cambridge: Ballionger, 1973, and Y. U. Chuyer and Y. B. Mikhaylor, Forecasting in Military Affairs. Moscow: Military Publishing House, 1975.

26. Vioti and Murray eds. The Defence Policy of Nations. Baltimore: The John Hopkins University Press, 1982: 5-7.

27. J. Garnett, "The Role of Military Power" in J. Baylis et. al. Comtemporary Strategy N. Y: Holmes and Meier, 1980.

28. S. Dalby, "Security, Modernity, Ecology: The Dilemmas of Post-Cold War Security Discourse" Alternatives 17, 1992:123.

29. R. Mandel, The Changing Face of National Security: A Conceptual Analysis. Ort: Greenwood Press, 1994.

30. T. Gurr, Minorities AT Risk: A Global View of Ethno-Political Conflict, Washington DC: USIPP, 1993.

31. P. Diehl, "Institutional Alternatives to Traditional U. N. Peacekeeping: An Assessment of Regional and Multinational Options". Armed Forces and Society. 19, No. 2, Winter 1993:211.

32. K. Knorr, Power, Strategy and Security, Princeton: Princeton University Press, 1983:22.

CHAPTER 2

NIGERIAN DEFENCE POLICY ENVIRONMENT: CONTINENTAL AND GLOBAL

OGABA OCHE

INTRODUCTION

Policies are essentially courses of action that are adopted by individuals, groups or governments, or they can be assumed to be the principles upon which such courses of action are based. Significantly, however, policies are implemented within, and have impact upon, a particular environment or ecology which also influences the substance of future policies. The dynamism of social environments necessitates their continual examination and analysis of policies in order to facilitate the formulation of improved and appropriate ones. With respect to defence policies the verity of this assumption is evidence. Defence policy has been described as being concerned with "the provision, deployment and use of military power to facilitate the protection and promotion of perceived national interests of the state in the international arena".[1] Because the destination of a country's defence policy is the international environment, analysis of this environment is crucial for the aforementioned reasons.

This chapter focuses on the continental and global environments of Nigeria's defence. The chapter adopts the period of the demise of the Cold War as a broad point of departure and does not make any strict demarcation between the continental and global environments largely because as a dependent subsystem, many developments on the continent are strongly influenced by developments in the larger global environment. A high degree of continental penetration by extra-continental forces and factors exist. This chapter focuses on five salient issues that, in the aftermath of the Cold War, have become significant features of Nigeria's defence policy and international security environment. These include the transformed character of international politics; conflict and international terrorism; globalization; trans-border crime; and the incursion of external interests into the West African region.

TRANSFORMED CHARACTER OF INTERNATIONAL POLITICS

The demise of the Cold War brought to an end a form of international politics that was given structural definition by the prevailing ideological antagonism between the erstwhile Soviet Union and the United States of America. Although the new power structure that has emerged in the wake of the Cold War is essentially unipolar, analysts have been challenged to provide a generalizable characterization of global politics in the post-Cold War era. One of the most influential thesis is that advanced by Samuel P. Huntginton[2] which argues that global politics is entering a new phase characterized and defined more by the salience of cultural and civilizational forces than ideology or economics.

This thesis argues that the dominating source of global antagonism and conflict would be essentially cultural. Although nation-states will remain the major actors in global politics, the principal conflicts in the international arena would have their genesis in differences between nations and groups of distinct civilizations. This form of conflict, which he labels the "Clash of Civilization", will be the dominant and defining features of post-Cold War global politics. He argues that the Cold War, and major wars that pre-dated that, typified conflict within western civilization. The post-Cold War period will, however, witness increasing intercourse and interaction between nations of Western and Non-western civilizations. With the growing power of non-Western nations the prospects for the occurrences of inter-civilizational clashes increases.

If the clash of civilizations theorizes that world politics will be defined by the contending forces of culture the end of the Cold War leaves the world with the United States as the de facto and pre-eminent global power. Proponents of structuralist analysis of international politics argue that war and the possibility of war among the great powers has been the driving and defining force behind world politics. Such contentions among the great powers have influenced the distribution of political values globally, as well as determining the fates of smaller and weaker members of the international community. The emergence of the US as the dominant global power also implies the global spread of its preferred political values and the penetration of American power into virtually every dimension of the global political system.

In terms of its preferred political values the world has experienced the widespread adoption of democratic systems of government with all its accompanying baggage of values as the most effective means for organizing the domestic politics of nation-states. The centralized single-party political systems are, to a very large extent, perceived as relics of the Cold War era. The pre-eminence of liberal democratic values can be seen as the ideological dimension of American Cold War victory over the erstwhile Soviet Union.

A further defining factor of world politics is American military dominance, it security agenda and the uses to which it is ready to deploy its forces. The very fact that the US possesses the most powerful military force in the history of mankind means that they have the capability to influence global security. The National Security Strategy of the United States essentially presets a new grand strategy for the US.[3] Although it is advanced primarily as a response to terrorism, it also constitutes a broader view about how the US should wield power and organize world order to the extent of its capability. According to this new strategy the US is less beholden to its partners, international law, norms, rules, regulations or institutions while it adopts a more unilateral and anticipatory role in attacking terrorist threats and confronting "rogue states" who are trying to obtain weapons of mass destruction (WMD). In essence the US intends to use its unparalleled military power to manage the emerging global order.

One of the core features of this grand strategy is the doctrine of preemption. This states that "To forestall or prevent hostile acts by our adversaries, the United States will, if necessary, act preemptively in exercising our inherent right of self-defence"[4] The thrust of this doctrine is the need to be preemptive, or even preventive, by taking on potential threats before they can present a major problem. This premise has been subjected to widespread criticism on the grounds that it completely disregards old international rules of self-defence and United Nations norms guiding the proper use of force. This doctrine emanated from the perception of, and arrogance associated with, the military dominance of the US over the rest of the world, in addition to providing a basis for American intervention in various parts of the world, including Africa.

CONFLICT AND INTERNATIONAL TERRORISM

The nature and character of conflict during the Cold War era was dictated to a large extent to be structural logic of the ideological antagonism between the rival East and West blocs as such conflicts were mainly inter-state in nature. The demise of the Cold War however altered the nature of conflict globally and on the continent of Africa in particular. Indeed, in Africa conflicts and their spread constitute one of the major features of the security environment.

A few facts may help to convey the immensity and scope of the problem posed by violent conflicts in Africa. By 1996 almost half of all war related deaths in the world occurred in Africa, and as at 1998 Africa had more armed conflicts than any other continent in the world. As a result of the pervasiveness of conflicts, Africa accounts for over 8 million of the 22 million refugees world wide.[5]

A close look at the conflict scenario in Africa shows that not only have conflicts risen in terms of numbers, there are also perceptible changes in the nature of these conflicts in various ways. Firstly, an ever-growing number of these conflicts tend to be intra-state rather than inter-state. Whereas during the era of the Cold War as lot of these conflicts could be traced to the rivalries and ideological competition that existed between the United States of America and the erstwhile Soviet Union with the support of their respective spheres of influence, the conflicts that occur in Africa today take place within individual states. Because of their nature these conflicts also affect neighbouring states either by way of spreading instability or by drawing these states into the conflict itself. For example, the civil war that ravaged Liberia from 1991-97 spilled over, on a number of occasions, into neighbouring Sierra Leone. The civil war in the Democratic Republic of Congo created a security complex that attracted the involvement of Angola, Namibia, Uganda, Zimbabwe, and Rwanda. The current crisis in the Darfur region of Sudan is feeding into rebel movements in Niger and Southern Chad. Thus, although a number of African conflicts are intra-state in nature, they posses the potential of becoming internationalized through linkages with neighbouring states.

Another characteristic of contemporary African conflicts is the widespread use of small and deadly arms such as the AK47 Kalashinkov assault rifle. The widespread availability of small arms on the African continent is directly traceable to the Cold War era. With the two superpowers, at that time, having achieved a state of mutual deterrence through their possession of nuclear weapons, the only way they could advance their interests in strategically important parts of the world was through the military support of proxy regimes and liberation movements. When the Cold War came to an end the massive stockpile of armaments that were amassed became readily available for disputes whose lines of conflict were now drawn along ethnic, regional, or religious grounds. Furthermore, the arms supply lines that were established during the Cold War era have continued to exist. As a consequence of this the availability of small arms have resulted in ever more lethal conflicts[6].

A further characteristics of African conflicts is that a number of them are causally linked to the erosion of state control or the phenomenon of "state failure". State failure or state collapse refers to a situation in which "the structure, authority (legitimate power), law, and political order have fallen apart…"[7] It represents a situation in which the old order collapses and there is a general retreat to ethno-nationalism as the residual and viable form of identity. Countries such as Somalia and the Democratic Republic of Congo provide examples of virtual state collapse as a direct consequence of internecine conflict.

The last two characteristics of African conflicts have been the growing involvement of children in conflicts as combatants, and the tendency for civilians to become targets of most conflicts. Increasingly, in various theatres of conflict in Africa, children are being used to augment the fighting forces of various warring groups. The phenomenon of the "child soldier" had manifest itself in conflicts such as those in Angola, Somalia, Liberia, Democratic Republic of Congo, and Sierra Leone. Apart from young boys being used as soldiers, young girls are also apprehended and sexually abused. This trend not only does psychological damage to the youngsters who are subjected to such abuse, on a broader societal level, the use of children as soldiers has long-term social and demographic implications that are detrimental to national development even in the event that the conflict abates.

Furthermore, while soldiers and military installations were, in the past, the primary targets in conflicts and civilians were seen as "collateral damage", today civilians are increasingly becoming the targets of belligerent groups. The genocide in Rwanda that resulted in the killings of millions of innocent civilians, and the Sierra Leonean civil war, in which the amputation of the limbs of innocent civilians became the instrument of conflict, provide us with vivid examples of the horrors that have become typical of African conflicts today. No less a personality than the former Secretary-General of the United Nations stated quite poignantly that:

> …the impact of wars on civilians has worsened because internal wars, now the most frequent type of armed conflict, typically take a heavier toll on civilians than inter-state wars, and became combatants increasingly have made targeting civilians a strategic objective,[8]

It is difficult to establish the precise causes of conflicts largely because conflicts differ from each other in terms of the combination of factors that give rise to them, and also because conflicts are social phenomena involving human beings and are not given to rigid scientific explanations. However, crises and conflicts in Africa, especially at the national and sub-national levels, can be seen to revolve around the four important issues of identify, participation, distribution and legitimacy.[9]

Identity Involves the self-conception and self-definition of an individual with respect to his/her membership in, and allegiance to, a particular community, which may itself be defined in social, political, economic or territorial terms. The issue of identify determines the extent to which an individual sees himself as being a member or non-member of a community. To the extent that the individual identifies with a particular community, that sense of belonging bestows upon the individual some psychological (if not material) gratification. The perception of identify also sets parameters to the extent of sacrifice that individuals and groups are willing to make for the benefit of the community. The issue of identity has been a major cause of violent conflicts on the African continent. According to Kofi Annan:

> The widespread rise of what is called identify politics, coupled with the fact that fewer than 20 per cent of all state are ethnically homogeneous, means that political demagogues have little difficulty finding targets of opportunity and mobilizing support for chauvinist causes. The upsurge of ethnic cleasing in the 1990s provides stark evidence of the appalling human costs that this vicious exploitation of identity politics can generate.[10]

Participation refers to voluntary actions and choice that are open to the individual for making demands of government and expressing support, or lack of it, for government policies.[11] The issue of participation can become problematic and lead to conflicts when individuals or groups attempt to monopolize all available avenues for meaningful political participation to the exclusion of others, which used to be the case with the prevalence of centralized regimes. The global spread of democracy represents an attempt to redress the problem of exclusivity in political participation.

The issue of distribution refers to the differential spread of, and access to, values and resources in society.[12] If politics can be defined in terms of "who gets what, when and how", then the allocation of values and resources may be said to lie at the very heart of politics. The manner in which values and resources are distributed determines the amount of justice, fairness, and equity that are attributable to a government. Conflicts that develop as a consequence of perceptions of inequality and relative deprivation are causally linked to the manner in which values are distributed in society.[13] The on-going spate of violence in the oil-rich Niger Delta region of Nigeria can be attributed to the perceived and actual inequality in the distribution of Nigeria's revenues, a large percentage of which is obtained from the region.

The issue of legitimacy involves "the individual's belief in the rightness of the rules governing political competition within a society"[14] The issue to legitimacy determines the extent to which a government is seen as acceptable or not, either by opposing groups or the population at large. Indeed, for conflicts to occur, either between groups or against the state, there must be deep-seated perceptions that the configuration of power within the country is unacceptable.

Another school of thought posits that economic decline is strongly associated with violent conflicts. The argument here is that the nature of politics that is associated with a receding or declining economy tends to be more conflict prone than the politics that is associated with a growing or buoyant economy. Thus, competition for increasingly scarce values tends to breed violence.

Finally, the process of political transition to democracy has also been identified as providing conducive contexts for the eruption of conflicts. Politicians, contenders for political power, ethnic and regional groups use the process of democratization and the political space that it opens up to justify protests and rebellions as struggles for individual and group rights which should be protected within a democratic political framework.[15]

Without doubt, if consideration is given to the frequency of conflicts across the African continent as well as their relatively protracted nature, conflicts can be seen to constitute a major threat to security on the African continent. African states are, by and large, fragile states and the meager development have been eroded by violent conflicts. The economic foundations of countries like Sierra Leone and Liberia have been virtually destroyed in their entirely as a result of conflicts, and the political superstructure of the state of Somalia has distintegrated as a culmination of civil war.[16]

Lastly, a phenomenon which dramatizes the adversity of conflicts in Africa and the fragility of human security are the large populations of refugees that have been generated by conflicts. According to a recent UN study Africa has the world's largest refugee population of 7.9 million, excluding internally displaced people. Out of this number 12 countries alone were responsible for over 6 million of the refugees.[17] Although environmental factors such as drought account for some of the refugees, the vast majority of the refugees are people that have been displaced from countries that are embroiled in conflicts.

The gravity of the impact of conflicts, which have been depicted above, brings to light the significance and salience of conflict resolution processes as means for the de-escalation and management of social conflicts, especially in Africa. At every level of analysis conflicts constitute a major problem in Africa. Overall, this dimension of the security environment has lead to an expected increase in demand for United Nations and regional peacekeeping missions towards which Nigerian has been a major troop contributing country over the years.

The phenomenon of terrorism, just like conflict, has been a feature of the global security environment right from antiquity. However, since September 11, 2001, the day America came under a series of devastating attacks from terrorists to date, the issue of terrorism was effectively brought to the forefront of international security discourse and simultaneously incidents of terrorism have climbed at an alarming rate. The aftermath has seen a global campaign by the United States of America against terrorism and the A1-Qaeda network to the extent that the war against terrorism has become a key component of that country's national security strategy, and by extension a major international security concern. A major reason for the upsurge in the level of terrorist violence and terrorist related incidents has been the availability of a huge-post-Afghanistan war "surplus". This surplus included combatants and military material. The majority of the combatants who took part in the war against the Soviet supported government, termed "Mujahideen" or freedom fighters, became socialized into a life of war. With the soviet forces having withdrawn from Afghanistan and a civil war there that threatened Islamic unity in the region, the unemployed guerillas sought new battlefields and new enemies to fight.[18]

The use of terror by a militant group as a means of overthrowing a government in power or forcing that government to change its policies can be dichotomized into direct and indirect forms of terrorism. In direct terrorism, the aim is to terrorize the actual wielders of power or political office holders.[19] Indirect terrorism on the other hand focuses on discrediting a government by demonstrating that the government cannot protect its own subjects and their property. It tends to demonstrate that such a government is not capable of maintaining law and order and as a result is unworthy of retaining power. In such cases the terrorists create chaos by bombing building and sundry forms of infrastructure. They also embark upon robbing banks, sabotaging industrial plants, kidnapping foreigners and prominent people.[20] This is the nature of terrorism applied by youths in Nigeria's Niger Delta region against the government of Nigeria and petroleum company workers in the area. In this setting, the Niger Delta region is made unsafe for government officials and foreigners , especially expatriates that work with oil companies and others in the area .

From the forgoing analysis terrorism can be adequately perceived as a form of asymmetric warfare, which are versions of not "fighting fair" that can include the use of surprise in al its operational and strategic dimensions and the use of weapons in ways that the unplanned by the terrorist or even a nation state actor. Not "fighting fair" also includes the prospect of a group designing a strategy that fundamentally alters the terrain on which a conflict is fought. Asymmetric warfare is, in its bare essentials, warfare between the very weak and the very strong. The weak actors in their quest to attain their objectives will employ unconventional weapons and techniques, which ultimately amounts to not "fighting fair". It is in this that terrorism can be seen as a form of asymmetric warfare in which the act of terror is instrumentalized as a weapon directed towards the achievement of a broader goal (political, economic, religious, etc).

The tendency is that asymmetric warfare makes a strong actor's power irrelevant.[22] Terrorism, however, is unique in its usage as an instrument of asymmetric warfare. The basic reason for this is the diversity of causes (political, religious, economic, etc) and people determined to achieve their objectives, even at the cost of their lives, in the contemporary world. As long as these are perceived as "just" causes, in a world of multiplying ethnic and religious divisions, there will be groups who will resort to terrorism because they believe that there are no legitimate ways to redress

accepted as a threat to international security. However, the largest populations of AIDS victims are in Africa and the disease is spreading more rapidly in Africa than all other parts of the world. The continent of Africa still retains the unenviable reputation of being conflict prone. The seemingly endless cycle of conflicts and complex emergencies such as the Darfur crisis in western Sudan will pose a serious test for the African Union and its conflict resolving capabilities. All these factors, intricately and dynamically linked, have a negative impact upon the process of development and influenced various facets of global and continental security.

TRANS-BORDER CRIME

An overlooked aspect of Nigeria's security environment is the phenomenon of trans-border crime. In definition terms trans-border crime refers not only to crimes that are international, or that cross existing borders between countries, they also include crimes that take place in one country while generating effects that are significantly felt in another country.[25] The beginning of the 21st century witnessed an escalation in the level of international organized crimes that had implications for security in Nigeria's immediate continental environment. Although not having proportionate impact upon the country's security such crimes ranges from arms, human and drugs trafficking, to smuggling, advance fraud, money laundering, armed banditry and military assault. Others are inter-communal conflicts, clandestine immigration and hostage taking.

Crime and conflict are highly interrelated in many cases in Africa, and this is no where clearer than in the case of arms trafficking. Guns imported for war, legally or illegally, can be used for crime, both during and after the conflict. They are also highly negotiable commodities international criminal commerce, and can be exchanged for a range of contraband, including minerals and oil, wildlife, and drugs. It is nearly impossible to estimate the number of small arms circulating in Africa, and attempts to do so are complicated by the fact that weapons are "recycled" in conflicts throughout the region. However, estimates of illicit weapons in circulation have been calculated to be as high as seven million.[26]

Arms trafficking extend from the North African countries of Libya and Algeria to Mauritania, Niger, Mali, Chad, Burkina Faso and Nigeria. Arms supply cells operate actively in Cote d'Ivoire, Liberia, Sierria Leone, Guineas and Gambia. The abundance of the supply cache from various countries has presented traffickers with a veritable source of supply.[27] The inability of governments in West Africa to bring an end to conflicts is partly a result of the free and unhindered proliferation of small arms and ammunition in countries such as Benin Republic, Togo, Ghana and Burkina Faso through to Cote d;lvoire and the Mano River Basin states of Guinea Bissau, Liberia and Sierra Leone.

The smuggling of natural resources, another trans-border criminal activity, is one involving both local and international trans-border organized crime groups. Africa is rich in natural resources, including oil, diamonds, other precious and strategic minerals, and timber. The theft and smuggling of these resources is a major organized crime activity, in countries at war as well as in countries at peace. For example, in Nigeria, criminal gangs steal large amounts of crude oil from pipelines and ship it on river barges to larger craft offshore in a practice referred to as "bunkering". It is a massive industry yielding massive profits for its participants in the Niger delta region of the country. It is an activity that provides finance for the violence being perpetrated by militia groups in the region.[28]

Oil-theft would, however, be impossible if it were not for willing buyers, the involvement of outsiders in the trade, and the collusion of security personnel. The oil bunkering syndicates are highly internationalized, including not only other West Africans, but also Moroccans, Venezuelans, Lebanese, French and Russians. By these means, oil bunkering links up with wider patterns of trans-border organized crime. Violence and insecurity, with cash, drugs and weapons all being traded in exchange for illegal oil.

INCURSION OF EXTERNAL INTERESTS.

An important structural influence on the security environment of Nigeria's immediate sub-region and the Gulf of Guinea is the incursion of powerful new external interests. While West Africa experienced the historical involvement of France and Great Britain, the post-Cold War era is witnessing the more robust involvement of China and the US in the affairs of the region.

With respect to China, their phenomenal economic growth, which has been predicated on the adoption of pragmatic polices has necessitated a shift in their focus away from ideology as the platform for their engagement with Africa to more practical desiderata dictated by their need for markets and natural resources. A major dimension of this change has been China's growing thirst for oil. As the world's second largest consumer of oil products after the United States, China uses 6.7 million barrels a day, and that level is projected to double to 13.4 million barrels per day by 2025. This growing need has led China on a relentless search for new sources of oil, of which Africa has many including the Gulf of Guinea region. Additionally China seeks markets for its flood of manufactured goods, especially textiles.

With respect to the US on the other hand Africa has assumed a more central position in her strategic calculations. The five factors which account for this change in American policy include international terrorism, HIV/AIDS, oil conflicts, and America's desire to expand global trade. International terrorism and HIV/AIDS, as stated earlier, have been identified as international security threats by both the United Nations and the US. The likelihood the Gulf of Guinea region may replace the Persian Gulf as the major source of oil for the US has led to the US declaration of the Gulf of Guinea as a part of her national security interests. The seriousness of America's intention in the region has been reflected in its formation of the African Command (AFRICOM), an arm of the US military dedicated primarily to the pursuit and protection of US interest, as well as forestalling the expansion of Chinese influenced in the region.

The incursion of competing foreign interests into a region that is already characterized by poor governance, instability and conflict constitute developments and dynamics that should be subjected to close observation in order to inform Nigeria's defence policy. The significance of this incursion lies in its propensity to generate rivalry that can compel the manipulation of domestic actors in order to attain pursuits or in an extreme scenario even lead to conflict. Lateral pressures theory argues that the aggressive pursuit of resources, as China and the US are engaged in for oil in the Gulf of Guinea, is a potential source of conflict between states, especially in instances in which at least one of the actors is a rapidly industrializing state.[29]

CONCLUSION

The Nigerian defence environment is clearly characterized by the dynamism and interpenetration of global and continental factors the most salient of which are features that have evolved in the aftermath of the Cold War such as globalization, incursion of new actors such as the US and China, and terrorism, and HIV/AIDS. Arguably the phenomenon of conflict is not new on the continent, rather it is its changed nature, as discussed earlier, and increased lethality that poses serious defence challenges. However, an overview of the continent does not suggest that the incidence of conflicts will significantly decline in the near future. Rather emergencies such as the Darfur crisis, which the US has described as genocide, should attract close attention by Nigeria's defence establishment because of its possibility of generating effects that can spill across borders. On the other hand the incursion of the US and China will definitely affect the continent's security environment. The introduction of the American military into West Africa could be defined as a challenge, and possible threat, to Nigeria's security interests or as military incursion by a great power towards which Nigeria has no feasible recourse other than passive acquiescence. Whatever perspective is adopted the facts are that the US is responding to a perceived intrusion by an emerging power (China) into a part of the world which it has described as being within its sphere of interest. It behoves on the Nigerian defence establishment to study and formulate adequate defence, as well as foreign, policy response to this emerging feature of the country's defence environment.

NOTES

1. Celestine Oyom Bassey, <u>Contemporary Strategy and the African Condition,</u> Ibadan: Macmillan, 2005, p.264.
2. Samuel P. Huntington, "The Clash of Civilization?" <u>Foreign Affairs</u> Vol. 72. No.3. 1993
3. <u>National Security Strategy of the United States of America,</u> March 16, 2006. Available on the Internet.
4. Ibid, p. 18
5. Greg Mills, "African Expectations and Priorities for the UN's Millennium Assembly: A View from South Africa" presented at a conference on <u>Priorities for Africa and the UN Millennium Assembly,</u> South African Institute of International Affairs, Wits University, Johannesburg, 18 November, 1999, p.3.

6. Sid Muni "Arms and Conflicts in the Post-Cold War Developing World' in Luc Van De Goor, Kumar Rupesinghe, and Paul Scilarone (eds) <u>Between Development and Destruction: An Enquiry into the Causes of Conflict in Post-Colonial States,</u> London: Macmillan, 1996, pp. 200-201.

7. I. William Zartman "Posing the Problem of State Collapse" in I. William Zartman (ed), <u>Collapsed States: The Disintegratioin and Restoration of Legitimate Authority,</u> London: Lynne Rienner, 1995, p.l.

8. Kofi A. Annan, <u>Preventing War and Disaster: A Growing Global Challenge,</u> New York: United Nations Department of Public Information, 1999.

9. Stephen Stedman, "Conflict and Conflict Resolution in Africa: A Conceptual Framework" in Francis Deng and I. William Zartman (eds), ibid, pp.374-383.

10. Kofi Annan, Op. cit, p.6

11. Stephen Steadman, op. cit, p.376.

12. Ibid, p. 3. 77.

13. For more on the theory of "Relative Deprivation" as it relates to violence see Ted Robert Gurr, <u>Why Men Rebel,</u> Princeton, New Jersey: Princeton University Press, 12974, p.24.

14. Stephen Stedman, op. cit, p. 377.

15. Ted Robert Gurr, "Peoples Against States: Ethnopolitical Conflict and the Changing World System" in <u>International Studies Quarterly,</u> Vol. 38, 1999, p. 361.

16. United Nations Development Program, <u>Human Development, Report, 1999</u> New York: Oxford University Press, 1999, pp.42-43. See also John Stremlau and Greg Mills (ed) <u>The Privatization of Security in Africa,</u> Johannesburg: South African Institute of International Affairs, 1999.

17. With specific reference to the case of Sierra Leone see Abiodun Alao "Diamonds are Forever Diamonds and the Actors in Sierra Leone's Civil War" in <u>Civil Wars,</u> Vol.2, No. 3, 1999, pp.43-64.

18. United Nations High Commissioner for Refugees <u>Protracted Refugee Situations</u> (2004) available on the Internet at http:www.unhcr.orgistatistics/STATISTICS/40ed5b384.pdf.

19. Gerard Chaliand, Terrorism: From Popular Struggle to Media Spectacle, London: Saqi Books, 1987.

20. Edward Hyams, Op Cit. p. 10. For a very comprehensive and detailed picture of the operations of terrorists see <u>The 9/11 Commission Report: Final Report of the National Commission on Terrorist Attacks Upon The United States,</u> New York: W. W. Norton, 2004.

21. Ibid

22. Ivan Arreguin – Toft: "How the Weak Win Wars: A Theory of Asymmetric Conflict", <u>International Security,</u> vol. 26, no. 1, 1992, p.93, and Robert A. Pape, <u>Bombing to Win: Air Power and Coercion in War,</u> Ithaca N. Y.: Cornel University Press, 1996, p.4. see also Glen H. Snyder and Paul Diesing, <u>Conflict among Nations: Bargaining Decision-making and System Structure in International Crisis,</u> Princeton, N. Y; Princeton University Press 1977, p. 190.

Katzenbaoh and Hanrahan, "The Revolutionary Strategy of Mao Tse Tung, Political Science Quarterly, vol. 70, no. 3 September 1955, pp. 325-326.

23. John Spanier, Games Nations Play, Washington DC: Congress Quarterly Press, 1990, p.367.

24. Jan. Art Scholte, Globalization: A Critical Introduction, London: Macmillan, 2000, p 26.

25. "Transnational Crime". Available at www.http//en.wikipedia.org/wki/ transnational creme.

26. "Estimated Distribution of Firearms in Africa" Small Arms Survey 2003. p. 80.

27. "West Africa: Small Arms Recycling Rampant", United Nations Office for the Coordination of Humanitarian Affairs, August 2004, p.l.

28. International Crime Threat Assessment. A Report by the United States Government on global transborder crime, available on the Internet at www. http//crimethreat.

29. Nazli Choucri and Robert C. North, Nations in Conflicts: National Growth and Industrial Violence, San Francisco: Freeman Published.

CHAPTER 3

GLOBAL AND REGIONAL SECURITY ENVIRONMENT

CHRIS A. GARUBA

PREAMBLE

The issue of global and regional security environment has become very important in recent times given new developments in the international system. The emergence of new states, the increasing role of multi-lateral order around the world, the emergence of new sources of conflicts in numerous manifestation to terrorism and suicide bombings/killings; and many more issues have generated growing concern for international peace and security. The concerns have arisen because the global system has moved from bi-polar to multi-polar system. Furthermore, new pressures on international cooperation, peace and security are also emerging from the realms of ideology, economy and technology. The profound structural changes in the international system combined with what appears to be turbulent crisis in the interstate system call for a re-examination of the global and regional mechanisms for the maintenance of international security.

However, there is an equally important concern that the growth tendency of American uni-lateralism if unchallenged may scuttle the emerging multilateral World Order. As can be seen in the dawn of the 21st Century, nations continue to uni-laterally and sometimes collectively compete, conflict, cooperate or interact with multi-lateral institutions [1]. This is perhaps why at the moment in the new millennium, the world is experiencing much turbulence with stresses and strains that could likely rock the global equilibrium [2].

There has been much advancement in science and technology which has led to unprecedented integration of the World economy with far-reaching results and consequences for different regions in the World [3]. These new challenges have no doubt compelled us to re-visit the concept of global and Regional Security. The African perspective in particular cannot address Regional Security without discussing the problems of underdevelopment and poverty alleviation. It goes without saying, therefore, that sustained regional security could ensure sound global peace and security. This overview will address the expectations of the global system in the new millennium, the African perspective on regional security and the place of our country, Nigeria in it.

THE PREVAILING WORLD ORDER

We are witness to the dawn of an era devoid of the ideological contentions that fuelled and sustained the Cold War for close to four decades. The collapse of the Union of

Soviet Socialist Republics (USSR) and its Warsaw Pact, could not have been more revealing than Boris Yeltsin's acceptance of the expansion of the North Atlantic Treaty Organization (NATO). With these developments, some observers argue that the only surviving power, United States of America (USA) is now in a pre-eminent and unassailable position in world politics.

A number of events support this assumption. After Iraq invaded Kuwait in September 1990, the US commenced mobilization for a counter offensive and only consulted close allies after making what was apparently, an irreversible strategic commitment. That the United Nations Organization (UN) endorsed the American led coalition, visibly reinforced the above assumption on Haiti in 1993. The Americans self-perception on this matter is instructive. President Bill Clinton, in his second inaugural address in January 1997, pointed out that US leadership of the world, at least up to the first fifty years of the 21st Century is a fait accompli. All that the country needs to do in order to achieve her strategic objectives, is to continue to direct and participate in actions that she designs to achieve "peace and security around the globe and particularly areas of her defined national interest" [4].

The above American perception is, however, debatable because there is a growing school of thought that sees the emerging world as basically multi-centric. The growing influence of national economy, particularly in the European Union and Japan, in shaping international diplomacy is sometimes cited as one factor that contradicts the above assumption. Nonetheless, we are mindful of the assertion of Gutteridge, that military power will continue to remain a symbol of national prestige which no self-respecting state can do without [5]. It is not just an accident of history that nations of consequence in the international system are also nations that were built on concrete military power foundations, or at least those with national power elements which "include the capabilities and capacities of their existing military that can he harmonized" [6]. It is indisputable that no country can unilaterally and successfully contest for power within the international system. This is the primary reason why alliance policies are pursued by states with a wide range of motives and interests. Although some writers have regarded alliances as major catalysts for war, most still hold that alliances are major fortresses of order and of national survival [7]. Indeed, the collective security goal of alliances constitutes the foundation block of the UN, and also serves as the guiding principle of Security Council.

In Article 1 of the UN Charter, the purpose of the Organization are stated as follows:

1. To maintain international peace and security and, to that end, to take effective collective measures for the prevention and removal of threats to the peace, and for the suppression of acts of aggression or other breaches of the peace, and to bring about by peaceful means, and in conformity with the principles of justice and international law, adjustment or settlement of international disputes or situations which might lead to a breach of the peace;

2.   To develop friendly relations among nations based on respect for the principle of equal rights and self determination of people, and to take other appropriate measures to strengthen universal peace;

3.   To achieve international cooperation in solving international problems of an economic, social, cultural or humanitarian character, and in promoting and encouraging respect for human rights and for fundamental freedoms for all without distinction as to race, sex, language, or religion; and.

4.   To be a centre for harmonizing the actions of nations in the attainment of these common ends. [8]

The diplomacy of nations is thus seen to be governed by Article 1.4 of UN Charter while Article 1.3 recognizes differences which implies a recognition of segmented interests and values. Indeed, the various actors in the international system find accommodation in the stated Charter. It is, therefore, not surprising that freed from the encumbrances imposed by the cold war, the UN is striving to justify the aspirations of its founding fathers. It is also understandable why powerful and prosperous states as the US, Germany, Japan, Britain and France still find the UN relevant while pursuing their national agenda. In a nutshell, as the 20th century draws to a close, the UN stands a better chance of recapturing its founding vision and successfully implementing its original objectives.

INTERNATIONAL PEACE AND SECURITY

As we enter the new century, there are enough indications to suggest that the nation-state will continue, as a prominent actor in the international system. However, non-actors will also continue to play increasingly critical roles in the management of international security. One area that deserves attention is the emerging trend of a growing America hegemony and a movement for multi-lateral activism in world affairs. In the first place, the developing nations need the support of multi-laterals which may undermine their own sovereignty. Indeed, no nation, developed or developing, big or small, powerful or weak, would willingly submit to the domination of any transnational organization in which it considers its vital interest.

The evolving trends so far identified show that great efforts are needed to harmonise the disparate interests of the various actors within the international system. As it were, ideology is no longer a protection for deviant behaviour in the conduct of politics. This pattern is already unfolding as former satellite states are left in their self-inflicted crises. For instance, Somalia which was desired as an ally by the two super-powers has degenerated into a state of anarchy and consequently become a pariah state. Zaire (presently D R Congo) which was once a major ally of the US in South Central Africa, was abandoned to the forces of change in the country.

The threat and use of mass destruction may not, from the beginning of the century, assume an alarming proportion. Indeed, the uni-lateral offer of Russian President Boris Yeltsin to reduce his country's nuclear war-heads could have mitigating effects on the nuclear threat. Somehow, the fear of actual use of the bomb was never really with the super-powers who had other capabilities to make them see the Atomic Bomb for what it really is – the ultimate weapon. It is the possibility of terrorist use of the bomb that poses the greatest concern to peace-loving nations. Yet technological explosion, which is anticipated for the next century, Regional arms races may replace the global one of the present; but the consequences for international peace and security will not be less severe.

What constitutes security will continue to be subject to debate, but increasingly it can no longer be narrowly defined. With the world increasingly becoming a global village, and with the developments in communication and computer technology, the behaviour of states can no longer escape global scrutiny. However, the ability to influence global events will increasingly become a function of national technological capability.

In the world of the 21st century, it would become increasingly illusory to conceive international peace in terms of the absence of a state of war. As noted by Holsti, there are issues which may ignite domestic revolutionary activities that could ultimately lead to external interventions. These issues include: explosive population growth rates, inequitable land-ownership patterns, alienation of prime agricultural land for export-oriented crops and meat production; deforestation and highly stratified social structures. All these would exacerbate problems of refugees and displaced persons which would continue to necessitate intervention of external actors in the world system. Other factors that could aggravate tension in the emerging world include: the use of armed forces against drug producers in other countries, and the mounting of armed operations against terrorist organizations in violation of the international integrity of other states. [10].

Perhaps Chisholm's observation on the major trends likely to shape the future is also appropriate. In his view,

1. Military intervention will be less focused;

2. There will be reduction in contribution to defence research and development (R&D): and

3. There will be greater access to technology [11].

What is discernable from this trend is that there will be increased emphasis on regional institutions to deal with threats to peace and security. Various actors would, therefore, require voluntary leadership to cope with the envisioned world.

HEGEMONS AND SECURITY REGIMES

The successful resolution of the Liberian conflict has shown that given the opportunity, African states under their own sub-regional security complexes, can build a sustainable security – regime capable of resolving conflicts. However, the example of Liberia has also shown that for an effective security-regime, there must be a regional hegemon, regionally influential or framework country which has the capacity to sustain the regime. For the seven years of the Liberian conflict, Nigeria was able to provide hegemonic leadership in articulating and supporting the goals of ECOMOG in Liberia. And through the co-operation of ECOWAS member states, the conflict was resolved without massive disaffection in the region. It was on the basis of the unity of purpose and spirit of co-operation demonstrated among ECOWAS member states themselves, that the international community was left with no other alternative than to endorse the sub-regional community's position on the resolution of the Liberian conflict.

Even so, the fact must be conceded that the creation of ECOMOG was not without some initial friction and constraints as already mentioned. Apart from the initial differences between states on how to resolve the conflict, there were also other countries outside the sub-region whose designs were based on their ulterior motives and which were not compatible with those of ECOWAS. These divergent interests informed the various approaches which were advanced towards the resolution of the conflict between 1990 and 1995. In the wake of these developments, there was the need for a country with the diplomatic skills, military strength and economic clout to build a consensus across the sub-region. Nigeria happened to be such a country, strategically located with its coastline enhancing its access to other parts of the West African sub-region, with a population which is about 55 percent of the West African total, with abundant resources, and with substantial military capabilities.

On the basis of the above attributes, Nigeria acting almost as a regional hegemon, succeeded in forging a consensus on the resolution of the Liberian conflict. Nigeria was able to employ her vast diplomatic, economic and military resources to get the ECOMOG initiative accepted eventually by the sub-region and prepared to play such a role, thereby relieving the other members of the burden of executing such a plan, it would have been difficult to attain the success recorded in Liberia today. As James L. Wood, the Africa Specialist at the US State Department stated in an August 1993 briefing of the US Congress.

> " The Nigerian contribution has been absolutely critical to the success of ECOMOG. Nigeria's manpower and logistics contributions are critical to the Operational capability of the entire regional force… Of course, ECOMOG's operation in Liberia have not been flawless from either a military or political perspective, but the Nigerians have demonstrated capabilities that few other sub-Saharan African militaries (with the exception of South Africa) have and none have ever been required to demonstrate: namely, the ability to deploy and logistically support a division equivalent. Additionally, Nigeria's ability to plan and conduct coordinated air, land and sea operations and to conduct a relatively effective counter – insurgency campaign has also been impressive….If we ever want to engage in PKO (peace keeping operations) using African troops, we should keep Nigeria's potential very much in mind".[13]

Flowing from the above, there are two options to creating an African security regime. The first is to widen the application of the experiences in Liberia, and build these experiences around the AU. In this context, unlike in ECOWAS, we should expect a number of sub-regional powers to play the role Nigeria played in ECOMOG. These powers should be allowed to exert greater influence over security and defence issues in the African region. In fact, acting as a concert of powers, we should consider constituting them into an AU security council, as Professor Ali Mazrui has already advocated, with the primary goals of executing preventive mechanisms against future developments on the continent. Mazrui has also identified 5 countries to play the role of members of the proposed African Security Council; namely; Nigeria, Egypt, Ethiopia, South African and Zaire (now Democratic Republic of Congo). In delegating the issue of conflict prevention, management or resolution to the proposed Security Council, the "AU will turn its attention to other neglected problem areas that are pervasive and contentious in the continent such as poverty, environmental issues, social and economic problems, humanitarian and development issue[14]". This perspective does not undermine the existing Peace and Security Council in the AU which has a membership of 15 members, 10 for 2 years and 5 for 3 years duration.

The second option is to leave the issue of security open to the sub-regional powers to fashion out measures towards the resolution of emerging conflicts within their zones. In relation to this option, Mazrui has advocated for a trusteeship system that is "more genuinely international and less western than under the old guise". [15] Here, the five hegemons or regional influential identified, are expected to play the role of benevolent international watch-dogs, intervening in all regional conflicts to restore order and stability. This, to me, is a better role than that of "benign" colonization by hegemonies, as suggested by Mazrui. This option has become necessary because, as we argued earlier, the Western powers are now more interested in resolving conflicts in their region than employing their human and material resources to resolve African conflicts. A clear example was their total commitment and dedication towards resolving the Balkan crisis of the 1990s in contra distinction to the lip service paid to the crisis in Liberia, Sudan Rwanda and other conflict situations in Africa.

From the above, we can argue that effective security – regimes in Africa must be anchored on the strength of benevolent hegemons and the co-operation of the smaller or less well-endowed states on the continent. In the developed world, security-regimes may not count on the stabilizing power of a hegemon but on the co-operation of member states through an institutional framework. [16] In Africa, the reverse must be the case. Given our weak economies and political instabilities, certain countries exist within the African region with resources comparable to those of hegemons elsewhere that can help build African security-regimes. And in line with Koeohane's position, hegemonic stability can bring about order in regional politics through the benevolent efforts of a single dominant power. [17]

The maintenance of this order requires an elastic hegemonic influence. It also requires political commitment and genuine interest in the peace and security of Africa on the part of all the countries concerned. It will demand, as well, on the part of a number of African states, the sacrifice of immediate but temporary and superficial gains, for strong and more enduring structures that will sustain real peace and security on the continent. This is important and timely, if we do not want to run into another process of external influence or the imperialism of conflict prevention and conflict resolution which some extra-African countries are already trying to foist on Africa.

NIGERIA'S ROLE

Nigeria, as a sovereign political unit, has the responsibility to protect her national interests and values. She also has the duty to play an active part in the management of international peace and security. The scope of her participation is strengthened not only by her status as a pre-eminent regional actor, but also by her membership in various international organizations.

The guidelines for Nigeria's participation in global activities of the 21st century should be governed by:

(i) A desire for internal cohesion through participation only in activities that enhance national integration;

(ii) Defining a common direction for both the nation and non-state-actors emanating from the country through consultations and coordination;

(iii) Embarking only on activities that enhance the national interests;

(iv) Adopting holistic approach to issues of international peace and security; and

(v) Avoiding strains and stresses by concentrating efforts on feasible ventures.

If the aspirations of the present Nigerian leadership are realised, Nigeria should be on the path of being a developed nation by 2020 at least during the course of the 21st century. The most basic requirement is an enabling environment which will assure the nation in three spheres of participation towards achieving international peace and security.

The first is the domestic scene where policies and programmers should not be such that excites the World into interference and intervention in the affairs of the country while providing a stable base for external commitment. By now, it should be clear that certain matters which are considered internal to nations have ways of resulting, first in local crises and then citizens displacement, which easily attracts attention in this growing world of electronics. Nigeria has a plethora of this issue-land, ethnic question, religion and so on which need tact to settle. A stable and peaceful Nigeria can then be in a position to fulfill its obligation to the outside world while avoiding threats to her internal peace and security.

The second is the envisaged status of the nation which appears capable of drawing her out of the crowd of needy nations in the African region in general and the West African sub-region in participation. Experience of the 1970s points at another round of immigration problems, given the pull effects of development on the nationals of less developed neighbours. The US is one country that continues to bear the burden of global development essential because citizens of other nations see in her a land of opportunities. In the years of Nigeria's prosperity, the nationals of other countries flooded her land, taking advantage of the porous international border and a weak immigration regime.

On the global scene, Nigeria may not catch up with the leading lights of development early in the century, but would become more and more strategic to their needs, as her exports acquire greater domestic value added. The reasonable step to take is to acknowledge that power bows to superior power and admit that what we can do to states in the African region, can be done unto us. With that at the back of our minds, it should be easy for us to fashion appropriate diplomatic, economic and military instruments of power for dealing with the developed states.

The nation's multi-lateral diplomacy, tailored to satisfy the five listed principles, should operate on the axion of no permanent friends but permanent interests. Yet, the need to share more enduring interests will grow. Alliance option is likely to feature more prominently in our conference diplomacy within organizations to which we belong. There is clearly the need to collaborate and cooperate with those powers whose interest are at congruene with our own in order that we can resist others whose interests compete and conflict with ours.

The economic realm is an area is which Nigeria's global influence could soar, given the nation's resource endowment. With the abundance of strategic minerals, a skilled population and a vast domestic market, the nation's economic development could be effectively accelerated. Whether we chart the course of political or economic diplomacy, we cannot escape from the threat from the country's potential adversaries. The most potent manpower against threat is a credible force.

Throughout the 20th century the Nigerian Armed Forces made useful contributions to international peace and security by engaging in their historical and non-historical roles. The nation's armed forces, diligently acquitted itself in the two great wars. But it is more in the area of peace keeping and peace enforcement that international recognition is pronounced. Nigeria over the years, has helped to redefine the theoretical concept of multilateral intervention through peace enforcement. This was the vision of the founding fathers of the UN. The Liberian experiment has since been played out in Bosnia-Herzegovina and Haiti and appears to be the model for the future. But this Nigeria's export to the international system, equally unveils the inadequacy of the existing peace enforcement machinery and the need to redirect doctrines and development of armed forces. There are other areas like operations against international terrorism, anti-drug campaigns and humanitarian missions for which military power will continue to be indicated.

While the Nigeria Military of the 20th century could afford to remain externally dependent, the same cannot be advocated for the military power that has to operate in the turbulent world of the 21st century. Moreover, the enhanced role of the United Nations in the global system dictates a firmer base for the Armed Forces. It is safe to assume that Vision 2020 of the present administration will examine the strategic environment, technological feasibility and resource availability to ensure the smooth growth of armed forces that is capable of discharging its obligations to the nation and the world, towards the attainment of the objectives of international peace and security. As Garnet once noted, military power "does not come into being by accident. It cannot be acquired without enormous resources, and its very existence is a source of worry for the government that controls it". [18] We may add that it is even more worrisome to do without military power or make do with a force that is glaringly inadequate. Nigeria cannot afford to be a regional power in the international community of the 21st century without a recognisable force.

CONCLUSION

This intervention has shown that security regimes are working elsewhere in the world and the experience of ECOMOG in West Africa has demonstrated that it is an option that can also work in Africa. It is an option that will reasonably deal with the familiar problems associated with the management of peace and security in Africa. The proposition here aims at building multi-polar centres of power in Africa. We have seen the crisis that a uni-polar system can cause, in the wake of the collapse of the Soviet Union. Such an arrangement threatens peace and stability. However, when power is shared, when power is benevolently guided, and when power is used for the collective good, it goes a long way in ensuring peace and security. It makes up for the inadequacies of the weak who are pulled along to levels that they would otherwise not have reached.

Further, we have attempted to review the dynamics of Nigeria's involvement in the management of international peace and security. It has been noted that despite the changing global environment, particularly the expanding role of multilateral institutions in world affairs, nations, particularly richly-endowed and active regional actors like Nigeria, have had to bear an ever-increasing burden in the management of international peace and security. Through her leadership of the ECOMOG operations in Liberia, Sieria-Leone and lately Darfur, Sudan, Nigeria has contributed immensely to the definition of the philosophy and practice of peace-keeping, and established the theoretical basis of peace enforcement.

These responsibilities trusted on Nigeria are likely to increase in the 21st Century. It is, therefore, imperative, that she invests maximally in the development of her human and material resources to a level that would enhance her continued operational effectiveness in the management of international peace and security.

NOTES

1. Rosenau, James E., "Armed Forces and Armed Forces in a Turbulent World," in James Burk (ed) The Military in New Times (Boulder: Westview Press, 1994).
2. Ibid
3. President Boris Yeltsin of the Russian Federation was at NATO Convention in Paris where he embraced East European countries' membership and announced Russia's unilateral decision to reduce its nuclear warheads.

4   The inaugural address speaks of America continuing her leadership roles for at least first fifty years of the next century.

5.   Gutteridge E., *Millitary Institutions and Power in the New States,* (London: Pall Mall, 1964).

6   Morgenthau H. J. & Thompson K. W. *Politics Among Nations* (New York: McGraw Hill, Inc., 1993)

7.   Booth, Ken, "Alliances" in John Baylis et al, Contemporary Stratey 1, (New York: Holmes & Meier, 1987).

8.   See the UN Charter for details on responsibilities for international peace and security.

9.   Holsti K. J. Peace and War: Armed Conflicts and International Order 1848 – 1989 (Cambridge: Cambridge University Press, 1992).

10.   Ibid

11.   Chisholm, J., "Reshaping the World Order" in Janes Defence 1997.

12.   Rosenau, James E., *op cit*

13.   Ibid

14.   Ibid

15.   Abacha, Gen Sani Address on the occasion of Inauguration of "Vision 2010 Committee" in November 1996.

16.   Ibid

17.   Ibid

18.   Shonekan, Chief E. A., Response to the C-in-C at the Inauguration of "Vision 2010 Committee" in November 1996.

19.   Nijman, Jan *The Geopolitics of Power and Conflict,* (London: Belhaven Press, 1993).

20.   Hedley Bull quoted Connaughton R., *"Military Intervention in the 1990s* (London: Routledge, 1992).

21.   Gernett John., "The Role of Military Power", In John Baylist et al., Contemporary Strategy I (New York: Holmes & Meier, 1987).

22.   Ibid.

CHAPTER 4

FORMULATION AND IMPLEMENTATION OF DEFENCE POLICY

N. UMARU

INTRODUCTION

The Armed Forces, established for national defence, are complex human institutions that are the most respected in any country because they serve with great courage, determination, zeal and cheerfulness. Serving in a dangerous environment with the willingness to accept death, what John Hackett calls a contract of *Unlimited liability"* makes them respected figures with strong public support[1]. They are a pivotal and relevant instrument of national power. However, the strength of the Armed Forces is not in their legitimate use of arms but in their neutrality to regime change and their focus on the defence of the nation, its citizens and its policies. As a results, it must be given the necessary support though good planning for effectiveness and must be guided by policy that may required institution changes from time-to-time. So, there is a need for the development of a military based on an articulated defence policy[2].

Strategy is the "art of creating power" (Lawrence Freedman)[3], "had to be grounded in military reality" (R. Holmes) *"is the vital controller of military behavioiur"* (Colin Gray) and it is policy expressed as ends, ways and means[4]. Strategy is continually being redefined by classical theorists, strategic thinkers, military historians and even political scientists. Its definition could be broadened, based on Clausewizian logic. Thus, "Strategy is the use of any available instruments, up to and including the threat of force or the use of force, for the ends of policy, in dialectic of two opposing wills, with the aim of imposing our policy and our will upon the enemy". (Chew Strachan & Andreas H-R)[5]. There is a connection between strategy and policy which supports the Clausewitzian assertion that "war…is an act of policy"[6].

However, the most gifted of Clausewitz's student, Molke, the architect of the Prussian/German general staff and military thought who also influenced modern military theory *"believed that policy should not influenced military operations"*[7]. This is because of the pride associated with decisive military victory and had its roots in the battle of Knoggratz in July 1866 – Bismarck, Napoleon III, Austria. Of all the Clausewitzian dicta, none remains hard on the military like their subordination (primacy of politics in waging war) to political authority *"because it is they who witness firsthand the price of military failure"*. The military is a versatile instrument of policy and there is a tendency for political leaders to use the military as a main policy instrument that can be manipulated decisively. It is attractive or even glamorous to easily use the military for resolving social problems because their loyalty is usually to the state and not any political party[8].

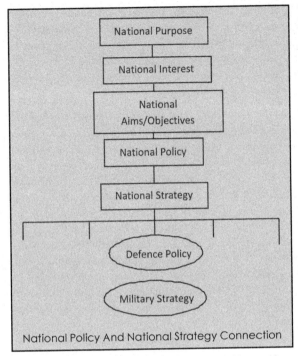

National Purpose

National Interest

National Aims/Objectives

National Policy

National Strategy

Defence Policy

Military Strategy

National Policy And National Strategy Connection

This chapter focuses on the "*formulation of defence policy.*" *National Defence Policy* is a continuous exercise to ensure a nation is abreast of matters of national security since it permeates and influences military operations. It must lay down a framework governing the conduct of defence in the country by highlighting the way the military and all other components of national defence can be used to protect, project, and promote national interest and contribute to international peace and security. We need a defence policy that will give us structures that will reduce the problems of resources, morale and politics through good national leadership.

Any national policy must take cognizance of national interest which can be pursued through real statecraft is about reality. "*Good statecraft maries objectives and means*". This requires real assessment of tangible objectives while at the same time "*identifying the means available for achieving them*" (TNI, Nov/Dec 07 figure 1). In formulating a defence policy, we must identify and highlight the type of military required to meet the spectrum of threats, risks and tasks. Consequently, I will be looking at the factors that are to be considered in the formulation of a defence policy and also look at effective implementation guidelines.

CONTEXT

A government policy is deciding and implementing a plan that will guarantee the well-being of its people. Different policies made by governments may overlap or interconnect with one another. Generally the following hierarchy may be established.

    a.   National policy
    b.   Foreign Policy
    c.   Security policy
    d.   Defence policy
    e.   Economic and Financial policies, etc.

A policy is usually a product of many inputs to ensure that many controversies are resolved due to varying interests. A policy cannot be perfect and once made will take some time to settle to a comfortable routine. Those who are aware of the processes involved with government's policy formulation and implementation know that a government cannot at once solve or take care of society's problem.

Generally policies come through political processes and are implemented by specific institutions of government. Policy making emanates from "good" analysis of articulated factors of concern and requires setting priorities where there is greater influence. A policy must take cognizance of innovative approach to critical national issues and co-operate on many spheres including military component of international security. Policies must of necessity contribute to national development. Although internal and external dimensions of policy are separates, they may overlap and complement each others with varying degrees of influence. Policy making in the security arena is very complex, difficult and hard to undertake successfully. National security policy, which should not be left to individuals, is determined by many factors cutting across all governmental activities: military, political, economic, social, environmental etc. *National security...depends on a sound economy, on civil liberties and human freedoms"* (RUSI, Feb 08). It is the most complex and difficult area of policy making. Indeed, security and stability are essential to development. Stability requires a strong and indispensable player[9].

DEFENCE POLICY

The defence of a nation is a complex business and cannot be easily reduced to ideas that are rational. However, in a democracy, policies have to be sustained by rational. However, in a democracy, policies have to be sustained by rational arguments or debates. Defence organizations are responsible for providing security response and freedom to a nation. Defence is an expression of sovereignty and provides services to the general public (e.g. aid to civil power, aid to civil authority, protection of civilians in times of disaster as the case in China). It is required to maintain a country's freedom and its ability to pursue its legitimate interests at home and abroad.

A defence policy must in essence support the wider foreign and security policies of a country. The politicians who have a strong attraction for the challenges of foreign policy use the military at any glimpse of crisis/conflict as a deterrence or show of force[10]. However, when forces are deployed for action, the politicians remain in a safe haven while the military men carry out what Clausewitz called "...*a continuation of political activity by other means*". Defining defence policy can be quite difficult and some early societies used it to justify policy can be quite difficult and some early societies used it to justify taxation. It is concerned with why we have armed forces, their nature and structure and how capable they ought to be based on the tasks they are suppose to perform and this is always primarily a political concern. It is laid down by political leaders for the military to act upon based on political and military situations. It is concern with general military strategy and other issues of collective security within given environment and will make the Armed Forces bring about an integrated approach to changing situations. Defence policy has linkages to foreign and other general government and deals with the co-ordination of military and non-military factors for war and peace.

We thus understand the interrelationship of various policies and their integration with national aspiration. For example, economic/financial policies and foreign policy are very closely related to the formulation of defence policy and therefore have the greatest effect on it. In reality, financial policy directly influences defence policy and in turn military strategy since it determines the expenditure profile for military commitments. Its influence thus extends beyond the cost of the Armed Forces. However, resources to the military.

Defence policy must ultimately highlight the preparation for and eventual employment of force as a legitimate policy option in response to security challenges (contingencies/threats). For this, there must be efficient management of resources in addition to flexibility to meet changing circumstances[11].

A defence policy is a product of many schools of thought and must focus on protecting national interest, which is over all other considerations, by ensuring national security. Adequate security is a pre-requisite for socio-economic development of a nation and requires the collective effort of government, communities and the wider civil society. The future security environment is hard to predict because of the new factors that are encroaching into international relations elements and security theory (e.g. technology, internet and climate change that transcend borders). Economies are slowing down and military structures and equipment are becoming more expensive. Yet request for use and employment of military power is increasing, with collateral damage frowned at, leading to demand for precision-guided munitions.

Managing a defence organization is a collective effort of military and civilian professional. For conduct of war, military plans are the direct responsibility of Ministry of Defence in association with the Higher Military Organizations. In the civil sector war plan is the responsibility of concerned Ministries at the national level. The strategic coordination of a war plan is achieved at the level of cabinet. Military strategy, within the directions provided by defence policy, is a military function; it develops the Armed Forces and formulates an integrated strategy to employ them to achieve set objectives. It provides direction and policy guidelines for Armed Forces and gives appropriate guidance to other agencies of government.

DEFENCE FORMULATION

A defence policy must be based on a vision that will ensure the use of power and influence to guarantee national survival and well-being based on key national values. The most important value for the nation is the ability to maintain its identity in terms of landmass, population and ethnic composition. Whatever will disturb the stability of a nation can easily be seen as a threat that must be dealt with through necessary means. The means may involve the use of the Armed Forces based on policy initiatives[12]. The duty of government is to provide for common defence for all by allocating adequate resources to sustain collective interest based on the situation of a particular environment. In general terms, the strategic environment comprises seven dimensions that will provide a framework for analysis (RUSI, Dec 2001) as follows:

a. Political
b. Economic
c. Military
d   Physical
e. Scientific and Technical
f.   Social and Cultural
f.   Legal, Ethnical and Moral.

These factors can be analysed for any country and their effects on the stability of the country assessed.

A key concern that will assist in the formulation of a defence policy is threat. Threat is characterized by the absence of freedom, lack of safety, absence of peoples' rights or even lost of live. Threats and challenges are diverse and multi-dimensional. Fundamentally, threat can be in two dimensions – external and internal. Externally, changes in international security environment will be main concern. Internally, political discontent and conflict over resources/export commodity should be given attention. These threats could be military or non-military.

Whatever it is, a defence policy must be aware of identified threats. Let's look at a list of situations that can bring about threats to a nation:

a. Regional Conflicts leading to cross-border banditry.
b. Illegal immigration
c. Weapon Proliferation. Small arms smuggling and gun-running.
d. Criminal activities of nationals abroad (international crime).
e. Volatile state of the global economy.
f.   Phobia (Anglo, Franco, Americo, Russo, Chino, Indo etc).
g. Economic crimes (careless drilling practices, broken promises, wide gap between rich and poor and corruption). *Corruption requires growth and structural change over a period.*
h. Environmental degradation (erosion).
i.   Population pressure/growth (Lagos will be the fastest growing city from now till 2015, with 58 new residents projected every hour – FP Jan/Feb 08)[13].
j.   Drug Trafficking (Excess cash can bring about corruption and extreme political influence.)
k. Hunger and Disease (Public health concerns). Hunger is an agent of mass revolt. High food price can lead to violence.
l.   Failure of state structures – poor governance, resource looting, poor leadership, abuse of power.
m. Ethnic conflicts (ethnic disintegration).- accumulated social stress and absence of social services and good infrastructure.
n. Piracy
o. Information warfare

p. Competition for scarce resources
q. Stress on government – weakening of state (threat multipliers).
r. Electoral Malfeasance.
s. Disruption of energy transportation (Somalian Coast).
t. Democratising nations. "Highly prone to both internal and external conflicts"[14].
u. Manipulation of Religion for political ends.
v. Lack of visionary leadership and capacity
w. Regional conflicts may lead to cross-border banditry.

All are above are ingredients for violence, crisis and conflict. The areas needing attention for policy design will be:

a. Clear Statement of needed roles for agencies concern.
b. Re-write and define organization.
c. Reserve forces for the Armed Forces
d. Resource for defence
e. Civil defence – Take over extra police duties: guarding, escorting and non-combatant activities.
f. Defence management including administration of military pension.
i. Policy guidelines
ii. Role monitoring – effectiveness of assigned roles.
iii. Issues of reform and re-organization
iv. Join civil-military structures to improve interaction.
v. Staff level review-Civil/Military
vi. Human resource development
vii. Finance and budgeting.

Today economic competition drives international relations. As a result there are new sources of conflict in areas with resources. The resources are: oil and gas (some supplier nation are prone to political and social disorder); water and forests. The monies obtained from sale of resources can be taken into poorly governed countries and used to fund civil wars and hostilities. Supplying resources to some countries and ignoring others e.g. oil, gas, timber can create threat situation. Lootabble resource –diamonds, timber and smuggled items sold in foreign markets can lead to tension. The resource factor on its own may not necessarily be the cause of violence or war. However, many of today's conflicts around the world are due to failure of institutions that govern how resources are utilized. The interacting factor could be ecological (water), institutional (failure of government), economic and political. Violence could erupt in form of insurgency, rebellion, gangsterism and urban criminality[15].

What processes are required for formulating a NDP? I have listed 4 stages as follows:

a. Interested parties, competent groups/individuals are invited or appointed for discussions and make submissions. Government must give an overview (TOR). Parties and individuals must seek access to wide inputs.
b. Submission made are critically looked at by government functionaries and those in the defence establishment before a draft policy is produced. The draft must be accepted by the parties concerned.

   c.   Draft is subjected to public scrutiny through general discussion and a final document is made available to government.

   d.   The final draft is critically discussed at the highest policy making organ of the government and a National Defence Policy is produced and issued for public consumption and implementation.

Because the processes require an integration of the academia, military , bureaucratic and political leadership, it becomes institutionalized and any change of key player should not bring a significant change to the defence policy. This is important since the processes received direction from the political leadership.

Let me look at a very relevant issue here – Security Sector Reforms (SSR). The reform of any activity of a government comes up when there is a disaster or catastrophe. Generally the fault areas are leaders, and policies. National security is too important to be left to amateurs and so the right people must be seen doing the right jobs. This requires constant education and training to bring about required skills and specializations. *"SSR is the complex task of transforming the organization and institutions that deal directly with security threats to the state and its citizens"* (Sean McFate). Nations in conflict that require SSR could be classified as follows:

   a.   Collapsed/collapsing states – Somalia

   b.   Failed/failing states (entities) – Zimbabwe, DRC, S/L, Liberia.

   c.   America, C. Asia, M/E.

Indeed even democratizing nations are sometimes prone to internal and external conflicts. Internal conflicts are difficult but can be resolved. External ones can be resolved through diplomacy or use of force. *"Successful SSR creates a security sector that is effective, legitimate and accountable to the citizens. SSR is a core component of peace building, as it allows a country to secure its own citizens and provides the exit strategy for costly peacekeeping mission[16]"*

There are many principles to be followed to arrive at an acceptable reform programme and end product to ensure success which is not usually very easy. For Nigeria, what we require is to focus on the area of operational effectiveness which is fundamentally a measure of success and invariably logistical. We will succeed in this area because of our President's appetite for reform. Due to its complexity in terms of resources, political processes, and local "ownership" SSR may take years to accomplish. The challenges of SSR are daunting.

The military profession is the most complex of all professions in the world. Its complexity demand extremes of technological expertise, mastery of human activities, a high degree of subordination, obedience and discipline in comparison to any other profession. It has an educational pattern and career structure that suits it. However, strong Armed Forces cannot be built without the political commitment of the people of the nation. The military organization has been central to the development of societies, the state system and defends the values of a civilization. The military professional is composed to *"an educated elite whose role in society is the organization, control and application of force in pursuit of democratic values as determined by the state"* (Sarkesian). Due to its varied activities, many join the Armed Forces for status, glamour and adventure.

Military professionals are consummate individuals who need and prefer weapons and support systems that are functional, reliable, come under their control and are effective under operational conditions. They like simplicity and precision in all they do akin to Jominian search for universal principles. Many other professionals learn and copy some of the military's principles and practices. Well, their integrity is above approach and most institutions of government are aware. The professional understand civil-military issues, political-military relations and employment of force. They reflect the political complexion of their nation and although we may not have an internationally acceptable standard for military professionalism, there are varying degrees of military usefulness. Military usefulness is derived through the pursuit of excellence based on evolving operational thought at theoretical and practical levels.

Due to globalization, civil supremacy over the military can be sustained with an appropriate constitutional and institutional framework. But their roles/mission must be clearly defined. However, not many political leaders are ready to appreciate their excellence or invest sufficiently in their development. Different attitudes to defence matters by various agencies of government can easily contribute to reducing their effectiveness. Defence usually partners with other government department/agencies to achieve strategic goals. Therefore, it is necessary that political leaders, citizens employment since they are usually established to deal with threats achieve political ends.

DEFENCE POLICY OUTCOME

A key outcome of a policy is to recognize the degree of the tasks and missions to be carried out. The Armed Forces, singly or jointly will have to be organized to carry out certain tasks and missions. These must be supported by a force structure based on threat assessment. Some of today's missions are support to wide security interests (internal and external), Peace Support Operations, Humanitarian Operations, Peacetime Security and Defence diplomacy. The military must be capable of carrying these out with some key pillars of military capability being:

a. **Force Generation** – Right numbers and quality. Quality of manpower is the most important and must be dependent on recruitment process, training, motivation, retention and resettlement (pension).

b. **Deployment, Tasking and Concept of Mobilisation.** Ability to move the Right Forces for the Right Missions at the Right Time.

c. **Effectiveness of Employed Force** – Doing the job using the necessary equipment for success based on a concept on arrival at location and fully supported.

d. **Sustainability** – Force readiness as long as necessary (difficult task). It is the totality of the logistics system.

e. **Defence Production:** Clear strategy must be in place to ensure local production of some key weapons requirement. For developing countries, there exists difficulty and foreign procurement is expensive and may carry a political prize.

FORCES REQUIRED

The forces to be employed under the direct supervision of the Ministry of Defence will be the Army, Navy, Marines, Air Force and for Joint activities. Some countries may have Coast Guards. Others simply have a Defence Force. Here are the key elements:

a. **Land Force (Army):** For the land force, number of boots on the ground is very important no matter how highly equipped and comprehensively trained. Today the land forces will have to combine many tasks: combat activities, support for civilians and co-operation the civilian organizations, repair and maintenance of infrastructure, etc Number is sacrosanct but there must be proper management. Irrespective of the assistance or support other Services can give the army, only land power can be decisive'.

b. **Maritime Force (Navy):** The oceans are a global route for commerce and are vital to economic prosperity of nations. A lot of the world's economy and political activity is conducted around the littoral. *Maritime activities of shipping, fishing and oil exploration are conducted within 200 miles of national coasts.* Providing maritime security is a key defence objective for littoral states. Maritime security responsibility is not only for navies. Indeed, maritime operations are resource intensive. Naval forces are a key asset to conduct defence diplomacy, expeditionary operations and amphibious operations, which requires the integrated and co-coordinated application of sea, land and air power. Today, more than ever before, naval forces need to be strengthened and made capable due to criminal activities by gangs around national coasts. Navies deliver influence from the sea.

c. **Marine (Naval Infantry):** Marines are naval infantry trained and organized to carry out amphibious operations (main purpose) and to fight from ships. Marines stress not only fitness but cunning in the conduct of operations and are the most naturally joint of the services, conducting the most complex land, sea and air operations. Their function has been significantly influenced by the technology and tactics of naval warfare at particular periods in history. In the 20th Century marines have regularly been used as elite infantry and gunners in major land campaigns. The complexity of their operations demanded a force trained and organized with specialist equipment and formed into self-contained all-arms formations dedicated to amphibious operations. Indeed Adm David D Porter commented, 'A ship without marines is like a garment without buttons' to show the importance and necessity for a marine formation[17].

d. **Air-Force:** When it first arrived, airpower changed the calculus of warfare and generated euphoria. It was highly praised and seen as a 'supreme expression of military power'. It is an effective tool of foreign policy if properly applied. It may not solve all military problems but it's the closest to doing it. It is a great contributor to the joint battle and an effective tool for managing the battlefield. However, its effective use must "be relevant to the desired political objective and appropriate to the strategic environment"[18]. Airpower has today become the *sine qua non of* modern armed forces. But for it to deal with the array of modern threats, it must be capable of dissuading, deterring and if necessary defeating the enemies. Airpower does not need defending because it has paid its dues in most operations. Tactically airpower is a 'victim of its own success' because the request for its support sometimes goes beyond what it can provide.

e. **Joint Force:** This is necessary for joint operation where all the elements of the Services come together as a cohesive whole. Joint operations is expected to permeate military thought. Here each Service with its attributes will play to its particular strength. What is necessary is to understand the differences between the Services and ensure application to patrol large spaces while the land forces may remain close to the edges of conflict. Doctrines, trust, personal contact, good leadership, change in thinking and attitude and clear understanding of the situation are key to success. Success demands that all forces must be able to operate together within a given command and control architecture where specific skills are required. Even if there will be a clash of culture; good education, training, proper orientation and requisite exposure for the right people, will remain the main sources of resolving differences amongst the Services for effective joint operations. Jointness requires 'sound comprehensive doctrine'. "The challenge of getting three distinct and proud Services, with individual interests and deep-rooted traditions, to agree to principles that have a fundamental effect on the conduct of their operations and training is not to be taken lightly[19].

The military requires clearly defined roles, missions or tasks from political authorities. However, not many political leaders are ready to appreciate the military's excellence or invest sufficiency in their development. Defence usually partners with other organs of government to achieve strategic goals. Therefore, it is necessary that political leaders, citizens and the government are conversant with the realities of military employment since they are established to deal with threats and achieve political ends. There must be a focus on operational effectiveness which is fundamentally a measure of material assets available and the ability to mobilize them and invariably logistical. Political and economic support determines military effectiveness. This emphasizes the need for a continuous and sincere interaction between the politicians and the military professionals on issues of resource allocation since modern conflicts or the employment of the military is complex and could even be destructive. To check emerging threats, equipments may need modernization to close identified gaps before troop commitments are made.

IMPLEMENTATION

Implementation of a policy is important to ensure effectiveness of assigned responsibilities because it must yield acceptable results. There must be a body charged with the implementation of a defence policy. It could be a board: that will comprise people from the strategic environment, academia, politics, military (retired and serving), members of Labour, NGOs and women organizations. This highlights the importance of a civil-military interface for effective defence policy implementation. It will be an advisory body and members must be those who have demonstrated competence not partisanship. The board is necessary because it is difficult to get decision taken in MOD even on issues that are not controversial. Personnel are important to success in any endeavour and so are key to the military's future. It is good to start with education and training as a key aspect including continuous professional development for individuals and groups within the services. Next is to look at the weaknesses in operational capabilities. Modern means must be employed to face new challenges bearing in mind development in military technology which is changing with time. Changes must be comprehensive, universal and consistent with global best practices and one's situation or circumstance.

National legislatures as separate arms of government must make input into the defence policy making process and must to a degree be involved with its implementation because of funds appropriation and authorization for military deployment. The defence committees should be knowledgeable on defence matters as they interact with military personnel, MOD staff and the general public. They are supposed to have sound advisers on defence issues to guide them. Interaction only on issues of project execution will not suffice particularly if it is not focused on strategic threat perceptions. A well articulated defence policy that is well implemented holds many possibilities for getting the right things done with the right people in place. It is an important goal in its own right and will help in solving most internal security problems. Therefore it must be responsive and accountable, provide a single military advice source and provide for an integrated policy/manning structure. In other words, the defence policy must give a military 'product' that a nation will be proud of and an example to neighbours. So an intellectual construct must be applied to get the desired result due to the innumerable inputs that will be made and will be required. Most importantly, there must be an interface between political authority and higher military organization which will retain and reinforce political control over the military rather than bureaucratic control.

An interface between military and political leadership is important to produce and implement a comprehensive defence policy. Government must ensure co-operation between all its relevant departments and agencies. For the Armed Forces to be effective, capabilities may be based on geographical and functional priorities and must provide for a variety of contingencies. Consequently, these areas will require attention:

a. **Force Structure:** An effective and functioning command structure must be designed since combat remains the fundamental task of the Armed Forces. The roles and missions envisaged must be fully accommodated including those for regional participation (strategic role sharing).

b. **Education and Training.** Full range of instructions in the art and science of war must be intensified in professional military education institutions.

Training must be challenging, continuous and geared towards readiness requirements,

c. **Equipping:** Force must be equipped to respond to situations that are complex and multi-dimensional. Forces must be configured to protect the country and its citizens. Varying phases of operations should be taken care of. Here, affordability must be squarely addressed.

d. **Re-orientation:** Forces need to be positioned to meet the challenges of changing security environment. Modern day military activities are sophisticated because the environment may be multinational and still requires effectiveness.

e. **Military Assistance:** The armed forces must be equipped to provide assistant to civil power (police), civil authorities (Ministries, government departments, civil communities) during riot, organized crime, strikes and during natural and humanitarian disasters like flood, earthquake, avalanche, volcanic eruption, etc. This assistance should also include participation in areas of development.

NIGERIAN CONTEXT

The constitution of the Federal Republic of Nigeria (FRN) 1999 recognises the need to have a legitimate and organized instrument of coercion within its borders that can be used based on identified threat-internal or external. The establishment of Armed Forces for a nation is the inherent right of self-defence to maintain sovereignty. Indeed section 217(2)[20] of the constitution encapsulates the essence and roles of the Armed Forces as follows:

a. Defendng Nigeria from external aggression.

b. Maintaining its territorial integrity and securing its borders from violation on land, sea or air.

c. Suppressing insurrection and acting in aid of civil authorities to restore order when called up to do so by the President, but subject to such condition as may be prescribed by an Act of the National Assembly; and

d. Performing such other functions as may be prescribed by an Act of the National Assembly.

Section 153 of the same constitution established certain Federal Executive Bodies, one of which is the National Defence Council that shall have power to advice the President on matters relating to the defence of the sovereignty and territorial integrity of Nigeria. The Council must give high-level direction and management of all defence activities. For the Armed Forces to perform their functions effectively there must be a policy put in place which will guide their operational conduct.

Due to our circumstances, a draft defence policy which should have been exposed to public scrutiny was handled mainly by the executive. The armed forces were directly involved with its review. In doing this the military high command tampered with some areas that to them could bring friction during operational situations. This tempering with created its own contradictions leading to unresolved issues of command and control. Public scrutiny is important because the will of the people is sovereign and any attempt to avoid this hurdle cannot be seen to be legitimate and brings about disconnect between policy makers, implementers and the people.

We now have a National Defence Policy which came out in 2004. It went through many reviews but did not go through the public debate I talked about earlier. Naturally some issues raised in the draft were dropped and few others added. That is why many within our strategic environment are not too comfortable with it due to lack of public exposure based on the absence of correct mechanisms for public participation in policy development. The public contribution is to ensure its legitimacy and make it accountable to the people of the country on whose consent power to use the Armed Forces is derived. One could compare a defence policy making process to Clausewitz's "paradoxical trinity – composed of primordial violence, hatred and enmity which are to be regarded as a blind natural force; of the play of chance and probability with which the creative spirit is free to roam; and of its element of subordination, as an instrument of policy, which makes it subject to reason alone"[21]. The essential elements; (the public/people, the military and the government/politicians) have unique roles to play.

All said and done we now have a NDP that could be reviewed from time to time. I want to believe that the MOD in conjunction with the military establishment under the policy and plan department are busy looking at areas that may require improvement and advice accordingly. The final policy[22] considered the following areas:

    a.   Strategic Review
    b.   Risks and Challenge
    c.   Strategic Response
    d.   Defence Management and Organization
    e.   Resource Support
    f.   Civil-Military Relation.

What is left is its implementation. The MOD and DHQ seem to be taking up this responsibility. I think as presently constituted they are not structured or adequately equipped to handle this issue; due to some inherent factors and contradictions that lower their performance. Working in the MOD (efficient bureaucracy) and DHQ (best and brightest of military minds) is a great challenge and is one of the most difficult and best jobs in government. MOD and DHQ need re-engineering to reduce institutional weaknesses. They need to be fused to become just one organ of government, new MOD. In doing this, we need a complement of staff (civil-military) to handle some key defence issues in addition to key recognized departments of a dynamic Ministry. The key areas should be:

    a.   Active Secretariat for Defence Council: to monitor implementation of defence policy and handle defence transformation. To quicken decision-making processes at the military and political levels and reduce bureaucratic sluggishness.

b. Strategy and Plans. Strategic direction of defence programmes; Preparation, Direction and Guidance of Operations; Operations concepts and thoughts; training matters and foreign deployment.

These complementarities of staff will look at core issues of military concerns and what the civilian authorities want them to do by providing link with main organs of government. It is here that the human dimension of combat that are difficult to measure can be looked into critically or even research sought on issues of leadership, organization, cohesion and morale, etc (socio-psychological variables)[23]. With these, a new MOD with rationalized staff, could put in-place structures that will contribute to strengthening our defence establishment. We must however keep in focus key offices that can be held accountable for certain responsibilities i.e. the Minister, Permanent Secretary, CDS and Service Chiefs. However, it must be very clear that only the CDS/Service Chiefs can be held responsible for the Service's fighting effectiveness, efficiency and morale in addition to the day-to-day activities and management of the military. How they get the resources to satisfy policy issues through the Ministry becomes their sole responsibility. They will have to constantly respond to changing internal and external environments as dictated by the political authority to enable the Armed Forces deliver requisite defence capability. Our Armed Forces have made positive contribution to our defence needs and have ensured regional stability. At all Higher Defence Organisation, personnel must understand national level decision-making processes. The civil servants must be experts in defence related issues and must properly understand the concept of national security, national interest and the place of defence in the national security equation.

MINISTRY OF DEFENCE

A defence organization, Ministry of Defence (MOD), must give the military institutional support and set priorities that are nationally affordable. It must quickly make and implement decisions in support of those engaged in operations. This will require adequate funding, comprehensive training of personnel, promotion for those who are competent at high levels and what the professional military institutions the academy, staff and defence colleges teach. Managing a defence organization is a collective effort of military and civilian professionals. However, military strategy, within the directions provided by defence policy, is a military function. It provides direction and policy guideline for Armed Forces and gives appropriate guidance to other agencies of government. However, defence planning is a key function of the MOD in supporting the Armed Forces for effective performance. A fully civilianized MOD may have difficulty understanding the nuances of the military professionals because they lack the skills that will enable them provide the necessary services and support for arming them, training them and getting them mobilized for good defence output. The bureaucrats may understand political direction sought by civilians but may not necessarily understand legitimate military concerns regarding operations. Therefore, there is need to inject some military minds into a New MOD to give it new orientation and understanding since military input may be necessary within a wider national policy construct.

Defence/Military issues are serious matters that require hard work and some degree of expertise. Defence planners must attempt to predict the future so they must be capable and posses certain expertise. Due to difficulty in predicting the future, "defence policy and plans and the equipment and forces they generate do not need to be in some absolute sense correct"[24]. However, to staff a modern MOD with purely civil servants may lead to the military losing sight of its fundamental purpose (its goal) of having such an organization in the first place. It may negate the military's utility since they become out of touch and become 'historical baggage' due to their minimal usage within the defence planner's realm. They may also distort the defence planning processes. We must establish a balance from many available options with those who are trained and understand the military instrument. This is an achievable goal and the civil servants, who should be well-trained, can be useful part of a defence planner's armoury. Civil service reform for effectiveness has all too often ignored the peculiarity of the defence institution and may even have a dysfunctional implication for military effectiveness.

In our situation, the MOD and DHQ are very complex organizations and any policy for fusing them will require comprehensive planning and dedicated implementation from a reservoir of experts. Openness is important in all areas of concern. A New MOD for effectiveness will require its roles and responsibilities clearly defined to avoid duplication and internal conflict. It must take care of the difficulties and structural problems of MOD and DHQ irrespective of the culture and bureaucratic interests of the Services and civilians. There must be room for an acceptable method to resolve conflicts between the Services when it arises. Organizational changes give more options for assigning the right human and material resources to achieve objectives. However, it is a delusion to think that changes will make an institution run smoothly. The benefits of change may come with inconveniences and risks which we must accept by testing the new system.

What is needed is a system that will bring out the best of ideas that will be profitable to the institution and the individuals. Re-organization is a dilemma that institutions or even governments face from time to time. Invariably the MOD should be an 'integrated politico-economic-military planning organization' to ensure military effectiveness and the understanding of all concerned, centred mainly on policy. However, "even the best structured organization cannot work effectively with unqualified people or with people who resist its central purposes and dynamics"[25]. The people must have proper orientation and the passion for what they are doing. Only the best will be good enough for the New MOD. Well, "change does not come easily-vision, commitment, trust and leadership are irreplaceable ingredients to sustain it"[26]. These are ignored at the organizations peril.

FUTURE DIRECTION

As instruments of national power, the armed forces must maintain their relevance and adapt to the changing global security environment. The security landscape of the future is most likely to be very different from today's. The global security environment is hard to predict because of the new factors of security: advanced technology, internet, globalization and climate change that transcend national borders. As a result, the character of war or conflict will keep changing; soldiers, states, sovereignty and borders are less defined and the rules of armed violence will remain unclear. Indeed globalization of goods, capital, services, people and intellect has often led to globalization of violence which inevitably requires a redefinition of the role of the military. The greatest challenge will be having a balanced and sustainable force posture with requisite strategic concept that will define the roles of the military in national policy.

A defence policy is a product of many schools of thought and must focus and remain capable for protecting national interest. Defence Policy must recognize the dangers of today and the challenges of tomorrow. The future direction of defence policy will primarily be based on the changing security environment and how the military can be employed. Trying to gaze at the future of the utility of force is a very hazardous undertaking. However, we must look at the past which may provide us some signs for the future since history remain our only guide. It is intellectually demanding but one could safely assume that irregular warfare or insurgency (4GW) will occupy a large part of the military's activities for the future. The armed forces must acquire counter-insurgency capabilities in addition to carrying out stability and reconstruction operations. So, training must focus on irregular warfare. Whatever it is, we must remember what Clausewitz said, "The first, the supreme, the most far-reaching act of judgement that the statesman and commander have to make is to establish by that test the kind of war on which they are embarking; neither mistaking it for, nor trying to turn it into, something that is alien to its nature". This is the first of all strategic questions and the most comprehensive[27].

Military transformation is today generally accepted. It involves new technologies, new operation concepts and radical changes in organizational workings requiring vision leading to new ways of thinking, fighting and doing things. Here one can see the footprint of irregular warfare. It requires sound institutional framework for success. Of utmost importance is the transformation of the mind; inside, within and outside. Many are however fearful of transformation because of its consequences since there is no end-state. For successful transformation, there must be a bond of trust between the military organization, the MOD and the office of the C-In-C. High standard is required between the civilian and military leadership. Future direction of defence policy will follow the key challenges of transformation and changing threats. Military "transformation is today a geopolitical reality, a strategic issue and a military necessity[28]. The military requirements will be:

a. Spectrum of Operation – equipment and training
b. Coherence of Operation and defence acquisition – existing capabilities, progress expected from technology, political directives (objectives and resources allocated), type of enemy.
c. Coherence of command and administration – coherence of command, neutrality of decision regarding fundamental values of military institution

in operation or in the barracks (courage, dedication, selflessness and solidarity).

Defence transformation as a policy must be accepted by political leaders. It should aim at getting the military institution effective, efficient, cost effective to society and sustainable in performing assigned tasks. An affordable strategy must be put in place through the collective will and courage of those concerned with implementation. Transformation should make Armed Forces more effective through strong policy instruments. Current policy and military posture due to obligations must not remain fixed. A widening of the "range of possible policy demands in the future"[29] must be anticipated a head of time through adequate projections for the future we know little about. The future will bring a lot of challenges for the defence institution. 100% accuracy will be hard but failure to predict the future correctly could be expensive. Well, all national militaries must be conventionally strong for the future with very well educated and trained officers/men and women who must be skilful and disciplined. The leaders at all levels must be competent and determined to respond to a wide range of challenges. They must also note that resources may not always be enough but governments can always make shift in priorities for national security.

A complex issue that will remain fundamental to ensuring national security for now and in the future is civil-military relations-the interface between policy leaders and military officers. The political leaders are masters of policy and the military are dedicated 'armed servants' who implement policy. The issue is that of balancing "military effectiveness and civilian control"[30]. Problems could arise in the relationship through poor civilian planning or attempt to micromanage military issues. What is required for good relationship is candid advice and vigorous exchange of views and insights about the varying "roles of military and civilian leaders in wartime decision-making". The best system is one that allows for substantial military autonomy in the military, technical, and tactical realms (how to fight wars) in return for complete subordination to civilian authority in the political realms (when and if to fight them)[31]. It is difficult to get "proper civil-military balance". Civil-military relations, "ultimately, it's about the interchange of viewpoints and the production of effective strategies and decisions about the use of the military instruments"[32]. So it requires vigorous discourse through varying education of future leaders.

CONCLUSION

Every aspect of state activity requires policy guidelines. Security, a pre-requisite for national development faces challenges that require comprehensive solution so we must pay attention to national security policy. Defence is a critical aspect of national security and a defence policy is necessary to guide the military on how to conduct their business efficiently. The making of defence policy entails many facets from a wide basket of issues with threat analysis being fundamental. The choice are complex and have tobe institutionalized requiring a lot of research. Threats may sometimes be difficult to identify, so capabilities must be made variable for responses to keep whoever is the enemy guessing. With all services being equally important for national security, robust forces must be maintained across a wide spectrum of capabilities and must be used as a tool of statecraft in pursuit of foreign policy goals and for internal tasks. Our main economic assets can be policy approached from the sea/air. Consequently, our military resources and capabilities should adequately manifest in these areas. Our force structure must match given missions. However, some threats could be real and many imaginary.

Matters of national defence require political direction from a stable political structure. The military's advice must be sought in the realms of strategy and employment of force. It is equally important that the academia be involved and the general public must also contribute from a position of knowledge and wisdom. Public opinion is important here and the press has a role to play through debates, discussions and interviews by those who hold national interest uppermost in their minds. A defence policy must be credible, have capacity for flexibility and responsive to change. A defence policy must be based on security challenges that threaten national interests and must be adaptable to changing security environment. It will require a list of activities with options to be adopted for national defence. Providing the requirements will make the military capable of defending the nation by acquiring the needed capacity and patriotism to implement the policy. To achieve this, a balance of influence between civilian and military elements is needed for increased integration of MOD. In this regard, it is important that military and civilian professionals are fused in the MOD with the civilians well managed and looked after in areas of training and exposure. This should aim at achieving operational effectiveness and economical use of resources.

Globally, nations are running out of resources leading to a global competition creating an arena for economic battle which may lead to crisis. Internally, budgetary considerations must be given careful study especially of the relationship between defence and civil/social service spending. It is always difficult to balance political ambitions and resources which is a fundamental problem of resource control at the centre government. Due to the unpredictable nature of their duty and the future, the military must be educated, trained and maintained with adequate resources. However, a defence policy must ensure efficiency in the use of resources and must be cost effective. This is because the Armed Forces cannot get all they wish to have; only what the nation can afford based on an adapted policy. They must be made more responsive when employed and it aiding civil power through necessary logistical reach for effectiveness. Manpower is vital to success in any conflict or given task and human resource development is a very key national security priority. However, there is a need to strike a balance between manpower requirement and equipment necessary for success in operations or given tasks. The greatest challenge will be to design a balanced, capable and sustainable force structures/levels shaped for envisaged threats of today and the future.

Looking backwards may or may not provide us with ideas to judge the future. However, we must not run away from bringing up good ideas even if there is institutional resistance to propositions that challenge existing policy. In implementing a defence policy, the military professional must not fail to highlight operational misconceptions that can lead to failure. The military professionals at high levels must exhibit intellectual ability and strategic vision based on positive arguments so that the organization can progress. Creativity must be rewarded for those who are ready to take intellectual risks and not be afraid of failure. Military professionals must understand civil-military relations be conversant with the fundamentals and ethics of the profession and their responsibility to society. There must be a decision-making set-up which will accommodate military advice and exchange of 'views and insights' between the military and civilian leaders. Therefore institutions of professional military education must carry out their mandates of sound indoctrination of upcoming officers.

Finally, constitutional provisions and the way agencies of government are organized must function well based on national aims, values and political arrangements. An unstable political structure cannot give the required direction on defence policy imperatives. Consequently, military leaders must be educated about duty and professional obligation to the state to enable them give purist military advice to supportive political leaders in the performance of their duty. That duty must be determined and guided by policy. Arriving at a sound defence policy requires great details; discipline, deliberate process, institutional innovation and interactive and continuous discourse on relevant issues and postulations. It is important to ensure that goals set by policy bring about the achievement of objectives at affordable costs. The public must know and understand the rationale for large defence allocation. Policy makers must understand the unique knowledge and attitude of the military professionals before setting achievable targets for them to implement. This is where AANDEC can play a critical role as a think-tank or an umbrella for the defence community to make input into not only issues of defence but also issues of security and strategic concerns to the nation. It could be an avenue where retired civil/military officers can express their views.

REFERENCES

1. Milan Vego, Operational Warfare at Sea: Theory and Practice, Page 19.
2. E. Christopher Dankeker, War, edited by Lawrence Freedman, Page 111.
3. Michael Clarke, "The Overdue Defence Review: Old Questions, New Answers", RUSI Journal, December 2008, Vol 153 No. 6, Page 5.
4. Colin S. Gray, Another Bloody Century Future Warfare, Page 364.
5. Beatrice Heuser, Clausewitz's Ideas of Strategy and Victory, Clausewitz in the Twenty-First Century, Edited by Hew Strachan and Andreas Herberg-Rothe, Page 161.
6. Carl Von Clausewitz, On War, Edited and translated by Michael Howard and Peter Paret, Book One, Chapter One, Para 24, page 87.
7. Michael I Handel, Masters of War, (Classical Strategic Thought), Third, Revised and Expanded Edition, Page xvii.
8. Carl Von Clausewitz,…Book Eights, Chapter Six, Page 608

9. Jim Storr, Neither Art Nor Science – Towards a Discipline of Warfare, RUSI Journal, April 2001, Vol 146 No 2, Page 42.

10. William Hopkinson, The Making of British Defence Policy, Page 67.

11. Nigel Essenhigh, Resource Accounting and Budgeting in the MOD, RUSI Journal, Dec 2001, Vol 146 No. 6, Page vii.

12. AA Milton, British Defence Doctrine and the British Approach to Military Operations, RUSI Journal, December 2001, Vol 146, No. 6, Page 42.

13. Richard Burdett, Foreign Policy, Jan/Feb 2008, Page 42

14. James Dobbins, Who Lost Iraq, Lessons from the Debacle, Foreign Affairs, Sep/Oct 2007, Page 72.

15. Mary Kaldor, New and Old War, (2nd Edition), Organized Violence in a Global Era, Page 9.

16. The Outcome of SDR, RUSI Whitehall Paper Series 44, Thursday 10 September 1998, Page 29.

17. Bartkett ML and Millett Allam R, The Oxford Companion of Military History, Edited by Richard Holmes, Pages 549/550.

18. Tony Mason, Air Power (A Centinnial Appraisal), Page 66.

19. Clive Loader, Is True Air/Land Integration Achievable? Defence Systems, RUSI, February 2009, Vol 11 No3, Page 50.

20. The Constitution of the Federal Republic of Nigeria, 1999.

21. Clausewitz,...Book One, Chapter one, Para 28, Page 89.

22. Defence Policy of Nigeria.

23. N Kinzer Stewart, War, edited by Lawrence Freeman, Page 145.

24. Colin S. Gray,... Page 47.

25. M. N. Umaru, The Fusion of Land, Sea and Air Forces for Joint Operations, Original Essay for the Award of fwc, March 1993, Page 13.

26. Akram Ghulam and Colonel Peter Tomlinson, RUSI Defence System, Oct 2008, Vol 11, No. 2, Page 80.

27. Clausewitz...Book 1, Chapter 1, Para 27, Page 88.

28. Jean-Louis Georgelin, RUSI Journal, April 2008, Vol 153, No 2 Page 56.

29. Britain's National Security (Compulsion and Discretion), RUSI Journal, December 2008, Vol. 153 No. 6, Page 17.

30. Desch, Salute and Disobey?, Foreign Affairs, Sep/Oct 2007) pages 154

31. Desch, Salute and Disobey?, Foreign Affairs, Sep/Oct 2007, pages 153/154.

32. Michael P. Noonan, Mind the Gap: Post-Iraq Civil-Military Relations in America, A Conference Report, FPRI Publication, Jan 8 2008.

CHAPTER 5

STRUCTURE OF DECISION-MAKING FOR DEFENCE IN NIGERIA

CHARLES DOKUBO

A critical challenge facing the modern nation-state is the creation of an environment of peace, stability and security. The problem of national security is complex and more apparent in a developing nation where the institutions and value goals of nationhood are fragile, unsettled and keenly contested among the competing interest or groups. In such a nation, there are numerous complications arising from the sad state of underdevelopment in the economic, political and social spheres. Nigeria has just emerged from several years of highly centralized military regime to a civilian participatory order. This arduous transition has unleashed an array of agonizing choices and responsibilities, ethnic political and economic.

The process of dissolution of the old decadent authoritarian order, on the one hand, and the emergence of a democratic alternative, on the other, is characterized by severe social dislocations, which poses serious dangers to national security. In this chapter, an attempt will be made to briefly explore the emerging concept of national security, the theoretical concepts of decision-making in Nigeria and the challenges of the process of decision-making to the Executive, the Legislative and the Armed Forces.

NATIONAL SECURITY IN PERSPECTIVE

Within modern international relations, security was initially looked at from a Western historical perspective. Between the First and Second World Wars, both sides of the realist-idealist debate were preoccupied with the concerns of a particular type of state and so security was defined as the relationships between the great powers and how these could be controlled more, or less, peacefully. As Ayoob suggests, since the debate was the product of a particular intellectual tradition, which faithfully reflected a particular process of historical and political development and could be traced at least to the Peace of Westphalia, this was entirely understandable.[1]

Because of World War Two and effective criticism such as Carr's critique of collective security, idealism was discredited and realism came to dominate the study of international relations in paradigmatic fashion. This dominance of the realist school in international relations was reflected in a continued bias in security definitions towards great powers and absolute security.[2] Security came to focus on war, the ability to fight wars and the external threats to the state which might give rise to them. Security depended on the ability of a nation to deter an attack or to defeat any that might come.[3]

The conceptual development of security was limited for a long time by the parameters of this tradition within which it evolved. Advances or changes, such as they were, remained located within the realist paradigm. An example of this is the development of strategic studies in the cold war era, strategic studies dominated investigations of security because the nature of superpower rivalry was such that it was absolutely vital to keep abreast of technical developments in weaponry, warning systems and so on. As a result, the development of security as a concept was considered unnecessary, and possibly dangerous, in that to change notions of security would tamper with the delicate balance which was claimed to have prevented nuclear conflict.

Fundamental problems for the Third World have scarely been considered within the context of realism. Work on security which took account of the Third World exhibited the tendency simply to adapt the concept applied to developed states. Walter Lippman noted that 'a nation is secure to the extent to which it is not in danger of having to sacrifice core values, it wishes to avoid war, and is able, if challenged, to maintain them by victory in such a war.'[4] To make this notion of core values applicable to the Third world it is necessary to reduce it to 'the minimum core values of any nation: political independence and territorial integrity'.[5] The maintenance of these values may have contributed to security at the level of the internation system but it has no meaning for those living in insecurity at the state level.

In the evolving literature on strategic studies, the Third World became a subject of focus, especially in the context of its attempts to acquire nuclear weapons. Analysis was based on the concern that certain Third World states would try to throw their weight around given their previous lack of power and influence. The growing military weight, economic power, and political influence of developing states require a re-examination of prevailing assumptions about their role and impact on global security.[6] The implication has been that Third World states would be less responsible than those involved in the "balance of terror" for many decades, since they have more to gain and less to lose.

The incorporation of the Third World into security studies was clearly inadequate from the point of view of developing states themselves. If security is seen as the maintenance of minimum values then it can be used to justify keeping internal order at any cost. This has led to policies of repression and patterns of expenditure that serve extremely narrow sectional interests. The survival of a particular regime became the essence the Third World security. Such an arrangement proved useful both to the super powers and Third World governments. If the interest of the regime in power is dressed up in the language of national security to lend it an air of legitimacy internationally, in reality, it is only possible to recognize regime security.[7]

The realist paradigm still predominates international relations theory and literature. However, realism no longer stands alone in international relations theory but is pitted against pluralist and structuralist approaches in a triangular debate. As with realism, these other approaches contain a variety of opinions within them, but have enough in common to be recognizable as distinct paradigms, and it will be important to bear in mind their possible implications for the study of security.

This chapter is part of the general orientation, throughout the 1980s and early 1990s, toward re-examining security as a concept, as well as how decisions about security are made. The process of security over the last decade has been facilitated by considerable changes in the world and in the nature of theoretical attempts to explain it. Whether security as previously understood is inadequate as a concept, or whether it has at least ceased to be adequate as a central organizing concept of international relations, has been increasingly questioned.

The end of the Cold War means that a whole range of issues that up until recently seemed absolutely critical has turned out to be of purely historical interest.[8] Endless organizing over the escalation of regional proxy wars between the superpowers and the likelihood or possibility of a first strike by one or the other are now irrelevant. Gorbachev's 'new thinking' with the Third World had only transitory importance in attempting to evaluate security in Third World. Gorbachev and his ideas have been superseded and questions about superpower rivalry in the Third World are of only historical interest. Consequently some work on security has become out of date very quickly. Calvert and Weiss & Kessler examine Third World insecurity in the context of relations between the USA and USSR, a relationship which no longer exists.[9]

In the 1990s, while the challenges facing most nations are not as immediately catastrophic as those confronted by the adversaries in the Cold War, actors at all levels of analysis face problems which may well be equally disastrous in the longer term and whose resolution may require international cooperation on an unprecedented scale.[10] Because of this, there has been a tendency to recognise the inadequacy of the previous definition of security and at the same time to maintain its centrality to international relations by revising rather than discarding it. The view can thus be taken that the study of security, without being restricted to a particular level of the international system, has been developing out of necessity.

Given the period of momentous historical change through which the world is passing, a reappraisal of security, particularly in a re-examination of the focus on military matters, seems entirely justified. However, the problems caused by the rapidity of change mean new and finished theories are unlikely. However, the security perspective adopted in this chapter is a broad one. Security is taken to be about the pursuit of freedom from threat and the ability of states and societies to maintain their independent identify and their functional integrity against forces of change, which they see as hostile. The bottom line of security is survival but it also reasonably includes a substantial range of concerns about the conditions of existence. Quite where this range of concerns ceased to merit the urgency of the 'security' label and becomes part of everyday uncertainties of life is one of the difficulties of this broad concept.

Thus national security will be defined as the ability of nations to prevent all forms of threats to its survival ranging from external aggression to threats of economic, political and environmental insecurities, whilst grappling with the challenges of nation-building and good governance.[11]

NATIONAL SECURITY DECISION-MAKING

There has been a great deal of activity in academic circles directed at developing and refining theories to explain how national security policy is made and why certain decisions emerge from the policy-making process. Some practitioners considered this to be purely academic exercise of little use in dealing with the pressures of the 'real world' of policy formulation and implementation. This criticism may be justified because in certain instances, policy theories have failed to develop practical recommendations to improve policy processes. But the value of concepts that lead to greater understanding of how process affect the quality and control of policy should not be underestimated. After all, it is the responsibility of the practitioners, not the academicians, to improve our policy-making mechanisms which require a more sophisticated understanding of 'what is' and a greater appreciation for 'what should and could be'.

Perhaps, the practioner's impatience with academic theories stems from the inherent nature of theory in the social sciences in general and complex policy-making systems in particular. A theory or model is an abstraction of reality and an attempt to reduce untidy complexity to regularize and rigorous relations. As the number of variables and the degree of uncertainty in a policy issue are reduced, the explanatory power of the model is increased and cause-effect relationship became easier to establish. Unfortunately, as this simplifying process continues, the model diverges significantly from reality, yet the practitioners must deal with issues in the real world.

Unlike the academicians, the practitioners cannot hold certain variables constant while he seeks solutions to perplexing problems. Nevertheless, it is useful to examine briefly some of the more popular models of the policy process. This section can be helpful to the participants and the practitioner because using various models to examine the policy process requires different 'thinking caps' – a venture that can broaden the perspectives of the participants interested in understanding national security policy.

The model highlighted here are the rational actor, bounded rationality and incrementalism, organizational maintenance and bureaucratic politics, presidential power, palace politics and domestic politics. This list does not in any way exhaust the theories of decision-making processes, but it is representative of the field and should give an impression of the advantages and disadvantages associated with decision-making models in general.

RATIONAL ACTOR MODEL

From this perspective, policy is made as a rational choice among the available course of action with the principle objective to maximize attaining clearly identified goals. Moreover, this approach that goals can be prioritized, so it is possible to select from among mutually exclusive goals.

Examing the national security policy process, the rational actor model assumes the following:

- Purposive action must be explained;
- The actor in the policy arena is the national government;
- The decision taken represents a rationally calculated choice with respect to be national security problem;
- The decision is explained when one can determine the principal goals of the actor when the decision was taken;
- The decision was reasonable considering the actor's goals.

The additional assumption that the policy maker has the necessary information and authority to make and implement a decision is inherent in this model. By extension, in a political system where power is divided among many actors and institutions, there must be a consensus on the nature of the problem, the goals of the nation, the criteria by which alternatives are to be judged, and a common understanding of the information available. A perfect decision requires perfect information. Most problem-solving models follow the general pattern of analysis suggested by the rational actor model.

The formal organization where policy is made at the top based upon objective information provided by subordinate organizations comes closest to a policy making orientation consistent with the rational actor approach. The ideal type of bureaucracy postulated by Max Weber describes the requirement for establishing a system of hierarchically-controlled policy formulation and implementation in a complex organization setting.[12]

The limited applicability of the rational approach to policy problems characterized by complexity and uncertainty has been addressed by several scholars. Herbert Simon criticized the assumptions and prescriptions of the rational approach to decision-making, arguing that objective depends on value judgements that are transferable among individuals, that complete information is never available, and that the human mind is incapable of conceiving all alternatives and their consequences.[13] The task of organizational leadership, therefore, should be to define the fact and value assumptions upon which individuals base their policy decision-making was more characterized by what he termed 'branch method' of successive limited comparisons than by the root method of rational-comprehensive choice. In addition to the limitations on individual rationality identified by Simon, Lindblom addressed the policy environment in which agreement over goals and their value preferences is not possible. He postulated that policy decisions are made by marginal analysis in which policies are compared to one another and agreement is made on means rather than on ends. This phenomenon, according to Lindblom, largely accounts for the incremental nature of policy changes, as only small departures from existing policies are acceptable in the face of uncertainties and unclear goals.[14]

Another variant of assault on the rational actor model in the literature is associated with the bureaucratic politics and organisation models. In this view, government agencies carve out and protect their organizational 'turf', becomes ends in themselves and controls many of the operational decisions that cumulatively define the nation's policy in specialized area of public concern. Policy is, thus, characterized as organizational output highly conditioned by the concerns and bureaucratic relationships of the agency. There can be no 'grand policy' effectively established and implemented by as central leadership. There are only narrow policies resulting from administrative decisions, and where organizational gaps exist, there may be no policy at all. The assumption is that Congress and the President may establish policy guidelines, but these guideline are too broad and vague to control administrative action on specific issues effectively.

The relationship between the bureaucracy and the political system that maintains bureaucratic power is characterized by an 'iron triangle' of an administrative agency, its clientele interest groups and congressional committee or blocs. Attempts by political leaders to impose broader policy constraints must penetrate the power of this relationship, which is used to foreclose outside interference in the specialized and closed system of influence. The phenomenon of issue networks can sometimes support the maintenance of this relationship, and at other times, challenge its authority as narrow interest-based groups seek influence over issues that cross agency lines. While most of the application of this concept is on domestic issues such as welfare, commerce, agriculture and natural resources use, some apply to national security issues. Perhaps the best examples are interservice and the influence of the 'military-industrial complex' in defence weapons decisions. International trade issues, particularly as they affect specific economic sectors, are also example.[15]

In certain areas of public policy, professional and specialized groups arrogate to themselves claims of unique competence to deal with issues. In the national security area, military officers, foreign service professionals, and intelligence specialists argue that their training, experience and responsibility for implementation mandate that they be consulted in policy deliberations and that detailed policies and implementation be left exclusively to their prerogative. Functional and geographic specialists in these groups also seek to carve out limited areas of discretion and to protect their prerogatives from other groups, even those groups in their professional community. Competition for specialized influence is further complicated by economists, systems analysts and management expert.

If specialized groups maintain credibility with political leaders and other sources of support, they can influence the parameters of or even foreclose policy debates. Policy, then, becomes the product of specialized judgement based on the perspectives, assumptions, values and norms of the profession. As such, it is likely to be slow to change, unresponsive to new challenges, and hemmed in by the traditional roles, missions, doctrines and specialized routine of the profession. While these effect may be similar to those of the Organizational Maintenance Model, the different origin of bureaucratic and professional power lead to meaningful distinction. Professionalism and expertise make broader claims to jurisdiction based on competence and unique responsibility, while bureaucratic 'imperialism' generally influences specific programmers.

Professions create carefully structured role definition and doctrines that significally affect the implementation of policy decisions. Since they perform essential functions, their essence cannot be eliminated or significantly constrained, as can specific agencies and programmers. Finally, professionals generally control employment standards, and therefore, are capable of maintaining their positions longer than political leaders.

The Organizational Process Model, therefore, treats policy decisions as the product of national leadership deliberations constrain by the influence of organizational and professional activities. The subtle difference is that, under the more traditional concepts, organizations and professionals tend to reserve for themselves the prerogatives of policy formulation and implementation. Government action is still seen as the output of organizations, but the President and his advisers seek to coordinate and control organizational actors and to set the policy framework in which organizational programmers will be carried out. The President and his policy advisers must deal with the realities of factored problems and diffused power, parochial priorities and perceptions and the tendency of organizations to filter information, offer options, and implement decisions that serve their own interests.

Organizations do not control policy directly as they do under the more traditional theories, but their routine operations uncover problems which are then presented in the context of the organization's own interests. Government leaders are not powerless, however, and can counteract many of the adverse organizational influences by seeking alternative information sources, choosing the organization to implement their decisions, and using their authority and influence to control implementation details. These activities are time consuming, however, and leaders must be able and willing to devote their full attention to the problem if they hope to control rather than be controlled by organizational influence.[16]

A second variant of assault on postulations of rational actor model, is the burecucratic model. In 1969, Graham Allison first published the conceptual framework that included the Bureaucratic politics Model. While many experts on this model have been treated in theoretical literature it sometimes get subsumed in the general approach.[17]

The fundamental proposition of the Bureaucratic Politics Model is that government decisions and actions result from political games played by individuals and group in positions and actions result from political games played by individuals and groups in position that give them the legitimacy and power to affect policy on particular issues. Policy is not a conscious choice among alternatives or the uncoordinated output of separate organizations. It is a political result of the contending forces attempting to solve different problems but engaging in political bargaining among themselves. Political power is shared among themselves. Other players representing different interests have the ability to affect policy outcomes.

National goals and the policy environment are uncertain and ambiguous, thus requiring that players focus more on power and politics than on the substance of their arguments. The positions taken and the stakes perceived are influenced by the position held. The phrase most often used to a player's viewpoint in "where you stand depends on where you sit." The key to predicting the results of a policy game is to identify a player's political bargaining advantage and his skill in using them. Government decisions and actions often result from the fortuitous coincidence of decision-makers with a problem seeking a solution and operators with a solution seeking a problem.[18]

Since the bureaucratic politics model assail the assumption (by the rational comprehensive model) that policy decisions are products of rationality and logic, several critics have argued that it underplays the President's role and the significant advantages his position provides in any political game, particularly one played in the confines of the executive branch. Most analyst of bureaucratic politics attribute the origin of the approach to Richard Neustadt's book, Presidential Power, yet they portray the president as only one among many players. Neustadt characterized presidential power not in terms of his formal authority, but as the "power to persuade others that what he wants of them is what their own appraisal of their own responsibilities requires them to do in their interest, not his". But the President's formal authority, including political appointees serving him, his reputation and public prestige, and his responsibility to a national constituency, all important sources of power, makes him first among the players in any bureaucratic political game.[19]

What distinguishes the Presidential Power Approach from those of Organizational Process and Bureaucratic Politics is that the President is not constrained by and forced to cope with existing processes in which others have the initiative. He has the power to choose the issues on which he will decide and to structure the channels through which others must gain his support. The centrality of the President's position ensures that his administration will reflect his priorities and his way of doing business. Differences in Presidential style are the key determinants of how policy will be made. These differences may lead to a system that resembles any of the above concepts or other variants described below.

ALTERNATIVE POSTULATIONS

If a President should choose to centralize as much decision-making as possible rather than delegate responsibility, to his Cabinet and the executive department, he will require a strong staff or personal assistants and advisers. There is a danger that individuals of such high ability and strong convictions will establish themselves as extensions of the President and may compete among themselves for influence with him. Policy decisions may be more a reflection of the outcome of personal power struggles than of informed deliberations.

The difference between Palace Politics and Bureaucratic Politics is that political games occur in a limited group through which other actors must attempt to influence policy decisions, rather than an open system in which each bureaucratic actor may choose his own tactics and action channels. While fighting among advisers for the President's ear may lead to dysfunctional filtering of information and oppositions, the President also has the power to establish the 'rules of the game' and to take advantage of the competition to ensure that valid arguments are presented to him.

This approach may cause "multiple advocacy" – a process in which important policy choices are made by the authoritative and well-informed President.[20]

A president may be primarily concerned with his political power base and may approach all policy issues, including those related to foreign and defence policy, from the perspective of protecting and expanding that power base in the general public and with congress. This is likely to occur in a President's first term when he is concerned with reelection. The major actor influencing the President's decision will then be his political advisers and political power brokers in congress, and public and private interest groups. Decisions are likely to reflect political support assessment and be coloured by domestic distribution of cost and benefits, instead of the effectiveness opinions in achieving more specialized national objectives like military preparedness.

While on the surface domestic politics domination may appear inappropriate as a basis for policy decisions, there are two schools of thought that argue otherwise: (1) influence of domestic interests in the foundation of the democratic pluralism theory; and (2) the political feasibility of establishing and implementing policy must be considered or the president will deny himself the prerogative of decision.[21]

Although this section was not intended to be a comprehensive deliberation of issues in decision-making theory, the major objectives was to introduce some concepts and considerations.

SECURITY DECISION-MAKING IN NIGERIA.

Nigeria has over the past forty years only had less than twenty years of democratic governance. Yet as a sovereign country, Nigeria has often had to address its national security problems. However, in doing this, the conception of national security is statistics, narrowly defined and the process of decision-making remained secretive. The long period of military rule, which reinforced a narrow military conception of national security, may be partly responsible for this situation. Whereas in the United States the long experience of democratic rule had enabled them to put in place an elaborate national security decision-making process complete with the key actors and a system of checks and balances, in Nigeria, it is still unclear.

NATIONAL SECURITY ORGANS

The following are the key national security organs under the Executive:

a) A central organ for coordination, control and supervision. The National Security Adviser (NSA) on behalf of the President, through the National Security Council, The Joint Intelligence Board (JIB), and the Intelligence Community Committee (ICC).

b) Specialized agencies for the collection of intelligence and the provision of security services. The SSS provides internal security, the NIA – external intelligence and the DIS for defense intelligence and security.

c) The Armed Forces, the Police and para-military organizations that have responsibilities for specific aspects of national security. They are tasked through the relevant ministries, service councils and established chain of authority.[22]

The National Security Adviser has the states and enjoys the privileges of a Federal Minister. He advises the President on national security and directs the NIA and SSS on policies approved by the President. He is a member of the National Security Council. The constitution prescribed a National Security Council composed as follows:

(a) The President as the Chairman
(b) The Vice-President who shall be Deputy Chairman
(c) The Chief of Defence Staff
(d) The Minister of Defence
(e) The Minister of Foreign Affairs
(f) The National Security Adviser
(g) The Inspector-General of Police
(h) Such other persons as the President may in his discretion appoint.

The Council has the power to advise the President on matters relating to public security including matters relating to any organization or agency established by law for ensuring the security of the Federation.[23]

THE JOINT INTELLIGENCE BOARD

The Joint Intelligence Board meets once a month or more frequently if the situation warrants. The composition of the JIB is as follows:

a National Security Adviser – Chairman
b Director-General, State Security Service
c. Director-General National Intelligence Agency
d. Chief of Defence Intelligence
e. Permanent Security, Ministry of Foreign Affairs
f. Permanent Secretary, Ministry of Internal Affairs
g. Permanent Secretary, Ministry of Communications
h. Permanent Secretary, Ministry of Finance
i. Permanent Secretary, Special Services Office
j. Comptroller-General, Nigerian Immigration Service
k. Comptroller-General, Nigerian Prison Service.
l. Comptroller-General, Nigerian Custom Service
m. Chairman, National Drug Law Enforcement Agency
n. Director, Naval Intelligence
o. Director, AIR Intelligence
p. Director, Army Intelligence

INTELLIGENCE COMMUNITY COMMITTEE

The Intelligence Community Committee (ICC) meets every week, it comprises the NSA, DGSS, DGSS, CDI, AIG, FCID and the PS, SSO. They discuss operational and administrative matters and coordinate the implementation of measures affecting public security.

HOUSE OF REPRESENTATIVE AND NATIONAL SECURITY.

Few developments in the national security arena have been so significant even in the developed nations in the past decades than the increasing assertion by the House of strong and continuing roles, indeed a full partnership in the policy process. In the main, the constitution presents to the House and executive an "invitation to struggle for the privilege of directing foreign policy". The House has both challenged the President's prominence across many of the important issues and has started acquiring the resources, information and the legal authority to do so on a comprehensive basis.

The claims of the House are soundly based in the constitution's deliberate distribution of powers among the three branches of government. The bulk of the enumerated powers related to "national security" powers were reserved for the House. The House is allocated the power to declare war, raise and support armies and the navy, makes rules for the government and regulation of the forces, and make all laws which shall be "necessary and proper" for carrying out these functions. Additionally, the advice and consent of the Senate must be obtained for treaties and the appointment of ambassadors, ministries, and other key officers of the government.

Whereas the President can at least in theory and subject to constraints as provided for in the constitution, move with dispatch and secrecy in the national security arena, the deliberative processes of the House are slow and open. Investigation hearings, debate, resolution of differences between the two Houses, all these take time. Hence in both emergencies and threat to the nation the public and often times of House itself traditionally has expected the President to take the lead.

The way members of the House have traditionally tended to define their roles and responsibilities are a third factor in explaining how the House handles national security. Basically, they have been concerned with subjects that personally affect their welfare, and also what directly impinges on their reelection. In general, members of the House do not consider questions of military policy in terms of their implications for strategic objectives. Instead they are focused on their personal well-being and constituency-related issues. Yet, while they explore the details of the defence budget in these areas they seldom question the strategy from which the structural requirement flowed.

Another reason offered especially in Nigeria to explain the House role in national security matters was lack of expertise and access to information on national security matters. The committee system tended to generate some expertise in the armed services or appropriation committees; members of that committee generally become well versed in some aspects of their committee work. Yet even those committee members seldom develop a full appreciation of all the full committee's concerns and often did not understand national security policy issues under consideration elsewhere in the House or Senate. A given number of the House might, for example, know a great deal about military personnel expenditure but relatively little about weapons procurement-let alone about strategy, mobilization, economics, warfare, or other aspects of national security.

Given the increasing complexity and vast amounts of information relating to any national security issue, the executive departments that controlled the information-producing and intelligence-gathering agencies had an advantage over the House. The Executive affixing a security classification to weapon system capabilities or to strategic intelligence further restricted access to information necessary to formulate and evaluate alternative proposals.

The House, however, could offset executive branch advantages to some extent by using its power to hold hearings and investigations, bringing executive branch witnesses before it to explain policies and programmers and to explore various points of view. Such hearings about national security matters often allowed inter-service rivalry to surface, giving legislators the opportunity to choose concepts or particular programmers that they found personally appealing or in the interest of their constituents. In any case, the hearings showed not only that the House can use its investigatory powers to acquire information needed to make strategic decisions but also that the House with its power of legislation and appropriation could be the place of final decision-even on matters of strategy.[24]

THE ARMED FORCES AND NATIONAL SECURITY

In a democratizing nation like Nigeria, the military's involvement in the national security process has been restricted to instrumental and administrative roles. By liberal democratic tradition, functional expertise, and professional inclination, the military had defined itself as a subordinate instrument of the policy process. "Grand strategy"-the first level of the policy process in which fundamental political goals are established has been largely "off limits" to the military officer. Ironically, and fortuitously, it is a restriction the democratic process has imposed in both its professional values and organizational purposes.

The military senior officers, particularly the Chief of Defence Staff, are trapped into secondary policy roles by their organizational responsibilities. As leaders and products of complex government institutions that increasingly display the appetites and characteristics of bureaucracies, the CDS has little time and perhaps of strategic goals. A close review of senior officers' schedules quickly reveals the established priorities. Far more time, energy, staff and imagination are dedicated to the mundane but essential tasks involved in running the armed services than are committed to the art of strategic thinking and planning. Few military officers think in strategic-political terms, but many have mastered the Byzantine intricacies of the planning, programming, and budgeting system that dominate the defence ministry's calender.[25]

The exclusion from the first or initiating level of the policy process is ironic because the very concept of "grand strategy" has a strong military connotation. In Western culture at least, significant advance in the development of strategic thought is associated with great military names e.g. Fredrick the Great, Napoleon, Clausewitz and Bismack.

In politics, thinking and acting are intimately related. Historically those military officers who have made the most vital contribution to strategic thinking usually had a large appetite for ultimate political power – the authority to choose their nation's strategic goals. Or they represented a military elite that was a close partner of an authoritarian ruling class. Defence of civilian authority on the ultimate political issue was not their paramount concern. Perhaps it is because they played such an important role in the formulation of the country's security goals that the great military strategists of the past have made such a significant contribution to the development of strategic thoughts.

It is, however, a price that few democracies are willing to pay. As a result, their military officers are consigned to narrower political functions at the instrumental and administrative levels of the policy process. Thus, the military in the contemporary democracy does not have a major contribution to make on the most critical policy levels-the national security debate.

CONCLUSION

The National Security decision-making is complex and fascinating because of the two worlds it involves: As Samuel Huntington explains:

> One (world) is international politics, the world of balance of power, war and alliances, the subtle and brutal uses of force and diplomacy influence the behaviour of other states. The other world is domestic politics, the world of interest groups, political parties, social classes with their conflicting interest and goals.[26]

National security affairs impact on and are influenced by both worlds, for national security involves the application of the national resources to the international arena in an attempt to make the domestic society more secure.

One way to characterize the national security policy-making process is a series of concetric circles. At the center is the President surrounded by his closest advisers. These are the people by virtue of their position or personal relationship to the President, are involved in the national security issue that require presidential decision. The inner circles of advisers usually include the Ministries of Foreign Affairs and Defence, National Security and Intelligence agencies. The composition of this "inner circle" will of course depend somewhat upon the issue and the desires of a particular President. Closely associated with this innermost circle are the organizations, such as the Finance Minister, budgetary planning department, are members of the President's personnel staff and among his most frequent advisers.

Beyond this circle lie the relevant departments of the executive branch and is the House ring with the organizations of the legislative branch. Beyond them lies the public arena consisting of the media, interest groups and the general public.

This concept of concentric rings in policy-making obviously focuses upon the President and executive branch, placing the House generally plays an important role, and in some cases, decisive role in national security affairs. Although it will be useful to pursue the concentric analogy for a moment, it should be recognized that in reality the House occupies a ring in another plane from the executive branch circles.

The boundaries between the policy-making rings should not be viewed as impenetrable barriers. Individuals and even organization can and do more from one ring to the other depending upon the issues. Most cabinet officers and their assistants, for example from the Ministry of Commerce – are part of the third ring of bureaucracies. When they are invited to participate in the deliberations of the National Security Council or its committees, say on a strategic trade issue, they become members of the second ring or even the innermost ring.[27]

There is no one way in which national security decisions are made. Issues range from the relatively mundane, such as how many separate agencies require representation at a foreign embassy, to the more critical, such as intervention in foreign crisis. There is regularized process for decision-making, but the issues themselves and the particular ways they arise often dictate the precise method by which they addressed. Factors such as secrecy, immediacy, political sensitivity and seriousness of impact tend to place decisions into either the "routine" or "priority" category. Routine decisions generally involve more of the circles of policy-making, while printing decisions especially those that require great secrecy and quick action, are often made in the inner two circles.

Finally, two trends are apparent in surveying national security decision-making and the actors and processes therein, namely, increasing centralization and the attempt by the House to strengthen its role. The trend towards centralization and the attempt by the House to strengthen its role. The trend towards centralization has been driven by the increased complexity and uncertainty in the international security environment, and has been fueled by the communication revolution that has permitted far greater central direction of large organizations than was possible in the past. It has occurred both within the individual departments and agencies in the decision-making process and also in the overall process itself.

The constitutional powers of the House blunt and diffuse the power of the President and his centralized decision-making apparatus. As party strength declined and the authority of the committee chairperson dwindles interest groups have multiplied and individual legislators have become less inclined to follow the leadership of the party and House leaders and the President.

The juxtaposition of these two trends poses the unwelcome prospect that the President and a well-informed Hours will continue to be at odds and that neither will be prepared to give way, short of major national emergencies.

ENDNOTES

1. M. Ayoob, Regional Security in the Third World (Croom Helm 1986), p. 129.
2. B. Buzan, People, State and Fear – An Agenda for Security Studies in the Post-Cold War Era (London: Harvest Wheatsheaf, 1991), p. 216.
3. A. Wolfers, Discord and Collaboration (Baltimore MD: John Hopkins University Press 1962), p.83.
4. W. Lippman, US Foreign Policy (Boston: MA: Little Brown, 1943), p.342.
5. T. Maniruzzaman, The Security of small States in the World (Canberra: Australian National University 1982), p. 363.
6. Koladziej and HarKavy: Security Policies of Developing Countries (Lexington, KT: Lexington Books 1982), p. 21.
7. Weiss, J. G. and Kessler, M. A.; Third World Security in the Post-Cold War Era (Boulder, Co. Lynne Reinner Publishers 1991), p. 163.
8. Freedman, L.; in Booth (ed). New Thinking About strategy and International Security (London: Unwin Hyman 1990), p.86.
9. Ayoob, M.; Regional Security in the Third World op. cit; Calvert; The Central American Security System; and Weis and Kessler; Third World Security in the Post Cold War Era, op. cit.
10. Booth, New Thinking, op. cit. p. 341.
11. Dokubo, C.; "African Security in the New Millenium" in Akindele R. and Bassey A. (ed.) Beyond Conflict Resolution *NILA and Vantage Publishers 2000), p.87.
12. Allison, G.; Evidence of Decision: Explaining the Cuba Missiles Crisis (Boston: Little and Brown, 1971), pp. 30-38.
13. Simon, H. A.; Administrative Behaviour: A Case Study of Decision-Making Process in Administrative Organizations, 2nd edition (New YorkL Free Press 1967), p. 211.
14. Lindblom, C. E.; The Science of Muddling Through Public Administration Review, Vol. 19, Spring 1959,p.79.
15. Halperin, M. H.; Why Bureaucrats Play Games, Foreign Policy no. 2, 1971, pp. 70 – 76.
16. Dixon, J. H. et al. National Security Policy Formulation: Institutions, Processes and Issues (National Defence University, Washington DC 1984),p. 143.
17. Allison, G.; op. cit, p. 217.
18. Ibid, p. 220.
19. Neustadt; R. Presidential Power: The Policy of Leadership (New York: Mentor 1960), p. 53.
20. Dixon, J. H., op. cit, p. 145.
21. Hoffman, S.; Gullivers, Troubles or the Setting of American Foreign Policy (New York; McGraw Hill 1968),p. 419.
22. Peters, J.; The Management of Nigeria's National Security, Nigerian Journal of International Affairs, vol. 3, 1982, p. 211.
23. Ibid, p. 215
24. Ibid, p. 217

25. Ibid, p. 219.
26. Huntington, S.; The common Defence (New York: Columbia University Press 1961), p. 1.
27. Hillsman, R.; The Politics of Policy-Making in Defence and Foreign Affairs (New York: Harper and Row 1971), p. 119.

CHAPTER 6

THEORIES AND MODELS OF STRATEGIC DECISION-MAKING

BAYO OKUNADE

PREAMBLE

This topic s apt as it addresses one of the basic ingredients of governance, decision making with particular reference to national security which I regard a the most fundamental of the defining elements of our national life and existence. It is one public good that we cannot even contemplate its privatization. In this age time, national security is not something to be taken for granted. It cannot also be left to chance.

This issue of mechanism for decision-making at the strategic level is no less fundamental. Ideally, every organization or institution constantly makes series of decisions that keep it going on daily basis, but the future of such organization like a nation largely depends on long-range planning which is what strategic planning/decision-making is all about. It might as well be that the activities at the non-strategic levels are just merely giving effect to decisions that have been taken years back.

CONCEPTUAL CLARIFICATIONS

While the various concepts and terms – decision-making, theory and model, strategic decision are not unfamiliar, a quick review is attempted in appropriate parts of this lecture as preambles to the core discourse here.

Decision-making: Decision making is a vital and intrinsic aspect of human, institutional and organization existence. It is a means to purpose accomplishments however defined. To Mintzberg et, al. it is a "specific commitment to action" which includes "all purposeful behaviour that concludes with a commitment to do something rather than merely to talk about it" Elsewhere it is "simply a moment in an ongoing process of evaluating alternatives for meeting an objectives and nothing but the moment of choice. The point has also been made that instead of just doing something "a decision to do nothing" is regarded as a decision.

The above presupposes that a decision follows a number of distinct stages or that there is a decision making cycle. It also assumes that behaviour is purposeful in that objectives are set and attempts are made to meet them within a wider decision process, whereas a broader concept of a decision may encompass the whole of the process of the process of decision making itself .

A decision process is concerned with the whole range of activities involved in making a decision, not merely the point of decision. Ti encompasses everything from the realization of the need for a decision through to the feedback from surveying events as a results as a result of the decision taken. Decision – making involves more then the choice of some preferred alternative. It also involves what can describe as a process that leads up to the choice situation and continue after the choice has been made. Usually, decision-making follows a somewhat continuous and not discrete set of processes and activities with possibility of revisiting previous stages.

ON DECISION-MAKING PROCESS

Because of the nature of decision making and the problem of perception there is no consensus process follows the path in FIGURE I below:

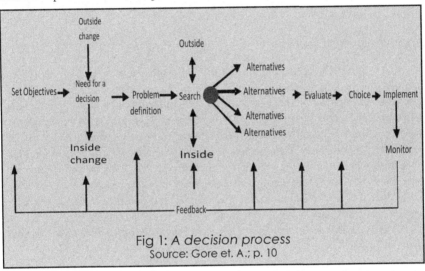

Fig 1: A decision process
Source: Gore et. A.; p. 10

These processes are discussed below:

1. *Objective Setting* which I considered to be very important as solution can only be seen a successful or not in the light of both the problem or opportunity and overall objectives of a firm or organization.
2. Recognizing a problem or need for a decision although not same as clearly specifying what is required. This stage can in fact determine the results looked for and so need careful attention.
3. *The search stage* – It is one that absorbs most time and can never be taken for granted.
4. The implementation and monitoring stage: these stages in practice are vital, for no matter how excellent a solution or decision is, if it is not translated into action and no attempt is made to ensure that implementation is in accordance with plans, the whole effort spent on the previous stages will be wasted.

Theories: strictly speaking, theories are "proposition(s) or set of propositions offered as a conjectural explanation for an observed phenomenon, state or affairs, or event". Within the context of decision-making, they relate to how decisions are made. This is the basis for models.

Models: are deliberately simplified and usually idealized and imaginary "representation of a "phenomenon; with fundamental properties that are explicitly defined (or physically built) and from which other properties can be deduced by logical reasoning (or by empirical observation if the model is a physical object). Similarly, Cooke and Slack described a model "as an explicit statement of our image or reality[4]. So, differences in models merely result from perception or different images of reality. A model therefore provides us with an organization of reality or links the theoretical world of our minds with the empirical world of our senses. This explains the existence of numerous alternative models of decision making exist. They are the result of different perception of ideal construct and of the application of these perceptions to diverse decision situation or diverse realities.

NATIONAL SECURITY

I have no doubt that you are familiar and fully subscribe to the non classical as against the myopic classical and state centered conception of national security. The orthodox definition as we know is not only unfashionable it is also untenable and unrealistic given the state of the literature and the reality of contemporary world. I will take it that the College's conception of security approximates what was espoused by the former Commandant at Ibadan when he elected the contemporary definition whereby national security is human centered. Relying on McNamara, he argued that in a modernizing society, security means development and without development there can be no security. He rightly submitted that "...security must be appreciated from both the military and non-military dimensions; hence it denotes the security of citizens as well as the state that provides opportunities for the well being of citizens'.

I do not intend to go into any theoretical exploitation of what security or national security is. I know we are on a familiar terrain when it comes to this. It is suffice here to state that, for us in Nigeria, security and national security is conceived in terms of current thinking though there is hardly any demonstration of this. The evidence for this lies in the disposition of former President Olusegun Obansanjo's to the contemporary thinking when he said "the primary objective of national security shall be to contain instability, control crime, eliminate corruption, enhance genuine development, progress and growth, improve the welfare and well-being and quality of life of every citizen". Though there are some disturbing and ambiguous element in the definition like 'contain instability', it is hoped that this will be done within the expressed provision in the Constitution especially its Chapters II and IV dealing with State Objectives and fundamental human rights respectively with the reviewing powers of the judiciary of the actions of government. One expects that the intention of the definition will be meaningful with the involvement of other relevant organs of state and responsible internal security institutions. Some of the development envisaged more so now under a regime that is committed to the rule of law is enhanced involvement of the Courts with the possibility of obedience by public authorities. It is in this context that the Supreme Curt ruling on Public Order Act is a welcome development. Though robust enough in term of its inclusion of some important aspects of security like the environment, some of the decision that are being taken though not strictly within the context of national security proper, some subsequent developments, for example, the decision recent decision at the last (6/2/08) National Executive Council meeting restricting harmful electronic substances that constitute unserviceable computers through tariff regime and the setting up of the National Council on Vision 2020 to prepare a technical economic blueprint to take us to the economic goal in 2020 to enable Vision 2020 project to be launched in 2020 next year (Punch, 7/2/08). Also important is the realization by President Umaru Musa Yar' Adua at the recently concluded AU summit in Addis Ababa (The Nation 2/2/08) that 'political stability was pivotal to real economic development and prosperity in African countries', and his admonition that 'an urgent action to overcome the recurring problem' problem should taken while calling for the enthronement of "true democracy" good governance, and the rule of law' which to him are 'essential ingredients for political stability in the continent'.

It is also very important to refer to the economic blueprint of the Federal Government as encapsulated in its seven-point agenda. According to the seven-point agenda, government's expenditure priorities are to be focused on areas of power and energy, food security and agriculture, wealth creation and employment, mass transportation, land reform, security as well as qualitative and functional education. All these have the capability for addressing the non military and human security elements of national security.

One other cheering development that will rub on the country's security is the renewed commitment by the current administration of NEPAD. The on-going Country Review Mission (CRM) of the New Partnership for African Development will put Nigeria on her toes on the four thematic areas – democracy and political governance, economic government and management of economic development.

ON STRATEGIC DECISION:

Any attempt at situating or understanding the nature or characteristics of strategic situations will necessarily involve a discussion of the various levels of decision making. While decision is a generic, ubiquitous, and imbued with common features, it is normally not taken at one singular point and has different ranges or decision span depending on the issue. It is this categorization that party determines the appropriate processes and method in decision making. The diagram below gives a vivid summary of the classifications.

There seems to be a considerable degree of consensus on what constitutes Strategic decisions in the literature but with controversy as to whether it could be a distinct or isolated aspect or stage in decision making. A good understanding of strategic decision has to be predicated on the discourse on levels of decision making which we attempt to do here.

The decision making architecture below is sufficiently informative on the nature of strategic decision making as it helps in locating the position of strategic decision in any organization. While Ansoff (1987) and Johnson and Scholes (1999) advanced three categories or levels of decision making with strategic decision making at the apex, in other classifications especially by Herbert Simon and Peter Drucker strategic decision are referred to as Non-Programmed/unique decisions provide a basis for understanding nature of strategic decisions at least at the basic or rudimentary manner.[6] To them, non-programmed/unique decision making which is the equivalent of strategic decisions is novel and complex with no predetermined or ascertainable system. They are also characterized by incomplete information and uncertainty. So they require judgement, creativity and customized solution. Furthermore, Simon's non-programmed and Drucker's unique decision is concerned with "objectives and long-range plans which are previously though, but no longer, to be exclusive to top management. This can be differentiated from the Programmed/Generic decisions which are routine, repetitive and predictable set of decisions. There also exist a definite procedure' or definite decision criteria or rules for handling them. It is essentially mechanistic and concerned with short term decisions mostly at the operation level.

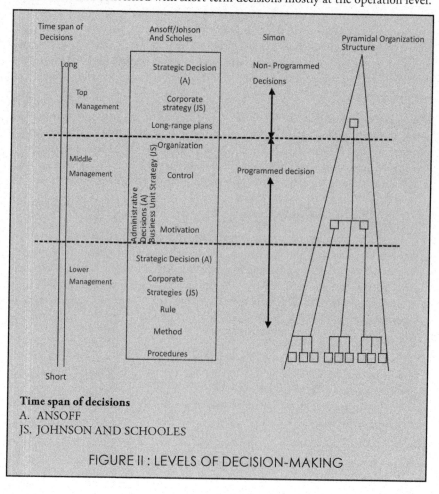

Time span of decisions
A. ANSOFF
JS. JOHNSON AND SCHOOLES

FIGURE II : LEVELS OF DECISION-MAKING

SOURCE: Gore, teal. (1992) and Johnson and Scholes (1999). In another set of classifications, Ansoff (1987), Johnson and Scholes (1999) suggest a three level classificatory schema. These are to Johnson and Scholes' Corporate Strategy' 'business unit strategy' and 'operational'. The equivalents in Ansoff's are 'strategic' 'administrative' and 'operating' decisions. In these classifications Johnson and Scholes, and Ansoff divide Simon's programmed and Drucker's generic level into 'business unit strategy' and 'operational' decisions and administrative decisions, and operating decisions while Simon's non-programmed' and Drucker's Unique level are the equivalent of Ansoff, Johnson, Scholes strategic level.[7]

It is important add that the categorization of decision making can be misleading. In real life situation, especially in the area of public policy, for example in a federal setting, each of the levels cannot be free standing and indeed are not free standing. It cannot therefore be exclusive responsibility for strategic or apex level of the organization. Apart from the importance of decisions taken at the so-called non strategic level which assist strategic decision 'intended' strategic decision can be 'unrealized strategies' as a result of interpretation or implementation problems. In reality, a web of relationship exists among the levels. In theory and practice, it is now accepted that strategic issue is not exclusive to the strategic level and personnel, all levels and are involved depending on the situation. (Johnson and Scholes, pp. xvi and 9). Given the nature of strategic decision as overall strategy, it cannot but affect other decisions and levels, vice versa.

STRATEGIC DECISION MAKING: THEORIES AND MODELS

Since our concern in this Lecture is about one of the levels of decision making which is at the strategic level, there is the need to discuss the basic theories and models of strategic decision model in order to facilitate our discussion in the next part on their relevance or appropriateness in 'Analyzing the Nigerian National Security Decision Making Process'. Of course, this assumes that Nigeria subscribes to a particular or set of these models. Given that the discussion here is on one of the levels of decision-making, the generally acclaimed theories of decision-making apply. While one can proffer specific models of strategic decision making, its underlying theories largely follow the general decision making theory. So we subsume our discussion of the theory of strategy decision making under the general decision making generally it can be somehow specific depending on the nature of decision and the decision making level.

THEORIES OF STRATEGIC DECISION MAKING

It is perhaps important to note the apparent confusion in the literature on decision making in the discussion of its theories and models. In many cases there are equivocations whereby the distinction between theory, approaches, models and methodology are blurred. These equivocations occasioned by the interchangeable use of these terms are evident in writings by most authors. The implication of these is that there is a short of ambiguity in drawing distinctions between theory and models of decision making. Also, there has been a lot of re-invention of the wheels. Some authors laid claim to particular theories or models while in actual fact they are replicating or describing existing works especially by the pioneers like Herbert Simon, Lindblom and Etzoni without acknowledge them. These authors can at best be original in the name(s) they attributed to the to the processes they are describing.

The conflict theory of decision making described a number of basic ways in which decision making cope with the threats or opportunities that are often part of crucial decisions. Often, decision makers defensively avoid the stress of difficult decision dilemmas by adopting coping pattern in their decision for a long time before thinking about the dilemma. Shifting responsibility entails passing the ultimate responsibility for the decision to other individuals or groups. Bolstering involves uncritically boostering the advantages of the least bad option of those options that are available – often the status quo or business-as-usual option. All these three coping patterns lower the stress inherent in facing up to difficult decision, regardless of which of these three defensive avoidance coping patterns are adopted, either singly or in combination, there are two common outcomes – incomplete search for, and evaluation of, incoming information that would aid choice, and lack of contingency planning in the event that the course of action being followed begins to fail badly[5].

MODELS OF STRATEGIC DECISION-MAKING

In specific terms, the concern here is to present some broad representative models that relate to the strategic level as a subset of decision making. Here one relies on the models of strategic decision as advanced by Gore et. al. because of their specificity. Not all paraded model of decision making really fit strategic decisions. The three models discussed below are representative of the two strands of approaches or methodology used in strategic decision-making. These that have been discussed earlier are the inductive an deductive which is Top-Down and Bottom-Up respectively.

A. RATIONAL SEQUENTIAL: 'TOP-DOWN' APPROACH TO STRATEGIC DECISION MAKING.

There are two variations of this model which have the semblance of Herbert Simon's Rational Comprehensive model or theory of decision making. These are Hofer/Schendel (1978) and the Higgins (1982) models. The duo advanced a rational sequential approach to strategic decision making which is necessarily 'top-down'[6]

I. HOFER/SCHENDEL STRATEGIC DECISION-MAKING MODEL

As shown below, to the model, the strategy formulation process largely excludes 'goal formulation'. The model is therefore of a general and of wider applicability and use. This model is based uncertainty, complexity of decision and bounded rationality, and provides a model for rational decision making that takes account of these features.

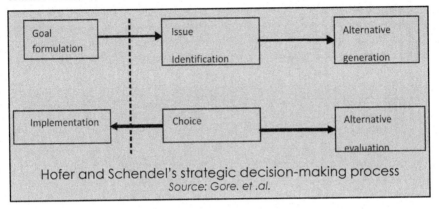

Hofer and Schendel's strategic decision-making process
Source: Gore. et .al.

Description of the model:

a. Issue Identification: This has do with identification of decision issue which is not 'simple or obvious' because of the problem of 'partial ignorance;. Because of the limitation, the inclusion of contingency planning in the strategy formulation.

b. Alternative Generation: this involved mapping out alternatives or options. This also includes social and political analysis as well as economic and market forecast.

c. Alternative Evaluation: These must then be evaluated; they suggest that it is difficult to look at problems or projects in isolation, because of the synergistic efforts among projects. Additionally, information especially those that concerned with the future, is unlikely to be reliable, so contingency planning at both a business level and an overall corporate level is advocated.

d. 147

e. Choice: making a choice in the most rational way, given the constraint on rationally, the choice situation will involve the use of criteria, or a choice 'model' like 'financial and risk appraisal models' the TOWS (threats, opportunities, weaknesses and strength) matrix, ' a stakeholder support evaluatory model' 'a strategic fit ranking matrix', These form part of what are called strategic tools.

The above model ends with Choice as Hofer and Schendel exclude implementation planning from the strategy formulation process.

II. HIGGIN'S STRATEGIC DECISION PROCESS

under this model, the critical issue in the strategic decision making process is the identification of information system needs which will over come the problem of assimilation that fully rational models would have. The model involves the setting of objectives and comparing them with required performance which comes from outside the model. This is followed by an examination of the (many) performance gap in the light of forecast which are themselves a result of an audit of the organizations present position (which may involve, for example, an analysis of strength and weaknesses compared with the results of an environmental analysis of the important factors likely to influence the Organization. From this comparison of different information on inputs on over all organizational results organization wide plan as well as plans for other levels using easily quantifiable data.

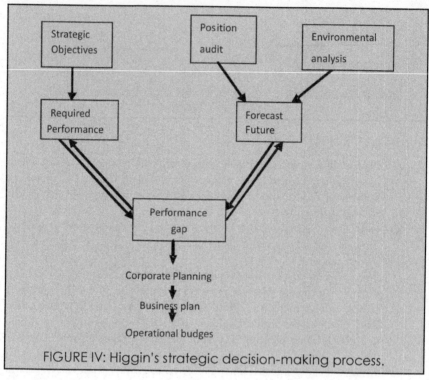

FIGURE IV: Higgin's strategic decision-making process.

B. LIMITED RATIONALLY OR BOTTOM-UP APPROACH

Mintzberg, suggested that limited rationality process is not sequential but involves considerable back-tracking or repetition of stages. Furthermore, there is not a firm distinction between the levels of decision-making.

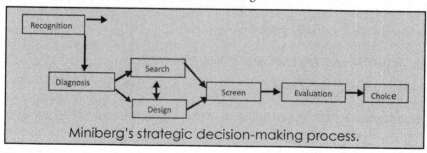

Miniberg's strategic decision-making process.

Because a number of operating or administrative decisions can eventually amount to a perceivable strategy. What emerges in such situation may not of course be desirable or what was really wanted. So for a bottom up approach to be successful in achieving overall objectives, it is essentially that an overall strategic direction is given from the top. The strategic management process must guide lower-level decision to ensure they are within the strategic objectives.

Mintzberg's approach unlike Hofer and Schendelor Higgins adopted a positive approach to theory formation and provies a rather richer model that not only recognizes limitations to full rationality but also incorporates practices that are adopted to overcome these limitations. According to the model, decision process fall into three stages. Identification, Development and Selection.

DEVELOPMENT AND SELECTION.

1. Identification consists of two part namely, the recognition of a problem and the diagnosis of that problem. Recognition of a problem is affected by the availability of an answer, or occurs if actual deviation from standard. The number of stimuli needed before a problem is recognized depends on whether the situation is perceived as being a crisis, a problem or an opportunity.

2. The second phase which is the Development also has two distinct parts, that associated with search and that associated with design. *Search* for solution begins with the organization's memory that I sits information systems, and the experience of established members of the organization . search is frequently passive in that for example, there are alternatives offered for by service organizations actively looking for organizations with problems. Finally, there is 'trap' search which involves letting others know that you require an answer to a problem. The *Design* of solution is a complex process. The problem is broken into smaller parts which are handled in a sequential manner with decisions to move on to the next stage effectively meaning that certain possibilities are ruled out as the decision progresses. To the model, solution may be custom-made or modified ready-made answer. The former approach is only used if the latter is not available, because it involves complex cycles of design and search activities which Mintzberg calls "nested cycles.

3. The last stage is that of Selection, as development which involves breaking a decision into a series of sub-decision, each of which requires a selection step, so selection in this case can be part of development. It involves screening to eliminate infeasible solutions and so this stage is often part of the search phase. Then evaluation under which judgement many of those responsible for making such decisions and not even strategic national security decisions are not aware of the need for their decisions to be aided by theory and models. However the description of the processed come in some cases within decision making theory and not the strategic decion modles. The impression

is that the reality of Nigeria's strategic decision-making did and does not allow for any comparison with idealized model to enable us establish whether certain stages have been missed out or disproportionate amount of time and resources have been devoted to one stage. It cannot also be established whether the process is unnecessarily erratic.[7] Let me put it crudely that the selected strategic models discussed among others are INAPPROPRIATE and IRRELEVANT in understanding Nigeria's national security decision making. (1) Thus Nigeria's national security decisions like most other decisions are not informed by any grandiose framework even some of the country's peacekeeping operation especially in the West Africa sub-region. So there is no identifiable model for taking some of these crucial decisions. It has however been suggested that most of these decisions have resulted fro some consultations, brainstorming, groupthink and scenario planning. Apart from the peculiarity of the country's decision making mechanisms including what Augustus Adebayo referred to as "decision making by laughter', there is the limitation occasioned by the nature of these theories and models especially their relevance to public policy which national security strategic decision is all about. These theories and model ignore the environment for decision especially the informally and the political contestation and negotiation which make decision making techniques which are more often than not mechanistic irrelevant. At best the models are 'aiders' of decisions. Somebody somewhere will have to take a decision which I largely judgemental. Though it can be argued that some of the national security related think tanks apply some of these in their decision making process, it has to be noted that the result ('decision') of such are just input into the decision making process and not decision as the final decisions are beyond them except to some extent at the operational level.[8]

More than anything, Nigeria's predicament especially her economic and political fortune and misfortune coupled with the character of her leadership and nature of security issues (secrecy), absence of democracy, and rule of law good governance among other factors are plausible explanations. It can also be said that strategic planning and techniques can only be credibly carried out in certain types of environment. Some degree of stability and availability of reliable data and information which Nigeria lacks are very necessary for such. It is an open secret that the country lacks reliable data even in respect of her demography and even the commanding heights of her economy and national finances. Only recently, the UN Under-Secretary and Administrator of the UNDP, Mr. Ad Melkert raise an alarm on the 'dearth of data' in Nigeria.

THE WAY FORWARD

In this concluding part of paper, the focus is on some categorical imperatives in favour of national security decision making in Nigeria within the context of contemporary world. In contemporary world, external factors have become more dominant in security thinking which is also being globalized in ways that shrinks national sovereignty and thwart any meaningful endogenous decision making at virtually all decision level. This to a large extent complicates the capacity of states especially the weak or failing states to engage in any meaningful strategic decisions. Even countries that have engaged in serious strategic planning in favour of national security and indeed the principal actors in the war on terror have had to go back to the drawing board since 9/11 to reinvent and reinvigorate their national security strategy. For example, the United States after 9/11 realized the need for a new thinking as a result of the new security threats. It had to review its reliance on the Cold War doctrines of Deterrence and Containment less than a year (May 2002) after 9/11. The new Strategic Framework involves 'reducing offensive nuclear weapons, creating defensive systems that protect against missile attack, strengthening non-proliferation and counter proliferation measures, and cooperating with Russia to combat terrorism'.

It is beneficial to turn our searchlight in some critical issues on Nigeria's national security and the need for strategic decision-making and not so much about the methodology or the mechanics that had informed national security decisions. It is my belief that after almost fifty years of ruderlessness characterized by wasted opportunities and squandered hope even under the eight years (preceding May 29, 2007) of supposedly democratic government, now is the time to address certain critical national issues especially that of national security on which our individual, collective and national survival hinge. From all indications, the on-going war against primitive accumulation called anti-corruption war will surely release the much needed fund for public goods while the commitment by the present government to the rule of law and good governance however rudimentary at the moment will be the bedrock for the much desired new Nigeria. Whatever shortcomings in Nigeria including the high rate of insecurity coupled with soliciting assistance or overtures from outside our shores to either train our police or support our security network, AFRICOM and all what not, are aspects of the various problems that have manifested in all facets of our national life. In fact, it will not be an overstatement that successive governments have failed in discharging their be an overstatement that successive governments have failed in discharging their fiduciary responsibility to the citizenry. Indeed, the Nigerian State and its successive governments whether military or civilian have failed to perform the three basic responsibilities of the State which are maintenance of peace, security and welfare of the citizens while the security of the Nigerian State is under threat. The fact the Nigeria remains one 'indivisible' entity is not necessarily an indication of a commendable system of national security. Both national and global communication networks are replete of information on Nigeria's fragile security or insecurity in Nigeria.[10]

Despite the changes in the past two decades especially since 0/11, the pillar of Nigeria's national security framework remains, safeguarding the sovereign independence and territorial integrity of the State with other guiding principle like African Unity and independence, non intervention in the internal affairs of other States and regional economic development and security cooperation. Though it could be argued that some of the country's international commitments within ECOWAS and AU have advanced these, but this cannot be adequate as these have to be domesticated within the reality of the country as these have many implications.

Even from what we know about the administration of Nigeria, one can say that if there had been previous attempts at reconfiguring Nigeria's national security such attempts can be conveniently ignored partly because in a corrupt ridden nation like Nigeria, the quality of public policy, decisions and implementation suffers. Many evidences including the mismanagement of the 50 billion naira Presidential Committee on Police Equipment Fund established in 2006 abysmal conduct and administration of the April 2007 elections and subsequent ones in which some security personnel were implicated, ridiculous and fraudulent sale of our nation assets in the guise of privatization, and the epileptic energy sector especially power supply despite the huge financial commitment to the sector. The ruling class/elite have been implicated in all these and it is this class we rely on as primary actors for strategic decisions in favour of Nigeria and Nigerians. As a matter of fact some of the crimes that threaten the country's national security including armed robbery could be said to be state induced. Given the above, it would appear as if our leaders constitute the greatest threat to the country's security.

In Nigeria, issue of national as against state or individual security is being seriously trivialized even under military regimes under which the military was virtually demobilized and security became avenue for private accumulation even now. Security votes are essentially used for anti-security purposes. In fact, the whole issue of security votes may have to be revisited in the light of the recent report that President Yar' Adua 'did not spend a single kobo from his security vote from May to December 2007'. Such colossal savings on personal security of certain public officers will be a substantial source of funding for other public programmes including security. After all, it may not be necessary in the face of responsive and responsive government that is committed to having functions security organizations.

National security cannot be overemphasized because for democracy and development to flourish and for sustainability, issue of national security must be taken seriously. Issues of national security are therefore intrinsically linked to democratic governance and the much desired democratic consolidation and development. Furthermore, if political violence, armed banditry, intra-boundary skirmishes, hostage taking and abductions, extra-judicial killings, sectarian crisis, cyber – and trans-border crimes that characterized Nigeria's recent history are to continue without adequate measures to curb them; if lives and properties of Nigerians are not safe and secured, democratic dividend and development would be a mirage or agenda for the future.

Under the new dispensation which hopefully will midwife a new Nigeria, the commitment constitutionalism and the various transformations at the global level especially the demise of the Cold War as occasioned by the lowering of the Berlin Wall, terrorism however defined and the involuntary phenomenon of globalization necessarily call for a rethink of the country's security policy. More fundamental is the need for a new national security strategic thinking. For decades, national security decisions have largely been at the operational, ad hoc, largely non-proactive and stunned and were not subject to any systematic review after the essential national and global factor have changes especially after the end of the Cold War. The strategic framework for such is non existing. The closest to strategic decisions are incidental through NEPAD, MDGs, Vision 2010 and now, NEEDS II which unlike NEEDS I has addressed the issue of security more significantly. Even then, these are largely on paper as they mean little in reality. They also address just a negligible aspect of national security in a non holistic or coordinated manner.

Under the present situation given the commitment to the rule of law, it is important that decision making follow due process as to do otherwise distorts adequacy of response to national security matters. Any meaningful attempt at national security planning will have to address the various composite aspects of security and will have to be based on wide consultation among the stakeholders. Now that the country is committed to launching the Vision 2020 and possibly a constitutional review is the time to set up in motion an appropriate mechanism for this.

The national security strategic plan will provide the framework for determining national security goals in Nigeria. This will involve political executives, Legislative bodies especially the relevant Committees, internal security forces and paramilitary like the police, SSS, NDLEA, NAFDAC, NSCDC; the military, military and non-military think-tanks (NDC, NIPPS, NISER) and non-governmental organizations and civil societies (NLC, TUC, SSANU etc). The task of addressing the issues is not for an institution but a collective one. Certainly the NDC is expected to be one of the key players in this task. Apart from the involvement of the public authorities, it will also include interest and pressure groups including NLC, TUC,ASUU, Nigerian youths and representatives of ethnic nationalities. The task will be to formulate a long term national security strategic plan based on national regional and global security issue and Nigeria's security commitment at sub-regional, regional and global levels. Of course this have to take cognizance of Nigeria's national interest, capacity and capability which one hope will develop with good governance and enhance national security.

Issue to be discussed on which strategic decision will also have to be made will include philosophy and aims of Nigeria's national security, infrastructures and institutions for national security, national image, military and non-military variables of national security, production, procurement and maintenance of military hardware and peripherals, internal and external security commitments, skills and re-orientation of security personnel, coordination of national security forces, appropriate responses to internal threats to national – security – sectarian conflicts, Niger Delta, brutality of security personnel, security to personnel, drug and child trafficking, appropriate responses to terrorism, security in the Gulf of Guinea and national borders and trans-border crimes, IT related crimes and local and foreign course opportunities for security personnel and Nigeria's response to the growing China/US rivalry. And of course the more specific issues of poverty and armed robbery, development, environmental degradation and pollution, legal issues in national security, involvement by non-governmental agencies, coordination and relationship among national security forces, international security cooperation, responsibility financing national security and the biggest of all CORRUPTION are also relevant issues to be discussed. We must add that the cross – cutting nature of national security issues have to be given some serious thoughts and should inform outcomes.

Obviously there cannot be any one model for doing this. So it might have to be sectoral and co-ordinated to reflect the country's national security goals in all these related areas. We need to move away from merely reacting to security issues on case by case basis as evident in AFRICOM, Gulf of Guinea, training of the Police, series of insurrections in the country and unabated military and hostage taking in the Niger Delta. The handling of some of these has caused some national embarrassments and avoidable complications. We have to note that most of these are not isolated cases and have to do with other aspects of national security issues.

While the framework cannot be easily advanced here, it is clear that such cannot be mechanistic. It has to be based on consultation and dialogue among identifiable stakeholders both within and outside government. Such also has to be knowledge based.

REFERENCES

1. Mintzberg, H. D. Rasinghani and A. Threat, 'The structure of unstructured decision process', Administrative Science Quarterly, 1976;21:246-75.
2. Gore. Chris, Kate Murray and Bill Richardson. (1992) Strategic Decision-Making Lond: Cassell, 1992 and Higgins J. C., 'Management information system for corporate planning', in B. Taylor and J. R. Sparkes (eds) *Corporate strategy and planning, Heinemann London, 1982).*
3. Colman, Andrew M. (2001) Oxford Dictionary of Psychology, Oxford: Oxford University Press.
4. Cooke and Slack and N. Slack Making Management Decision, Practice-Hall International Englewood Cliffs, NJ 1984.
5. Wright, George Strategic Decision Making: A best practice Blueprint, West Sussex: John Wiley & Sons, Undated and Mintzberg, H., D. Rasinhani and A. Threat, "The structure of unstructured decision processes, *Administrative Science Quarterly, 1976; 21:246-75.*
6. Hofer, C. N. and D. Schendel, *Strategy Formulation: Analytical Concept,. West Publishing St. Paul, MN 1978) in p.14.*
7. Ekpo, Akpan U and Daniel A. Omoweh in R. A. Akindele and Bassey E. Ate (ed.) Beyond Conflict resolution: *Managing African Security in the 21ˢᵗ Century,* Vintage publishers, Ibadan. The African security Project: NIIA Security Studies Series.
8. Castles, F. G.; D. J. Murray andD. C. Potter, (1971) *Decisions, organization, and society, Penguin, Harmondsworth.*
9. Drucker, P., (1976) *The Effective Executive* , Harper, and Row, New York.
10. Isa, A. A. M. (2007) *National Defence College and Nigeria's National Security,* First University of Ibadan/National Defence College Distinguished Lecture, 16 November, 2007, Department of Political Science, University of Ibadan and Kupolati, Taiwo, (2007) Remaking of the Police: *A Kaleidoscopic Inquisition,* Lagos.

CHAPTER 7

NATIONAL SECURITY AND DEFENCE

O. A. AZAZI

INTRODUCTION

In the state of affairs of nations, many issues would usually contend for government and popular attention often at the same time, and one of the most engaging of such issues globally is security. If we consider security simply as well being and freedom from threat, it would obviously be the foundation for survival and progress of mankind. It is such that once a threat or the potentials for threat exists, the need to define and provide security against such threats occupy the minds of stakeholders, and the means for providing such security could be as varied as our imagination. In Nigeria for instance, even a cursory observation of our media nationwide will show a preoccupation with politics, economics, religion, health, leadership and an array of social matters (mostly discussed as our relative national well being, i.e. how Nigeria, and Nigerians fare in relation to others). The concerns may be domestic, but are often analysed relative to the wider international setting within which the country exists. Thus our domestic and foreign responses derive from and are moderated by an accumulation of universal human experience in a world under continuous geo-strategic change.

The ability to respond to our advantage within this setting is in direct proportion to state power. For ease of analysis, let me note that state power in contemporary times is conveniently deployed via the indices of politics, economics, military and informational functions. Accordingly, success is contingent on the skills, the will and the strength to use them. These skills, will, and strength together with the structures, processes and procedures through which they are applied reside in the domain of national security. It is within this context that the wider sense of national security and defence is to be appreciated, and this enhances our understanding of the environment of national security.

Irrespective of borders, we may consider the total resources of the world as one unit from which individual states draw their needs in contest with other nations. Notably, the challenges of sovereignty mean that this contest resolves into confrontation and collaboration as nations jostle for survival and growth. For the sovereign state, therefore, the fundamental first joint of reference in this scheme of survival and growth is its territory and people. These constitute its critical bargaining resource from which all other forms of bargaining powers are derived and therefore must be secured. Stretching beyond this will be found a complex interplay of many issues both concrete and abstract that have implications for national survival. In direct terms, the purpose of the Nigerian state as with other states is to guarantee the survival and growth of the nation through the attainment and sustenance of national goals.

National defence which I would refer to as the cumulative policies, resources, and actions that could be devoted to a nation's military is a veritable, but not exclusive, means of ensuring national survival.

In this short address I will attempt to examine the context of national security with some examples, and the nexus between national security and defence within the international system of states. It will then discuss the structures and institutional arrangements for national security and defence in Nigeria. I may not be able to give you specific national security indices but I will address a number of issues hoping that it provokes our thoughts sufficiently on the role of defence in national security.

CONTEXT

The aim of this chapter is to discuss national security and defence - linkages within the epistemic context of policy debate in the literature.

NATIONAL SECURITY

I want to start examining national security by stating that the term security itself is a contested concept. Academics have differed on whether it is all about freedom from threats to core values and therefore could be protected by military force or should focus on the individual and several considerations of the international system. Suffice, however, to state that the concept has stretched across a wide spectrum of elements common to the survival and growth of human civilizations. Thus we are familiar with references to such security concepts as food security, economic, political, energy, industrial, human, environmental and sundry other considerations. For instance, the Grand Strategy for National Security of Nigeria defines national security as: ..."*the aggregation of the security interests of all individuals, communities, ethnic groups, political entities and institutions that inhabit the territory of Nigeria.*

It is the motley of security perspectives that aggregates to forge the somewhat amorphous, albeit critical elements of national security that embeds the national interests. In this respect, national security itself characterizes the spirit and form of the modern nation state. It is "the maximum possible reliance on a state's own resources and the support of its allies[2]". It struggles for survival and growth within the international system of states. Existing as root to national interests, therefore, there is little wonder that nations build their survival and progress within a reasoned expression of national security policy that embodies the manner in which the elements of national power (political, diplomatic, military and informational) are integrated and applied in pursuit of the expressed objectives of national well-being. This pursuit of national well-being is done within the frame work of a geo-strategic environment in which there are other state and non-state actors. Often, this environment breeds conflict which may open the precious flanks of our national security interests to assaults. Being of critical value to the nation, therefore, national security deserves protection within an environment assuredly characterized by conflict, albeit some cooperation.

At this point, it may be germane to give some historical insight into the formal institutionalization of the term national security. The idea of state security itself dates back to antiquity. However, the modern connotation of national security has been traced to the 19thh Century. Official first time use of the of the term national security is attributed to J. Reuben Clark, US Under Secretary of State in his so called Clark Memorandum of 17 December 1928.[3] To this day, methodologies to achieve and maintain the highest possible desired state of national security have been consistently developed over the modern period. In brief, some of these methodologies and measures include the following[4].

    a.   Using diplomacy to rally allies and isolate threats.

    b.   Maintaining effective armed forces.

    c.   Implementing civil defence emergency preparedness measures (including anti-terrorism legislation).

    d.   Ensuring the resilience and redundancy of critical infrastructure.

    e.   Using intelligence services to detect or avoid threats and espionage, and to protect classified information.

    f.   Using intelligence services or secret police to protect the nation from internal threats.

It will be noted that national security interest are multifarious and they bestride both the domestic and foreign domains. The Grand National design for national security therefore operates a bundle of mutually supporting strategies to secure national security interests. Within this bundle of mutually supporting strategies to secure national security interest is found the defence component, which may gain prominence depending what is at issue. This is a survival necessity in an international system which confers legitimacy on states to resolve conflict by the legitimate means at their disposal. Very often the armed forces of a nation play prominent role as instruments or legitimate means.

For obvious reasons then, as long as the nation-state system is the prevailing form to political organization, the emphasis will continue to be on national security rather than on international cooperation. However, it must be noted too that these two ideas are not necessarily mutually incompatible. At least, the popularity of military alliances and regional associations suggest that the goals of national security can partly be promoted by adopting means which result in cooperation between and among states. In the final analysis, however, military power is an intrinsic part of the delicate international order associated with the international system[5].

DEFENCE

Defence refers to the military arrangements at the service of the state. Defence is thus one elements in the national strategic efforts, being coterminous with military, in reference to the political, economic, diplomatic, military, and information array. The preference for the term defense is acknowledged by Baylis[6]. Largely for political and propaganda purposes, War offices have been retiled Ministries of Defence in most countries, and the use of the term military policy has generally been dropped in favour of defence policy. This is partly at least because of its more favourable connotations in peacetime.

Thus defence policy is defined in general term as: "*the provision, deployment and use of military resources to facilitate not only the protection but also the pursuit of the perceived national interests of the State*". At least two specific elements of use are implied in this:

a. To secure the protection of the homeland and people from both internal and external threats.
b. To safeguard the political and economic interests of the state in the world as a whole.

In general, there is a strong aversion particularly in democratic states, for the use of military force as an instrument of domestic policy. However, we are also aware that in most evolving democratic states the military is an instrument at their disposal. However, defence policy in a classic sense operates predominantly as an instrument of foreign policy to check external aggression and in support of political and economic interests of the State. Nations with global interests would have expeditionary defence policies, while others focus on defence of homeland. These interests of different nations are the seminal agents of national security which must be sought within the existing geo-strategic environment. Baring a totally isolationist policy, the interests can hardly be confined to the domestic arena.

It is hardly surprising, therefore, that the bulk of a country's national security challenges often find expression in the external domain. Consequently, there is an inextricable association between national security and defence. This association is not limited to the traditional war fighting functions of defence. It extends to some innovative ways of applying the defence function to overall national strategies including new concepts like Military Humanitarianism or force for good. This association embraces some or all of the following:

a. Confrontation with neighbours such as:
   i. Territorial and sovereignty disputes
   ii. Competition over natural resources
   iii. Managing bordering ethnic peoples
   iv. Dealing with refugees
   v. Instability of a neighbour
   vi. Nationalistic and political posturing.
b. Regional power relations, in cooperation with other states.
c. A desire for prestige.
d. Cooperative efforts with the UN and other coalitions and countries including peacekeeping operations, humanitarian assistance, and disaster relief.
e. Obligations of treaty commitments.
f. Negative transnational issues such as terrorism, drug trafficking, and environmental issues (e.g. pollution, deforestation, oil spills)
g. Protection of microeconomic factors, such as watersheds, sea-lanes, Exclusive Economic Zones (EEZs), marine resources and fisheries.

h. Protection of macroeconomic issues, such as market access to trade, investment, energy, food and other vital resources.
i. Maintaining domestic law and order.

The spectrum and size of the national security needs of a state tend to correlate with the defence effort required to gain and sustain them. In this respect, states like the US, with a large demand on world resources to support their survival, growth and way of life also deploy great defence and diplomatic effort to pursue their goals. Quite often, the issues that melt down to a defence and security issue can come from even obscure areas of the national security agenda. Even when such conflicts are resolved diplomatically, there is always a conscious, even if muffled reference, to the military parity of contenders. In this way, defence assumes the position of a critical driver of national security policy. It is instructive then, to note that many nations enjoy a high level of national attainment also display elevated levels of defence posture. For those nations that lack the defence capacity, many of their interests remain an aspiration.

The link between national security and defence arguably reveals the intrinsic values of military power in the international system of states. In spite of avowed global aversion for armed coercion and its associated violence, it is doubtful if the world could have been a better place without defence. In his book war as an instrument of National policy, Shotwell has noted that:

> War...has been the instrument by which most of the great facts of political national history have been established. It has played a dominant role in nearly all political crises; it has been used to achieve liberty, to secure democracy, and to attempt to make it secure......

Wright captures the same theme thus:

> It may be superfluous to remind anyone that the great states of modern times have been the product of war....England, France, Spain, Russia, China, Japan and the US acquired their domains and their territorial integrity through war...The resources of weaker lands and peoples have been made available to the stronger ones through exploitation made possible by the force of arms. Markets too, have been opened by the British Royal Navy...and by the fleets and soldiers of many states in a hundred lands. The technological progress of mankind has involved the use of raw materials from every section of the globe, and many of these have been surrendered at sword's point.[12]

PERSPECTIVES IN NATIONAL SECURITY AND DEFENCE

This part of the presentation takes an exploratory glimpse at some national security and defence issues of the US and India. This is to appreciate the nexus between national security and defence. Developments in the geo-strategic circumstances have always provided the trigger of events in the national security and defence matric. America claim is that the US entered the First World War to spread democracy to the world. While this may sound appealing as theme for US involvement in the war, it is pertinent to note the underlying issues that bordered on her national security. The security unease in the US in 1914 was hinged on economic depression and widespread unemployment. Unemployment meant low levels of consumption. As a neutral state in the war, her right to trade with the belligerents was jeopardized by German indiscriminate attacks on shipping across the Atlantic. Swayed by the need to carry on export trade in order to mitigate recession, together with cultural reasons, President Wilson diminished trade with Germany in favour of Britain. In this process the US abandoned her policy of neutrality in the war and drew the belligerence of Germany. Subsequently, the US decided for war in March 1917. Events followed such as the sinking of the Lusitania in May, German unrestricted submarine warfare and the German-Mexican Alliance.

US neutrality in the Second World War was broken by the Japanese attack on her naval bas at Pearl Harbour. While the naval presence secured US interests in the South East Asian region, it formed an impediment to Japanese expansionist economic forages in the area. By Japanese calculations, only that sort of "unprovoked" and surprise attack as unleashed on Pearl Harbour could neutralize the prohibitive US threat to their economic ambitions. The US joined the war on the part of the allies. Subsequently, the demand for unconditional Japanese surrender ultimately brought nuclear capability into the national security-defence calculus in the bombing of Hiroshima and Nagasaki. After the war, US promise for continued post –war cooperation between the allies began to wane following Russian behaviour. For example, before Russian territory was physically threatened, she had referred to the war as the Great Imperialist war. However, as the homeland was threatened following invasion by Germany, Russia appealed to the sentiments of the Russian people and the motherland for resistance. Emphasis was shifted from the imperialist war to the Great Patriotic War. These nuances were to clearly explain the dualism in Russian wartime cooperation and the quick change to post-war confrontation.

In reality Russian national security interests had remained rooted in the ideological framework of Marxism-Leninism, founded on the principle of inevitability of conflict between communism and capitalism. For the US and her allies, an early demonstration of the unfolding scenario was the Russian siege of Berlin. These developments were to define not only the communist-capitalist divide, but with it the global geo-strategic tenor called the cold war. This formalized the US adoption of the atomic bomb as a military weapon in her defence policy. The US runs an industrial economy that leverages on global sources for raw materials, energy and markets. Therefore, the spread of communism threatened US survival to the roots. The US challenge was, therefore, how to counter the spread of communism. From the US perspective it was evident that diplomacy alone could not achieve this. Therefore, US national security act number 68 of 1947 acknowledge this state of affairs, and in line with President Truman's domino theory of communist spread it proposed the doctrine of containment as the means of checking soviet power.

From this time onwards, US foreign policy was defined by the containment of communism until the demise of the Soviet Union in 1990. It is noteworthy that the entire containment apparatus was defence backed. Although no direct battlefield confrontation ensued between the two nations, the world was held hostage throughout by their posturing as they used their defence capabilities to shape and to respond to global geo-strategic conditions. It is instructive to recall some of the events that constituted this endeavour. These are considered here in outline.

a. Korea. The invasion of South Korea by North Korea in 1950 inspired the first Communist expansionist agenda in the region. The US quickly rallied the support of the UN and intervened to force an armistice along the 16th parallel. This parallel remains the boundary between the two Koreas as they remain officially at war till date.

b. Viet Nam. In 1953, the French lost in the bid to re-colonise Viet Nam after their classic defeat in the hands of General Giap at Dien Bien Phu. To stem communist complete takeover of Viet Nam, the US propped up the regime of Signam Rhee in the south, and officially from 1969 to 1972 fought a highly debilitating anti communist war.

c. Cuba (Bay of Pigs). The Bay of Pigs invasion was an unsuccessful attempt by US-backed Cuban exiles to overthrow the communist government of Fidel Castro in 1961.

d. Iran. Iran is worthy of note here because it was the significant event of the hostage crisis of 1979 that the "communal antagonism of Islam versus America that eventually collapsed the World Trade Centre and punctured the Pentagon on September 11, 2001, came out of the closet'[8] To recall, In 1951, to guarantee Iranian oil supplies the US had consolidated Rheza Phalavi's hold on Iranian power against popular will. On his death, his son Muhammed Rheza Phalavi was equally entrenched in the throne with American support. His overthrow by the clergy led by Ayathola Khomeini was followed by rumours that the US planned to forcefully reinstate him. This drew the irk of a group of students from a Tehran university who stormed the US embassy taking Americans hostage. The hostage crisis lasted 444 days and involved a failed but disastrous US attempt to rescue the hostages by force.

e. Proxy Wars. The US and USSR sponsored proxy wars in places like Nicaragua, El Salvador, Angola and Afghanistan in continuation of their proxy wars.

f. Military Assistance Programmes. In addition to military advisory support, both the US and the USSR employed arms sales and arms transfers to bolster the military capabilities of their allies.

The Kuwaiti expedition of 1990 was successfully executed to check Iraqi domination of Arabian oil sources. Currently, US defence and security interests are also playing out in the ongoing coalition wars in Iraq and Afghanisan expressly to defeat Al Qaeda and the Taliban. In the present times, US defence and security concerns as summarized by the National Security Strategy of the United States establish eight national security objectives:

a. To champion human dignity
b. To strengthen alliances against terrorism'
c. To defuse regional conflicts
d. To prevent threats from weapons of mass destruction.
e. To encourage global economic growth
f. To expand the circle of development
g. To cooperate with other centres of global power
h. To transform America's national security institutions to meet the challenges and opportunities of the twenty-first century.

The defence component of the associated national security strategy is espoused in the current US naval and military strategies. Essentially, these two strategies emphasize the development of combat capabilities across the entire spectrum of conflict including the asymmetric conventional and non-conventional. They also specify global strategic cooperation to sustain regional stability.

INDIA

India's strategic interests in Asia are two-fold[9] :

a. Ensuring security in its immediate neighbourhood
b. Protecting India's interests, including economic and energy interests in the rest of Asia and the Middle East.

There is a belief that the most likely military contingencies India faces in the medium term are 'Kargils and Tsunamis" in the form of sharp limited land engagements on the borders and broader humanitarian problems in the extended region.

India's national security policy is based on a premise that its immediate neighbourhood is dangerous and that regional instability from neighbouring countries fuels her internal insurgences. Her relationship with Pakistan has been troubled from the start. Also, insurgents in Kashmir have close ties with their counterparts in Pakistan. Revolutionaries in central India are said to have loose ties with the erstwhile Maoists in Nepal. Beyond the immediate South Asian region, India's broader concerns include ensuring the security of her lifelines for trade, investment, and most importantly, energy. India require 10% annual GDP growth rather than the current 6% (now 8.5%) rate to achieve primary goal of social stability, especially the reduction of poverty.[10] Given a small budget, about 3% of GDP, the military relies on nuclear deterrence. This is considered cheaper than conventional arms. This approach is similar to that of the Eisenhower administration's use of the massive retaliation doctrine to avoid high defence spending. Nevertheless, it must be noted that uncertainty over the will to apply nuclear capability not only tends to lower credibility, but encourage elevation of spending on conventional capabilities.

In an effort for self-reliance after the 1962 confrontation with China, India created a widespread defence industry that includes 39 ordnance factories and 8 defence public sector undertakings. These include the Hindustani Aeronautics and Bharat Electronics. India's missile and nuclear production facilities are a contentious point in international relations. She sees herself as a rising regional actor, and considers military power as one elements in this process. Thus as any aspiring regional player, she identifies potential partners as well as potential enemies.

NATIOAL SECURITY AND DEFENCE IN NIGERIA

In line with the preceding pattern of analysis, this part of the presentation deals with a consideration of Nigeria's goe-strategic circumstances within the scope of national security imperatives that it generates. Safeguarding the sovereignty, independence and territorial integrity of the state has been the central pillar of Nigerian national security policy. This policy also includes the guiding principles of African unity, independence and regional economic development and security cooperation. Let's, however, not forget that emphasizes individuals, communities, ethnic groups, political entities and institutions.

A discussion on the environment of Nigeria's national security, and defence should focus on the structures and institutional arrangements as well as the challenge we contend with. We may want to concentrate on the challenges, because they determine the real issues in national security. Some global issues are also relevant in Nigeria, but sometimes in different dimensions.

Nigeria's geo-strategic situation is defined by the fact that she is located in the Gulf of Guinea, and straddles western and equatorial Africa. Its long land and coastal boundaries, and offshore oil deposits now emphasize her global geo-strategic situation. The current geo-strategic appraisal may be further captured from the draft National Military Strategy as submitted by the Armed Forces Transformation Committee.[13] Thus, Nigeria's geo-strategic location in the Gulf of Guinea and the fact that she is bordered by francophone countries may not pose an immediate threat. However, the increased international interest in the crude oil deposits in the Gulf of Guinea, and the use of neigbouring countries as staging posts for subverse activities or prosecuting proxy wars cannot be discounted. The Nigerian Military must be ready to actively participate in the protection of the Gulf of Guinea in concert with allies, and to face series of low intensity conflicts such as proxy wars, insurgencies aided and abetted by foreign interests[14]. Other issues factored into the security environment include the following:

    a.   Nigeria's littoral location, land mass, population ethnic diversity, cultural and multi religious disposition which pose a unique challenge to its security.

    b.   Being the most populous black nation naturally imposes on her some obligations to the black race.

There are several issues associated with social wellbeing, like employment, food, heath, gender, the environment, leadership, governance, rule of law, and diverse issues which in indirectly affect defence because its presence ensures relative stability for addressing them. The following could be specific to defence:

a. Nationalism: Nationalism in this sense would refer to our collective experience as a nation, the vision of the future, and a collective resolve to achieve the state of that vision.
b. Domestic insurrections.
c. Energy, (and the protection of energy resources)
d. Humanitariansm and human rights.
e. Terrorism
f. Drug interdiction
g. Small arms and light weapons
h. Robbery (including piracy)
i. Communication and the internet revolution.

We should be reasonably conscious of how national defence could safeguard or offer reprieve to some if not all of the above factors.

CONCLUSION

The crux of national security is concerned with the totality of issues that build into the survival and growth of a nation. The land, its resources and people of a country constitute its primary resources. For this reason the protection usually engages prominent attention in the country's national security efforts. Beyond this, everything that a nation requires for survival and growth whether they exist in abstract or concrete forms is gained within the competitive framework of the international system.

The fact remains that sovereign states have yet to find conflict resolution mechanisms that create a real obsolescence of armed force. They therefore rely ultimately on defence capabilities and arrangements to support and secure their national security objectives in conjunction with other elements of national power. Since national security demands span both the international and domestic domains in survival of individual nations have come to be intrinsically linked to the capacity to derive from the competitive geo-strategic government, the vital elements required for survival and growth.

Nigeria's national security interests enlarge as she rallies to implement the 7-point agenda of the current administration, and as she aspire to be counted amongst the world's first 20 economies. These have great implications for defence. The reality is that the opportunities to be appropriated for this growth will at least equal those to be lost by other contenders within the international system. While globalization has entailed negative consequences in some countries. It has equally improved the capacity of many others as contenders in the global system. Nigeria can be under no illusion that her national security aspirations will be met without stiff competitive resistance. In an uncertain global geo-strategic setting, the best insurance still remains a dependable defence capability. From this perspective therefore, it strikes the mind that the proposed transformation of the Nigerian armed forces is a project that must be vigorously pursued in tandem with national security aspirations.

ENDNOTES

1. Nigeria, Grand Strategy for National Security.
2. Palmers ND and Perkins HC (eds) International Relations. (Delhi: AITBS) publishers & Distributors, (2004) p.xxix.
3. National Security. http://en.Wikipedia.org/wiki/national security 2008-06-14
4. Ibid
5. Garnet J. Booth, K. and Baylis J. (eds.) Contemporary Strategy. (New York: McGraw Hill Inc, 1985) p.139.
6. Baylis J. (ed) British Defence Policy in a Changing World. London: Croom Helm, 1977) p.13
7. Ibid.
8. Harris D. (ed) The Crisis New York: Little Brown & Co p.5
9. South Asia Momitor No. 105. centre for Strategic and International Studies Washiongton DC.
10. Defence Resource Allocation in India – http://www.pacom.mil/publications/apeu02/s07 Defencon8.pdf.
11. Palmers ND and Perkins HC (eds) op. Cit. P.193.
12. Ibid.
13. Draft National Military Strategy, April 2008.

CHAPTER 8

MACRO FACTORS DEFINING NIGERIA'S NATIONAL SECURITY DECISION-MAKING PROCESS

ALIYU MOHAMMED

PREAMBLE

The world is undergoing a series of processes which define the parameters within which countries, big or small, rich or poor, can operate. Nations of the world find themselves, increasingly in an environment of interdependence. Old enemies realize that in order to survive, they have to cooperate with their adversaries. This is very different from the experience of the past where might was right and peace can only be enjoyed if imposed on others through overwhelming military might. This is no longer the case. We have now seen where non-state actors, without standing armies, continue to threaten the national interests of the current most powerful country in the world. Yet we have also seen that some strategic problems can only be solved by the use of military force, (e.g. Iraq)[1].

Some issues have also been of greater importance than they used to, in the security context. Such macro factor includes Economy and Energy Issues. The world is contending with the threat of recession in the United States of America and the impact of environmental unaffected if the America economy crumbles? The answer is obvious, based on the proportion of our national income which is tied to the prosperity of the USA. Energy, especially oil is also a major factor. Nations have demonstrated the extent to which they are willing to go, to defend and protect their sources of supply of energy. These and other strategic consideration should shape our policies and guide our national security process[2].

Internal factors are crucial to the security process. Nigeria continues to contend with security threats and challenges which are home based. Nigeria's ranking in the world is usually based on indices taken from the domestic environment. Only if a country can manage its internal space well, would it enjoy the respect of others. Let me add as a side-note: *no power has ever long sustained its position, when it has not been self-sufficient in food production. We are no longer self-sufficient in this arena. This should be a clear warning signal to us[3]*. In Africa, Ghana and Rwanda are shinning examples of nations that are currently managing their internal space well. Some of internal threats which have been with us for a long time are yet to subside. They are either compounded or are giving rise to new ones in interaction with the global situation. Our policy makers have to be aware that the effectiveness of security controls, to moderate the behaviour of residents of the country's territorial space, has been diluted by the effects of globalization. Technology and systems, like the world-wide-web, make methods and capabilities available to individuals whether in urban or rural settings, individuals are also empowered to carry on tasks, involving others across national boundaries, with greater ease, to threaten national interests[4].

The macro factors, which impact on National Security, can be global, regional or local. They can be digital or analogue, modern or primitive, with each segment of the threat population having attained different stages of development and sophistication. This reality provides challenges and opportunities to our national security decision-making process in order to consider, adopt and pursue to right policies in sustaining Nigeria's national interest[5]. The aim of this chapter is to present comprehensive perspectives of the factors which determine Nigeria's national security decision-making process. It focuses specifically on grand strategy, components of national security external dynamics, internal dynamics and challenges.

CONCEPTUAL CLARIFICATION

Gregory Copley, the President of the International Strategic Studies Association (ISSA), told a gathering of senior Australian military officers earlier this month that *"Grand Strategy is about the total function of the state within the total context of the world"*. The world determines what pressures and opportunities come to bear upon the state. That eternally-changing context determines our field of operations. This is in line with Archimedes who said: "Give me a place to stand, and I will move the Earth." It is a given, then, that in grand strategy the exponent must first understand his own position in relationship to the Earth, as well as his own position in relationship to history. The national grand strategy which we develop determines how the state anticipates; pre-empts; plans-for; creates; or responds to those pressures and opportunities over the longest possible time frames.

Grand strategy, like good military strategy, is predominantly about intangible elements, although modern political life, like modern military life, has become fixated heavily on tangibles, such as technology and visible strengths. Whatever way we look at it, however, it is the non-military factors which ultimately, usually, drive the employment of the armed forces. As Napoleon, cautioned "the moral is to the physical as two is to one" meaning that the psychological and intangible aspects of the strategic environment are twice as important as the physical. Grand strategy, in other words, provides the contextual environment in which military strategy and operations occur[6].

The prevailing definition of National Security for Nigeria is that which applied during my tenure as the National Security Adviser. This was contained in the President's Grand Strategy for National Security issued in 2001. It 2001. It articulated national security as *"the aggregation of the security interests which inhabit the territory of our great country Nigeria"*. This definition gives a holistic perspective rather than the narrow prescription of national security which other countries adopted[7].

Our concept is similar to the that articulated, for the sake of comparison, by the United States of America. It defined national security to include *"the defence of the United States of America, protection of its constitutional system of government, and the advancement of United States interests around the globe and the creation of opportunities for America to prosper in the world economy"[8]*. In summary, the concept of national security is the management of safety and prosperity and the advancement of a desired way of life. Until recently, America's national security did not include internal security, law and order. Now it does.

Security, or lack of it, is the driver of development or underdevelopment. Robert McNamara, Kennedy's Defence Secretary said *"Security is Development"[9]*. In a democracy it is the elected leaders who determine what is vital to national interest and they allocate the resources to implement security policy initiatives. Where there is an absence of a proper understanding of the security needs of the country, the security system will decay and be ineffectual. Security is also an expensive venture which requires constant and steady investment in infrastructure and the upgrading/modernization of existing facilities in order to cope with emerging threats. *Without resources, not much can be achieved!* Security Operatives have a clear role. *They can influence but should not determine security policies.* It is to be assumed that security policies would be articulated in the national interest and not to serve parochial or vested interests.

In May 2000, when the democratic dispensation was barely a year old, the Office of National Security Adviser conducted a comprehensive National Security Review which identified the lapses in the system and recommended appropriate remedies. Unfortunately, the memorandum was defeated by bureaucratic opposition from ministers and services which felt challenged by the initiative. However, some of the suggestions, such as the new defence policy, were implemented piecemeal, while the core issues remain unattended to up till now. Therefore, *impediments to the policy process qualify as factors to be considered when evaluating the national security decision-making apparatus.*

National Security objectives for Nigeria include:

- a. The enthronement and protection of democracy
- b. Promotion of true federalism, rule of law, secularism and other core values.
- c. Defence of territorial integrity and sovereignty.
- d. Enhancement of economic prosperity
- e. Promotion of peace, law and order within the country.
- f. Promotion of stability and peace within West Africa in general.
- g. Enhancement of world peace.
- h. Development and prosperity through technology, industrial growth and the expansion of infrastructure.
- i. Safety and the preservation of lives and prosperity[10].

The policies to be considered to attain these objectives are the substance of what should engage the national security process. It is obvious that the security objectives constitute a wish list which can only be realized through programmed, systematic and sustained efforts. It is paramount for all those participating in the security decision-making process to be conscious of the security objectives which are ultimate.

COMPONENTS

National Security is a broad concept which affects many facets of the national life. The components of national security represent the various sectors or segments impacted upon by national security policy initiatives. These components also influence the national security process as factors. At the same time, the national security activities can also determine the course of events in these sectors. The main components of national security are:

  a. Politics
  b. Economy
  c. Justice, Law and Order
  d. State Security
  e. Foreign Policy.

Agencies of government have overlapping responsibilities for these components. One agency can be the lead agency for a particular component but others still have contributions to make.

Politics: The conduct of politics affects every aspect. National Security suffers if there is imbalance in the political organization or development of the country. *The conduct of security operations is also cognizant of the supremacy of politics and political authority.* The form of political organization, the relationships among the political entities, federal, state and local governments or Executive, Judiciary and Legislature, all affect peace and security. In Nigeria, like in other developing states, the conduct of elections is usually a critical crisis point. The outcome sometimes results in disorder which could create short or long term instability depending on how it is managed. The disputed elections in Kenya and the violence before the elections in Pakistan are contemporary pointers to the importance of politics as a security factor. Locally, we have seen the importance attached to the outcome of the verdicts of election tribunals in various states of the federation. Another important aspect is that of governance. *It is argued that good governance is an essential strategy for enhancing national security.* Equally important is the settlement of disputes using the machinery of politics and governance to achieve compromise and peace. We may ask ourselves, how well has Nigeria fared in the aspects listed above, and what do we need to do, to achieve better results?.

Economy: Resources are cardinal to progress. The efficient management of the economy creates as conducive atmosphere for prosperity and development. Studies all over the world indicate that greater prosperity reduces the tendency for dispute and crime generally. *Many of the threats to security in Nigeria are induced by economic factors.*

Justice, Law and Order: The maintenance of peace, law and order is the most apparent index for measuring security. An understanding of the system will portray the linkage between effective policing. The neglect of the judiciary and the penal reformation system resulted in situations where neither the courts nor the prisons could cope with the crime situation despite the multiple increases in policing capacity over the last decade. Part of this understanding must include an appreciation of the crime situation, causes and possible remedies and the strategies for crime control. The importance of this component is evidence in the fact that crime discourages the inflow of foreign investments into the economy thus impeding economic prosperity which is a vital national interest. The most paramount issue for national security is the enthronement of the rule of law through justice, law and order. We should here draw attention to the expectations of distributive justice-the question of who gets what within the national confines. The agitation for resource control and the hustles for the equitable distribution of the national income are ample manifestations.

State Security: The protection of the country from its enemies internally is usually referred to as state security. The American version which is the latest admission of the importance of internal security is referred to as *homeland security.* A strong internal security system is required to help the country cope with the stresses and processes of nationhood. A good surveillance network keeps leaders abreast of the state of affairs in every aspect while enforcement capacity enables the system to identify threats early and neutralize them before they blossom.

Defence: The use of military means to secure and protect national interests is part of the national security strategy. The armed forces have always played an important role in the maintenance of security. It is therefore appropriate that the armed forces are organized and equipped to respond to the ever dynamic threat situation when required to do so. The major areas of employment of the Nigerian armed forces remain the provision of aid to civil authority in the maintenance of internal security and the fulfillment of the international obligations of the country in international peace keeping.

Foreign Policy. Nigeria's relationship with the out side world is governed by its foreign policy. Nigeria should be appreciated for what it is – a giant of Africa – through natural endowments. It has a huge population hungry for development and the improvement of the quality of life of every resident. This implies that its relationships with the world should be guided by economic interests too. Nigeria plays the leadership role in west Africa and shares continental leadership of Africa with Egypt and south Africa. This leadership role attracts certain demands and expectations. Thus, while Nigeria has her own burden locally, she has to continue to devote resources to meeting international commitments and obligation. Nigeria's quest for permanent membership of the UN Security council is a Major foreign policy initiative which should influence national security decision-making[11].

DYNAMICS

Many external factors determine the shape of Nigeria's security decision-making process. Among these I would like to discuss the following:-

    a.   Global approach to peace,
    b.   The place of Africa in the world order,
    c.   Border Security,

  d. Foreign Military Influence,

  e. International Terrorism.

More than ever before, the great powers are desirous of peace. The eagerness for global war has diminished especially given the high costs of such wars, the instinct of the International coalition in Afghanisation and Iraq have proved. Even with local wars, the instinct of the International community is not to jump into the fray, unlike in the past. This explains why it has taken so long to deploy UN forces in Darfur. The tendency these days is to envelope regional civil conflicts whenever they occurs, circumnavigate and ignore such crisis with the hope that they would not affect vital interests. The influence of the Domino theory which normally propels military intervention by great powers has been replaced by the concern for markets and economic interests. It is only the Israeli-Palestinian crisis which continues to command international interest and attention. The implication of this trend for our national security is that we should not expect much help or support in dealing with national security issues of a local or regional nature. We should also not be too eager to jump to the aid of warring parties in the sub-region, as we did in the case of Liberia or Sierra Leone. But, if we are to intervene successfully, we have the capability to do so.

Africa continues to lag behind other continents in terms of economic development. Its share of world trade is less than 1 percent. The UN has more peace-keeping operations in Africa, currently, than in any other part of the world. Yet the spectre of instability continues to rage in Africa. The problems in different parts of Africa even in countries far away from Nigeria should interest Nigeria's security planners because she will be expected to play one role or the other in solving such problems. Nigeria has extensive land and maritime borders, most of which is undemarcated and unprotected. Relations with neighbouring countries are relatively calm. The dispute with Cameroon over Bakassi has been resolved but remains a region of potential.

Volatility: Up north, crisis continues to brew in Chad between government and rebel forces. Africa is attracting the attention of great powers that have identified its energy sources as vital to their national interest. The main contenders for influence in Africa are United States of America and the Peoples Republic of China. The deployment of foreign military elements into Nigeria's sphere of influence should warrant consideration by security planners. The implications would be the ability to deploy commensurate platforms and units to cooperate with these foreign troops where required or to monitor and check their activities so that they do not see themselves as having a free rein. In either case, the quality and level of preparedness required by the security forces may be quite daunting.

The probability of war between Nigeria and another country is low. Equally minimal is the threat of military invasion. Despite these probabilities, Nigeria is still required to deploy forces regularly to satisfy existing and anticipated international obligations. As at today, Nigeria has 6 Battalions, I signal squadron, several observers and Staff Officers on international duty. To continue to service regional and continental peace keeping operations or to accede to fresh demands are factors which would impact on the national security decision-making process[12].

The threat of international terrorism seems to have subsided but remains a factor of importance to national security. This in particular concerns public safety and the institution of control measures to reduce that threat. *The character of the threat requires appropriate mechanisms to understand and detect the threat, and for the timely deployment of specialized forces to respond to incidents of international terror should they occur.*

The internal dynamics of the national security environment is familiar territory although opinions might differ. Therefore, it would suffice to summarize the most salient aspects. Irredentist movements such as MASSOB continue to pose threats to national cohesion and integration. The agitations of similar outfits representing other aggrieved ethnic groups seem muffled but certainly not fully resolved. Niger Delta remains a zone of instability with negative effects on the national image and revenue earnings. There are many other issues which threaten internal security. These include economic and political grievances over marginalization, unemployment, violent crimes, armed robbery, cultism, ethno-communal clashes, and so on. *To manage or solve the security problems arising from these threats is the responsibility of the national security decision-making process[13].*

Some factors also affect the ability of the security forces to contend with internal threats. One such factor is the politicization of issues. Ready examples are the attempt to tackle the imposition of Sharia in some states and the creeping scourge of terrorism in those states. Some of the measures by government were termed anti-Islamic or anti-North. Similar exploitation of ethnic or parochial sentiments manifest in the portrayal of security operations in the Niger Delta and against MASSOB as genocide. *Internal political dynamics are therefore parts of the process of threat curtailment.*

There is *infrastructural constraints which hamper the effectiveness of national security.* These constraints can only be addressed by us. In other countries, civil infrastructure is available as backbone to security or military operations. In Nigeria, the services have to virtually provide for everything they need to facilitate their operations. This makes the cost of defence and security high. Yet, these needs have to compete with other more demanding sectors of the national economy for resources. Most times, priority goes to the sectors with the potential to add electoral or political value to the government of the day. In the process, the long term strategic development of the security sector suffers. There is apathy of citizens towards leaders. There is also the issue of feeling of alienation by most citizens from the structures of governance. In such circumstances, public support for security measures and policies is manifesting in resistance by average citizens to the imposition of law and order.

CHALLENGES AND OPPORTUNITIES

The improvement of the security situation in the country and the enhancement of the ability of Nigeria to achieve her national security objectives abroad remain the main challenges. *These challenges can be met through the articulation and implementation of short, medium and long term strategies, based on the detailed consideration of each issue.* There is no magic wand or cure – all solution.

The promotion of national integration is a major challenge to help Nigeria endure as a polity and overcome divisive tendencies which weaken the national fabric. *The revival of policies which foster unity and national integration and security awareness is essential. Equally management and peace building.* The use of force does not solve problems and can only be regarded as part of the arsenal to encourage parties to dialogue so as to attain peaceful resolution.

Another major challenge is that of capacity building for the nation's defence and Security Forces in order to be able to cope with their enormous responsibilities. If we agree that the current state of readiness is far from optimal, then more has to be done positively and systematically over the coming years. The intelligence capabilities of the services needs to be strengthened so that accurate and timely information will be available to pre-empt threats and conflicts before they develop. Local and International defence obligations provide challenges to our armed forces and other services to be able to project adequate and effective forces levels in good time to meet unfolding requirement. This can only be achieved through adequate force development and effective strategic operational planning.

The security situation; external and domestic, is dynamic. The challenges of unpredictable occurrences and the scarcity of resources to cope with all eventualities have to be factored into security considerations. The trend in the world in the world is towards integration where regional allies can work together through seamless interaction. The cooperation among ECOWAS and African Union Security Forces needs to be improved and strengthened. Various ongoing initiatives have to be pursued practically and with vigour. The same is true of the challenge of *improving the integration of communications and procedures among Nigerian security forces to enhance inter operability and effectiveness of joint operations.* The protection of our oil resources is vital to Nigeria. *The security of oil assets which is the major source of national income can be regarded as the most cardinal challenge to national security management. The challenge includes deliberate sabotage and the theft of Nigerian oil*[14].

CONCLUSION

The contemporary national security situation is dynamic. The international environment affects and determines the ability of any country to manage its national security. *Many of the threats arise across boundaries.* Globalization has also weakened some of the barriers which countries can use to protect their territories and security interests. However, globalization also presents opportunities which can be utilized to advance national security objectives[15].

The *macro factors which mould national security consideration can be globa,l regional or local.* These have to be considered in detail in the process of decision-making on any security issue. Also worthy of consideration as factors are: *the quality of inputs into the decision-making process; and the impediments to implementation.* Security decision making is a continuous process that requires constant proactive fine tuning and improvement in order to be effective.

We need to further develop within our defence capabilities, proactive thinking and planning capabilities. We need to be comprehensive in our approach, working with our intelligence, information and foreign policy communities to fashion a unified capability to shape our strategic environment. Finally, we need to frame our national security needs for the forthcoming decade, and perhaps even further into the future, within the framework of the nations goals, while taking into cognizance the capabilities and development possibilities of Nigeria's major soft-power projectors such as culture, values, and creative ideas that can often successfully preempt more direct coercive had-power measures such as military action or economic sanctions.

CHAPTER 9

NATIONAL SECURITY COUNCIL, AND INTER-AGENCY PROCESS IN NATIONAL SECURITY DECISION-MAKING.

L. K. K. ARE

INTRODUCTION

National Security Decision-making thrives on the application of statutory rules to the conduct of the chief executive, leaders and principal officers of security agencies. The process depends on formal and informal interaction among statutory bodies and agencies. The framers of the Constitution and the laws which define the responsibilities of agencies and principal actors in the national security setting prescribe how these institutions or statutory organs should function[1]. Sometimes, they do function as prescribed. Most times they do not. Where the dysfunction is so evident, because of major changes in the system. Amendments become inevitable. Experience has, however, shown that individuals who participate in the process including the Commander-In-Chief, Ministers, Service Chiefs and secretarial staff play significant roles in shaping the effectiveness of these institutions.

Observations on the functioning of national security process in the last decade yield certain conclusions. The first reality is that some of the decision-making structures have not grown beyond mere prescriptions on paper to become the productive vehicles for vital decision-making which they were meant to be. Secondly, most of the actors or participants do not receive adequate briefing or education on how these institution function after they have been appointed or elected into office. Their participation is therefore structured on the basis of personal interpretation and not adherence to any rule book. The performance of the national security decision making structure therefore depend too much on the experience and disposition of the Chief Executive.

In certain circumstances, the functioning of the statutory bodies have been relegated to the background or made perfunctory. In which case, process of governance and decision-making continue without the inputs expected of these bodies. In other cases, the functioning of statutory bodies were replaced by informal meetings comprising essentially of the same participants but without the formalities associated with the statutory meetings. In one particular year, the National Security Council met only once.

Ideally, the national security process recognizes that the decision of the Commander-In-Chief is paramount. The terms of reference of NSC and NDC, prescribed that their role is to advice the C-In-C on specific issues. Therefore, they are simply advisory bodies, although in reality, they carry out executive functions. It can then be argued that it does not matter how, but as long as the Chief Executive is advised correctly on the issue at hand, the purpose has been served. This is however not as simple as it sounds. Sometimes, bureaucratic bottle-necks to not allow the Chief Executive to receive the best advice. Secondly, certain officials can use their personal influence to prevent the views of other institutions and principal officers which might present superior and more viable options from being heard.

The foregoing observation validate the assumption that the national security decision-making process would gain tremendously if the statutory bodies are allowed to function as they should. The bodies proved platforms for political leaders to hear directly form the Chief Executives of the action agencies. The Chief Executives are forced to defend their submission and to benefit from the inputs of other. Conflicting information from different agencies can also be resolved, instead of the eventual decision being based on one-sided or misleading perspective. The bodies provide the avenue for integration of efforts and the coordination of policy action.

Fundamentally, national security decisions have broad impact across the intelligence, defence and security establishments. Sound decisions can only be taken and implemented effectively through collaboration with various parties inside and outside the decision loop. Sometimes, agencies are under the misleading impression that the decisions in question affect their responsibilities alone, until they share with others to find unknown common grounds. Leadership is important in driving the interactive process among agencies. Equally of importance are the expectation and influence of the consideration by the appropriate statutory body. The role of the Chief Executive at the national, state and the institutional level is therefore very crucial to the national security decision making process[2].

ROLE PRESCRIPTIONS

Section 130 of The Constitution states that the President is "the Chief Executive of the Federation and Commander-In-Chief of armed forces" are vested in the President. As far as National Security Decision-making is concerned, the Chief Executive is the President.

While the executive powers of the President are absolute, the national security decision process recognizes that other players or smaller chief executives, also have their part to play. The process flows as follows.

a. Policy decisions by elected chief executives based on the advice of the relevant institutions.
b. Legislative action by the National Assembly, and State Houses of Assembly, were prescribed.
c. Administrative / operational decisions of the higher command authority.
d. Operational decisions by field commanders to execute the directives passed through their chain of command.

The success of the national security policy process depends on constant consultation, coordination and harmonization of policies among the various stakeholders. However, clear lines of authorities and responsibilities have been specified in other to avoid confusion. The process flow is designed to achieve cooperation while respecting the identity and independence of each level or entity.

At the state and local government level, the processes and responsibilities are not well defined. In the case of local governments, security is not part of their schedule prescribed by the Constitution. Indeed, all the issues which are pertinent to security are in the Exclusive legislative list. This means that states and local governments cannot legislate on them. However, the Constitution (Section 11(2) does not preclude State Assemblies from making laws in respect of essential services and supplies affecting public order and security. This notwithstanding, the operation of the security decision process at the state and local government level remain discretionary depending on the preferences or sentiments of the elected Chief Executives[3].

The processes at the state, local government and community level still rely on the use of federally controlled forces and units for the implementation of their security programmes. In this regard, the Constitution specified the authority of a State Governor to issue instruction to the State Commissioner of Police regarding public safety and security. Security, is therefore. by law a federal responsibility, but in reality, everybody's business.

THE PROCESS

A complex web of interaction occurs at various levels. A subject comes to the attention of the process through several sources. The Chief Executive can decide that an issue deserves priority and tabled before the relevant council or body for deliberation. The decision to consider may also be triggered by the submission from State Governors or other sources. Submissions by services, can also spur action on a particular subject.

The formal method of presenting issues before Council is through memorandum. The circulation of memoranda gives participants ample chance to prepare contributions. In general, participation is determined by the statutory composition of the bodies. Occasionally, non-members are invited to participate in the deliberations of specific agenda items which the Chief Executive or his principal advisers consider appropriate. Emergency sessions do not give room for lengthy papers and memoranda to be circulated to members before the meeting.

The Constitution created the National Defence Council and the National Security Council to advice the President in making decisions on National Security. However, other bodies created by the Constitution such as the Nigeria Police Council and National Economic Council and National Councils of State sometimes but rarely consider issues with security ramifications. The feedback from these bodies is passed into the security chain through the Office of Secretary to the Government of the Federation (OSGF).

Some characteristics of the operation of the national security decision-making process can be summarized as follows:

a. The main vehicle for national security decision-making is the National Security Council.

b. The National Defence Council considers only issues of relevance to defence policy and the administration of the Armed Forces.

c. Some of the decisions of the NSC may be referred to other bodies.
   - In the case of the National Assembly for ratification, as necessary;
   - Where the issues are beyond the NSC, It is referred to the appropriate body such as NCS, FEC, NPC or NEC.

d. The implementation machinery is usually based on the resolutions of the Council which are later authenticated in the minutes.

e. Decisions which mandate the use of force are normally conveyed through an operational directive issued by the National Security Adviser on the authority of the President, or through the relevant Minister.

f. In special circumstance, the President issues orders directly to the service or agency concerned.

g. When so required, the implementation of Council decisions is overseen by an ad hoc committee of service chiefs or their representatives under a Chairman assigned by the Chief Executive[4].

Observe that in contrast with what operated under military rule, the decisions of the NDC and NSC are not supreme. In practical terms, under civil rule, the FEC is considered a higher decision-making.

NATIONAL SECURITY COUNCIL

The composition of the NSC is prescribed by the Constitution which also allows the Chief Executive to appoint members other than those prescribed into the Council. The composition of the NSC from 2001 – 2009 is as follows:

a. President-   Chairman
b. Vice-President -   Deputy Chairman
c. Chief of Staff to Mr. President
d. Secretary to Government of the Federation
e. Head of Service of the Federation
f. National Security Adviser
g. Honourable Minister Internal Affairs
h. Honourable Minister of Defence
i. Honourable Minister of Foreign Affairs
j. Chief of Defence Staff
k. Chief of Army Staff
l. Chief of Naval Staff
m. Chief of Air Staff
n. Inspector General of Policy
o. Director General State Service
p. Director General National Intelligence
q. Co-opted members.

The function of NSC is to advice the President on matters relating to public security and the management of the structure, staff and other matters relating to agencies established by the National Security Agencies Act 1986. The role envisaged for the NSC is that of an apex body to discuss security policy. The enlarged composition did not allow it to provide strategic directive to the intelligence agencies as provided by the act. This function fell largely to the National Security Adviser whose ambit of authority depends on what the Chief Executive allows[5].

NATIONAL DEFENCE COUNCIL

The composition of the NDC as stated in the Constitution is as follows. It has not varied in practice except the inclusion of two members; COS to Mr. President and SGF.

a. President   - Chairman
b. Vice President   - Deputy Chairman
c. Chief of Staff to Mr. President
d. Secretary to Government of the Federation
e. Honourable Minister of Defence
f. Chief of Defence Staff
g. Chief of Army Staff
h Chief of Naval Staff
i. Chief of Air Staff
j. Co-opted members

The function of NDC to advice the President on matters relating to the defence of the sovereignty and territorial integrity of Nigeria, and the administration of the armed forces. The Council meets when necessary.

NDC ministers to policies across services. While the Chief Executive often delegates the Chair of Service Councils to the Minister, he is likely to always chair the NDC himself. Some prefer only the CDS among the service chiefs be a member of the NDC. However, some cases in the early life of the last administration revealed occasions when the CDS failed to carry service chiefs along on certain policies. The reaction to decisions without the concurrence or support of the Services Chiefs made it expedient for the COAS, CNS and CAS to be members of the NDC. The head of each service tend to focus on service interest while the CDS as the Principal Military Adviser to the President focuses on national and joint service interests. Service Chiefs retain the right to disagree with the CDS on policy issues and make their case direct to the Chief Executive through the Minister of Defence and the forum of the NDC[6].

NATIONAL ASSEMBLY

The legislature is a pillar of democracy. The role of legislature in the national security process in terms of decision-making and the implementation of decisions are very significant. It is important to understand the avenues by which the National Assembly influences the national security process as follows:-

a. **Appropriation.** Through the instrument of appropriation, the National Assembly can enhance or frustrate the implementation of a national security initiative. Operations which were not already catered for in the budget cannot be sustained except through supplementary appropriation. (Sections 80-83). Funding would affect the level of operational readiness and equipment availability.

b. **Emergency Rule.** In the case of wide spread disturbances or riots, the Constitution empowers the President to proclaim a state of emergency in any part of the country. The proclamation is however subject to the endorsement by 2/3 majority of both chambers of the National Assembly. (Section 305).

c. **Declaration of War** The President cannot declare a state of war between Nigeria and any other country without the support of a resolution of both houses of the National Assembly sitting in a joint session. (Section 5 (4)).

d. **Combat Duty Abroad.** No member of the armed forces can be deployed on combat duty outside Nigeria without the consent of the Senate. The President is allowed to do so in a situation where national security is under imminent threat but has to seek the consent of the Senate within seven days of actual combat engagement. Senate has to give or refuse consent within fourteen days of receiving the request. (Section 5 (5))

e. **Force Structure** The National Assembly has the power to create new services or branches of the armed forces. The President cannot do so without an act of the National Assembly. (Section 217). It would be recalled that the last National Assembly created the Nigeria Security and Civil Defence Corps[7].

The National Security decision-making process has to take the powers of the national assembly into consideration in its deliberations on certain issues. Where necessary, influential legislators are briefed and persuaded to promote the acceptance of proposed policies among their colleagues.

INTER-AGENCY INTERACTION

There are several steps in the policy process. A decision can be triggered by a report, policy paper or memoranda. The Chief Executive can decide on the basis of the information he has to summon a meeting of the NSC or NDC for broad –based consideration of the matter. A member can also request a meeting, but only the Chief Executive can summon the meeting and determine its agenda.

It follows therefore that information is the basis for action. Requisite information should be made available to all participants for them to make informed contributions based on correct understanding.

Liaison is important to the exchange of information and the establishment of rapport. Liaison can be through formal and information channels. Good liaison is important at all stages but more so during the implementation state. The producers of information need to get regular feedback from the users of the information they provide. Feedback should include the use to which the information is put and assessment of the relevance of the information the gaps if any in the coverage.

Leadership has a very important role to play in the degree of cooperation among agencies working towards the fulfillment of a common objective. It is the perception of leaders which shape the agenda and the choice of options to be decided upon. The mood and reputation members of his service may receive from participants from other services in carrying out the mission assigned by the national security decision process.

Other measures which could promote healthy interagency interaction include regular meetings at the Chief Executive and directors levels, fostering of informal network among officers of various services and the joint preparation of plans and activities possibly under unified leadership.

INFORMAL PROCESS

An understanding of the National Security decision machinery would be incomplete if due cognizance is not given to informal aspects of the process. Sometimes, especially at odd hours, the Chief Executive can summon some of his principals who are members of the NSC or NDC to deliberate upon germane issues. Such meetings are official but informal in the sense that it would only involve the principals with out the presence of secretarial staff.

No minutes are taken, therefore contributions can be more candid. The absence of memoranda or prepared position papers also means that participants are more open-minded. The drawback is that the short notice or informal setting might deny the participants, opportunity to come to the meeting with relevant data. They only have to depend on their memory and personal ability and not staff support.

Informal meetings to consider security decisions are occasional but equally significant. Their frequency depends on the mood of the Executive. The principals get the opportunity to hear the Chief Executive's definition of the problem, to make their contribution and then receive instructions on what to do. In the absence of minutes, sometime informal meetings are followed up with written instructions to give effect to the decisions taken. At other times, the verbal instructions issued at the meeting suffice.

CONCLUSION

The national security decision making process is designed to advise the President, who is the Chief Executive of the Federation of Nigeria. This process includes the integration of inputs and perspective from various sources and organs with a view to assisting the Chief Executive make the best decisions. It is also designed to enhance the articulation and implementation of national security policies issued by the relevant authorities.

The system thrives on the application of statutory rules and formal and informal interaction among the participating elements. Better results may be achieved through adequate education of participants on roles and expectations. Aspects of the functioning are subject to change or revision based on the preferences of the Chief Executive.

To make the national security decision-making machinery work well statutory prescriptions have to be translated into reality through diligent staff action and bureaucratic support. It is not always that the Chief Executive with accurate information and well considered options based on professional consideration and the national interest.

The best decisions are of no use if they are not implemented properly through the integration of inputs, consultations with Stake holders and the coordination of the various agencies involved in the process. Effective interaction among security agencies through liaison, regular meetings and networking and joint effort will enhance process of policy development and policy implementation thus ensuring that national security policies and decisions achieve their stated objectives.

REFERENCES

1. The Constitution of the Federal Republic of Nigeria, 1999.
2. Nigeria Defence Policy, Abuja: MOD, 2006.
3. O. Aguda Understanding the Nigerian Constitution of 1999, Lagos: MIJ Professional Publishers Limited 2000: 259 – 260.
4. Alaba Ogunsanwo "The Constitution and National Security" Proceedings of the National Conference on the 1999 Constitution, NIALS, Abuja, 26 – 28 October, 1999:5.
5. The Constitution of the Federal Republic of Nigeria (1999) section 3 (1) and (2).
6. See Istifanus Zabadi, "Nigeria and Security Sector Reform" African Strategic Review Vol.1, No.1, Nov/Dec 2007.
7. See O. Aguda Op: Cit.259 – 266.

CHAPTER 10

MECHANISMS FOR ACCOUNTABILITY, CONTROL AND DEFENCE POLICY MAKING PROCESSES IN NIGERIA

GANI YAROMS

INTRODUCTION

A statement made by Richard Akinjinde, one of the cabinet ministers in the First and Second Republics states thus;

> *Talking on the first coup, Balewa got Missing…We nominated Acting Prime Minister among us… Having nominated Zana Dipcharima as our Acting Prime Minister… We approached the Acting President, Nwafor Orizu, to swear Him in because He cannot legitimately act as the Prime Minister except he is sworn in. Nwafor Orizu refused. He said he needs to contact Zik who was then in West Indies… The Acting President Nwafor Orizu who did not cooperate with us cooperated with the GOC. Dr Orizu and the GOC, prepared speech which Nwafor Orizu broadcast handing over the government of the country to the Army. I State here again categorically as a member of that cabinet that we did not handover voluntarily. It was a Coup. (Akijinde, <u>Sunday Punch</u> 200:15).*

From this statement, it is discernible that lack of *esprit de corps* among political leaders necessitated the derailment of the democratic process of the first republic; indicating that there were problems with enforcing mechanisms for democratic accountability and control in the past. The impression given by Akinjinde is that Nigerian problem is more of state-society relations rather than civil-military relations. Thus, the continuous military reengagement is as a result of faulty nature of how the Nigerian state was founded. It is on this plank that this work attempts to explain how state-society relations defines or affects the ability of the political class to control the military and set out the parameter for determining national Defence Policy process. What these work has done at the moment is to first conceptualize patterns of democratic accountability and control and defence policy processes in Nigeria political system.

The second part of the work attempts to situate these terms within the cultural perspectives of Nigerian politics. While the third section isolates the strength and weakness of the mechanism for democratic control of the defence and security sector in Nigeria, particularly , the experience with the democratic rule that ushered in the regime of Chief Olusegun Obasanjo's regime and that of his immediate successors. The conclusion presents an open-ended approach for stakeholders to begin to think of the fundamental rudder to democratic accountability, control and defence policy making processes in Nigeria.

CONCEPTUALICING DEMOCRATIC ACCOUNTABILITY AND CONTROL

The danger poised to democratic rule in the third world countries has always been pointed more to military authoritarian rule than civilian autocracy. Accordingly, military interventions and re-engagements in politics have succeeded in establishing certain features which invariably have affected accountability and control. These features are:

(i.) violent approaches to overthrowing civilian and democratic government,

(ii) Rationalizing military rule on the fact of civilian incompetence, maladministration and corruption;

(iii) Legitimizing military rule on the basis of being the custodian of national interest;

(iv) Promoting militarism as an ideology that believes on military perfection, was given its efficiency, competence and patriotism

(v) Developing a pattern of civil-military relations characterized by military supremacy over civil institutions;

(vi) using stat power as an instrument of corruption and private enrichment thus, making political power highly attractive and thereby promoting a cycle of coups and counter coups,

(vii) Gross violation of human right through prejudicial actions, repressive policies and practices, and

(viii) Putative efforts by the military to disengage from politics and often willing to return to power after disengaging.

(ix) Turning of the military institution into *militics* and building a corps of *militicians* in place of politicians and the electorates (*see: Agbese*, 2000, lhonvbere 2000, Luckham 1996, Kieh 2000, Fayemi 1998, Olaniskin: 1999).

If these features are seemingly becoming permanent in Nigerian politics, it is equally difficult to expect total democratic accountability and control in an unstable political environment. Democratic accountability and control presuppose some measures put in place to avoid misrule, abuse of human rights and authoritarian tendencies which undermine democratic consolidation. Accountability and control are two separate concepts.

`However, both are mutually reinforcing and do provide the basis on which governance remains consistent with the consent of the people. In the light of this, accountability is first seen as the ability of democratic institutions to render stewardship creditably without which governance can be impaired . Hence democracy itself is a system rooted in. The greater the level of accountability the stronger the consolidation of democratic foundation. Democratic control on the other hand is dependent on the strengthening of democratic accountability. According to Luckham, democratic control is "how to prevent military intervention or re-intervention against established institutions" (Luckham 1985: 56). However, as much as control is important, it is not just containing the military but how the social forces could break the continuation in which civilian and military regimes alternate as "a basic strategy to safeguard the material interests of the dominant class and… to legitimize perpetual military intervention" (Luckham 1994: 65)

Thus both accountability and control are twin products of not only preventing military intervention and re-intervention against established democratic institutions but subjecting and engaging the military to its constitutional role and responsibility. Secondly, as much as the military is under the control of civil supremacy it is equally an accountable establishment, of government, military professional autonomy not withstanding. Third, the occupants of democratic establishments must also demonstrate a perfect example of accountability to the electorate and the entire society in terms of transparency, to the extent that any military contemplation for coup and intervention would not only be highly doubtful but resistible by the society. In the same line of though, military interventions occur when attitudes and behavior of the social force are not framed and focused on the template of collective social whole. In other words, authoritarianism emerges often in culturally fragmented social system. In a fragmented social system democratic landing becomes hard rather than being soft, in view of the in- built anti-democratic culture. This therefore calls for an explanatory theory of soft landing. According to the theory, the state is an organic structure built on a weak foundation (Yoroms: 1999: 2000). The possibility of it collapsing is apparent if no attention is taken to provide some supporting pillars. The Nigeria state is seen in this light after the June 12 presidential election crisis. In order to avoid total collapse of the system the elites in the North in collaboration with their international networks began to search for a personality that would land Nigeria softly as against any possibility of crash landing.

Therefore, to avoid a tempestuous storm and subsequent eruption of the Nigeria state there is need for an insurmountable and towering personality or group of people whose participation in political system would be like standing pillars, holding a house that is about collapse. Even if the house would eventually collapse, the strength of the pillars would be such that the landing process would not be disruptive, catastrophic nor of earth quaking proportion. It is on this ground that Obasanjo was throw up. (see Adekanye, 1999). With Obasanjo, the North was confident that its interest would be protected, given his initial management of stat affairs between 1976 and 1979 which favored the North. In the same vein, the South particularly South West, too can not disown him because he is a symbol of power shift, being a southerner. In a way it psychologically cushions the southwest over the June 12 palavers which Chief MKO Abiola fought and died for.

The agitating question therefore, is whether Obasanjo has landed softly in the wake of the crisis Nigeria went through, or whether he has crash landed the country after 8 years in office? If he has landed softly, then it is possible to focus the discussion on civil military relations by identifying mechanism that will strengthen democratic accountability and control. If not, the basis for starting the discussion would have to begin from state-society relations. This position is taken based on the fact that civil-military relations have more roots in developed countries which have sorted out the basic differences between state and society. Unlike in Africa where the relationship is asymmetrical and dysfunctional, in the developed world it is mutually interactive. In the light of this, it is important to understand the nature of the Nigerian political culture which affects the dynamics of State-society relations.

NATURE AND CHARACTER OF NIGERIAN POLITICAL CULTURE

Democratic accountability and control cannot be conveniently evolved without a properly understanding of the nature and character of Nigeria political culture. Following after Almond and Verba civil or political culture is understood within the context of democratic imperatives especially habits, value and principles that induce tolerance and fair play (Almond and Verba 1963). However, within the Nigeria context, the civil democratic culture has been overshadowed by long period of military rule shortly after independence.

The military institution is seen rightly by Ekeh as part of "migrated social structures developed around models of social organization imported to colonized Africa...virtually disembodied of their moral contents, of their subtraction of implicating ethics. And yet the imported models were never engrafted onto any existing indigenous morality" (Ekeh 1980:17). This structure, from Adekanye's perspective, has led to military occupation of power rather than military professionalism (Adekanye 1993;3). The military succeeded in establishing its political weight shortly after independence because the nationalist movement were essentially a coalition of desperate groups untied by their common grievances against colonial regime; their group relationship with one another was never free from tension and conflict" (Ake: 1996:4). Each group was moving with its ethnic culture into the civil arena. Because there was no synthesizing process, the arena became a cultural garage tensed with conflict. At the end, as Ekeh noted, the civil institutions suffered from "organizational fixation and becomes actually fixed" (Ekeh 1980: 18). In this case, Ekeh's treatise, on the "two publics" becomes relevant. According to him, there exist primordial and public realms in African politics, where resources are transferred from the public realm to the primordial realm without qualms (Ekeh 1975).

Thus, Nigeria's major problem with democratic construct is not institutional but attituditional: shaping cultural values of the society. Thus, according to research findings conducted by the defunct Centre for Democratic Studies, four sources of anti democratic attitudes and behavior were identified as being the causes of democratic breakdown in Nigeria. These sources are: (Omoruji: 1992):

(a) lack of trust among political actors which on further investigation is acquired in the child socialization

(b) lack of faith in the regime in power. Citizens do not have faith in the regime or its laws; do not even believe that the system would last,

(c) low threshold of tolerance – what makes one laugh in one setting could provoke violence in another, and

(d) people see politics as business proposition and see investing in politics as a business or family venture.

Based on these sources, Nigeria has experience electoral malpractice, abuse of political office as avenue for gross personal enrichment in the face of an abject mass poverty, political intolerance, lack of intra-party and inter-party democracy, blatant manipulation of religion, ethnicity and geographical factors as spring board and handle to personal political ambition and disregard to continual rule of the game (Omoruyi 1992:9). The military emerged by successfully establishing a culture of violence which helped to perpetuate military rule.

From the above analysis, the experience with long period of military rules varies in the society. First, the militarization of the society led the civil population to turn to a reactive force, lacking patience. As Omoruyi pointed out, Nigerians are not gifted with the attribute of patience, which is a precondition for the development of democratic culture. Nigerians would ask, for how long? To many Nigerians, to wait for the emergence of the civil culture is to postpone indefinitely the attempt at democratization (Omoruyi 1992:11). Second, the absence of civil culture has affected the level of elite accommodation. The Nigerian elite lack the spirit of socialization with engrained norm of mutual respects and tolerance, sense of fair play and readiness to compromise. The fictionalization of the elite (along ethnic and primordial cleavages) has made those who have lost out of the corridors of power to influence, support and sponsor the military to take power to their own advantage.

Three, the imbalanced nature of recruitment into the military creates fear, insecurity and estrangement among some segments of the country who have been putting pressure for regional military. That is, because the military being alternative means of accessing power, cannot be left to one segment of the society. This trend is not only dangerous to democracy, democratic control and military professionalism. Once the military is polarized the basis for sustaining national integrations becomes difficult.

Four, the political structure and institutions, though in existing, are incapable of enforcing the rules of the game because of lingering anti-democratic attitudes and behaviors of the power players. The three arms, the Executive, Legislature and Judiciary are like strange bed-fellows. Their failure to be separate but interact makes it difficult for them to understand the working mechanism of the system. Given the in-fight within the three arms, the military is not only distanced but finds it useful to intervene to take control of state power.

Five, military rule has not only underdeveloped the political institutions which it has used to ascend to political power. Budgetary allocation to various military formations was misappropriated by unit commanders without developing the military institutional infrastructures like the barracks, (equipments, materials) and logistics research and development. Furthermore staff allowance, welfare packages and pension benefits were embezzled by office's corps who had no opportunity to occupy political offices. The apathy and lack of trust among officers and between them and the soldiers, have not only led to the weakening of the military institution but its criminalization. The effort to weaken military institution is deliberate because key professional appointees of various military formations are made by military political office holders otherwise known as *militicians* who wanted collaborators to defend their corporate interests within the military system. The in-fights and the fear of what the institution could turn out to be, had led various incumbent military regimes to ensure that the Air Force was grounded, the Navy was anchored and the Army equipment folded up and/or rendered non-functional. The weakening of the institution makes a deal for the perpetuation of the military rule than the respect for the institution. Six, it has also affected the processing of policy formulation and policy making including budgeting, national planning and defence management. It is difficult to expect a democratic regime emerging without being militaristic in decision making. This has recently affected the Executive – Legislature relationship.

Seven, the growing strength of ethnic and religious conflicts across the country are grievous to, rather than reinforcing, democracy. These include the agitations by the restless youth in the Niger Delta among others groups like Odua people's Congress (OPC), the *Yan banga,* and the *Bakassi Boys.* The long period of military rule which suppressed people's view threatened rather than providing building blocks for democracy. Lastly, the long period of military rule has bastardized the concept of federalism. Nigeria, though a plural society was forced into what one might call unitary federalism rather than systemic or functional (or in Nigeria parlance) true federalism. This has led to several agitations for resource control and regional ethnic police and army.

Given these problems, attempts to stamp out military re-engagement in politics would depend on restructuring the state – society relations and strengthening the mechanisms for democratic accountability and control.

STRENGHTENING DEMOCRATIC ACCOUNTABILITY AND CONTROL

Democratic control and Accountability are seen more of witch-hunting than system-induced mechanism in Nigeria. Nevertheless, the process of democratic accountability and control is trial-run and should be developed to reinforce the mutual relations between the state and the society. It is much more difficult as Oyovbaire points out, that the character and performance of the emerging democratic institutions and arrangement in Nigeria is still informed by the phenomenon of praetorians (Oyovbaire 2000:5). This notwithstanding, there is the need to strengthen what exist as appearances of democracy to avoid a relapse to deeper authoritarian rule. Some aspects of these mechanisms are considered.

CONSTITUTIONAL ENGINEERING

Constitutional Engineering is an important aspect of democratic control and Accountability. It remains a supreme legal binding force for any given country. The strength of a constitution determines the effectiveness of state – society relations and its capacity for democratic control of the military. The 1999 Nigerian constitution, like the previous ones, in section 1 (2) forbids the forceful take over of the government of Nigeria or any part thereof, except in accordance with the provision of the constitution. This constitutional framing does not have biting teeth because several coups have been staged and democratic regimes have been overthrown with reckless abandon. If the 1963 and 1979 constitutions did not stop making coups, what magic will the 1999 constitution perform?

It is further problematized by lack of faith by the citizens on the system and its constitution. This is because since 1922, Nigeria had up to 17 constitution and constitution making processes respectively. However, none had been subjected to thorough public debates, discussions, referenda and/or plebiscites. Constitution making in Nigeria has been elitist. This might have informed the reasons for less expensive ways coups have also been successfully affected. Secondly, because the people are not totally part of the constitution making process they are always defenseless when coups occur. They have seen copies of the constitution not even its content which would give them strength to defend it (Ihonvbere 2000). To overcome this, Obasanjo's leadership set up a Constitution Review Committee to revisit and revise the 1999 constitution which, in all intents and purposes in military in nature. However, for the committee to produce an acceptable constitution that will control the military, the people must be involved in deciding the type of constitution which would be accountable and could as well meet their requirements. Nigeria needs a living constitution engineered only by the people.

Unfortunately the Technical Committee on the Review of the 1999 constitution made itself too technical for the participation of the people. As Ihonvbere pointed out, no Nigeria can afford to go through the pains of expressing their views on the type of constitution they need if the process is not less tasking (Ihonvbere 2000:32). More fundamentally, the Mantu led parliamentary committee on the review of the 1999 constitution focused more on elongation of Obasanjo's regime than the fundamentals of the institution. As a result the effort to revise the 1999 constitution was overturned. The current attempt by the National Assembly to make use of internal process of constitutional amendment/review is still skeptical because most of the members of National and State Assemblies were rather appointed than elected. This raises serious credibility issues on the process of the constitutional amendment/review.

MILITARY REORGANIZATION AND REPROFESSIONALISM.

The long period of military rule in politics has advertantly affected the civil respect for the institution? At the return to civil rule in 1999, there were several insinuations against the military. The National Assembly adopted a motion on relocating the military barracks around the presidential area (Three Arms Zone) to other places outside the seat of power. In addition, there were resolutions that past military heads of state or presidents should not be paid gratuity. Also during the political reform conference, members seriously criticized the military for political and economic suffocation Nigeria has gone through. This made the retired military officers who were members of the conference to apologise on behalf of the military leadership and military institution for the damage they had caused the nation. The MPRI report on Civil – Military relations as at 1999 was so bizarre:

> The Nigerian armed forces do not currently enjoy a favorable reputation in the urban and elite sectors of the Nigerian society. Discussions with several legislators, educators, and non governmental organizations indicated a lack of understanding of the need for and value of military capacity in a country of Nigeria's size, wealth and location. Many military members are themselves discouraged by their public image and asked if the Joint Planning Team could mitigate the **"war"** declared on them by the rest of the country. They have not been invited into a partnership with other important sectors of Nigerian society or government (MPRI 1999: 48)

This worry is genuine because as it also noted:

> "… there is an entire generation of people who do not know how a democracy should work and who have grown up under military rule in a society where government and military services are seen primary as a means to acquire wealth and power. The legacy of this past is a governmental structure and ethnic environment which have been so fundamentally weakened that it is arguably incapable of healing itself, regardless perhaps of the will or good intentions of the current political leadership. The NAF suffers accordingly" (MPRI: 1999:10).

It is as a result of this that the reorganization and re-professionalization of the military became part of the panel-beating process to enhance civil control of the military. According to the former Minister of Defence Lt. –Gen. T.Y. Danjuma (Rtd), Nigeria does not have the skills, experience or the material resources necessary to effect re-professionalism without external assistance. Therefore, in order to establish effective civilian control through re-professionalism "the Ministry of Defence has sought the assistance of the United States Government in the task of re-professionalizing our armed forces" (Danjuma: 2000:4). Before we take on the issue of external assistance, the Obasanjo's government embarked on reorganizing the military, in such a way that it has drawn a lot of comments and criticism.

The regime embarked on a deliberate project of re-organisation and re-professionalization. The first step was to retire some military officers otherwise known as *'militicians'* who were in political office between 1985 and 1999. The retirement of these 93 officers was necessary because they have been smeared by politics which has damaged both the military professionalism and military institution in particular. Thus, leaving them in the military would mean creating powerful force within the organization whereby a segment which has been performing its pure military duties would be perpetually left groaning. The second step taken was the seizure of properties and finances of the *militicians* who have corruptly enriched themselves during military rule. However, while backing out of his promise to reduce the strength of army, from 80,000 to 50,000, government has instead decided on measures towards implementations of demobilization based on enforcing rules of 35years mandatory retirement age, poor disciplinary records and unproductivety. To cushion the effect of demobilization, the government has promised to provide attractive packages to avoid its effects. Recently too, in line with general review of salaries and wages in the country, salaries of officers and men have been skyrocketed, above that of civil servants, with further increase in wages. The Obasanjo's regime had completed plans for further pay rise for the military before his exit in 2007. Presidents Umar Yar' Adua had began giving attention to military welfare and military Pension reform, which the government of President Goodluck Jonathan is seriously consolidating.

The above measures taken by government are laudable but not adequately challenging. First, there are a lot of atrocities committed by officer corps against the Non-Commissioned Officer (NCOs) under the guise of regimentation, command and control. When welfare packages for soldiers are appropriated by officers it creates restlessness as they become potential coup recruits. Second, the treatment which retired officers and men receive in pursuing their pension and gratuity is scaring to serving military personnel. This has created divided loyalties among their families after retirement. This undermines their interest in professionalism. Government must delineate properly national defence policy in the context of sorting out the militicians from the professionals. This policy could form the basis for either a sweeping demobilization of the politically oriented officers or provide a rational right – sizing retirement, on the basis of age, indiscipline and proper placement of officers among others. If this is not done, the retirement of 93 officers and a further decision to retire up to 5,000 would not actually sensitize the military to perform its professional role. The military institution was deliberately bastardized and underdeveloped by successive military regimes as a means of mitigating the occurrence of coups by one military regime or the other. That is, as an institution, the military can be a breeding ground for coup plotters, if not weakened.

During military rule, a process of co-option was put in place, where resources allocated to unit commanders, considered as professionals were not accounted for. There was no process for questioning this. The political office holders would not question this because they would not like an opposition within the military that would lead to a coup. At the same time the commanders would not think of plotting a coup because were beneficiaries of military regimes. For instance it was alleged that Gen. Abacha was given N400m in the early 19990s by Gen. Babangida for the construction of the Directorate of Military Intelligence Headquarters (DMI) in Abuja. The money was misappropriated as the project was not carried out until he (Abacha) became the Head of State.[1] There were similar cases like this that ruined the military structure. This apart, the Nigerian military is a welfare organization. Welfarism is promoted as a means to sustain and cushion those not holding political appointments from planning coups. The concept of welfare as gratification should be separated from the general welfarism of the military men and officers. The non-political officers are involved in contracts, running their own businesses and engaging in other means of gratification like material and financial assistance from their *militician* colleagues. In running for contracts and pursuing business, there is no doubt that professional officers could have amassed wealth which might be equal to or more than that of political soldiers. Therefore, the distinction between political officers and their professional colleagues should not be seen as very gravious.

The entire military needs restricting to eradicate a "group of disorganized cow boys" (cited in Jega 2000:8) who have turned "the military into an army of anything" and becoming each others enemy "through rope in, set up and framed up, abuses and infringement of rights of innocent men and officers; as lying becomes official military policy" (Ibrahim: 2000:14).

This is a major problem in the military. The institution has been smeared and it cannot be made better by distinguishing between professionals and *militicians* or that the institution is political but the men and officers are bad. It is difficult to separate the wheat from the chaff. The issue involved is systemic. It is the parts make up the whole and the whole is also affected by long participation, of military in politics ii This call for massive reorganization and demobilization of the military to be followed with good promises so as not to rock the system. The only sacrifice the nation can pay is to offer a fat welfare package for the military which the former Minister of Defence Gen. Danjuma earlier promised but later declined. Indeed the military, in the last 9 years, has witnessed serious conscientisation and improvement in imbibing the tenets of democratic control of the military. The political fact remains that the political system is still turbulent. The political class still lacks the managerial ability to govern. Corruption and bad governance are still found in the art of governance. This does not auger well for a society where, inspite of the failure of the military in governance, it is still seen to be relevant compared to the political class. Nevertheless, there is need to focus on downsizing and right sizing of the military to meet expectation as a professional body in the course of the defence of the nation.

In the process of right sizing, government needs to provide adequate cushioning package, to those to be affected. The MPRI in its report has also recommended the importance for the military welfare package (MPRI;1999). Therefore, the following packages are suggested as measures to cushion the military from the effect of right-sizing:

Rank	Amount	Rank	Amount
Major Generals:	N20ml	Brigadier Generals	N18ml
Colonels	N15ml	Lt Colonels	N12ml
Major	N10ml	Captains	N8ml
2nd Lt – Lt	N5-6 ml	Others	N1-4ml

The justification for this sweeping right-sizing benefits is to ensure that the retirees are cushioned to start a new life in the civil realm without many difficulties. This would keep them away from contemplating taking on actions that are irrational and are at the risk of the security of the country. It would also appreciation to citizens who signed out their lives to defend the country; and having successfully been demobilized, it becomes an honor to be reciprocated. This argument has been debunked by critics who see the military as consisting of people who wrecked and corrupted the economy and needed no further cushioning but prosecution (see Adekanye; 1993). However, if the recommendation is accepted, it could be applied discreetly. It is the part of the sacrifices we have to make in order to build confidence within the system. If this is done we can develop a new corps of military force that would be effective for democratic accountability and control. Indeed, as Adekanye agreed, this suggestion is too critical to be accepted by the public as it seems unimaginable to pamper a repressive organ of the society. This, not withstanding it is also advisable that apart from maintaining a sound pension scheme, there is need to establish a credible social security system in the country to take care of both the military and the general public service. There are current efforts to this effect, like the retired officers housing schemes among others, which are quite commendable. The new pension scheme is also a good step in the right direction. Government has put up a pension scheme where it bears ½ of the military pension but it can also delete the military from the contributory pension scheme in order to assure the military of its strategic role in the society. In addition, senior military officers have been given car loans to ensure their confidence. Though this has been seen as an official bribe, a trend which was started by the Ibrahim Babangida regime has served as a means to forestall coups.

Thirdly, the Nigerian military still maintains the classical rigidity of a soldier seen as a war maker. He is taught, trained and debriefed to believe that he is a superman. He is half-human and half-beast, with the target to fight and win war; and not peace making. In this light, he takes order and command from his superior officers and not from any "bloody civilian" political class. In a situation where his boss already has a framed opinion against the political class, it is doubtful whether civil command would be saluted with dispatch like in the military. As much as training of soldiers for national security is important, the new millennium of military training is re-focusing on soldiering for peace, which Nigeria must not be left behind.

In views of this, the military does not only need reprofessionalisation. In fact the reprofessionalisation process must go along with political as well as civic education of the military on the supremacy of civilian control of the military. The political and civic education should be taught as part of military orientation towards accepting political control over its activities. In revisiting the question of external support for reprofessionalism, the training so far offered by the US based Military Professional Resources Incorporate (MPRI) was far below expectation. The cultural basis of the training was very weak as it failed to touch on the realities of civil-military relations in Nigeria. As argued by Amoda and Chinwezu, "external inputs whether contracted or philanthropic ought to be facilitative and not determinative; and they should not be a condition for receiving aid. When external inputs take determinative or conditions forms, the government so aided suffers a diminution of their sovereignty" (Amoda and Chinwezu: 2000:27). Thus, General Danjuma reliance on external support for professionalism is questionable. In fact, the officer corps of the military was opposed to MPRI because they were not taken along when the policy was being formulated.

Therefore, for effective political education and orientation of the military to be apolitical and to demonstrate their loyalty to civil supremacy, there is need to create a (structure of) training Organ around the retired Nigeria military officers. Nigeria has highly respected retired military officers like Lt-Gen. Salihu Ibrahim, Maj-Gen. Isola Williams, AVM A. Bello, Rear Adm. Aduwo, and Major-Gen. Ejiga among others. The experience they acquired is very important in terms of building a restricted cult of military officers who would operate like MPRI in defending our security interest. [2]Unfortunately, the Army HQs has recently banned soldier from further training because they often turn out to be arrogant among their contemporaries and dysfunctional to the institution (National Concord, August 22, 2000, p. 12). At this age of technology, Nigeria can not afford an educationally bankrupt military. The directive is fraudulent and undermines the input of the soldiers who are still largely uneducated.

Above all, the question of reprofessionalisation is very fundamental to the question of democratic accountability and control which Amoda and Chinwezu queried;

(i) How will the reduction of the strength of the armed forces from 80,000 to 50,000 institutionalize:
  (a) The prevention of the unconstitutional seizure of government by the military,
  (b) The mobilization of the Nigerian populace to frustrate the armed seizure of the people's government by an armed section of the military, and
  (c) to re-institute democratic government when ever it is subverted by the military?

(ii) what prevents the Armed Forces, even when reduced in strength, from effecting the overthrow of the civilian government?

(iii) is professionalization of the armed forces synonymous with their subordination to civil democratic control?

(iv) what kind of reconstitution would make it a matter of institutional survival for the Nigerian Armed Forces to accept their subordinate to civil democratic control? And

(v) how are the Armed Forces to be organized in order to inhibit the formation of coup driven cells within .

These questions are relevant if we are to take the professionalization exercise seriously, especially when involving external support and establishing credible civil-military relations.

It is in light of this that the services have began to look at how to reorganize the armed forces. Unfortunately, the services are carrying out the reorganization independent of each other. Except the Defence Headquarters is involved in harmonizing the reforms, the Nigerian Armed Forces will experience reorganization crisis. However, of all the services, Nigerian Army (NA) is outstanding in its reorganization programme. Accordingly, the NA sees its reorganization as a transformation process intended to provide the basis for the army to be well organized, trained, equipped and readily available for rapid development. The architect of this transformation, the former Chief of Army staff, General A.O. Azazi who later became the chief of Defence Staff (CDS) has ensured that this transformation is generalized for the Nigerian military. Already, the Ministry of Defence has taken over the transformation programme which all the services have been properly brought into it as part of government restructuring of the military. As Bassey(2000;303) pointed out the reorganization or transformation of the armed forces must be based on ;

a. Organizational decisions concerning the methods and forms by which Nigeria's armed forces are organized and administered
b. Personnel decisions concerning the number retention, pay and working conditions of members of the military service
c. Material decisions concerning the amount of procurement and distribution of equipments and supplies
d. Budgetary decisions concerning the size and distribution of fund made available

THE THREE ARMS OF GOVERNMENT AND DEMOCRATIC ACCOUNTABILITY

The three arms of government are the Executive, Legislative and Judiciary. The long period of military rule has led to executive recklessness excessiveness and autocracy. It has weakened judiciary review as a result of extra-judicial and ouster clauses. In the same way, the legislature is not only also weakened but paralyzed. It is difficult to implement legislative oversight, checks and balances in a country like Nigeria where transition to civilian rule has occurred again, only after a period of 15 years of repressive military rule.

Among the three arms, the legislative which is supposed to be endeared to the people is rather distanced and detached. The legislature must be strengthened. First, the parliament must have confidence in its itself and must draw the support of the people. The people must be encouraged to interact and make enquiries through their elected members. In the same way, the parliamentarians would also be required to pay frequent visits to their constituencies and interact with other social forces in the society in order to create a rapport and interactive confidence. The populace needs to be encouraged by the civil society organizations to know that members of NASS are elected to serve them and that they have the rights to reach out to various committees to express their grievances. Secondly, for the legislature to perform its constitutional duties, the executive must not always see the actions of the parliament as confrontational. Politics is about contradictions and how to resolve them to the advantage of the society. The inability of both executive and the legislature to understand this has made any meaningful progress in Nigeria's democratic process difficult since 1999.

Thus, the Executive-Legislative relationship should be embedded on the depth and craft of interactive lobbying rather than confrontation. The consequences of the legislature pitching battle against the executive and vice versa call, for rationality in behavior from both arms of government as it affects the overall development of democracy and especially legislative oversight, on governance generally. The presidency needs to create more informal interactions like breakfast meeting, dinner, telephone calls, visits and other necessary measures with members of NASS, once a while. This seems to have paid off after the 2003 election then President Obasanjo was re-elected. There is need to strengthen the legislature because a weak legislature creates a basis for civilian autocracy. It takes time to notice the existence of civilian autocracy, because it is colored with democratic gerrymandering. At the end, civilian authoritarianism only provides an opening for military intervention.

A strong parliament is therefore, preferred because it could establish the democratic recipe for accountability and control. Apart from its constitutional power the moral strength of the legislature creates a liberal environment for democratic accountability and control. The use of state power by the executive to disregard legislative immunity is dangerous to democratic rule. For instance, the undue invasion of the official residence of Chuba Okadigbo, the former senate president by the police, the sacking of the Abia State Assembly by some hoodlums suspected to have been sponsored by the state Governor Dr. Chris Ngige for the fear that the state legislature had concluded plan to impeach him, and other related cases are danger signals to democracy in Nigeria. Through it could be argued that it is a learning process, it must be done with civility.

As much as impeachment and recall system are constitutional measures for checking the excesses of the elected members of government, the executive should not be threatened with impeachment simply because the legislators have power to do so. In the same vein the executive must not take up the rule-making functions and should appreciate that democracy triumphs with "minimal executive proclamation". While the legislature must give the executive the latitude within which they can function effectively in executing the law, the executive must learn to respect the legislative constitutional power as much as the legislature must not be seen to be sentimentalizing constitutional issues.

This is the first time in Nigeria's political history that the National Assembly (NASS), though dominated by the ruling party, is defining its independence without due regards to party control or presidential influence. In the period, leadership of NASS under Chief Ken Nnamani and Alhaji Aminu Massari has demonstrated some level of competence which the succeeding leadership of David Mark and Demiji Bankole has imbibed under the dispensation of the president Umar Yar' Adua and President Good luck Jonathan. NASS should be encouraged by the social forces to stabilize. The important aspect is the self-cleansing exercise which the senate began with a probe of itself. The confidence it creates for itself can be sustained if the Kuta-led investigation panel stands the test of credibility.[iv]

This will give NASS the ability to exercise democratic oversight and control over executive autocracy and check military itching to re-engage in political governance. The nation is alert today because of the spate or call for probe panels across the country, which has started with the Senate. This is the beauty of democracy because such a thing cannot happen under the military. This is the more reason why NASS must be supported by all primordial forces of democracy and democratic forces. However, the strength of support from the aid society for NASS depends on its members' code of conduct in the society. If as educated as they are, they could still carry anti-democratic cultural traits, then Nigeria would require the rule of Angels.

Nevertheless, as earlier noted, the legacy left by the leadership of Ken Nnamani and Bello Masari between 2005 and 2007 has impacted on the current leadership of NASS under Senator David Mark and Hon. Demiji Bankole. The National Assembly has continued to exert its influence as an important arm of government.

PRIMORDIAL SOCIAL FORCES OF DEMOCRACY

Democratic accountability and Control is not only a state affair. It also involves "forces of democracy and democratic forces." (Yusuf: 2000). Primordial social forces of democracy means primordial civil society organizations that are rural or urban based like cultural, ethnic, market women, farmers and others that live in associational life community based organizations (CBOs). Whereas democratic forces are the civil –civil society organizations like the press, labour and students union, human rights activists and other prodemocracy movements like the Non-Governmental Organizations (NGOs). While the forces of democracy are always available for democracy rule, it cannot be without the backing of democratic forces which are the politically conscious organs of the society. They contributed immensely towards the struggle against military rule and fought for the enthronement of democratic rule. What they did was to demilitarize the government by civilianizing it. The greater task now is how to democratize it. And with the take over of the stage by the political class the civil-civil society groups are weakened to play any significant role, especially with donors withdrawing financial supports and sponsorship shortly after the civilianization of the governmental process. However, if they will be relevant, they must target the primordial organizations by giving them political education and indoctrination in order to enhance they ability to protect democracy.

Therefore, the task of "takeoff stage" to democratic rule lies with the primordial forces of democracy. The ability to nurture these groups would further sustain the course of democracy. In short, the ethnic militias could be turned to defenders of democracy if only the Nigerian state under Obasanjo's regime was able to meet the yearnings of the ethnic communities that had suffered under military rules. These groups can as well support military reengagement if the civilian regime is not prepared. For instance, fear is still hanging in Jos where armed military forces have been dispatched to contain the Jos crisis. Government must not be seen to be sweeping grievances under carpet by using military arbitrarily to silence those involved in communal conflicts. These conflicts must be properly addressed under the democratic norms and practice.

MASS POLITICAL AND CIVIC EDUCATION

Political and civil education is other important issues for building a culture of democratic control and accountability. The government owned National Orientation Agency (NOA) has embarked on creating peoples parliament in some states. In Lagos State for instance, NAO organized public fora where local government Councilors and Chairmen gave account of their stewardship. Increasingly too, in public and private televisions and radios, elected members have often appeared in live radio and television discussions. For the first time under the present dispensation Nigerian public has access to contribute to discussion with public officers without fear. These trends must be sustained by civic and political education measures among the grassroots people if we want to make meaning out of democracy. The people must be properly educated not only by NOA but also active non-governmental organizations and institutions, on how to resist coup such as staying away from work place, market place, and lecture hall and down tooling of all labour working implements.

Therefore, the efforts of NOA not withstanding, it can not provide a holistic approach to political and civic education because of its governmentarian appearances. The onus falls back to civic-civic organization to indoctrinate the people against illegitimate government.

THE POLICE

The concept of the police is intended to create a civil defence force that would protect the society and keep it as partners in governance. The long period of military rule has equally militarized the police in its dealing with the public. The police needs restructuring if we expect to use it to enforce democratic control. The police must see itself as a civil defence corps and not as military institution. There is need to reprofessionalise it and equip it to support the civil defence of the constitution anytime coups occur. After the overthrow of Alhaji Shehu Shagari in the Second Republic, one of the first targets of the coup plotters was to seize the equipment the civilian regime had purchased for the police. The military fear a strong police force because it could be used to control the military. As a checker against military re-entry, the police should be equipped only to the extent that they maintain democratic vigilance and not to intimidate the society. This can only be possible if corruption and professional abuse in the force is tackled. Or else, as it is, the police are not yet prepared for democratic control of the military. Therefore, government must facilitate the institutionalization of police trust fund.

PARTY SYSTEMS

Another important mechanism is the weak development of party system in Nigeria. The formation of political parties are not based on the aggregation of interest but regulated by the state as stated in sections 221 and 222 of the 1999 constitution. Political parties are supposed to be hallmarks of democracy. The sustenance of any established democracy is based on stable political parties. Parties should be allowed to grow from among the political entities either on the basis of ethnicity, religion or ideology. On the basis of this, it is possible for local parties to emerge controlling their local affairs while larger ones seeking state and national offices would have to negotiate with the local parties. In the light of this every ethnic group, every religion and ideology would feel relevant. This will reduce the culture of election irregularities and violence experienced in the past.

In allowing parties to grow from within the people it would equally reduce the financial burden of funding parties by individuals or by government through the Independent National Electoral Commission.(INEC). The initially legislated three political parties were:

> *"(H) Urriedly assembled the purpose of getting rid of military rule and for electing officials to government office; we ended with having political parties without a party system. Curiously, while they could not be settled down before the elections of 1998 to early 1999, they still have not settled down the year after. If there is no party system, it is difficult to see how the vital role of political parties can be discharged in the democratic system. Individually and collectively, the three political parties can hardly be described in any successful terms. Where they are not organized they are simply an assemblage of personalities with little or no impact on the political process. (Oyovbaire 2000:17).*

It is in the light of this that party system should be structured on the basis of multiple systems instead of regulated and imposed three-party system. As noted by a party chieftain recently the parties are motley assemblies, as they don't have manifestoes and programmes. The Electoral act 2006 has improved on party registration from 3 political parties in 1999 to 50 by 2006. However, the fact remains that none of these parties are based from the grassroots. This makes proof the doubt that massive rigging may still be with us in spite of the attempt to introduce the electronic voting machines.

MINIMAL STATE.

In reflecting on the nature of the problem affecting democratic governance in Nigeria, it is important to note that the Nigerian state is too big. It has appropriated a lot of power and resources that nobody thinks he can do well outside the state arena. The state is an arena of contestation because of enormous resources at its disposal. It is hoped that when the state becomes minimal it is possible to expect that many of the elites who think their survival is dependent on the state would realize that it no longer glitters. This is likely to reduce some of the contentious problems of state-society relations; thereby sustaining and consolidating democratic accountability and control. Indeed, more than two-thirds of Nigerian elites made their fortune from the state without contributing to the production of state. In view of this, everyone is interested to get into the state arena whether as a governmentarian or governmentariat.[v]

As Ake notes the bloated nature of the state has become a strategy for corruption and should be trimmed by reducing its extent of economic ownership and control

(Ake: 1991:38). This does not however mean the state would abandon its primary responsibility to the people. But its primary responsibility should not be a caveat for corruption and abuse of office. The efforts of government through the Economic and Financial Crimes Commission among others are commendable. However, there is need to reduce the pay package of the ruling political elite. Political officers should only be for service and not wage-paying. In this way only those that are called to service should be respected and honored .

THE PRESS

Above all, the measures taken so far, the press remains the foremost cardinal *defecto* in determining whether the system would last or not. The survival of media houses is dependable on their oversight on the three arms of government and the military. As the fourth estate of the Realm the Nigerian press succeeded in helping in the struggle for the termination of military rule. However, the press cannot help its struggle further if by its reportage, overtly or covertly, create the conditions for military reengagement. We need a cautious press with democratic consciousness that would go a long way to meet the yearning of the population and not only the financial gains. The press should learn from the experience of 1983, 1985 and the Abacha's 1993 coups in which the regimes were repressive to the press , in spite of supports given by the press and public, overtly or covertly. The press must continue its fight to indoctrinate the public that the worst civilian regime is better than the best military junta. This does not mean supporting corruption but it must be exposed as an aspect of checks and balances in the system without giving an open invitation for military intervention. One of the reasons why the press speculates is because government makes it difficult for them to access information. A society that is misinformed is indeed sufficiently endangered. Therefore, NASS can help to strengthen the power of the press by passing into law the freedom of information bill . However, the fear about the bill is that if endorsed into law, government is;(i) doubtful of the maturity of the press to be entrusted with national security information and how (ii) the bill will favor a section of the country which has the concentration of the press more than others. Hence, information in the hands of such a sectional press may jeopardize governance. As a result of these key issues, it is believed that the Freedom Information Bill may be delayed except assured by the press, which is the major benefit of it.

OMBUDSMAN SHIP

There are in existence some ombudsman institutions which need to be strengthened. These are the Code of Conduct Bureau, Code of Conduct Tribunal and Public Complaint Commission among others. Recently USAID/OTI has been working with the Code of Conduct Bureau, providing it with capacity building mechanisms. Further more, the setting up of Human Rights Violations and Investigation Commission (HRVIC) Independence Corrupt Practices Commission (ICPC) and Economic and Financial Crimes Commission (EFCC) amongst others are major steps taken by the civilian government to address some of the Corruption tendency and repression unleashed on the society. What gives confidence to the democratic process is how the people could trust the government to provide sound and credible reports. Government too, as part of the democratic accountability should be willing to implement the reports of these organizations. These institutions must be allowed to function without prohibition. In fact, these institutions should be seen to be active in serving as watch dogs of Nigeria democracy.

DEMOCRATIC CONTROL AND DEFENCE POLICY MAKING PROCESSS

Given the foregoing tabulations of democratic accountability and control, it also remains that the success depends on concrete defence making process. Therefore the 1999 constitution by section 218(1) authorized the president of the republic to assume control of the military. The president according to section 218(2) has the power to appoint the Chief of Defence Staff (CDS). He could also by section 218(3) delegate power to the member of the armed forces of the federation. Meanwhile, in these wide ranges of power, the National Assembly by section 218(4) has the power to make laws to check and regulate the ability of the president to exercise his powers including appointment, promotion and disciplinary control of members of the armed forces of the federation and even to deploy troops and declare wars.

The same constitution also sets out the hierarchical order of authority relating to defence policy issues. While the CDS exercise his executive command over the military, he does so based on the direction and delegate power or discretion of the Minister of Defence who does not necessarily require having a military background. The constitution also made provision for a National Defence Council; made up of the President of the republic as the Chairman and the Minister of Defence, CDS, Service Chiefs as members. This council advises the president on defence matters. The National Security Council is a bigger council made up of Minister of Defence, State Governors among others with the President as chairman. It is also an advisory council. This means the issues of defence policy lies with the president and his minister of defence who could be civilians without military background. It is in the light of the above that the National Assembly (NASS) has been given enormous power of legislative oversight over the Ministry of Defence and the armed forces in the area of defence policy formulation and implementation. The Ministry of Defence (MOD) must be ready to give enough and adequate information when required by the parliament. The purpose of defence policy is to improve civil – military relations and not to undermine it. Thus the President Olusegun Obasanjo (1999) summarized this fundamental doctrine of civil – military relations to include:

- accepting the constitution as the sole and supreme document defining the role of the armed forces;
- accepting elected civilian president as commander-in-chief of the armed forces and of the supremacy of the elected officials of state over appointed officers at all levels;
- accepting civilian headship of the ministry of defence and other strategic establishments;

- accepting civilian or legislative deliberation and decision making over the military budget;
- accepting decision regarding the goals and conducts of military operations as serving political and strategic goals established by the civil authority;
- accepting the application of civilized principles to all military investigations and trials, and
- accepting the right of civil (supreme) court authority to review any actions or decision taken by military judicial officers

These points are indeed fundamental to defence policy process in terms of maintaining civil – military relations especially in the military aid to civil authority. In responding to call to assist civil authority, the military must keep to civilized rules of enforcement especially when it intervenes in communal conflicts. Measures should be taken to ensure that the military does not embark on ethnic or communal cleansing as it was in the case of Odi and Zaki Biam and the controversial military deployment to quench the recent crisis in Jos .

While the military succeeded in creating the corridor of tranquility in Kaduna, the Odi and Zaki Biam ordeal were eye sores. The standard rule for military assistance to civil authority should, when police humanitarian actions fail, include (i) operational justification based on the rule of law and rule of engagement. (ii) not escalating a crisis situation in the process of intervening; (iii) apply minimum force to restore order (iv) assuring the people of government goodwill and not alienating the people from the government; (v) safeguarding the lives and property of loyal and law abiding citizens, and (vi) ensuring that all the property seized, persons arrested, and those killed are properly documented and accounted for after the operations. However, the killing field exercises in Odi and Zaki Biam might have been politically dictated or tolerated, but the 2010 involvement of the military in containing the Jos crisis was an entire effort by the military not willing to work within the framework of democratic control. The GOC, Major Sale Maina was making political statements that set the military against the other security forces while heating up the political system. Apparently the nation was consumed by the 'political economy of President Yar A'dua's health' that no body, including the President, Dr Goodluck Jonathan , then Acting President; was ready to generate a controversy that might lead to heating up the political system further. Indeed, there were calls from Northern Christian Elders for the removing of the Chief of Army Staff, Lt General Dambazzau .This was countered vehemently by the Sultan of Sokoto, Alhaji Sa'ad Abubakar in a widely publicized press statement. Though the religionisation of the military operation in Jos tore the nation apart but for President Yar'Adua's health and his subsequent death the government took a casual stand on the action of the military

The Nigerian military elites are conservatives and have regards to their role in the system. As much as one may not say much about young revolutionary officers who may emerge to surprise both the civilian and military elite in any coup (we are yet to experience a successful revolutionary coup), the elite officers must be taken into consideration in policy making and should be encouraged to interact with the parliament especially the defence committees, to ensure familiarization process between the military and the National Assembly. As Fayemi pointed out, "the process of agreeing on appropriated role for the military can only be successfully achieved in a climate of mutual confidence and dialogue between the civil and military elites" (Fayemi 1998 : 96). The military interest must not be aggrieved with the wider political implications of state policies. What is required is entrusting the military elite with the confidence of being a stake holder in the political processes. While the military is being involved, it should also cultivate the process of learning how to open up its tight-fist on some contending military issues like budgeting; expenditure and some basic information, which the NASS and the public require for effective Defence Policy Making.

The issue of budgetary oversight to the military is very crucial. The Nigerian military would prefer a concealed oversight because where military budget appears along with other budgets in the policy it is a lot easier for the public to understand a tractor or a stethoscope, and their cost and uses than a tank, a ship or a fighter aircraft: "the nature of security is such that it cannot be subjected to the same type of assessment and evaluation as other services, nor can it be subjected to the same type of public knowledge or public debate". (Shiyanbade 2000:31). The position of the military is that it needs the cooperation of the legislature and the executive to recognize that not all matters of the military budget can be defended in public as even in advanced country like Britain where about 7 billion pounds were spent in developing the Trident submarine before it was made known to the public. Equally too, the US B-2 stealth Bomber cost a lot of money which the public did not get to know. But the fundamental issue in Nigeria's defence expenditure is the competing interest by individuals in the public office to misdirect the government. For instance, a source alleged that if not for General Danjuma's intervention one of the Defence Ministers of State, (junior ministers) under him; who acted in his absence nearly committed Nigeria to buying a refurbished armored tank from Poland, though they were cheaper but cannot last longer than 10 years. Meanwhile, what is fundamental to the defence policy process is how the National Defence policy was couched to meet the reality of the preparedness of the armed forces in accordance to the available resources.

REVISITING THE ISSUE OF STATE SOCIETY RELATONS

Given the parade of discourse unveiled in this research, can we be at rest that our democracy could be guaranteed and be made accountable as measures to control the military. In our conceptual approach we noted some features of military re-engagement and argue that if they are becoming permanent features it would be difficult to establish the basis of and for democratic accountability and control. There are some sections of the civil and primordial societies which see the military as the hope of their salvation. This shows that they still have issues to contend with the Nigerian state. The military is only a means to engaging in politics and the demands of these sections of the society are not properly addressed; control and accountability will be mirage. The military will always re-engage because the foundation of the state is still weak. The military as an institution will only find ways of meeting its own needs, and more particularly the interest of the corps of political class or a particular region within society which it stands to protect its political interest. This tends to perpetuate the crisis of state-society relations. This has been revealed by the statement made by the the Chairman of the Northern Elders Forum, Alhaji Abdulrahaman Okene that "the military is not only the protector and defender of the Northern interest in the past and today, but that the military would continue to be the protector and defender of the Northern interest in the future"(cited in Bassey;2001;301)

Therefore, we must go back to the basics. It is here that we further contextualized the question of state-society relations. The success of democratic accountability and control is dependent on the nature of state society relations. What we have so far is a dysfunctional federalism, where people were forced to live together for the benefits of colonial economic interest. The military perpetuated this by creating states to satisfy their clientele interests. Thus, state power is acquired to satisfy ethnic or primordial interests. This had led to massive corruption of the system. While some have continued to dominate political power to the disadvantage of others, those who are kept outside the corridor of power have continued to struggle to take possession of their shares by other means. This has not only led to cut throat competition but communal conflicts which have affected the process of democratic governance. The space occupied by the state is predominantly dominated by a section to the detriment of others in the society. This does not augur well for democracy. The state is supposed to be an arena for reconciling differences based on general will and not a preserve of some few elites.

The advent of civilian rule after another long period of military rule has opened up a new dimension of ethnic restlessness. The oil states want to control their land, resources and security. While still initiating that process, some states in the north have gone ahead to establish Sharia with its enforcing agencies which Bolaji Akinyeni said is amounting to establishing state police (Akinyemi 1999). In the light of this many states are unilaterally taking unconstitutional actions which would inevitably lead to sovereign national conference. Already, pockets of ethnic crises like the Ife-Modakeke, Jukun-Tiv, Chamba – Kuteb, Igbura-Bassa and Agulere-Imulere, the reawakening of Biafra sovereignty under the movement for the actualization of the sovereign state of Biafra the movement for the actualization of the sovereign state Biafra (MAOSSOB), the pressure from Ijaw and Ogoni nationalities, and the search for regional autonomy from the middle belt among others have opened doors for multi-oppositions. This shows that Nigeria is yet to negotiate its destiny and the federal government cannot claim ignorance of this restlessness simply because of a constitution, which the elected officers swore to protect and defend. However, a constitution should be an instrument made for the people and not the people for the constitution. The clamor for the restructuring of the state and its security system must be addressed.

If states in the north have set up Sharia with its enforcing agencies what stops others from making their choice in accordance to their whims and caprices? It shows that the constitution is faulty and something has to be done about state-society relations before its final collapse. Sharia issue raises a fundamental question from citizenship and indignity. Sharia can not be applied selectively. For political reason it can be selective, monumentally but as it becomes established it would no longer be so. It applies automatically to an offender irrespective of whether one is a Moslem or not, as it is in Islamic countries. Those who can not comply would have to leave the state. The Sharia debate has resurrected the question of indigeneship which has been buried for long. It rises the question of what other avenues of justice are available for the minorities to express their fundamental rights as minorities.

The quest for restructuring and subsequent pressures for sovereign national conference is becoming glaring as Richard Akinjide (former Federal Attorney General) who had all along identified with the north throughout his political career has turned out to be the advocate of the entire southern interests. According to him:

> .....nobody can terrorize any body in this country today. It is not possible.... At the moment 90 percent of the revenue of the country comes from Delta State, then how can you now say a section of the country should be ruling the country perpetually? Nobody is going to accept that. It is not possible. You see it is very easy to make this country ungovernable and no section should think they are the only one with the monopoly of power to make the country ungovernable. But we don't want to do that.... I've always been patriotic... but it's now got to a stage whereby they think the southerners are fool. Now we want to tell them the southerners are not fools. (Vanguard July 25, 2000:71).

The above statement insinuated how the elections of 2003 and beyond are going to be critical only if the federation remains as it is. This may be seen as mere threat but the fact remains that things which were previously neglected turn out to create dispenses in the society. Therefore, no amount of discussion about democratic accountability and control can be successful of we do not begin with the discussion on the shape and structure of the state-society relations, which is a bigger question than civil-military relations or civil security relations. At this point, we must commend the government of the late President Yar'Adua for initiating the amnesty programme for the Niger Delta .This is now being considered by NATO for adoption to resolve the protracted crisis in Afghanistan. Even so, the Niger Delta amnesty was only a palliative measures as the basic issues of national question must be addressed within the context of democratic practices and the rule of law.

CONCLUSION

Let me conclude by referring to the most noted stated of a famous Nigerian military officer, General Theophilus Yakubu Danjuma who once said that no nation survives a second civil war. Nigerians must therefore seek to renegotiate their collective mandate to avoid the collapse of the state and the society. What this work has done is to problematic the scenario of democratic accountability, control and defence policy processes. At the end it leaves the reader and stakeholders to decide where to begin the processes of democratic control. This can be done from either the civil military relations perspective or state-society relations. Therefore, from either way not only the military but every Nigeria elite owe Nigerian people and the future generation a large debt which they must pay up. This can be done not only by giving democracy a chance but by being accountable and being subject to its control

REFERENCES

1. **R. Akinjide** "Amalgamation was a fraud", Lagos, Sunday Punch, July 9, 2000.

2. **K.J. Fayemi** "The Future of Demilitarization and civil Military Relations in West Africa: Challenges and Prospects for Democratic Consolidation" African Journal of Political Science, Vol. 3 Nos. 1988 82-103.

3. **B.R. Luckham** "Democracy and the Military: An Epitaph for Frankenstein Monster?" Democratization Vol. 3 No. 2 summer 1996 Pp. 1-16. "Dilemmas of Military Disengagement and Democratization" Ids Bulletin Vol. 26. No 2 April, 1995 and "The Military, Mobilization and Democratization in Africa: A survey of Literature and Issue" African Studies Review Vol. 37 No.

4. **G. J. Yoroms** "Transition to Democratic Rule in Africa: The Case of Nigeria and South Africa in Comparative Perspective" Scandinavian Journal of Development Alternative and Area Studies Vol. 18 No. 2&3, & September, 1999 and "Obasanjo and the Theory of Soft Landing" community Vol. 5 No. 1 pp 13-14

5. **B Adekanye** "Military Occupation and Social Stratification" inaugural lecture, University of Ibadan, 1993, "Civil-Military Relations and Consolidation of Democracy" in Nigeria", IDEA Project, Lagos March, 22, 2000 and The Retired Military As Emergent Power In Nigeria, Ibadan, Heinemann Books

6. **G. Almond and Verba, M** The Civil Culture: Political Altitutdes And Democracy In Five Nations, Princeton University Press, 1963

7. **P. Ekeh** "Colonialism and Social Structures" Ibadan, University Inaugural Lectures, 1980 and "Colonialism and the two Public in Africa: A Theoretical Statement" in Comparative Studies In the Society and History 17, 91 -112, 1975.

8. **O. Omoruyi** "The Armed Force Must Reflect Ethnic Nationalities" the Guardian, Lagos, July 13, 1998. Also see **Olanisakin, F.** Democratic Transition In Nigeria. Will The Military Stay Out Of Politics? African Insight Nos. Vol. 29, 2000.

9. **S. Oyoivbaire** "Consolidating the Gains of Democracy in Nigeria" Paper Presented at The National Conference On Consolidating Democracy in Nigeria: Promoting Stable-Civil-Military Relations Organized By Yakubu Gowon Centre, Abuja 4-7 July, 2000.

10. **J. O. Ihonvbere** "the Military and the Nigerian Society. The Abacha Coup and the Crisis of Democratization in Nigeria" in Eboe Hurchfall and Abdulaye Bathily (eds) The Military And Millenarianism In Africa (CDDESRIA Dakar), 1998.

11. **J.O. Ihonvbere** "Towards a Constitutionalism in Africa" CDD Occasional Paper Series No. 4 April, 2000.

12. MPRI Report, 1999:48
13. MPRI Report, 1999:10
14. **T.Y. Danjuma** "Role of the Military in the New Democratic Dispensation" Paper Presented At the National Conference on Consolidating Democracy in Nigeria. By Yakubu Gowon July 407, Abuja, 2000.
15. **A. Jega,** "Implications of the Military in Governance: the Nigeria Experience", Paper Presented At A conference on Consolidation Democracy In Nigeria: Promoting Stable Civil Military Relations, Organized By Yakubu Gowon Centre, Abuja, 4-7, July 2000. Also see **Jinadu, A.** (1999) "Nigeria: Path to Entering Democracy" Vanguard, December 6.
16. **S. Ibrahim,** "Nigeria Democracy: Regionalism, the Military and Ethnicity" Paper Presented At the International Conference on the Military in African and Latin America, Abuja, 7-11th August, 2000.
17. **J. Amoda, and Chinwezu** "External Interests In The Professionalism Of Our Armed Forces". Vangard, Friday July 21-27, 2000.
18. **Amoda and Chinwezu**, Ibid:28
19. **C. Bassey** "The professionalization of the armed forces: Challenges and Prospects in Okon Uya (ed) **Taming the Wilderness: Two Years of Obasanjo Administration** see also Huntington, Common Defence. New York: Columbia University press, 1996. Also see **Y. Bangura** "The Crisis of Underdevelopment and The Transition to Civil Rule Conceptualizing The Question Of Democracy In Nigeria", Africa Development Vol. Xiii, No. 1, 1997.
20. **Oyoivbaire,** Op. Cit: 17
21. **O. Obasanjo,** (1990) Speech at the Graduation Ceremony Course 7, National War College, Nigeria July.
22. **Fayemi,** Op. Cit 1998:96.
23. **G. Shiyandade,** "The Military in a Democratic Nigeria: Institutionalizing Professionalism" Inaugural Lectures, National War College, Course 9, September 18, 2000.
24. **Bassey** Op. Cit:301.
25. **B. Akinyemi** "Democracy and restructuring" Lagos, The Vanguard, December 6, 2000.
26. **P. Agbese,** "The Politics of Stable – Civil Military Relations: African Transition Seminar 490, June, 2000 and "Containing the Nigeria military: the role of civil society", paper presented at the conference on consolidating democracy in Nigeria: promoting stable-civil-military relations organized by the Yakubu Gowon centre Abuja July 4-7.
27. **A. Momoh and Adejumobi, S.** (1999) The Nigerian Military And The Crisis Of Democratic Situation: A Study In The Monopoly Of Power, Lagos Civil Liberties Organization.
28. Vanguard, July 25, 2000. Also see **J. Paden** "African in the past Cold War Era: Military Cultures and Transition to Democratic Processes", African Studies Association Meeting, December 4-7, Boston, Mass USA, 1993.
29. **See C. Welch** "Civil-Military Agonies in Nigeria: Pains of an Unaccomplished Transition" The Armed Force And Society 21, 4Summer, 1995.

30. **C. Ake,** <u>Democracy And Development In Africa</u> The Brooking Institution, Washington DC, 1996 and "Rethinking Africa Democracy" <u>Journal Of Democracy</u> Vol. 2, No. 1 Winter, 1991

31. **G. Kieh** "Military RE-Engagement in African Politics" Paper Presented at Ford Foundation <u>Workshop on the Military Question in West Africa: Option for Constitutional and Political Control,</u> July 15, Jos, Nigeria, 2000 and **F. Kramer** "Vision Of A New US-Nigeria Relationship" Lectures Delivered At The National War College, Nigeria By US Assistant Secretary Of Defence For International Security Affairs Published in <u>Vanguard,</u> Lagos, October 2, 1988.

PART TWO

STRUCTURAL COMPONENT

CHAPTER 11

SYSTEMIC CRISIS AND THE CHALLENGES OF MILITARY MODERNIZATION

CELESTINE BASSEY

One of the most problematic and intractable areas of public in Nigeria since the civil war concerns the development of a professional defence establishment adequate to meet the challenges arising from the altered parameters of our security environment.

The drastic and elemental alteration in the perceived threat to Nigeria's security since the early 1970s-largely a function of the traumatic civil war experiences and adverse continental developments that shattered the naïve optimism of the immediate post-independence era – engendered a significant disharmony between its declared policy goals and the operational ability of its defense establishment to provide the means for their actualization. Since at any given point in time, capabilities limit the range of choices that are available to decision-makers, this inadequacy in force structure and striking power neutralized to a considerable extent the projection of Nigeria' military power into continental troublespots (e.g., Angola and Zambia, the "Rhodesia" frontier).

The correction of this condition is the primary motivation of an armed forces' modernization and augmentation program that touches upon all elements of Nigeria's military power: its size and composition; quantity and performance of equipment or hardware; logistical reach; capability of performing sustained, active operations; mobilization resources and productive capacity; leadership and doctrine; communications and control; military intelligence effectiveness; and manpower quality in terms of skill, training, physical stamina, and morale. The operative criteria (as stipulated in an official policy paper)[1] are the needs to meet the capabilities of potential adversaries and to economize resources. Satisfying these criteria may be extremely difficult in a complex, dynamic domestic and external environment because of contingencies that necessarily have "uncertain identities and properties."[2] And this fundamental difficulty in defense planning has been magnified in recent years by the rapidity of change in the relevant environments. An accelerating external military presence in the continent (euphemistically captioned the "new scramble for Africa" by the *London Economics*)[3] and unrelenting military buildup by apartheid South Africa made the specification of options by Nigerian defense planners very risky and rendered available choices quite unattractive.

This chapter is at once a review and a critique of the major facets of this modernization and augmentation process of the Nigerian armed forces within the operative context ("the goal oriented guidance")[4] of the new dimension of threat perception and the strategic parameters that have guided Nigeria Military Planning since the civil war in 1970. The major focus, therefore, will of necessity center on the structural decisions concerning the procurement, allocation, and "organization of the men, money, and material" that sustain the units of Nigeria's military power and not on the strategic decisions concerning "the commitment, deployment, and employment of these forces, as manifested in military alliances and war plans."[5]

In other words, following Samuel Huntington's disquisition,[6] among others, a necessary distinction is made in this article between the "structural" and "strategic" components of defense policy. The former involves the "procurement, allocation, and organization of the men, money, and material which go into the strategic units and use of force."[7] The latter, on the other hand, focuses on the "particular need and implicity or explicitly prescribes decisions on the uses, strengths and weapons of the armed services"[8] Since the latter has been adequately dealt with elsewhere, I will, in this chapter, concentrate on issues in Nigeria's military statecraft bearing on the former: the conditions for possessing the ability (structure, magnitude, and institutional parameters of Nigeria's defense establishment) to meet specified functions and challenges[9].

Before dwelling on these structural problems, however, it is proper to offer an examination of the context and operative variables (the threat dynamics) that both necessitated and conditioned the military modernization process, as a basis for the critique that follows.

CHANGING STRATEGIC PARAMETERS AND RESPONSE

As persuasively argued by Samuel Huntington, the military establishment of any country is conditioned by two primary forces: "a functional imperative stemming from the threats to the country's security and a societal imperative arising from the social forces, ideologies, ad institutions dominant within the security."[10] The threat-factor constitutes a major dynamic in defense strategy and force planning. This is particularly so because any security decision inevitably hinges on the threat perception and definition of the relevant strata of policy planners of the state involved; and how the 'threat issue' is defined for decision may well influenced what the decision is. It is in this respect that the analytic conceptualization and visualization of the international environment as a "threat system" impinge upon and to a considerable extent determine the magnitude or level of a national defense effort.[11].

Because the nature of the threat confronting different countries varies widely over time, whether considered objectively or subjectively, the determination of the resources available to the government and the allocation of these resources to defense purposes is also bound to vary considerably. This complex, variable, and evolving dynamic between threat perception/threat manifestation and the expansion or regression of national military power is clearly evident in the development of Nigeria's defence system.[12] In the pre-civil war period (1960-1966), an introspective security concern and posture resulted in a largely ceremonial army of 10,500. The recurrent expenditures on defense varied just below 4.5 percent of the total Federal and Regional budgets between 1959 and 1966 although it rose in money terms from about 4 million pounds in 1959-1960 to nearly 8 million pounds in 1965-1966.[13]

The relatively low priority accorded defense in the budgetary allocations of the First Republic was hardly surprising: the threat to the Nigerian state was largely perceived as internal, arising from fissiparous discharges associated with the struggle for ethnic self-determination.[14] As a consequence, by 1966, the Nigerian military ranked as one of the smallest war machines on the continent engaged in border patrols and policing duties.

Conversely, the drastic alternation in perceived threat to Nigeria's security since the late 1960s (largely the function of traumatic civil war experiences and continental development that shattered the naïve optimism of the immediate post-independence era of the early 1960s) engendered unprecedented commitment to the qualitative and quantitative expansion of its military forces. This expansion marked, and was in turn sustained, by the incorporation of the West African subzone and the continent at large – especially Southern Africa – into Nigeria's vision of systemic security.[15] Thus, judging from policy statements and the direction of its foreign and defense policy planning since 1970, it may be valid to assert that the "territorial frontier" no longer constitutes the exclusive radius of security concern as was clearly the case in the First Republic (1960-1966).

On the contrary, unlike the prevailing attitude, perception, and complacency that characterized the security posture of the Balewa administration, the dominant mind-set in Nigeria's governmental circle since the civil war was well-expressed by a former Head of State, Yakubu Gowon, who said that "...the survival, security and independence of Nigeria cannot be assured as long as any part of Africa remains under colonial rule, or an apartheid regime."[16]

As a consequence of these developments, the parameters of Nigeria's security boundaries have been reconceptualized in terms of three concentric circles. The inner circle is the territorial threshold: the protection of the life, property, and resources of the state from internal and external subversion. The protection of this frontier, as Margaret Vogt has argued, constitutes the single most important preoccupation of the Nigeria military and as such presents the "most basic of the functional duties of the military establishment."[17]

The second circle consists of the ring of countries (Cameroun, Chad, Niger, and Benin) that surround Nigeria's borders. The major consideration here is that the existence of foreign military presence in any one of the neighboring countries "creates a situation whereby the Nigerian defense establishment has to take into consideration the power potential of an extra force in its defence calculus."[18] It was for this reason that the Chad-Libya merger was declared unacceptable by the Shagri administration.

The outermost circle of Nigeria's security frontier has been seen to encompass Economic Community of West African States, and second, the rest of the continent of Africa this is affected and conditioned both by intraregional and extraregional (global) processes of intervention interaction. According to the Federal Government White Paper of March, 1976, the proximal interests of the country are best served by limiting the political, economic, and military activities of non-African actors in Africa.[19] This explains why French activism in West-Central Africa has been a constant source of attention and irritation for Nigerian governments.

It is to be expected from this expansive redefinition of threat to the Nigerian state (a consequence of both domestic fissure and systemic pressures), and the representation of Nigeria's strategic environment and defense policy posture, that the conditions for possessing the ability to meet these challenges resides in the development of "usable military power."[20] Because a chosen design of military forces and equipment has consequences for the range of alternative defense policies available to decision makers, the largely "light infantry" force of about 272,000 in 1972 provided limited military options for the kind of missions envisaged in reformulations of Nigeria's security and foreign policy objectives.[21]

The Nigerian armed forces has grown more by accident than by design during the civil war. "Its growth," as former Chief of Army Staff Danjuma, put it, "was not based on any strategy. It was just dictated to us by the battlefield needs of the war."[22] Such a phenomenal expansion of the armed forces within a span of three years would present a formidable problem for any army, because it inevitably reduces the level of professionalism-its corporateness, expertise, skill, discipline, and experience. This was even more true in the Nigerian Military, in which these basic prerequisites of operational efficiency and cohesiveness of action were already seriously impaired by the disintegraton of the military command into what Mazrui termed "militarized ethnicity" during the traumatic months of January to September 1966.[23]

In overall terms, the uncoordinated and overexpanded armed forces had all the makings of a paper tiger by 1975, and was of marginal utility in terms of externally projectable military power. Crucially absent in its organizational structure were such indispensable specialist units as paratroopers and armored and mechnanized formations; marine amphibious assault forces; and search and rescue squadron and transportation arms in the Air Force. Furthermore, even though the strategic and operational value of the MIGs and Illushins proved to be one of the decisive factors in the civil war, they are, nevertheless, essentially combat aircraft of the 1960s vintage and patently inadequate for any future role in Southern Africa, for instance.

Understandably, the conditions under which the three services had expanded to meet the exigencies of the civil war precluded a systematic and phased development of specialist units. However, these extenuating circumstances were no longer an excuse for the distressing state of the armed forces by 1975. It was in the context of this unsalutary condition of the armed forces and its attendant dissatisfaction that the modernization program emerged in the mid-1970s as the primary focus of defense planning.

The operative principle of the program has been, as its chief architect, General Danjuma – the former Chief of Army Staff – explained, the "synthesis between the requirements of the combatant and specialist units admitting this need for greater mobility and armaments."[24] Given the confines of existing budgetary allocations, this could be achieved by "substituting fire-power and mobility for excess manpower."[25] Thus, Danjuma maintained, "Nigeria could not afford to keep her army at its present size, because to arm and equip the existing divisions with sophisticated weapons would absorb sixty percent of the country's national income"[26]. Between 1975 and 1989, therefore, an imperative need to economize resulted, as will be seen below, in major structural decisions directed toward achieving maximum military worth from a given volume of inputs.

Broadly considered, these complex programme decisions concerned the strength of the armed forces, their composition and readiness, and the number, type, and rate of acquisition of their weapons. In turn, these decisions presupposed a broad range of related decisions concerning type, procurement, allocation, and organization of the men, money, and material on which force levels and readiness crucially depend.[27]

The various elements – men, money, material, and organization – of this program may conflict with each other, as Danjuma has noted. Obviously, a major action in any given area implies demands upon the other areas. A decision, for instance, to augment the fire-power and mobility of the Nigerian armed forces army inevitably impose policy decision on the budget (increasing capital expenditures on weapons and support systems either by raising the total military budget or reallocating resources from other services), on personnel (extensive demobilization , such a the reduction of navy personnel from 8,000 in 1980 to 4,000 in 1983),[28] on material (changes in procurement and base construction policies), and possibly on organization (enhancing the position of the armored and mechanized division in the Army, for instance, or establishing relative parity between two previously secondary services – the Navy and Air Force – and the Army within the overall defense organization). A review of this exercise, and the conceptual, administrative, and strategic factors guiding both options and planning is the subject of the next section.

THE ARMED FORCES MODERNIZATION PROGRAM

From an institutional viewpoint, there are three essential aspects of military establishments. One involves organization: how forces are raised, trained, and identified. A second involves doctrine: how forces will fight, and how to conceive of war itself. And the last is the nature of the instrument, as driven by changing technology: the weapons and the supporting systems of war.[29] As prerequisites for a modern, efficient and effective war machine, none of these facets can be considered in isolation. A modernization program concentrating on firepower augmentation (the weapons and supporting systems) to the exclusion of both organizational reforms and doctrinal innovation in response to challenges in the environment can produce unpleasant surprises in a combat situation.

For example, it is the purpose of military doctrine (strategic and tactical) to guide procurement, organization, and operations, and to do so based on certain assumptions about enemy planning and the strategic environment in which military forces would operate in wartime. Thus, in modern military thought, the crux of any modernization program necessarily spans the military's three basic facets: organizational structure, doctrine, and instruments. The determination of the tempo, direction, and consequences of national military power (assuming the viability of the economic base): the political determination to generate and use military strength, and the administrative and managerial skills to produce military strength from the available resources. As Knorr has rightly argued, "how well this task is performed greatly affects the usable military power that is generated."[30]

However, designing military forces and equipment is anything but a perfect art: it is inevitably affected by nonmilitary factors in preparing for and the selecting of the "cheapest" set of alternative means toward performing them effectively."[31] Apart from the central administrative problem of making choices for an uncertain future, "bureaucratic manipulation, strategic accounting errors, and self-centered orientations of individuals representing conflicting interests," can make defense planning a fickle activity, "something far removed from the precise base-line for planning which dedicated empiricists would like."[32] The structural decisions that informed the modernization process and the major policy alternatives entailed are considered below.

MAJOR POLICY ALTERNATIVES

A variety of sources – presidential addresses, ministerial lectures, and presentations by senior members of the armed forces[33] – attest that the armed forces modernization scheme is a major endeavour touching upon all elements of Nigerian military capability. This, as alluded to above, involves fundamental structural decisions in four critical areas designed to improve the quality, firepower, and maneuverability of the three services, while reducing the army's personnel strength. Involved are: a) *Organizational decisions concerning the methods and forms by which* Nigeria's armed forces are organized and administered; b) *Personnel decisions concerning the number, procurement, retention, pay, and working conditions of members of the military services)* Material decisions concerning the amount, procurement, and distribution of equipment and supplies) *Budgetary decisions concerning the size and distribution of fund made available.*

These structural categories are by no means exclusive. They are interdependent: a major policy action in any one area demands compensatory adjustments in others to ensure equilibrium in force planning and readiness. However, for analytical reasons these four facets of the modernization scheme will be considered sequentially.

ORGANIZATIONAL REFORM

The rapid, uncoordinated, and spasmodic growth of the military during the civil war had made organizational reform an indispensable prerequisite of operational effectiveness. Four of the basic issues involved were:

i.   The structure and composition of the military command;
ii. The nature and scope of demobilization

iii. The creation of specialist formations; and
iv. Reorganization and management of military intelligence.

In the first issue-area, two interrelated sets of problems confronted the planners. The first was a more complex and integrated organizational structure that included the creation of the office of the Chief of Defense Staff (15 April 1980) to preside over the Joint Chiefs of Staff Committee (JCSC), which was also established to ensure routine and coordinated planning between the three services, including "force development, joint training and exercises, formulation of joint operational plans, standardization and centralization of procurement processes."[35] This arrangement (although yet to fully implemented) was meant to supplant the unhealthy situation in which the defense establishment was a loose confederation of independent fiefdoms, uneasily presided over by the Minister of Defense. The Army, the Navy, and the Air Force controlled their own budgets and determined their own force structures , with a minimum of coordination, although the Prime Minister (later the Military Head of State) did determine goals.

The second problem area involved the distribution of authority in the high command, which, like the issue of demobilization considered below, was among the more sensitive and intransigent problems in the reorganization exercise to confront the military administrations of Gowon and Mohammed /Obasanjo in the post-Civil war era. The root difficulty was essentially that of striking a new balance among the various military constituencies. The first set of constituencies involved the unconcealed mutual antagonism between the "task specialists" and "social specialists" (as Adekunle, Mohammed, Bissalla, and Haruna), who bore the brunt of the fighting in which they distinguished themselves for higher positions in the military hierarchy. The latter's primary responsibilities were political and social: presiding over the Federation in the capacity of either federal or state functionaries.[36]

The second set of constituencies spans the first and concerns ethnic distribution in the high command. By 1970 officers from the Middle Belt had reached the top of all three divisions of the Army, while officers from the dominant Yoruba and Hausa constituencies dominated the support units (Engineers, Medical, Signals, Transport, and Ordnance) and Army Headquarters, Lagos. With the expected return to civilian rule, first in 1976, then in 1979, the centrifugal aspirations and collective/syndicalist interests of these constituencies became a major obstacle to reorganization.[37]

The potentially destabilizing implications of these divergent aspirations engendered a paralyzing inertia, indecision, and equivocation in the military hierarchy under Gowon. This crippling condition bedeviled general public perceptions of military reorganization in the post-civil war era (as stipulated in the Second National Development Plan initiated in 1970) and was supplanted only after the 1975 coup, which, among other things, saw the retirement of the "social specialists" who owed their promotions to political consideration rather than to functional competence. The concomitant emergence of such "task specialists" as Mohammed, Obasanjo, and Danjuma to top command positions set the stage for the sweeping organizational reform and demobilization exercise between 1975 and 1980.

Allied to the issue of the structure and the composition of the military command was the exceedingly urgent and thorny question of demobilization: that is, the drastic reduction in the size of the army from a quarter of a million to around a hundred thousand. From a military and policy stand point the necessity to trim the army to manageable size was indisputable, but demobilization proved to be an extremely sensitive and hazardous issue, as the abortive but bloody Dimka Coup of 13 February 1976 showed. The fissiparous and potentially explosive ethnic and factional centrifugences, which delayed implementation between 1970 and 1975, was unmistakably real: any "appearance of discrimination against any section whatsoever was likely to precipitate civil as well as military unrest."[38]

Nevertheless, under the judicious and imaginative scheme developed by its architect, T. Y. Danjuma, the demobilization process was implemented. Its prime objective, as he intimated in December 1975, was to create a balance in the entire defense system in:

i The size of the armed forces,
ii. The rate of personnel turnover,
iii. The distribution of ranks, and
iv The proportion of civilians in the defense establishment. [39]

As the trend in the 1980s indicates (e.g., the Nigerian Navy was pruned from 8,000 in 1980 to just below 4,000 1988 to allow for a further increase in delivery systems), this model, clearly designed to combine the capabilities of a highly mobile and proficient volunteer force with the massive manpower supply of a large reserve force, may well be on the way to becoming the dominant form of military manpower system in Nigeria, as in some European countries.[40]

In the third issue-area – the creation of specialist formations – one of the glaring structural weakness of the Nigerian armed forces by 1975 was the virtual absence of specialist formations such as an armored division and paratroopers in the Army, amphibious assaults force in the Navy, or reconnaissance and search and rescue squadrons in the Air Force.[41]

By 1982, however, this structural flaw had been remedied with the formation of one armored division (comprising four armored, and one mechanized brigades); two mechanized divisions (each with three mechanized brigades); and one composite division (consisting of one airborne, one air portable, and one amphibious brigade).[42] Similarly, the amphibious assault capability of the maritime arm has been enhanced by the acquisition of two tank landing craft (LCT) from France and two modern roll-on, roll-off type tank landing craft (LST) built to Nigerian specifications in Germany. These ships are the core of an amphibious assault force having the ability to transport armor, men, and equipment anywhere on the West African coast. The sea mobility was designed to complement the air mobility to transport armor, men, and equipment anywhere on the West African coast. The sea mobility was designed to complement the air project the country's military power over a considerable distance.

In the final issue-area (reorganization and management of military intelligence) estimates derived from military intelligence provide the basis for operational engagement. This is so because the "management of violence" is a composite activity involving the collection, evaluation, analysis, integration, and interpretation of information concerning an enemy's "order of battle," as manifested in war plans and force movements. In addition, information regarding the likely combat performance of adversary forces, military geography, arms transfer patterns, the war-fighting role of indigenous arms industries, great power interventions, and surrogate forces are normally considered as part of the "current reportorial" – "keeping track of the modalities of change" – underlying operational planning. This is the domain of military intelligence.[43]

Prior to the late 1970s, intelligence activity of the Nigerian armed forces was largely a stepchild of operational planning; it did not crystallize out as a separate activity and remained "uncoordinated and conceptually undefined."[44] This unsatisfactory state was squarely confronted under the reorganization and augmentation scheme of the military intelligence management system.

In structural terms, this involved the creation during the Second Republic of a Directorate of Intelligence in the office of the Chief of Defense Staff to coordinate the activities of the specialized intelligence units in the Army (DMI), the Navy (DNI) and the Air Force (DAI).[45] This Directorate was later superseded in 1984 by another body – the Defense Intelligence Agency (DIA) – located in the office of the Minister of Defense .[46] The activity of the Agency in the field of Strategic Intelligence is presently complemented by the National Intelligence Agency responsible for external intelligence[47].

In operational terms, the redevelopment of the military intelligence system had as its express purpose the qualitative expansion of estimating capabilities, including the development of specialized capabilities for both verbal and physical intelligence. [48]

Finally, the necessity for "conceptual and structural rethinking" about information evaluation and policy formulation has also been widely revisited in the Nigerian intelligence community. This consideration is critical because the pervasiveness of errors of judgement is often partly attributable to the "group-think factor". The collective systems of thought of intelligence officers that set the "parameters for diagnosis of problems, interpretation of information and formulation of options."[49] A need then arises for a continuous re-examination of the organizing hypotheses that guide the processing of information and the estimate of likely action of the opposing forces.

A related issue was the need to begin an irreversible dynamic towards professionalizing the intelligence management system through astute retraining programs and perceptive personnel policy. The management of large volumes of information, while filtering and coordinating stress-induced properties of the international environment, call for a premium on quality, dexterity, and professionalism in recruitment. In the Nigerian context, this consideration has so far led to the deployment of some of the best officers to the various intelligence units by the military command. However, the prevailing realities in the country – the need to contain military system syndicalism and coup d'etat – have allowed political factors to take premium over professional requisites.

PERSONNEL POLICY

Related to organizational reform was personnel retraining and recruitment policy. Demobilization is primarily a quantitative issue, affecting postwar armed forces, but training is a qualitative problem affecting the degree of professionalism of the forces – their corporateness, skill, expertise, and dedication to common goals. As noted previously, the military coups of 1966 and the wartime expansion left a legacy of shattered military professionalism.

One of the fist priorities of the modernization program, therefore, involved parallel efforts to "clean up" the armed forces – beginning with the purge of some 216 officers on grounds of indiscipline and incompetence – and a major retraining and evaluation scheme for all battlefield commissions. As part of this policy, the Nigerian Army Command and Staff College (NACSC) was set up at Jaji (currently known as Command and Staff College – CSC) to improve leadership quality among the senior cadre of officers. A conversion exercise, entailing a reassessment of each officer's intellectual and military potential through a series of examinations and practical tests, was introduced by the Chief of Army Staff towards the end of 1975. Although it was unpopular among many affected officers – "veterans of the civil war who were now to be judged by criteria which were unfamiliar and therefore suspect"[50] – it provided a reliable basis for pruning incompetent elements from the officer corp.

As a complementary development (for officers of junior rank), the Nigerian Defense Academy has been modernized and raised to Technical University status, underlining the new emphasis on quality rather than quantity. To complement the initial phase of training for cadets, twenty-four army training centers were established in 1978 to provide instructions to about 25,000 officers and men.[51] Upon completion of this training, personnel involved are subsequently assigned to operational units advanced tactical training at regimental levels. Similarly, the Navy has established training schools for qualified officers at Lagos, Port Harcourt, Calabar, and at a new base in Bendel State. The Air Force training schools are sited in Kano, Jos, and Kaduna, where clear skies and low humidity facilitates pilot training and aircraft maintenance.

To augment interservice coordination and planning, as well as to provide candidates for high-level military command, a National War College has been established in Lagos (now National Defence College, Abuja) to prepare, as the current commandant put it, "selected officers of the armed forces for higher level policy, command and staff functions by giving them the necessary expertise and knowledge needed to exercise these functions in their services, joint services and to hold extra regimental military and civilian appointment at national and international level."[52] As made public by the Miniter of Defense, only graduates of the Defence College can in the future be promoted to the rank of Brigadier or its equivalent in the Navy and Air Force (Commodore), as well as qualify for further training at the National Institute for Policy and Strategic Studies.[53]

The extent to which these qualities – high combat expertise, morale, endurance of trails of war, and an ability to maintain combat activeness and an unshakable will to win under the most difficult conditions – presently obtain in Nigeria's defense establishment as a result of the intensive conversion exercise, training, and education since the mid-1970s is clearly subject to speculation. They certainly cannot be determined a *priori, without* the aftersight of actual combat engagements. Nevertheless, case evaluation reports of recent large –scale annual military exercises and maneuvers of Nigerian armed forces, as well as peacekeeping duties in Chad and Liberia, suggest a high degree of combat coordination and mastery of fundamental operational art and tactics. Such complex exercises permit the creation of instructive situations, facilitates practical checks of operational-tactical calculations, and serve as a good basis for investigating intricate current questions covered by combat and command training schedules.

However, if adequate manpower training and acculturation in the "military ethnic" remain decisive factors in war, actual performance of personnel cannot be separated from the nature of the instrument (equipment). This is why the constant development of weapons and combat equipment complicates the process of training personnel, presents increasing demands on officers, and makes the improvement of existing methods of conducting warfare necessary. The effectiveness of operational training, as well as the level of combat, might depend inescapably, therefore, on the nature and quality of the instrument.

MATERIAL PROCUREMENT

The ability of any armed forces to provide a military underpinning to a country's defense and foreign policy objectives depends crucially also on the nature of the instrument, as it is driven by changing technology: the weapons and the support systems of war. And in the 1980s, if not in the 1970s (largely because of the personnel retrenchment) material decisions concerning the amount, procurement, and distribution of major weapon systems to the armed forces became the centerpiece of the modernization program.

According to official sources, these essentially involved two principal policy focuses:

1.   Direct acquisition of major weapons platforms (such as ship, aircraft, and tank) and weapons (missile, gun, and torpedo),
2.   Import-substitution industries for weapons production, which combine assembly of imported subsystems with indigenous research and development of new weapons.

The material program for the government and distribution of weapons systems to the Nigerian armed forces may be examined from two interrelated standpoints. The first is both quantitative and qualitative: an assessment of weapon plaftforms so far acquired and their heightened effect, if any, on the operational and projectable power of the armed forces. The second is the compatibility or divergence of arms acquisition patterns and political purposes: whether policy considerations (security and foreign policy objective) guide or follow current structural decisions involving arms procurement for the Nigerian military. This issue will not be addressed in detail here as it has already received extensive examination.[55]

Similarly, the issue of development of a local "military-industrial complex" has been considered elsewhere.[56] We note, however, that in order to reduce the present inordinately high level of dependence on foreign sources for equipment, maintenance, and modification, the Fourth National Development Plan called for the expansion of Nigeria's defense industry. Because the impact of this military-industrial development on the capability of the Nigerian armed forces is largely long-term (subject unavoidably to current structural limitations on the defense budget), the primary focus of this section is on the procurement agenda involving direct major weapons acquisition.

Significant policy reorientation and adjustment in defense allocation in favour of weapons procurement was one of the major highlights in defense planning during the Second Republic. The Fourth Plan (1980) allocated over N7 million (out of overall projected capital expenditures of N70.5 billion) for military equipment over five years in an efforts to make Nigeria's military, in the words of President Shagari, "an effective force second to none in Africa and comparable to the best in the world….. to defend the largest black nation on earth."[57] Accordingly, the period spanning 1979-1985 witnessed a concerted effort aimed at heightening the combat capabilities of the armed forces, involving actual expenditures of 6.9 billion Naira.[58] Despite the national economic crisis arising from significant decline in oil revenue, defense allocation continues since 1986 as a significant percentage of sectoral allocations, averaging 9.2 percent by 2009.[59]

Despite this appreciable amplification in the striking power of the Nigerian armed forces, crucial structural and doctrinal problems remain. First, although the diversity in sources of supply has insulated the military from the whim of any one supplier, heterogeneity of equipment and shortages of skilled maintenance technicians have constituted formidable logistical problems. Second is the apparent indifference of Nigeria's defense community to the potentially paralyzing consequences of current schizophrenic tendencies between its foreign policy aspirations and its military policy concerning patterns of arms acquisition. I have argued elsewhere that this constant disregard for the political component in defense planning owes its from and tragic dynamism to the double antimony of class and function bearing on Nigeria's position in the international division of labour.[60] In other words, Nigeria's defense problem is fundamentally a result of its political economy: even the decisions Nigeria could make on defense ("what weapons it buys abroad for instance, how much and from whom") are "closely related both to its development policy and its earning of surpluses from the international economy."[61]

Finally, the overall magnitude of the military modernization and augmentation effort (in terms of force level and force strength) depends on decisions concerning the size and distribution of funds made available to the armed forces. The determination of the defence allocation and its distribution among different armed services in the race of competing national demands was, along with demobilization, one of the most controversial issues in Nigerian public policy planning from the late 1970s through the 1980s to the year 2009

BUDGETARY DECISIONS

The recurrent debate in the Nigerian press about the rationale for the "disequilibrium" between the dominant goals of domestic policy, on the one hand, and security and foreign policy objectives, on the other, since the end of the civil war in 1970.[62] During the thirty nine years since the end of the war, defense has absorbed an average of 16 percent of the Federal budget. This has undoubtedly imposed limits on the resources available to competing demands in society.

Conversely, the tremendous upsurge in demand for other social needs (agriculture, education, health, industry, communication, and so forth) had by late 1970s unleashed an unprecedented groundswell of controversy about priorities in national planning and resources allocation. As a consequence, the magnitude of the defense effort became a key issue in the new patterns of fiscal politics, focused upon the allocation of resources between the military and nonmilitary sectors of the society and among the various purposes of government .

As seen in the direction of this debate, there were persistent tendencies – despite the interdependence of budgetary components – either to treat each segment in the equation separately, "something to be considered on merit without reference to other goals," or to assume that one goal was of overriding importance and must have absolute priority over the other.[63]

As seen in the direction of this debate, there were persistent tendencies – despite the interdependence of budgetary components – either to treat each segment in the equation separately, "something to be considered on merit without reference to other goals," or to assume that one goal was of overriding importance and must have absolute priority over the others.[63]

In practice, however, no single elements (the absolute limits of the economy) could determine the level of defense spending necessitated by the modernization program. Neither do spurious charges – disguised as a dispassionate policy critique – such as Bayo Adekson's Military Extractive Ratio (MER) thesis contribute significantly to understanding the complex issues involved.[64] It can hardly be disputed that a number of elements in the domestic political and economic constellation may have a significant effect on military expenditures, in this case the characteristics of leadership and the process of recruitment and tenure maintenance.

It may be speculated that the military as the dominant actor – the "sole judge" of the allocation societal values – in the period 1966-1979 and 1984 to 1998, allowed a disputable degree of resource allocation to defense. Adekson's explication, however, fails to explain the defense spending hikes under the civilian administration (1979 -1983 and 1999-2009) with a qualitatively different and more complicated budgetary process.[65]

A more informed analysis, therefore, of the resources available to the military government and the allocation of these to military, domestic, and foreign purposes, has less to do with self-aggrandisement of a military "power elite," compelled by the "logic of the situation to satisfy members of their profession with increased donatives and benefits, whatever the economic conditions prevailing in the society."[66] Adekson's thesis is basically defective. He utilize fragmentary and circumstantial evidence and a fallacious conceptual apparatus (Military Extractive Ratio) to produce a highly biased view of the military era.

An alternative conceptualization and explanation of the high level and rate of fiscal outlay for defense was, and still is, in part the consequence of the altered position of Nigeria in a regional subsystem deeply unsettled by pressures of decolonialization, regional revalries, and external intervention. It was also partly a result of the military – institutional imperative of providing infrastructural facilities and support (barracks, logistical bases, training centres, airfields, defense industries, and so forth), for a military that has expanded more by accident than by design from 8,000 in 1967 to 272,000 by 1972.[67]

This functional reconceptualization notwithstanding, the inevitable impact of high defense spending on the social and economic sectors cannot be minimized or ignored. However, the extent to which the current level of defense spending can be maintained will depend, first, on Nigeria's balance-of-payments positions, as it is affected especially by the volatility of the oil market: second, on the extent to which the government is able to satisfy competing national demands: namely, social welfare and development plans for industrial expansion; and third, on the degree to which the IMF (its principal external creditor) enforces its "military conditionality" of reduction in defense spending as a prerequisite for loans and developmental assistance.[68]

CONCLUSION

The phased and planned modernization of Nigerian armed forces which began in the mid-1970s is still in the process of completion. Although beset by major problems and challenges (severe shortages of semi-skilled and highly skilled manpower and substantial shortfalls in oil revenues that prompted cutbacks in government expenditures across the board), considerable progress has been made in the targeted areas. Both vertical and horizontal reforms of the military organizational structure have been largely accomplished. Apart from a more composite redesign of command structure, extensive personnel retraining, and demobilization exercises, a considerable amount of hardware has been acquired by the services, although certain organizational and maintenance problems remain. As Nelson has observed:

After a concerted reorganization effort since the mid-1970s, the size
of Nigeria's army has been reduced by nearly 50 percent, and efforts
were under way to improve the combat capabilities of its field units.
The air force was adapting to as one analyst put it?

Seen in such terms, it becomes a problematic exercise to prejudge the operational effectiveness (decisiveness in attaining policy goals) of the Nigerian armed forces at the present stage in the modernization process. While certain variables of the program previously analyzed that contribute to operational ascendancy are amenable to quantitative statistical measurement, others are not. The former include force structure and weapons platforms. The latter involve sustainability and readiness.

Considered together, these factors as they are ultimately manifested in human resources (technical skills, leadership, morale, unit cohesion), logistics (supply and maintenance), mobility (rapid movement of troops and equipment, projection of power outside state boundaries), firepower (weapon systems), manpower (number of personnel under arms, level of organization), and command and control (communications facilities and administrative expertise) constitute major determinants of the operational effectiveness of national armed forces. deficiency in such components may adversely affect both the micro-competence (the ability to operate and support modern weapons) and macro-competence (the ability to organize and manage forces for military ends) of defense establishments.

In the Nigerian context, the question as to whether the capacity of its armed forces to provide military underpinning for the realization of policy objectives has improved considerably as a result of the program is necessarily contingent upon the nature of systemic challenge and actor(s) involved. Tentatively, however, there is sufficient evidence from annual military exercises and maneuvers, combat in the Lake Chad Basin, peacekeeping duties in Chad, Lebanon, and Liberia, Sierra Leone and logistical support operations in Southern Africa in the late 1970s and 1980s to indicate considerable improvement in the decisive prerequisites for high combat effectiveness and readiness in the Nigerian military.

Nevertheless, as some observes have rightly noted, crucial problems remain affecting both the micro-and macro-competence levels of the Nigerian Armed Forces. These are rooted preeminently in atavistic social forces arising out of pristine ideologies and institutions dominant within the Nigerian social system. Although they vary over time, these problems include:

i   The tendency of social objectives to override strategic considerations as criteria for top command positions;

ii.   Insecurity of the regime "which leads to distrust of independent power centres," and certain attitudes and mindsets which arise out of the traditional cultures;

iii. Persistent problems of building a reliable logistics system;

iv. Broadening repair and maintenance programs; and.

v.   Continuing difficulties with developing the capacity to absorb and operate complex systems [71]

As this analysis suggests, Nigerian defense planners are not unaware of these problems, although finding solutions to them resides in the level of development in the economic, educational, social, political, and cultural spheres of the Nigerian society. As Raymond Aron once put it: "An army always resembles the country from which it is raised and of which it is the expression."[72] The extent to which the ongoing modernization program produces the desired result in Nigeria's defense capabilities will depend, among other things, on the transformation of its socio-economics technological, and cultural fabric such a transformation is a sine qua non for sustainability and force readiness as well as for the generation of a viable military industrial base, which is indispensable for the "relation of force to national purposes." The tragedy of Nigeria's military development, as could be so far observed, is that productive capacities have lagged behind organizational and doctrinal innovations.

NOTES

1. See Audu Tijjani and David Williams (eds) *Shehu Shagari (London: Frank Cass, 1981)*: pp. 167-192. Also see General I. B. Babangida, "Defence Policy in the Frame-work of National Planning" (Gold Medal Public Lecture Series, Lagos, March 1984), and W. I. Aleyideino "Modernization of the Armed Forces of Nigeria" Unpublished Manuscript (SEC-2, 07). National Institute Library, Kuru, Nigeria.

2. Oskar Morgenstern et. al., Long Term Projections of Power: Political.

3. The Economist, 19 September 1981, 44

4. Yu. B. Mikhaylov, Forecasting in Military Affairs (Moscow: Military Publishing House, 1975), p. 9. Forecasting (Cambridge: Ballinger, 1973):3.

5. Samuel Huntington – The Common Defence (New York: Columbia University Press,)

6. Ibid. 1 – 24

7. Ibid, 4.

8. Ibid., 4. In practice, however, no sharp distinction can be drawn between strategic and structural elements in a defense policy decision. As Huntington has noted, "the determination of the magnitude of the (defense) effort combines strategy and structure and also transcends them." Huntington, Common Defense, 5.

9. See Celestine Bassey "Nigeria's Defense Policy in a Future Continental Order," Nigerian *Journal of International Affairs 13,2* (1987): and C. Bassey, "The Military Instrument and Strategic Policy in a Democratic Order: A Theoretical Reconsideration of Some Unresolved Issues Concerning Nigeria," *The Journal of Political Science XIII, 1 and 2 (1990): 15-31.*

10. Samuel Huntington, *The Soldier and the State (Cambridge:* Harvard University Press, 1957*).*

11. See K. Knorr, *The Power of Nations (New York: Basic Books, 1975),* and H. Brown, Thinking about National Security (Boulder: Westview, 1983).

12. For the evolution of Nigeria's military power and situational conditions that fuel it, see, among others, N. J. Miner's The Nigerian Army, 1956-1966 London: Methuen, 1971), and T. A. Imobighe, ed. *Nigerian Defence and Security (Lagos: MacMillan, 1987),* Part Two, 53-104.

13. Figures from Accountant-General's Annual Reports, as presented in Miner's, Ibid., p. 251.

14. See Sam Ukpabi, Strands in Nigerian Military History (Zaria: Gaskiya Corporation, 1986), Chapter Six, and Margaret Vogt, "Nigeria's Defense Policy: A Framework for Analysis" in *Nigeria's External Relations, ed. Gabriel O. Olusanya and Rafiu A. Akindele (Ibadan: University of Ibadan Press, 1986), 459-476.*

15. See Margaret Vogt and A. E. Ekoko eds. Nigerian Defence Policy: Issues and Problems (Lagos: Maltnouse Press, 1990).

16. Long live African Unity, text of the statement by Yakubu Gowon at the seventh OAU Assembly of Heads of State and Government, Addis Ababa, 1-4 September, 1970 (Lagos: OAU, 1970).

17. Vogt, "Nigeria's Defence Policy: A Framework for Analysis," 465.

18. Thomas Imobighe, "Libyan Intervention in Chad: Security Implications for Nigeria," *Nigerian Journal of International Studies* 4, 1 and 2 (January and June 1980): 23.

19. See Federal Ministry of Information (Lagos), *News Release No. 780, 29 June 1976.*

20. See B. Brodie, War and Politics (N.Y.: Machmillan, 1973); H. Kissinger, *Nuclear Weapons and Foreign Policy (N.Y. Harper, 1957);* and K. Knorr, *The Power of Nations, Chapters Three and Five. See also C. Hitch, Decision-Making For Defense (Berkeley: UCLA Press, 1965).*

21. ISS, Publication of the Institute for Strategic Studies, London. Military Balance, 1972-1973 (London: ISS, 1973).

22. See the summary of Danjuma's interview on Radio/Television, Kaduna (RTK) Programme, "Meeting Point," in Daily Times 13 December 1975, 5; African Confidential 24,12 June 1975:8.

23 See R. Luckham, *The Nigerian Military: A Sociological Analysis (Cambridge: University Press, 1971).*

24. Daily Times (Lagos), 13 January 1986; *New Nigerian (Kaduna) 13* January 1976; also see Sunday Times, 18 January 1976.

25. Daily Times, 13 January 1976, 5. Also see Edgar O' Balance, "Nigerian Armed Forces" *Armed Forces 6 (December 1987): 558-561.*

26. Daily Times, 13 January 1976, 5.

27. See M. I. Wushishi, "The Nigerian Army – Growth and Development of Combat Readiness" In Imobighe, ed., *Nigerian Defence and Security,* 53-71.

28. ISS, Publication of the Institute for Strategic Studies, London *The Military Balance 1972-73; 1980-81; and 1988-89.*

29. An institutional perspective implies that the study of military systems requires an analysis of the "organization of military forces and the manner in which they are used in the pursuit or the avoidance of conflict." See M. Janowitz, Military

Conflict: Essays in the Institutional Analysis of War and Peace (Beverly Hills: Sage, 1975). Also see Orbis 27, 2 (Summer 1983): 245-300.

30. See K. Knorr, Military Power and Potential (Lexington: Lexington Books, 1970), Chapter Four; and S. Enke, Defense Management (Englewood Cliffs, NJ: Prentice-Hall, 1967).

31. See K. Knorr, *Military Power and Potential (Kexington: Lexington Books, 1970), Chapter Four; and S. Enke, Defense Management (Englewood Cliffs, NJ: Prentice-Hall, 1967).*

32. K. Booth, *Strategy and Ethnocentrism (N.Y.; Holmes and Meier, 1979): 117. Also see W. Boucher* and E. Quade, eds. Systems Analysis and Policy Planning (N. Y.: American Elsevier, 1968).

33. See Oniyangh Akanabi, "Technology and National Defence Capability – Policy Options" (paper presented by the Minister of Defence at the NIIA, 1982); also see the collection of presentations by Senior Members of the Armed Forces in Imobighe, ed. Nigerian Defence and Security.

34. See Imobighe, ed. *Nigerian Defence and Security. For a conceptual clarification of these categories, see Huntington, Common Defense, 3-4.*

35. Ibid, 6, National Defence Policy for Nigeria (Lagos: JAD, 1978).

36. For the conceptual distinction between a "task specialist" and "social specialist," see Norman Dixon, *On the Psychology of Military Incompetence (London: Futura, 1983): 216ff.*

37. See K. Panter-Brick ed. Soldiers and Oil (London: Billing Ltd., 1978): 92ff; *African Research Bulletin 20, 5,(June 198): 6826.*

38. Lan Campbell, "Army Reorganization and Military Withdrawal" in Panter-Brick ed. *Soldier and Oil, 61; African Research Bulletin 20, 5, (June 1983): 6826.*

39. See W. A. Ajibola, "Reducing the size of the Army," Daily Sketch 16 (June 1977): 5; Femi Otubanjo, "Functionality of Quantity" paper presented at the Nigerian Political Science Association Conference, University of Ife, Ile-Ife, Nigeria, April 1978; and Imobighe ed. Nigerian Defence and Security.

40. See E. Hackel, Military Manpower and Political Purpose (London: IISS, Adelphi Papers, No. 72, December 1970).

41. ISS, Publication of the Institute for Strategic Studies, London. *The Military Balance 1975-76 (London: ISS 1976).* An armored corps existed in the Nigeria Army before 1975-76. However, it was equipped mostly with armored cars rather than battle tanks, and therefore, did not have the specialized capability to operate in a modern warfare condition.

42. See Vogt and Ekoko eds. *Nigerian Defense Policy; A. L. Aminu, "Nigeria's Defence Preparedness and Planning," Nigerian Journal of International Affairs 12, 1 and 2 (1986): 77-87; and Harold Nelson ed. Nigeria: A Country Study (Washington D. C.: American University, 1982).*

43. See, inter alia, A. Dulles, The Craft of Intelligence (London: Weidlenreld, 1964); and H. Ransom, The Intelligence Establishment (Cambridge, Mass: Harvard University Press, 1970).

44. See Major O. O. Oladoyin, "Management of Nigeria's Intelligence Community: An Alternative Option." Defence Strategy Review Vol. 11 No. 11 (4 November 1985); and Olisa Agbakoba, "In Defense of National Security: An Appraisal of the Nigerian Intelligence System," *Spectrum January / February, 1984.*

45. See Vogt and Ekoko eds. *Nigerian Defence Policy.*

46. See. J. Peters, Defence "Intelligence Agency" (DIA) was established under Decree 19 of 1986 (National Security Agencies Decree).

47. The National Intelligence Agency (NIA) was established under Decree 19 of 1986 (National Security Agencies Decree).

48. Verbal intelligence derives from "work" if the object of intelligence is a "stolen plan, a report on troop morale, or intercepted orders". Physical intelligence concerns entities: "bodies of troops, aerial photographes of fortifications, the noise of tank motors," etc. see D. Kahn, Hitler's Spies (London; Anow, 1980): 39ff.

49. J. Stein, "Intelligence and Stupidity Reconsidered Estimation and Decision in Israel, 1973," *The Journal of Strategic Studies 3,2 (September 1980): 147.*

50. Campbell, "Army Reorganization and Military Withdrawal," 62.

51. These include the Nigerian Army School of Armour (NAS), the Nigerian Army School of Artillery (NASA), the Nigerian Army School of Military Engineering (NASME), the Nigerian Army School of Signals (NASS) and the Nigerian Army School of Infantry (NASI). See, among others, M. I. Wushishi, "The Nigerian Army-Growth and Development of Combat Readiness", H. Nelson, ed., Nigerian: A Country Study (Washington D. C.: American University Press, 1982); and A.B. Mamman, "Force Readiness: Nigerian as a Case Study" (SEC-4, 24) National Institute Library, Kuru, Jos.

52. See "Meeting the Defense Needs of Nigeria," *The Nigeria Economist (Special Supplement 12-25 September 1990): 19-34,* and Lt. Gen. J. T. Useni, "National War College" *SOJA (special edition) July 1992:* The Establishment of a War Academy (as was the case of the Command and Staff College) is also meant to localize training and profoundly reduce the financial burden of training personnel abroad (U.S., USSR, Britain, West Germany, and India). This does not, however, eliminate the extensive Military Assistance Programme to the various services that has been a salient feature of the modernization process (see Imobighe, 1987; Vogt and Ekoko, 1990). The latter took the form of assistance in the training of 4,000 officers yearly by 1982 in the United States (IMET programme), the USSR, Britain, India, Australia, Canada, and West Germany. In addition, a U. S. Technical Assistance Field Team visited Nigeria to train Nigerian naval officers as hydrographic engineers, while a Soviet team trained the MIG fighter pilots and ordinance team for the armoured and mechanized divisions. Similarly, a British team of 78 officers rendered help as technical advisers at the Command and Staff College, Jaji, Kaduna.

53. See Eunice Damisa, "War College begins classes June 16," National Concord 19 May 1992:2.

54. Wushishi, "The Nigerian Army: Growth and Development of Combat Readiness," 65-67.

55. See Bassey, "Nigeria's Defence Policy in a Future Continental Order"; and Celestine O. Bassey, "Nigeria and Inter-African Peacekeeping Approach to Conflict Management," Calabar,' *Journal of Liberal Studies 3,2 (1991): 21-42.*

56. See Celestine O. Bassey, "Nigeria's Quest for a Military-Industrial Complex," Nigerian Journal of Internationals Studies 12 (1988): 46-55; Sunny Biaghere, "Nigeria: Creating a National Defence Industry," *African Defence Industries Corporation of Nigeria;'* Current Research on Peace and Violence 4 (1983): 258-269.

57. Tijjani and Williams, eds. Shehu Phagari: 33.

58. See Celestine O. Bassey, "The Political Economy of Defence Expenditure in Nigeria: The "Gun" or "Gari" Controversy Revisited," Proceedings of the 15th Annual Conference of the Nigerian Political Science Association, ed. Sonni Tyoden (Ibadan: University of Ibadan, 1988). Between 1979 and 1985, the strength of Naira varied from 1.50 to 1.00 U. S. dollars. In the post 1984 structural Adjustment policy, the value varied from N5 in 1988 to N180 to the dollar in 2009.

59. Vogt and Ekoko, eds, *Nigerian Defense Policy; "Budget 89" Newswatch 16 January 1989: 13-19; "Budget of Two Races." The African Guardian Guardian 14 January 1990:29-37; and Federal Government Budget Fiscal Years 1986-1991 (Lagos: Ministry of Finance) Unprecedented provision for "defence" and "Security" in the Niger Delta was made in the 2009 fiscal year a amounting to over 450 billion Naira.*

60. Celestine O. Bassey, "Nigeria, African Security and the Nuclear Option," Bodija Journal 1, 2 (1989): 61-70.

61. R. Luckham, "Armaments, Underdevelopment, and Demilitarization in Africa" Alternatives 6,2 (July 1980): 179-245.

62. Bassey, "The Political Economy of Defence Expenditure in Nigeria".

63. See Adekson, Nigeria in Search of a Stable Civil-Military System; O. Kamanu "Nigeria: Reflections on the Defence Posture for theh 1980s" Gene-Afrique 6, 1 (1977-78): 27-42; and I. Nximiro, "Militarization in Nigeria: Its Economic and Social Consequences", for theoretical exposition, see Huntington, Common Defence, op.cit.

64. Adekson, Nigeria in Search of a Stable Civil-Military System.

65. See Thomas Imobighe, "The Defence Budget: Analysis of Content and Process" in Imobighe, ed. *Nigerian Defence and Secuirty, 12-36.*

66. Adekson, *"Nigeria in Search of a Stable Civil-Military Systems, 55.*

67. By January 1966 (when the first military coup took place), the combined size of the army, navy, and air force stood at 10,500. This size was reduced to 8,000 before the advent of the civil war, when officers and men of Eastern Region origin withdrew into what later became the "Republic of Biafra" following the pogrom of July and September 1990. see Robin Luckham, The Nigerian Military (Cambridge University Press, 1980).

68. See World Development Report 2009 on the issue of military conditionality.

69. Nelson, ed. Nigeria 257-258; Olatunde Oladimeji, "Nigeria on Becoming a Sea Power," United States Naval Institute Proceedings, 115 (March 1989): 69-70; Bruce

Arlinghaus and Pauline Baker, eds. African Armies: Evolution and Capabilities (Boulder: Westview, 1987); and Jimi Peters and A. L. Amunu, "The Armed Forces and Nigeria's Foreign Policy; Reflections on Past Experience and a Note on the Future" Nigerian Journal International Affairs 12, 1 and 2 (1986): 88-99.

70. Arlinghaus, *Military Development in Africa 2-3; also see Sunny Biaghere, "Nigeria's Rapid Deployment Force: How Viable? African Defence Journal 1121 (December 1989): 38-39.*

71. See Arlinghaus, ed. *Military Development in Africa 64-91; Vogt and Ekoko, eds. Nigerian Defence Policy, 171-175.*

72. Raymond Aron, The Imperial Republic (Washington D. C.: UPA, 1974). 99.

CHAPTER 12

MILITARY SYSTEMS AND THE NIGERIAN ARMED FORCES

O. A. AZAZI

INTRODUCTION

The Military as a profession is relatively modern, but the art of warfare and the business of soldiering are as old as recorded history. Biblical records have it that "there was war in heaven, and the archangel Michael fought against the dragon (Lucifer) and his angels" – Rev 12:7. Again, history has it that the Romans were keen on military matters, leaving for posterity many treaties and writings as well as a large number of lavishly carved triumphant arches and columns celebrating their victories. The Chinese and the Russians have equally impressive antecedents.

The word Military has two broad meanings: first it refers to soldiers and soldering and second, it refers to the armed forces as a whole. In the second sense, the military is usually organized in components and over the years, military units have come in all shapes and sizes. They have been as small as a handful of medieval peasants banded together for battle under their feudal lord or as large as the invasion force created in 1944 for D-Day. They can be rigidly organized as the Impis of Shaka the Zulu or virtually autonomous like the knights Templar during the crusades, who being organized into small bands of fighters, with farmers supporting, and the religious for spiritual may have influenced modern military organizations[1].

Fredric Engels specifically described the military as "the organized association of armed men maintained by the state for the purposes of defensive and offensive warfare". Edomwande also agrees with Engels when he described the military as "a group of people assembled, drilled, disciplined and equipped by a nation for offensive and defensive manoeuvres in warfare". These definitions are not completely inclusive of all purposes for keeping a military. The role of the military today is as central of society as it ever was. With the advent of Peacekeeping Operations, the role of the military has been expanded to accommodate the noble role of managing varied complex emergencies.

In our own era, world wars and countless other major conflicts have changed the political landscape beyond recognition. We are all familiar with the concepts of globalization, multinational environment and liberalized economies which give the impression that wars in their old sense may become extinct. In fact Thomas Friedman, in two of his books, "The Lexus and the olive tree" and "the World is Flat" argues that democracies may not wage war against each other[2]. We however know that enormous social changes have been wrought and military power continues to dominate international politics. The role of the military today is as central to society as it ever was. As professionals, we therefore need to understand and be constantly abreast of what the military means to the societies in which we live.

Perhaps a relevant starting point would be to discuss, the purpose of a military organization in society. In my view the purpose of a military is essentially the employment of force to produce successful outcomes in war for achievement of political objectives or otherwise. In modern times we could translate this to the conduct of all types of military operations i.e warfare and operation other than war[3]. Defining the standards of successful military operations in the face of lethal modern weapons is what Stephen Biddle refers to as the modern system which he traces to the First World War. Add the military operations conducted to relieve burdened societies in the face of opposition from other sections of the same societies and their leaders. We, however, have since moved from cover, concealment, dispersion to combined arms integration, the employment of joint components, and the generation of forces for peace building.

Military systems, I do observe is a very wide subject, because in my little research, I found that we could organize a whole one year course on military systems. I will, therefore, restrict myself to certain basic ideas which I believe are key to a professional military. I will discuss few elements that I believe are critical to a military system. I will also take a look at the challenges facing the Nigerian military and then, finally, briefly address my pet subject, the transformation the Nigerian Armed Forces and how we could enhance its efficiency and effectiveness.

ELEMENTS OF A MILITARY SYSTEM

The word system refers to a set of interacting or interdependent entities forming an integrated whole. Systems therefore have component parts but are designed to work as a objectives. We could therefore talk of an educational system, judicial system and the security system of a nation. The total national security management system could comprises so many organizations amongst which are the military, police, customs immigrations and several security and intelligence agencies. The components of any system that blend to make it function are what I refer to as the elements of a system. Today, we are interested in the military system which has several components or elements as we choose to refer to them.

There is certain difficulty in discussing military systems because, we could very safely identify basic areas which are indeed themselves part of the whole, e.g., military human resource management system, and even fire delivery system of a particular weapon. This could be confusing, so we should move on to certain aspects which for want to better description, I would refer to as tangible and intangible elements. In the tangible and what appear to be universal components, nations seem to have armies or land forces, navies or marine forces, the air force and in few cases, other variants. In some of the nations the National Guard is part of the military while in others it is more of a para-military establishment. In non-littoral (landlocked) nations, the Navy is often completely absent.

What we should see as the tangible systems is, therefore, mostly their weapon systems, or the implements of warfare e.g. aircraft, warships, ground systems (tanks, artillery pieces etc), surveillance systems, and munitions of these components, as well as the industries that produce such components. Military combat system includes offensive and defensive weapons and platforms as well as C41SR equipment. Air forces can boast of attack/fighters/interceptors, transport, air borne early warning, helicopters and unmanned aerial vehicle. While the navy has in its inventory aircraft carries, submarine destroyers, frigates, mine sweepers, LSTs and other platforms of various classes. The army in its case has in its inventory, tanks, APCs, anti-tank weapons, artillery and anti-aircraft guns, its missiles system include surface-to-air, air-to-surface and surface-to-surface (tactical weapons). These platforms must be integrated for optimal benefit of the user[4].

The intangible elements of a military system refer to those aspects of the military system that determine the potency of the tangible aspect. They differentiate the different category of militaries. Again, they are very many, so I have chosen to identify a few that are critical for success in the Nigerian Military. These include elements such as higher defence management, manpower planning, training, education and leadership development, combat systems, military logistics systems, defence budget, defence industry, and technology[5].

HUMAN MANAGEMENT OF NATIONAL DEFENCE

Higher Defence Management is regarded as the process undertaken by the state to control, coordinate and manage the national defence organization i.e., the processes as well as the human and material resources to meet national objectives of defence. Higher management of defence is a concept that outline the organic framework through which the entire spectrum of defence management and operations are carried out. Implicit in this definition is the need to ensure close interaction between the civilian bureaucrats and military personnel in order to give the desired support to the political decision makers in this vital sector. Higher Defence organization in any particular nation refers to the powers of the Head of State, Legislature, the Defence Ministry hierarchy in the management and regulation of national defence.

I will go on to give few examples of how it works in a few countries. Egypt has Army, Navy, Air Force and Air Defence Forces. The President of Egypt is the Supreme Commander C in C and, often the Minister of Defence. He can declare war or emergencies, although subject to concurrence by the Peoples Assembly. The Armed Forces have a Commander in Chief, who doubles as Minister of the Armed Forces and Minister of Defence Production. He has under him a Chief of Staff and the various Service Chiefs. There is also a para-military force known as the Central Security Forces who come under the Ministry of Interior. The Indian system is more intricate with supreme command of the Indian Military vested in the President while responsibility for national defence lies with the cabinet committee for political affairs under the Prime Minister. The Minister of Defence is responsible to Parliament. India is about the only big military without a Chief of Defence Staff. For now decision making is done at the Chief of Staffs Committee which has the oldest service Chief as Chairman. There is however an integrated joint headquarters which is the precursor to having a CDS. South Africa has Army, Navy, Air force and Medical Service. The SANDF works under the Defence Command Council made up of the four Service Chiefs, the National Defence Planning Staff and the Military Inspector General.

From the above examples, it is obvious to me that activities of the political authority in defence management can only achieve success if properly articulated, coordinated and managed to protect the core values and national interests from domestic or international threat. Since capabilities limit the range of choices which are available to decision makers, any inadequacy in the structure of defence management, force structure and force level would neutralize, to a great extent, the projection of a country's military power needed for the emerging strategic environment. In line with global best practices, an integrated MOD (civilians and military personnel) has been quite successful in the management of defence and further entrenches civil democratic control of the military.

MANPOWER PLANNING

In any organization, the set objectives determine the human resources requirements, their management within the organization to better fulfill their roles. This very appropriately applies to any military organization. According to the British Defence Doctrine, 'the fighting power of a military force is dependent on conceptual, moral and physical component all of which are interrelated". The moral component is described as the ability to get people to fight and this is composed of equipment, logistics, training and manpower. McBeath described manpower as "the number of people in an organization in the desired quantity and quality". He postulated that the right quantity was important because having too many people would impair productivity while having the right quality was crucial to efficiency. A proper articulation of the responsibilities of the Armed Forces and the specific role of the Services will determine force structure, Order of Battle (ORBAT) and the manpower requirements to implement them. However, the rationalization of manpower and role of the armed forces has always been associated with tri-Service integration at the national level. The specific objectives of a military force at whatever level will determine requirements and consequently the level of manpower its employs. However, in a benign international environment, characterized by shrinking defence budgets, the economics of defence has always emerged as a dominant factor. Dual consideration of cost reduction and affordability would therefore influence the quantity and quality of Armed Forces, rather than purely the nature of the threat faced.

TRAINING (EDUCATIONAL SYSTEM) AND LEADERSHIP DEVELOPMENT

Training and leadership development starts from an entry point (recruitment or enlistment) through a training/developmental process to an exit point (disengagement/

separation). After the enlistment/selection (officers) and recruitment (soldiers/ratings/airmen) stages, the professional development of the individuals begins with skills acquisition training and continues through professional military education and other forms of education, career progression, motivation and deployment. All these are aimed at developing the right quality of manpower. Training blends competent individuals into effective military organization, and its primary aim is to meet manpower requirements. Individual Services have peculiar Service training for its personnel; however, basic military training is often done together by all the Services. For instance in the Israel Defence Forces, joint training is for the Army, Navy and Air-force personnel before they split into their various Services. The harmonization of recruitment ensures that the same entry criteria are used for all members of the Israeli Defence Forces. The use of established selection centres also facilitates vetting of personnel, thus ensuring that undesirables are excluded from becoming members of the military.

The military education system is very important in producing good quality manpower and the type of leaders we want. Both the military and the society have responsibilities, but we must acknowledge, generally we are starting off better than most because of the system of selection. It is very difficult to rise above the society in all areas of education except in purely military areas. The quality of higher education especially in this era of technology will determine what the military has. Rule of thumb is to seek for the best that is available and take advantage of it[6].

MILITARY LOGISTICS SYSTEM

Military logistics concerns itself with the allocation of scare resources within the defence sector. It embraces generic management fields such as budgeting, project management and decision-making relevant to both the balance of armed forces and deployment. Efficient management of defence resources must also be lined to the supply of underlying civil-military technologies, enabling the development and systems integration of modern weapon systems to occur. Contemporary defence management techniques highlight commercialization, fostering cost saving through operational efficiencies. Such techniques streamline the acquisition cycle, promote incremental innovation, and encourage economic efficiency through exposure to the fierce gales of competitiveness[7].

With ongoing pressure on defence budgets, there is need for greater economy and efficiency at the logistics end to maintain military operational capability. The potential for logistical savings is enormous. In the US, for example, more than one third of the total budget of the Department of Defence is accounted for by logistics spending while nearly 50 percent of manpower is in support activities, with logistics personnel outnumbering combat troops by 2 to 1. The response to improving logistical and general resource management efficiency pressures has been the introduction in the UK of the Smart Procurement Initiative (SPI) and in the US the Defence Acquisition Reform Process. The common policy thrust has been towards faster, cheaper and more effective weapon systems. The policies are multi-dimensional, focusing on partnership, industrial participation, incremental technology insertion, long-term ownership of project management, application of commercially off the shelf (COSTS) technologies, concurrent engineering, systems engineering, empowerment and commercialization particularly through completion, collaboration and the contraction of procurement cycles[8].

Traditionally, the policy thrust of defence production has been indigenization, thereby creating massive military industrial complexes but few countries now subscribe to this goals. Adams Smith, for instance, believes that "defence is the ultimate public sector good and not subject, therefore, to the iron laws of commercialization"[9]. The trend now is towards cost reduction, in which an open-trading environment leads government to purchase abroad, promote collaborative programmes and foster traditional integration.

Competitiveness through globalization will ensure equipment and component acquisition at the lowest cost. Outsourcing from specialist off shore supplier, joint venture and foreign subsidiaries will facilitate the process of cost reduction. There will be significant emphasizes on inter-service jointness and multi-national operations. The defence industrial base must also be transformed into one which is competitive state of art, international, information-intensive, low costs, and with a capability for rapid response, and one which is heavily dependant upon civil-military integration, even including the remaining few large systems integration firms.

CHALLENGES TO THE NIGERIAN ARMED FORCES

In view of the complex nature of the external and internal threats, the Armed Forces of Nigeria would be confronted with the following potential challenges.

I. DEFENCE MANAGEMENT

Since independence Nigeria has been operating a Ministry of Defence that is fashioned along the Federal Civil Service structure, manned by civilian technocrats. In the same vein since 1979, the nation has operated a variant of the Pakistani and USA Defence Headquarters structure with some success. Constitutionally, the President is the C-in-C of the Armed Forces and he is empowered to appoint Federal Ministers. The Ministers of Defence is the Political head of the Ministry; he provides policy direction for the Armed Forces and participates is Government's wider policy making process.

The MOD is composed of the civil and military components. The civil component is headed by the Permanent Secretary (PS) who is responsible for the managerial support as well as policy initiation for the ministry. He is, therefore, the Chief Accounting Officer of the Ministry. The military component consists of the Armed Forces (DHQ and the 3 Services) and is headed by the CDS. The Minister of Defence is required to act through the CDS for the implementation of the defence policy. Both the PS and the CDS are answerable to the Minister of Defence.

In the same manner both the Third Schedule of the 1999 Constitution and the National Defence Policy (NDP) 2006 mandated the National Security Council (NSC) and the National Defence Council (NDC) to act on behalf of the President in formulating the Defence policy. This provision implies that the command and control of the Armed Forces is vested in C-in-C who delegates authority through the Minster of Defence to the CDS and the Service Chiefs. The NDP 2006 succinctly explained that:

> ...the chain of command for planning and conduct of military operations flows from the NDC to the Honourable Minister of Defence to the CDS and from the CDS to either the Service Chiefs or the Commander Joint Task[10].

Furthermore, the control of the Armed Forces, joint operations and the training are vested in the CDS who is also responsible for coordinating the 3 Services.

The MOD as currently structured does not allow for proper integration of the civilian and military components as well as jointness within the Armed Forces. The civil and the military components of the MOD are working in parallel and almost independent of each other. The separate workings of both the MOD and the DHQ seem to hamper efficient management of the Armed Forces as it does not lend itself to support or encourage any coordination between MOD, DHQ and the Services as well as other stakeholders. Therefore , there is need to integrate the structure of the MOD and DHQ as well as the Services for effective and efficient performance of the Armed Forces within the context of the Nigerian Constitution 1999 and the NDP 2006.

II. LACK OF DOMAIN AWARENESS/ICT

The key to containing the threats in this dynamic multidimensional battle space is a "Total Domain Awareness' concept. This would entail creating an effective and efficient national C4ISR (command, control, communication, computer, intelligence, surveillance and reconnaissance) capabilities to monitor all land, sea and air spaces within the confines of Nigeria's territorial land, air and sea areas.

In modern warfare, successful operations are no longer primarily a function of which nation puts the most personnel and equipment into the battle space. As Sun Tzu noted, "the acme of military skill is the ability to win without fighting"[11]. It is therefore necessary, to develop an effective Information and Communication Technology (ICT) base, that would enhance our operational efficiency to even win wars without fighting. In this regards, both the human and material resources in our Armed Forces would be mobilized to ensure we attain a satisfactory level of ICT. We need to cooperate with other agencies, especially NITDA and NIGCOMSAT, to put in place a deliberate policy in this direction.

An integrated Command and Control Centre is critical to our own developmental efforts. Accordingly, our ICT programme would be flexible enough to keep pace with the dynamics of technology and focus on Data Management, Battle Space and Routine Communications, Command and Control, Logistics, Intelligence and Tele-Medicine.

The defence sector lacks an integrated network that is effect based and ICT driven hence it will be difficult for it to gather information, process it into actionable intelligence and disseminate it in a timely manner. Defence Intelligence would have to be developed to meet the requirements of modern warfare and also provide the necessary guidance in the restructuring and development of Service's intelligence outfit with the sole aim of contributing effectively into the overall national security network.

III. HARMONIZATION OF COMBAT SYSTEMS/JOINTNESS

Today, we uniquely have joint training facilities at different levels, but we do not have a commonly identified national military strategy. If properly articulated, this will influenced that combat doctrines, combat systems, procurement policies and even our manpower planning to objectively improve joint operational capabilities.

This level of disharmony has affected about all our capabilities including the management of emergencies, i.e., the conduct of our Armed Forces in Military Aid to Civil Authority/Military Aid to Civil Power (MACA/MACP). Issues of inadequate equipments, lack of training and effective coordination due to absence of a defined command structure and inherent incapacities derived from our core competence have adversely affected the conduct of these operations. The armed forces would have to evolve new strategies that would provide the right mix of a well trained and motivated force to effectively conduct MACA/MACP in ensuring internal peace and security. Thus harmonized control and capacity building are the main issues that would need to occupy the attention of the Armed Forces.

IV: INADEQUATE PEACE SUPPORT CAPACITY

General insecurity in the region or sub-region would have indirect implications on national security as envisaged in the Gulf of Guinea Guards, ECOWAS Standby Force and the African Standby Force. The armed forces would require an enhanced PSO capacity building in terms of mission oriented training, rapid mobilization, robust logistics structure and human resource development mechanisms.

Since independence, Nigeria has used the military as an instrument of national power in furtherance and protection of her foreign policy. This has been done, through our contributions to global peace, by our participation in Peace Support Operations (PSOs). The nature of challenges the military faces in these PSOs, change from time to time given the highly dynamic, unpredictable and complex environments in which we live and operate. Nigerian's contribution to international security is legendary, but we may not have optimized the benefits accruing there from. The requirement is for well prepared and adequately equipped troops that would not only demonstrate national resolve, but show the quality of a well organized force.

The multi-national, multicultural and multidimensional nature of PSOs presents unique challenges and there is the need to deploy well-trained and robustly-equipped troops with minimum delay and without ambiguity of mission objectives. The deployed troops must be familiar with contents of multi-national doctrine to enable them function with greatly reduced form of friction and ensure cohesiveness towards achieving set common objectives. It will also allow them to uphold their professional ethics as well as act within defined legal limits in the conduct of PSOs. The aspects of multi-nationality and joint forces in Peace Keeping Operations (PSOs) are vital issues that demand careful attention to details. The Nigerian Armed Forces Doctrine for PSOs 2007 will however proved effective guidance for Nigeria Armed Forces troops launched into PSO assignment(s). It highlights the land, the Maritime and the Air component aspects of deployment of joint force in a multi-national PSOs environment.

V. INADEQUATE DEFENCE APPROPRIATION

Defence allocation in recent times has been reduced due to other competing interest in the national economy. However, the threat scenario is ever increasing and becoming more dynamic. The ability of the Armed Forces to contain these threats would depend on funds available to improve its capability in procurement of new platforms, training, equipment and R&D. While the Armed Forces have been able to perform its constitutional roles relatively well with the limited resources provided, more stringent measures are still required for the Armed Forces to sustain Nigeria's national security objectives in military terms. The table on the screen is comparison of our defence spending with that of Egypt, India, Brazil and South Africa.

DEFENCE EXPENDITURE AS % OF GDP

Country	2004	2005	2006
Brazil	1.5	1.6	1.6
India	2.6	2.8	2.9
Egypt	3.0	2.8	2.9
South Africa	1.5	2.5	1.5
Nigeria	0.7	0.7	0.7

Source – SIPRI Yearbook 2008.

The deficiency in defence appropriation could be blamed on us recommending the budget, and also different other, but it directly incapacitates the Armed Forces and the nation in several areas. A good example is securing our marine environment. Considering Nigeria has enviable natural endowment and with her commitments to global, regional and sub-regional issues, friction may arise out of competing interests. The situation necessitates the Armed Forces developing capabilities for the proactive response.

VI. DEFICIENCY IN MANPOWER PLANNING

The REHTACOS for Officers 2007; HTACOS 2006 for soldiers /Rating and Airmen; the Armed Forces Act CAP A20 Laws of the Federation, the TACOS and the respective Manning Plans or Establishments of each of the Services stipulate the criteria for enlistment of personnel into the Nigerian Armed Forces. The recruitment of soldiers and selection of officers encourages fair representation of all states of Nigeria including the Federal Capital Territory (FCT). It also takes into consideration the requirement of the Federal Character Commission. However the system is fraught with many abnormalities. Despite these provision, it has been observed that the Armed Forces still lags behind in HRD to meet with emerging challenges. The AFN needs to transform its HRD programmes in order to optimize the benefits of technological developments. Currently there is no standardised joint manpower planning effort to determine future manpower requirement for the military. This informs the present individual Services recruitment efforts.

WAY FORWARD

The desire to reposition the Nigerian Armed Forces towards meeting the emerging global security challenges resulting from the dynamic and complex nature of the geo-strategic environment necessitated the setting up of a committee on the Transformation of the Armed Forces of Nigeria by me. This desire was reinforced by observed structural lapses created by the military's past experience and more importantly, the need to optimize the opportunity presented by the President's Vision 2020 within the context of the seven Point Agenda of which national security is considered a core factor[12].

In transforming the Nigerian Armed forces, the under listed aspects would have to be addressed:

a. Geo-Strategic Environment
b. Higher Management of National Defence
c. Manpower Planning and Leadership Development.
d. Joint logistics Management Structure
e. Defence Space Command
f. Medicare.
g. Proposed Military Strategy.

GEO-STRATEGIC ENVIRONMENT

An appropriate starting point discussing the way forward would be to acquaint you with the contemporary strategic environment. This environment is dynamic and complex hence determining how it could evolve up to 2020. I want to believe that this audience is very conversant with our internal environment no matter how dynamic it has become in recent times. In assessing the external environment I want to remind you of issues such as global economic imbalance, ICT, international terrorism, and HIV/AIDS.

But, specifically let us address the following issues. We need to objectively consider the place of Nigeria in global politics and especially Africa. What is Nigeria's political and military sphere of influence and what should it be? Today, in the African Standby Force arrangement Nigeria is critical to ECOWAS Standby Force (ESF). Are we ready: We are discussing the Gulf of Guinea Guard Force to protect our oil resources. We want to spearhead, but we are doing it with lot of suspicion from the rest of stakeholders, and the partners may not be helping the situation. Recently, we have had and we are going to have bilateral military engagements. We are undertaking all these in spite of the views on the US AFRICOM.

HIGHER MANAGEMENT OF NATIONAL DEFENCE

The activities of the political authority in defence management can only achieve success if properly articulated, coordinated and managed to protect the core values and national interest from domestic or international threat. The political authority alone cannot effective in defence management hence the military and civilian personnel are integrated in the MOD of most countries. However, the integration of armed forces personnel and civilian bureaucrats in MOD cannot be achieved easily or sustained for long without friction, which may arise due to fundamental divergent interests and perspectives of both parties.

A transformed MOD would seek to combine the political offices and those of the civil servants supporting the Honourable Minister of Defence (HMOD) and the Ministers of State with Senior Armed Forces personnel as staff officers. Initially, this may not easily fit and some discomfort may be created which could potentially paralyze defence management and military-strategic guidance. However, the resentment and friction that the initiative would generate could be greatly reduced through clear cut channel of communication and schedule of duties. It is expected that a unified MOD will be better placed to provide the strategic guidance to the military and steer the national defence effort in a joint and integrated manner than the current practice.

Hence it is appropriate to examine the current structure of higher management of defence in Nigeria and then considered other successful models in order to determine the most suitable structure for the country. In considering other models, due consideration was given to those countries that operate popular representative democratic political system that assign broadly similar direction and oversight roles to legislative arms of government for defence activities

MANPOWER PLANNING AND LEADERSHIP DEVELOPMENT

The HRD approach adopted by each of the Services were designed to attract and retain suitably qualified Nigerians, train them to attain their full potentials, provide adequate compensation, maintain conducive living and working conditions as well as implementing a total welfare package for the overall well being of the personnel. The HRD of the Services cover the requirement of an establishment or effective manning plan, recruitment, training utilization or deployment, performance evaluation, promotion, motivation and separation. A balanced manpower programme is aimed at developing the individuals through adequate selection/recruitment, training, motivation, stabilization and retirement[13].

Generally, military personnel are deployed for a specified period but this could be extended or shortened based on service exigencies. Consideration is given to seniority, experience, specialization and previous deployments. Ideally, individual qualifications are matched with job specifications to ensure that personnel achieve progressive self-actualization. However, where appropriate rank and experience are not available, personnel of the immediate relatively lower experience and status could be deployed to fill such vacancies. The process, unfortunately, is sometimes compromised as factors such as political considerations and quota systems determine who gets deployed to special positions. Retention of personal staff by some commanders and irregularities in deployments associated with manual record keeping have caused overstay in one deployment and location. Similarly, there is sometimes the problem of individual qualifications not matching with job specifications, which such individuals are expected to discharge. All these factors affect career progression and create loss of enthusiasm.

JOINT LOGISTICS MANAGEMENT STRUCTURE

The proposed Joint Logistics Management Agency (JLMA) shall comprise of elements from the 3 Services and MOD whose responsibilities will be to collate and assess the acquisition requirements for the Service to meet the imperatives of interoperability in equipment and also determine the requirements for joint operations.

The general concept of Nigerian Armed logistics structure would be based on the top-bottom and bottom-top approaches. These two broad approaches will provide the framework for the articulation of the Nigerian Armed Forces logistics planning and execution. Hence the proposed concept for equipment life-cycle would outline the procurement, maintenance and disposal policies.

It is within this context that the joint logistics management agency would be driven by some imperatives in the discharge of their duties. These include analysis/determination of Defence requirement/acquisition and procurement method/model/option. Others are logistics re-supply chain, inspection and maintenance procedure, inspection and disposal procedure.

These structures when fully developed would ensure enhanced efficiency in logistics management of the Armed Forces. In this regard, it is proposed that a Joint Logistics management agency with its logistics tenders board be established at the MOD[14].

DEFENCE SPACE COMMAND

Nigerian satellites are national strategic infrastructure that could transform the Nigerian Armed Forces into the information age. A technical collaboration between NASRDA and the Nigerian Armed Forces is needed to utilize the transponders of both the Nigeria Sat-1 and NigComSat-1 for the defence and security of Nigeria. Such partnership would provide a critical ICT framework needed to enhance military operations in areas of communications, imagery intelligence, and surveillance and action information organization. Other areas are Search and Rescue (SAR), R&D and rocketry. It will also support our military strategy through enhancing our early warning system and provision of situational awareness.

It has to be stressed that the issue of Defence Space Command is still under consideration by a committee. Models from other countries and reports of previous committee on this subject have been examined and a number of consultations are being made with some resource persons in this area. The potential benefits of Nigerian space and satellite programme have been identified and the Committee is working on a coordinated programme of action that will culminate in the long term to the establishment of the Defence Space Command. In the short term, however, the Nigerian Armed Forces will seek to have a cell under the current structure of Nigerian Air Space Research Development Agency. (NASRDA).

Technical partnership with the Agency should be the guiding principle for the Armed Forces at this stage. Thus, the nucleus of the military component in the NASRDA will be made up of personnel already trained in space technology. In order to maximize the benefits from the programe and ensure proper coordination with NASRDA, a Defence Space outfit under the office of the DHQ is being considered. It is this outfit that would eventually metamorphose into the Defence Space Command in the long term[15].

DEFENCE INDUSTRY AND TECHNOLOGY.

In the first part of this discussion I used countries like India, Egypt, Brazil and South Africa as examples. I don't want the popular trap of how we all started together and how Nigeria has been left behind. It is true, we have not made much progress, but we did not start together. The Brazilian and South African arms industriues galvanized existing privately owned assets which have made massive progress. We can used the examples of DENEL in South Africa, and Embracer in Bazil. Today, the Hindustani Aircrafts Ltd and different shipyards inherited from the British are making giant strides. Egypt has 26 different factories which have adopted dual use technology.

Until about a year ago, DICON was moribund. There was an injection of one billion Naira which has improved capacity by over 90%. Beyond, DICON is seeking 2.8 billion Naira to establish lines for AK 47 rifle and 7.62 special ammunition. It is heartwarning that it is doing further research in different areas. I also commend the recent efforts by the Navy. We probably need to do more at DANA. The important thing however, is to address our objectives to take advantage of all defence related undustries[16].

MEDICARE

The disbandment of the Armed Forces Medical Services in 1976 encouraged the duplication of health facilities by the Services resulting into poorly funded, equipped and staffed facilities with an attendant sub-optimal service delivery in the Armed

Forces. The integration of health care service at the tertiary level would translate to having fewer tertiary hospitals with concentration of manpower and equipment thereby improving service delivery in the Armed Forces. The re-establishment of the AFMS would ensure joint training in support of the combat arms and better coordination of medical support to the Armed Forces among others. There is also the need to have dedicated funds through legislation for the rehabilitation of the medical facilities in the Armed Forces. The following recommendations would address the observed problems in the medical department of the Nigerian Armed Forces.

a. Medical Service in the Armed Forces should be integrated at the tertiary level.

b. Individual Services should retain their primary and secondary health facilities.

c. Tri-Service facilities and programme should be placed under the AFMS for effective coordination.

d. The Medical schools for the NA and NN could be merged into an Armed Forces Medical school and the NAF will be incorporated as well.

e. The MOD should advocate for a dedicated fund backed by appropriate legislation for the massive rehabilitation and maintenance of all Nigerian military health care facilities.

f. The office of the Chief of Armed Forces Medical Service should be establish at DHQ in order to articulate and coordinate medical issues across the 3 Services.

The approval for the construction of a 50-bed hospital for the Armed Forces is a step in the right direction.

STRUCTURAL TRANSFORMATION

a. *Active Defence Flexible Response:* The Armed Forces will have to possess a professional and integrated force that can respond effectively and timely to a variety of threats and challenges of the security environment.

b. *Cooperation and Partnership:* The Nigerian Armed Forces will be actively engaged in bilateral and multilateral cooperation as well as joint and combined training activities, including Peace Support Operations. The Nigerian Armed Forces will have to integrate into its doctrine and plans, the employment of the Armed Forces in the emerging Gulf of Guinea Guard Forces, ECOWAS Stand-by Force (ESF) and the African Stand-by Force arrangement.

c. *Operational Structure of the Nigerian Armed Forces.* The National Military Strategy will ensure a balanced structure to reduce redundancy and promote cohesion in the Nigerian Armed Forces. In view of the gradual response concept, the Nigerian Armed Forces will be structured for operations into quick reaction force, follow-on force and a main defensive force. This operational structure is flexible enough to adapt to variety of security situations. The outline structure includes:

1. *Quick Reaction Force:* The force will be linked to the early warning system for quick response. The force will be capable of responding promptly to and adequately containing all the identified potential threats and tasks.

2. *Follow-on Force:* The follow-on will exploit the success of the quick reaction force and its state or readiness time will be based on 20 days and above Notice to move. They could be involved in stability operations.

3. *Main Defensive Force:* These are the main force mainly from the reserves. They reinforce the follow-on force.

d. *Funding Imperative:* The success of the National Military Strategy (NMS) will be hinged on the availability of the required financial support. The armed forces globally are expensive to build and maintain and would require high investment especially in the face of competition for funds with other sectors. However, the NMS will assist in the long term funding of the Nigerian Armed Forces, as this will require setting long term funding of the Nigerian Armed Forces, setting a long term goal and expenditure plan. A modernization fund for the Nigerian Armed Forces could be established and an annual increment of the budget for the fund applied. Also, application of effective and efficient procedures and best business practices will help to reduce financial leakages and unnecessary overheads.

CONCLUSION

Military systems are designed to achieve desired outcomes. Therefore, the architecture of the Nigerian Armed Forces system ensures that forces are focused on achieving the objectives set out for individual services. Thus far, we have performed quite well within reasonable limits, but we could do much better as a nation. The desire for optimal productivity has necessitated the need to consider transformation of the military. The focus is to evolve better ways of doing the business of the military. The dynamics of the environment where most military assignments are conducted suggests a critical assessment of existing Nigerian Armed Forces with a view to achieving standards that are obtained in other militaries of repute around the world. What I have seen of the transformation draft is an impressive document. We need to articulate to get by in within the military and by the larger society. We are starting somewhere; there is no end state in transformation, but I expect a lot of progress.

REFERENCES

1. See D. Morris, The Washing of the Spear, London: Sphere Books, 1976.
2. T. Friedman The Lexus and the Olive Tree: understanding Globalisation. London: Pengum, 1999 and T. Friedman, The World is Flat. London: Penguim, 2006.
3. B. Brodie, War and Politics N. Y: Macmillan, 1973.
4. S. Bidwell, Modern Warfare. London: Allen Lane, 1973.
5. J. Keegan, War and Our World. N. Y: Vintage Books, 2001

6. See J. Downey, Management in the Armed Forces. London: McGraw-Hill, 1977.

7. S. Enke Defense Management. N. J. Prentice-Hall, 19167.

8. P. Sarin, Military Logistics. The Third Dimension. New Delhi: Manas Publication, 2000.

9. A. Smith, An Inquiry into the Nature and Causes of Wealth of Nation's, ed. by Edwin Cannan – New York: Random House, 1937.

10. National Defence Policy. Abuja, Ministry of Defence, 2006.

11. Sun Tzu, The Art of War. Oxford: Oxford University Press, 197.

12. Vision 2020 Document Presidency, Abuja,

13. S. Huntington, Common Defence Columbia University Press, 1966.

14. See Report of Armed Forces Transformation Committee (April, 2008).

15. Report of Armed Forces Transformation Committee (Defence Space Doctrine) April, 2008.

16. J. Adekanye, "Domestic Production of Arms and the 'Defence Industries Corporation of Nigeria", Current Research on Peace and Violence. No. 4, 1983:258-269.

CHAPTER 13

DEFENCE MANAGEMENT IN THE MINISTRY OF DEFENCE

H. U. SANUSI

PREAMBLE

Three issues have featured prominently in national security matters since the end of the Cold War. These issues are globalization, democracy and Security Sector Reforms (SSR). Globalization influences national security in so far as national borders are gradually disappearing and national security issues are attracting more regional or global interest. Consequently, issues such as size of troops, equipment holding and proliferation or acquisition of certain as size of troops, equipment holding and proliferation or acquisition of certain types of weapons including deployment and usage become the focus of managers.

This interdependence necessitated the global call for a common best practise in defence management under the initiative of SSR requires that the military, beyond the traditional functions, should be used to assuage the burden of development by improved efficiency, transparency, improved Civil-Military Relations, subordination to civil authority and also act as catalyst for industrialization where they are so fashioned. Implicitly, the military must protect democracy and be an agent of economic development.

In this wise, Nigeria like other developing nations, has continued to reposition its Armed Forces through various reforms and modernization which includes attitudinal change, accountability and reprofessionalisation based mostly.

EPISTEMIC CONTEXT

The term defence connotes different meaning to different people depending on the field of study or the situation or circumstance in which the term is used. As military men and technocrats involved with the military aspect of defence matters, defence can only be translated in the perspective of making strategic plans to ward off enemy attack or prevent aggression. Defence, therefore, refers to military measures and manoeuvres for protecting a State, its core values and national interest from internal and external threats.

Resource can simply be defined as a person, material or capital which can be used to accomplish a goal. Resource is used mostly in the plural form resources, and it applies to a wide array of matters. Thus we have human, natural, material, financial, mineral and other types of resources. This chapter will however consider the management of resources available for the defence of the nation, which in this regard include human, material and financial resources.

From the foregoing, defence resources could therefore be defined as the human, material and financial assets at the disposal of a nation, which it can use to protect the State from internal and external threats. Similarly, management is regarded by some management scientists as an encompassing process by which scarce resource – human, money, materials and time are skillfully deployed to achieve set targets and objectives by an organization. This implies that the manager must possess the intellectual and physical capability for conceptualizing, planning, organizing and controlling the establishment, as well as its resources[2]. Therefore, managers are responsible for optimizing all of the resources available to them, be it material, human or capital. The management tool of any organization would therefore include:

a. Conceptualizing
b. Planning
c. Budgeting
d. Staffing
e. Organising
f. Coordinating
g. Directing
h. Coordinating
i. Monitoring
j. Reporting
k. Feedback[1]

Specific to the defence organization, however, Defence Management deals with theories, concepts and techniques for forecasting, planning, directing, coordinating and controlling human, physical and information resources for achieving the aims of national security through operations on land and / or sea and / or air, and being prepared for all these aspects at all times by creating the infrastructure for waging a war (through training, logistics and intelligence)[2]. In line with the general concept of defence, Defence Management cannot be treated without treating the details of resources available for defence. Defence Resource Management covers the strategic, operational and tactical plans put in place to ensure the success of deterrence, defence or even war. It presupposes therefore, that military success is dependent on teamwork by the military and civil arms of the Military. Furthermore, it becomes clear that the machinery of Defence Management revolves around the dynamics of balanced organizational structure and the prudent utilization of human and material resources. It is apt at this stage to examine the defence structure and the management framework in the Ministry[3].

STRUCTURE AND ROLE OF MINISTRY OF DEFENCE

The Ministry of Defence is the headquarters and the central coordinating body for the operations and administration of the Armed Forces of Nigeria. The Ministry comprises civil and military arms with the Honourable Minister of Defence (HMOD) as the Head and the Chief Executive Officer. The HMOD is vested with the requisite authority for controlling the 3 Services (Army, Navy and Air Force) through their respective Councils/Boards, acting through the Chief of Defence Staff (CDS). The civil arm of the Ministry is headed by the Permanent Secretary who is the principal policy adviser to the Honourable Minister of Defence. The Chief of Defence Staff (CDS), is the Chief Coordinator of the military arm and all Armed Forces' Joint activities. He is also the Chief Adviser to the Honourable Minister of Defence on defence related and joint operation matters. The CDS carries out this assigned role in consolation with the Service Chiefs. Both arms of the Ministry work closely together to achieve the overall national defence objectives and functions, which are clearly outlined in Section 217 of the Constitution of the Federal Republic of Nigeria.

Accordingly, the Ministry of Defence is responsible to the Federal Government for the formation and execution of the Defence Policy. It is the political, operational, and administrative headquarters of the Armed Forces. The statutory functions of the Ministry of Defence, as spelt out in Federal Republic of Nigeria Official Gazette No. 15, Vol. 76 of 3rd March, 1979, are as follows:

a. Armed Forces Development Projects
b. Clearing Foreign Military aircraft and warships
c. Defence
d. Procurement of Defence equipment
e. Welfare of Ex-service men
f. Liaison and Armed Forces of foreign countries
g. Recruitment of local forces, including Armed Forces and Cadets.
h. Matters of policy on establishment, recruitment, finance, training and operations connected with the Nigerian Armed Forces.
i. Resettlement Scheme for Armed Forces Ex-Servicemen and;
j. Maintain relations with Armed Forces Institute of Nigeria (AFIN), Defence Industries Corporation of Nigeria (DICON), Military Pension Boards (MPB) and the Nigerian Legion.

STRUCTURE OF THE CIVIL ARM

The civil arm of the Ministry of Defence is currently structured into two major departments: the Common Service Department and Operation Department. The former is further divided into three departments, while the latter comprises four as follows:

a. Common Service Department
   (1) Department of Administration and Supplies
   (2) Department of Finance and Accounts
   (3) Department of Planning, Research and Statistics
b. Operations Department
   (1) Department of Joint Service
   (2) Army Affairs Department
   (3) Navy Affairs Department
   (4) Air Force Affairs Department.

The three Common Services Department provide essential services to the Ministry. They act in their respective areas of jurisdiction only at the request of the Operations Departments. For example, the Department of Administrations is not expected to commence the process of filling vacancy, or employing a staff, if not requested by the department with the vacancy. Similarly, the Department of Finance and Accounts cannot place an order to make payment a formal request from any of the department. The work of the operation department includes, not only policy execution, but also policy initiation and policy development in their respective areas of concern. They take care of issues of common concern to the Services [4].

Each department is structured into Divisions, headed by a Deputy Director. Each Division is further divided into Branches, such that each branch is headed by an Assistant Director. The Branch is further divided into sections and headed by an officer of Grade level 14. There are also four (4) units, which work directly with the Minister and the Permanent Secretary. These units are the Internal Audit, Protocol, Press and Public Relations, and the Legal Units. More recently, Ministerial SERVICOM Unit was created as part of the Administration's reform agenda. The Departments and their functions in areas of defence resources management are as follows:

i. The Department of Administration and Supplies is responsible for:
    a. Establishment matters
    b. Appointment, Junior and Senior Staff Committee; Staff training and welfare.
    c. Secretariat of the Ministry's personnel management and its committees.
    d. Maintenance of personnel records.
    e. Liaison with relevant bodies outside the ministry e.g. the Federal Civil Service Commission, National Planning Commission, and Establishment and Pension office, etc.
    f. Budgeting for recruitment and capital expenditure.
    g. Procurement of supplies such as stationary, office equipment, materials furniture, etc.
    h. Stores
    i. Management and transport facilities
    j. Maintenance of equipment, furniture, office space, etc
ii. The Department of Finance and Accounts is responsible for:
    a. Revenue and Financial Administration
    b. Accounts, and
    c. Liaison with relevant bodies outside the Ministry such as the Ministry of Finance and Economic Development, Central Bank of Nigeria, Office of the Account-General of the Federation, etc.
iii. The Department of Planning Research and Statistics is responsible for:
    a. Development of Rolling, Medium and Perspective, Plans for the Ministry.
    b. Monitoring and evaluation of plan implementation

c.   Secretariat of the Ministerial Tender Board.

d.   Research into the Sectors over which the Ministry has jurisdiction.

e.   Research into the Internal organization and operational Modalities of the Ministry.

f.   Setting and Monitoring of performance and Efficiency Targets for the various sub-Divisions and Staff of the Ministry.

g.   Regular Collection and processing of Data and Statistics relating to the Ministry.

h.   Secretariat of the Ministry's Records and Information Resources such as the Registry, Library, Computer Services and the Data Bank, when established.

JOINT SERVICE DEPARTMENT

The Joint Service Department's areas of responsibility include the following:

a.   Secretariat for the Boards of Nigerian Defence Academy (NDA), Armed Forces Command and Staff College (AFCSC) and the National Defence College (NDC). The Department represents the Ministry on the Board of the Defence Industries Corporation of Nigeria (DICON) and ensures the follow-up/implementation of decisions of the four bodies.

b.   Processing the training requirements of the Armed Forces personnel, as well as training and technical assistance requirements for other African countries.

c.   Providing secretariat for the Ministry of Defence Committees on all disarmament matters and, with DHQ representing the Ministry on the United Nations Conferences on Nuclear, Chemical and Biological Weapons negotiation.

d.   Representing the Ministry on all joint Commissions on Military co-operation and negotiations between Nigeria and other countries, including UN sponsored peace keeping or peace enforcement missions like United Nations Mission in Sierra Leone (UNAMSIL).

e.   Processing payment of compensation on land acquisition and rent on requisitioned properties.

THE LEGAL UNIT

The Legal Unit performs the following functions:

a.   Representing the military or any of the Services or organs of the military in any civil action pending in any court of law in the Federation. It also represents the officials of the Ministry, the Army, the Navy and the Air Force in civil actions where the action complained are performed in the course of their normal duties.

b.   Preparation of drafts and vetting of all contract agreements involving the Ministry, or any arm thereof, as well as the Service organs and parastatals.

c. Rendering of advisory opinion on all matters referred to it for legal opinion e.g. contract, torts, personnel, compensation/rents for acquisition and requisition, international relations, military co-operation, etc.

d. Representing the Ministry or any arm of the Services' organs or parastatals before all arbitration tribunals set up in or outside Nigeria to determine any issue where the interest of these bodies is at stake[5].

PRESS AND PUBLIC RELATIONS UNIT

The press and public relations unit is under the general direction of the Honourable Minister. It is responsible for formulating and articulating a dynamic strategy for achieving effective press and public relations for the Ministry. It is also saddled with the overall responsibility of projecting the programmers, policies, plans and activities of the Ministry through press releases and statements, brochures, posters, file photographs and public lectures. The Unit monitors all shades of public opinion and reactions to the Ministry's plan, policies, as well as projects and respond to opinions and reactions. It organises and covers familiarization tours, facilitates visits and also carry out evaluation of enlightenment campaigns.

MINISTERIAL SERVICOM UNIT

The Ministerial SERVICOM Unit in the Ministry is headed by a Deputy Director, who serves as the Nodal Officer and the Head of the Unit. He is expected to report directly to the Honourable Minister through the permanent secretary. The unit performs the following functions:

a. To spearhead the Ministry' Developments and Parastatal's Service Delivery initiative through SERVICOM compliance.

b. To produce, review and monitor performance of charters of the Ministry and its parastatals.

c. To manage the Ministry's Customer Relations Policy including providing opportunities for customer feedback on service.

d. To institute appropriate Market Research techniques in identifying customer needs and expectations.

e. To ensure the promotion of quality assurance and best practices in the Ministry's performance of its functions.

f. Provide a comprehensive and effective training policy for the frontline staff.

g. Disseminate best practice and other tips on service delivery improvement.

h. Serve as a link between the Ministry and SERVICOM office in the Presidency.

i. To serve as the Secretariat of the Ministry's Service Delivery Committee.

Inspite of the positive intentions in the structure of the civil arm, a lot of shortcomings still exist, particularly in the areas of retention of knowledgeable and professional civilian staff. One of the major constraints in this regard is the pooling system whereby highly experienced middle and top management personnel are periodically moved around the ministries. The policy ought to be officially re-examined to re-align it with the imperative of professionalism and the need to enhance competitiveness in a rapidly globalizing world.

STRUCTURE OF THE MILITARY ARM

The military arm of the Ministry comprise the Defence Headquarters (DHQ) and the 3 Services – Army, Navy and Air Force. It is structured for the purpose of the defence of our territorial integrity on land, sea and air.

DHO Suffice to note that the DHQ is responsible for joint operations and coordinates the activities of the three services. Each of the three services departments responsible for the following for its respective service:

(a) Provision of secretariat for the services board/council.
(b) Monitoring of Defence projects as they relate to the particular service.
(c) Vetting of the Armed Forces Tender's Board meetings;
(d) Processing of end users request for each service for equipment; logistics support or training;
(e) Processing of contractor's claims etc[6].

NIGERIAN ARMY

The Nigerian Army is organised into five divisions: four infantry and one armoured division. All the divisions operate combined-armed forces structures with the compliments of combat supports services. Each division is designed to operate, either on its own in special operations or, conventionally, in conjunction with the Navy and Air Force. The national resource base is, however, not strong enough to fully equip the size of force required to attain the capabilities already mentioned. The immediate concern of the army, therefore, is to attain about 80% overall readiness level and to have one brigade group fully prepared as part of a Rapid Response Force (RRF). The essence is to assure rapid deployment and response capabilities in order to protect the nation's territorial integrity and assist the Police in overcoming problems of internal security.

The Nigerian Navy provides the maritime elements of the nation's defence forces with the general responsibility of meeting contingent and actual maritime requirements. The Navy's ability to undertake missions at sea is its unique contribution to national defence. For the Nigerian Navy, this entails the defence against for seawards and the protection of the resources in the nation's maritime environment up to the limit of our Exclusive Economic Zone (EEZ). This vast maritime environment harbours abundant natural resources, including hydrocarbon, which now account for about 90% of the nation's foreign exchange earnings. Other maritime resources include the numerous offshore and coastal oil platforms, loading terminals and coastal industrial towns that harbour some of the country's vital installations like tank farms, petro-chemical plants, thermal power stations and rolling mills. Others are the Aluminum Smelting plant and the Calabar Free Trade Zone (FTZ). Nigeria's

Sea Lane of Communication through which her maritime trade is conducted is equally important, as over 85% of the country's imports and exports pass through this SLC.

NIGERIAN AIR FORCE

The priority of the Nigerian Air Force (NAF) is the defence of the nation by air, especially the protection of vital national economic interest that are spread across the country. The NAF maintains this capability to deny the enemy the ability to attack strategic assets through constant surveillance and rapid response of forward deployed counter air assets, This "active-defence" posture constitutes part of the first line of defence in order to ensure that no damage is inflicted on national interests. NAF has also been employed, either singly or jointly with other services, in regional and sub-regional operations. Nigeria continues to provide and apply military force in support of her regional peace efforts. Such crisis response capability is dependent on a developed "Forward Engagement' policy by always retaining the ability to project force within the region. Having listened to the functions and management of the services. We will now proceed to discuss resource management in the Military.

DEFENCE RESOURCE MANAGEMENT

Resource management in defence is, often under extreme conditions, informed by military operational exigencies. In this wise, defence resource management must be with considerations for efficiency and economy within the dictates of the defence objectives. Materials Management, as part of Logistics Management, is that coordinated function which is responsible to plan for, acquire, store, move and control materials to optimize usage of facilities, personnel, capital and provide services to the user in line with the organization's aim. The magnitude of materials management can be gauged from the fact that materials costs constitute 50% to 75% of the total cost of a finished product or good. For instance, the materials budget of the three services in the past couple of years has been very enormous and this underscores the importance placed on effective management of materials.

To be effective, materials management at the MOD and the three services has been tailored to meet the primary objectives of achieving the right quality, quantity, price, source, and delivery at the right time. Additionally, the Ministry ensures that material management at the MOD meets the secondary objectives of having reciprocal relation; new materials, processes and products; economic 'make or buy' decisions; standardization; product improvement; inter-departmental harmony; and forecasts. At the MOD, the management of materials resource comes under the purview of the Department of Administration and Supplies. As I earlier stated, the department handles such issues as procurement and storage of supplies; management of transport facilities; maintenance of equipment, furniture, office space etc.

Human resources are key organizational assets since the performance of any organization depends, amongst other things, on the quality of employees, their ability and motivation. According to Kreitner, management of human resources of the MOD is undertaken by the Department of Administration. Issues related to the appointment, staff training, welfare, records and pension are handled by the department.

Financial Management in the MOD is undertaken by the Finance and Accounts Department. The Department handles the procurement, budgeting, accounting and auditing of the Ministry's expenditures. Beside its traditional financial control mechanism, the MOD also operates its financial management within the provisions of the Due Process Procedures facilitated by the Resident Due Process Team (RDPT) and or the Budget Monitoring and Price Intelligence Unit (BMPIU) in the Presidency. The MOD also maintains constant liaison with the Ministry of Finance and Economic Development, the Central Bank of Nigeria (CBN), the office of the Accountant General of the Federation in its financial processes. Among the financial management activities in the Ministry are defence procurement, budgeting, accounting, auditing and due process[7].

Procurement in the Ministry is ideally initiated by the NA, NN and NAF or the civil departments. The usual practice is for a particular unit or formation to send forward request of its operational or administrative request through appropriate channels to its individual service headquarters. The process follows the national procedure for procurement, which starts with the identification of needs by units, formations, or department based on tasks and mission. Advertisement or invitation letters are sent out for tenders for the contract after which a pre-qualification exercise is conducted for the prospective contractors.

The ministry conducts a bid opening and financial evaluation, where the successful contractors are selected for the ward consideration. Thereafter, negotiations for price reduction and discounts are undertaken with the companies before the final contact award. It is worth mentioning that the defense procurement through contracts is done at the instance of either or both the Resident Due Process Team (RDPT) and the Budget Monitoring and Price Intelligence Unit (BMPIU), which ensure that the contract pricing is appropriate. The functions of these two bodies will be mentioned in the course of the lecture. The RDPT issues the Due Process Certificate for contracts less than ₦50 million while the BMPIU issue same for contracts above ₦50 million. The instance of due process competence certificates leads to the signing of the contract agreement. The contract agreement and the Military Due Process Certification (MDPC) are sent to the office of the Account-General of the Federation for final procurement processes.

The annual budget preparation of the MOD starts with a Budget Call Circular issued by the Budget Office of the Federation to all federal ministries, parastals and agencies, with the year's guidelines and timeline for the submission of the budget proposals. Prior to the budget call, the Budget Division of the MOD usually sends out internal Budget Call Circular on behalf of the Honourable Minister of Defence (HMOD) to the services, department, MOD civilian establishments and units, reminding them of the need to set in motion the process for preparation of their annual budget proposals.

The corps commanders, formation commanders and commandants of the tri-service military training institutions as well as Defence Advisers abroad send their proposals to their services headquarters and the DHQ as the case may be. Budget officers collate all the submissions for the approval of their respective department heads, the service chiefs or the CDS before they are forwarded to the MOD for the preparation of the entire Ministry's budget proposal by the Budget Division.

At this stage, in order to reconcile the Military's budget proposals with the ceiling and other administrative guidelines stipulated in the Call Circular from the Ministry of Finance, an in-house meeting of the Military Budget Committee is usually held under the Chairmanship of the Honourable Minister of Defence or the permanent secretary. The Committee further deliberates on the entire proposals submitted and further adjustments are made where necessary, before the proposals are forwarded to the Federal Ministry of Finance. It is however not unusual to exceed the Call Circular ceiling but such excesses have to be justified when the Ministry's budget is being discussed at the Federal Ministry of Finance and/or any other subsequent levels.

Like the other Federal ministries, MOD is usually invited to defend its budget before the relevant Committees of the Senate and House of Representatives that have oversight responsibilities over the Ministry. In our own case, the relevant Committee is the Senate and House of Representatives Committees on Defence. A joint sitting of the National Assembly then considers the budgets of the various Ministries and the result is an Appropriation Act that is sent to Mr. President for his assent.

Defence accounting broadly entails payment and accounting of all charge pertaining to the defence services, including bills for supplies and services rendered and for construction and repair works, pay and allowances, revenue, miscellaneous charges, etc. Further to the accounting functions is the internal auditing responsibilities, which also include the audit of cash and stores, auditing of accounts kept by various units and formation of the three services and the civil departments in the Ministry.

In line with the provision of the Financial Regulation, the Internal Audit Unit carries out complete and continuous audit of the accounts and records of revenue and expenditure planned and allocated as well as unallocated stores. It also carries out management audit encompassing all areas of activities and functions of the Ministry. The internal audit periodically visits formations for resident auditors to audit accounts and records of revenue and expenditure etc. This is a marked departure from the past, where auditing procedures were not being fully adhered to.

Other adhoc assignment carried out by the Internal Audit Unit include:

a. Verification of promotion arrears of teachers
b. Investigation into alleged cases of fraud.
c. Developing and auditing the books of accounts and records at MOD liaison office, Lagos.
d. Maintains collaboration with the services and the office of the Accountant-General of the Federation. The Internal Audit also carries out detailed auditing and review of the accounts and records of the Directorate of Ministry Pension.

DUE PROCESS PROCEDURE

It is pertinent to mention at this point that there is, in the office of the President, a unit designated as the Budget Monitoring and Price Intelligence Unit (BMPIU). The Unit, as its name implies, is involved in the monitoring of Federal Government projects nationwide, and ensures that the cost of projects, contracts, and services are reasonable and competitive. The Due Process Certification must be obtained before the award of contracts for projects and services and processing of payment. There are two types of Due Process Procedures, viz:

A.   RESIDENT DUE PROCESS TEAM

Each Ministry has a Resident Due Process Team (RDPT) comprising the Permanent Secretary as the Chairman, the Directors of Administration, Finance and Accounts and Planning, Research and Statistics, as well as a Sector Specialist representing the Budget Monitoring and Price Intelligence Unit (BMPIU). The Due Process Team issues certification for projects/contracts/services whose value is not more than ₦50 million.

B   BUDGET MONITORING AND PRICE INTELLIGENCE UNIT.

This Unit is located in the Presidency. It has the Senior Special Assistant (Budget) to the President as its Head and the Principal Secretary to the President, two Special Assistants and two sector specialists as members. Projects/contracts/services worth over N50 million are approved by the Federal Executive Council. Thereafter, the BMPIU issues Due Process certificates on them.

Similar to the practice in other ministries, Defence Management in MOD has its own challenges. These challenges include inadequate funding, inadequate integration of staff, lack of effective defence industrial complex and lack of appropriate R & D structure. The challenges will be briefly discussed[7].

CHALLENGES

Major challenges confronting the Ministry of Defence

i. Inadequate Funding: Conflicting demands for scarce national resources within a democratic setting, connotes less allocations to the military, especially in peace time. The overhead requirements of the Ministry are grossly under funded. Consequently, most of the defence equipment, facilities, vehicles, buildings, and other structure cannot be properly maintained. In essence, MOD's submissions for overhead costs appear to have become a matter of yearly routine because its proposals are never considered item-by-item, or at least Department by Department, as submitted.

ii. Inadequate Integration

The effective control of the military by the civil authority requires a good working knowledge and relation between the two sides. This could be achieved through a good mix of civil and military staff in the MOD. There is the need for MOD to be restructured to absorb some military officers to work in the ministry in conjunction with their civilian counterpart, as it is done in most democratic countries. The effective and efficient mix of these officers will not only foster trust and cooperative integration, but will help in facilitating policy implementation.

iii. Lack of Defence Industrial Complex

The result of lack of either a Defence Industrial Complex or even a national industrial base is the importation of most of our military equipment from foreign countries. The availability or otherwise of such equipment depends on the political and economic relationship with the producing countries. The military industrial complex in the country, to say the least, cannot cope with the present level of our military requirements. Over-dependence on external sources for military needs like we do could result in serious consequences if met with disappointments especially in crisis period.

iv Lack of Appropriate Research and Development Structure.

The need for an effective R & D cell as a major and important in all aspects of defence management cannot be over-emphasized. All nations that have developed to an appreciable level of self-sufficiency have placed adequate attention to R&D. Currently, R & D in Nigeria's military can be described as virtually non-existent. There is nevertheless, the need for an effective Research and Development (R&D) network to support an industrial base as well as service the needs of the services. To this effect, individual services R & D cells would need to be well established and programmed to collaborate with a joint service R & D Cell which would in turn be part of the national cell. The absence of such a structure and the levity with which issues of R&D are currently treated in the country would be inadequate to support the industrial base required for a strong and prudent military. No single sector of the country could get the fund it requires, but there is still need to service critical areas within available resources. Considering the dynamic nature of defence requirement, especially within the context of current national and global security issues, funding the Defence Sector requires some priority. It is my considered view that it is in best interest of Nigeria and its people that our national defence policy objectives are attained. This view may sound ambitious, especially to those outside the Defence Ministry who may feel that, rather than allocating more funds to defence and security, more funds should be allocated to the production and service sectors of the economy. It must be emphasized that in the absence of peace and stability, there could be no realistic expectation for sustained social and economic development. There should however be judicious management of resources, to be ensured by adherence to financial policies and efficient oversight.

The need for the right caliber of staff in a good mix to manage defence resources cannot be overemphasized. A good mix of military and civilian staff at both MOD and the DHQ would provide the desired cooperation and integration for better understanding and control. A deliberate policy of retaining military staff trained civilians permanently in the Ministry would also be worthwhile.

To ensure the efficient and economic management of defence within the current global perspective, where acquisition of military stores and equipment is becoming more complex, requires a reasonable level of self-sufficiency. The current revitalization effort at DICON could therefore be pursued with a deliberate policy to attain a set level of self-sufficiency in military equipment production within a time limit.

Similarly, there cannot be a viable industrial complex no matter how sophisticated that would provide self sufficiency without a well funded R&D base. One cannot overemphasis the importance of R & D, and its contributions to all sectors of defence resource management. It will be necessary to reiterate however, that R & D requires more attention, if there is to be any meaningful effect in the defence management. R&D would also need to be integrated into the overall national R & D policy.

CONCLUSION

This chapter discussed the contemporary issues in Defence Management and the MOD's effort in keeping with these challenges. The discourse covered institutional framework of the Ministry and the ways human, material and financial resources are managed in the MOD. It also emphasized the essence of the Due Process (facilitated by the RDPT and the BMPIU) as the structures employed to ensure efficiency and economy in defence management.

Four major challenges, among some minor ones, militating against resource management in the MOD were highlighted. They include poor funding, inadequate mix of civilian and military staff at the higher defence management levels; the lack of necessary military industrial complex supported by a well coordinated R & D Cells to provide and sustain self sufficiency in military equipment. Accordingly, proper and timely funding of the MOD, proper mix of civilian and military and support of well integrated R & D Cells were suggested as the way forward.

REFERENCES

1. R. Grant Contemporary Strategy Analysis Malden: Blackwell Publishing, 2005.
2. J. C. T. Downey, Management in the Armed Forces: London: MaGraw-Hill, 1977.
3. S. Enke and C. Hitch, Decision-Making for Defence, Berkeley: University of California Press, 1965.
4. See I. S. Zabadi, "The National Security Decision-Making Process in a Democracy Lecture Delivered at NWC on 12 January 2000.
5. Report of Armed Forces Transformation Committee, April 2008.
6. S. V. L. Malu "The Nigerian Army "Lectures delivered at NWC on 12 October 1999.
7. See "Guidelines On the Operation of the Defence Budget" issued by the Permanent Secretary of MOD, 1992.

CHAPTER 14

THE POLITICS OF DEFENCE APPROPRIATION

CELESTINE BASSEY

INTRODUCTION

The debate in the Nigerian defence community about the rationale of the present level of defence spending since the end of the civil war in 1970, is a palpable reminder of the continued "disequilibrium" between the dominant goals of domestic policy, on the one hand, and defence and foreign policy objectives, on the other. Since the end of the civil war, defence has consumed an average of 16 percent of the Federal budget each year[1]. This has undeoubtedly imposed limits on the resources available to other competing interests and demands in society, especially in the wake of proactive strategic engagement in Liberia, Bakassi and Sierra Leone.

As a result of the foregoing, the magnitude of the defence effort became a key issue in the new pattern of fiscal politics, focused upon the allocation of resources between the military and non-military sectors of the society, and among the purposes of government. As seen from the direction of this debate, there were (and still are) persistent tendencies either to treat the defence component in the budgetary equation separately, something to be considered on merits without reference to other goals; or to "assume that one goal was of overriding importance and must have absolute priority over the other".

This chapter is essentially a synthesis and evaluation of this controversy within the context of the organic and conjunctural crisis in Nigeria's economy. It argues essentially that, in practice, no single element-the absolute requirements of security or the absolute limits of the economy – could determined by itself the level of defence efforts necessitated by the armed forces modernization programme. Consequently a more informed analysis of the determination of resources available to the military/ civilian government and the allocation of these to defence, domestic, and foreign purposes, has only partly to do with self aggrandisement of military "power-elite" as Adekson and Nzimiro, among others, have claimed. It is on the contrary, partly rooted in the prebendal structure of primitive accumulation in Nigeria and partly the political resultant of the functional imperative and dynamics of developing national defence system in a regional sub-system deeply unsettled by pressure of decolonization, regional revalries, external intervention, political instability and civil strife.

CONTEXT: COALITION AND CONSTITUENCY

The tremendous upsurge in demand for other social needs (agriculture, education, health, industry, communication, etc) had by late 1980s and 1990s unleashed an unprecedented groundwell of discontent and controversy about priorities in national planning and resources allocation. Thus, unlike the civil war period when military needs became overriding, taking more than 35% of the Federal budgets, each administration since 1970 has had to balance an uncomfortable equation in which the major elements were:

i. Domestic Schemes for agriculture, housing, highways, education, health, etc., loosely identifiable as serving the welfare purposes of the country.

ii. Foreign Programme, including expansion of diplomatic missions (from six in 1960 to eighty-two in 1980), military – strategic commitments (e.g aid and logical support to liberation movements, and peace-keeping in Chad, Lebanon, Liberia and Sierra Leone loosely related to the goals of diplomacy and security).

iii. Tax Limitation and Reduction, justified in terms of private consumption and investment; and

iv. Balanced budgets, justified since in the 1980s by a number of goals, including the prevention of inflation and the reduction of the national debt related to the value of fiscal integrity[3].

These four elements constitute the primary underpinning of the "Gari versus Gun" controversy (the Nigerian variant of the guns or butter debate) which profoundly influenced budgetary decisions concerning the size and distribution of funds to the armed forces. As reflected in the direction of this controversy, there are persistent proclivities – despite the obvious interdependence of these budgetary components – either to treat each segment that "one goal was of overriding importance and must have absolute priority over the others". For example, a number of critics of defence spending have conveyed the erroneous impression that domestic needs could be met independent of security needs – that an absolute limit existed on what the economy could afford for defence – despite the lesson of the civil war era and the enormous fiscal outlay involved in Ecomog operations in Liberia and Sierra Leon.

Conversely, institutional and public defenders of relatively high defence expenditure often seemed to underestimate pressing domestic needs engendered by the "revolution of rising expectations". They assumed that the requirements of security were absolute and that the only legitimate limit on their fulfillment was the physical capacity of the economy. In other words, the general tendency among this group of analysts was to balance the "requirements" derived from legitimate but competing expectations of government and society[4].

However, in practice, no single element – the absolute requirements of security or the absolute limits of the economy-could determine by itself the level of defence efforts necessitated by the armed forces modernization programme. In this regard, Bayo Adekson's Military Extractive Ratio (MER) thesis contributes partially to the understanding of the complex farrago (of sometimes confusing and confounding contradictions) of issue involved. As Adekson himself explains:

The military has for some time now been the government... and with this the legislative function, as we know it ceased, while open party politics was proscribed. The implication of the latter for fiscal policy was that the military as an interested and the more organized sector, was also the sole judge of how much went to it vis-à-vis other competing sectors, such as agriculture, education, heath, labour, and community development. Nor were auditor generals' offices permitted to function effectively in monitoring how a given defence ministry spent its allocations. Besides, even if they did not want to, soldier-rulers often found themselves compelled by the logic of the situation to satisfy members of their profession with increased donatives and benefits, whatever the economic conditions prevailing in the wider society... I submit that the foregoing state of affairs invariably resulted in a skewed budgetary distribution in favour of the military.[5]

It is hardly to be disputed that a number of elements in the domestic political economic constellation may have a significant effort on military expenditures. In this respect, it may be hypothesized that the military, as the dominant actor – the "sole judge" of the allocation of societal values – in the periods 1966 – 1976, 1984-1998, ensured a disputable degree of resource allocation to defence. All decision regarding defence policy, including the shape of the defence budget, were taken within the Supreme Military Council (later the Provisional Ruling Council) that served as the Federal Military Government's Chief Executive body. The incapacitation of the office of the Auditor-General and that of the Accountant-General in the process frustrated transparent accounting system resulting, for instance, in extra-budgetary spending by the Federal Military Government of some N100 billion in the first three months of 1999 fiscal year (January – March, 1999). The inevitable consequence, as one commentator puts it, is that:

The worst case scenario is that the figure which represents 80 percent excess spending or about 50 percent of the ₦202 billion deficit projected for the whole year could not be pinned down to any specific project. But the danger signals which have already started to show the rising rate of inflation. It has now hit two digits.[6]

Adekson's explication however, failed to explain the defence spending hikes under the civilian administration (1979-83) with a qualitatively different and more complicated budgetary process. What is more plausible is the accumulative tendencies of the galaxy of policy elite representing military and civilian fractions in terms of inflated contracts tied to brazen consumption pattern rather than production. A more informed analysis, therefore, of the determination of resources available to the military, domestics, and foreign purposes, has only partly to do with self-aggrandizement of military power-elite, "compelled by the logic of the situation to satisfy members of their profession with increased donative sand benefits, whatever the economic conditions prevailing in the wider society", but also to the imperatives of evolving adequate defence establishment to cope with challenges to national security.

Adekson's thesis was basically defective. He utilizes fragmentary and circumstantial evidence and a fallacious conceptual apparatus (Military Extractive Ratio) to produce a biased view of the military era. To this extent he failed to appreciate the dynamics of an expanding national defence system in a post-colonial state. He also ignored the fact that the drastic changes in Nigerian foreign and security policy since the civil war reflected the altered position of Nigeria in a regional sub-system deeply unsettled by pressures of decolonization, external intervention and intra-and inter-state conflict spiral. For example, the Federal government spending (1999 fiscal year) which was reported to have exceeded ₦224 billion by the end of March (involving a deficit of ₦100 billion over the ₦124.5 billion expenditure projected for the first quarter of that year) is only explicable, among others, in the context of ECOMOG operation in Sierra Leone and the sudden escalation of the war since January 1999. This virtual paralysis of the ground (MBT, APC, and IFV). Air (Alpha Jets) and sea platforms of the Nigeria Military (the backbone of ECOMOG) contingents in Sierra Leon as a result of dearth of spare parts and munitions entailed furious extra-budgetary acquisition following the rebel (RUF) incursion into Freetown in January 1999[7].

Hence, an alternative conceptualization and explanation on the high level and rate of fiscal outlay for the defence was, and still is, in part the consequence and requirement of building to use Shagari's word, a "well-equipped, mobile and virile defence force" on a meagre legacy (at the time or independence) within a short span of time, to meet systemic challenges. It is also partly a result of the military–institutional imperative providing infrastructural facilities and support (barracks, logistical bases, training centres, airfields, defence industries etc.) for a military that had expanded more by accident than by design from 8,000 in 1966 to 170,000 by 1980 after extensive demobilization from the 272,000 level of 1972[8]. The determination of resource available for public purposes and the allocation of those resources to defence, domestic, and foreign policy objectives, therefore, cannot be sufficiently explained in Machiavellian categories as Adekson proffered.[9] Such a perspective may be elegant in its explanatory simplicity but hardly does justice to the complex array of issues involved. Rather, the fundamental issues of institutional policy have always focused on the problems of balancing the functional and societal imperatives – that is, the objective of developing a stable system of civil-military relations which will maximize defence or security at the least sacrifice of other social values. Samuel Huntington explains why:

> *The military institutions of any society are shaped by two forces: a functional imperative stemming from the threats to the society forces, ideologies and institutions dominant within the society. Military institutions which reflect only social values may be incapable of performing effectively their military function. On the other hand, it may be impossible to contain within society military institutions shaped purely by functional imperatives. The interaction of these two forces is the hub of the problem of civil-military relations. The degree to which they conflict depends upon the intensity of the security needs and the nature and strength of the value pattern of society[10].*

This functional conceptualization of the imperative of military institutional development notwithstanding, the negative impact of high defence expenditures on social and economic sectors cannot be minimized or ignored". The implication of this concern has been a rationalization which maximizes the utility of available resources without sacrificing either efficiency or competence. In other words, there has been a concrete trend under the Shagari administration and thereafter towards defence planning which sought to create a proper balance between recurrent budgetary expenditures (salaries and overhead costs of military personnel) and capital expenditures (on equipment, support systems, and R. & D schemes).

Thus, unlike the decade of the 1970s when, according to the former Chief of Army staff, Danjuma, only about 10 percent of the budget for the armed forces has been going on equipment while the remaining 90 percent is spent on salaries and emoluments of the personnels", legislative intervention during the Second Republic resulted in a significant diversion of funds for military hardware (N7 billion designated for the fiscal period of 1980-85, under the Fourth National Development Plan). This was possible no doubt largely as a result of the determined and extensive demobilization exercise conducted under the Muhammed/Obansanjo military administrations as the approved Federal Budgets on subsequent fiscal years suggest[12]. However, the commitment of the Nigerian Armed Forces to a major and protracted operational engagement in Liberia and Sierra Leone resulted in the 1990s in a parallel extra budgetary outlay for the defence under the syndrome of "security vote". Billions of dollars of unbudgeted funds were committed both by the Banbangida and Abacha regimes to peace – enforcement operations in both countries. The net outcome was the systemic neglect of infrastructural development, health, education, economic and welfare programme with attendant deepening crisis of mass poverty and unremitting inflationary scourge.

However, the extent to which the level of defence spending can be maintained in future will depend, first, on Nigeria's balance-of-payments positions, as it is affected especially by the volatility of the oil markets; and second, on the extent to which the present and future government is able to satisfy competing national demands; namely, social welfare and development plans for industrial expansion. These and related issues will constitute the subject of the final section below.

POLICY IMPLICATIONS

Since the production, maintenance, competing social and economic demands – especially in a developing polity such as Nigeria – set definite limits to decisions concerning the direction, and magnitude of effort in the defense sector. The opportunity costs of generating and employing the military, as Knorr has succinctly argued, equal the alternative uses of productive capacity (Labour, technology, natural resources, real capital – in the form of factories, power and dams, communications networks, investors of material, educational establishments, etc) that have been foregone[13]. The invariable reason is that defence policy (the relation of forces to national purposes) inescapably hinges on the structural decisions involving the procurement, allocation, and organization of the men, money and material which "go into the strategic units and uses of forces"[14]. In a condition of limited resources, especially in foreign exchange reserves, such an allocation invariably engenders fundamental conflicts between those purposes which relate to the achievement of security objectives and those which relate to achievement of domestic goals (economic development, inexpensive government, low taxation, political stability and social welfare)[15].

However, Knorr's position as elucidated above no doubt represents the conventional wisdom in defence analysis. As the literature debate in this "issue-area" indicates, the empirical analysis of the mutual relationship between defence and social welfare questions the assumption that expenditure on defence entails a net withdrawal of the corresponding amount of resources from circulation. The reason is, of course, that defence expenditure itself produces both beneficial (e.g., participation of the Nigerian Army Engineering Corps in "civil action' programmes and the development of local government areas) and detrimental effects upon the economy. Stephanie Newman has argued, for example, that 'despite the volume of writing on the subject, we still do not know whether there is a causal relationship between military expenditures and development, much less what the relationship is"[16]. In much the same manner, Gavin Kennedy noted that for the developing countries during the 1960s, "there was not obvious relationship between growth rates and percentage allocated to defence". Based on this observation, he further suggested instead that the relationship between military expenditures and economic growth will "depend upon circumstances and will not follow some general law applicable to all times and places"[17].

The controversy in the literature clearly reflects differences in epistemology, methodology, and ideology concerning the nature, decision and magnitude of impact of military expenditure on economic performance and whether it can be mitigated or compounded by government policies and socio-economic conditions. As one analyst has aptly noted, to tackle these questions one "needs dynamic analysis to determine temporal leads and lags, the reciprocal influences parameter"[18]. It is arguably in this context that the analytical challenge of a valid causal inference – "whether and how a change in defence spending causes a change in economic performance" can, if at all, be arrived at.

As a whole, while most analysis of the impact of defence expenditure on the economy in LDCS generally seem to corroborate Knorr's thesis stipulated above, there has nevertheless, been econometric analysis in the form of stepwise regression estimates for all the core variables based on 44 LDCS to produce a positive conclusion about the net impact of higher defence spending on the economies of the developing countries[19]. A closer examination of Benoit's study, however, reveals disturbing theoretical assumptions, methodological flaws and statistical discrepancies. For example, Nicole Ball argued that "the positive relationship found by Benoit between defence burden and economic growth could be spurious because economic growth could be caused instead by the inflow of all sorts of foreign resources in the aggregate"[20]

The tentative assumption and analytical position of this paper is unequivocally in the mainstream tradition. If increased effort is made to augment the fighting capability of national armed forces through higher defence spending in a comprador economy (such as Nigeria's) then the compression of civilian consumption, investment and non-military public expenditure would tend to be politically harder, especially with a population of over 100 million, and a phenomenal and menacingly high birth rate of approximately 3.7 per annum. The reason for this compression, as Ogbemi Omatete has observed, is that:

> *The military expenditure in a country where all the equipment is produced within that country and the personnel are trained within goes directly into the national economy. The expenditure circulates within the country, producing multiplier effects.. where the equipment is imported and most of the high – level personnel are trained in foreign countries, a high bulk of the military expenditure is outside the country... The Nigerian intellectuals maintain that such spending depletes the small foreign exchange needed for development and results in a negative multiplier effect.*[21]

In latent terms, however, the Nigerian economic base appears, at first glance, to be impressive and should be able to support a "well-equipped, mobile and virile defence force" without the concomitant risk of compromising basic development programmes. The country is endowed with a variety of industrial minerals and its agricultural potential is obvious from the number of years Nigeria relied on agriculture both for domestic consumption and export. Her energy base – oil, gas, coal and hydro-electric power – is abundant and potentially supportive of a vibrant industrial economy. In short, as Jean Herakovits observe, Nigeria appears to have "the economic base to classify as a significant regional power"[22]. Nevertheless this seemingly encouraging picture by itself is misleading for a number of reasons.

First, the transformation of national economic potential into usable resources is not an automatic process; it depends critically on interlocking administrative, scientific and technological skills; the sine qua non of modern industrial state which so far has eluded Nigeria's inept and hedonistic officialdom as a recent study by the United States Centre for strategic and International Studies (CSIS) conclude. These skills of labour and management are integral to any efficient and fruitful implementation of the series of aborted national development plans initiated in the country since independence in 1960. Administrative skills, for instance, is required in making the numerous and complex decisions concerning strategies and targets of industrialization. In Nigeria, as in other LDCS, the operative criteria for such planning are the need to diversify the economy and create an irreversible dynamics towards sefl-sufficiency in basic industrial sectors, thereby brearing the paralyzing cycle of dependence on external sources. Although for apost-colonial state like Nigeria, satisfying these criteria can be extremely difficult in a global capitalist environment, these problems have been undeniably compounded by organizational incompetence, the "cult of mediocrity", and petty – and large-scale graft, all of which have become the norm for government operation rather than as the occasional exception. This deep and ubiquitous problem in the Nigerian body politics may be considered the "most fundamental obstacle to national development (Onimode, 1985), as could be seen in the series of official investigations by the current National Assembly.

As a result, nothing short of a pervasive social transformation will suffice; "a wholesale metamporphosis of habits, money work; a wrenching reorientation of values concerning time, status, money, work; an unweaving and reweaving of the fabric of daily existence itself"[23]. These transformations are ultimately a function of how motivational resources are structured and managed. For such social reorientation to take place, a precondition must be the replacement of regimes based on a perpetuation of the status quo by alternative regimes "audacious enough to unleash social changes". This is all the more urgent in an elistist, and semi-feudal, social order such as exist in Nigeria, confronted as it is simultaneously with the horrendous problems of development within the context of ethnic fragmentation, political instability, explosion of communal violence and infrastructural collapse.

And second, a corollary of the preceding consideration is that Nigeria's low-level industrial capacity (especially in vital areas of machine production and related infrastructural system) has largely negated the substantive hearing of her economic potential on her capacity to maintain expensive defence system. However, this relatively fragile industrial base would have been less damaging to the effort currently underway to upgrade the conventional capability of the Nigerian armed forces if the huge spin-off in foreign exchange earnings from oil production had continued over time. As the cases of Libya, Saudi Arabia, Iraq and Iran (under the Shah) demonstrate, the balance-of-payment position and reserves of international liquidity (gold and foreign exchange) impinge on the defence potential of states, allowing for acquisition of massive offensive platforms without compromising social and welfare responsibilities.

The ability of a country to run a substantial import surplus – on the strength of either large holdings of foreign currencies and gold, or borrowing power – permits it, for a time at least, to accelerate the build up military strength accordingly. In this respect, the astronomical increase in Nigeria's foreign-exchange reserves from 1973 to 1981 as a result of the oil bonanza saw a step-level increase in defence expenditures. Conversely the traumatic decline in Nigeria's foreign exchange earning following world-wide recession and increased conservation especially in the West, plus the vigorous entry into Western markets of non-OPEC Oil producers such as Britain, Mexico and the Soviet Union, compelled a cutback on the five-year defence procurement plan valued at N6.4 billion adopted under the Shagari administration from 1982 to 1983.

One of the profound and inescapable consequences for Nigeria's defence policy of the above factors (frail socio-economic and technological base) has been a noticeable discrepancy between its foreign policy posture and actual behaviour in crisis situations. For Nigeria's underdeveloped and primarily "mono-cultural" economy the paralyzing effect of accelerated defence spending and protracted involvement in combat would have a catastrophic effect on its domestic programmes in the absence of remedial measures. Such measures might involve, inter alia, curtailing types of outlays such as merchandise imports, health, education, housing, agriculture, as was the case in Nigeria following the peace enforcement operations in Liberia and Sierra Leone.

However, the drastic alteration in the perceived threat to Nigeria's security – largely the function of traumatic civil war experiences and continental developments which shattered the naïve optimism of the immediate post independence era of the early 1960s – engendered unprecedented commitment to the qualitative and quantitative expansion of her military forces. This expansion marked and was in turn sustained by the incorporation of the West African subzone and the continent at large – especially Southern Africa – into Nigeria's vision of systemic security. This expansive and elemental reformulation of Nigeria's security environment, nevertheless, highlighted the incongruity between her declared policy goals and the operational ability of her defence institutions to provide the means for their actualization.

The magnitude of this mismatch between security aspirations and military capabilities is reflected in the huge disparity between extant and projected weapon systems level of the Nigerian armed forces on the one hand, and the balance of potential adversary forces in its security environment on the other[24]. Since at any given point in time, capabilities limit the range of choices which are available to decision-makers, this inadequacy in force strength neutralized to a great extent or provided limited military options for the kind of missions envisaged in the reformulation of Nigeria's security and foreign policy objectives alluded to above. The correction of this enervating condition constitutes the primary motivation of the armed forces modernization and augmentation programme that touches upon all elements of Nigerian military power. These include size and composition (in terms of balance or allocation of resources to the three military services, and within these services); quantity and performance of equipment sustained, active operations; mobilizable resources and productive capacity; leadership and doctrine; communications and control; military intelligence effectiveness; and manpower quality in terms of skill, training, physical stamina and morale. The operative criteria (as stipulated in official policy speeches) are the need to meet the capabilities of potentials adversaries and to economise resources. These entailed major spending on defence (largely unacknowledged through the mechanism fo "Security vote") which by the end of the Abubakar regime in May 1999 nearly pushed Nigeria to the brink of bankruptcy with an external reserve of barely 3.1 billion dollars. This alarming insolvency prompted defence policy adjustment by the Obasanjo administration in the period 1999 to 2007.

CONCLUSION

The nature and range of the armed forces modernization and augmentation programme highlited above necessarily required accelerated increase in defence spending in the 1970s through 1990s if the goals of policy are to be met. Although such a hike in defence appropriation and expenditure inevitably impact on resources available for other competing domestic programmes, the charge of self-aggrandisement of military power – elite by critics such as Adekson oversimplifies the issue.

The step-level increase in defence appropriation was rather partly a political resultant of a functional imperative stemming from the expansive redefinition of the perceived threat to Nigeria's security and the need to develop the institutional parameters to meet these challenges. It was also partly the need to provide support facilities (barracks, bases, training centres, airfields, etc). To sustain the phenomenal expansion of the armed forces from 8,000 in 1966 to 272,000 by the end of the civil war. The former consideration was particularly preeminent, as the determination of resource allocation to defence by any state inevitably hinges on the three perception and definition of the relevant strata of policy planners; and how the "threat – issue" is defined, for decision may well influence what the decision is. In the case of Nigeria, accelerating external military presence in the continent combined with pressures of decolonization and unrelenting military build up by the South African Reich, made the specification of options by Nigerian defence planners very risky, and rendered available choices quite unattractive in the "cold war era". The response to this adverse, complex and evolving dynamics in her security environment essentially thus required a magnitude of military effort by the Nigeria State.

However, the era of proactive military engagement (spanning the Babangida and Abacha period) also, initiated an unprecedented process of spending of public funds which certainly reinforced Adekson's earlier observation that "soldier – ruler often found themselves compelled by the logic of the situation to satisfy members of their profession with increased donatives and benefits, whatever the economic conditions prevailing in the wider society...." Thus, the politicisation of state structures and social exchange processes under Babangida and Abacha became painfully obvious in the appropriation and spending of oil sale surpluses of 12.1 billion dollars by the former and possessive individualism of the later which dollars by the former and possessive individualism of the later which exercised no restraint in the importation of military hardware were only symptomatic of deep structure of crisis in state management in Africa. As the CODESRIA Bulletin recently notes:

> The African State is changing and evolving in multiple directions, which are simultaneously contradictory and non-linear. These intricate disjunctures are articulated in the strategies of identity – formation, forms of social mobilization and new dynamics of exclusion that form part of the emergent dynamics of re-territorialisation in Africa. These recombinations arise from the decisive issue in contemporary Africa: the struggle over the appropriation of resources and over the control of spaces[25].

The politics of defence appropriation in the period from 1985 to May 1995 was essentially reflective of the pattern of military institutional domination of the state and society in Nigeria. This praetorian domination of the state may be characterized as "infection by, and the generalization of, practices whose criminal nature is clear whether according to the national juridical definitions and standards in force, or more particularly, according to the norms of international law and international organizations..."[26]. These include large scale graft at the highest level of leadership illegitimate and arbitrary uses of the coercive apparatuses of the state, the "proliferation of privatized means of violence such as specialized security forces" and the widespread violation of human and civil rights manifested in politically motivated and arbitrary killings, torture, disappearances, and illegal detentions". As Ogoh Alubo succinctly observes:

> Within this period Nigerians have been bled dry, not only by corruption or its less poignant appellation, mis-application, but also by the war, first in Liberia and now in Sierra Leone. No one is telling the people the human and material costs of this long drawn war. Strongly, when the minimum wage was reversed, the adduced reason was that the government could not afford it. No one is asking whether or not we can afford the war in Sierra Leone[27].

Alubo's observation underscore the fiscal subordination of contending social needs to military – institutional imperatives. The attendant consequences by the end of the military rule in Nigeria have been the legitimating of corruption, mass immiserization, stagflation, alienation, armed robbery, mounting external debt and periodic outbreak of social crisis as could be seen in the Niger-Delta vortex. How these systemic discharges are handled in the Fourth Republic will determine the trajectory of civil – military relations in Nigeria in the next millennium. Certainly at this historical conjuncture, the threat to the core and context – specific values of Nigeria is preeminent rooted in these multiple symptoms of underdevelopment (joblessness). This structural condition finds fiscal expression in the direction of public policy, if stability and the democratization process to prevail.

REFERENCES

1. C. Bassey "Nigeria's Quest for a Military – Industrial Complex Nigeria Journal of International Studies Vol. 12, 1988:46-55 and J. Peters, The Military and State in Nigeria. London Vantage, 1996.

2. I. Nzimiro, "Militarization in Nigeria: Its Economic and Social Consequences" International Social Journal, 35, 2, 1983:21-43.

3. A. Omede "National Defence Spending. An Analysis of High Military Expenditure (MILEX) in Nigeria". African Journal of International Affairs and Development Vol. 3 (1) 1998:55-68, B. Onimode, (1985): Imperialisation and Underdevelopment in Nigeria: the dialectics of mass poverty London: Zed. 1985

4. J. Adekanye Nigeria In Search of a Stable Civil-Military System: Boulder: Westview, 1981:55, AT. Aluko, I. The linkage between disarmament and Development" Nigerian Journal of International Affairs Vol. 8. No 1982:11-59, B. Arlinghaus, Military Development in Africa. Boulder: Westview, 1984.

5. Omede, Ibid:62.

6. R. Adesina, Reversal Victory, Ibadan: Heinemann, 2002.

7. Luckman, The Nigerian Military
8. Adekson, op.cit.
9. S. Huntington. The Soldier and State.
10. S. Deger: Military Expenditure in Third World Countries London: Rouledge; 1986; and Military Expenditure and Economic Development" World Bank Research Symposium on Military Expenditure. Washington DC: World Bank, 1990; and Deger, Saadet and Sommath Sen (1983): "Military Expenditure, spin-off and Economic Growth" Journal of Development Economics 13 (August - October): 67:83.
11. C. Bassey "Defence Planning and the Nigerian Armed Forces Modernisation process, 1970 – 1991: An Institutional Analysis" Armed Forces and Society 19, 2, 1993:253.
12. K.Knorr, The War Potential of Nations Westport: Greenwood, 1979. Also see H. Nelson Nigeria: A Country Study Washington: American University Press, 1982
13. S.Huntington, The Common Defence N. Y. Columbia University, 1966. see also T. Imobighe, Nigerian Defence and Security: Issues and Options for Policy. Kuru: NIPSSS, 1987.
14. S. Deger "Optimal control and Differential Game Models of Military Expenditure in Less Developed Countries" Journal of Economic Dynamics and Control 7, 1986 153-169
15. S. Newman, Defence Planning in Less-Industralised States. Lexington: D. C. Health; 1982.
16. G. Kennedy, The Economics of Defence, London: Faber and Faber; 1975; The Military in the Third World N. Y. Charles Scriber, 1974.
17. S. Chan "The Impact of Defence Spending on Economic Performance" Orbis 29 (Summer): 1985 403-434.
18. Benoit, Defence and Economic Growth in Developing Countries Lexington: Lexington Books, 1973. Growth and Defence in Developing Countries" Economic Development and Culture Change 26 (January)1978, 271-80; and M. Brzoka, and Wulf, H. (1979): "Rejoinder to Benoit's Growth and Defence in Developing Countries – Misleading Results and Questionable Methods" University of Hamburg, M. Mimeograph.
19. R. Dorfman, "A Comment on Professor Benoits Conundrum' International Development Review. 14, 1972: 10-12. Grobar, L. M. and Porter, R. C. Benoit Revisited: Defence Spending and Economic Growth in LDCs" *Journal of Conflict Resolution 33 (June) 1990 : 318 -343 and I. B.* Haruna, (1981): "Nigeria Military and Social Expenditure "The Punch" October: 3-5.
20. O. Omatete, "The Security of the Nigerian Nation: in J. Okpaku (ed.) Nigeria: Dilemma of Nationhood Estport: Greenwood; 1972.
21. Herskovits, "Deterline Nigeria: A back power" Foreign Policy, winter 1977/78 39-53; and M. Hobkirk, (1983): The Policies of Defence Budgeting. Washington, D. C. National University Press.
22. R. Heibroner, (1983): *The Great Ascent N. Y. Harper 1983.*

23. C. Bassey "Nigeria's Defence Policy in a future continental order". Nigerian Journal of International Affairs Vol. 13,1987:83-105; Also see M. Vogt and A. Ekoko, Nigerian Defence Policy. Lagos: Malthouse, 1990.
24. CODESRIA Bulletin, No. 2, 1998:29
25. Ibid:29
26. O. Alubo

CHAPTER 15

DEFENSE SPENDING, SAVINGS AND ECONOMIC DEVELOPMENT IN NIGERIA

MICHAEL O. NYONG

INTRODUCTION

Interests in defense economics by economists is of recent development. Previously, the subject was considered as peripheral to economics and falling within the mainstream of political science. It was felt that there are limited outlets for research in the field within the economics profession coupled with the fact that there are limited courses involving defense economics in most universities. Hence, there are few, if any mechanisms, to attract new people into the field.

But defense economics is far too important, particularly in developing countries, to be given so scant attention by economists. According to Intriligator defense economics is concerned with the overall economy including the level of defense spending , both in total or as a fraction of the entire economy as well as the effect of defense expenditure on output and employment. "The reason for the existence and size of the defence sector; the relation of defence spending and defence sector for international stability or instability[1]". Given the widespread presence of the military in government in developing countries, defence economics can no more be relegated to the background of mere scholastic interest by economists.

Recent interests in defence economics have focused on the effect of defence spending on output and employment. However, the results of these studies have been controversial and disquieting. Rothschild investigated the defence-development relationship using a sample of fourteen (14) OECD countries over the period 1956-69. His results led him to conclude cautiously that increased military spending tends to reduce export and to lower economic growth[2]. But Benoit using a correlation analysis involving growth rates, investment rates, foreign aid receipts and other variables, and a sample of forty–four (44) developing countries pertaining to the period 1950-65 produced unexpected results. The results led him to conclude that defence spending helps economic development. Specifically, he found that "countries with heavy defence burden generally had the most rapid rate of growth and those with the lowest defence burdens tended to show the lowest growth rate[3]". A previous study by Benoit also indicated positive effect of military burden on growth. Therefore, Benoit findings in 1978 reinforce his results of 1973[4].

The results by Benoit were confirmed four years latter in Frederickson and Looney. Using a sample of seventy-four (74) countries they found that defence spending helps economic growth in resource-rich LDCs. The results obtained by

Benoit, Frederickson and Looney were based on supply-side[5]. Harrod - Domar framework and for countries during the period 1965-74. But there are other empirical studies (to be reviewed shortly) which show that defence spending hurts economic development. Consequently, there are conflicting results from the various studies that have investigated the military spending- economic development nexus.

In an attempt to provide greater insights into the defense-development relationship, Biswas and Ram based on an augmented neoclassical growth model re-examined the studies done by Benoit, Frederickson and Looney (1982) and Lim, using a sample of fifty –eight (58) developing countries for the period 1960-70, and 1970-77. They found that military expenditure neither help nor hurt economic development in developing countries. They concluded that "one can have a positive or negative relationship by focusing on certain time periods, limiting the sample to countries with certain characteristics, or adopting certain types of specification alternatives"[6]

In a related research Deger re-examined Benoit results using a sample of 50 developing countries for the period 1965-73 and found evidence opposite to Benoit's results. Deger's study raises an important methodological issue that provides a serious challenge to previous studies that were based on single equation estimation approach. It recognizes the possibility of interrelationships among defense spending, growth and other intervening variables which must be taken into account before we can be certain whether an increase in defense spending will decrease (or increase) the growth rate of an economy.[7]

He explicitly considered the existence of multiple conduits by which defense spending affects economic development, the existence of intermediate effects and feedback's between defense burden and creation of new resources or between investment/ saving and growth that needs to be explored. He emphasized that once the direct and indirect effects are considered, "overall, military spending will reduce growth rate and retard economic development"[8]. Accordingly he suggested the adoption of simultaneous equations model in future studies to uncover and analyse the complex interrelationships that need to be explained.

In spite of the rich analytical insights provided by his study Deger's study suffers the basic defect as in those of others. Deger and others used cross sectional data. The assumption underlying cross sectional analysis is that the countries included are homogeneous. This may not be true. Countries differ in their levels of socio-political development, structure of growth –defence relationship, resource availability (i.e. resource rich as opposed to resource-constrained), and absorptive capacity. Thus, the lumping of these countries together as if they are homogenous may produce misleading results. The limitations of previous studies in this regard is the point of departure of this study.

The specific objectives of this study are to:

i.   To investigate the effect of defense burden on the average propensity to save;
ii. Determine whether military spending promote or hamper economic development;
iii. Determine the sensitivity of the result obtained into administrative regimes in Nigeria; and
iv. Identify the productivity of the defense sector, if any.

The rest of the study is organized as follows: Section II provides a brief discussion of defense spending and the military industrial complex in Nigeria. In section III we present analytical framework and methodology by which we identify the various channels by which defense spending affect economic growth as well as the model specification based on the underlying theory. Section IV provides the empirical results and analysis. We conclude the study in section V with a summary of the main results and some policy prescriptions.

II DEFENSE SPENDING AND NIGERIA'S MILITARY INDUSTRIAL COMPLEX

The main industry in Nigeria statutorily charged with the responsibility of manufacturing arms and ammunition is the Defense Industries Corporation of Nigeria (DICON). Established under the Defense Industries Corporation of Nigeria Act 1964 for the purpose of building and manufacturing arms and ammunition and other military-related products, it played a major role in the prosecution of the Nigeria-Biafra civil war 1966-1970. Thereafter, not much have been done to stimulate the industry for greater performance and realize its wider objectives. We shall return to this issue latter.

In 1981, the Shagari democratic civilian administration expressed government intention to reactivate the corporation to play an important role in the economy. It seems that the Shagari administrative regime 1979-1983 did little to position DICON on the path of greatness. DICON, as is the case with most state-owned enterprises (SOE) in Nigeria suffered neglect and underfunding. Adekanye noted that since its inception in 1965 DICON had been active only once. This was during the Nigeria-Biafra War when it assisted in the production of ammunition and explosives shells for the Nigerian army.[9]

The Eastern Nigerian (Biafran) army, on its part, relied extensively on local made arms, ammunition, bombs, landmines grenades and tanks. Local scientists and engineers were challenged to produce weapons of war to prosecute the war. Indeed, the defense industry in Eastern Nigeria made significant impact in the conflict. However, after the war in 1970, the military made no effort to translate the "Biafran" side into a dynamic postwar programme of research and development. To-date, DICON does not have an active R and D unit staffed with scientists, engineers, technologists, and economists.

However, various development plans have shown great interests in the expansion of the activities of DICON to meet commercial and industrial needs for tools, locks and keys as well as spare parts. The Third National Development Plan 1975-1980 directed attention of the DICON to the manufacturer of rifles, heavy weaponry and the establishment of factories for explosives, military uniforms, boots and heavy caliber ammunition. The Fourth National Development plan (1981-1985) extended the scope of DICON to include the manufacture of strategic weapons and equipment not only for the military but also for the police. Adekanye noted that government paid lip services to DICON but provided little funding to the corporation for its development.

For instance the yearly capital expenditure of DICON between 1975 and 1980 was only N25.7 million or about three-quarters less than the total investment initially earmarked for DICON projects under the Third National Development Plan. Adekanye also observed that much of DICON's actual capital outlays, as with those of many other Federal government agencies, tended to be used for the purchase of office equipments, including furniture, staff accommodations -cum -comfort, and new official cars, rather than devoted to serious domestic arms production purpose"[10]. There is renewed interest in the reactivation of DICON's a defense industry. Recently, DICON in addition to production of hand-pumps and furniture and other related civilian products has begun to produce AK-47 rifles.

Over the years government expenditure on defense has been on the increase in absolute terms. Defence spending is set to rise in Nigeria as the government pursues a transformation project aimed at improving professionalism within the military and expanding the country's role in international peace operations. Spending on equipment and training will rise in the coming years as the government comes under increasing pressure to enhance its defence capabilities by the international community in terms of both improving capacity for international and regional peace operations, and to provide greater security for international oil interests in the Niger Delta region. Budgetary allocations for the army, navy and air force reflect the new emphasis on improving, training, living and working conditions of members of all three forces, especially the army. The far greater allocation to the army reflects not only the country's overwhelming reliance on the army for both internal and international deployments, but also the targeting of the army for professionalisation due to it being historically highly politicised. The army is likewise facing an ongoing domestic deployment to the oil-rich Niger Delta, in the south of the country, due to persistent insecurity in the region.

Under military rule, actual Nigerian defense expenditure tends to outstrip allocations due to supplementary allocations. Under civilian rule, governments have not necessarily been able to deliver on budgetary allocations.

TABLE 1: DEFENSE SPENDING AND
SELECTED MACROECONOMIC AGGREGATES

YEAR	DEFENSE N m	GOV N m	GDP Nm	DEF/ GDP	DEF/ GOV	REGIME	Saving Rate
1961	26.8	170.0	2,378	1.13	15.76	CDR	5.27
1962	34.3	168.0	2,516	1.36	20.42	CDR	7.64
1963	33.4	183.0	2,946	1.13	18.25	CDR	9.96
1964	45.8	218.0	3,145	1.46	21.01	CDR	11.55
1965	48.0	236.4	3,361	1.43	20.30	CDR	14.84
1966	48.0	255.1	3,614	1.33	18.82	MR	13.56
1967	71.8	258.0	2,950	2.43	27.83	MR	10.53
1968	159.3	350.0	2,878	5.54	45.51	MR	9.53
1969	191.15	556.2	3,851	4.96	34.37	MR	9.81
1970	603.27	1,130.0	5,621	10.73	53.39	MR	6.21
1971	601.9	1,092.4	7,098	8.48	55.10	MR	16.12
1972	701.25	1,863.7	7,703	9.10	37.63	MR	13.4
1973	801.75	1,778.8	10,991	7.29	45.07	MR	20.7
1974	955.6	4,260.1	18,811	5.08	22.43	MR	28.2
1975	522.2	8,258.3	21,779	2.40	6.32	MR	25.8
1976	864.4	9,701.5	27,572	3.14	8.91	MR	28.31
1977	777.9	11,695.3	32,520	2.39	6.65	MR	18.78
1978	716.3	12,337.1	35,540	2.02	5.81	MR	24.11
1979	493.5	13,191.4	43,151	1.14	3.74	MR	12.7
1980	781	23,695.7	49,755	1.57	3.30	CDR	27.3
1981	821	21,238.8	56,602	1.45	3.87	CDR	15.2
1982	745	15,368.2	60,483	1.23	4.85	CDR	11.4
1983	736	11,525.0	63,293	1.16	6.39	CDR	10.3
1984	607	11,686.4	69,950	0.87	5.19	MR	10.9
1985	688	14,828.8	78,776	0.87	4.64	MR	8.7
1986	951	16,773.7	79,704	1.19	5.67	MR	4.3
1987	737	22,018.7	108,885	0.68	3.35	MR	3.28
1988	1,101	27,749.5	145,243	0.76	3.97	MR	9.6
1989	1,081	41,028.3	224,797	0.48	2.63	MR	26.74
1990	1,607	60,268.2	260,637	0.62	2.67	MR	28.85
1991	2,245	66,584.4	324,010	0.69	3.37	MR	22.41
1992	2,706	92,797.4	549,809	0.49	2.92	MR	13.36
1993	4,171	191,229	697,095	0.60	2.18	MR	6.37
1994	5,492	160893	914,900	0.60	3.41	MR	9
1995	7,375	248,768	1,977,700	0.37	2.96	MR	8.7

1996	14,196	337,218	2,823,900	0.50	4.21	MR	4.05
1997	15,428	428,220	2,939,500	0.52	3.60	MR	7.33
1998	21,279	487,110	2,837,000	0.75	4.37	MR	12.5
1999	32,947	947,690	4,780,000	0.69	3.48	CDR	19.72
2000	40,074	701,000	6,850,000	0.59	5.72	CDR	29.73
2001	63,472	1,018,000	7,055,000	0.90	6.23	CDR	10.5
2002	108,148	1,018,200	7,984,000	1.35	10.62	CDR	7.27
2003	61,724	1,226,000	10,136,000	0.61	5.03	CDR	5.4
2004	76,057	1,426,000	11,674,000	0.65	5.33	CDR	11.9
2005	111,868	1,822,000	14,325,000	0.78	6.14	CDR	12.4
2006	98,360	1,938,000	18,223,000	0.54	5.08	CDR	18.7
2007	121,146	2,450,900	20,558,000	0.59	4.94	CDR	16.4
2008	111,011	3,241,000	23,842,000	0.47	3.43	CDR	17.0

Table 1 indicates trends in military expenditure and defense burdens between 1961 and 2008. *Notes: Defense is military expenditure (million naira); Gov relates to government total expenditure in million Naira; DEF/GOV is ratio of military expenditure (recurrent and capital) to total government expenditure (%); DEF/GDP is ratio of military spending to GDP in percentages or military burden; REG is regime type while CDR is civilian democratic regime while MR is military regime indicating periods when each is in control of government; GNSY is national saving rate in percentages.*

Sources: i) CBN Economic and Financial Review (1970); ii) CBN Annual Report 1977; iii) CBN Statistical Bulletin 1995 and 2008; iv) CBN Annual Report 1995 and 2007; v) IMF International Financial Statistics *Year* book 1988, 1999; vi) World Bank: African Economic Indicators (various years).

The picture that emerges is that defense burden measured by defense spending to GDP ratio increased dramatically during the civil war period 1967-1970 when it attained the highest rate of 10.73 percent in 1970. Thereafter, military burden was on a decline falling to 1.14 percent in 1979 when the military handed power over to the civilian government headed by Shehu Shagari. Military burden rose from 1.14 percent in 1979 to 1.57 percent in 1980 under the civilian administration but fell to 0.87 percent in 1984 during the military regime of Buhari/Idiagbon which overthrew the civilian democratic government of Shagari.

There was a marginal increase in defense burden from 0.87 percent in 1984 to 1.19 percent in 1986 during the Babangida military regime which overthrew the Buhari/Idiagbon regime in a swift military counter-coup d' Etat. The military government reduced the military burden to 0.48 percent in 1989. The Babangida military administration thereafter maintained a low defense burden at 0.60 percent or lower. Between 1994 and 1998 (the Abacha military regime) and 1998/1999 (the Abubakar military regime) the defense burden stayed below 0.80 percent. A low military burden was still maintained by the civilian democratic government that took over government from June 1999 such that by 2008 military burden has fallen to a mere 0.47 percent of GDP which is about a third of its 1986 value.

From the results in the Table we find that increases and declines in military burden cut across both military and civilian regimes. There is no definite pattern in the trends in military burden with respect to civilian democratic administration or military regimes. This is further illustrated in Figure 2.1.

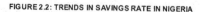

FIGURE 2.1. TRENDS IN THE SIZE OF MILITARY BURDEN (DEF/GDP) IN NIGERIA 1961 - 2008

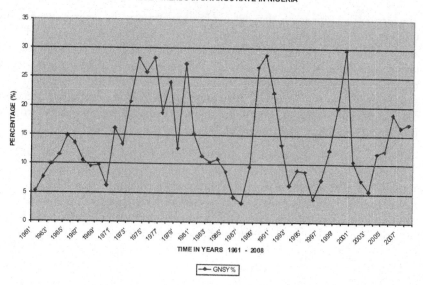

FIGURE 2.2: TRENDS IN SAVINGS RATE IN NIGERIA

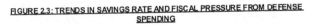

FIGURE 2.3: TRENDS IN SAVINGS RATE AND FISCAL PRESSURE FROM DEFENSE SPENDING

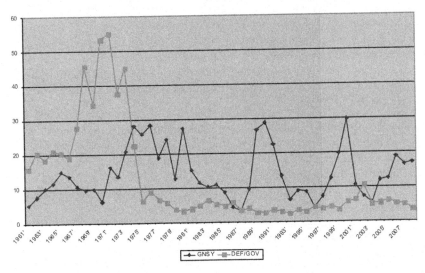

From Figure 1 we fine that military burden rose to all time high value of 10.73 in 1970 and fell drastically in the 1990s. The fall in 1990s is rather surprising given the involvement of the country in the Liberian conflict under the umbrella of ECOMOG and in the Bakassi Peninsular in the dispute with Cameroon. Perhaps, this surprising result is either a result of weaknesses in our database or absence of transparency and accountability on the part of the regime in power. There is strong reason to believe that both are applicable. It is possible that military spending takes place outside the national budget beyond the scrutiny of Nigerians. The penchant for extra budgetary allocations for which the Babangida administration (1985-1993) was notoriously famous is a case in point. Without the integration of such allocations into the budget there is no way of knowing how much was spent and on what. Both the World Bank and the International Monetary Fund have on several occasions advised the government on the need to eliminate extra-budgetary allocations or integrate all government projected expenditures and revenues into the budget. This aspect of accountability and transparency in government transaction cannot be over emphasized given the need to drive towards good governance in Nigeria.

Turning now to the savings rate we fine that there seems to be an inverse relationship between the average propensity to save and military burden. For instance in 1965 when the military burden was only 1.43 percent the average propensity to save was as high as 14.84 percent. In 1970 when military burden rose to 10.73 percent the average propensity to save fell to 6.21 percent, which is less than half its 1965 value. However, the results obtained are on the basis of casual empiricism which cannot be relied on for policy purposes. A more systematic and rigorous analysis is provided in section IV.

With respect to defense spending relative to total expenditure, Table 1 (column 6) shows that substantial investment was made in defense sector during the civil war years. With 18.82 percent in 1966 it rose to 55.1 percent of total government expenditure in 1971 . Since then it has been below 9 percent of government expenditure up to 2001. Besides the slight increase to 10.62 percent in 2002, defense spending as a proportion of total government expenditure thereafter had been minimal, less than 6.2 percent of total government expenditure. Defense spending as a proportion of total government expenditure attained the lowest value at 2.18 percent in 1993.

In the next section we provide the analytical methodology in our analysis of the interrelationship among defense spending, savings and economic development in order to unravel the various channels by which defense spending impact economic development. The approach, hopefully, will provide us with richer and better insights on the detrimental or beneficial effect of defense spending on economic development.

III THEORETICAL FRAMEWORK AND METHODOLOGY

There are four main channels by which defense burden can influence growth or development. These include stimulation of aggregate demand, spin-off, diversion of resources away from potential civilian investment, and creation of new savings. On creation of additional demand, exponents of beneficial effect of military spending on growth have argued that a rise in military spending on goods and services may lead to an increase in aggregate demand, thereby 'exerting a Keynesian impact on the growth rate by inducing a rise in capacity utilization.[11] The increase in capacity utilization may also lead to greater employment of labour. An increase in demand that leads to more efficient capacity utilization may lead to a rise in profit rate and to increased investment and ultimately to faster growth.

The economic spin-off of defense spending has many ramifications. The argument is that the military through R & D may foster faster technological progress which affects civilian economy indirectly. Other direct and indirect spin-offs include provision of technical skills, educational training and medical care, and creation of infrastructure, all which are beneficial to economic development. Military training contributes to improving the educational level and discipline of the labour force and hence acts as a stabilizing force. Thompson submits that military expenditure can be economically productive to the extent that it enhances national security and improves the enforcement of property rights which encourage private investment and growth[12].

Moreover, in an underdeveloped country, the military remains the most modern institutions. They help create the sociopolitical structure conducive to growth by destroying questionable acceptance of local customs and tradition and substituting national for a local, ethnic, or tribal consciousness. The allocation of resources away from more productive investments has generated much debate. While agreeing that defense burden may have detrimental effects on economic growth because military expenditures may divert resources away from productive civilian investment, Benoit and other exponents of the beneficial effect of military spending on growth and development argue that the negative impact is more than compensated by such positive effects as stimulation of demand, modernization of the economy, efficient organization of production, and increased availability of foreign resources.[13]

To back up this claim, Benoit further submits that if a developing country spends less on defense, it does not mean that the shortage will be spent on more investment. Rather, the additional resources released by decline in military expenditure may be frittered on non-productive expenditure such as extravagant consumption, or imported luxurious goods.[14] In studies by Benoit, Kennedy, Benoit who tested the relationship between defense spending and economic development, they generally arrived at results which show that military spending helps development[15]. A recent study by Ferda indicate results that were in agreement with Benoit. Ferda examined the defense expenditure –economic development nexus for the case of Turkey for the period 1950 -2002 using multivariate cointegration analysis. His results show that there exists a positive and stable long-run relationship between defense spending and economic development in Turkey.[16]

However, there is counter view that defense spending hampers economic development, and that an important consequence of defense spending is its indirect effect on the savings rate or saving-income ratio and hence investment spending particularly in developing countries. In such countries an increase in defense spending may lead to reduction in expenditure in health, education, water, electricity, transportation, and communication. This may lead to corresponding increase in private sector spending on these items. But since income is inelastic, aggregate consumption expenditure increases, and more is spent on education, health care services, transportation etc., all of which significantly increases consumption. This means a reduction in the national saving ratio and hence in investment. This point is extremely important in developing countries where majority of the people are already living on subsistence level. For this group of people, a reduction in government expenditure on social services will force them to "reduce their meager savings in order to finance current expenditure".[17]

The debate on the effect of defense spending on economic growth and development is far from settled. Rothschild, Deger, Deger and Smith, Faini et al, Deger and Sen, Frederickson and Looney, Lim, Deger, Biswas and Ram indicate negative relationship. These studies indicate that defense spending hinder economic growth in the sense of slowing down the development process.[18]

First, they argued that in less developed countries, the military industrial complex is almost non existent. This means that equipments, machinery and ammunition among others have to be imported rather than manufactured locally, thereby worsening the balance of payments problems and reducing the multiplier effect on employment generation.

Secondly, they maintain that defense spending crowds out private sector investments and leads to slower growth. Defense spending, by diverting resources away from civilian uses, reduces the level of resources available for private sector investment, and enlarges the savings-investment gap with adverse effect on economic development. They insist that military spending is not governed by any market processes. Hence it tends to be distortionary resulting in deadweight loss to total productive capacity and to negative externalities on capacity output. These include military procurement preferences for certain companies and industries, and the existence of rent seeking activities around the military because of the noncompetitiveness in allocation of resources.

Perhaps, far more illuminating is the study by Kentor and Kick. Using a cross sectional regressional analysis of 71 countries from 1990 to 1997, they found that military spending hampers economic development by slowing the expansion of the labour force because of the capital intensive nature of the military organization. They insist that the relatively capital intensive military organization limit the entry opportunities for the unskilled and under- or unemployed people for whom a more labour intensive military had previously provided a pathway for upward mobility.[19]

From the foregoing controversy on the empirical and theoretical findings, our model used to test the relationship between defense spending and economic development consists of three interdependent equations, the economic development equation (GPCI, equation 1), the savings equation (SY, equation 2) and the defense spending equation (MB, equation 3). The economic development equation is specified as a function of military burden (MB, and one period lagged value of MB), savings rate (SY, and one period lagged value of SY), and growth in the exports (GEXP). In Nigeria, exports constitute an important factor in development process. All the variable in the growth equation are expected to be positive. However the military burden variable may carry a negative sign in line with the theoretical controversy discussed earlier.

The savings equation is specified as a function of defense burden, economic growth, dependency burden (DPEN), inflation (INFLA), and foreign capital inflow as a percentage of GDP (FAY). This specification also takes into consideration the Coale-Hoover hypothesis, and the life cycle hypothesis[20]. The inclusion of military burden in the saving equation captures "the mobilization or resource creation effect, by which the increase in militarism may increase or decrease the available resources of the economy"[21.], Deger also noted that while inflation may lead to forced savings, and an increase supply of new resources induced by high prices or rise in profitability may lead to higher investment, it is also possible that the expectations of continued inflation might cause spending spree, lead to conspicuous consumption, and investment in low priority sectors that have little growth potential. Fontanel showed that for Morocco, military spending depresses growth through the inflationary process it generates.[22]

Thus, in the savings equation, economic growth is expected to enter with a positive sign, but military burden may carry positive or negative signs. Foreign capital inflow may also carry positive or negative sign in line with the theoretical controversy on the effect of foreign capital inflow on savings in developing countries. However, inflation and dependency burden are expected to carry negative signs.

For the military burden equation, the factors hypothesized to influence the defense spending in equation 3 include War, or the involvement in wars against neighbors, the type of administrative regime in place (military or civilian), the level of per capital income (PCI), and government size (GOVY, i.e. government expenditure as a proportion of GDP). Since defense is a public good, it should be influenced by government expenditure.

The specification of our model is as follows:

$$GPCI_t = \alpha_0 + \alpha_1 MB_t + \alpha_2 MB_{t-1} + \alpha_3 SY_t + \alpha_4 GEXP + u_{1t} \quad \ldots\ldots\ldots\ldots 1$$

$$SY_t = \beta_0 + \beta_1 GPCI_t + \beta_2 MB_t + \beta_3 MB_{t-1} + \beta_4 INFLA_t$$
$$+ \beta_5 FAY_t + \beta_6 DPEN_t + \mu_{2t} \quad \ldots\ldots \quad \ldots\ldots\ldots 2$$

$$MB_t = \pi_0 + \pi_1 SY_t + \pi_2 GPCI_t + \pi_3 GOVY_t + \pi_4 WAR_t + \pi_5 REGIME_t + u_{3t} \ldots.3$$

where $GPCI_t$ = Growth rate of real GDP per capita at time used as proxy for economy development;

MB_t = Defense burden at time defined as the ratio of military expenditure (both recurrent and capital) to GDP; MB_{t-1} = one lagged value of MB_t;

SY_t = Savings-income ratio at time t indicating the resources available to the economy;

$GEXP_t$ = growth rate of export in time t;

$INFLA_t$ = Rate of inflation at time t;

FAY_t = Foreign capital inflow at time t a percentage of GDP;

$DPEN_t$ = Dependency burden at time t or ratio of population aged 0-14 years and 65 years and above to the population; WAR_t = dummy variable taking value of 1 when war occurs and otherwise;

$REGIME$ = Dummy variable with value 1 for military administration and 0 for civilian administration;

$LPCI_t$ = Logarithm of per capita income at t;

$GOVY_t$ = Government size at time t measured by government expenditure to GDP. The u_{it}, i=1.2, 3, are the stochastic error terms with the usual properties. In the empirical implementation of the study we use the change of the log of per capita GDP (LPCGDP or LPCI) as a proxy for economic development.

DATA SOURCES, LIMITATIONS AND ESTIMATION

Data were collected from various publications of the Federal Office of Statistics, CBN Annual Reports (Various issues), CBN Statistical Bulletin (various issues including the 2008 edition), IMF International Financial Statistics Yearbook (various issues) and African Development Indicators (various issues). One of the most difficult problems in less developed countries is the reliability of the data, an issue we have earlier identified. Pertaining to data on defense spending it is possible that official data cover only part of actual military spending. Important items can be hidden under non-military budget headings or may have even been financed entirely outside the government budget. These limitations should be borne in mind as we present the results.

Two-stage least squares method was used in estimating the parameters. The advantage of two-stage least squares is the fact that we need not know the mathematical formulation of the whole system of interdependent equations in detail, but we must have a knowledge of all the exogenous variables.[23]

We use the term economic development and economic growth interchangeably. However, the two terms are not exactly the same. While economic growth is possible without development it is not a sufficient condition for development. However development is not possible without economic growth. Thus, growth is a necessary but not sufficient condition for development. Development involves change in attitude and customs together with structural transformation of the economy. It involves three components. First, life sustenance or provision of adequate food and clothing, housing, health and education. Second, self esteem or self respect and independence. Third, freedom or freedom from want, ignorance and squalor. The three components are interrelated. Economic growth of its part refers to sustained increase in real per capita GDP[24]. This limitation should be borne in mind as we interpret and analyze the results. Absence of self-esteem and freedom result from low levels of life sustenance. But a lack of self-esteem and economic imprisonment are the link in a circular, self-perpetuating chain of poverty by producing what Galbraith calls the "accommodation of poverty"[25]

IV EMPIRICAL RESULTS AND ANALYSIS

The empirical results are presented in Table 4.1 and Figure 4.1. In Table 4.1, the t-values, the standard errors of the regression and p-values are included as well as standard errors of the regression (SER) and Durbin Watson statistic (DW). In the development equation all the variables are statistically insignificant at conventional levels except the saving rate variable which is statistically significant at better than 2 percent level and have expected signs. Increase in the mobilization of savings may lead to higher level of economic development in Nigeria through its canalization into productive investment. However, military burden, both in current and previous year have no statistically significant effect on economic development in Nigeria. The results for Nigeria are consistent with those of Biswas and Ram who found that military expenditure neither help nor hurt economic development in developing countries.[26]

TABLE 4.1: PARAMETER ESTIMATES AND RELATED STATISTICS

	Coefficient	Std. Error	t-Statistic	Prob.
Estimation Method: Two-Stage Least Squares				
Sample: 1962 2008				
Total system (balanced) observations 141				
Instruments: MB(-1) GEXP DPEN INFLA GOVY WAR REGIME C				
Economic Development Equation = Equation 1				
Constant	5.576208	0.536878	10.38636	0.0000
MB	-0.196462	0.190747	-1.029963	0.3050
MB(-1)	0.134528	0.183273	0.734029	0.4643
SY	0.090858	0.038223	2.377064	0.0190
GEXP	0.000213	0.001758	0.121170	0.9038
	SER=0.797	DW=1.025		
2. Saving Equation				
Constant	-73.87842	41.28505	-1.789472	0.0760
LPCI	7.643620	2.880718	2.653373	0.0090
MB	-0.478397	1.832655	-0.261040	0.7945
MB(-1)	0.572795	1.661536	0.344738	0.7309
INFLA	-0.131803	0.075816	-1.738450	0.0846
DPEN	0.798558	0.641477	1.244874	0.2155
	SER=7.038	DW=1.027		
3. Defense Burden or Military Spending Equation				
Constant	-0.004448	0.139114	-0.031973	0.9745
SY	-1.982315	0.200046	-9.909275	0.0000
LPCI	0.116148	0.064203	1.809088	0.0729
GOVY	0.769932	0.745179	1.033218	0.3035
WAR	-0.423110	0.581149	-0.728056	0.4680
MB(-1)	0.872701	0.143722	6.072149	0.0000
Determinant residual covariance	2.314160	SER=1.285	DW=2.22	

In the savings equation the results indicate that neither current defense burden nor its previous year value has any statistically significant effect on savings. Thus, defense burden neither affects savings nor economic development in Nigeria. The results also show that per capita income makes positive contribution to savings in Nigeria. The higher the level of per capita income, the higher the savings likely to be mobilized. Inflation, on the other hand, has a negative coefficient in the savings equation. The results show that an increase in inflation rate by 1 percent may lead to a fall in savings rate by 0.13 percent, all things remaining the same.

Turning now to the determinants of defense spending we find that neither war nor regime type exerts any statistically significant effect on defense spending as to be expected by visual inspection of the data. We found that for the defense spending equation, the critically important determinants are the savings rate (SY) and government size (GOVY). While higher saving rate may lead to decline in military burden, higher per capita income may lead to higher defense burden. Specifically, the empirical results indicate that an increase in per capita income by 1 percent may lead to increased military burden by 0.116 percent, all things remaining the same. The income variable was significant at better than 7.5 percent level.

Overall, the estimated economic development equation is well determined and provides a good tracking performance with respect to the underlying trend of economic development in Nigeria. Figure 4.1 indicates the forecasting power of the growth equation. Although the tracking ability is low in the 1960s, it performance improves progressively with time. The root mean squared error (rmse) and the Thiel inequality coefficient are low and reasonable. The distribution of the residual errors as shown in Figure 4.2 indicate that they are mean riveting and hence that the residual errors from the regression are integrated of order 1 (0).

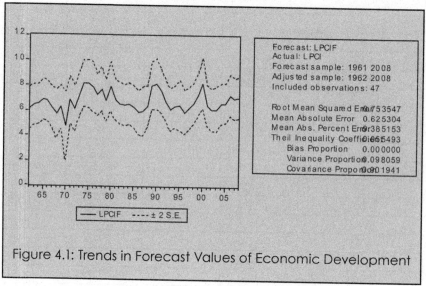

Figure 4.1: Trends in Forecast Values of Economic Development

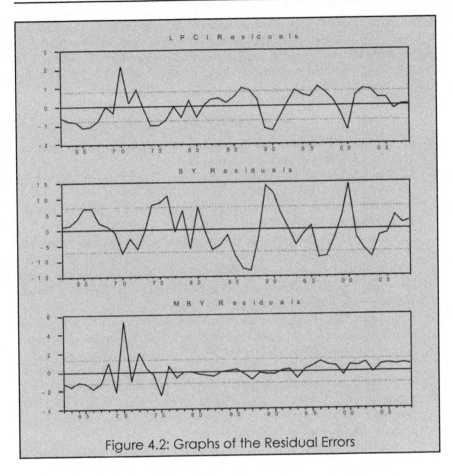

Figure 4.2: Graphs of the Residual Errors

V CONCLUDING REMARKS

The objectives of this study have been to investigate the effect of defense spending on the average propensity to save, determine whether military burden hamper or promote economic development, assess the sensitivity of the results to administrative regimes in Nigeria and lastly identify the productivity of the defense sector in Nigeria. Our results show that the effect of military spending on average propensity to save is weak and statistically insignificant. Military burden neither hampers nor promote economic development in Nigeria. This goes against the findings by Benoit and others with respect to the positive effect of defense burden on growth in developing countries. The evidence that increase in defense spending will raise the level of economic development does not exist as at now given the low level development of the military industrial complex reflected in the role of DICON in the Nigerian economy.

Defense burden is not sensitive to administrative regimes in Nigeria. In our regression results, the administrative regime variable was not statistically significant, and was deleted in the reported result. The significance of the regime type variable is further confirmed by an inspection of the defense expenditure and military burden in Nigeria across the two regime (military and civilian democratic regimes) as seen in Table 1. There is no definite pattern in military burden across the various regimes in Nigeria.

REFERENCES

1. M. Intrilligator, D. Econometric Models, Techniques and Applications. Prentice-Hall, Inc., Englewood Cliffs, New Jersey, 1978.

2. K. Rothschild: "Military Expenditure, exports and Growth" *Kyklos* 26 (December), 1977 pp.804 -13.

3. E. Beniot, Growth and Defence in Development Countries" *Economic Development and Cultural Change* 26 (January) 1978 pp.271-80.

4. E. Beniot, Defence and Economic growth in Developing Countries. *(Boston: D. C. health & Co) 1973)*.

5. P. Frederick and Robert Looney (1982): "Defense Expenditures and Economic Growth in Developing Countries: Some Further Empirical Evidence" *Journal of Economic Development* 7 (July) pp. 113 – 26.

6. B. Biswas and Rati Ram" Military Expenditure and Economic Growth in Less Developed Countries: An Augmented Model axed Further Evidence" *Economic Development and Cultural Change* Vol. 34, No. 2 (January) 1986pp.361-372.

7. S. Degar, Economic Development and Defence Expenditure" *Economic Development and Cultural Change* vol. 35, No. 1 (October)1986 pp. 180-196

8. Fatini, Ricardo, Patricia Annez, and Lance Taylor (1984):" Defense spending, Economic Structure, and Growth: Evidence among Countries and Over Time" *Economic Development and Cultural Change* 32 (April), pp.487-98.

9. B. Adekanye, Domestic Production of Arms and the Defense Industries Corporation of Nigeria" *Current Research on Peace and Violence* 4 1983 pp. 258-269.

10. Ibid: 261

11. M. Knight, Norman Loazyza and Delano Villanueva (1996): "The Peace Dividend: Military Spending Cuts Economic growth" *IMF Staff Papers* Vol. 43, No. 1 (March), pp.1-37.

12. Thompson

13. Ibid:26

14. Benoit, (1978) op. cit. 276.

15. Kennedy, The Military in the Third World. (Duckworth), 1974.

16. H. Ferda, Defense Spending and Economic Growth in Turkey: An Empirical Application of New Macroeconomic Theory", *Review of Middle East Economics and Finance* Vol. 2, No. 3. 2007.

17. A.Koutsoyiannis: Theory of Econometrice. Second edition, 1985 and D. Lim, David "Another Look at growth and Defense in Less Developed Countries" *Economic development and Cultural Change* 31 (January), 1983 pp.377-84.

18. Smith," Military Expenditure and Capitalism" *Cambridge Journal of Economics* (March) 1970 pp.61-76.

19. J. Kentor and Kick, E. "Military Spending and Economic Development: A New Perspective", paper presented at the annual meeting of the American Sociological Association, Marriott Hotel, Loews Philadelphia Hotel,Philadelphia,on linehttp:/www.allacademic.com/meta/ p23123_index.html, 2005

20. Nyong, M.O. (1996a): "Population Growth, Savings Rate and Economic Development in Nigeria" *Research Report submitted to Union for African Population Studies (UAPS)*, Dakar, Senegal.

Nyong, "Saving Mobilization"Saving Mobilization for capital Formation and Growth in Africa: The Case of Nigeria" Research Report submitted to International Centre for Economic Growth (ICEG), California, USA, 1996, Nyong, "The Dynamics of Savings in a Deregulated Economy Some Theoretical and Empirical Extension" *NDIC Quarterly* (1996).

21. S. Degar op. cit: 191

22. J. Fontanel, Military Expenditure and Economic Growth (France, Morocco)" (report written for the United Nations) 1982.

23. M. Intrilligator op. cit: 66

24. A.Thirwall, A.P. (1983): growth and development with Special Reference to Developing Economics. ELBS. MacMillan.

25. J. Galbraith, (1980): The Nature of Mass Poverty. Penguin. Intriligator, Michael D. (1990):"On the Nature and Scope of Defense Economics Defense Economics", vol.1, pp. 3-11

26. Biswas and Ram op. cit.

CHAPTER 16

DEFENCE INDUSTRIAL DEVELOPMENT: THE CHALLENGES OF DICON

CELESTINE BASSEY

National Self-defence is too important to be subjected to the whims and caprices of foreign States.[1] **Col. Oduwole**

An army always resembles the country from which it is raised and of which it is the expresion.[2] **A. Aron.**

One of the bitter and unforgettable lessons of the Nigerian civil war, 1966-1970, was the inexorable realisation that as a state whose military power critically depends on externally acquired weapons systems, Nigeria cannot exercise independent initiative on matters relating to war and peace as suppliers retain veto power through their ability to withhold essential hardwares. The correction of this enervating condition constitutes the primary motivation of the modernization and augmentation programme that touches upon all elements of Nigerian military power, particularly in relation to the development of one of the critical foundations of national military power, namely the local "military-industrial complex".

Thus, the current transitional plannig in the defence sector involves a projected endeavour towards the expansion of the Defence Industries Corportions of Nigeria (DICON) through a combination of indigenous research and development of appropriate/intermediate military technology and collaborative and licensing agreements on basic weapon systems production with foreign agencies operating in the country. The "goal-oriented guidance", as stipulated by the former Defence Minister in the Second Republic, has been the imperative necessity to "reduce and eventually eliminate our dependence on foreign manufacturers and suppliers of military weapons and equipment."[3]

The palpably limited publications in this crucial issue-area of Nigeria's defence planning process have so far focused on either official pronouncements or sought to describe the characteristics and products of current defence related industries in the country. Beyond these descriptions of motivation and inventory of present infrastructural base of Nigeria's nascent "Military Industrial complex", however, the vital question" (for short and long-term planning and projection) is inescapably thus: is Nigeria capable of sustaining large and diversifed military industries as official policy pronouncements invariably assume?.

Utilising statistical data from the comparative experience of other "Third World" countries concerning intermediate rather than advanced or lead-edge technology, this paper argues (with some qualification) in the affirmative. Nigeria seemingly possesses the combination of socio-economic preconditions for a viable military industry. This contention is generally consistent with findings which establish a significant correlation between factors of scale and military-industrial production. However, before delving into the core-complex of this issue, the first section below establishes the analytical context of the defence policy planning objectives within which the debate on the feasibility of military-industrial complex in Nigeria can be readily comprehended.

CONTEXT: DEFENCE EXEGESIS

The ability of any national armed forces to provide a military underpinning to a country's defence and foreign policy objectives depends crucially, among other things, on the nature of the instrument, as it is driven by changing technology: the weapons and the support systems of war. It is in this regard that in the 1980s, if not in the 1970s (largely because of the immediate and pressing problems of providing accomodation and the retrenchment exercise) that material decisions concerning the procurement and distribution of major weapons system (such as ship, aircraft, and tank) and weapons (missile, gun, and torpedo) to the Nigerian armed forces became the centerpiece of the modernisation scheme.

However, under the conditions created by the configurations of international power (dominated by two major military blocs of NATO and Warsaw Pact), the successful exploitation of utilization of instrumentalities of war by militarily dependent states such as Nigeria poses a special problems. This is because as a state whose military power critically depends on externally acquired weapons systems, Nigeria arguably cannot exercise independent initiative on matters relating to war and peace as supplier retain veto power through their ability to place embargo on vital supplies. As one analyst aptly noted: since arms transfer has become one of the most handy instruments of persuasive or coercive diplomacy, "the promise or initiation of arms supplies or its reduction, stoppage as well as the provision or denial of spare parts; ammunitions, ancilliary supplies, training or technical assistance can be used and routinely utilized as political leverages for controlling or shaping the policy of recipient states.[4] This was the bitter lesson the Federal Government of Nigeria had to endure at the onset of the civil war. It was also the unforgettable lessons of the Middle East War of 1973 as well as the more recent Argentine and British confrontation over the Falkland/Malvinas Islands. As one of the leading figures – Moshe Dayan – in the former has vividly chronicled:

> *The intensity of the fire power, the prodigious quantities, and the lethal quality of the weaponry also have far-reaching political significance. The dependence on outside sources*

> *... the Soviet Union and the United States as suppliers of arms – was so great in this war that it would have been impossible for the fighting to continue in defiance of the decisions of Washington and Moscow... Israel and the Arabs were dependent on their will. They were not their own masters, neither in the opening stage of the war, nor in its conduct, nor, above all, in determining its end.[5]*

The ECOMOG Operation in Sierra Leorne (1997-2000) also suffered a near catastrophic reversal with the imposition of sanctions on the Federal Government of Nigeria following the execution of Ken Saro-Wiwa and the "Ogoni g" (the executive of the Movement for the survival of Ogoni people). According to General Rafiu Adesina, the sanctions imposed by NATO countries was so effective that it crippled the operational capacity of ECOMOG to defend territories occupied by its forces, and strengthened the insurgents counter – offensive which resulted in their incursum into the capital Freetown[6].

Seen in the context of these disquieting developments, it may be contended that unless and untill fundamental changes are initiated in the nature and structure of arms procurement pattern, the ability of Nigeria's defence establishment to provide policy means will remain in a state of suspended paralysis. This is particularly so because the need to keep up with the changing dynamics of conventional military technology and gadgetary ties the "recipients indefintely to the apron strings of the suppliers." Along with such a dependence is the inescapable erosion of the ability to respond independently to challenges in the security environent. What is critically needed in transitional planning in the defence sector, therefore, is an integrated "goal-oriented guidance" for short as well as long term projections. In other words, the selection of the direction in arms procurement and the adoption of soundly based decisions with respect to policy objectives constitute the crux of viable defence planning.

The basic task (indeed the critical factor) for Nigeria is to recognise the trend and the logic in the evolution and correlation of forces in its strategic environment thus making it possible to minimize uncertainty ("friction" to use (clausewiz's category). This inescapable prerequisite for military effectiveness in industrially backward countries is the direct consequence of existing "patron-client" international dependencies "a reciprocal, durable, and sometimes personalized relationship between states comanding unequal resources of status, and power."[7] In specially military terms, for the dependent party such patron-client relations evolving from arms acquisitions and economic links invariably entail greater sensitivity to the desires of the superior power in military terms she is not" as sovereign as are the more developed nations", and she is "incapable of protracted warfare without riverting to more primitive modes, as they do when engaged in civil war."[8] This condition, therefore, dimished somewhat the utility of military power for Nigeria and states in similar circumstance.

It is in the unsalutory context of the preceding considerations that the defence production in developing countries, based on a strategy which combines assembly of imported sub-systems with indigenous research and development of new weapons. These facets include maintenance and overhaul facilities for the services and repair of imported arms, gradual domestic production of components (either under license or through co-production, co-development or copying), modifications in systems manufactured under license, and production of domestically designed and tested systems such as was undertaken in Eastern Nigeria during the civil war.[9]

To this end the 1980-81 defence budget allocateed N19 million for renovation of the country's Defence Industries Corporation (DIC), while considerably more money has since been chanelled into the corporation to meet its expansion.[10] Set up in 1964 as a joint ventures between Nigerian government and the West German firm of Fritz Werner the DIC is expected to "act as overseer for specifically set up private economic ventures related to defence equipment," but also to conduct research into new weapons for the armed forces. Thus, the current Director – General of DICON has noted that:

> *The concept for the establishment of DICON in 1964 was based on the premise that, the small arms and ammunition factories would be the nucleus of a conglomerate of defence industries. These industries were to be located nationwide for the eventual productin of all defence and security needs of the country. It is the momentum was not sutained after the civil war as Government lost interest in DICON. This peirod would have been used by the Government to nourish the young industry to world standards, instead, stunted growth despite it 42- year existence. The imperative need for a defence industry to meet and sustain the operational needs of the Nigerian forces was justified during the Nigerian Operations in Liberia and Sierra Leone when the "fledging industries small arms and ammunition" There is also the further expectation that DICON will provide the nucleus for the "operation, maintenance and control of ordinance factories for the manufacture of defence-related material, operation of these factories on sound commercial basis and the utilisation of excess capacity for civilian goods"*[11]

Two plants so categorised are already operational in Bauchi (Steyr Daimler Puch of Austria) and Fiat of Italy in Kano. Other subsidiary companies include Leyland vehicles of the U.K., and Daimler – Benz of West Germany. According to the former director of the DIC, Brigadier David Jemibewon, local production of some basic components for weapons and military vehicles have een stipulated as a high-priority objective for these companies.

Systems currently under production include armoured personnel carriers (Steyr), military and special range vehicles (Fiat), while plans are reportedly in place for the assembly of main battle tanks at the Steyr plant in Bauchi.[12] Furthermore, the Leyland Plant in Ibadan is expected to assemble Land-Rovers using locally produced chases, truck cabs, and pressings. The version being considered (101 Forward control Military Land-Rovers), apart from its proven tactical value for support units, also tow a range of artillery pieces (such as the 105mm), guns (e.g. Rapier SAM systems' all currently in service with the Nigerian Army. Also part of the production inventory is the British Shortland armoured patrol car MK3 and its APC model (SB.301), both of which consist essentially of modified long-wheel-base Land Rover chassis with an armoured body.[13]

Two other major arms of the military-industrial complex involve the proposed ship-building and aircraft industries.[14] The latter is still largely on paper, although negotiations with Brazil and India have been underway since 1979 for the establishment of a possible Nigerian aircraft industry as part of a $3 billion trade deal.[15] Given the current trend in joint ventures between the two programme with India which has developed her own jet fighter HALL HF-24 Marut as well as building British Gnat MK1 fighters and Soviet MIG21 fighters under license.

In the former case-ship buidling – several infrastructural facilities (ship assembly and building plant as wel as three dock repair yards) started under the military government of Olusegun Obasanjo are nearing completion. These are intended to set the foundation for the development and expansion of marine engineering, repairs and refitting of the growing armada of naval and commercial (Nigerian National Shipping Line) vessels currently in service.[16] Beyond this cursory appraisal of present infrastrural base of Nigeria's nascent "military-industrial complex", inescapably thus: is Nigeria capable of sustaining large and diversified military industries as official policy pronoucements invariably assume? This quintessential policy question will be the subject of analysis in the subsequent section.

QUESTION OF FEASIBILITY

From a hypothetical standpoint, and concerning intermediate rather than advanced or lead-edge technology, the answer to the above questions is arguably in the affirmative. Nigeria seemingly possesses the combination of socio-economic preconditions (financial resources, a large military, and a sizeable pool of trained manpower and market) for a viable military industry. Although the conversion of such putative resources into actualized power is highly contingent on a number of intervening variables, Nigeria's endowment of these "socio-economic sources of national military-industrial capabilities" place it in the rank of potential LDC weapons producers. What remains problematic are those two other foundations of national military power: the political determination to generate a military-industrial base and the crucial elements of administrative and management skills involved in producing military strength from the inputs drawn from society.

This argumentation is generally consistent with findings (Neuman, Peleg, Wulf, Harkavy, etc)[17] which establish a significant correlation between factors of scale and military-industrial production. The hypothesis here is that although political factors may indeed be important stimulants (as in the case of Israel and South Africa) or constraints (as in the case of Egypt after the Camp David Accords and Iran subsequent to the 1979 revolution), determining both the initiation of and the short-term success or failure of LDC military production effort; in the long-term it is factors of scale that account for the quantity and quality of industrial production and the ultimate success of national defence industries.

For example, Neuman's analysis of 26 LDC producers reveals relatively high and positive correlations among size of military, GNP, and military industrial capability across arms producers:

What emerges within the Third World from these data is hierarchically shaped arms production system based largely on factors of scale. Generally, for each region countries with the largest populations, producing the highest GNP, and sustaining the largest military forces are also the largest and most sophisticated producers of weapons. Land size is also strongly correlated in Latin America and South Asia but not in the Far East, where small states such as Taiwan the two Koreas, and Singapore out-produce larger states in the region such as Philipines, and Indonesia.[18]

Given the obvious and unavoidable deficiencies in the data-base (especially the exclusion of such cogent factors as *leadership and* political will) the validity of Neuman's empirical analysis may be deemed suspect. As Klaus Knorr has rightly noted: "the actualization of putative power crucially depends on the will, manifest or presumed... Without will, there may be power potential in terms of technological, economic, and administrative capabilities, but there can be no power. This will can either be inspired by deliberate response to a specific international situation or be rooted in pre-existing attitudes."[19] Such a consideration is no doubt important in explaining, for example, why some state produce arms while others do not. Or why even among the industrialized countries some states support large and diversified military industries while others do not.

This reservation notwithstanding, general and qualitative consideration derived from research such as Neuman's lead to acceptance of the original hypothesis establishing a positive correlation between factors of scale and military-industrial production. The existence of a large military to provide an adequate domestic market, combined with sizeable national income and population to support the necessary industrial infrastructure, significantly affect a state's long-term ability to produce major weapon systems as well as the quantity and sophistication of these products.

What this conclusion essentially implies in the context of Nigeria is that, given a adequate time-frame, administrative competence (required in making numerous inter-locking decisions), enlightened and determined leadership, proper allocation of existing resources and fundamental reforms of existing structures along functional lines, the development of a viable and sustained military-industrial complex" is a distinct possibility. Nigeria possesses both the structural and material prerequisites to develop into a major military and industrial actor in the region. However, such a transition is not ineluctable but highly contingent on a number of intervening factors, both national and systemic. As the DG DICON regrettably Observes:

It is disheartening that forty-two years after the establishment of DICON, we are thousands of miles behind some other Defence industries of the World established about the same time. It is on that opened up for further the initial successes during the Nigerian Civil War were not utilized by successive Federal Governments. There lost opportunities included the oil boom period of the 80s when the Nigerian currency Dollar, the ECOMOG Operations in Sierra Leone and Liberia (1990-2000). Another cost opportunity was the arms embargo imposed on Nigeria by the West during General Abacha's military rule (1993-1998). Ironically, other countries like South Africa, Israel and Brazil took advantage of similar peculiarities to develop their military industrial capabilities[20].

However, experimentation in Research and Production in the Biafran enclave (1967-1970) adequately demonstrated the feasibility of local military –industrial complex if the crucial precondition exist: political determination and elements of administrative and management skills involved in producing military strength from resources available in the society. As Biersteker and Schatz, among others, have acknowledged, Nigeria's potential for generating and indigenous economic and industrial base through structural reforms and intermediate technology is considerable. The former, for example, has reasoned that:

The presence of necessary conditions for feasible indigenous production in Nigeria and the demonstration of local capabilities during the civil war suggest...that feasible alternatives to the multi-national corporation exist in Nigeria. These alternatives would not necessarily provide a superior product or a greater output than the multinationals, at least at the outset. But the example suggests that whatever losses might initially take place in economic terms would probably be smaller and short-term than predicted by neo-conventional writers and would be compensated for by immediate gains in terms of technological innovations and employments effects[21].

Indeed, an interim report issued by the OECD Development Centre on the development of low-cost or intermediate technology is largely supportive of Biersteker's conclusion. The ingenious technical designs and managerial competence in the former Eastern Region ('Biafra') of Nigeria during the civil war was cited as a case suggesting 'that isolation can have positive effects on the development of technology, and notably on a society's ability to rely on its own inventive force'.

First, several industrial units were kept operational after the mass departure of their expatriate staff. Spare and replacement parts were 'machine-tooled locally, as ingenious cannibalization and mechanical miracles' substituted for the dearth of imported parts. Second, new intermediate production technologies were 'developed and employed in indigenously organized firms even as the war progressed'. Third, an extensive experiment in weapons research and production programme was initiated, also utilizing 'intermediate technologies based on Local innovative capabilities. These include the construction of armoured vehicles along with a variety of guns, ammunition, land mines, rockets, grenades, stand-cannon, and even aerial bombs.

Biafran defence industry also reactivated also reactivated damaged weapons captured from federal forces and copied and mass produced some of their latest equipment. As Frederick Forsyth has noted, perhaps the most famous (and the most feared by the Federal forces) of these weapons was the Ogbuniqwe or "mass destroyer" developed by Biafran Scientists and engineers. With a killing range of 200 yards (covering goto 180 degrees arc), this remote – controlled land-based system is normally capable of destroying a company of attacking forces, this considerably heightening the tactical position of defence:

Finally, and most significant perhaps (since petroleum refining is generally considered among the highest technology industries) was the demonstrable capacity to refine petroleum and related products by Biafran scientists and engineers, 'on a large scale, in numerous and widely distributed locations, and without the assistance of expatriate technicians or direct supervision'. As the sea, air and land blockade of the federal forces tightened around 'Biafra', these petroleum products from locally designed plants kept essential transport and military machines moving throughout 'Biafra' until its final collapse in 1970. Again as Barstaker notes:

> *The Biafran refiners, many of them trained in the Port Harcourt plant, effectively set up refineries under war-time conditions. They undertook research to improve quality and extend the range of products. These efforts went some way towards dispelling the myth that refining technology was beyond the immediate capacity of Nigeria.[22]*

Although these unprecedented achievements in black Africa in a short period of three years (1967-1970) were largely ignored by the comprador bureaucratic elite (fuelled as it was by ethnic jealousies) who dominated critical federal policy planning agencies in the 1970s, comprehensive measure designed to utilize and expand indigenous technological and innovative capabilities now constitute the centerpiece of the new Nigerian strategy on industrialization based on the policy of self-reliance[23]. The magnitude of the current effort – succinctly described by Adedeji as "increasing substitution of factor inputs derived from within the system for those derived from outside'---is evident in the proliferation of scientific and technological planning and policy-making bodies. These include the various R&D establishments under the Ministry of Science and Technology[24].

However, while these endeavour may be considered an impressive beginning in the African context, the actual spin-off for the Nigerian economy—both in terms of the translation of research into practical application and the necessary multiplier effect- will depend on the extent to which extant organizational and attitudinal problems are confronted and resolved. Apart from critical factors influencing the output of R&D units (co-ordination, finance, underutilization and misuse of science and technology manpower for activities not relevant to S&T development), incisively analysed in the Nigerian context by Babatunde Thomas, Teriba and Kayode and NES (2004), fundamental social and psychological problems remains[25].

At the national level, these potent intervening factors include: (a) retention and productive use of available manpower (research scientists, engineers and technicians) in the various institutions supportive of the development of defence; (b) expansion of the crucial determinant of national technological capacity in the modern era: organized Research and Development (R &D); (c) the proportion of national revenue devoted to basic research, since technological innovation tends to flourish in proportion to national revenue devoted to basic and applied research, and to the rewards innovators receive for achievement; (d) the parallel or concomitant development of economies of scale since the production of "building blocs" of modern defence systems within a single economy largely depends on the composition of national output, and the structure of production capabilities behind it; and (e) the degree to which the present and future regimes in Nigeria succeed in eradicating pervasive social and institutional inertia and erroneous values (e.g. the low status until recently accorded research scientists in the social culture of Nigeria) inimical to scientific enterprises[26]. In concrete terms, there is an imperative for some radical institutional shifts in values from the traditional ascription to legitimacy based on the principles of meritocracy, efficiency, productivity and reward, supportive of industrial culture:

> *Until this radical shift in value is effected, science and technology research work may not attract the right calibre of citizens and the vertical transfer of technology may be deprived of one of its central elements: human resources – research scientists, engineers, technicians, managers. At a time when the cascading brain drain to Europe, North America, Asia has deprived Nigeria of approximately some 50,000 professionals and executive grade personnel, some real financial incentives might have to be introduced to starve the tide of the mass exodus...[27]*

At the global level, crucial factors relating to technological transfer remain. The difficulty of access to military technology by Nigeria is not only occasioned by a weak local science and technology system, but also by economic need and pressures to protect relevant know-how in the industrialized countries (the potential sources of military and industrial technology).[28] However, as competition intensifies among the dominant weapon – exporting countries (exacerbated by the aggressive entry into the international market of relatively inexpensive systems by NIC arms producers – Argentina, Israel, Brazil, China, India, South Africa, Korea and Taiwan) there is an increasing, if not inexorable, tendency on the part of these states to enter into co-operative ventures with potential LDC manufactures, through various "offset arrangements": Licensing, coproduction, codevelopment, off-shore assembly etc.[29] As Neuman aptly observes, "European manufactures have accepted these arrangements as part of the price of doing business...Judging by the plethora of agreements, both the Europeans and the Third World are finding the marriage of their mutual needs in the defence sector to be compatible"...[30]

Nevertheless, despite this emerging disposition on the part of arms producing state, the extent to which Nigeria can successfully exploit opportunities may depend on its development of appropriate negotiating skills, its strengthening of relevant policy instruments, and the effective use of bargaining power and political will. Finally, the rapidity with which Nigeria achieves significant domestic capability in the military-industrial sector will also depend on degree of access to international credit and finance. In this regard, the continuation of the present paralysis engendered by the combination of Political instability and IMF preconditions for finance may turn out to be the most formidable barrier to Nigeria's dream of self-sufficiency in defence acquisitions.

These critical intervening factors notwithstanding, there is no gainsaying, as Arthur Nwankwo explicitly contents, that if Nigeria's goal of developing a viable military-industrial base is ever to be consummated, both the short and long term panacea resides in harnessing its growing army of scientists and technicians. This will in turn depend on fundamental reorientation in structural and value parameters through comprehensive corrective strategies such as those attempted in the past by Mohammed and Buhari military governments. However, despite the widespread pessimism and projections of some dependency scholars, to admit the existence of multiple dysfunctions in the socio-economic order of Nigeria is not to foreclose the possibility of evolutionary change.[31]

In conclusion, however, even if Nigeria emerges successfully as the "Brazil" or "India" of Black Africa in the Military-industrial field, certain pertinent questions which continue to bedevil most LDC arms producers remain, these include: (a) the question of dependence: would the shift from imports of weapons to imports of technologies to build weapons merely change the form of Nigeria's dependence and represent a new instrument through which industrial producers exert leverage over her policies", (b) the question of military effectiveness, and (c) the question of economic return.[32]

The first consideration is particularly worrisome, since besides engine and avionic systems, Nigeria will of necessity depend indefinitely on external sources for critical electronic components concerning new battlefield technologies: Precision guidance; remote guidance and control; ammunitions improvements; target identification and acquisition; command, control and communication; and electronic warfare equipments[33]. Since these issues are more relevant to the political economy of Nigeria's defence acquisition strategy, they cannot be satisfactorily examined here. Suffice to note, however, that, as the case with other issue-areas, the question of meeting defence needs, through indigenous production is complex and problematic. Even if military criteria and sound economic principles cannot be seen as rational bases for any decision to develop a local "military-industrial complex" in Nigeria as critics proffered, political or prestige considerations may prove too overriding to ignore.

By 2006, after the trauma of the Babaginda-Abacha years, less than 15% of DICON machinery was functional. However, by 2008 after sustained and accelerated process of rehabilitation through the mobilization of Nigerian Engineers and Technicians, 95% of machinery capacity has been restored. Currently, the installed "production capacity stands at 14,000 x FN (LAR) Rifles per year, 7,000 HP pistols per year, 12 million rounds of 7.62mm x 51 per year and 4 million rounds of 9mm x 19 per year: other weapons (cited in the DICON DG Report) include sub machine guns general purpose machine gun and hand grenade:

With about 95% machine capacity, DICON has repositioned itself for higher productivity. Achievement includes production of the OBJ-006 Assault Rifle, 7.62mm x 39 ammunition, welding centre for oil and gas sector.[34]

Future projects listed in DICON's DG's report include improvement on the locally manufactured mortar tube, rocket propelled grenade launcher, a more aggressive support for our local industries, production of higher caliber weapons, production lines for 7.62mm x 39 ammunition, local manufacture of field kitchen, APC (Nigeria's version) and fast Assault craft. It is also projected that in "order to meet up with other world-class Defence Industries in the field of arms and ammunition production, DICON will have to embark on: (i) Comprehensive upgrading of the existing infrastructure and support facilities (ii) establish more functional research and development centres (iii) Exploit areas of cooperation with the private sector (iv) Initiate more purposeful and concrete partnership with other advanced defence industries.

To this extent, if the present concentration on the development of indigenous capabilities supplemented by vertical technological transfer generate a viable military industrial base then Nigeria's exercise of independent initiative on matters relating to war and peace will arguably be less subject to adverse systemic forces than is currently the case. Otherwise, Nigeria's sobriquet as a "problematic power" may outlive even the most pessimistic of projections in the current literature.

REFERENCES

1. Col. Oduwole quoted in Daily Times, editorial, (Lagos), (November 19, 1982).

2. Raymond Aron, The Imperial Republic. (Washington, D. C.: UPA 1974), p.99

3. Akanbi Onlyangi, "Technology and National Defence Capability Policy Options," Unpublished MS., Lagos, NIIA, 1982.

4. O. S. Kamanu, "Nigeria: Reflections on the Defence Posture for the 1980s" Genave-Afrique, 1 (1977-1978), p.39.

5. Moshe Dayan, The Story of My Life, London: Sphere Books, 1978), p. 629.

6. R. Adesina, Reverse Victory, Ibadan: Heinemann, 2002.

7. For an excellent analysis of international political clientelism, see Robert Rothetin, Alliances and Social Power, (New York: Columbia University Press, 1988).

8. Klaus Knorr, The Power of Nations, (New York: Basic Books, 1975), p. 10.

9. The ambiquities of the term "military-industrial complex" (MIC) necessitate some clarification. As used here, it simply denotes the existence in a contry of an integrated military-industrial firm (MIF), which may be defined as any organization that acts as a supplier of basic inputs to the defence establishments, See Inter alia, Sam Sarkesian (ed.), The Military-Industries' Complex: a Reassessment (Deverly Hills: Sage, 1972), pp, 3-52.

10. See K. Gooding, "Nigeria's Drive for Self-Sufficiency", Financial Times, (London) (25 March, 1976) and R. Handerson "Perspectives on Nigeria Defence Policy," Paper presented at the 8th Annual Conference of the Nigerian Society of International Affairs, NIIA, Lagos February, 1980.

11. D-G, DICON, NDC Lecture, Course 16, 2008, Abuja.

12. See "Made-in-Nigeria Armoured Cars Soon" Daily Times, (20 September, 1976).

13. Henderson, "Perspective on Nigerian Defence Policy".

14. Nigeria to Assemble Ships," Daily Times, (27 February, 1979).

15. Pauline Baker, "A Giant Staggers: Nigeria as an Emerging Regional Fower," in B. Arlinghaus (ed.) African Security Issues. (Boulder: Westview, 1984), p. 92.

16. Gooding, "Nigeria's Drive for Self-Sufficiency," p.6.

17. Stephanie Neuman, "International Stratification and Third World Military Industries" International Organization 38 (Winter 1984): 167-197; Ilan Peleg, "Military Production in Third World Countries," In McGowan and Kegley (eds.), Threats, Weapons and Foreign Policy, (Beverly Hills: Sage, 1980); Herbert of Hamburg, Study Group on Armaments and Underdevelopment, 1980); and Robert Harkavy, The Arms Trade and International Systems, (Cambridge: Ballinger, 1975).

18. Neuman, International Stratification and Third Military Industries," pp. 184-185.

19. Knorr, The Power of Nations, p. 41.

20. D-G DICON, NDC Lecture 2008

21. Thomas Biersteker, Distortion or Development Cambridge: MIT Press, 1978:92

22. Ibid:100

23. Ibrahim James, "Impediments to Vertical Transfer to Technology in Nigeria," Nigerian Forum, 2,5, (May 1983): pp. 114-116; also see J. Adekanye, "Domestic Production of Arms and the Defence Industries Corporation of Nigeria" Current Research on Peace and Violence. No. 4 1983:258-169.

24. A. Adedeji, "The Crisis of Development and the challenge of a New Economic Order in Africa." Africa currents 9 (Summer, 1977) 11-17

25. See NES, Challenges of Nigerian Industrialisation: University of Ibadan, 2005.

26. James, "Impediments to Vertical Transfer of Technology in Nigeria," p. 115; See also F. O. Fajana," The Nigeria Economy," Nigerian Forum, 3, 1 (January 1983); pp. 956-964.

27. See Harkavy, The Arms Trade and International System, esp. chapter 5.

28. For an analysis of these various modes of arms transfer, see Harkavy, Ibid; Un Ra'anan et. al. (eds) Arms Transfer to Countries: The Third World (Boulder: Westview, 1976), chs. 4 and 5; and H. Tuomi and R. Vayrynen, Transnational Corporation: Armaments and Development, (Tampere: Tampere Peace Research Institute, 1980).

29. Neuman, "International Stratification and Third World Military Industries,"p. 193.

30. See, for example, Segun Osoba, "The Deepening Crisis of the Nigerian National Bourgeoisie" Review of African Political Economy, (13 May-August, 1978): 63-77; and Okwadiba Nnoli (ed.) Path to Nigerian Development (Dekar: Cordesria, 1981), and Bade Onimode, Imperialism and Underdevelopment in Nigeria. London: Zed, 1985.

31. Thomas Biersteker, Distrotion or Development, (Cambridge: The MIT Press, 1978), p. 100. Also see Sayre Schatz, Nigerian Capitalism, (Berkeley: University of California Press, 1977), Nicholas Jequier, Low-Cost Technology: An Inquiry Into Outstanding Policy Issues, An Interim Report of the Study Sessions, Held in Paris, 17-20 September 1974, (Paris: OECD Development Centre, 1975). P. 17.

32. The complex variegations of these new battlefield technologies can, for example, be seen in ad domain of guidance technology breaker guidance, precision positioning and correlation guidance). This includes laser designation electro-optical infra-red seeker, and satellite position fixing: For the descriptions and characteristics of these systems, see Weapons technology: a Survey of Current Developments in Weapons Systems, (London: Brassey's, 1975). See also Gen. 1.1. Anureyev et. al. Scientific – Technical Progress and the Revolution in Military Affairs (A Soviet View); James Digity, Precision-Guided Weapons, Adephi Paper No. 18, (London: 11SS. 1975).

33. DICON DG Report, NDC Lecture, 2008.

CHAPTER 17

MILITARY LOGISTICS IN THE INFORMATION AGE

O. L. ABIDOYE

PREAMBLE

The Military activity termed logistics is perhaps as old as War itself. It, however, gained general usage in the United States Army during the Second World War. The word itself could be traced to the Latin word logistics meaning skilled in calculating, which is derived from the Greek word logos meaning reckoning or calculation.[1] The first usage of the word with reference to military administrative science is traceable to the French writer Jomini who served as a staff officer in Napoleon's Army.

He defined logistics as the "practical art of moving armies". It is perhaps on account of this that logistics is defined as the *"Movement, Storage and Supply of Troops and Equipment"*[2] However, the term and its associated techniques are widely used in public and private enterprises today. To the economists, the whole business of logistics is one major factor in calculating the cost of war to an entire nation. In private enterprise it involves the planning and control of the flow of goods and materials through an organization or manufacturing process.

This encompasses functions such as warehousing supply chain management, inventory management and transportation. These processes are today receiving serious attention from management experts on account of their importance in cost reduction strategies. It is against this background that a management expert remarked that: "as we enter the 21st century the greater need for greater focus on the logistics process that underpin supply chain effectiveness becomes even more apparent"[3].

Military logistics is, however, the means by which operations are sustained and linkages provided between those forces on active duty and their national strategic resources. It is the process of planning for and providing goods and services in the support of military forces. That is moving, supplying and maintaining military forces. It is very basic to the ability of armies, fleets and air forces to exist and operate. Logistics in this respect becomes a continuum: an uninterrupted and orderly flow. It is against this perception that logistics has been described as the "bridge connecting a nation's economy to its war fighting forces". It is apparent from the foregoing that military logistic in its widest perspectives include the ability of the national infrastructure and manufacturing outfits to support and supply the armed forces deployed in the field using the national transportation system. Logistics is not about the supply of men and material but the effective application of these resources in a timely manner to favorably affect the outcome of battle as well as the provision of food, clothing shelter and entertainment to troops in order to safeguard morale and discipline.

Henry Eccles is of the view that there is no magic in word logistics. He states that the word logistics can disappear from the military vocabulary without altering the nature of war or the manner in which the various means of war operate in relation to strategy, organization and combat effectiveness[4]. He, therefore, concludes that logistics is merely a convenient term used to encompass the problem of controlling all the means of war as appropriate at various levels of command. This is understandable since all concepts are convenient capsule-form phraseology for explaining often complete phenomenon. In outlining the concept of military logistics, no attempt is made to provide a working definition but to bring the fundamental relationships, principles and functional application, which would endure regardless of administrative decisions.

The difficulty in agreeing on a single precise definition notwithstanding, it is possible to recognize a definite structure in logistic generally as a term. Such an approach would give an understanding of the fundamental realities of the concept irrespective of terminology. Every logistics problem can be approached in the simple terms of four broad categories, three fundamental elements and four basic aspects. Starting from a basic definition of logistics as "the provision of the means to conduct military operation; we can proceed to identify four broad categories that make up the means of military operations as: men, *materials, facilities and services.* In providing these categories of military means there are three fundamental elements, which are determination of requirements, balanced procurement and timely distribution[5]. These management and command processes in turn involve organization, planning, execution and supervision, which constitute the basic aspects of logistics. These categories, elements and aspects make up the heart of logistics regardless of the level of command. They are present in every logistics problem and they blend and overlap in accordance with the nature and circumstances of each particular situation.

It is against this background that some of the established definitions of logistics will make sense. Jomini saw logistics as the "art of moving armies". It comprises the "order of details of marches and camps, and of quartering and supplying troops". This definition contains some essentials but we must agree that with sophistication in weapons as well as changes in battle space, logistics concerns have gone beyond order of marches, camps and quartering. It is perhaps in realization of these developments that US Military defines logistics as "the science of planning and execution of all military matters not included in tactics and strategy". This definition goes further to identify the concern of logistics as "movement and maintenance of forces". Lt Gen William Pagonis (USA) emphasized that dimension of integration and coordination when he defined logistic as "the careful integration of transportation, supply, warehousing, maintenance, procurement, contracting, and automation into a coherent functional areas: and in a way that prevents sub-optimization in any of these activities; and in a way that permits and enhances the accomplishment of a given goal, objective, or mission" [6].

In terms of dimension, logistics discourse generally covers pure and applied logistics. Pure logistics also regarded as the science of logistics, is concerned with the scientific inquiry into the theory of logistics, its principles, scope and function in the science of war. The first formal attempt at establishing pure logistics was in 1917 when Lt Col Cyrus Thrope of the US Marines published a book titled *Pure Logistics: The Science of War Preparation*. This initial attempt made to develop theory and principles of logistics attracted little attention, but today it forms a large segment of the science war[7].

Theories and principles can neither prepare a nation to fight nor win a war. Rather, their benefit lies in their application towards understanding respective war problems and solving them. Applied logistics is concerned with the practical application of the functions of logistics. Such a function is an art not a science. In order to prepare for war, practical tasks and logistics functions must be assigned to specific organizations and individuals. It is this consideration that has given rise to the logistics corps or services and logistics staff appointments in the various arms of the military.

Integral to logistics management in modern warfare is the application of computers to defence planning and the conduct of warfare. Information is becoming an increasingly vital national resource that supports economic activities, politics and the effective employment of military forces[8]. In military operations, useful information would include troop movements, the number of fighter aircraft involved in an air raid, or the number of naval ships involved in an amphibious operation. The information revolution has affected weapons, weapon platforms, military strategies and operations in the developed armies. The reform that the military is undergoing as a result of the information revolution can be captured under revolution in military affairs (RMA) as is being experienced in USA Army.

Terms like information operation (IO), information superiority and information warfare have unfolded in military lexicon. Over the last 25 years, a rapid evolution of information, information systems and communication systems has occurred. Ayo in his book, *Information Technology: Trends and Applications in Science and Business*, asserts that information is processed data[9]. It is also the knowledge gained and supplied about something or somebody[10]. Raw data such as the number of fighter aircraft in a squadron could be of value in warfare. Similarly, the data on the serviceability status of naval ships in a country is equally important in strategic and operational military planning.

EVOLUTION OF MILITARY LOGISTICS

Logistics as a human activity is as old as mankind. From the time man found succour, comfort and convenience in the use of implements for hunting, fishing and other activities, logistics as functions of efficient utilization of materials for livelihood came into play. Unarguably a historical human activity, the recognition of logistics as a field of study only became prominent as a result of the anatomy of past military failures. However, today, logistics is receiving greater acknowledgement and credit for many successful campaigns and operations. The concept of logistics has not, however, attained unanimity as it is still evolving. Logistics is, therefore, a relatively new word used to describe a very old practice, the supply, movement and maintenance of an armed force both in peacetime and under operational conditions.

Following the dramatic evidence of the dominant influence of logistics in the Second World War and other campaigns, the study of logistics is now concerned with looking ahead and projecting how the tremendous technological progress will impact on its future. Operations during the Second World War are noted to have been characterized by novel logistics techniques as forces were maintained by versatile and mobile logistics support. Subsequent wars such as the Arab – Isreali wars, the Falkland War (1982) and the wars at the Gulf (1991 & 2003) have also witnessed tremendous increase in quanta and sophistication of the logistics armada. Consequent upon this realization logistics consideration are now vitally considered in the making of battle plans because without logistics the tanks, armoured personnel carriers, artillery pieces, helicopters and aircrafts are just numbers on a TOE[11].

In the 21st Century, when warfare became characterized by high technology, precision-oriented logistics became inevitably the way forward. Precision-oriented logistics aimed to achieve effective support with relative small input, but relative high efficiency. The focus of logistics support shifted from reliance on quantity to reliance on speed and information, making full use of information technologies and delivering an appropriate amount of resources to the front in the right place at the right time feasible. The degree of precision of logistics support in terms of time, space, variety, quantity, and the deployment in strength becomes a prerequisite for effective support.

Humankind entered the information age with the advent of computer and the subsequent evolution of computer connectivity and this change has revolutionalized the activities of man in all facets. Most aspects of states economy, from the entertainment industry, to manufacturing, banking, retailing and defence are now largely dependent upon revolutionary modern information processing. As the revolution provides its products for application in theatres of modern warfare, battles are becoming more fluid, complex, ambiguous and uncertain. A commander must, therefore, have the capability to assess speedily the relative positions and strength of both sides and also have the capacity to deliver material precisely and timely where they are required in the battlefield.

The evolution of IT characterized by development and application of microchips and integrated circuits have been the basis for the recent challenges and opportunities confronting military logistics in the information age. The military might must, therefore, draw on new technologies and strategies of the information age which is pivoted on IT evolution. The military logistician is therefore further challenged in the information age to leverage the abundant information technologies of the 21st Century in order to be empowered for the challenging task of supporting her fighting force in a modern battle characterized by speed, precision, guided munitions, sensors, computers, intelligence, surveillance and reconnaissance but with very limited time available for decision making. The information age requires a military logistician that will not rely on historical data, but real-times, predictive information to enable him make intelligent decisions and optimize force readiness.

One way of discussing the evolution of military logistics is by tracing the development of military logistics over time by undertaking a chronological survey of the practice of logistics from medieval time to the present modern military establishments. It should, however, be noted that time, space and my modest knowledge would limit this attempt to a selected but significant campaigns within the second period with his army on campaign away from a seaport or navigable rivers. Where necessary, Alexander developed dumping sites to shorten distances to his seaport resources. The Roman legions were later to employ the techniques pioneered by Philip and Alexander and also took advantage of improved infrastructure including the roads they constructed as they expanded their empire. They also improved on ship building in sustaining logistics support to distant operational theatres. However, economic decline and the determination to have soldiers live on the land were later to reduce logistics to the level of pillage and plunder. Some inventions and innovations that later revoluntionalized logistics included the steamship, fossil fuel and improvement in weapons. This improved the efficiency and endurance of ships and, thus, the sustainability of forces.

This period in the development of military logistics may be regarded, as the period of the tyranny of plunder.[12] As a result, the armies of this period were probably the worst maintained with marauding bands of armed ruffians devastating countryside they crossed. Nevertheless, the need to furnish the soldier with at least his most elementary needs including food, arms clothing was established.

As centuries passed, despite new tactics, the improvement in gunpower and the railway system, the problem facing armies remained the same: sustaining the forces while campaigning. Napoleon took advantage of the improved road system of the early 19th Century and the increasing population density in designing a sustenance scheme for his forces. Ultimately, he still relied on a combination of magazines and foraging. At a stage, many Napoleonic armies abandoned their tents pior to combat engagements. However, in the long run, the numbers of Calvary and artillery pieces grew as well, thus, defeating the objective of being light. Consequently, Napoleon failed the logistics test when he crossed the Nieman in 1812 to start his Russian Campaign. He started with over 300,000 men and reached Moscow with just 100,000. Napoleon had known that the logistics system would not support and sustain his army on the road to Moscow continually. He, therefore, gambled to force the Russians to the negotiation table and dictate terms but was indeed defeated by "General Winter" of Russia as his army were found unprepared for the long and severe Russian Winter and so had to retreat. The pursuing Russian Army did not fare better as they started at Koluga with 120,000 men and reached Vilna with only 30,000 men.

The important development that this period bequeathed on the practice and study of logistics arose from the realization that mere plunder was an unsatisfactory method of feeding an army. Some generals, therefore, began to use requisitions; purchase orders and contracts to exploit the resources of occupied territories. To this must be added the use of the magazine system and forward bases. The system whereby armies advance with eight days provision, halt, take stock and establish a new base where stock is replenished before further advance was contemplated and developed in this period. The importance of national infrastructure to logistics build-up and support was also established.

Logistics in the American Civil War that ended in 1863 foreshadowed its impact on future warfare. This was a large conflict between big populations with mass mobilization armies. It was, therefore, necessary to set up logistics infrastructure to cater for the training, equipping, movement and sustenance of these armies. Railways played an important part in this war, speeding up the movement of troops and supplies. The railways also dictated, to a great extent, the axis of advance, the sitting of defensive positions and locations of battles.

One significant observation is that it was the first large scale war in which deliberate combat measures were taken to interfere with the enemy's communication and supply centres. It emphasized the importance of sea blockade as employed by the forces of New England against the confederates along the coast of Virginia. It was also in this conflict that canned food was used to feed troops for the first time. Another significant logistic legacy of this period was tremendous increase in ammunition expenditure supported by a local production line, which the National Army used against the Confederate Forces.

The First World War was, in its very scale, unlike any thing before it. It was a war in which the forces outstripped the logistics support available. In particular, ammunition demand outstripped pre-war estimate.[13] Another logistics nightmare of this war was the vast resources required to build fortification in Europe. To this must be added the unprecedented scale of casualties, which contingent force were unable to cater for, leading to the introduction of neutral medical support. The slow pace of the war in the first four years was, ascribed to the numerous logistics problems encountered. It was only from 1981 that the British, with the help of tanks, motorized gun sleds were able to maintain the pace of the advance and maintain supply well away from railheads and seaports. Expansion in the industrial capacity and transport lift of the belligerents ensured the supply of armies on the move.

The Second World War was logistically the most testing war in history. The cost of technology had not yet become an inhibiting factor and only the industrial potential and access to raw materials of belligerents limited the amount of equipment, spares and consumables that were produced. The war was global in size and scale. Combatants had to be supplied at ever-greater distances from the home base. The war tended to be fast moving and voracious in the consumption of fuel, food, and water as well as ammunition. Railways, again, proved indispensable but sealift and airlift made even greater contributions as the war dragged on. The large-scale use of motorized transport for tactical re-supply helped to maintain the momentum of the offensive operations, and most armies became more motorized as the war progressed. The principal logistic legacy of the Second World War was expertise in supplying combat forces from far-off operational theatres and a sound lesson in what is and what is not administratively possible. This was specially highlighted in the campaigns conducted in the Sahara, which further stressed the impact of environmental factors on logistics. The restrictions imposed on Rommel by the environment in North Africa also depicted the importance of infrastructure to logistics. Although Rommel employed the blitzkrieg, it was found to be ineffective due to uncertainty of resource available rooted and the absence of modern mechanical consumables. The need to have secure and realistic lines of communication was also brought to light in this war.

The Gulf wars of 1990 and 2003 amply demonstrated what a well coordinated logistics chain, supported by modern management techniques, can achieve. The first was started with an initial build up of American-led Allied Forces in what was known as OP DESERT SHIELD. In the first 30 days of the build up, well over 38,000 troops and 163, 581 tons of equipment were delivered to the theatre.[14] This involved the handling of about 35 planes and 2 vessels on a daily basis. When compared to the Second World War, (within the same time frame) these were significantly larger. The Second Gulf War in March 2003 was not different. The place of air and sea logistics support was further consolidated during these wars. The art and science of logistics was indeed taken to greater heights during these wars, as nothing was left to chance-not even a pint of water that the average soldier needed.

That the two wars ended successfully can be understood from the perspective of logistics planning and execution that characterized them. The wars also emphasized the need for the centralized control of logistics resources for effective management. Indeed, a number of writers have stated that the Gulf wars were essentially logistics wars. Without the painstaking planning and execution that was the hallmark of the wars, no success could have been achieved.

LOGISTICS AND WARFARE IN THE INFORMATION AGE

The nature of warfare in the information age is characterized by speed, accuracy and precision. It is a period of widespread electronic access to information through the use of computer technology. Effective conduct of warfare in the information age is significantly dependent on timely processing distribution and receipt of data using computer hardware and software, telecommunications, and digital electronics. It could be referred to as warfare pivoted on the use of technologies from computing, electronics, and telecommunications to process and distribute information in digital and other forms. This is different from warfare in the pre-information era. As Du Fu (a Chinese Poet) in his book, *The Ballad of the Army Wagons* put it "Warfare in the pre-information era was largely characterized by din of wagons, and whinnying horses. Each marcher at his waist has bow and quiver, Old people, children, wives, running alongside, who cannot see, for dust bridge over river."[15]

Modern warfare could be categorized into six generations in time. These are the first, second, third, fourth, fifth and sixth generations. While the first and second generations were distinct, the third through to the sixth were interwoven. The first generation began with Peace of Westphalia in 1648, which ended the thirty years war.[16]". It also marked the State's assumption of monopoly of warfare, that is, war became something waged by states, with the armies and navies doing the fighting. The second was developed by the French Army during and after World War I. It was best summed up with the French saying "the Artillery conquers, the infantry occupies".[17] It was also known as firepower/attrition warfare as decisions making was central and hierarchical…success was measured by comparative body count.[18] The third generation was the manoeuvre warfare developed largely by the German Army and perfected with the Blitzkrieg during World War II. The fourth generation which is the main focus of this paper is the IT warfare which is propagated over long distances with pinpoint accuracy and limited collateral damages.

Information age warfare could be traced to the outbreak of World War I (1914-1918) when wireless transmission proved an invaluable military tool on land, sea, and air in Europe. Impressed by its strategic applications, and wary of its potential as an instrument of espionage and mass propaganda, US President Woodrow Wilson banned non military broadcasting when the United States entered the war in 1917.[19] The war also aided the development of radio technology, as governments on both sides of the conflict poured money into research. Armstrong, a decorated military pilot who served with U.S. forces in France, is credited with having made great improvements in air-to-ground and air-to-air radio systems.

In the information age, accurate target acquisition and bombing precision is the hallmark of military operations as was witnessed when the Israeli attacked Hezbollah targets, including weapons, storehouses and missile launching points, across the country. Also precision attacks continued to be decisive as in 2003 when United States and British forces invaded Iraq to depose the regime of President Saddam Hussein. The U. S. – British alliance began its air campaign on 19 March 2003 with limited nighttime bombing of the capital Baghdad, followed days later by intensive bombardment. Nearly 14,000 sorties were flown, and more than 800 Tomahawk cruise missiles were fired at Iraqi targets from March 19 until mid-April when Iraqi resistance largely ended.[20]

In addition to the intensity of the bombardment, the air campaign was also notable for its use of a new generation of precision-guided bombs which were tracked, controlled and guided by computers located thousands of miles away. Precision-guided bombs used in the conflict included Joint Direct Attack Munitions (JDAM), conventional bombs outfitted with a device that uses the global positioning system to home in on targets. The Predator drone provided U.S. forces with real-time images of Iraqi troop movements and positions, especially the location of antiaircraft weapons. Infrared cameras on surveillance aircraft also enabled U.S. and British forces to track Iraqi movements at night. These are characteristics of warfare in the information age.

Future developments in military aviation in the information age are likely to include smaller guided bombs and the wider use of stealth technology. In late 2001 Lockheed Martin started work on the biggest ever fighter project, the F-35 Joint Strike Fighter. The United States planned to build 3,000 of these stealthy, supersonic fighters, some of which will be able to hover and land vertically, the aircraft prototype version has already been tested.[21] Also in the planning stage is a military space plane, a reusable spacecraft that would be smaller but more reliable than the Space Shuttle and designed for reconnaissance and attack missions. The US Air Force is also seeking cruise missiles that can fly at 6,400 Kph (4,000mph) – more than twice as fast as any previously tested cruise missile and Unmanned Aerial Vehicles (UAVs) equipped with radar that can find targets hidden under trees from 16 km (10mi) above the ground.[22] More than ever, air and space power will continue to dominate future wars in the information age.

In the area of logistics, warfare in the information age would require more of just in time delivery of material than use of clearly defined logistics chains of delivery. Since weapons of the information age would be capable of delivering munitions to targets thousands of kilometres away, the need to move heavy ammunitions to combat zones would be greatly limited. In the area of personnel and supplies movement, satellite tracking would be employed to guarantee prompt and safe delivery from home bases or depots.

As precise and accurate warfare in the information age could be, it is still far from perfect. Despite the improved precision of U.S. weaponry, errant missiles landed in the neighbouring countries of Saudi Arabia and Turkey and reportedly in civilian residential areas of Iraq's capital. United States officials, however, maintained that only a tiny percentage failed to hit their targets. These and many other events confirm the ever evolving nature of warfare in the information age.

TAXONOMY

I. FOCUSED LOGISTICS

A distinct characteristics of military logistics in the information age is the art of focused logistics. Focused Logistics is the ability to provide the fighting forces the right personnel, equipment, and supplies in the right place at the right time, and in the right quality, across the full range of military operations. It entails the fusion of logistics information and transportation technologies for rapid crisis response, deployment and sustained, the ability to track and shift units, equipment and supplies even while en route, and delivery of tailored logistics packages and sustained directly to the warfighter.[23] The technology underpinning the Focused Logistics operational concept rely predominantly upon the flow of information back to the operational commander. Sophisticated, technologically advanced computer and information systems are required not only to provide the necessary command and control of the forces but also identify and ascertain availability of provisions and supplies during combat and non-combat operations (operations other than war.) Morgenstern recognized this need for the operational commander when he stated that"...the deeper analyses of the problems of military logistics will show that most difficult and most important aspects lie in the field of information and in the flow of messages and papers." [24]

The Nigerian Armed Forces Joint Vision 2020 document recognized that modern warfare depends increasingly on an increased tempo of operations.[25] Hence, the logistics system must ensure delivery of the right equipment, supplies and personnel, in the right quantities, to the right place and at the right time to meet operational requirements. Improvements in information systems, innovation in organizational structures, improved processes and advances in transportation technologies would result to logistics agility. Logistics agility means linking all logistics functions and units through means of information (computer and communications) systems that will integrate "real-time" logistics asset visibility with the common and current, operational picture. This would allow providing logistic support in time and at the right locations to support joint operation. The primary goal is to improve the linkage between operations and logistics while at the same time increasing efficiency and reducing vulnerability. Not only will this system support the Joint Force in war, it will provide the primary operational elements in the delivery of humanitarian or disaster relief or other activities across the range of military operations.

There are many examples of how technological advancement affects logistics and logisticians today. Consider bar coding products and components-electronic scanners that capture product location and send the information directly to systems that log and check inventory and order level. Automatic ordering and continuous replenishment with just-in-time delivery have completely changed manufacturing procurement cycles, distribution centre requirements and retail operations. War bar coding and electronic scanning, tracking and dynamic rerouting of orders and deliveries are relatively easy. Enterprise Resource Planning (ERP) systems also enable full tracking and availability of information for real time management of inventory and supplies.

II. JUST-IN-TIME LOGISTICS

Total asset visibility coupled with enhanced situational understanding and knowledge of the operational plan could result in the army's ability to accomplish predictive or "just in time" (JIT) re-supply. The smart push of critical supplies by rear-based logistics specialists close to supply sources is the most efficient process. JIT is a concept of logistics where demand in the logistics chain pulls productions towards the market and the flow of components is also determined by that same demand. It is a technique that is based upon the principle that wherever possible, no activity is to take place in a system until there is a need for it. JIT manufacturing seeks to minimize stock levels and to optimize the manufacturing process delivering stock "just in time". The absence of traditional buffer stocks requires reliable production of high quality goods.

The supply chain starts with the provision and procurement organizations whose job it is to determine what is required, the quantities to be procured and any limitations which may be put on the use of materiel once received from industry. It ends with the unit which consumes or uses the materiel passed down the chain. Tri-Service linkages in-theatre could be developed to ensure optimum effectiveness. Key tools in the process are Asset Tracking and Total Asset Visibility (TAV).[26] TAV is a principal logistic element of digitization of the battlefield." It can only be effected by the full integration of the myriad special-to-purpose logistic IS among the services. The overall aim is to provide a fully integrated system in which data is only input once, there is only one terminal per staff officer and from that terminal the staff officer can access the whole database.

LOGISTICS MANAGEMENT

The first major phase of logistics is the process of procurement. All the provisions and facilities required by the military are acquired or obtained or produced in-house. These include goods and services, weapon systems and various other commodities. The procurement process involves budgeting, contracting, production, evaluation and trials. The second phase involves transportation, storage, inventory control, distribution and supply management. The third phase involves sustaining the defense forces through maintenance, replenishment, servicing of equipment and weapon systems. It is, however, quite evident that the economic resources of the state influences its entire logistics process.

As a nation goes into war, the economy transit into a wartime economy. Industrial activities swiftly shift to war production and national resources including manpower and manufacturing effort naturally tilt towards meeting the emerging demand of war. Automobile makers turn to production of tanks and warplanes just as others go into production of weapons, ammunition, food, clothing etc. Contacts for delivery of services or other items locally or from international market place are also embarked upon. The aggregate of all the activities and effort directed at creating, producing, manufacturing, procuring, transporting, concentrating resources or requirements for war effort may be termed production logistics.

It is a truism that no country can assemble and make organic to her armed forces all that is required to prosecute war in the prevailing global economic circumstances. Therefore while the advanced and industrialized nations such as USA would rely more on manufacturing for war production, less developed nations and developing countries depend more upon acquisition through international market place for the material needs of its armed forces with its accompanying setbacks. Some of these are the lack of or difficulty of reverse logistics, insensitivity to surge and susceptibility to conspiracy amongst others.

Reverse logistics refers to the flow of materials from the users back to depots for repair, modification and reissue. The international market place has little or no place for reverse logistics. Availability to cope with a surge in demand on the battlefield is equally questionable. There is also the likelihood of conspiracy by the developed world or the supplier clique to frustrate efforts by a developing country or buyer nation in the battlefield through sanctions or other repressive policies as experienced during the Nigerian Civil War. The production for war system or mechanism must therefore be more inward looking and designed to counter the inherent dangers on the reliance on the international market place. There is need for more reliance on local production which is dependent on the local industrial capability. The military must collaborate with the industrial sector in its strategic planning for war.

Whether military requirements are sourced from the international market or the local industry, the question still remains as how they reach the soldier in his trench to enable him live and fight to project the interest of the country. Modern day operations have revealed various methods of delivery of war production in the logistics system. These ranges from trucking, sea lift, air lift as well as rails and pipelines amongst others.

In the early 1980s, trucks were used primarily for local deliveries and limited interstate commerce. This was because roads were poor and rail roads controlled the long distance shipping of freights. Today, trucks have proved to be an invaluable means for delivering soldiers including their supplies during war as was exemplified by the Americans in Operation Desert Storm in the American led Coalition Iraqi War. Infact, by the end of World War I, more than 600,000 trucks were in use for war delivery in the USA.[27] While civilian haulage trucks were vital to lift materials from the industries and air and sea ports, military controlled haulage vehicles took care of delivery and distribution within the battlefield area. This exhibits the shared responsibility in war deliveries between the civil sector and the military.

In terms of sea lift, the American Strategic Sealift Force deploys and sustains military forces wherever needed, through the delivery of materials, petroleum, equipment and other supplies. The Sealift Force comprises the Afloat Pre-positioning Force made up of 25 ships loaded with military equipment and pre-positioned around the world to achieve five days sailing time to potential trouble spot.[28] For rapid deployment and sustenance of a division, fast sealift ships, the fastest cargo ships in the world deliver tanks, helicopters and other military supplies to where they are required from the home base or industries.[29]

In the less developed countries where the navy may not be so organized, the maritime sector is exploited for military sealift functions. Sealift, however, has some limitations including sea blockades as witnessed during the Coalition-Iraq War as well as more deliberate enemy offensive activities such as mining and submarine action. It, nevertheless, remains an invaluable means of war deliveries in the production logistics system which must be complemented by other means.

Airlift is not limited to the use of aircrafts and helicopters alone for the delivery of troops, equipment and supplies but encompasses other forms of air supply such as parachuting. During Second World War, armies made extensive use of parachutes to drop heavy equipment, tanks, trucks as well as guns. Today, the design of parachutes has become increasingly sophisticated as they are now designed to achieve control of descent, reduce wind effect as well as maintain stability according to the weight and shape of the object being conveyed.[30] While the importance of airlift in logistics requires no further emphasis, it is however limited by infrastructure requirement and scope of utilization.

It is apparent, therefore, that effective war production itself does not contribute any value to the war effort except material and others so produced or acquired reach the battlefield. To this extent, the logistics system must coordinate the various means of delivery, as well as integrate not only military assets but those in the civil sector as well.

LOGISTICS IN LIMITED AND GENERAL WARS.

National strategy is defined as "the art and science of developing and using the political, economic and psychological powers of a nation, together with its armed forces, during peace and war to secure national objectives"[31]. Military strategy on the other hand will be confined to the development and employment of the armed forces for the attainment of national objectives. Consequently, strategic calculations from the perspective of the military will refer to those key considerations leading to a choice or decision on such issues like force posture, size of forces as well as platforms, force mix and design for battle among other things.

While the national threat will dominate the consideration of strategic calculations highlighted above, it is unthinkable that options would be adopted without sparing a thought for the "means and ways" of the nation. An example from the events in our sub-region will bring this point home. When Nigeria started massive purchase of armoured vehicles in the late 70s, our neighbours especially to the West and Northern boundaries felt threatened. The most desirous strategic calculation on the part of these countries would have been to match Nigeria tank for tank. However, weighing their national "means and ways" led to a cheaper yet effective option of massive procurement of Rocket Propelled Grenades (RPG), which were deployed down to section level.[32] You would agree that this is a case of strategic consideration being conditioned by logistics realities.

The strategy adopted by a country is a function of the anticipated threats and its endowments. The economic situation of a country and the technology available in the realm of the future will eventually decide on the size and mix of the military forces.[33] Any national strategy formulated, therefore, which is not supportable by the national economy, is not achievable. What this means is that there has to be a sound logistics disposition and plan to support several strategic and as well as tactical plans. The key thing to note is that all strategic and operational plans must be logistically supportable. This is so because, not only are strategic plans limited by the feasibility of logistic support, logistic plans are themselves limited by the national economy. This is understandable if we consider the definition of logistics from the perspective of an economist, which is that logistics is the total cost of war to a nation. Infact some well known economists have stated that strategies are ways of using budgets or resources to achieve military objectives. [34]

As soon as strategic aims and objectives are formulated, the next logical steps are to undertake a comprehensive analysis of the technology and economic capability that would support and sustained them. This analysis would expose the mismatch between what is desired and what is achievable within the national economy. Factors such as funds, materials and technology would be considered, and ways and means found towards meeting those requirements that provide the right kind of national defence. Herein lies the importance of logistics to strategic calculations in any form of conflict be it limited or general warfare.

JOINT OPERATIONS

Logistics planning for joint operations may be discussed from the strategic and operational levels. At the national level (strategic), the sum total of the nation's economic resources is crucial in achieving the nation's strategic objectives using the military forces. At this level, therefore, resources such as the national infrastructure including hospitals, depots, defence industries, research organizations, civil and military industrial bases are crucial in the logistics planning calculation. In short the whole spectrum of the country's infrastructures become the bedrock on which logistics planning at this level is hinged upon. Logistics at this level means therefore providing for and sustaining the combat effectiveness of the military forces wherever they operate. It is obvious from the foregoing that logistics planning can be used to indicate the incorporation of logistics considerations into the formulation of strategic plans. If the nation's industrial, technological and economic capabilities do not support the strategic plans, then the plans are futile. This is why as a country we have to worry since we depend for most of our requirements on foreign suppliers who do not owe us any allegiance.

At the operational level, the emphasis is on ways and means of supporting a force at the place of military intervention. Logistics planning at this level aims at supporting operational plans using and deploying forces in a well-defined manner. Issues such as regional depots, repair facilities, medical and supply facilities are critical towards meeting the logistics requirements of the force.

Logistics planning at this level considers the factors of distance, destination, demand and duration what is referred to, as the 4 DS.[35] They are crucial to predicting logistics requirements. These factors can be applied to established men and material requirements. The consideration to distance is imperative in terms of the strategic and theater lines of communication (LOC) before, during and after the operation. The capacity, length (in terms of distance and time) and topography of the LOC ultimately would decide the size, shape, structure and balance of logistics resources committed to it. The destination on the other hand gives an overview of the environment in which the operation will take place. The effect of this environment on equipment in terms of wear and tear, and the psychological demands on personnel would be determined. The strategic LOC, the overall type of the regenerative loop and the resources needed to prime it would be defined by the destination of the resources and distance involved. The pattern, rate of change and variability as well as the aggregate consumption or usage of material constitutes the demand. The duration connotes the length of operation and together with the rate of demand determines the overall volume of material necessary or the size of logistics problem.

In joint and multi-national operations such as our recent ECOMOG operation, consideration has to be given to the local support that may be available to the force operating in foreign lands. This is termed host nation support. It encompasses both civil and military assistances that can be rendered in peace, crisis and war by a host nation. For instance during the planning stage it should be possible to ascertain in detail the physical infrastructure and material resources available to support operations in the host nation. Another major consideration in planning logistics support for joint as well as combined operations is the availability of strategic lift. The military must retain the capability for initial insertion of a reasonable size of the required force in the crisis spot by air, sea or land. Subsequent build up of forces and the logistics trail may be boosted by mobilized civil resources.

CONCLUSION

The relevance of logistics to warfare has been noted to be as old as warfare itself. Logistics support, however, is becoming increasingly complex due to the demanding nature of modern warfare. Modern warfare is characterized by arrays of sophisticated weapon system and high battlefield fluidity. Hence the evolution of information technology and it's application in modern warfare has impacted tremendously on effective logistic support. The modern concept of manoeuvrist approach to warfare has also further heightened the need for the military to keep abreast with the dictates of modern logistics.

I have in this chapter tried to conceptualize military logistics as the means, method and mechanisms by which operations are sustained and effective linkage between forces on active duty and national strategic resources. Attempt was thereafter made to trace the evolution of military logistics from the medieval period to date.

The pivotal roles of logistics were vividly identified in the campaigns discussed. The chapter particularly noted the very indispensable role of logistics in the Gulf war as was expressed in the words of Lt. Gen Pagonis when he stated that, "It was a 5 months logistics miracle followed by a one hundred hour tactical exercise". The nature of warfare in the Information age was also discussed with particular emphases on Focused Logistics and Just-in-time logistics. Production and delivery in modern warfare preceded the discussion on the importance of logistics calculation in limited and general warfare. The modern trend of logistics as noted in the lecture calls for desirable evolution of a joint logistics structure for the Nigerian Armed Forces. This call has become louder with our adoption of the manoeuverist approach to warfare with its attendant consequences of jointness in all operations.

REFERENCES

1. William G. Pagonis with Jeffrey L. Cruikshank, Moving Moutains-Lessons in Leadership and Logistics from the Gulf War, (Havard Business School Press Boston) 1992, Page x.
2. Ibid
3. M. Christopher, Logistics and supply Chain management Strategy for Reducing Cost and Improving Services.
4. Henry E. Eccles, Logistics in the National Defence (Newport, The stock Pole Company) 1952.

5   Ibid
6   William G. Pagonis with Jeffery L. Cruikshank, Moving Moutains-Lessons in Leadership and Logistics from the Gulf War. (Havard Business School Press Boston) 1992.
7   Burch JG, jr, Strata F. R, Grudnitski G, Information Systems: Theory and Practice 2nd Edition (New York: John Willey and Sons Ltd 1979) P27.
8. G. Stem, Information Warfare, (http:#www.airpower.maxwell.af.mil/) PL.
9. Lik, Information Technology Trends and Applications in Science and Business, (Lagos: Concept Publications, 2001) P 105.
10. Microsoft Encarta Encyclopaedia 2007.
11 David M. Moore, Learning from the past Defence ExperienceL Is What is past Prologue? (London Royal United Services Institute for Defence studies) 2000.
12. Martain Van Creveld, Supplying War, Logistics from Wallenstein to Patton (London, Cambridge University Press) 1997.
13. B. Duniya, The Logistics Arts, A Lecture Delivered to Participants of NWC 13 Abuja 2005.
14 William G. Pagonis with Jeffrey L. Cruikshank, Moving Moutains-Lesson in Leadership and Logistics from the Gulf War, (Havard Business School Press Boston) 1992.
15. I. A. Yammah, Manouevrist Approach to Warfare: Implications and Challenges on Logistics for the Nigerian Army. (Unpublished Research Project NWC 14) 2006.
16. Ibid
17. Ibid
18. Ibid
19. Weiss, Egon A. et al, Warfare at Microsoft Students 2008, Redmond WA: Microsoft Corporation 2007.
20. Ibid
21. F 35 Lightening II www.lockheedmartin.com
22. Weiss, Egon A. et al, Warfare at Microsoft Students 2008, Redmond WA: Microsoft Corporation 2007.
23. John J. Cusick, Quted in Doctrine for Logistics for Logistics Support of Joint Operation (JP 4-0) 6 Apr 00.
24. Oscar Morgenstem, "Note on the Formulation of the study of Logistics" RM 614, Santa Monica, (California: Rand, 28 May 1951), P10.
25. Nigerian Armed Forces Joint Vision 2020.
26. US Army Doctrine for Logistics Support for Joint Operation, JP 4 – 0.6 Apr 00. PGL-9.
27. Military Transportation Microsoft (R) Students 2008, Redmond, WA, Microsoft Corporation 2008.
28. Parachute Microsoft (R) Students 2008, Redmond, WA, Microsoft Corporation 2008.
29. Sweetman, Bill 'Unmaned Aerial Vehicles, Microsoft (R) Students 2008, Redmond WA Microsoft Corporation 2008.
30. Ibid.

31. The Logistics Arts, A Lecturer Delivered to Participants of NWC 13 Abuja 2005.
32. Ibid.
33. Ibid
34. Big Parmodh Sarin (Indian Army), Military Logistics. The Third Dimension, (Manas Publication New Delhi) 2000, Page 38.
35. Brig Gen B. Duniya, The Logistics Arts, A Lecture Delivered to Participants of NWC 13 Abuja 2005.

CHAPTER 18

LOGISTIC PLANNING IN JOINT MILITARY OPERATIONS

F. N. N. OSOKOGU

When the battle is going well, the strategists and tacticians are lionized, however, when the tanks run out of fuel it is heads of the logisticians that are hunted

PREAMBLE

History is replete with proud and aggressive military commanders who focused enormous attention on their operational plans; but neglected the basic logistic requirement for sustaining the forces deployed in combat. The results were that brave soldiers could not fight because they lacked basic logistic like water, ammunition, food, medical supply, clothing, transportation and spares among many others. The failure to provide these basic requirements would no doubt lower the tempo of operation and subsequently lead to loss of battles and lives. Logistics, which some writers defined as the science of planning, carrying out the movement and maintenance of forces is an important war-winning factor. Its importance was further emphasized by Field Marshal Lord Wavell during the Burma Campaign when he said:

> *The more I have seen war, the more I realize how it all depends on administration and transportation (what our American allies call logistics). It take little skill or imagination to see where you would like your army to be and when; It takes much knowledge and hard work to know where you can place your forces and whether you can maintain them there. A real knowledge of supply and movement factor must be the basis of every leader's plans[1].*

Golushko also stated that;

> *"In modern warfare, no success is possible unless military units are adequately supplied with fuel, ammunition and food and their weapons and equipment are maintained"[2].*

Logistics in its earliest form simply had to do with an individual warrior carrying sufficient food and weapons to support him for the duration of the battle; only to forage in the battle space if his supply is exhausted. This is what is call living off the land or combat survival in modern warfare. But as warfare became more protracted and complicated; more elaborate methods of providing and sustaining forces emerged. Today, the complexity of modern warfare demands vast logistics support ranging from creation of logistics in industries to Host Nation logistics support, maritime pre-positioning of logistics ships, super cargo aircraft and fleet hospital ships amongst

258

other logistics arrangements. Of course, the synergy of a nation's logistics capability must be located at the highest strategic levels and superintended by the political and industrial stay powers[3].

A classic example of modern application of logistics in recent times was the mobilization for operation Desert Storm in the Gulf War of 1991 by the coalition forces. In the preparation for that battle, there was extensive provisioning and lifting of resources over long distances. Within one month, 100,000 troops and assorted equipment which in due course increased to a total of 350,000 troops, 2,500 armored vehicles, 46,000 tones of ammunition, thousands of tones of other war fighting equipment were flown into the Gulf. The magnitude and effectiveness of the Allied logistics build-up created an atmosphere of fear and defeat among the Iraqis even before the war began. An analyst of the Gulf War once observed on the logistics build up of the coalition forces at the beginning and end of the war effort for the Iraqis when he stated that:

> *The Iraqi army stood by and watched on the television as American Army assembled a sophisticated combat force in front of them with efficiency and dispatch. The act of building the logistics infrastructure during the Desert Shield created an atmosphere of domination and a sense of inevitable defeat among the Iraqis long before the shooting war began[4].*

On the other hand, instances abound where failure had resulted from non application of sound logistics concepts. The German invasion of Russia in 1941 failed due largely to poor logistics planning and application, despite eight months of preparation. Failure to equip the German troops for winter operations adversely affected the troops. Infact the invasion of Normandy by the Allied Forces in 1944 had to be delayed for about 3 months for logistics reasons. Suffice to say that, logistics dictates the pace and sets the operational limits of military operations[5].

At the strategic level, logistics creates the capability that facilitates the conduct of military operations by mobilizing and transforming national power, natural endowment and industrial capacities etc into weapons, equipment and supplies in support of a joint force commander. At the operational level, it delivers these elements in optimal operational state to the theatre of operations and ensures continuous operational availability.

The Nigeria Armed Forces since its inception, have been involved in military operations other than War (MOOTW), Internal Security (IS), Counter Insurgency CI, Amphibious and Peace Support Operations (PSOs). These operations have required extensive logistics support to prosecute. Meanwhile, DHQ remains saddled with the responsibility of coordination and prosecution of each of these operation. How then has the Defence Headquarters faired in the provisioning of logistics and combat support for military operations in the Nigerian armed forces? This is the main thrust of this chapter.

CONCEPTUAL CLARIFICATION
LOGISTICS

The origin of the word "logistics" could be traced to the Latin word logistics meaning skilled in calculating, which is derived from the Greek word "logos" meaning calculation[7]. It however gained general usage in the US Army during the Second World War. The modern word "logistics" was coined from Marechal General de Logis by the French strategic Baron Antoine Henri Jomini who defined logistics as:

> ...the art of moving armies. It comprises the order and details of marches and camps, and of quartering and supplying troops; in a word, it is the execution of strategic and tactical enterprises.[6]

It is perhaps on the account of this that some have defined logistics as movement, storage and supply of troops and equipment. In general terms, military logistics is the means by which operations are sustained and linkages provided between those forces on active duty and their national strategic resources. It is the process of planning for and providing goods and services in support of military operations. The science of logistics therefore concerns the integration of strategic, operational and tactical sustainment efforts within the theatre.

Based on historical analysis, logistics is accepted as a dynamic term which has no single definition. The difficulty in agreeing on a single precise definition of logistics notwithstanding, it is possible to recognize a definite structure in logistics. Such recognition gives understanding of the fundamental realities of the concept irrespective of terminology. Starting from the basic definition of logistics as the provision of the means to conduct military operations, we can proceed to identify four broad categories that make up the means of military operations as, men, material, facilities and service. In providing these categories of military means, there are three fundamental elements namely: determination of requirements, balanced procurement and timely distribution. These management and command process in turn involve organization, planning, execution and supervision, which constitute the basic aspects of logistics.

It is against this background that some established definitions of logistics will make sense. For example, Newton believes that logistics is the forgotten dimension and the inseparable component of military strategy[7]. Logistics according to him governs how military units can be moved to a theatre of operations and maintained there subsequently[8]. He believes that logistics governs the phasing of battle plans and often the selection of tactical objectives. The US military on the other hand defines logistics as "the science of planning and execution of all military matters not included in tactics and strategy"[11]. The definition goes further to identify the concern of logistics as movement and maintenance of forces. William Pagonis recently emphasized the dimension as integration and coordination of "transportation, supply, warehousing, maintenance, procurement, contracting and automation into coherent functional areas into the definition of logistics. This in a way prevents sub-optimization in any of these activities and in a way permits and enhances the accomplishment of a given goal, objective or mission"[9]. Logistics in its widest perspective therefore, includes the ability of the national infrastructure and manufacturing outfits to support and supply the armed forces deployment in the field using the national transportation and communication system[10].

The relative combat power that military forces can bring to bear against an enemy in its entire ramification is constrained by a nation's capacity to plan for, gain access to, and deliver forces and material to the required points of need across the range of military operations. The purpose of logistics according to White and Hendrix primarily is to facilitate the achievement of the objective of a battle, war or campaign which in turn is derived from the national purpose[11]. In this paper, therefore, logistics will be viewed as the process of planning, executing the projection, movement and sustained, reconstruction, and redeployment of operating forces in the execution of national security policy.

MILITARY OPERATIONS

For a comprehensive understanding of this chapter, it is important to take a cursory look at the concept of military operations. This is necessary because of the influence of logistics in achieving its success and the need to distinguish it from joints operations. Strategy, military operation and tactics are the three components of war. Military operation is however the component that I will be concentrating on in this chapter. Military operation as a concept first appeared in the 20th Century in the Soviet Union as 'operational art' according to Newell[12]. The concept at tactical level is the principal tool of the commander for integrating all elements of his forces in a unified effort against an enemy. It is a concise statement of how the commander plans to fight and win the battle.

Military operation as a concept is the application of policy, planning, management, and administration principles in employment of military forces and resources in daily formation and unit activities to achieve a specific goals[13]. While the first aspect is a concept, military operation itself can involve the carrying out of a strategic or operational manoeuvre through management of logistics movement of forces. In general tactical use, it refers to military combat operations or military missions which are the subset of military operations.

In the process of carrying out an operation, the forces may require provision of services, training, or administrative functions to allow them to commence, continue and end combat. This may also include the conduct of movement, supply, attack, defense, and maneuvers needed to achieve operation's objectives in a battle or a campaign. Military operations can be classified by the scale and scope of force employment, and their impact on the wider conflict. The scope of military operations can be: theatre, campaign, operation or battle[14].

It is a well known fact that the ultimate objective of war is for one nation to compel another to do its will by the use of military power through military operations. Ogwu posits that countries use military operations for power projection which requires the political will and material to project the national interest[15]. According to Clausewitz, he posited that before the commencement of every war, its character and main outline should be defined according to what political reasons led to the commitment. This according to him was to ascertain the scale of the means (logistics) to be put forth for that particular war to achieve the objective[16].

Cushman also believes that military operations cannot be conducted without the full range of logistics support which include; airlift, sealift and operational bases[17]. It is, therefore, crystal clear that for any military operation to be successful, logistics plan must be fully and intelligently articulated, developed and executed. Montgomery buttressed this when he said that "there must be a clear cut, long term relationship between operational intentions and administrative resources"[18]. The import of logistics on military operation therefore need not be over emphasis as without adequate and timely delivery of logistics at the right place, military operation would not be successful.

FORCE CAPABILITY AND READINESS

Capability of a force refers to its degree of combat superiority over the adversary in battle. Operational capability is driven by four components: force structure, modernisation, sustainability and readiness[19]. A military should have a force structure that allows for flexibility to perform offensive, defensive and supportive roles. While modernisation is the upgrading or outright acquisition of weapon systems with improved firepower and combat efficiency over previous systems in the inventory, sustainability connotes the ability of the force to absorb, operate, maintain and support equipment and personnel. Force readiness relates to the effectiveness of a force. Capability further manifests in chasing the human development index of the military to prosecute and manage equipment and logistics. Factors such as quality of the available human resources both skilled and unskilled, level of training, frequency of exercises and provision of logistics are some of the fundamentals that affect the readiness of a force for operation.

Readiness, according to the USAF Joint Publication 1-02, is the:

> *Ability of forces, units weapon system or equipment to deliver the outputs for which they were designed....to deploy and employ without unacceptable delays.*[20]

Readiness of a force therefore connotes the possession of the required manpower, the right equipment and training and maximizing the taken for such a force to undertake its assigned task(s). Closely linked to force readiness is operational readiness. Though they differ in the sense that readiness is concerned with effectiveness of a force while operational readiness lay emphasis on the efficiency of a force. Operational readiness is a critical factor in responding to major and sudden contingencies in the country and in our peace support operations around the world. It is an important tool used in the military to measure efficiency of a force in conformity with their constitutional roles. The DHQ and the Service Chiefs are responsible for the operational readiness of the Armed Forces. I suppose you are by now wondering what is the meaning of all these. Note that readiness will involve high logistics demand on the military. Peace time logistics will have to be separated from wartime logistics. The military forces have been tasked to do hard and dangerous jobs and in the process, may put their lives on the line. It is, therefore, necessary to provide them with the best possible equipment and logistics to make their task less hazardous and more enthusiastic to undertake.

Modern battle-winning forces need equipment which will give them a decisive technological edge at critical points in the theatre of battle. Logistics as co-determinant of successful operations provides the means to create and to support combat forces. Logistics limits the combat forces which can be created and in its operational sense, it limits the forces which can be employed in combat operation[21]. There is the urgent need for investment in DICON, to increase R&d funding, all in the effort to enhance our state of readiness. Single service skills and ethos that remain the essential foundations will be conducted by joints forces composed of fighting units from the different services. DHQ, therefore, has the enormous task of harnessing the logistics requirements of the military at the Joint Forces level to synergies the country's total resources and ability to prosecute successful operations.

Since war or conflict could suddenly occur, all services need to be combat ready at all times. The Navy should practice the techniques of sailing, replenishment at sea and tactical response to hostile or belligerent entities. The Army develop and practice logistics exercises while the Air force should improve their method of re-supply, refueling among others. All these could be seen as logistics which could be called the logistics aspects of a force combat readiness. "It is the ability to undertake, to build up and thereafter to sustain, combat operations at the full combat commanders in those areas that are vital to the security of the nation"[22]. In achieving this state, the following factors need to be considered: mental attitude of commanders, the balance of forces, logistics plans, logistics organization, the state of material readiness, training and exercises of the force.

Worthy of note also, is the aspect of economic blockade as a major means of logistics denial to the enemy forces. This invariably reduces the effectiveness and efficiency of the opposition. While every effort is on to improve own capability and force readiness, a total or partial blockade of adversary sources of logistics are areas the higher management of Defence organisation must exploit in their future operations, as logistics remains the live wire of combat forces. This was attested to in the Joint Logistics Warfare Publication 4 – 00, which noted the failure of an enemy operations to have been caused by logistics. It reads thus;

> *Throughout the struggle, it was in his logistics inability to maintain his armies in the field that the enemy's fatal weakness laid. Courage his forces have in full measure, ammunition and food alike ran short and the dearth of fuel caused their powers of tactical mobility to dwindle to the vanishing point. In the last stages of the campaign*

263

they could do little more than wait for the allied advance to sweep over them[23].

Logistics in the Nigerian Armed Forces can be categorized into two: peacetime and wartime logistics. The peacetime logistic comprises those efforts embarked upon to ensure that the Nigerian Armed Forces attain adequate capability required to meet its constitutional responsibilities. This entails provision of adequate working and comfortable living environment, provision of necessary working and combat equipment. The mechanism for provisioning of combat equipment is usually through upgrading of existing equipment, the procurement of new equipment or exploring other possibilities through research and development to meet operational challenges of the future[24].

The logistics for military operations (wartime) in the Nigerian Armed Forces on the other hand entails the assembly and delivery of combat material in the right quantity, to the right place at the right time in order to maintain a force in an operational theatre. In the conduct of any methodology of logistics requirements, therefore, the motivating factor is often the existence of logistics problem. This also involves the urge for a multi-dimensional concept embracing a host of procedures, like the means and ways of proffering solution, and the degree of the problem as well as the outcome of the investigation. In essence, the various procedural steps employed in addressing logistics problems depend heavily on the nature, objectives, available resources, (human, financial and material) and the possible outcome of various steps taken. Thus, administration of logistics services can be simple or complex, depending on its nature and other available resources[25]. For instance, the initial logistics support for the joint operations of the Nigerian Armed Forces in ECOMOG was not as complex as it became when the mandate change from peacekeeping to peace enforcement. This was a clear demonstration of the inadequacy of the existing method of administration of logistics[26].

The Defence Headquarters, should be a policy making and coordinating headquarters during tri-service operations. DHQ through its Department of Logistics should collate and assess logistic requirements from the services. This includes arrangement for land, air and sea transportation. Thus, the main approach of assessment is purely through coordination of requirements of the services particularly in a tri-service setting.

Experience in the peacekeeping operation in Liberia has shown that the present logistics support for joint operations in the Nigerian Armed Forces is not the best. For example, when the mandate given to ECOMOG changed from peacekeeping to peace enforcement, the need to introduce more troops, combat supplies, arms and equipment into the operational theatre to effectively enforce the new mandate became necessary. However, there was a noticeable shortfall in logistics support in the operational area because of inadequacies. The lack of proper coordination coupled with misconception of the operational procedures of the services including personal interests of some individuals, prevented the NN and NAF from being approached to provide sea and airlift necessary to meet the enforcement action in Liberia. DHQ was therefore forced to charter aircraft and ships to effect the bulk delivery of arms and equipment to Liberia. This is attributable to poor assessment/preparedness for logistics requirement.

It is well known fact that wars are not fought and won by single service alone. This therefore calls for the need for a well coordinated logistics chain among the three services in order to achieve success in operation. This coordination in this case should cover procurement, acquisition and maintenance of services equipment without necessarily losing the independence, which each service requires to guarantee and preserve its identity. In this regard efforts are still modest but the spirit and principle must be sustained and even extended to cover other areas of cooperation and jointness[27].

The establishment of a logistics intelligence cell will ensure accurate and timely identification, classification and codification of equipment and materials needed by the various services. Furthermore, the envisaged intelligence cell will ensure accurate and timely determination of true requirements and condition of the equipment required for production. It has also become imperative for the CDS to be empowered constitutionally or through the National Defence Policy to have full authority in all ramifications over the Service Chiefs. This is currently lacking and could be said to have affected greatly the ability of the DHQ to coordinate and integrate the logistics system of the Armed Forces. Each service presently procures their logistics requirement without recourse to DHQ[28].

THE PROCESS OF FUNDING

It is logical to state that the liability or burden of processing bills for funding any logistics consignment lies with the initiator of the consignment. As earlier mentioned, most of the procurements of equipment and materials for the Nigerian Armed Forces are still being done independently by each service or the MOD. Consequently, the funding of such material is equally initiated by the services with the exception of those specifically sponsored by DHQ. However, with the current transformation process, it is hoped that this situation will change in the nearest future to ensure jointness and centralisation in areas that are necessary.

The present peacetime process of logistic procurement and funding is decentralised to the Services and MOD. MOD would have been able to reduce mismanagement and duplication of purchases if it has used DHQ to harmonize the procurement of military requirement. The Due Process Certification system introduced by the Federal Government for all contracts allows each Service to award a contract of not more than 20 million naira through their In-house due process committee known as Residence Due Process Team (RDPT), while those above 20 million but not more than 50 million naira would be awarded by the MOD Residence Due Process Team. A contract of above 50 million naira is awarded by the Presidential Contract Monitoring Committee with the funding centralized. Each of the committees would issue Job Completion Certificate after a contract has been completed satisfactorily and later issue Due Process Payment Certificate to Accountant General of the Federation who would in turn raise cheque in the name of the contractor to MOD for onward transmission to the service involved for payment. It is note worthy, however, to state that contracts executed by the MOD on behalf of the services are confirmed to be of acceptable standard by DHQ basically for professional reasons[29].

The associated problem with this method of procurement and funding is that each Service forwards its logistic requirements to its Department at MOD who independently processes it with HMOD and presents it as budget for that Service. Untill now there is no budget committee that harmonizes all the Services requirements at MOD but it is understood that the Federal Government is coming up with such committee in all ministries including the Presidency. Presently, jointness and interoperability are thrown to the dustbin because of lack of centralise procurement policy. Uniform standard of material and equipment is impossible under the current system where different contractors for example tenders for the same item under the Services and the contract won by different companies. The possibility of an improvement in defence production is reduced due to low patronage of individual service production outfits. A joint production capacity will ensure economy of production, when resources are pooled together for the production of common user items.

The unfortunate aspect of this abnormality is the duplication of facilities that could have been jointly funded and the surplus directed to other important areas of need of the armed forces. An example of this duplication is the setting up of food canteens at the Army and NAF Headquaters, while the Defence Headquarters, is about completing a new canteen within a distance of less than 100 metres between them. We have not been able to address this issue nor overcome and evolve the spirit of collective responsibility in the allocation of scarce resources for now. However, with the funding of items of commonality to the services for joint operations, procurement is expected to be slightly different as this should be exclusive DHQ responsibility. But even in this case, the Department of Joint Services that could unify the procurement has not helped the matter. Some of the time, the department awards contract for an operational logistic requirements to a contractor before directing the same contractor to DHQ for specification. One then wonders about the specification used in awarding the contracts in the first place. Until the Joint Services Department is staffed by either serving or retired service personnel, this problem would most likely persist. On the other hand, one wonders the need for Joint Service Department at MOD which, in my opinion, is a duplication of the role of DHQ. The beginning of effective logistic coordination in the Armed Forces depends on the differentiation of the roles of DHQ and Department of Joint Services at MOD.

SUPPLY LINES AND PROCEDURES

The Nigerian Army logistics supply lines are still mainly through overseas purchases. However, to some extent, local purchases are now being carried out. Ironically, the current local purchases system is not exempted from the foreign influence as they are merely handpicked off the shelf. Although there is a documented procurement policy, however, there still exists indiscriminate procurement of items for the Nigerian Armed Forces. The problem associated with the procedure of buying off the shelf is that, the materials and equipment are manufactured in environments different from where they are used. This has also led to the accumulation of all sorts of arms and ammunition, some of which had become obsolete. There is, therefore, a clear wastage of logistics efforts and multifarious equipment problems resulting in unnecessary large inventory. A further disadvantage of the existing procedure is lack of control over specification, drain in foreign exchange, and unguarantee sources of supply. Also, subsequent maintenance become more difficult and the nation's research and development efforts are invariably inhibited, as they are not encouraged to produce new things. Worst still is the fact that equipment security for the country cannot be assured as dependence on foreign import give political leverage to the seller both in peace and war.

To avert these problems, the guiding principles for logistics planners in the dynamics of successful delivery of logistics services should be simplicity, flexibility, economy, foresight and integrated efforts of all vital sectors. These sectors could be those to be involved in the final production and delivery of the logistics hard and software's servers. Supply lines would have to be streamlined to attain set objectives. It is also necessary to look inwards to source for supplies of equipment and the subsequent maintenance. It is my belief that this approach will encourage development of local skill and ensure the security of equipment.

TRI-SERVICE LOGISTICS SERVICE

The latest trend in logistics management is the relevance of acquisition of materials and equipment in line with technological changes. For example, modern combat ground forces will require sophisticated close air support for effective movement of troops. Therefore, DHQ's view on the scope for further tri-Service logistics service is to position DICON and other military related industries for the 3 Services in contemplation of technological changes. The presidential directive to reorganize and reactivate DICON to be able to produce small arms and ammunition in large scale is already being implemented; it is a welcome development in our effort towards self-actualisation and sufficiency.

The logistics branch for example has forwarded proposal for mass production of uniform and accoutrements for the three services through local manufacturers. As a follow-up, there is the need for effective coordination at DHQ level for the purpose of standardization. This will involve determining the broad outlines of logistics requirements, formulation of logistics policy in line with operations and maintenance plans for the Nigerian Armed Forces. It will also involve preparing appropriate strategies for the acquisition and provision of materials, equipment tools, documents and certain performance target for the Services in order to succeed in military operations.

It is however, to be noted that unless DHQ which should be the apex of defence organization in Nigeria is given constitutional backing, its ability to coordinate the activities and functions of the Armed Forces may not be effective. There is also the need for more regular joint training and exercises to include joint logistics practice to enhance the combat readiness of the Nigerian Armed Forces. To achieve this, I am of the view that logistics intelligence unit be established to guarantee accurate and timely identification, classification and codification of equipment and materials. There are many visible challenges confronting the management of logistics system at DHQ level for the Nigerian Armed Forces. Among these challenges and constraints are training, funding, doctrine, Services individualism sourcing of material, communication, transportation, storage and low level research and development (R&D). The greatest challenge to effective logistics management could however be said to be lack of technological base needed to produce most of the sophisticated equipment, arms and ammunition required by the Nigerian Armed Forces. As earlier mentioned, the over reliance on foreign acquisition of military hardware and software has pervaded the fabrics of the nature of our purchase to the extent that the country has become a dumping ground for all types of goods and services. Since the Nigerian Armed Forces aspiration is to achieve self-reliance, dependence on import for military equipment should not be practised indiscriminately or indefinitely. There must be justification for any procurement contemplated through imports. In order to maintain prudence, we should be able to accurately identify the requirements and develop their technical specifications. While importation may not be totally eliminated, the need to step up effort in area of R & D is imperative.

It is also clear that the military is yet to take advantage of the potentials of the local industries. The Armed Forces is in the best position to further the capacity utilization of the DICON that is currently responsible for the production of small arms and ammunition in the country. This could be done by redefining the present status of DICON by developing it in to a large-scale industry that could produce soft and hardware equipment for the three services through a long-term plan and genuine development of R & D sector. The cottage industries need also to be encouraged to produce accessories as is practised in some developing countries e.g. Indonesia and India. All that is needed are commitment, incentive and encouragement. In essence, the Nigerian Armed Forced need to:

a. Improve on logistics practices, human development and training of personnel.
b. Relate logistics to the needs and aspiration of the troops.
c. Appreciate the effects of modern technology on the logistics requirements of the fighting forces.
d. Rationalizing choices in the use of resources available for logistics services.
e. Adjust operational strategies with complexity of the modern times logistics management.

Other areas of challenges include the need for doctrinal guide for the operation of logistics in the three services, clear cut system of mobilization, contingency plans, integration of some logistics services in the three service and the national resources. The factory production lines and transport network would have to be coordinated in such a fashion that they meet the requirement of a National Defence Logistics Planning Cell at DHQ as was advocated by Maj. Gen. Duniya in a paper he presented at National War College, entitled 'The Logistics Art'. This cell he proposed should include all stakeholders in the productive economic sector. The aim would be to ensure interoperability and compatibility through similar procedures and processes of logistics requirements needed to be known, develop and pre-plan as part of contigency[26]. For example what it entails to convert civilian transport plane to military use if the need should arise.

CONCLUSION

I have to a large extent brought out the complexity of the subject matter and the inability of the current existing provision to adequately effect an efficient administration of logistics services in the Armed Forces. There is also evidence of lack of awareness of the magnitude of uncoordinated logistics system in the Armed Forces. The poor technological base and lack of adequate research and development capability are part of the challenges confronting logistics in the Armed Forces and subsequently military operation. This situation has virtually forced the Armed Forces to remain on a long-term reliance on foreign products, leading to the accumulation of all sorts of arms and ammunition in the nation's inventory. The unharmonized manner of purchases has equally worsened the problem of large inventory of equipment that are not interoperable and obsolete in nature. The poor state of R & D, lack of joint tri-service doctrine on logistics, general logistics mobilization and contingency plans are still areas of challenges that needed to be tackled by the DHQ in its effort to improve the logistics state of the Nigerian Armed Forces.

DHQ is of the view that the Armed Forces cannot continue to live with these problems indefinitely. To address this issue, the National Defence Policy has recognized the need for centralised procurement. In line with the above, there is the need to evolve a well-articulated procurement policy and also set up a centralised procurement organ in DHQ to co-ordinate all defence requirements of the services.

Finally, it is important for MOD to develop a well-coordinated logistics policy among the three services at DHQ level. This is to facilitate standardization of equipment, minimize the cost of logistics services and enhance the Nigerian Armed Forces efficiency and effectiveness in military operation. As a consequence, the following recommendations are therefore proposed:

a.   That Nigerian Armed Forces should take stock of weapon systems in its inventory with a view to standardizing them.
b.   A uniform procurement policy should be put in place by MOD.
c.   That logistics requirement of the three services should be harmonised and procured centrally.
d.   That R & D should be encouraged to improve local production of equipment and goods.
e.   A logistics doctrine should be fashioned out for the three services by HHQ.

NOTES

1. ACP Wavell, in Foxon PD. Powering War, Modern Land Force Logistics (London: 1994) Vol 2 p. 15

2. Julian Thompson, The lifeblood of logistics of war, logistics in armed conflict (UK > Brassey's 1991) pp 9.18.

3. TRADOC, Military History 'Lecture and notes' 3 and 4 vol.2, (Minna: HQ TRADOC NA DATSC, 2002).

4. William G. Pogonis with Jeffrey L Cruikshaunk, Moving Mountains-Lessons in Leadership and logistics from the Gulf War, (Havard Business School Press Boston) 1992. http:/www.2 World War 2.com/principles – of – war htm.

5. US Armed Forced Doctrine for logistics support for joint operations Microsoft Encarta Encyclopaedia standard 2007

6. Jomini HA, The Art of War, translated by Model GH and Graighill WP (US Army) in Julian T, Life Blood of War in Aondo J, "Logistics for the Armed Forces", Lecture delivered at NWC on 1 Mar 06.

7. Clayton Newell, The Framework of Operational Warfare (London and New York: Routledge, Chapman and Hall Inc, 1991), p 101.

8. Ibid

9. William G. Pogonis, Op. Cit.

10. Ibid

11. Eston T. White and Val E. Hendrix, National Security Management: Defence Acquisition and Logistics Management (Washington DC: National Defence University Press, 1994), p. 3.

12. Clayton Newell, Op. Cit p 16

13. Ibid

14. www. Wikipedia.org/wiki/military-operation.

15. Joy Ogwu, "Power in International Politics" in KE Ekwo "Logistics in Military operations: The Nigerian Army Experience"; Research Project submitted to NWC in partial fulfilment of the requirements for the Award fo Fellow of the NWC, (Abuja Jun 2001) p.20.

16. National War College, Precise on Military Strategists for Course 9 (Karl Von Clausewitz and JFC Fuller), p 66.

17. John H. Cushman, Thoughts for Joint Commanders, in KE Ekwo "Logistics in Military Operations: The Nigerian Army Experience"; Research Project submitted to NWC in partial fulfilment of the requirements for the Award fo Fellow of the NWC, (Abuja Jun 2001) p. 21.

18. PD Foxton, Powering War: Modern Land Force Logistics (London: Brassey's UK Ltd, 1994).

19. Arhinghaus B., Military Development in Africa: Political and Economic Risk of Arms Transfer, (Colorado: West View Press, 1984)p.6.

20. Basic Aerospace Doctrine of the United States Air-Force, Air Force Manual 1-1 Vol. II (Washington DC. US Government Press 1992), p. 298.

21. Henry E. Eccles, Logistics in the National Defence (the Stackpole Company Harrisburg Peensylvania USA 1959)p.315

22. Joint Logistics, Joint Warfare Publication 4.00
23. B. Duniya, The Logistics Art, lecture delivered at NWC on 22 Feb. 05.
24. J. Aondo Logistics for the Armed Forces, Lecture delivered at NWC on 1 March 06.
25. J. L. Cruikshaunk and Pogonis WG, Moving Mountains-Lessons in Leadership and Logistics from the Gulf War. (Havard Business School Press Boston) 1992. Cushman USA Army (ret), Thoughts for Joint Commanders, (Maryland: Annapolis press, 1993).
26. B. Duniya, The Logistics Art, lecture delivered at NWC on 22 Feb. 05. E. Ekwo KE "Logistics in Military Operations: The Nigerian Army Experience"; Research Project submitted to NWC in partial fulfillment of the requirements for the Award of Fellow of the NWC, (Abuja Jun 2001) p. 21.
27. C.E. Hendrix and White ET, National Security Management: Defence Acquisition and Logistics Management (Washington DC; National Defence University Press, 1943). Henry E. Eccles, Logistics in the National Defence (the Stackpole Company Harrisburg Pennsylvania USA 1995).
28. National War College, Precise on Military Strategists for Course 9 (Karl Von Clausewitz and JFC Fuller).
29. TRADOC, Military History 'Lecture and notes' 3 and 4 Vol.2, (Minna: HQ TRADOC NA DATSC, 2002). UK, Strategic Defence Review, 1998. US Armed Forces Doctrine for Logistics Support for Joint Operations and www.2World War 2.com/principles –of-war htm. www.wikipedia.org/wiki/military-operation.

CHAPTER 19

NAVAL TECHNOLOGY APPLICATION IN MARITIME INDUSTRY

V. O. S. OLUNLOYO

INTRODUCTION

The sea "serves the dual purposes of harvest and transfer". Harvest refers to a nation's efforts to reap the resources at the sea while transfer involves transportation of goods and services. The quest by the early explorers to harness resources in the sea necessitated evolution of different technologies and capabilities. Apart from the Biblical account of Noah's Ark, the ancestors of the Australian Aborigines and the New Guineans went across the Lambok Strait to Sahul by boat over 50,000 years ago. Moreover, evidence had it that early Egyptians developed the technologies of assembling planks of wood into a watertight hull. The Greek and others introduced multiple banks of oars for additional speed. As technology advanced, Britain built an entirely iron constructed ship. Since 1940, ships have been constructed almost exclusively with welded steel. Essentially, ship construction and repair have been carried out in shipyards and dockyards.

The Dockyard is an important and strategic industry in a number of countries around the world. A nation's need to build and repair its own naval and commercial vessels that support its primary industries cannot be over emphasized. Japan used her dockyards in the 1950s and 1960s to build its industrial structure. Korea made shipbuilding a strategic industry in 1970s and China is now in the process of achieving the same models. South Africa, a littoral state with good technological base has a 25,000 tons Naval Dockyards. The dockyard recently refitted French Naval Warships. The Indian Naval Dockyard is proudly responsible for the building of her submarines and other naval vessels. In addition, the facilities offer commercial services to other shipping outfits. It, therefore, follows that Naval Dockyards are the bedrock for an accelerated growth of the maritime industry.

Nigeria, having realized the importance of developing a naval dockyard, acquired from Elder Dempster line in 1965, a modern engineering outfit to construct small vessels/boats among others. This has since metamorphosed into the present day Nigerian Naval Dockyard. Moreover, as a way of empowering local maritime operators, the Federal Government of Nigeria enacted Cabotage Act of 2003. The aim of this chapter is to highlight the importance of naval dockyard to the growth of a nation's maritime industry.

STRATEGIC RELEVANCE OF NIGERIA'S MARTITIME INDUSTRY

Nigeria's maritime environment is endowed with petroleum and other rich natural resources that support industries and lives of the people. These resources include fish, manganese noodles and shrimps. The maritime environment also facilities the movement Nigerian needs to develop a virile Maritime Industry. Consequently, the Federal Government of Nigeria enacted the Cabotage Act of 2003 which is broadly aimed at promoting the growth of indigenous shipping and the overall development of the maritime Industry in Nigeria.

The itemized objectives of the Cabotage Act are:

    a.   Cargoes originating from Nigerian coastal boundaries/waters are to be exclusively carried by Nigerian ships,

    b.   Such ships are to be wholly owned by Nigerians,

    c.   Building and repair of such ships are to be carried out in Nigeria.

    d.   Such ships are to be crewed by Nigerians.

Prior to the enactment of the Cabotage Act, it was believed that wealth from the Nigeria's maritime resources was eluding Nigerians due to the dominance of foreigners in the country's domestic water borne commerce. The Act was therefore meant to be a means of empowering local operators by guaranteeing a captive local market for Nigeria's fledgling maritime industry. The thinking was that by servicing this captive market, Nigeria's Maritime Industry, particularly its ships building and maintenance capability would be greatly enhanced. Naval technology had earlier been defined as the application of scientific knowledge through devices, machines and techniques for manufacturing and maintaining warships. However, naval technology application could then be adjudged as the key component of realizing the objective of the Cobotage Act and ultimately the development of Nigeria's Maritime Industry.

The Naval Dockyard as earlier defined is an area with docks and equipment for repairing and maintaining warships. This implies that the Naval Dockyards's operation is wholly dependent on the application of naval technology. In view of the previously highlighted importance of naval technology to the development of the maritime industry, the Naval Dockyard would play a pivotal role in the development of the Industry, particularly in achieving the objectives of the Cabotage Act.

ORGANIZATION AND FACILITIES

The Nigerian Naval Dockyards was acquired from Elder Dempster Lines in 1965 and upgraded to its present state in 1990. The objectives of acquiring and modernizing the dockyard are to enhance the Nigeria's strategic self reliance in the maintenance of vessels, develop expertise and embark on design and building of ship and craft. Thus, the NND was set up to acquire and apply naval technology. This acquisition and application are to be achieved using the Dockyard's Manpower organization and its facilities. The Naval Dockyard is the area with dock and equipment for repairing and maintaining ships, while Maritime Industry "includes all enterprises engaged in the business of designing, constructing, manufacturing, acquiring, operating, supplying, repairing and /or maintaining vessels or component parts thereof: of managing and /or operating shipping lines, stevedoring arresters and customs bookerage services, shipyards, dry docks, marine railways, marine repair shops, shipping and freight forwarding services and enterprises. Both the dockyards and maritime industry provide the infrastructural basis for the development and integration of naval technology, defined as "The Study, Development and Application of Scientific Knowledge through devices, machines and technique for manufacturing, producing and maintaining warships".

MANPOWER ORGANIZATION OF THE NND

The NND is managed and run exclusively by professional NN personnel and civilian workforce. The Chief Executives is the Admiral Superintendent who is responsible to a Board of Directors which has the Chief of Naval Staff as the Chairman. The 5 departments of the yard, each headed by a General Manager, in Planning, Yard Services, Finance/Business Affairs and Sea Trials.

The present strength of staff stands at 41 officers, 164 ratings and 186 civilians. The organization encourages division of labour. It is result-oriented and tailored to suit functional management and administration of its hybrid of naval and civilian workforce.

FACILITIES OF THE NND

The NND has excellent facilities that could aid the achievement of its mission. They include graving docks, slipway, various workshops/laboratories sand Yard support services:

i. *Main Graving Dock and Twin Docks:* The graving docks undoubtedly remain the nerve centres of the NND. The well equipped main graving dock, with a dimension of 180m x 24m x 12m is capable of accommodating large vessels up to 10,000 tons for dry docking. There are also 2 smaller docks, each capable of accommodating vessels up to 250 tons, with a dimension of 50m x 15m x 6m. The main graving dock is serviced with a 40 tonne crane while the twin docks both use a 12 tonne crane, with its associated auxiliaries.

ii. *Slipway:* The Dockyard also has a slipway capable of handling up to 5 boats at a time. It is used for slipping small vessels that may not be economical to dock. This slipway is not operational now, however, effort is being made by MOD to replace it with a 500 tonne travel lift or refurbish same.

iii. *Steel Workshop:* The Steel Workshop is equipped to carry out different functions which include circular cutting of steel rod up to 300mm diameter, cold bending and straightening of sections up to 16 mm thickness as well as precision cutting using plasma flame. Its other capabilities are the dishing of plates up to 9 mm thickness as well as MIG/MAG and TIG welding machines for inert gas welding of errous and non-ferrous materials.

iv. *Electrical Workshop:* The Electrical Workshop provides facilities for rewinding of motors, alternators and transformers of up to 500 KVA. The workshop also handles electrical installations onboard ships.

v. *Arsenal Workshop:* Arsenal Workshop houses the facilities for the repairs of ships' electronic system such as navigational aid, presently carry out repair of communication equipment and Decca navigational radars, especially TM 1226 series, which are being phased out, to be replaced with Decca Bridge Masters.

vi. *Mechanical Workshop:* The NND mechanical workshop is equipped with modern machines and equipment of provide excellent engineering and technical services. It is capable of repairing ships' propulsion and auxiliary machinery. There is an engine test bay where engines can be tested after major overhaul. The workshop can also machine components such as shafts, bushings and other complicated fittings.

vii. *Foundry Workshop:* Facilities to cast non-ferrous materials are available in the foundry workshop. It is equipped for melting, moulding and casting.

viii. *Glass Reinforced Plastic Workshops:* The Glass Reinforced Plastic (GRP) Workshop is capable of constructing and refurbishing GRP boats and other ship fittings. The workshop is also equipped to manufacture components for automobile and communication industries e.g. car bumper, mud guards and satellite dishes etc.

ix. *Galvanizing and Electroplating Workshops:* The Galvanizing and Electroplating Workshops handle surface treatment of ferrous materials which are extensively used in ships and industries. It is one of the most modern in West Africa.

x. *Carpentry Workshop:* The Carpentry Workshop is well equipped for carpentry, joinery and cabinet works. It can process wood from timber to finished product.

xi. *Quality Assurance Laboratories:* There is a quality control outfit, which ensures that production procedures and quality of work follow acceptance standards. The outfit has at its disposal facilities for destructive and non-destructive tests. Among the facilities are tensile, compression and torsion test machine, notch impact test machines, hardness test machine, ultraviolet crack detection apparatus, industrial x-ray/photo facility and ultrasonic test equipment.

xii. *Design Offices:* The design offices of the Dockyard are equipped to produce vessel and other maritime platform designs. It also produces all naval architectural drawings needed for the operations of the Dockyard. The designs for ferry passenger boat and water ambulance have been produced, and can be easily adapted for construction of boats suitable for landing operations within the vast waters of the region.

xiii. *Yard Support Services:* A number of support facilities and amenities have also put in place to enhance the performance of the Dockyard. These support facilities include:

a. Alternative Power Plant (Diesel Generators).

b. Compressed Air System.

c. Sea Water and Fresh Water Systems.

d. Material handling and lifting equipment such as cranes, forklifts among others.

e. Fire fighting and Rapid Damage control services section.

    f.   A well equipped Medical Centre including a dialysis section.

    g.   Library.

xiv. The manpower and facilities in the Dockyard make it stand out as an integrated ship repair yard in West African Sub Region- it is indeed a veritable repository of naval technology which could be harnessed towards the development of Nigeria's maritime industry. Given the opportunity, it would compete favourably with other dockyards within or outside Nigeria in the refit and maintenance of Nigerian Navy Ships and ships in the maritime industry. It could also develop the capacity for ship design and construction.

CONTRIBUTION OF THE NND TO THE NIGERIAN MARITIME INDUSTRY

The activities of the NND have impacted positively on NN operations in particular and the maritime industry of Nigeria in general. Some of the feats accomplished are regular maintenance and refit of NN Ships for operations as well as docking and repairs of commercial vessels. Others are the construction of other marine platforms and training.

I.   REGULAR MAINTENANCE AND REFIT OF NN SHIPS.

The NND has refitted and repaired the over 60 NN ships and craft with the attendant savings in foreign exchange and improved availability of the vessels. The result showed during the successful deployment of NN ships to ECOMOG operations and other duties within our territorial waters. Over 72,000 refugees were sea-lifted from Liberia to Nigeria by NNS AMBE and some merchant ships.

The Naval Dockyard also carried out the major refit of NNS ARADU, the flagship of the NN, two Mine Counter Measure Vessels (MCMVs) and six Fast Attack Craft (FAC) Missile. Infact, the refit of NNS ARADU enabled her to participate in the bi-centenary celebrations of the battle of Trafalgar in Portmouth, UK, in 2005. This was achieved despite the contrary predictions of Janes Fighting Ships, an international military publication. Also, NNS ARADU just returned from her recent participation in the bi-centennial celebrations of the Brazilian Navy at Rio de Janeiro last September.

Major refit of two ocean going tug boats is presently at completion stage. This is a singular exercise since the inception of the dockyard that is close to new shipbuilding. This is because except for the hull design and inherited hull frame, virtually every other aspect of the projects was undertaken by NND from scratch including structural works, complete fitting out of all machinery, shafting works, installation of gadgets, power distribution and interfacing functions.

II. DOCKING AND REPAIR OF COMMERCIAL VESSELS.

The Dockyard has docked and repaired over 150 ships belonging to private ship operators and owners in the last decade. Some of these vessels did not require docking to carry out the desired repairs.

III. CONSTRUCTION OF OTHER MARINE PLATFORMS

NND contributed to the fabrication of components for BONGA project. BONGA is the first deepwater project for the Shell Nigeria Exploration and Production Company Limited (SNEPCO) and for Nigeria as a country. Excess NND capacity was utilized by Dorman Long Engineering in the fabrication of some vital components for the project.

TRAINING

NND has contributed to youth and manpower development schemes such as the Industrial Training and National Youth Service Corps (NYSC) Programmes at an average recruitment of 20 persons per year.

The milestones attained by the NND have enabled the NN to justify her existence and relevance as a stakeholder in the economy of the nation. Furthermore, these achievements constitute major contributions in the quest for self-reliance in maintenance of ships and skilled man-power development. However, the NND is yet to attain its full potentials due to some challenges.

CHALLENGES

The NND has been faced with various challenges that prevents it from attaining its full potential. Some of these challenges are inadequate electric power supply, degraded facilities, shortage of skilled manpower, under-development of capacity, insufficient funding, adverse environmental impact as well as inadequate Research and Development (R & D).

I. INADEQUATE ELECTRIC POWER SUPPLY

Regular electric power supply is essential to the operations of an engineering outfit like the Naval Dockyard. Electric power is a major operational input to the main graving dock and the twin docks, the workshops and Yard support facilities such as pumps, capstans etc. To forestall a breakdown of operations due to power outages, the Naval Dockyard was connected to the 33 KV line of the National Grid. The Yard also has three main generators of 900 KVA each and other smaller generators scattered around the Yard to complement the power supply for Power Holding Company of Nigeria (PHCN). Regrettably, the NND connection to the 33KV priority line is defective.

A short term remedy to the aforementioned power supply problems would be the continuous operations and maintenance of the NNDs generators. For the long term, the Dockyard would need to replace its two defective 7.5 MVA transformers on the 33 KV line. These two solutions are presently unachievable because of the lean financial resources of the NND. Hence, the resultant power outages have led to increased downtime and reduced productivity.

II DEGRADED FACILITIES

The NND is a complete and comprehensive engineering outfit with large capital investment outlay. It facilities have to be properly maintained to sustain operations. Presently, the Yard is grappling due to frequent breakdowns of aging facilities and equipment due to inadequate maintenance and unsustainable requirements for repairs warranted by obsolescence owing to fast changing technology. Allied to this is the necessity to upgrade facilities such as slipways and crane capacities to meet the increased demands of production.

The graving docks have been in operation for close to fifteen years and now need refurbishment. The evidence of wear and tear is visible along the dock concrete walls and at the gate's seat/sealing edges. The assessed cost of maintaining and upgrading the facilities of the Yard is beyond its financial resources. However, the degraded state of facilities has continued to lower the productive capacity and revenue of the Dockyard. Hence, the Yard urgently require assistance in order to sustain its aging facilities.

III. SHORTAGE OF SKILLED MAN POWER

The dockyard requires skilled manpower to work, coordinate and manage its activities at all levels. However, many of the qualified officers, ratings and civilian technical staff who specialize on critical systems have either retired or discharged from the Service. Others have migrated to better paying jobs in the oil and gas industry where they would be better remunerated than in the military or civil service. Furthermore, the Naval Dockyards Apprentice School is de-commissioned and has been dormant for over a decade.

A study two year ago indicated that out of about 3,041 technical staff required to carry out maintenance on board NN ships, at the FSGs and NND, only 312 are available. This is only 10% of the requirement. For the NND in particular, the ratio of designed (i.e staff establishment billet) to actual technical strength was 14.1. This depicts a very acute shortage of technical manpower. In order to reverse the current trend, there is need to plan for enlistment of artisans, technicians and engineers in the relevant fields of ship building, systems engineering and dockyard management. The Yard could partner with other companies to jointly develop the common manpower skills required. Presently, NND and Dorman Long Engineering Limited are negotiating with INTSOK of Norway with support from PTDF to set up a fabrication training centre at NDAS.

IV UNDER-DEVELOPMENT OF CAPACITY

The NND faces a major challenge of putting its existing facilities into optimal use. For instance, parts of the Arsenal Workshop meant for the maintenance of combat systems of naval ships are yet to be commissioned thereby limiting the capacity of NND to undertake such jobs. This under-developed military aspects of dockyards facilities which have been neglected for many years is a significant requirement of NND operations given that naval ships are incomplete without functional combat systems.

Similarly, other dormant facilities in the Yard such as the destructive and non-destructive testing laboratories as well as the oxygen and acetylene plants would have improved the industrial output of the Yard if operational. Therefore, there is need to hasten the development of these abandoned facilities for ship maintenance and ultimately shipbuilding. It is heartening to note that the Gas plant and the material testing laboratories have recently receiving attention from prospective private sector partners.

V INSUFFICIENT FUNDING

Another major challenge of the NND is inadequate finding. Funding for the defence sector was very low between 1992 and 2000. During the same period, the European Union placed arms embargo on Nigeria (1995-1999). The effect was a noticeable decline in the ability to maintain military asset. This applied equally to the NND. Although partially commercialized, the NND can hardly break even to have the kinds of profits required to maintain its facilities and equipment and undertake other projects. The establishment cannot afford the 10-15% of acquisition cost of assets to be made available annually for upkeep of facilities.

It has become clear that without massive injection of funds, some of the visions of the dockyard will remain dreams. Therefore, there is urgent requirement for funds to prompt address maintenance problems before they deteriorate, phase out obsolete equipment, upgrade facilities, perform credible R & D studies, train specialists as well as develop the existing but latent ship building potentials. However, government cannot do it alone, hence the need to throw this challenge at the private sector. With the repositioning of the financial sector, the banks are now in a position to assist credible investors. However, the benefits that will accrue from such investments would not manifest immediately as they are for long term results.

VI. ADVERSE ENVIRONMENTAL IMPACT

Equally crucial are the Environmental factors affecting NND operations. These factors include tidal surges, wind, industrial effluent, high traffic density as well as Ships bilge and sewage discharges around the NND. Toxic industrial effluent within the basin could be the cause of the high rate of corrosion experienced in the Dockyard.

The NND experiences tidal surges and turbulence periodically which damages its infrastructures and ships berthed alongside its jetties. High deposits of debris and situation severely affects planning due to long periods of clearing and cleaning of graving docks. These environmental problems also block high capacity drainage pumps as well as damage the caisson gates, berthing hawsers and bollards.

VII. INADEQUATE RESEARCH AND DEVELOPMENT.

There is little or no R&D activity at the NND. Usually, improvements in ship construction and maintenance result from R&D efforts during post design maintenance activity on these ships. Potential areas of R & D in the NND, include foundry products, appropriate paint schemes and applications, environmental studies on corrosion control, fabrication works and maintenance of database for ships. The R&D Department is supposed to champion the improvement of naval technology at the Dockyard, towards solving identified ships problems. Presently, these R & D subjects are not being tackled at NND. In view of Nigeria's low industrial base, there is need to step up R & D activities, in order to promote self-reliance, self sufficiency and efficiency in the quest to acquire naval technology.

Developing countries such as India, Pakistan, Argentina and Brazil identified the centrality of R & D to the achievement of technological transfer. Hence, they have been able to grow their military industrial capacity with a follow up effect on their overall industrial sector. Of significance, R & D has been identified effort. Lack of proper R & D slows down the transition from one level of production to another, such as from assembly to parts production, affect quality of products and inhibits the emergence of local ability to modify or design equipment.

THE WAY FORWARD

The previously mentioned challenges of the NND are not insurmountable. In fact, it behoves on the Dockyard to seek ways of overcoming them in order to ensure that it performs its paramount role of applying naval technology to guarantee the operational availability and readiness of the NN as well as the growth of Nigeria's maritime industry. The proposed solutions include joint venture partnership as well as increased funding and upgrading of facilities. Others are training and sharing of experience as well as outsourcing.

I. JOINT VENTURE PARTNERSHP

The NND needs a technologically competent private concern interested in genuine development, partnership and investment. Such venture must build on the existing potentials of the NND, add value to the primary pre-occupation of applying naval technology, which will lead to self reliance in local production.

The specific aims of such partnership could be to strengthen the indigenous design and development capability through joint R & D; to stimulate transfer of technology and managerial competence for sustained growth in the maritime industry; to improve human resource development and to increase local input in ship construction and maintenance.

II. INCREASED FUNDING AND UPGRADING OF FACILITIES

The NND is presently funded by the Nigerian Navy in accordance with the Federal Government Defence allocations which is not sufficient. There should be greater synergy between NND, industry (equipment manufacturers) and financial institutions aimed at improving productivity. While equipment manufacturers could support the funding of NND indirectly through subsidized logistics supplies, financial institutions on the other hand, could finance maritime industry projects being executed at NND. Such funding would create the opportunity for improved contract planning management of capital projects of the maritime industry such as new constructions.

Obsolete equipment remains a major threat to NND sustainability due to financial constraints. These facilities could be concessioned to private investors on a Rehabilitate Operate and Transfer (ROT) basis. These private investors could also have the privilege of joint venture partnerships in addition to the concessioning.

III. TRAINNG AND SHARING OF EXPERIENCE

Highly skilled manpower is the most important resource in any organization. There is need to pursue a deliberate policy on training at the highest level to cover all areas of naval technology such as hull construction, hull protection, maintenance of machinery and propulsion control systems as well as electronics.

The NND could collaborate with the local shipyards for cost effective training packages and concessions from the manufacturers of such equipment. Furthermore, our shipyards could share relevant expertise on common systems to support each other in the areas of Dockyard Management, Systems Engineering and Shipbuilding Technology.

IV. OUTSOURCING

Outsourcing is a situation whereby some aspects of the operations are contracted out to relevant firms with superior expertise to handle. Such services cover areas from consultancy services to maintenance of facilities. For example, the South African Naval Dockyard at Simons Town out-sources most of its maintenance activities to competent companies and manufacturers for agreed periods and subject to contract renewals. The NND could take a cue from this by identifying major local contractors to out-source the maintenance of some of its facilities for enhanced operations. This would also aid in the spread of naval technology.

CONCLUSION

Nigeria's maritime environment services the dual purposes of economic lives of the people and means for transportation of goods and services. Realizing the importance of these roles, the Nigerian Government acquired the Nigerian Naval dockyard from Elder Dempster Shipyards in 1965 as a basis towards promoting naval technology as a tool for accelerating the growth of maritime industry in the country. As a follow up, Cabotage Act of 2003 was also aimed at empowering local maritime operators and protect the industry from being dominated by foreigners.

The Naval Dockyard is equipped with a graving dock, twin docks, slipway, different workshops among others for repair of equipment and ship's structures. The NND as a custodian of naval technology has refitted and repaired over 62 NN ships and about 150 merchant ships in the last decade which confirmed its pivotal role in the development of Nigeria's Maritime Industry.

Nevertheless, these feats are not without challenges. Among the problems faced by the Yard are inadequate electric power supply, degraded facilities, shortage of skilled manpower, poor funding, adverse environmental impact as well as inadequate research and development. To this end, joint venture partner, increased funding, upgrading of facilities, training and sharing of experiences as well as outsourcing would be a panacea, in ameliorating the problems facing the Naval Dockyards.

PART THREE

ORGANIZATIONAL DEVELOPMENT

CHAPTER 20

PROFESSIONALISATION OF THE NIGERIAN ARMED FORCES

CELESTINE OYOM BASSEY

Treating the military profession as an object of social inquiry enables a fuller and more accurate assessment of its power position in society and of its behaviour in international relations (Morris Janowitz, The Professional Soldier, 1964).

INTRODUCTION

Military sociologists have invariably attributed the multiple and complex problems associated with military institutions in Africa to the perceived abysmal level of professionalism generated by a convergence of systemic and institutional factors and development in these post-colonial states. The general assumption in this classical literature is that military professionalism – in terms of expertise, corporateness and responsibility – is not only the antidote of "aberrant" behaviour (such as military coup d'etat), but the guarantor of military effectiveness and combat efficiency.

In this context, the institutional catharsis of the Nigerian military under prolonged period of military rule (engendered by its distinctive praetorian philosophy of governance) has been widely considered the source of its multiple disorders, over-politicization and low coefficient of combat power. The effective policy response to this unsatisfactory state of the Nigerian military establishment, as seen by the Obasanjo administrarion, resides in the imperative need to institute an irreversible dynamics towards a programmatic professionalisation of the military that touches upon all elements of its institutional ethos and mission: its value structure (ideology), size and composition, quantity and performance of equipment of hardware, logistical reach, capacity of performing sustained, active operations, leadership and doctrine, communications and control, military intelligence effectiveness, and manpower quality in terms of skill, training, physical stamina and morale[1].

Thus, from the policy standpoint of the current administration, professionalisation of the Nigeria military in the post-Babangida-Abacha era (1985-1998) involves two fundamental and interrelated structural decisions: ideological reorientation (professional socialization) of the officer corps and establishing the minimum basis for military organizational effectiveness through a programmatic development of elements of combat power. This chapter is a seminal review of this policy direction of the Obasanjo administration in the last two years within the operative context of policy stipulations of the Minster of Defence, General Danjuma (Rtd.). Such a review, however, could benefit from a preliminary clarification of theoretical and institutional parameters bearing on military professionalisation as the basis for analyzing and comprehending the Administration's effort.

THE CHALLENGE OF MILITARY PROFESSIONALISM

The central problematique of military professionalism remains, in the words of Peter Feaver, how to "reconcile a military strong enough to do anything the civilians ask them to with a military subordinate enough to do only what civilians authorize them to do"[2]. The first element of the problematique – "a military strong enough to do anything the civilians ask them" belongs to the provenance of strategy:

> *Program decisions concerning the strength of the military forces, their composition and readiness, and the number, type and rate of development of their weapons. Use decisions concerning the deployment, commitment and employment of military force, as manifested in military alliances, war plans, declarations of war, force movements and the like*[3]

On this view, strategic decisions identify a particular need implicitly prescribe modalities on the "use, strength, and weapons of the armed forces" in a given security environment. These involve force structure and weapons platforms as well as sustainability and readiness. Considered together, these factors as they are ultimately expressed in human resources (technical skills, leadership, morale, unit cohesion), logistics (supply and maintenance) mobility (rapid movement of troops and equipment, projection of power outside state boundaries), fire power (weapons systems), manpower (number of personnel under arms, level of organization), and command and control (communications facilities and administrative expertise) constitute major determinants of the operational effectiveness of national armed forces as a function of professionalisation[4].

Deficiency in such components may adversely affect both the macro-competence (the ability to organize and manage forces for military ends) and micro-competence (the ability to operate and support modern weapons) of defence establishment. Both are vectors of national military power as determined by combat power of the armed forces: a "combination of the physical means available to a commander and the moral strength of his command". This involves the "total of quantitative and qualitative coefficients" that characterize national military power, and hence capability, to "fulfill particular missions in the required time and situation"[5]. As is generally recognized in defence studies literature, the effectiveness of any national military organization as a function of combat power is a product of the threshold of professionalisation[6]. Hence, Morris Janowitz's contention that:

> *The military face a crisis as a profession: how can it organize itself to meet its multiple functions of strategic deterrence, limited warfare, and enlarged politico-military responsibility? First, there is the complex task of adapting the military establishment to continuous technological change. Second, there is the necessity of redefining strategy, doctrine,*

> *and professional self-conceptions. Maintaining effective organization while participating in emerging schemes, such as regional security arrangements, will require new conceptions and produce new tasks for the military profession[7].*

Professionalism, therefore, remains the hallmark of modern military institutions. The armed forces is, as Samuel Huntington notes[15], "strongest and most effective when it most closely approaches the professional idea; it is weakest and most defective when it falls short of that ideal"[8]. The distinctive sphere of military professionalism resides in "the management of violence" and the functional imperative of the armed forces is combat. In this institutional context, the "modern officer corps is a professional body and the modern military officer a professional man: as a professional, his sphere of operation falls within the first line of defence of the core and context – specifics values of the state. His duties, as Huntington argues (1957:11) notes, spans the "direction, operation, and control of a human organization whose primary function is the application of violence" and central operational task, namely:-

    i.   The organizing, equipping and training of this force.
    ii. The planning of its activities, and
    iii. The direction of its operation in and out of combat.[9]

As will be amplified upon below in the Nigerian context, the protracted involvement of the military in politics (praetorian Army) inexorably compromises professional ethos as several examples from Africa, Latin America and Asia demonstrate. The "military mind" and "military ethics", more often than not, give way to military greed and psychosis of power as in the case of Mobutu Zaire and Abacha Nigeria. As Amos Perlmulter concludes, "on the whole praetorian conditions affect the military establishment negatively, lowering the standards of professionalism and resulting in fratricide as family feuds break out, coup occur, and officials are assassinated". Since the "praetorian's mobility is very high compared with that of the classical professional soldier, corporate orientation, status and military ideology supercede skill and knowledge as professional requirements. Political loyalty and coup-making skill supplant the traditional skills of the professional soldier". Hence, under General Abacha (1993-1998), political generals supplanted combat generals as promotions became routine, tribalised, and in many cases, a travesty of military ethos"[11].

The second element of the problematique – "a military subordinate enough to do only what civilians authorized them to do" – borders on the intractable problem of "civilian control" (or "civil supremacy") of the military and its subordination to the "public will". This is a central consideration in democratic governance and the paramount objective of the process of professionalisation of the armed forces in a constitutional order. As the experiences of emerging democracies of Latin America, Africa and Asia in the 1970s through 1990s show, the weakening of civil supremacy and the wider involvement of the military in domestic politics often forewarn of demise of such experiments in constitutional practice, as in the First and Second Republic of Nigeria. The answer to this political melodrama, as several theorists of civil-military relations contend, is to maximize "military professionalism" as a function of institution and acculturation. Thus, ideally, in terms of professional socialization, the military officer is "above all, obedient and loyal to the authority of the state, competent in military expertise, dedicated to using his skill to provide for the security of the state, and politically and morally neutral[12]".

While this ideal typology of the officer corps is often seen as a characteristic of professional military systems (a product of protracted and complex sociological developments in Europe and North America), its emergence in the contemporary Third World condition cannot be taken for granted. In other words, comparative experiences in the Third World since the 1960s have sufficiently demonstrated that the central assumptions of "theoretical practitioners" such as J.J. Johnson, Lucian Pye and Guy Pauker (Literature on the military as political agents of modernization) are logically unsound and sociologically untenable. As Robert Price incisively observes:

> *A striking characteristic of the literature on military rule in developing countries is the gap between theoretical expectations and political, social and economic reality. For when the organizational forms of European armies are copied and transplanted to a "transitional" social and cultural environment they may undergo transformations in the process: transformations that may seriously alter the behaviour of the organization and its members. By the failure to take account of these transformations, the explanatory power of the formal organizational model is severely weakened[13].*

To argue, for instance, that the Nigerian or Ghanaian military is a product of Western organization and technology and is, therefore, an "ideologically and structurally cohesive organization capable of high levels of internal discipline and … whose members share a professional belief system combining the elements of secular rationality, puritanical asceticism, patriotic nationalism, dedication to public service", and an apolitical orientation (as was widely assumed in the immediate post-independence era), is rather an act of value judgment and preference rather than sociological contestation. The African condition in general and the Nigerian experience in particular embody the negations of such ideal-type neo-Weberian demarche.

In his premier work on *Political Order in Changing Societies*, Samuel Huntington explains why:

> *As society changes, so does the role of the military. In the third world of oligarchy, the soldier is a radical; in the middle-class world he is a participant and arbiter; as the mass society looms, the conservative guardian of the existing order. The extent to which a politicized officer corps plays a conservative and reform role in politics is a function of the expansion of political participation in the society[14].*

Huntington's caveat has been reechoed in a number of empirical studies such as Bengt Abrahamson's Military Professionalisation and Political Power (1972), William Gutteridge's Military Institutions and Power in New States (1974), Claude

Welch's (ed) Soldier and State in Africa (1970) and Eric Nordlinger's Soldiers in Politics (1977). The arguments proffered in these literatures are generally the same: the social and political condition of a society will "determine the role played by the military, not the armies' organizational characteristics". In other words, the professional military and the professional soldier are quintessential products of the "secularization of society and the economic and legal rationality...provide the setting for the professional military organization as well as for the modern bureaucratic state structure with its norms of coercive, legal and rational order[15]" Thus Amos Perlmutter has trenchantly argued that:-

In most aspects of its development the modern professional organization has generally emulated staff was contemporary with the rise of modern corporation and its elaborate system of planning; in fact, the former contributed to the rise of the latter. Feudal Patrimonialism had influenced the professional army. The economic captain of industry, not the heroic soldier; the career officer, not the old feudal chief; the rational authoritarian leader, not the feudal warrior – these became the models of the new armies[16].

The "materialization" and "condensation" of the doctrine of civil supremacy and civilian control cannot, therefore, be taken for granted, especially in the context of nascent democratic systems. The "maximization of civilian power" will depend critically, on the one hand, on the threshold of military professionalisation and, on the other hand, on the extent to which the constitutional order – the rule of law – is promoted and defended by practitioners in government. On this premise, there is fairly high degree of consensus in the literature that in "modern civil-military relations there is a high correlation between the type of nation-state and the type of military organization". Hence, Perlmutter contention that:

Political conditions dictate the nature of civil-military relations. A stable, sustaining, and institutionalized civil regime can hardly succumb to military pressure and rule. Nor can the military establish–the most dependent bureaucracy of the modern nation-state, challenge a well established political order. The military is motivated to intervene only when its corporate or bureaucratic roles seem threatened, a condition that does not usually exist in highly institutionalized and complex political systems. And even if it has such intentions, the military must be aware of the futility of challenging such a regime[17].

Perlmutter's observation basically reinforces the theoretical conclusions of Samuel Huntington's institutionalization theory which attributes the ubiquity of military interventionism in the politics of Third World social formations and the resultant instability of the political order to the rapid mobilization of new groups into politics coupled with the slow development of political institutions[18]. Military intervention in African as well as in Asian and Latin American countries, therefore, is primarily the inexorable consequence of failure to develop political institutions sufficiently adaptable, complex, autonomous and coherent to cope with the emergence of new and variegated social forces resulting from profound changes in these societies. Thus, the failure to establish and sustain "civilian supremacy" over the military in the First and Second Republic in Nigeria, from this standpoint, is precisely a systemic resultant of this development: "Social forces were strong, political institutions weak. Legislatures and executives, public authorities and political parties remained fragile and disorganized. The development of the state lagged behind the evolution of society[19]"

In this regard, one of the major casualties of interventionary behaviour of "rambunctious colonels" is military professionalism. In stable political order, on the other hand, the greater the rationalization of military profession and therefore the greater its professionalisation, the "more politically responsible it becomes" – the more oriented toward a role subordinate to the civilian control of the military which new democratic dispensations such as Nigeria seek to promote rest on both "subjective" and "objective" foundations:

    i.   The maximization of military professionalism (objective principle), when the potential for military intervention is low; and

    ii.   The maximization of civilian control (subjectivity principle), when the potential for military intervention is high.

In both contexts, the armed forces as a profession is subordinate to civilian authorities. As Christopher Gibson and Don Snider suggest, from epistemic standpoint, this calls for two levels of analysis of civil-military relations: "one, subordination to authority; the other, compatibility of the professional military ethic with the prevailing political ideology in society[20]".

Although Huntington's thesis, that professionalism and political intervention are antithetical, has been subjected to devastating criticisms, on methodological and substantive grounds, it still provides a useful and theoretically defensible framework for the analysis and comprehension of the Nigerian condition[21]. B.J. Dudley contended, for instance, that "the institutionalization theory, has "no scientific status; it is neither applicable to the world nor useful to understand it[22]". By explicating political instability and military intervention in Nigeria largely as a function of political "modernization" and "development", the institutionalization perspective poses a veritable form of reductionism which sees disorder as a defined stage in an established progression towards an assumed model of stable political institutions: the competitive capitalist state or the "open market societies", in the words of C.B. Macpherson. In this respect, the conceptual bias of the institutionalization approach misleads by seeking to parade what is patently ideological as a "theoretical", "conceptual" construct.

In specific terms, several other critics have castigated the tautological character of Huntington's reasoning. S.E. Finer raised trenchant issue of empirical validity and theoretical adequacy of Huntington's thesis in an observation that such armed forces as the German or the Japanese (before the Second World War), with highly professional officer corps, would have to be declared "non-professional" simply because they intervened in politics in violation of the principle of civilian supremacy[23]. Furthermore, both Janowitz and Sarkesian have demonstrated that:

> *In many armed forces the professional orientation of the officer corps is associated with a political outlook distinctly different from the dominant view prevailing in civilian society. Such a dichotomy, if strong enough and left unchecked, tends to produce tensions and in an extreme case may even push the military into open rebellion "against" the civilian authorites[24].*

Empirical support for this view derives from the French military revolts of 1958 and 1961, the behaviour of the highly professional Chilean officer corps in the 1973 coup and the Greek military coup d'etat, which resulted from a "basic incongruence between the "military mind" and the democratic ethos of Greek society". Common to those criticisms is the assumption that "alienation of the military in its professional capacity from the general moral orientation of the state can lead to severe tension" and even intervention (Van Doon, 1969:55). Although these caveats cannot be lightly discounted, Huntington's thesis has also received extensive support from a wide range of historical and sociological studies[25].

In analytical terms, what this controversy seems to suggest is a theoretical synthesis in Hegelian tradition: that truth is to be found neither in the thesis nor the antithesis but in the emergent synthesis that reconciles elements of both. Amos Perlmutter (1978) and Charles Moskos ("Pluralistic model" of civil-military systems) have both reasoned along this line: that the "controversy can be resolved by emphasizing the two key concepts of corporate professionalism – the maintenance of expertise standards and the defense of corporateness or exclusivity[27]". Hence, Perlmutter contention that:

> *Huntington is, however, generally dismissive of these efforts at theoretical synthesis or, to be explicit, epistemic compromise. As he puts it: "all this extraordinarily suggestive. Professionalism involves a balance among expertise, responsibility, and corporateness, and the corporatism which leads to intervention represents a perversion of Professionalism, in which the corporatist element overbalances the components of expertise and responsibility"[28]*

In the final analysis, it seems reasonable to underscore Huntington's conceptualization of civil-military relations as a paradigmatic context of the Nigerian condition. First, is his ..... that the officer corps and civilian elites constitutes distinct groups; second, that the relations between these groups are "inherently conflictual in nature"; third, that "what keeps the conflict within bounds is subordination of the officer corps to civilians except on matters requiring military expertise". Finally, "the perceived shifts in civil-military relations over time is a function of the degree of effectiveness of civilian control"[29]

Accordingly, in a nascent democratic experiment such as Nigeria, the consummate goal of armed forces professionalisation is not only to restore the fighting power of the military establishment – "a military strong enough to do anything the civilians ask them to" – but also institutionalizing civil control (irrespective of provocative societal conditions) over the military and the subordination of the latter to "public will". This means a "military subordinate enough to do only what civilians authorize them to do" by setting the "proper limits to the activities" of the Nigerian officer corps.

NIGERIAN MILITARY: IMPERATIVES OF PROFESSIONALISATION

It could hardly be contested that the Nigerian military was in a state of crisis at the inception of the Fourth Republic. Systemic development in the Babangida-Abacha era (coups and preemptive coups, aborted national elections and the June 12 crisis, the collapse of the Transitional Government of Shonekan, the Diya Saga, Abiola and Abacha's death) had a convulsive and traumatic impact on the corporate structure (group consciousness and bureaucratic organization) of the Nigerian armed forces. At Abacha's death, the military was beset by manifest syndicalism, hatred and mistrust (as could be seen in empty officer's messes throughout the country), collapse of *esprit de corps* (camaraderie), virulent ideological cleavages and obnoxious system of patronage and nepotism. In short, the armed forces, in Ali Mazrui's words, reverted into "militarized ethnicity":

> *Their hubris in entering politics so violently brought the wrath of the gods upon them – unlocking further terrible conflicts over which they could have little control, and in which so many of them were destroyed. As Max Weber put it, "whoever contracts with violent means for whatever ends – and every politician does – is exposed to its specific consequences*[30].

Thus, in his incisive survey of the political environment at the beginning of the Fourth Republic Omo Omoruyi's verdict on the state of the Nigerian armed forces was unapologetic and unequivocal: "Nigeria does not have a 'Nigerian' military and Nigeria does not have a 'professional' military. This is the history of Nigeria since 1966". Copious evidence adduced by the former Director-General of the Centre for Democratic Studies (CDS) include the composition and structure of the military high command; the process of officership recruitment which turns the Nigerian Defence Academy into training ground for political ('militicians') rather than combat officers; officers who prefer to remain colonels and military governors, instead of being promoted to a higher rank only to be sent to command troops; officers who preferred being made to retire and continue as ministers. As a consequence, "professional military titles were dying while political ones were becoming the preferred ones"[31].

Given this development, the threshold of military professionalism which was a central focus of the armed forces modernization Programme initiated in 1975 under the Mohammed-Obasanjo regimes, fell to the lowest ebb in terms of the indices of control and discipline, as General Diya's recent utterances on Major Mustapha before the Oputa Panel and his incarceration experience suggest. Ladipo Soarse has noted in this regard that the intervention of the military in politics "brought adverse political consequences on its professionalism and ethics. It brought demands and pressure;

the cohesion cracked along ethnic and sectional cleavages which led to further coups and counter-coups". Furthermore, "the military values of discipline, puritanism and modesty" have been replaced by "greediness, materialism and indiscipline" which have had adverse effects on professionalism[32]. In effect, military regimentation and military ethic gave way to a culture of indiscipline, arrogance, hedonism, favoritism and nepotism. The military "came to believe", as Julius Ihonvbere laments, "that there were two political parties in Nigeria: the military and the people; since it, the military, monopolized the means of coercion, it was the superior party[33]".

The collapse of organizational cohesion (both horizontal-solidarity-and-vertical-authority and discipline) of the Nigerian military in the period June 1985-1998, no doubt resulted from institutional politicization under the military autocracy (rather than Junta rule) of Babangida and Abacha and the extent to which primordial sentiments and cleavages were manipulated to perpetuate personal rule. As the current commandant of the National War College, Rear Admiral Gabriel Shiyanbade, has noted:

> In an era of regime of absolutism, no sector is safe. Because power is not exercised according to any laid down or established procedures, power itself is held hostage by fear. Every sector is considered a threat, including the military. Indeed, in a non-democratic environment, the military finds itself in double jeopardy[34].

This is so because, as Shiyanbade argues, on the one hand, "it stands the risk of becoming the instrument for the coercion of the wider society and thus being viewed by society as an enemy". On the other hand, "because it is the most credible instrument of organized violence in society, absolutism is uncomfortable with it, and so spends so much effort in watching it and, as much as possible, weakening it…. We dare say that the military is always the first casualty when democracy is overthrown"[35]. Hence, the traumatic attrition suffered by the Nigerian armed forces in the Babangide-Abacha era as a result of regime insecurity and syndicated process towards self-succession[36]. The imperative for re-professionalisation of the armed forces in the Fourth Republic arises from the systemic need to establish a value congruence between the corporate orientation of the military and the state in the new democratic dispensation, as a praetorian "army amidst a democratic people will always be a source of great danger". From the policy speeches of both the President and the Minister of Defence, it could be asserted that it was in the context of the above unsalutary condition of the armed forces and its attendant dissatisfaction that the scheme of professionalisation emerged at the beginning of this Administration as the operative principle of defence management.

POLICY DIRECTION

As earlier noted, the two key issues in the armed forces professionalisation Programme are the twin pillars of "control" and "skills" as the "two key qualitative variables of military professionalism[38]". That is, how simultaneously to subordinate a praetorian military to "public will" and how to ensure that it has the requisite resources (expertise and hardwares) to "do anything the civilians ask them to".

Regarding the first issue – area ("Control" or Civil Supremacy"), the challenge, as articulated by Admiral Shiyanbade, is "to redefine an approach to the promotion of military professionalism with ...., in such manner as shall be consistent with the dictates of democracy, the constitution and international standards". This, in specific terms, as President Obasanjo outlined in his address at the Course[7] graduation ceremony of the National War College, requires that officers and men of the Armed Forces must embrace in "its totality, the fundamental doctrine of military subordination to civilian authority" as stipulated in the 1999 Constitution of the Federal Republic of Nigeria.

As a consequence of the Administration's awareness that one of the major obstacles to the achievement of the subordination of the military to civil authority in the Fourth Republic lies in what Omo Omoruyi termed "ethicized and politicized character" of the Nigerian military, its first decisive action was to retire those officers whose role as political appointees, helped to sustain the obnoxious system of patronage and nepotism in which they were primary beneficiaries. Given their enormous personal wealth and hedonistic life style, their presence in the military definitely constituted a source of indiscipline and professional decay.

A related problem area of concern to the new administration is the issue of "injustices from the highly regionalized and highly politicized military"[39] (Tell, April 5, 1999:26). This structural problem of the armed forces command was given graphic expression by Abdulrahman Okene of the Northern Elders' Forum when he defiantly stated that "the military is not only the protector and defender of the Northern interest in the past and today, but that the military would continue to be the protector and defender of the Northern interest in the future[40]". Such morbid and inflammatory utterances only added significance to the widespread popular reason given to the annulment of the June 1993 presidential election and reinforced the conviction of those calling for a total restructuring of the military.

In this regard, the current administration had to face squarely a multiple of policy options ranging from:

i. Recommendation that recruitment into the officer corps must be on the "basis of local communities and not state representation".
ii. The application of the 'federal character' provision in the 1999 Constitution to the military: "the composition at all levels of the armed forces and the recruitment, promotion, deployment and the location of the armoury should reflect the federal character weighted by the population of the states in the federation".,
iii. "Scrapping of the highly-politicized and highly-regionalized military and replacing it either with "State armies or commencing a new Nigerian armed forces as was the case during post-World War II reconstruction in Germany and Japan"[41].

In the end, the administration decided that both the corporate existence of the country and the professional integrity of the military will only be best served by a

Programme of cautious reform involving purging the military of "political" officers and balanced appointments to the military command reflecting as much as possible the geopolitical realities of the country.

The administration's cautious and minimalist approach has not, however, gone down well with a significant section of the civil society. In a recent appraisal of the state of army, Adegbenro Adebanjo noted that:

> *The revelations at the Oputa Panel have shown that the army still harbours elements with the tendency to rock the political boat. While it may be impossible to follow the Tanzanian example, where the whole army was disbanded, the current administration can still take certain steps to save the Nigerian Army from itself and the nation from another misadventure as it marks the 35th years of the army's first incursion into the political arena"[42]*

This public apprehension concerning the military, heightened by events in Pakistan and Cote d'voire, was given extensive public expression in the workshops on the review of the 1999 Constitution in January 2001. Perhaps Richard Joseph's article "Nigeria and the challenge of leadership" best sums up the depth of popular feelings:

> *The Nigerian military must itself become a constitutional entity. The gap between such an ideal and the reality has grown even larger. Since the first intervention of the military into political life, Nigeria has seen the military emerge as the central political institution in the nation. The mere handover of power from a general to a retired military general, and the retirement of several top military officers, do not ipso facto alter this reality. Demilitarization of the Nigerian polity is one of the most important and difficult exercises the Obasanjo administration must perform. This project has to be thorough, comprehensive, and even radical in conception. Unless the Nigerian military is transformed in this way, the country will never become a constitutional democracy[43].*

While significant players in the current Administration do not underestimate the substantive and residual powers of the military institution in the current dispensation, it is, nevertheless, their view that fundamental transformation of the system can only be generational rather than abrupt and episodic given the fragile nature of state and Nigerian society. As the Director of Army Public Relation, Colonel Felix Chukwuma, put it, the "Army is back to basics". Ultimately, only "good government prevents coups". In this regard, as Admiral Shiyanbade notes, "the quest for greater professionalism and for a new orientation in civil-military relations also requires mutual education between military and civilian authorities"[44].

The related policy direction in the military professionalisation programme of the administration, noted above, is to restore the fighting power of the military – "a military strong enough to do anything the civilians ask them to" – after a protracted period of attrition in major weapon platform (such as fighter aircrafts, Naval vessels and army weaponry) – arising either from the cumulative effect of international sanctions on the Abacha regime following the execution of the "Ogoni Nine" or the conscious policy of the military regime (such as the grounding of Air Force planes by General Babangida after the alleged Vatsa coup plot) or strategic engagement in Liberia and Sierra Leone. This parlous situation was heightened in the Report of the Senate Committee on Defence and Security after an extensive tour of military installations in the country.

The correction of this condition necessitated fundamental structural decisions in four critical areas designed to improve the quality, fire power, and maneuverability of the three services, while reducing the army's personnel strength. They are:

a). Organizational decisions concerning the methods and forms by which Nigeria's armed forces are organized and administered;

b.) Personnel decisions concerning the number, retention, pay, and working conditions of members of the military services;

c). Material decisions concerning the amount of procurement and distribution of equipment and supplies;

d.) Budgetary decisions concerning the size and distribution of funds made available[45].

As to be expected in any fundamental decisions concerning the direction of defence policy of any country, the policy options of the administration quickly became a subject of extensive debate in the policy, academic and media circles. This was not surprising as designing military forces and equipment is anything but a perfect art; it is inevitably affected by non-military factors in preparing for and the selecting of the "cheapest set of alternative means toward performing them effectively"[46]. Apart from the central administrative problem of making choices for an uncertain future, "bureaucratic manipulation, strategic accounting errors and self-centered orientations of individuals representing conflicting interests", can make defence planning a fickle activity, "something far removed from the precise base-line for planning which dedicated empiricists would like"[49].

The first area of major controversy was the size of the armed forces, following the Defence Minister's pronouncement about a drastic reduction in the strength of the military (especially the Nigerian Army) to 50,000. General Danjuma of course had in mind his traditional concern with substituting "fire power for excess manpower" in an unstable economy: that is, the "synthesis between the requirements of the combatant and specialists units admitting the need for greater mobility and armaments". Given the confines of existing budgetary allocations, this could be achieved by "substituting firepower and mobility for excess manpower"[47].

Critics of this policy position, mostly from Danjuma's military constituency, have generally seen it as myopic and an affront to the corporate integrity of the armed force. As Oluwole Bright, a retired lieutenant-colonel has argued:

> *Loyalty and dedication to duty within the armed forces or any other*
> *corporate body for that matter waxes stronger to the degree that they*

are made to believe that real importance is attached to their work. Conversely, a continual fluctuation and unnecessary changes endanger the overall integrity and well being of the force[49].

However, as it is fairly well understood by defence analysts, the key issue concerning the size of any national armed forces is not a mathematic question (of the size of the military in relation to the population of a country), but a political one. As a number of participants in the recent workshop on "Nigeria's Defence Policy and Challenges of the Twenty First Century" (28 February – 1 March, 2001) noted, the determination of the size of the armed forces involves complex geopolitical and economic issues related to:

    i.   Making explicit judgment (the possibility of confident prediction) about anticipated challenges from Nigeria's politico-military environment ten, fifteen years hence;

    ii.   Whether the forces and procedures developed to meet these challenges are adequate; and

    iii.   How to draw the necessary distinction between what is desirable and what is feasible within the overall context of Nigeria's current and projected economic potentials[50].

Considered together, these factors even determine the military manpower system of any country concerning the size of the armed forces, the rate of personnel turnover, the distribution of ranks, and the proportion of civilians in the defence establishment[51].

The second dimension of the program involved restoring the fighting resources of the armed forces. The problem here was epitomized by the outdated squadrons of MIG 17 and 21 fighter planes and the equally aging Alphas and defective Jaguars. Scrap and replace them or upgrade the existing aging fleet? The Administration eventually decided in favour of the later option and awarded the contract to an Israeli firm. The reason for this policy option is fairly obvious. Given the capital-intensive nature of the Air Force, the quantum of financial outlay needed to develop a first rate air power, even by Third World standard, is too prohibitive for the Nigeria economy in the light of current cost of fighter planes and bombers[52].

The injection of offensive arsenal into the Air Force inventory can only be achieved with a collateral cost since the overall magnitude of such modernization and augmentation effort depends on the determination of defence allocation and its distribution among different services in the face of competing national demands. In this regard, a modernization state-of-the-art aircraft (F- 16 or MIG 29 or 33) will certainly impose policy decisions on the budget, increasing capital expenditures on weapons and support systems either by raising the total military budget or allocating resources from other services.

A third, a highly controversial, policy decision of the Administration, was the entry into a "military assistance" arrangement with the United States of America – The Military Professional Resources Initiative (MPRI). Under the arrangement, Nigeria was to provide a counterpart funding of $3.5 million, while the US promised a yearly grant of $10 million in its Foreign Military Financing and another $800,000 in international Military exchange Programme (MEP). This has made it possible for about 20 Nigerian officers to resume training in the United States since the beginning of Obasanjo administration in May 1999[53].

Criticisms of the agreement ranges from concern about the military dimension of "structural imperialism" (Galtung's thesis) which availed the United States of enormous leverage over political development in Latin America and Asian countries to questions of doctrine and strategy. Thus, for Omo Omoruyi, the "use of the U.S. Marines to undertake the assignment of professionalising the Nigerian military is the wrong step and a recipe for disaster; and decision to use the U.S. Navy to monitor the oil producing areas after the genocide in Odi in Bayelsa State is Ominous"[54].

Ominous Omoruyi is of course concerned about the structural subordination of the Nigerian military establishment to the United States and the effect a future US embargo on spare parts for the current equipments it is supplying to Nigeria could have on the ability and latitude of the Nigeria Government to take vital decision on matters relating to war and peace in the face of such veto. A dimension of this problem is the question of indoctrination which may spell disaster for any nationalist regime in Nigeria as was the case of Argentina (under Peron) and Chile (under Allende) even in a post-cold war era. Hence, General Malu's observation that "our interplay with any such country should not in any way compromise our national security, national military strategy, national interest and objective from which our sovereignty as a nation is sustained[55]". Finally, for others, defence is equated with national pride and a "beggar military" should be a cause for utmost concern. Thus, for Louis Odion, the "challenge of professionalisation before Danjuma today should not just stop at issuing the members of the armed forces with new weapons donated by Western nations and teaching them their use. The psychology also has to change"[56].

CONCLUSION

The quest to consolidate the process of democratization in the Fourth Republic necessarily entails also a value reorientation of the military institution in line with the democratic tradition and dictates of constitutional practice. This involves a process of reacculturation of the Nigerian officer corps (reprofessionalisation) in the values and principles of military professionalism which promote expertise and corporateness while at the same time sensitizing it to its responsibility as a "servant" rather than a "master" of the State. In this regard, G.A. Shiyanbade has noted that the task of improving civil-military relations "requires that members of the Armed Forces show greater commitment to the restoration of professionalism in their service .... Can be no "gainsaying the fact that stability in civil-military relations depends largely on the sustenance of a high degree of professionalism within the armed forces itself"[59].

However, the sustainability of this process will also depend on the current political actors' willingness to advance the process of democratization through the politics of compromise. A crisis environment in any country automatically heightens the profile of the military as a social force and as an arbiter in the political process.

Although the administration has taken significant steps to ensure an irreversible process of military professionalism, certain problems still remain relating to the tendency of social objectives to override strategic considerations as criteria for top command positions. This is the cancer of ethnicity which "remains a factor to reckon with within the Nigerian military and in the society as a whole[58]" (Welch, 1995:611). Nevertheless, if the democratic structures remain in place, the generational dynamics of national political process could confound even the worst pessimist and the course of armed forces professionalisation may be determined less by the consciously adopted plans of the government than by the "cumulative influence of day-to-day pressures and case-by-case directions"[59].

REFERENCES

1. C. Bassey, C. "Defence Planning and the Nigerian Armed Forces Modernization Process (1970-1991): An Institutional Analysis", *Armed Forces and Society* 19, 2 Winter 1993:253-277. Bassey, C. "Retrospect's and Prospects of Political Stability in Nigeria", *African Studies Review*, 32, 1, 1989:97-113.

2. P. Feaver, "The Civil-Military Problematique: Huntington, Janowitz and the Question of Civilian Control", *Armed Forces and Society*, 23, 2, Winter, 1996 and Finer, *The Man on Horseback: Military Intervention in Politics*. Harmondsworth: Penguin, 1975.

3. S. Huntington, *The Common Defence*. N.Y.: Columbia University Press, 1966:6

4.

5. A. Millet, et al, "The Effectiveness of Military Organizations", *International Security*, 11, 1, 1986:37-71.

6. J. Lepingwell, "The Laws of Combat", *International Security* 12, 1, Summer 1987:89-139.

7. M. Janowitz, (ed.), *The New Military: Changing Patterns of Organization*. N.Y.: Russell Sage, 1964: vii. Also see Johnson, J. J.,   (ed.), *The Role of the Military in Underdeveloped Countries*. Princeton: Princeton University Press, 1962. *see* Joseph, R., *"Nigeria and the Challenge of Leadership", Tell*, July 5, 1999:48-50 and R. Joseph, R. *Democracy and Prebendalism in Nigeria:* Ibadan: Spectrum, 1993

8. S. Huntington, S., *The Soldier and the State*. Cambridge: Harvard University Press, 1960:11

9. Ibid:13

10. A, Perlmutter

11. Tell Magazine, September 8, 1997 and Newswarch, October 12, 1998.

12. Huntington, The Soldier and State:20

13. R. Price.

14. S. Huntington, *Political Order in Changing Societies*. New Haven: Yale University Press, 1972:222.

15. Perlmutter.
16. E. Nordlinger, *Soldier in Politics:* Military Coup and Government. N.Y.: Printice-Hall, 1977.
17. Perlmutter.
18. Huntington, Political Order in Changing Societies:4.
19. Ibid:11
20. Gibson & D. Snider., "Civil-Military Relations and the Potential to Influence: A Look at the National Security Decision-making Process" *Armed Forces and Society*, 25, 2, Winter, 1999:193-218. Gutteridge, W., *Military Institutions and Power in New States*. London:
21. F. Nunn, *The Military in Chilean History: Essays in Civil Military Relations*, 1810-1973. Albuquerque: University of Mexico Press, 1976. Pall Mall, 1976.
22. Dudley, *Instability and Political Order*. Ibadan: University Press, 1973 and Dudley, B.J., *Nigerian Government and Politics*. London: Macmillan, 1985.
23. B. Abrahamson, B. *Military Professionalisation and Political Power*. Califonia: Sage, 1972.
24. M. Janowitz, N., *Military Institutions and Coercion in the Developing Nations*. Chicago: University of Chicago Press, 1977 and Janowitz, *The Professional Soldier*, N.Y.: Free Press, 1960.
25. K. Lang, K., *Military Institutions and the Sociology of War*. California: Sage, 1972 see Lasswell, "The Garrison-State", American Journal of Sociology, 46 (January 1941): 455-58.
26. Moore, *Social Origins of Democracy and Dictatorship*. London: Oxford University Press, 1970.
27. C. Moskos, C. & Harris-Jenkins, G., "Trend Report: Armed Forces and Society", *Current Sociology*, 1982.
28. Perlmutter.
29. Albright, D. "A Comparative Conceptualization of Civil-Military Relations", *World Politics* XX, 1, 1980:555
30. As quoted in R. Luckham, *The Nigeria Military*. Cambridge: Cambridge University Press, 1980.
31. O. Omoruyi, O., *Tales of June 12*. Ibadan: Spectrum, 1998. see also Omoruyi, "Only True Federalism Can Save Nigeria", *Tell*, April 5, 1999:18-29.
32. *Newswatch Magazine*,
    "The Army and the Abacha Presidency", October 27, 1997.
    "On Death Row", May 11, 1998.
    "War of the Generals", November 29, 1999.
    "Bamiyi", November 15, 1999.
33. J. Ihonvbere, "A Radical View of Nigeria's Political Development" in O. Oyediran (ed.) *Governance and Democracy in Nigeria*. Ibadan: Agbo Areo Publishers, 1996. and Ihonvbere, J.A. & Falola, T. *The Rise and Fall of Nigeria's Second Republic*: 1979-84. London: Zed Press, 1985.
34. G. Shiyanbade, "The Military in a Democracy" in Uya, Okon E. et al (editors), *Nigeria: A People United, A Future Assured*. Abuja: Federal Ministry of

Information, 2000, and Wiatr, J., "The Military in Political Realities and Pass", *International Journal of Social Sciences*, 1981:97-106.

35. Ibid

36. Tell Magazine (Special edition) August 1997; September 8, 1997.

37. De Tocqueville A., *Democracy in America*. N.Y.: Knopf, 1955.

38. Perlmutter.

39. Tell Magazine, April 5, 1999:26

40. Tell, April 5, 1999:26

41. O. Omoruyi, Tales of June 12. Ibadan: Spectrum 1998.

42. Tell, 22 January, 2001.

43. Tell, 5 July, 1999

44. Shiyambade, "The Military in Democracy"

45. See Bassey, "Defence Planning and the Armed Forces Modernization Process".

47. K. Boothe, *Strategy and Ethnocentricism*. N.Y.: Holmes and Meier, 1979:117. Decalo, S.,Coups and Army Rule in Africa. New Haven: Yale University Press, 1977.

48. Bassey, C, "The Military Instrument and Strategic Policy in a Democratic Order: A Theoretical Reconsideration of Some Unresolved Issues Concerning Nigeria", *The Journal of Political Science* XIII, 1 and 2 (1990: 15-31). Bland, D., "A Unified Theory of Civil-Military Relations", *Armed Forces and Society*, 26, 1, Fall 1999: 7-26.

49. S. Enke, S., *Defense Management*. N.J.: Prentice-Hall, 1967.

51. Hackel, E., *Military Manpower and Political Purpose*. Adephi Papers, London 1155, 72, December, 1970.

53. *Newswatch Magazine*, "Obasanjo Turns to America for Help", 26 February, 2001.

54. *The News, 26 February 2001:19*

55. *Ibid*

56. *The Guardian Newspaper, 20 September, 1999:63.*

57. *Shiyanbade op.cit: 464.*

58. Welch, (ed.), *Soldier and State in Africa*. Evanston: North Western University Press, 1970 and Welch, C. (ed.), "Civil Military Agonies in Nigeria: Pains of an Unaccompanied Transition", *Armed Forces and Society*, 26, 4, Summer 1995: 593-614.

CHAPTER 21

NIGERIAN ARMY:
THE CHALLENGES OF PROFESSIONALISATIONS

CHARLES DOKUBO

INTRODUCTION

A review of the literature has shown that the study of professions over the past century has been incoherent and partitioned according to extant disciplinary approaches. This chapter will survey the various approaches to studying the professions in most parts of the Western world, highlighting those which are most relevant to the study of the army. Recent studies of professional developments suggest that the concept of a profession changes over time based on social, economic, cultural and historical contexts. Accordingly, there is agreement among scholars that a profession is a kind of work, but disagreement about what actually distinguishes it from other kinds of work.[1] Despite these disagreements, however, the following definition of professionalism is typical of those most commonly found in the literature:

> *Professionalism is official recognition that the occupation uses in its work a complex body of formal knowledge and skill that commands abstract concepts or theories and requires the exercise of a considerable amount of discretion.*[2]

Although its origin extends well into the past, the real beginnings of military professionalism, as we understand it today, are to be found in the late 19th century. While the first professions, in the modern sense of the word, emerged in 12th century Europe when church and state set standards to regulate the training and behaviour of practitioners, professions only appeared in the United States 700 years later with the formation and restructuring of the legal and other professional associations at the end of the 19th and the beginning of the 20th centuries.[3] The nature of the military as a profession today is a direct result of that era's drive for increased professionalism.

This study deals mainly with the military profession in the context of the army or land force because the vast majority of the literature is based on examples taken from this service. Many articles in American professional military literature have titles referring to military - not just army - professionalism, but there is no detailed discussion of the differences among the American services based on their organizational cultures, and this work make it clear that their professional competence are varies[4] Huntington also speaks of "specialists in the management of violence on sea, on land and in the air ..."[5] but, to date, no significant body of knowledge exists on the professional differences between these specialists. Before examining the professionalism of the Nigerian army, a brief examination of the conceptualization of professionalism will be made, followed by the place of professionalism in the Nigerian army. The last section will look into the professionalisation of the Nigerian Army.

CONCEPTUALISING ARMY PROFESSIONALISM

The early work of writers like Huntington and Finer on theories of professionalism hypothesized that civilian control over the armed services "was best served by maximizing professionalism" because it "recognized and encompassed" civilian control. Central to Huntington's search for an answer to his question as to whether or not American liberal ideals of democracy had been compromised by an increase in the size of its peacetime armed forces was the concept of professionalism. Military professionalism, according to Huntington, was the key to civilian control over the armed forces. He argued that it was far more preferable to professionalise the armed forces as an objective method of control than by maximizing civilian authority over them. He believed that with professionalism the armed services themselves would promote military efficiency whilst at the same time recognizing their subservence to the state. In his view, this was better than imposing civilian values and directives on them, which might impair their efficiency.

Huntington identified three criteria for a profession and indicated that the military profession met all of them. The first is expertise. Plainly stated, it means that the professional military officer is an expert in the management of violence. This expertise is "acquired only by prolonged education and experience", and there are "objective standards of professional competence which are applicable cross-nationality". And this is true whether the soldier is an American, a Nigerian or a South African.

The second characteristic of military professionalism, according to Huntington, is responsibility. The professional performs a service "essential for the functioning of society; the client of every professional society... The social responsibility distinguishes the professional man from other experts". In anticipation of a later point, Huntington notes that, "financial remuneration cannot be the primary aim of the professional man" - or professional woman. This does not mean that financial considerations are irrelevant. There has to be a certain level of support which will affect recruiting, retention and morale.

The third characteristic is corporateness. This is partly a sense among professionals themselves that they are in a profession, with certain standards of admission to their ranks and a set of competencies that should be exhibited by its members. As Huntington stated, "the members of a profession share a sense of organic unity and consciousness of themselves as a group apart from laymen". This is fostered by the length of training and discipline, and the sharing of their "unique social responsibility".

Civilian control of the military, in Huntington's terms, is what is called "objective control", as the tenets of military professionalism themselves keep the military apart from prevailing currents in society. In this view, military professionals do not need to be civilianized in order to be controlled. Military professionalism and service to society will take care of that, he opined. He believed that, with professionalism, the armed services themselves would promote military efficiency whilst also recognizing their subservience to the state. In his view, this was better than imposing civilian values and directives on them which might otherwise impair their efficiency. Huntington's ideas were in tune with the "new conservatism" of post-Second World War America, where the need for a large and efficient standing army was recognized. Professionalism would ensure that the US armed services embraced both the highest standards of performance and an obligation to serve society.

Finer, one of Huntington's fiercest critics, noted, however, that in certain circumstances the armed services of a state may be constitutionally required to intervene in government as a measure of last resort and a matter of professional duty. On the other hand, research on Latin American militaries has shown that professionalism alone was not a guarantee of non-involvement in politics. Civilian governments tended to be supreme until the military acquired the capacity to usurp civilian control of the state.

Huntington acknowledged that, in some states, the prevailing ideology was wholly incompatible with the Western concept of professionalism, except in terms of the military being composed of paid experts. However, the universality of Huntington's theory of military professionalism has been challenged because certain ideal conditions, such as a balance between the requirements of the armed forces and the values of society, would have to prevail for it to apply in all cases.[23] Feaver observed, in his 1977 revision of *The Soldier and the State*, that Huntington did not discuss his earlier characteristics of professionalism - expertise, responsibility and corporateness - but adopted "the Janowitz's vocabulary of "cognizance/convergence".

Janowitz's study of the post-Second World War American armed services concluded that, while there had been changes in the professional officer corps and the armed services' organizational structure, the American armed services had maintained their professional distinctiveness and integrity. Their professional ethic, he concluded, was adequate to maintain civilian political supremacy without compromising professional autonomy.[25] Feaver suggests that, for all their conceptual differences, Janowitz and Huntington used the same "values-based" mechanism, i.e. professionalism, to explain how civil control of military forces can best be maintained in the West.

Abrahamson, on the other hand, building on Finer's work, has provided the most detailed critique of professionalism as a basis of the contemporary civil-military relationship. He argued that, like all organizations, the armed services are concerned with growth, improvement and their own survival. A professional army, as a well-organised and conservative institution, is likely to be effective in resisting civilian direction or looking after its own interests. He contended that they should be seen for what they really are: not disinterested professionals but a politicized, highly active interest group with strong political views.

Abrahamson's critique of Janowitz and earlier writers' works highlighted the fact that, even though professional armed forces might declare their disinterest in civil affairs, they were nevertheless often "politicized, highly active and motivated" interest groups possessing strong political views and prepared to compete with civilian groups in the political arena.[27] Recent struggles over US defence budget allocations where the US military has defied the secretary of defence's orders to cut certain weapons' systems by appealing for congressional support demonstrates the late Carl Builder's assessment that the "most powerful institutions in the American national security arena are ... Army, Navy and Air Force – not the Department of Defence or Congress or even their commanders-in-chief, the president, still appears to be accurate".

However, Perlmutter's work builds on that of the authors mentioned above. He challenges the idea of a clear distinction between the armed services and other state institutions, emphasizing that, in the modern state, there is a wide area of overlap between the two, only varying in degree according to "ideologies, orientations, and organizational-structures". His "fusionist" model holds that all states are to some degree praetorian given that professional military officers are drawn into national policy-making even in advanced Western democracies. For Perlmutter, the key to the interaction between armed services and the state is the fact that the modern armed services are characterized by their corporate professionalism. As a corporate entity they work to maintain themselves in existence and to protect their exclusivity. Perlmutter devised three broad categories of armed services: 1) the professional corporate, which is found mostly in Western democracies; 2) the praetorian, which is found in those states where civilian authority is weak; and 3) the revolutionary, which is found where there is a strong ideological component which encompasses the whole society.

One of the greatest weaknesses of Huntington's work is his methodology. While few would argue with his view that people, events, beliefs and institutions do not fit into "neat logical categories and therefore scholars are forced to generalize if they wish to derive lessons for broader application," most historians would take issue with generalizations that are not supported by facts. Kaplan tells us that Huntington was a political scientist who was comfortable producing *The Soldier and the State* as "a book of relentless empirical generalization".[30] If one accepts that "empirical" here refers to making generalizations based on observation or experience and not rigorous research[26] then those scholars who have recently taken issue with him appear to have a point.

In *The Long Shadow of the Soldier and the State* Coffman gives examples of how lack of historical data can lead to faulty assumptions. Historians have found that, contrary to Huntington's assumptions, there "was no great gap between (American officers) and the propertied class" in the late 19th century, and that "the drive for military professionalism" was no different than that found in civilian professions at the time.

In fact, rather than epitomizing a civil-military gap, the officer corps of the late 19th century American army shared many characteristics with urban reforms in America – they were white Anglo-Saxon protestants from the middle class who believed in "character, fair play, progress, the betterment of mankind, and the democratic mission of their nation". Furthermore, in the decades from 1880 to 1920, military leaders "maintained close social and intellectual ties with America's business, professional, and political elites and shared their outlook".

In the main, studies have shown that Huntington's model does not correspond to "the realities of American life" and, in some ways, were almost a "literary construct". American army officers were not polarized ideologically from their contemporaries but shared the values of the class from which they came. This raises the question of how Huntington arrived at his conclusions.

However, in this chapter professionalism will be defined in Mosko's analysis, where he tries to distinguish between what he calls "institutional" as opposed to "occupational" motives for military service. Institutional considerations include patriotism, love of service and dedication. Occupational considerations, by contrast, include material reward and career advancement. A combination of the two was the bedrock of professionalism in the Nigerian army.

THE MAKING OF THE NIGERIAN ARMY

To argue in favour of African militaries upholding professionalism it is first necessary to examine how they have thwarted it. In this regard, Nigeria provides a perfect case study, and with it a virtual museum of pathological civil-military relations. This is a tragedy of immense proportions. Few African nations hold more promise than Nigeria. It is the most populous nation in sub-Saharan Africa by far and its extensive oil and gas reserves give it a rare level of economic potential. Moreover, unlike some other states that have economic or military power without the will to use them, Nigeria considers itself a model for sub-Saharan Africa and a spokesman for the Third World in general. For instance, it has participated in many UN peace-keeping operations, including those in the former Yugoslavia, Somalia, Cambodia, Angola, Rwanda, Mozambique, Namibia, and Zaire[11]. More recently, Nigeria led a major peacekeeping effort in Liberia and has provided military advice and training to other African states such as The Gambia and Sierra Leone[12]. When a Liberian peace agreement was arranged in 1995, George Obiozor, director-general of Nigeria's official foreign policy think tank, said, "By brokering a successful peace among the warring factions of Liberia, Nigeria has reconfirmed her primacy in the West African sub-region in particular, and Africa in general"[13]. Nigeria currently holds one of the rotating positions on the Security Council and is actively seeking a permanent seat.

Unfortunately, much of the country's potential and the immense energy of its people have been wasted through misgovernment. Since independence, Nigeria has made several attempts to build democracy but all have been thwarted by military intervention. The army has directly ruled the country for 27 of its 50 years of independence; it has also exerted a powerful influence over policymaking, even during the brief periods of civilian government. There have been seven successful military coups and many failed ones.[14] Throughout Africa, statist economic policies, weak political institutions, and what Samuel Decalo refers to as "an internally fractured army composed of personal loyalty pyramids," have led to military coups.[15] Nigeria epitomizes the pathology of civil-military relations in Africa.

Nigeria is an artificial state created according to colonial exigencies rather than ethnic coherence. It has three main groups: the largely Christian Igbo in the southeast, the Yoruba in the southwest, and the Muslim Hausa-Fulani in the north. Together, they constitute 65 percent of the Nigerian population. During the colonial period the British governed through local political structures (particularly in the Muslim north) in what became known as "indirect rule." The emergence of the military in governance was spurred by the Civil War (1967-1970) as the army grew from a light infantry force of about 8,000 to over 250,000 equipped with heavy weapons and supported by air and naval power. The war also saw the sharp erosion of the military's trust in civilian leadership. Despite training in the British notion of professionalism that stressed subordination to civilian control, the Nigerian army seized power in January 1966.16. Thus began a dismal tradition of military intervention in politics. In 1975, General Yakubu Gowon, who had ruled Nigeria since late 1966, was overthrown by reformist senior officers and a new regime headed by Brigadier Murtala Muhammed began a managed transition to democracy. He purged the military and civilian bureaucracy of inefficient or corrupt officials and instigated a five-stage programme for restoring civilian, democratic government. The first steps were the creation of new states to better distribute political power among the competing ethnic groups, and the writing of a new constitution modelled after the American. The culmination was the transfer of power to an elected government in 1979. Although Muhammed was assassinated during a failed coup attempt in February, 1976 his successor, General Olusegun Obasanjo, completed the transition.

Despite (or because of) the opportunities provided by the oil wealth that flowed into the treasury during the Second Republic, the civilian government proved massively corrupt. Much of the bonanza was squandered on useless projects or stolen when it wasn't simply looted.[17] When the military again seized power again on December 31, 1983, there was celebration throughout the country.[18] Major-General Muhammadu Buhari, the new Head of state, launched a "war against indiscipline" which met with initial approval but its repressiveness soon eroded the regime's popularity.[19] On August 27, 1985 Buhari was overthrown by Army Chief-of-staff, Major General Ibrahim Babangida. According to Habibu Idris Shuaibu, a Nigerian officer who had backed Babangida, the driving force behind the coup was not the public's discontent but Buhari's failure to appoint junior and middle-ranking officers to political office.

Babangida instigated a second managed transition to democracy designed to avoid the problems that plagued the earlier one. All previous Nigerian political leaders were banned from participating. Babangida also sought to craft nothing less than a new political culture devoid of corruption and ethnic conflict.[20] In practical terms, his greatest innovation may have been the creation of a mandatory two-party system. Throughout Africa, the serious shortcomings of both one-party and multi-party systems were evident. Having one slightly-left-of-centre and one slightly-right-of-centre was seen as a palliative (and was a direct emulation of the American political system)[21]. Babangida attempted for the first time in Nigerian history to disperse real political power to local governments. And recognizing the key role that competent and effective civilians played in democratization, the military government created the Centre for Democratic Studies to help train local elected officials.

Mismanagement of the economy and endemic corruption during the Second Republic had led to economic crisis and a precipitous decline in living standards. By the time the military seized power in 1983, Nigeria had amassed an external debt equal to its gross domestic product, and suffered widespread unemployment, underutilized industrial capacity, high inflation, substantial budget deficits and a declining currency exchange rate.[22] Babangida attempted to ameliorate this through an economic emergency involving pay cuts and a reduction in government subsidies, currency devaluation, privatization, deregulation, and an economic adjustment programme designed by the International Monetary Fund and the World Bank.[23]

Unfortunately, these badly needed steps complicated democratization as the hardships imposed on the Nigerian public eroded support for the government. Corruption quickly returned and even escalated. Dr Pius Okigbo, a Nigerian economist, estimated that $12.4 billion of the country's oil revenues was stolen unaccounted for in the course of Babangida's eight-year tenure. By the end of the 1980s, Nigeria had fallen from a middle income country with a per capita income of around $1000 per year to one of the world's poorest, with an estimated per capita income of $250.[24]

Babangida recognized that Nigerian democracy would be unsustainable without serious reform of civil-military relations and the professionalization of the officer corps.[25] However, he quickly discovered that this was easier said than done. After nearly 20 years of involvement in politics, all memory of British-instilled military professionalism had faded. Nigeria faced no serious external or internal security threat to provide the incentive for professionalization. And Babangida's use of officers as political administrators gave them a taste of corruption's rewards. By the early 1990s, it was no longer possible to classify officers as "political" or "professional" since only a minority remained outside the patronage system.

Throughout Babangida's rule, military morale declined precipitously. An organizational pattern emerged in which corrupt senior military "godfathers" built and used networks of lower ranking clients.[26'] Junior officers without a patron were unhappy with the system, but this was often due less to commitment to the national interest than jealousy and resentment. For enlisted personnel, conditions were dire. While most senior leaders were multimillionaires living in mansions and driving Mercedes Benzes, lower ranks were victimized by Nigeria's economic collapse and lived in crushing poverty.[27] The handful of officers who did seem committed to democratization and the broader national interest were co-opted or eliminated. A failed coup in 1990 signalled the cancerous condition of the military and sparked suspicion, fear, and purges.[28]

Growing ethnic conflict also heightened existing schisms. While the majority of officers were southern or middle-belt Christians, the source of deep resentment came from non-northern officers and civilian elites. Both Muslim and Christian fundamentalism had been growing for some time in Nigeria, largely as a response to the wider social decay. Following Babangida's 1986 decision to seek full membership of the Organization of Islamic Conference, religious tensions flared up, particularly in the middle and northern segments of the country. More than 5000 died in religious violence between 1990 and 1994, with 1000 killed in April 1991 alone during riots in Kaduna and Bauchi states.

"Probably no democratic transition," Larry Diamond posited, "has ever been beset by such a massive gap between the elaborateness of its engineering and the cynicism of the public's expectations".[29] Events justified this. As preparations for the final stage of the transition programme approached - election of a national president and a handover of power from the military - Babangida became increasingly "corrupt, manipulative, unpredictable, ambitious, unreliable and uninterested in leaving office". Although he initially promised to restore civilian rule by 1990, he eventually postponed the date four separate times.[30] The presidential campaign between Moshood Abiola of the centre-left Social Democratic Party and Bashir Tofa of the centre-right National Republican Convention failed to generate public enthusiasm. Most Nigerians considered the election as simply one more in a long series of charades staged by the elite. Neither Abiola nor Tofa were known as political leaders and both were considered allies of Babangida.[31] The general's obsessive desire to control the political transformation and his endless manipulation of the process further jaded Nigerians. Corruption and vote-rigging during the presidential primaries "alienated virtually the entire electorate."

There were no civil-military relations in Nigeria in the sense of discrete military and civilian institutions with a structured relationship. There is no discernible difference between the corrupt, co-opted senior military leadership and the equally corrupt and co-opted civilian elite. Abacha's dictum that, "during the transition period, particular attention will be paid to the orientation of the military to inculcate the spirit of subordination to the civil authority" is utterly ludicrous considering the general's own extensive involvement in coups. While the Nigerian military retains a war-fighting capability that makes it a major regional power, professionalism in the Western sense of holding politics at arm's length has totally disappeared from its senior ranks. While the threat of a coup from junior officers persists, it will most likely be driven by personal aggrandizement and the settling of scores. The military is incapable of self-reform and cannot lead successful democratization; civil-military relations are beyond reform. Claude Welch put it, "Nothing less than a revolution in attitudes will suffice". The only way that democracy can be built and sustained is through a radical transformation of the military to include the wholesale replacement of the officer corps.

THE NIGERIAN ARMY AND PROFESSIONALISM

At independence Nigeria inherited an army that was equipped to play an essentially internal security role. It was relatively small and immobile with little in the way of a logistical base. It was more akin to a constabulary force without even the capacity to operate beyond the country's borders. The colonial administration also failed to develop a national officer corps, the edifice on which military training and professionalism could have been built. The crucial point here is that the Nigerian officer corps that should have been the major force in professionalizing the army had little time to do so. Any sense of cohesion, authority and *esprit d'corps* was destroyed with the 1966 coup.

There is little doubt that Nigerian officers at Sandhurst, Mons, Fort Benning, Quetta or the Staff College, Camberley learnt their jobs well and acquired all the correct social rituals to accompany them. But they returned to play their newly acquired role in an army in which the social structure had been distorted. The normal relations of command and control were undermined because there was little difference in age and experience between officers at the upper and lower levels. Career expectations had to be adjusted to a situation in which promotions were alternately fast and slow, and in which mobility from posting to posting was rapid and organized career lines difficult to establish. It was the pace at which military institutions were transferred and the way they took place, rather than the failure to internalize and uphold one's professional calling, that were largely responsible for the demise of professionalism after the fall of the First Republic.

The coup sounded the death knell of professionalism in the Nigerian army. Professional standards coexisted with increasing politicization in the years after 1966 as the focus shifted to internal security and national development. This was what Alfred Slopan referred to as the "new professionalism". He stated that, while professionalism was rooted in the assumption that armies developed their skills for conventional warfare against foreign armies, the new professionalism led to a belief that there was a fundamental inter-relationship between the two spheres, with the military playing a key role in interpreting and dealing with domestic political problems owing to its technical and professional skill in handling internal security issues. The latitude of military concern for politics became unlimited. The new professional military man was highly politicized.

DEMOCRACY AND RE-PROFESSIONALIZATION

After years of military rule, it was widely believed that the "new professionalism" has impacted negatively on the "old professionalism" of external defences, hence the need by the new democratic administration to revisit the concept of professionalism.

Reorientation of the military was at the forefront of the drive for re-professionalisation. The then commandant of the National War College, Rear Admiral G.A. Shiyanbade, was one of the first to articulate the basic assumptions of this programme in a paper captioned "The Military in a Democracy" on 13 September 1999. He pointed out the following:

- The first assumption was that it was in the best interest of the armed forces to preoccupy themselves with the function for which they were established.
- The second was that the use of the armed forces for internal security on a sustained basis carried with it the danger of weakening their combat readiness, morale and capacity for effective external missions.
- The third was that there must be a balance between defence spending and other competing needs. Both the armed forces and the larger society need to appreciate that too much spending on defence can lead to a situation where there may be nothing for the armed forces to defend. At the same time, not to provide for effective defence will be to return society to anarchy.
- The fourth was that military professionalism thrives best under democratic rule; in his own words:

  Indeed in a non-democratic environment, the military finds itself in double jeopardy. On the one hand, it stands the risk of becoming the instrument for the coercion of the wider society and thereby viewed by society as an enemy. On the other hand, because it is the most credible instrument of organized violence in society, absolutism is uncomfortable with it, and so it spends as much as possible weakening it. So many dictatorships in Latin America, Asia and Africa related to their armed forces with such suspicion that they almost in all the cases had to build alternative or parallel forces at the expense of the regular one. I dare say that the military [as an institution] is always the first casualty when democracy is overthrown.

Furthermore, the agenda for re-professionalization should include re-orientating military personnel, carving out a sphere of responsibility and autonomy for the military, and protecting it from unwarranted interference by politicians; in short, military subordination to civil authority.

STRENGTHENING ARMY PROFESSIONALISM

Although the army has historically survived periods when its professionalism has been questioned, especially after the fall of the First Republic, today's situation is complicated by the "new demands" of the international community. Globalisation, economic interdependence and coincidental societal changes are influencing its legitimacy and capability.

However, a key factor in the rebuilding of the army after the third wave of democratization is the revalidation of its status as a profession in two critical ways. First, it should re-intellectualise its professional expertise through effective training and a need for internal dialogue amongst the officer corps on issues of strategic and doctrinal focus. Within the next decade, middle-level officers should understand and identify their role as "collective skill trainers" creating a "trained and ready army".

Second, the army should examine, and then revamp, many of its management systems (particularly those for human resources) to reinforce professionalism rather than diminish it.[41]

Through this systemic emphasis of being a profession, the army should renew its professional identity, which in turn will enable its members to align their personal and professional self-concepts. This is a critical connection, and one which is increasingly missing today. The alignment between individual officers and the profession's identity is critical for long-term viability, since professionalism ultimately resides in expert knowledge, character and personal motivation.

The traditional conception of army professionalism paralleled the broader investigation of professions taking place in the Western industrialized world. Early in the 1930s, professions were identified as a unique means of organizing and controlling work which were inherently different from the more common formal organisations and labour unions. Research into professions began as descriptive case studies of professions, progressed through the identification of professions' differentiating characteristics and, by 1960, modelled the professionalization process by which occupations were converted into professions. The characteristic which separated professions from occupations was the application of abstract knowledge to specific situations. Others included: organization of the occupation, extensive education of its members, service to society and shared ethics. Professionalization was seen as a one-way street; an occupation's status as a profession was relatively static, something to be maintained over time through its unique characteristics.

Classic writings on the military profession, including Vagts, Huntington, Janowitz and Abrahamson, drew on this more general studies. Most important were the characteristics that identified the military as a profession. As succinctly summarized in the late 1970s by Allan Millett, the attributes and character of the military occupation which cause society to give it professional status includes:

> *The occupation was fulltime and stable, serving society's continuing needs, it was regarded as a life-long calling by practitioners, who identified themselves personally with other vocational sub-culture; it was organized to control performance standards and recruitment; it required formal theoretical education; it had a service orientation in which loyalty to standard of competence and loyalty to clients' need were paramount; [it] was granted a great deal of autonomy by the society it served, personally because the practitioners had proven their high ethical standard and trustworthiness; and overall, the profession's work was the systemic exploitation of specialized knowledge applied to specialized problems.*[42]

From this tradition's conception of the military profession came the self-concept of the individual professional.

> *[The officers] identity is partly inherited, partly self developed. He inherited the broadly defined characteristics of his career and the*

special institutional setting within which he finds himself. He must develop stable and lasting concepts of self that are compatible with his profession. This transformation or "professional socialization" is not taken lightly by the other practitioners with whom he begins his careers.[43]

This conception also fits the military's understanding of war as a subordinate instrument of policy to be exercised by a democratic government - the Clausewitzan duality of war. As explicated by Huntington, and widely accepted by the Nigerian army before 1966, objective control of the military meant that, in return for limited autonomy in which to develop their expert knowledge and conduct their professional duties, the army's natural self-interested role would be self-policing, non-political and internally focussed on its expertise and moral responsibility.

CONCLUSION

After years of political involvement, there are indications that the army has not only lost its professionalism but has also suffered from a weak relationship with the Nigerian public. Furthermore, the end of the Cold War and the emergence of democratic government has been one of massive change to which the army has yet to fully adapt. Simply stated, the end of the Cold War, which also coincided with the demands of democratization and globalisation, has drastically altered the expectations of where and how the profession of arms will apply its expertise.

In today's evolving security environment, the army's professional situation has become far more complex. Quantitatively, the amount of work has increased dramatically, as measured by numbers and duration of deployments. Qualitatively, extensive objective and subjective changes have taken place in the army's tasks. The fall of the Berlin Wall, the demise of the Soviet Union and the shrinking of the defence budget caused objective changes for the army. More subtle influences, such as the evolving regional security structure and the army's expanded jurisdiction across the spectrum of conflict, are particularly critical because. Unlike most other professions, the military does not independently select its jurisdiction. Instead, selection results from negotiations with its client, the Nigerian government and people.

The new professional framework establishes that almost everything the army does is part of the institution's expert work – the application of its specialized knowledge to new situations – and therefore its professionalism. And therein lies the conclusion. Who should decide what army professionalism constitutes at any point in time and what priority issues affecting it should be addressed. It has been observed that discussion of these issues has been largely carried out by Nigerian academics. The army has played a passive role in the public discourse. This must change.

Finally, in an uncertain and dangerous world, the army in a free society is a vital part of its strength – not only the strength of physical power, but also of moral force. The the military shares the vision that its purpose is not personal advancement or the personal and professional satisfaction of a job well done but the defence of freedom itself. There is no conflict between military professionalism, properly understood, and patriotism, humanism and support for the democratic state.

REFERENCES

1. J. Burk, : "Expertise, Jurisdiction, and Legitimacy of the Military profession", paper presented at the Inter-University Seminar on Armed Forces and Society, Baltimore, MD 19 – 21 October 2001, p. 4.
2. E. Freidson,: *Professionalism: The Third Logic* (Cambridge (UK): Policy Press 2001), p. 27.
3. M. Burrage, "Introduction: The Profession in Sociology and History", in Burrage and Torstendah, R. (eds.): *Profession and Theory and History* (London: Sage 1990), p. 11.
4. C. Builder,: *The Icarus Syndrome: The Role of Air Power Theory in the Evolution and Fate of the US Air Force* (London: Transaction Publishers, 1994), pp. 5–6.
5. S. Huntington,: "Officership as a Profession," in Nakin (ed.): *War, Morality and the Military Profession* (Boulder, Colorado: Westview Press, 1986), pp. 27–28.
6. S. Metz,: "A Wake for Clausewitz: Towards a Philosophy of 21st Century Warfare," *Parameters* (Winter 1994 –95), pp. 126–132.
7. J. Lynn, "The Evolution of Army Style in the Modern West, 800 – 2000," *The International History Review*, vol. 18, no. 3, August 1996, p. 505.
8. J. A. Keegan: *History of Warfare* (Toronto: Vintage Books 1994), p. 227.
9. R. O'Connell: Of Arms and *Men: A History of War, Weapons and Aggression* (New York: Oxford University Press, 1989), pp. 45–50.
10. Keegan op. cit., p. 231.
11. E. T. Ricks: "On American Soil: The Widening Gap between the US Military and US Society", in John, M.: *Olin Institute for Strategic Studies Project on US Post Cold-War Civil-Military Relations* (Harvard University Press 1996), p. 281.
12. Keegan op. cit., p. 228.
13. Ibid, p. 231.
14. C. Dokubo, "An Army for Rent: Private Military Corporation and Civil Conflict in Africa: The Case of Sierra Leone," *Civil Wars*, vol. 3, no. 2, 2000, p. 55.
15. Keegan op. cit., pp. 228, 233.
16. Ibid, p. 234.
17. Ibid, p. 235.
18. Ibid, p. 236.
19. S. Huntington, *The Soldier and the State: The Theory and Practice of Civil Military Relations* (Harvard University Press, Cambridge Mass., 1957), p. 211.
20. Ibid, p. 217.
21. Ibid, p. 218.
22. Feaver: "The Civil-Military Problematique: Huntington, Janowitz, and the Question of Civilian Control," in *Armed Forces and Society*, vol. 23, no. 2, 1996, p. 163.

23. M. Edmonds, *Armed Services and Society* (Boulder, Colorado: Westview Press 1990), p. 82.

24. Feaver, op. cit., p. 176.

25. Edmonds, M., op. cit., p. 83.

26. Feaver op. cit., p. 165.

27. Edmonds, M., op. cit., p. 169.

28. Ibid, p. 170.

29. Edmonds, M., op. cit., p. 83.

30. R. Kaplan, "Looking the World in the Eye," *The Atlantic Monthly*, 280, no. 5 (December 2001), p. 72.

31. M. Coffman, "The Long Shadow of the Soldier and the State", *Journal of Military History* 55 (January 1991), p. 78.

32. Ibid, p. 79.

33. Coffman, ibid, p. 81.

34. A Lecture delivered by Gen. Bamaiyi, Chief of Army Staff, 30th Anniversary Conference of the Nigerian Society of International Law, June 1998.

35. R. Luckham, *The Nigerian Military: A Sociological Analysis of Authority and Revolt 1960 –67* (Cambridge: Cambridge University Press, 1971), p. 85.

36. Ibid, p. 90.

37. Ibid, p. 108.

38. Ibid, p. 121.

39. S. Alfred, *Authoritarian Brazil.*

40. Shiyanbade: Lecture delivered to the participants of Cause – National War College, Abuja.

41. M. Snider, and Watkins, G.: "The Future of Army Professionalism: A Need for renewal and Redefinition", *Parameters*, Autumn 2000, p. 16.

42. R. Millet: "Military Professionalism and Officership in America", Mershon Centre Briefing Paper No. 2, (Columbia: Ohio State University, May 1977), p. 2.

43. Ibid, p. 5.

CHAPTER 22

NIGERIAN ARMY – CHALLENGES AND RESPONSE

LUKA YUSUF

INTRODUCTION

As you may be aware, the Nigerian Army (NA) dates back to 1863 and is an offshoot of the West African Frontier Force (WAFF), a colonial creation. Since the country's independence in 1960, the NA has grown in shape and size. It has also been tested on all fronts including the prosecution of civil war from 1967 – 70, which resulted in no victor no vanquished" in the spirit of national unity.

The primary security objective of any nation is to ensure the defence of its territorial integrity, with a view to advancing her interests and ensuring the safety of the citizens. This is amply captured in the NA mission statement thus: 'To win all land battles in defence of the territorial integrity of Nigeria, protect and advance her national interests and accomplish other tasks as may be assigned in aid to civil authority".

The foregoing mission statement derives from the constitution of the Federal Republic of Nigeria, which also stipulates the roles of the military under section 217 to include:

a. Defence of Nigeria from external aggression.
b. Maintaining our territorial integrity and securing our borders from violation on land, sea or air.
c. Suppressing insurrection and acting in aid of civil authorities to restore order when called upon to do so by the President, but subject to such conditions as may be prescribed by an Act of the National Assembly and:
d. Performing such other functions as may be prescribed by an Act of the National Assembly[1].

These Constitutional imperatives are by extension the roles of the NA. They are complemented by the National Defence Policy, which is the broad articulation and specification of the way the nation plans to use its military and other components of national power. The policy provides the official guidelines military capabilities in line with identified national objectives. The NA, therefore, is an instrument of the Nigerian state charged with the responsibility of protecting the territorial integrity of the nation among others. This function of course, is to be undertaken as part of the Armed Forces of the Federal Republic of Nigeria. Inherent in the protection responsibility is the defence and security of the nation people and wealth. The implication of the roles is therefore that the NA is expected to be apolitical and to diligently perform these constitutional roles under appropriate political directives and within the dictates of the National Defence Policy[2]. It is the desire to effectively perform these constitutional roles that informed my vision for the NA thus: "To consolidate on the gains of the recent past and lead the Nigerian Army that has discipline as is watch word: an army whose moral, human rights and professional conducts are without reproach while strictly adhering to its constitutional roles".

In this Chapter, I shall attempt to share, with you the challenges and responses of the NA in the discharge of its constitutional roles. In doing this, I intend to look at the threat to Nigeria, outline the force structure of the NA, identifying the challenges before it and then present the NA's responses to these challenges. It is my hope that at the end, you will appreciate the challenges facing the NA and be better prepared to contribute more meaningfully to its evolution, to the end that it would be a professional force by every account.

THREATS TO NIGERIA: EXTERNAL AND INTERNAL

The Nigeria policy of good neighbourliness has largely contributed to the relative peace, harmony and mutual trust existing between her and her Francophone neighbours. However, areas of potential threats still exist arising primary from unresolved geographical issue. This is as a result of, Nigeria's extensive international borders with her contiguous neighbours. Until these borders are properly defined. Demarcated and protected, Nigeria will continue to operate on the basis of the expectation of threats in the form of border violations and conflicts. Other areas of external threat include cross-border crimes, local conflicts civil strife and unrests in neighbouring countries that could either have spill-over effects on Nigeria or directly affect Nigerians resident in those countries. The recent crises in Chad offer an easy example[3].

The internal threats are those issues that could distort the socio-political and economic balance of the nation[4]. These include the following:

a. Ethnic and religious militias that are well-armed and semi-trained to carryout raids, ambushes and even assault against law abiding citizens.
b. Inter-border and inter-communal conflicts.
c. Unemployment especially among the youths with subversive and criminal behaviours leading to economic sabotage and threatening of civil economic installations especially in the oil sector.
d. Influx and proliferation of sophisticated weapons in the society. Given this position, I do not agree with Claude Ake's assertion that "in the absence of a credible external threat the African Military is redundant. Against a credible external threat it is expensively useless"[5]. I believe that even in times of absolute peace the army still has its relevance. Our situation to say the least, is far from absolute peace. I will argue that real politics makes the contend further that democracies, the world over need the military to grow and Nigeria is no exception.

FORCE STRUCTURE

The structure of the NA has undergone various transformations in line with the challenges over a given period. Currently, the NA is organized into 5 fighting divisions and transiting to 4 fighting divisions. These transformations are critical responses to building a force that is strategically positioned to act as demanded by the Constitution. The 5 divisions are 1 Division with its headquarter in Kaduna, covering the North-West geo-political zone, 2 Division with its headquarter in Ibadan an covering the South-West geo-political zone (less Lagos area) and part of the South-West geo-political zone, 3 Division with its headquarter in Jos covering the North-East geo-political zone and part of the North-Central zone, the 81 Division covering the Lagos area and 82 Division with its headquarter in Enugu and covers the South-East zones and a greater part of South-South geo-political zone. The Brigade of Guards covers the Federal Capital Territory, Abuja. The transition earlier mentioned will see the exist of 81 Division. The Area of Responsibility (AOR) of 81 Division will then be subsumed into 2 Division.

CHALLENGES

To fully appreciate the challenges to be outlined in this lecture, it is important to present a digression in the discourse. Human interactions are conflict prone and have been accepted as inevitable. Zartman for example, observed that "conflict is an inevitable aspect of human interaction, an unavoidable concomitant of choices and decisions"[6]. Benneth adds that "conflict in various forms is to be found all around us, in international relations, in politics, in economic (and in biological) competition, in relationships between individual people in a more general sense is a natural consequence of our power to take actions that affect others". Therefore, it is the inevitability of conflicts inherent in human interactions and the need to manage the conflicts to ensure a peaceful environment that forms the cornerstone of the challenges facing the NA. The Nigerian civil war readily comes to mind in this case.

While it is the traditional role of the military to ward off external aggression against the state, the Army is implicitly relevant in checking the activities of various actors in the domestic sphere that manifestly pose danger to the society. Moreso, the paradigm shift of conflicts from interstate to intrastate has aggravated internal conflicts. For this reason, the challenges faced and are being faced by the NA are largely internally based. I shall now discuss these challenges.

To the average Nigerian pubic, the NA is a symbol of brutality, a tool for destruction of the national fabric and above all, an instrument for melting the democratic value-system. Our past national failures have been erroneously attributed to the Army. The reason for this could be the long years of military involvement in the political administration of the country. Even though it was expedient at the time and that the military involvement in politics impacted more negatively on the military itself, hardly can most people be convinced that the occurrence was part of the national political evolution and not a sole creation of the military as an institution. This erroneous perception by the public is one of the greatest challenges facing the NA today. It must be noted that issues of national development and progress cannot be relegated to the level of one sector of the society being held responsible for the woes of the society. I would crave the good understanding of every Nigerian to the fundamental issues of statecraft. The military and by extension the NA cannot be held responsible for our past failures.

I, however, note very profoundly that military involvement in political administration is an aberration. I must equally note with pride and satisfaction that we have long past that era. The NA as a major component of the military in Nigeria is on a totally professional path and its leadership is consistent with this commitment. We have in the past 9 years worked hard as an institution to clinically purge and sanitise the NA of every political leaning and desire. I am confident and proud to report that the present NA is wholly subordinated to the political class.

Closely related to the challenge of poor public perception of the NA is the problem of gaining the trust of the political class. The NA is on transformation programme aimed at re-positioning itself to playing its roles in line with constitutional mandates and in the most professional manner. The requirements for fulfilling this goal are enormous. In the spirit of the manoeuvrist approach to Warfare, defence and security of the nation must extend its frontiers to exploring means of fostering peace. In unattractive adventure that peace becomes inevitable. This should be focus of sound, professional soldiering. The strategy must have collaboration with the political class. However, there is a need to gain the absolute trust of the political class for total support of this new thinking. It is, therefore, our desire to continue to assure the political class that we have been purged of any political cleavage and leaning.

I am happy to note the commitment of The President, C-in-C to ensuring that the focus of the NA leadership hierarchy in sustaining the professional drive of the Army is on course. The National Assembly is also doing very well to give the desire support. I cannot but ask for greater support. Other stakeholders must also build on the values of the President to support the NA to effectively meet its constitutional mandates. We do require as stable and peaceful environment within which to push for the national vision of being among the first 20 leading economies of the world by the year 2020. A properly equipped and focused NA would be key in providing the embience for this undertaking.

The greatest internal security problem in the country is the insecurity in the Niger Delta. As you know, the region is the economic base of the nation with about 90 percent of our national wealth coming from the region. Oil and gas being our mainstay, account for this wealth. The magnitude and character of the insecurity in the Niger Delta has led to the deployment of troops in the Area. The NA provides over 90 percent of the troop requirement in the area. Accordingly, one would be right to suggest that the insecurity in the Niger Delta is a major problem confronting the NA.

The problem in the Niger Delta is multi-dimensional. While it is true the problem is resource-related and requires a political solution through development, it is equally true that criminality is beclouding the struggle. There is, however, no doubt, that there is a serious demand for development in the Niger Delta. The issue of environmental degradation is equally worth mentioning. These deep imbalances have helped to create the violence and extremism being witnessed. The situation cannot be left unattended, hence the deployment of the NA to contain the insecurity to allow the government to tackle the aspect of development. In the words of Kofi Anan, the former UN Secretary General, "There can be no development without security and long term security can only be achieved through development and respect for democratic values"[7]. Whatever is reason for the violence and insecurity in the Niger Delta, it must be noted that violence is negative-sum game. It promotes dysfunctional pluralism and issues are usually misinterpreted to the disadvantage of various groups of the society. I am, however, hopeful that the attention being given to the Niger Delta problem will reverse the losses so far recorded and set an acceptable platform for improved life for all stakeholders.

DIFFICULTIES

In today's world, every responsible institution must be well equipped to meet its challenges that are largely imputed upon it by the vagaries of globalization. He NA cannot afford to be oblivious of this fact. It must be ready to shift from the attritionist strategies of operation to the manoeuverist concept. In this wise, there is a requirement for deliberate programmes of re-equipping the NA to meet these challenges. This requirement is resource dependent. In the face of dwindling resources and in a competitive democratic environment, getting the required funds is a daunting task.

Globally, military hardware are expensive. The competing demand for development and other social needs in the country present daunting challenges. Suffice it to say that the NA would have to compete with other sector of the economy in the quest to re-equip. This imperative is predicated on the wisdom of Kofi Anan earlier alluded to in this chapter. Security drives all other sectors under the current setting in Nigeria and indeed in other climes. At the international relations level, there is a greater need more than ever before for Nigeria to continue to maintain a credible defence force that is capable of supporting our national aspiration of an economically viable, stable and effective player in the new world order. Notwithstanding our principle of peaceful co-existence and pacific settlement of international disputes, the reality is that security challenges are on the increase. A deliberate planning and allocation of resources for a potent military force must be undertaken. Our vibrant democracy must be backed by a credible military as exists elsewhere. Democracy must have potent fangs capable of biting hard whenever necessary. I would therefore appeal that we see the challenges within the prism of a share value system. To this end, every sector of the economy must do well in giving credible support to re-equipping the NA.

DEMAND FOR PEACE SUPPORT OPERATIONS

The global nature of threats and the cost of terrorism are beginning to reshape international politics, peace and security arrangements. The character of global insecurity that attended the immediate post-cold war years is gradually shifting to other forms. While intra-state wars are beginning to abate except for DR. Congo, Sudan, Chad and Somalia, other forms of insecurity are fast gaining untold proportions. These include violence arising from human rights violations, criminal gangsters operating beyond the control of central governments and terrorism among others. Terrorism is a globalized phenomenon. Nigeria cannot afford to be complacent with efforts at curbing its surge. Equally, politically motivated violence as was recently witnessed in Kenya adds to the list of the growing need to join in peace support operations (PSOs) as part of coordinated efforts at ensuring global peace and security.

The Nigerian Army has excelled in PSOs. Our gains however, would need to be consolidated. The demands for NA involvement in PSOs are enormous. The NA only succeed with strong political and economic support. Besides, the enviable status of her performance would need to be sustained. Additionally, the global nature of PSOs demands that best practices should guide actions. In this vein, a balance and well structured force with modern equipment becomes an imperative. The high cost of these equipment need not serve as an insurmountable barrier to our quest to continue to excel in PSOs[8].

RESPONSE

I have so far attempted to highlight some of the major challenges before the NA. We have constructively proffered strategies for meeting these challenges. I shall now take a look at these strategies which are our responses to the challenges.

The NA on realizing the need for re-professionalization and the huge task of repositioning herself, embarked upon a transformation process. A Change Management Committee was set up to fashion a roadmap upon which the NA is rapidly building upon for more efficient and service-oriented soldiering. The committee identified and service-oriented soldering. The Committee identified attitudinal change as the foundational basis for every other aspect of the transformation process to thrive[9]. An Attitudinal Change campaign was, therefore, launched in 2006 to sensitise officers and soldiers on the requirements for change. This has progressed satisfactorily.

It should be noted that the transformation process has no terminal point in mind. It is rather a continuous process designed to achieve a lighter, yet lethal, sustainable and more rapidly deployable and responsive force, better able to meet the diverse challenges now and in the future. On assumption of office, I realized that a solid foundation has been laid for a better service. It is my belief that building on this solid foundation was essential to attaining our institutional goal.

Our image is changing for the better. Our human rights disposition has been rewarded. The UNESCO rewarded the NA recently in recognition of her efforts. It is our belief that professional competence and strict adherence to our constitutional roles will earn us respect locally and internationally. It is worth mentioning that the NA would need cooperation of all and sundry in order to give greater meaning to her efforts. Offering adequate publicity on the positive changes in the Army is critical to the way we will be perceived by the Nigerian people. This, we hope to explore. Equally, this respected audience may wish to note that 4 out of squad of the recent U-20 World Cup Champions that did the nation proud are products of our Barracks. To further encourage this endeavour, the Barracks Youths Foundation is being set up to fully exploit the rich potentials that lie across NA Barracks.

The NA of today operates an 'Open Door' Policy. We have realized the need for closer interaction with the political class and the public in general in order to gain their trust. Besides, it will make NA activities more transparent. We have shifted from the era of the military being seen as a 'closed society'. This does not however mean that issues bordering on state security are to be compromised. The NA has increasingly engaged the political class in our training and operation activities. The last EX EAGLE RING V was witnessed by both the various arms of Government at every level and the public including the traditional rulers. It is our hope to make the NA leadership very transparent. We believe that the process will galvanize the much needed trust from the political class. The trust is envisaged to inject the quantum leap needed in our re-professionalization efforts.

INTEGRATED APPROACH TO OPERATIONS

Following the insecurity in the Niger Delta and some other parts of the country, the NA is re-organising to meet the challenges of internal security (IS) duties. The re-organization is also to conform to the roadmap of our transformation process. Equally, there is a change in our concept of operations in IS duties. We believe that IS duties would require a more people friendly approach for greater results. In this wise, we are collaborating with the Niger Delta Development Commission (NDDC) and other stakeholders in the Niger Delta to ensure that our efforts are complimentary to theirs. This is predicated on the fact that the insecurity in the Niger Delta is mostly development related. Given the right development injects; the problem will be greatly minimized.

The NA is equally in sympathy with greater political involvement as part of the comprehensive plan for an enduring solution in the Niger Delta. I am glad that the government is on the right course in this direction. The listening posture of President Yar' Adua's administration is unprecedented. We can only hope for the good understanding of our brothers and sisters in the Niger Delta. The promises from the government will be actualized with their understanding. On our part, we shall remain rebust in our disposition in order to create the security imperatives for developmental plans to take root and become concretized.

As earlier mentioned, the modernization of the NA is imperative in terms of equipment and weapon systems. The NA equipment should meet requirements for the new mission and the force structure. The factors to consider in re-equipping the army are portability, ease of maintenance, reliability, durability, necessity and affordability. The huge cost implications for military hardware in the midst of other competing demands nationwide would mean a different approach to the funding issue. Accordingly, the NA has embarked upon a robust sensitization of the various stakeholders. Also, budgeting for equipment the army has taken a new turn. It has become more deliberate and active and is set to achieve the desired goals considerably. Besides, a consortium of Banks is being engaged to fund part of the re-equipping plan. The re-payment under this regime will be through receipt from the NA participation in UN missions.

The NA will continue to participate in PSOs in line with her constitutional mandates. The participation will be with a renewed vigour and greater drive towards professionalism. We are set to sustain the international trust and confidence in our abilities. The glory and accolades to the country that have been garnered so far from our international engagements would be harnessed to the advantage of the NA and the Nation. We are seeking actively to become even better at PSOs. The adoption of the Continental General Staff System (CGSS) is largely designed to bring us at par with other armies of the world with whom we work together under the auspices of the UN. The NA has continued to train and reequip. Presently, we are focusing on II training that will ensure a seamless transition into CGSS. To this end, laptop computers have been purchased and are being distributed.

The welfare of personnel is critical to the success of our response strategy. Within the framework of the strategy, welfare has been given a pride of place. All the welfare schemes in the NA are being strengthened. The Post-Service Homes Ltd (PHL) has been designed to enable NA personnel to own houses within the period of engagement at the locations of their choice. Mortage loans schemes are being pursued for troops to ease the payment plan to the ownership of houses. On medicare, 2 hospitals are being upgraded to functional referral standards to handle all serious medical cases. This will reduce the number of cases for medical evacuation of Nigerian Medical practitioners, Vesta Healthcare International Limited. The result of this partnership is beginning to be felt throughout the NA.

Equally, kitting of troops has received tremendous support from Mr. President. All personnel of the NA will receive two pairs of uniforms every quarter in the first instance. Therefore, the old practice of exchange of worn-out uniforms will be re-introduced. All these welfare initiatives are sure to reshape the NA for a balanced output in all its undertakings.

CONCLUSION

I have attempted to give you some understanding of the challenges and responses of the NA in this chapter. The NA has continued to justify her existence in line with constitutional provisions. Our performances in IS operations and at international engagements have been remarkable. I wish to indicate that the present NA leadership will continue to lift the army to higher heights. The support and cooperation of all stakeholders are essential and are hereby solicited. We can only hope that the new Army would meet the aspirations of all Nigerians.

REFERENCES

1. Constitution of the Federal Republic of Nigeria, 1999.
2. National Defence Policy, Ministry of Defence, Abuja.
3. J. E. Dougherty and Pfaltzgraf, R. Jnr. Contending Theories of International Relations: A Comprehensive Survey, Second Edition, (Ny: Harper and Row, 1981).
4. L. Coser, The Functions of Social Conflict, (New York: The Free Press.
5. C. Ake, "The causes of Conflicts in Africa: A Research Proposal" (Port Harcourt: CASSS) 1995.
6. I. Zartman, Conflict "Reduction: Prevention, Management and Resolution" in F Deng and I Zartman (eds), *Conflicts Resolution in Africa,* Washington DC, 1991.
7. K. Annan, "The Causes of Conflict and the Promotion of Durable Peace and Sustainable Development in Africa" (New York: UN) 1998.
8. L. Irabor, "Conflict Management Resolution: A case study of the Bakassi Peninsular Conflict Between Cameroon and Nigeria". Thesis presented to Legon Centre for International Affairs, University of Ghana, 2002.
9. S. Huntington, The Soldier and the State (Vantage Books: Belknap Press).

CHAPTER 23

THE NIGERIAN NAVY: CHALLENGES AND RESPONSE

G. T. A ADEKEYE

PREAMBLE

The immense importance of the sea to mankind is underlined by the fact that over 70% of the World's surface is covered by sea, 80% of countries have a coastline and most of the World's population live within 5000km of the coast[1]. The traditional use of the sea is as a medium of transport; especially maritime trade, which constitutes 80% of world trade and remains the principal means by which raw materials and manufactured goods are transported between supplier and consumer nations[2]. Additionally, the sea contains immense natural resources such as hydrocarbons, large quantities of fish, manganese nodules, cobalt and nickel[3]. It is estimated that fish from the sea provides about 25% of the world supply of animal protein[4]. It is also estimated that maritime nations earn a total of about £1,950bn from the sea annually[5].

The benefits of the sea, predicated on its large size and the natural resources therein, have made it a most attractive environment for illegal activities for criminals and saboteurs to explore the sea for their selfish ends[6]. Consequently, most maritime nations have established one or more agencies such as the navy and the coast guard to police their maritime environment. However, with an exclusive economic zones of up to 200 nautical miles (nm) seawards for each littoral state, the policing of the maritime environment has been known to be a Herculean task by most nations due to its sheer size.

Nigeria has a coastline of about 420 nautical miles (nm) and an Exclusive Economic Zone (EEZ) of 200nm which translate to an area of 84,000sqnm. Please permit me a slight digression here. This is just to explain some comparative data. Do you know that 84,000sq nm translates into some 284,000 sq km to EEZ. That is almost 1/3 of the total land mass of Nigeria and the NN has to patrol that! It is instructive to note that over 70% of Nigeria's crude oil lie offshore. Beside crude oil, there are other abundant mineral resources such as calcium, manganese nodules, cobalt, nickel, uranium, copper and natural gas as well as being a rich source and haven for marine life and foods. That is not to talk of other economic activities like shipping, including others on innocent passage which we have responsibility to protect.

On account of the expanded economic activities in the EEZ and the renewed global interest in the Gulf of Guinea, new challenges have correspondingly been thrown up to the NN. Besides, the growing threat of trans-national terrorism is of serious concern to Nigeria since most of the new large oil exploration fields are in isolated waters, many miles offshore. In particular, sabotage of these vital assets by an external adversary or any of the growing groups of militant youth in the Niger Delta cannot be discountenanced. These new challenges have presented more tasks in addition to those envisioned by the statutory roles of the UN.

EPISTEMIC CONTEXT

The aim of this chapter is to acquaint you with the NN's challenges with a view to highlighting appropriate reaction strategies to ameliorate them. Navies are one of the policy instruments of the state and the maritime service of a nation's defence force[6]. Thus, they represent a critical factor in the equation of any maritime state. Specifically, they allow states the use of the sea for their own advantage, while at the same time attempting to prevent use of the sea by others to its disadvantage[7]. Bear in his submission enthused that a navy is a state's main instrument of the maritime force and what it should do, what doctrine it holds, what ships it deploys, and how if fights are determined by practical political and military choices in relation to national needs[8]. From the foregoing, it follows that navies reflect the totality of a state's aspirations and well being of the maritime frontier.

In the categorization of navies, Morris divided navies of the world into nine ranks [10]. His naval hierarchy comprises Major Global Force Projection (complete), Major Global Force (partial), Medium Global Force Projection, Medium Regional Force Projection, Adjacent Force Projection, Offshore Territorial Defence, Inshore Territorial Defence, Constabulary and Token Navies.

Morris ranked the US Navy as the only complete major force projection navy, USSR as partial force projection while Britain and France were placed at the third rank of medium global force projection navies. The NN was placed in the sixth rank, that is, offshore territorial defence navies[11]. The other navies in the West African sub-region are placed lower than Nigeria as constabulary and token navies. Booth offered another classification of navies based on geographical reach[12]. He classified them as Global, Ocean Going, Contiguous Seas Coastal Sea Navies.[13]

The classification of Morris and Booth show that the navies in Sub-Sahara African are ranked in the 3 lowest cadres of the world's maritime forces. And that should not be surprising. Captain Tom Crychton, in his book Pegasus Book of Naval Warfare (US Naval Institute, 11969) stated that *"Of all the great nations of the world, only Negroes of Africa and the Indians of North America never really mastered the use of the sea. It they had, the history of the world in the last 4000 years would have been very different"*. Hence the NN is the only navy in West Africa categorized as Offshore Territorial and Coastal Sea Navy. In consideration of its status, the NN has the potentials of adequately safeguarding Nigeria's maritime environment from multiple challenges.

Challenge is generally understood as the assertion of opposition against an individual or a programme by a challenger who believes victory is possible. It means a summon to take part in contest or trial of strength or a summon to prove or justify something, a demanding or a difficult task, or a call to respond.[13] The foregoing definition implies that challenges is all about a call to rest. It is an opportunity to assert oneself.

Challenges could also mean objection, opposition resistance, to confront, defy, offer resistance and thwart.[14] It follows that challenge is a threat to the attainment of objectives. Hence, the challenge of the NN are those factors, internal and external, detrimental to optimal use of its human and material resources to attain Nigeria's maritime defence objectives.

Response is something done in reaction to something else. It is also a reaction to stimulus.[15] It means reply, answer, acknowledgment, rejoinder, retort, riposte, return and comeback.[16] Thus, response is a counter to challenge. From the foregoing, let me submit that this chapter is all about identifying those factors detrimental to the NN's attainment of Nigeria's maritime objectives and how it is responding to or countering them.

NIGERIA'S MARITIME ENVIRONMENT

The British Doctrine Handbook (BR 1806) defines maritime environment as the coastal sea areas and that portion of the land which is susceptible to influence or support from the sea, generally recognized as the region which horizontally encompasses the land- water mass interface from 100km ashore to 200nm at sea, and extending vertically into space from the bottom of the ocean and from the land surface.[17] This area is often referred to as the "littoral'.

As earlier asserted, Nigeria has an expanse of about 84,000sq nm of maritime environment. Indeed, the extent, variety and value of the resources in these waters are so enormous that they are not easily quantifiable. These resources range from shrimps and fish to oil and gas, including avenues for maritime trade. Also, embedded in Nigeria's internal waters as a vast network of pipelines mostly ubiquitously located in the complex network of creeks, flow-stations and many other oil/gas installations. Petroleum accounts for over 90% of Nigeria's total export and about 80% of her budgetary revenue is maritime-based. These installations are thus the nation's prime assets and need to be protected by the NN from theft, vandalism and sabotage.

The preservation and defence of the economic lifeline of Nigeria is one of the country's core interests. According to Admiral Gorshkov, *"the strength of a maritime state is its capacity to place al resources and possibilities offered by the Ocean at the service of mankind and make full use of them to develop its economy and the health which finally determines all facets of the life of the country including its defence capability".[18]*

The vast majority of goods that Nigeria exports or imports for industrial, services and commercial activities are transported through the sea. Additionally, a considerable proportion of the world's sea trade passes though Nigeria's waters. The safe transit of the ships and their goods is among the nation's foremost maritime interests. Thus, any attempt to block Nigeria's sea lanes constitutes a serious threat to the country. In addition, any activity that would undermine effective harvesting of the maritime resources, is considered a threat.

Threats: threats to Nigeria's maritime interests represent those things that endanger or undermine the pursuit of the security of the Nigerian State or its survival as a corporate entity. Such threats could be either internal or external.

    a.   *Internal Threats:* Internal threats to Nigeria's maritime interests include political and communal conflicts, smuggling, piracy and sea robbery, poaching and marine pollution. Others are illegal bunkering, pipeline vandalism, sabotage; and maritime terrorism.

   1. *Political and Communal Conflict:* Political or participation based conflicts have to do with partisan political identification and politicking, centralizing tendencies, decentralization and creation of constituent units such as states, local government and chiefdoms. Communal conflicts could be identify-based or resource-based.[19] These conflicts have manifested themselves in ways that disrupt economic activities and destroy lives and properties.

   2. *Smuggling:* Smuggling, as defined by United Nations Law of the Sea Conference (UNCLOS) is the act of taking or bringing people or goods secretly and illegally into or out of a country[20]. This act has grave consequences on the economy and security of the nation as it precipitates loss of revenue to government and encourages trafficking in illegal drugs, arms and ammunition. It also aids the closure of industries by stifling the patronage of domestic products.

   3. *Piracy and Sea Robbery.* The International maritime Organization (IMO) defines piracy as any illegal act of violence or detention, or any act of deprivation, committed for private ends by the crews or passengers of a private ship or a private aircraft and directed by the high as against another ship or against persons or property on board such ship.[21] Sea robbery, on the same note is the commission of these acts in ports or terminal waters[22] Unfortunately, the incidence of piracy and sea robbery have been on the increase in Nigeria. This development, if unchecked has the potentials of giving Nigeria a very negative global image that could impact on the inflow of foreign investment.

   4. *Poaching:* Poaching is the act of fishing in a nation's waters without permission or licence. The Food and Agriculture Organization states that one-quarter of all fish stocks worldwide are being increasingly overexploited largely due to poaching[23]. For many littoral states, fishing represents a substantial part of their feeding and economy, hence poaching is inimical to their livelihood and development.

   5. *Marine Pollution:* Marine pollution is the discharge or dumping of toxic or hazardous waste in the maritime environment. The 2005 Abuja Declaration reiterated issues highlighted by the Food and Agricultural Organization which indicates that on account of pollution, fishery resources have experienced stock depletion, distorted ecological balance and environmental degradation.

6. *Illegal Bunkering:* Illegal bunkering is the illegal transfer of fuels and other petroleum products between vessels, from storage facilities to vessels and vice versa. This criminal activity has severe implications for our economy since the oil industry accounts for 90% of our foreign earnings or 80% our GDP. In Nigeria however, illegal bunkering has taken a new dimension as well as new sense of urgency as the perpetrators deal in illegal crude oil exports while they source their cargo from vandalized pipe lines to steal the products. The NN is, however, unrelenting in its efforts to reduce illegal bunkering activities in the Niger Delta.

7. *Pipeline Vandalism and Sabotage:* Further to the above the increase in public awareness of the monetary value of oil and gas products coupled with the remote location of most of the facilities associated with them, have ensured a rise in the spate of pipeline vandalism and sabotage. The quest to unscrupulously make earnings through compensations arising from oil spillages and siphoning of product from the pipeline have encouraged the destruction of pipelines and flow stations.

8. *Maritime Terrorism:* The International Maritime Organisation (IMO) defines maritime terrorism as the use of threat or violent action in the maritime environment against person, installations and shipping in order to achieve political or socio-economic aims or to force government to act in accordance with terrorists' dictates[24]. Youths in the Niger Delta Area have persistently engaged in maritime terrorism and this has become a major operational challenge to the Nigerian Armed Forces, particularly the Nigerian Navy.

9. *External Threats:* External threats manifest in various forms. These include hostile propaganda, threat of force by unfriendly states, sabotage of sensitive military, economic or other strategic installations (such as oil platforms and export terminals) as well as the denial of access to markets, especially crude oil markets. External threats to Nigeria are likely to be within the areas of the overlap of WWZ between countries of the Gulf of Guinea, weak and vulnerable neighbours, maltreatment of Nigerians in the Diaspora and the actualization of an independent and robust foreign policy. However, most of the present challenges are from internal threat.

Roles and Capabilities: The roles of the NN were derived from the Constitution of the Federal Republic of Nigeria 1999, Nigeria's Defence Policy, and the Armed Forces Act Cap A20 Laws of the Federation of Nigeria 2004. The roles assigned to the NN by these documents could be classified into 3 prominent aspects. These are military, policing and diplomatic roles.

a. *Military Role:* The military role includes:
1. Force projection functions
2. Balance of power functions

b. *Policing Role:* The policing role of the NN is concerned with the maintenance of law and order within the internal waters, territorial waters, contiguous zone and EEZ.

c. *Diplomatic Role:* Diplomatic roles include:
   1. Negotiation from position of strength
   2. Manipulation
   3. Prestige.

There is also the need to maintain law and order within the EEZ since a coastal state has exclusive access to the living and non-living resources within this zone. The functions of the NN under this role are in the areas of coast guard and nation building.

Coastguard Functions: The coastguard functions of the NN include:

a. Prevention of infringement/violation and enforcement of customs, immigration, fishery and pollution laws and regulations.
b. Protection of the nation's merchant shipping and sea lanes.
c. Ensuring that the exclusive rights of exploration and exploitation of resources within the territorial seas are preserved.
d. Prevention of drug trafficking and dumping of toxic wastes in Nigerian waters and seaports.
e. Maintenance of good order.

Nation Building Functions. Nation building functions are inform of aid to civil power and such other functions, which are mostly limited to the maritime environment and they include the following:

a. Organization of Search and Rescue (SAR) operations, especially at sea or in the riverine areas.
b. Patrol of coastal areas during Internal Security (IS) operations to prevent infiltration of saboteurs.
c. Provision of relief for people and their evacuation from disaster areas.
d. Provision of skeletal services during strikes by dockworkers and other government parastatals.
e. Organization of landing parties in support of civil authorities during IS operations.

CAPABILITIES

The NN Fleet is capable of dealing with surface, air and underwater threats, and is particularly effective in conducting coastal patrols of Nigerian waters to protect the nation's vast oil/gas installations and pipelines. The NN is not only concerned with blue water operations, it also maintains special squadrons to protect coastal approaches and numerous creeks where oil and gas installations abound. In general, the NN capabilities include:

a. Maritime Combat

b.   Sea Lift.
c.   Offshore Patrols
d.   Inshore Patrols
e.   Hydrographic Survey
f.   Aerial Surveillance.

Force Structure: At inception, the NN had limited coast guard duties with limited hydrographic survey capability, while the colonial Royal Navy was performing the blue water tasks. However, continuous upgrading of equipment and adequate training of personal have greatly improve the operational readiness of the fleet. In order to sustain this arrangement and ensure uninterrupted operations, the NN is structured into a Naval Headquarters, four Commands and a few autonomous units.

   a.   Naval Headquarters: The NHQ is the administrative and policy making organ of the NN. It has seven branches each administered by a branch chief who is of flag rank. The organization of the NHQ is as shown:

   b.   Commands. The NN has four Commands. These consist of two operational commands and Western Naval Command and Eastern Naval Command. They are all headed by Flag Officers Commanding (FOCs). The two Operational Commands are responsible for the protection and policing of the nation's maritime environment. They have fleet, operational bases and forward operating bases under them. Additionally, the Commands have fleet support groups, for effective maintenance of their fleet in order to support the execution of their responsibilities.

Autonomous Units: The autonomous units include the Naval Dockyard, Naval Shipyard and the Naval Ordance Depot (NOD). The NN has the largest Naval Dockyard in West Africa located in Lagos as well as a shipyard at Port Harcourt. The Dockyard and Shipyard build small craft and carry out third line maintenance and docking of NN ships while the NOD provides storage for arms and ammunition. The NOD provides storage for the NA, NAF and some paramilitary units. These units are facilities enable the NN to maintain the fleet for sustained operations.

NIGERIAN NAVY FLEET

The NN Fleet consists of mixed classes of ships as follows:

   a.   *Offshore Vessels.*
      1.   MEKO 360 Frigate   -   1
      2.   MK9 Corvettes   -   2
      3.   Fast Attack Craft (Missile) -   6
      4.   Mine Countermeasure Vessels (MCMVs)- 2
      5.   Landing Ship Tanks   -   2

   b.   *Inshore/Coastal Patrol Vessels*
      1.   River/Town Patrol Craft (PC) -   4
      2.   Defender Class Boasts   -   15
      3.   Inshore Patrol Boasts (IPC) -   29

    c.   *Auxiliary Vessels:*

      1   Tug Boats   -   5

      2. Hydrographic Survey Ship   -   1

      3. Cat Class Ships   -   4

      4. Training Ship   -   1

    d.   *Naval Air Arm:* The NN Air Arm has 5 Agusta helicopters in its inventory with another 4 to join soon.

Most of the aforementioned ships were commissioned into the service of the NN in the early eighties, hence they are averagely over 25 years old. However, the Cat class ships, 15 Defender Class boats and 4 Agusta helicopters are recent additions which have helped to reinvigorate NN operational readiness. All these new addition have been injected into the NN orbat specially to enhance its policing operations. There is, however, the need to enhance fleet balance to sustain the NN Concept of Maritime Defence In-Dept. This is because, Nigeria must retain her blue sea capabilities and regional maritime capabilities, even if there are no immediate challenges there.

POLICING MARITIME ENVIRONMENT

The primary objective of policing the Nigerian maritime environment is to be able to monitor activities within the EEZ and maintain saboteurs now employing high-technology equipment, it would be desirable for the NN to acquire effective counter-measures and policing capabilities.

DETECTION AND RECORDING SYSTEMS

Detection and recording systems comprise radars, night vision equipment, photographic and video cameras. High probability of prompt and early detection is a strong deterrence to intruders. Additionally, recording equipment are required to provide data which could be used as evidence against offenders. To this effect, the NN proposed the installation of radar stations at its 5 FOBs. Each station is capable of acquiring signals at a range in excess of 200nm, which will be well beyond our EEZ.

Platforms

The detection systems used for surveillance and recording must be mounted on suitable platforms for their deployment and operation. Such platforms include coastal observation posts, patrol, Maritime Patrol Aircraft (MPA) and helicopters.

    a.   *Coastal Observation Posts:* Coastal observation posts are shore-based facilities housing detection equipment such as Over-The-Horizon (OTH) radars, cameras and electro-optical equipment. They provide a cost-effective means of EEZ surveillance since they have low personnel and maintenance needs. The transit time of NN ships from their present operational bases at Calabar, Port Harcourt and Warri to sea is very long. It takes not less than 5 hours for NN ships to sail from these naval bases to the open sea. This greatly reduces the reaction time of the naval ships and helicopters to emergencies at sea. Consequently, Forward Operating Bases (FOBs) were established at Bonny, Ibaka, Igbokoda, Formoso and Escravos, closer to the open sea. A new FOB is being proposed for Topo Island off Badagry. The FOBs are in various stages of development. The present focus is to provide them with essential facilities such as jetties, POL reservoirs, armouries, helicopter landing pads, offices, and accommodation quarters. In line with its plans to actualize a more effective coverage of the Nigerian maritime environment, the NN intends to establish Fast Reaction Posts (FRPs) at Ikot Abasi, Sambreiro River, Funiwa, Ramos River Aje Ogheye, Epe/Lekki and Agbara before 2020.

b. *Patrol Boasts:* The term "Patrol boasts" covers a wide range of vessels ranging from inflatable dinghies to fully armed corvettes.[25] The choice of which size of boat to use is dictated by the perceived threat and the section of the maritime environment where it is situated. Larger vessels such as Offshore Patrol Vessels (OPVs) are particularly suitable for patrolling deep into the EEZ because of their low operational costs and endurance. Patrol of coastal waters are best effected with smaller coastal vessels, while the creeks are best patrolled with small boats and Flat Bottom Boats (FBBs). The NN has had to contend with an ageing fleet and this has necessitated intensified local refit of ships. The successes recorded have been a great source of encouragement and has led to the ongoing exploratory building of Seaward Defence Boats and other platforms at the NND, Lagos. The NN is developing a 5 – year Ship Maintenance and Operational Circle (SMOC) to strike a balance between deployment and maintenance of ships. The NN is also making efforts to acquire new vessels to enhance patrols of our maritime environment. To this end, I can happily state that the Federal Government has approved a fleet renewal for the NN. The first set of boats will join us in May/June this year 2008.

c. *Maritime Patrol Aircraft:* The large area of the ocean to be policed makes the use of fixed-wing MPA logical. Park asserts that the MPA is the most versatile platform for covering a large EEZ[26]. He lists the advantages in using MPA as including its all weather capabilities, speed and the surface search, detection, location, identification, speed and tracking systems that can be installed in it[27]. It is essential that the MPA is adequately armed with weapons such as machine guns, rocket launcher; and marker buoys in order to enforce any instruction it might give a suspected vessel. The MPA is either operated jointly by the Navy and Airforce or solely by the Navy. Apart from inter-service rivalry that manifests in the acquisition of such platforms, it is most logical to have such an aircraft in NN inventory even if they will be flown by the Air Force.

d. *Helicopters:* Helicopters are best used for patrolling coastal areas, from bases, preferably FOBs, for refueling and basic maintenance[29]. They can also operate from helicopter-carrying ships in which cases they act force multipliers. Their major advantages include their ability to hover, and cover large areas at high speed when compared to large surface vessels[29]. The acquisition and subsequent deployment of helicopters in the NN Fleet has helped NN operations. However, two squadrons of helicopter currently operated by the NN is grossly inadequate to effectively support the other assets operating within the vast Nigeria's maritime environment. In order to effectively discharge its statutory roles, the NN envisions the development of 2 other air stations at Calabar and Warri and 5 flying units at the FOBs.

Command, Control, Communication, Computer and Intelligence (C⁴I). C^4I are essential for effective policing of the maritime environment because they allow a naval force commander to make optimum use of available maritime policing resources. The BRI806 defines command and control as the process through which a commander exercises command or operational control to organize, direct and coordinate the activities of the forces allocated to him[30]. It states further that it must be robust and flexible and must support the principle of centralized direction and decentralized execution, thus allowing freedom of action within the overall concept of operation[31]. The importance of intelligence lies in its ability to provide vital threat information on the location, capabilities and intentions of economic saboteurs which could facilitate tailoring and directing adequate platform to meet the threat. Over the years, the NN has improved its information gathering capacity and this has reflected in the successful conduct of patrols.

Concept of Operations: Concept of operations is a clear and concise statement of the line of action chosen by a commander in order to accomplish his mission; it stipulates the ways an operation should be carried out. The main objective of policing the maritime environment is to deter economic saboteurs and if this fails, to detect, intercept, arrest culprits/perpetrators and hand them over to the appropriate authorities for prosecution. It is therefore essential that patrols are not predictable.

Training: According to Hattendorf, policing of the maritime environment involves specilised procedures and legal requirements[32]. These demand that personnel engaged in maritime policing duties are well trained on these procedures and legal requirements so that they thoroughly understand the laws they are enforcing. Through its various professional schools, the NN ensures adequate training for its personnel. The Naval Training Command administers all the NN professional schools and the Sea Training Unit, which is responsible for exercising and evaluating the performance of our Fleet and the ships' company as appropriate.

CONSTRAINTS

The constraints to NN's operational efficiency are in the areas of old and degraded platforms, inadequate ship support facilities and low level research and development efforts, low national industrial capacity, poor marine domain awareness and funding.

Old and Degraded Platforms: Most of the ships in the NN Fleet were commissioned into the Service in the early eighties and have had no major refit or upgrade prior to recent local refit efforts. They have indeed become more expensive to operate and maintain. The challenges of securing Nigeria's maritime environment and assets, especially the offshore oil and gas installations calls for newer and more modern ships that have the capability for sustained patrol for a period of at least 3 weeks.

Inadequate Ship Support Facilities: The NN's capacity to meet the logistics requirements of vessels in the bases is impaired by the serious state of disrepair of support facilities. The NN cannot utilize its POL depots because they are unserviceable. The challenges of the increasing pace of NN operations, especially in the Niger Delta Area and our EEZ have brought to the fore the need to have a vast reserve of POL to adequately cater for the Service. This is made more compelling by the current spate of pipeline vandalism that leads to the shortage of POL products . The major constraint of the NND and the Nigerian Navy Shipyard (NNSY) is the age of the facilities. The maintenance cost of these facilities has risen and constitutes a drain on the resources of the NN.

LOW LEVEL RESEARCH AND DEVELOPMENT EFFORTS

The Navy is a highly technical establishment that needs to constantly adapt to developments in or maritime environment. NN ships are saddled with the problems of corrosion and undergrowth that require a novel home-grown efforts to tackle effectively. There is also a need to help enhance the operational efficiency of our platforms. There are however efforts to establish a well-equipped research and development unit in the NN to stem the tide.

Low Industrial Capacity: Another problem the NN contends with is the low industrial capacity of the country to help in the maintenance of equipment and fabrication of spare parts for platforms. The low industrial capacity has also seriously stunted the efforts of local shipbuilding. For example turn around of our ships are hampered by lack of very basic maintenance needs like steel plates, welding equipment not to talk of replacement of machinery spares.

Poor Maritime Domain Awareness: It is now common knowledge that while Nigeria is a well endowed maritime nation, the nation's pervading lack of a maritime culture tends to undermine every efforts of both the government and private practitioners, to fully develop the potentials of her maritime wealth. Also, despite the tremendous dependence of the strategic sectors of our national economy on the maritime environment, Nigerians, regrettably remain largely unaware of the full potentials and benefits of the sea. This general lack of interest about the sea particularly by our elite, policy formulators and decision makers have adversely affected the funding and provision of equipment to the NN. This lack of domain awareness portends grave adverse consequences for the nation. For example, go to the NNPC or Ministry of Transport and find out how many of their executives have been even on a pleasure visit to the sea.

Inadequate Funding: Over the years, the NN has been stretching its meager resources to contend with the enormous responsibilities of safeguarding Nigeria's maritime frontiers. These responsibilities have been growing exponentially particularly in the light of recent developments in the Niger Delta and the Gulf of Guinea. Adequate funding of the Navy is imperative in consideration of the insecurity resulting from the smuggling of arms and ammunition and the colossal loss of revenue by the government predicated on the lack of credible naval presence in our maritime environment.

Future Policy Direction: The future policy direction of the NN takes cognizance of the growing importance of the Gulf of Guinea in the socio-economic well-being of Nigeria. The latest discoveries of large oil/gas deposits far offshore, such as the Bonga, Agbami, Ekoli and Akpo and Mistra in Nigeria (which are at distances of not less than 120nm from any of the NN Bases), Bogi in Sao Tome and Principle, Zafiro and Alba in Equatorial Guinea amongst many others, underscores the need for credible naval presence within the Gulf of Guinea:

> *To have a navy that is rational and sustainable through a planning function that is holistic in approach. A navy that will be equipped, well trained, well led and well motivated to achieve success in the tasks it undertakes, respond decisively to tasks that might arise and build its capacity to respond to long-term defence and national security challenges.*

The hub of the vision embraces a credible NN with the requisite details needed to meet its mission and in particular, the contemporary maritime security challenges it has to face now and in the nearest future. It captures the requirements for an effective Service that is versatile, proactive, resilient and adaptive to an ever-changing socio-political and economic environment. Consequently, the vision requires that we train, equip and emplace a highly motivated and operationally combat ready naval force that is poised to:

a. Contribute meaningfully to the security of Nigeria and its citizens in peacetime including providing military aid to the civil authorities.

b. Participate in the National Defence Diplomatic initiatives through the building of international trust.

c. Support Nigeria's interest, influence and standing abroad, especially in the West African sub-region and within the AU.

d. Participate in peace support and humanitarian operations.

e. Maintain a naval capability to mount a response to any conflict that could adversely affect Nigeria's interests.

f. Provide forces needed to respond to any sub-regional and regional conflicts as may be required under the ECOWAS and the AU charters.

Nigeria's leading role in the sub-regional and regional affairs in Africa will often necessitate her participation in most security operations particularly peacekeeping, as the need arises. This further underscores the need to adequately maintain and sustain the existing platforms in addition to increasing the Fleet appreciably with new ships, in order to enhance NN operational capabilities.

It is obvious that the present equipment holding of the NN cannot adequately meet the emerging threats for the effective maritime defence of Nigeria as envisaged in the National Defence Policy. Efforts are, therefore, being made to update NN facilities in order to meet future challenges. For instance, the Navy is sourcing for foreign technical partners for the Nigerian Naval Dockyard and the Shipyard, so as to further improve their maintenance capabilities, as well as provide a viable basis for ship building in Nigeria. The delay in executing this scheme is dictated by the need to build such capacity for the Naval Dockyard so that she can be a viable partner to the foreign investors.

Projection of Ship/Fleet Mix: Driven by the consideration for an effective coverage of our maritime environment, the NN has made projections into the future. In this vein, the NN proposes the acquisition of vessels that would ensure a balanced Fleet in the following mix:

a. 4 x Meko Type 200 Frigate.
b. 6 x Offshore Patrol Vessels
c. 14 x Squadrons of Helicopters
d. 2 x Landing Platforms Docks
e. 2 x Landing Ship Tanks
f. 4 x Corvettes
g. 4 x Ocean-going Tugs.
h. 2 x Logistics Ships
i. 2 x Fleet Tankers.
j. 2 x Conventional Submarines

It would be expedient for the appropriate authorities to grapple with this vision and commence action on the acquisition processes, considering the lead time which could be as far as 5 – 15 years if action commences immediately. I do not wish you to look at this projection as over ambitious, or expensive if you can see our challenges especially if it is noted that the incursion of the US and other Western Navies into our waters is because they know we are not effectively there.

Logistics Assets. In tandem with the NN's vision of a balanced fleet and the necessity to ensure credible presence in our EEZ, there is the need for strategic logistics reserves to ensure sustained operations. In this regard, the NN plans to build strategic logistics depots at Lagos, Calabar, Sapele and Port Harcourt in addition to developing an integrated logistics system to enhance its operations.

Diversification of Training and Specializations. The focus for the future is to ensure that the training institutions are well equipped and staffed to be able to meet the modern trend. Training aid upgrade, accreditation of courses as well as training institutions and proper staffing are being pursued vigorously. The joint concept of operations, which is the thrust of modern military doctrine, is being entrenched in our training programmes. Naval personnel undergo professional training with

Service especially in areas where there are commonalities. In addition to these efforts, the NN is intensifying efforts at seeking billets for training abroad. This is desirable to enable us keep abreast of developments in other parts of the world. Currently, officers and ratings of NN are being trained abroad where billets are available anywhere on the globe.

Welfare: Motivation of personnel is being addressed from 2 perspectives. Firstly, to ensure that the work environment is conducive for trained personnel to effectively practice their skills. Secondly, to ensure that personnel are relieved of such welfare needs as education and medicare for their families so that they could concentrate on their work. Also, concerted efforts are being made to ensure that personnel are deployed appropriately. Appointment cycle of officers and draft cycles of ratings are constantly being reviewed in order to minimize the relapse syndrome in their performances.

CONCLUSION

Nigeria has an expansive maritime environment of about 84,000 sq nm, rich in installations, and living and non-living resources. The internal threats Nigeria contends with include political and communal conflict, smuggling, piracy and sea robbery, poaching and marine pollution. Others are illegal bunkering, pipeline vandalism, sabotage and maritime terrorism. Some of the external threats are sabotage of sensitive military, economic or other strategic installations and hostile propaganda.

The roles of the NN are military, policing and diplomatic. These are beside its coastguard and nation building functions. In a bid to effectively address its mandate, the NN in structured into a Headquarters, 4 Commands and a number of autonomous units. The Fleet comprises offshore, inshore/coastal patrol and auxiliary vessels, and an air arm of 5 helicopters.

The requirements for an effective policing of the Nigerian maritime environment include detection and recording systems, platforms C⁴I, concept of operations and training. Some of the constraints to the operational efficiency of the NN are old and degraded platforms, inadequate ship support facilities and low level research and development efforts. Others are low industrial capacity, poor Maritime Domain Awareness and Inadequate Funding.

The future policy direction of the NN takes cognizance of the growing importance of the Gulf of Guineas in that socio-economic well-being of Nigeria. The vision of the NN is predicated on the need to have a credible navy, with the requisite wherewithal to meet its mission and in particular, the contemporary security challenges it has to face now and in the nearest future. To this effect, the NN has projected for new ships to enhance her fleet mix. It also plans improvement of its logistics, assets, diversification of training, specializations, and welfare.

NOTES

1. Janes Intertional, Janes Amphibious Warfare Capabilities (Couldson: Jane's Information Group, 2006)
2. Royal Navy, British Maritime Doctrine Manual, (BR 1806), (Second Edition).
3. Ibid
4. Ibid
5. British Department of Trade and Industry, British Maritime Industry Catalogue, 1999 Edition.
6. SA Afolayan, "The Nigerian Navy", Lecture delivered to NWC Course 11, 9 October 2002 pg 1 – 2.
7. GTA Adekeye, "Nigerian Navy in National Defence". A paper delivered to participants of NWC, Abuja, January 2007.
8. GW Baer,One Hundred Years of Sea Power: the US Navy 1890-1990, (Stanford University Press, 1993), p.1.
9. AT Morris, Expansion of Third World Navies (London:Macmillan, 1987). P.24.
10. Ibid. p. 25.
11. K. Booth, Navies and Foreign Policy, (New York: Holms and Meier, 1979) p.258.
12. Ibid. p. 260.
13. Microsoft Encarta Encyclopaedia, 2005 Edition.
14. Ibid
15. Ibid
16. The New Penguim Thesaurus (Middlesex: Penguin, 2000).
17. Royal Navy, British Maritime Doctrine Manual, BR 1906, (Second Edition).
18. O. Ibeanu, "Communal Conflicts and Population Displacement in Nigeria: An Exploratory Analysis" in O Nnoli (ed). Communal Conflict and Population Displacement in Nigeria, Enugu: PACREP Books Series.
19. United Nations Convention on the Law of Sea (UNCLOS III), 1982.
20. UNCLOS III, Article 101 quoted on IMO website, *http://www.imo.org/facilitation.mainframe.*
21 Ibid.
22. Du Plessis L, "The Challenge of Effective Sub-Saharan Maritime Defence" in Du Plessis and Hough M (eds), Protecting Sub-Saharan Africa: The Military Challenge (Pretoria: HSRC Publishers, 1999).
23. IMO website, Op.cit
24 British Department of Trade and Industry, Op cit.
25. British Department of Trade and Industry, Op cit.
26. Ibid
27 Bennet C, "The Patrol Corvette and Organic Air" in South African Maritime Interests Papers, working paper No 2, June 2001.
28. British Department of Trade and Industry, Op cit.
29. Royal Navy (BR 1806), Op cit.
30. Ibid
31. Hattendorf JB, "Maritime Strategy in the Twenty-First Century" in Mills G (ed), Maritime Policy for Development Nations (NATAL:Sila, 1995).

CHAPTER 24

THE NIGERIAN AIR FORCE IN A CHANGING SECURITY ENVIRONMENT

CHARLES DOKUBO

INTRODUCTION

Airpower took a quantum leap in credibility and perceived importance after the opening days of Operation Desert Storm in 1991. The convergence of high technology with intensive training and determined strategy that was attested by the allied coalition's successful air campaign against Saddam Hussein's Iraq bespoke a breakthrough in the strategic effectiveness of the air weapon after a promising start in World War II and more than three years of misuse in the Rolling Thunder bombing campaign against North Vietnam from 1965 to 1968. Indeed, the speedy attainment of allied air control over Iraq and what that allowed allied air and space assets to accomplish afterwards by enabling the prompt achievement of the coalition's military objectives on the ground marked, in the view of many, the final coming of age of airpower.

There was no denying the effect that initial air operations had in shaping the subsequent cause of the war. The opening coalition attacks against Iraq's command and control facilities and integrated air defences proved uniformly successful, with some 800 combat sorties launched in the darkness of night in radio silence against Iraq's most militarily critical targets and only one coalition aircraft lost – a U.S Navy F/A-18 presumably to a stray infrared missile shot from an Iraqi MIG-25. Over the next three days, the air campaign stuck at the entire spectrum of Iraq's strategic and operational level assets, gaining unchallenged control of the air and the freedom to operate with impunity against Iraq's airfields, fielded ground forces, and other targets of military interests.

In the aftermath of the war, the predominant tendency, not just among airmen, was to credit the coalition airpower with the bulk of responsibility for having produced such a lopsided win. Senator Sam Nunn, initially a doubter about the wisdom of the Bush Administration's going to war for the liberation of Kuwait, hailed the result as attesting to the advent of a "new era of warfare."[1] Three years later, Elliot Cohen of the Johns Hopkins University's School of Advanced International Studies observed that:

> *Although ground action necessarily consummated the final victory for coalition forces, airpower had made the final assault as effortless as a wartime operation can be.*[2]

Cohen, who earlier had led the U.S Air Force's Gulf Airpower Survey, went on to note that airpower had all but taken on a mystique in the public mind as result of its success in the Persian Gulf. Since then, a high-stake controversy has emerged in major capitals around the world centering on how best to apportion operational roles and budget shares among the services at a time of uncertain challenges and near-unprecedented fiscal constraints. Naturally, given the predominant role played by the allied air campaign in Desert Storm and the far-reaching claims made on behalf of airpower as a result of its performances, the roles and resources controversy has gravitated towards airpower as the principle lightening rod for debate. At its core, this debate has come to concern the extent to have even Third World countries can now rely on air-delivered precision stand-off attack weapons in lieu of ground forces to achieve battlefield objectives and minimize the incidence of high casualty rate of their armed forces.

However, if the pronouncement that "airpower had won the Gulf War is indeed valid, the premises underlying it, is that airpower suggests a wider evolutionary development, and that it has attained relative dominance vis-à-vis land and naval forces as the "fulcrum" in modern warfare, has the NAF come of age? Bearing in mind the changing security environment in the continent and sub-region and the nature of post-modern warfare.[3]

Against this background, this Chapter seeks to offer a perspective on the nature and meaning of the qualitative improvements that have taken place in airpower since the mid-1980s, with a view towards offering a measured portrait of airpower's newly-acquired strength and continued limitations. The Chapter concentrates on the development and capacity of the NAF in the context of its assets, and its role in new emerging face of warfare in the 21st century.

AIR-POWER: SOME CLARIFICATIONS

Three binding rules need stipulating at the outset to clarify what is meant in this Chapter by airpower. First, airpower does not refer to merely to combat aircraft (the glamorous 'shooters' that performed so unexpectedly well in Desert Storm) or to the combined hardware assets of an air arm, even though these may seem at times to be the predominant images of it held by both laymen and professionals alike. Rather, in its totality, airpower is a complex amalgam of hardware equities and les tangible but equally important ingredients bearing on its effectiveness, such as employment doctrine, concepts of operations, training, tactics, proficiency, leadership, adaptability and practical experience.[4] These and related "soft" factors vary enormously among air arms around the world operating superficially similar kinds, and often even identical types of equipment. Yet more often than not, they are given little heed in what typically passes for air capability analysis. Only though their combined effects can however, one ultimately determines the extent to which raw hardware will succeed in producing desired combat results.

Second, airpower is functionally inseparable from battlespace information and intelligence. Thanks to the dramatic growth in the lethality and combat effectiveness of airpower since the late 1980s, it has become both correct and fashionable to speak increasingly not of numbers of sorties per target killed, but rather the number of kill per combat sortie. Yet airpower involves more than merely attacking and destroying enemy targets. It also involves knowing what to hit and where to find it. It is now almost a cliché that airpower can kill anything it can see, identify and engage.[5] Airpower and intelligence are thus opposite sides of the same coin. If the latter fails, the former is likely to fail also. For that reason, accurate, timely, and comprehensive information about an enemy and his military assets is not only a crucial enabler for allowing air power to produce pivotal result in joint warfare; it is an indispensable precondition for ensuring such results. This means that tomorrow's air campaign planners will have an ever more powerful need for accurate and reliable real-time intelligence as a precondition for making good on their most far-reaching promises.

Third, airpower, properly understood, knows no colour of uniform. It embraces not only Air Force aircrafts, munitions, sensors and other capabilities, but also naval aviation and the attack helicopters and battlefield missiles of land forces. In this regard, it is worth highlighting that the first allied weapon impact in Operation Desert Storm was not a laser-guided bomb delivered by an F-117 Stealth Fighter, but a Hellfire missile launched against an Iraqi forward air defence warning site by a US Army AH-64 Apache attack helicopter. As was borne out by that example, airpower entails a creative harnessing of all combat and combat support elements, including space and information war adjuncts that exploit the medium of air and space to visit fire and steel on enemy targets. Recognition and acceptance of the fact that air warfare is an activity in which all services have important roles to play is a necessary first step towards a proper understanding and assimilation of airpower's changing role in joint warfare.[6]

THE NIGERIAN AIR FORCE (NAF)

The Nigerian Air Force (NAF) as part of the nation's Armed Forces is under the control of the executive arm of government. Thus, like all other arms of the national defence force, it does not have autonomy of action in defining its role in society at large except in cases where such actions or roles are within the guidelines of national policy objectives. In the recent past, national policy and objectives have undergone fundamental changes as a result, the role, tasks, and mission of the NAF is also undergoing substantial and to an extent a painful adaptation.

The principle of self-defence as it is stipulated in the United Nations charter provides the moral justification for maintaining an Air Force as part of national defence. Though the realities of power, politics and national interest have often superseded this moral ideal, it still provides the general constitutional basis for the establishment and deployment of an Air Force. The Air Force as other branches of the Armed Forces within a democracy exists to deter and if deterence fails defend the country against external and physical attack.

The success of airpower during operation Desert Storm was part of the inspiration for this chapter, but a little preamble is necessary. Air power as it was employed in the Gulf, exemplified classic textbook prescription with all the awareness that it implied. The centrepiece of Desert Storm, the air campaign, was clinical and brutally executed; achieving such success that the assertion was subsequently made that "air power" had won the Gulf War.[7]

If the pronouncement that "airpower had won the Gulf War" is indeed valid, the premises underlying it is that air power suggests a wider evolutionary development, and that it has attained relative dominance vis-à-vis land and naval power as the "fulcrum" in modern inventorial warfare. Has the Nigerian Air Force come of age? Bearing in mind the changing nature of warfare, and security.

Thus, this chapter will speculate in the challenges facing the NAF in the light of the recent dramatic changes in the international, regional and national environment within which it exists, it will also try to investigate the application, vulnerabilities and doctrine of the NAF in the context of the security architecture of the early -mid 21st century and the argumentation it may entail.

THE EVOLUTION OF THE NIGERIAN AIR FORCE

The mission of the NAF derives from the National Defence Policy. By the statutory Act of Parliament establishing it in 1964, four goals were specifically highlighted by this Act:

a. To achieve a full complement in the military defence system of the Federal Republic both in the air and on the ground.
b. To ensure fast versatile mobility of the Armed Forces.
c. To provide close air support for the ground forces in all phases of operation and to ensure the territorial integrity of a United Nigeria.
d. To give the country the deserved prestige which is invaluable in international matters.

ROLES OF THE NIGERIAN AIR FORCE

The mission of an Air Force further determines its equipment and its roles. The Nigerian Air Force being a defence-oriented force is essentially a Tactical Air Force, and not a strategic one. Although defensive in nature, the edifice stone of NAF operational doctrine is offensive response with emphasis on counter air operations. The NAF is thus organised to carry out the following roles:

a. **Air Defence:** Air Defence is attained by maintaining air superiority over Nigerian air space through interception, point defence, and combat air patrol.
b. **Counter Air Operations:** Counter Air Operation is performed either through preventive or retaliatory attacks against enemy targets and installations.

c. **Interdiction:** Interdiction is carried out against hostile forces and supply activities in the battlefield.

d. **Close Air Support:** This is performed through concentrated air attacks against enemy forces within the Forward End of Battle Area (FEBA) as requested by friendly forces.

e. **Air Transport:** This provides tactical mobility for troops and equipment. It includes air combat support, medical evacuation, search and rescue and movement of VIPs.

f. **Maritime Operations:** Maritime Operation involves aerial patrol of own territorial waters for security and information gathering purposes.

g. **Air Recce:** Air recce involves aerial reconnaissance mission flown for the purpose of gathering air intelligence.

The NAF prior to the civil war was in the process of being established. During the crisis that led to the war, it lost, like the other services, highly trained Igbo officers. After the war, the Air Force remained for a long time underdeveloped in relation to the two other Services. Nevertheless, it acquired some systems to add to its civil war stock. It took delivery of some F-27 medium transport aircraft in 1971; Soviet-built MiG-21 Fighters in 1975, C-130 transport aircraft in 1976, and acquired helicopters, and training aircrafts.

The NAF was restructured into three major commands – The Tactical Air, Training and Logistics. Infrastructural developments further led to an increase in operating stations. In 1975, it was observed that the NAF structures did not reflect the roles it had to play in providing not only air defence and air support duties, but also in achieving air superiority in any conflict in which Nigeria was involved. The 1975 – 1980 NAF development plan, therefore, 'restructured the NAF field formations into units of group status that reported directly to HQ, NAF. This structure, however, proved too cumbersome, and led to the creation of the Tactical Air Command and the Training Command in 1978. In 1980, however, the support changed to Logistics Command. Soon after that, strategic planning was made a permanent feature of NAF with the establishment of the Forces Structure and Establishment Committee in 1981.[8]

In spite of all these restructuring, the Air Force nevertheless, still felt inadequately equipped. A former Chief of Air Staff, Air Vice Marshal Bello lamented in 1982 that 'the Air Force lacks aircraft in the strike or counter-strike role which could provide the necessary defence, and if need be, the offensive force against any potential enemy.[9] The importance of air defence strategy and the need to develop Nigeria's air defence network was strongly pushed by the Air Force during this period. The fact that the Army and Navy budgets were always higher irrespective of need, worked against it; and an argument was put forward for this to be changed to reflect the changing face of Nigeria's defence requirements.

From the perspective of the Air Force at the time, it required:

At least, three Squadrons of modern fighter-bomber aircraft capable of making about ten short ton of bombs within a radius of about 250 nautical miles. Such an aircraft must be equipped with self-navigational system and aerial refuelling system for improved range, and should be capable of night operations with defence suppression capability.[10]

THE CHANGING SECURITY ENVIRONMENT

The uncertainty of events in the former Soviet-Union, Eastern and Central Europe and the war in the Gulf would appear to dash the hopes that the new world order is in any way a safer place than the previous era. In retrospect, the international bipolar structure may have provided a greater degree of stability than the uncertainty of present and expected future changes in regional and global balances of power. In fact, recent events in the former Soviet Republics and Yugoslavia have given rise to concern about the stability and nature of the "New World Order".[11] It is of course certain that new international "rules of the game" will certainly emerge, but this will not happen over night nor will acceptance of, or adherence to the new power structures be unanimous.

These events are disheartening as they make it obvious that the world has not yet entered a golden age in which military power and armed conflict are something of the past. In the first world communities recognition is, however, being given to the declining utility of armed conflict in favour of economic instruments of power. In contrast considerable value is still attached to the use of armed forces and coercion in what is generally termed the Third World. Since the majority of the peoples of the globe live in the Third World, this situation is a cause of great concern.[12]

This assessment is illustrated by the fact that most of the wars which have occurred since 1945 took place in the Third World, whilst in this period Europe and North America experienced an unprecedented era of peace. The last three decades have seen the major conventional conflicts in the Middle East alone, namely the Arab-Israeli conflict, the Iran-Iraq war, and most recently, the unequal test of strength between a First World coalitions of the willing against Iraq.

Even though First World rivalries and competition have played no small part in most of these Third World conflicts, the origin of these wars cannot simply be attributed to external involvement alone. Much of Africa has no political tradition of accountability as a result; leaders are often in business for themselves and a rather small group of supporters. Although governments do change, the processes of election are neither free and fair nor free from fear.

To a degree these developments may support the role of a regional power such as Nigeria. Rather than run the risks inherent in direct involvement in the often-messy conflicts and problems in a region such as West Africa, the developed world may attempt to enhance regional stability through regional arrangements. However, lasting cooperation on such sensitive issues as security in West Africa can only succeed if built upon a shared value system, common interest and cooperation. This, in essence is the implication of President Bush's (Snr) New World Order.

Multinational involves sharing the burden of defence while at the same time promoting common and regionally acceptable political and economic aims. In military strategic terms it implies that mobility be accepted as a strategic principle which guides force structure and doctrine considerations. Consequently, military forces should have the ability to react quickly and appropriately to a crisis, i.e implying lighter, multi-role air force capable of executing a variety of tasks,[13] which are not limited to those on conventional armed conflict alone. Along with these developments go the obvious requirement for strategic mobility and support, propositioned stocks, and multinational cooperation etc.

THE REGIONAL CONTEXT

In broad terms, Jenny Macgregor's description of Africa also holds true for West Africa:

> *Most African states are suffering from high population growth rates, declining per capital, food production, severe land degradation, declining export revenue, worsening trade balances and enormous debts.*[14]

From a regional perspective, West Africa remains a cesspool of conflict as was stated by Nowamagbe Omoigui in a lecture delivered to the National War College on the 19th of January 2005:

> *Sub-Saharan Africa is mired in bitter ethnic feuds and has the world's lowest growth rates in per capital Gross Domestic Product (GDP). Similarly, life expectancy, the rate at which children are immunised against disease and ration-in-take in Africa are the lowest in the world. Consequently, Africa has the highest percentage of people living below the international poverty line. In recent years, its economic performance has been the worst in the world. Africa cannot adequately feed, educate or maintain the health of its rapidly expanding population, many of whom are internally and externally displaced persons. To compound the problem, there are limited opportunities for extra-governmental acquisition of sustainable wealth. Instead private wealth is accumulated largely as a result of access to state power. This confluence of power, wealth and social mobility within the state structure, set up a rat race of gargantuan proportions for control of government.*[15]

To a large extent much of rural West Africa has deteriorated to the point where in countries such as Liberia, Sierra Leone and Cote d'Ivoire, Central government have lost control over much of the countryside, either to armed opposition movements or warlords. In a once prosperous country such as Cote d'Ivoire, urban neglect and decay has reduced the modicum of central government control over the rural areas to an alarming degree.

In Nigeria, the expansion of the democratic space has let loose pent-up frustration and agitation contained by years of military rule as the fourth republic got on track. There is nothing new about communal conflicts in Nigeria. The country's diverse ethnic groups have always lived somewhat uneasily together, and there has been terrible outbreaks of violence in the past, although the current tension does not remotely compare, for instance with the situation in 1966, when ethnic pogrom helped spark off the Nigerian civil war. But the recent upsurge in violence coming so early in President Yar' Adua's tenure has provided a gruelling examination of his government's ability to assert its authority, whilst not being seen to be favouring one group over another.[16]

Like a Bulgarian bear at bay, tormented and cut to pieces by a thousand bloodhounds, the Nigerian state has borne the brunt of a dramatic upsurge of ethnic militias, particularly since the restoration of civil governance. The names are often as bloodcurdling as their stated missions. The Egbesu Boys of Africa; Oodua Peoples Congress, Movement for the Actualisation of the Sovereign State of Biafra, the nascent Arewa Peoples Congress and the Niger Delta Volunteer Force which has made resource control its main agenda.[17]

CHARACTERISTICS OF THE PREVIOUS THREAT ENVIRONMENT (TYPICALLY PRE-NINETIES, AND ESPECIALLY PRE-EIGHTIES):

- Mode of conflict were primarily interstate in nature and one against another;
- Conflict manifestation and the underlying strategic philosophy on conflict were predominantly conventional;
- Order of battle (ORBATs) of opponents were mainly static in nature, this become less the norm as we moved into the modern era, but even recent conflicts still made use of trenches and fixed positions from which to wage war (e.g the Gulf War and the Angolan War);
- Force design patterns of war-fighting parties assumed linear proportions, with equipment procurement and ORBATs developing in line with perceived changes in threat variables, of which opponent capabilities were the most important;
- Reasonably fixed and clear cut rules of engagement (ROE) existed; Opposing doctrines and tactics were well-known to the various parties in a conflict; and
- Strategic early warnings of an impending attacks was **generally** possible, due to the time it took to move large bodies of men and equipment into position for attack.

CHARACTERISTICS OF THE EMERGING THREAT:

- Conflict are assuming an increasingly intra-state nature, although spilt over potentials remains high in most cases;

- Conflicts are becoming increasingly non-conventional in nature, as they are fought more often in developing countries with limited conventional forces, however, it needs to be stated that the danger of nuclear, biological and chemical (NBC) proliferation is real;
- ORBATs are becoming dynamic and random and hence difficult to predict, mainly due to the fact that forces are no longer organised along predominantly conventional lines;
- Non-linear force structure increment are becoming increasingly apparent this is mainly the result of the greater availability of ultra-sophisticated weaponry on the world's arms market, such as missiles systems, chemical weapons, computerised planning systems and systems and systems which embrace the greater use of micro-technology;
- Doctrines are becoming increasingly vague and fused, being tailor-made to suit specific operational requirements;
- Strategic early warning is becoming increasingly difficult to obtain, mainly among less technologically developed opponents, due to the unconventional nature of systems and doctrines involved in combat, and due to the unique and non-traditional triggers which often initiate conflict.
- More pressures are being exerted on defence forces to be involved in peace support operations.[18]

The above may be summarised by stating that traditional doctrine and force structures has remain the same as most modern defence forces have been directed towards the use of over-whelming force to achieve victory. As should be already apparent from the above, and as will be argued further in this chapter, this is hardly a formula for coping with the wide range of new threats, which are presently emerging.

This seriously hampers the development of air forces; force design and force structures in most countries. How does one plan for such a volatile environment? How does one go about acquiring equipments for threat, which are vague and unmanifested? How does one achieve the optimal balance in one's force design between catering for expected minor contingencies, but simultaneously remaining, prepared for major conflicts, however rare these may be? And what about the trade-offs for peace support operation? Does one prepare for visible threats, or to counter potential capabilities? Intent can change more rapidly than military capability, so the clever solution would seem to be to design one's air force according to perceived opponent's capabilities, and not according to threats. There is obviously a careful balance in approach required, driven mainly be considerations of cost and effectiveness.

The changes in the security environment can only have an impact on the nature of future conflicts, and on the resulting nature of forces, which will take part in such conflicts. The question is, though, what a nation will require from its air force in the evolving security environment. Viewpoints differ, especially in an era of greater openness, which surrounds defence debates in most countries. In most cases, there would seen to be some agreement that the following should be the major drivers which need to underpin the formulation of defence forces' vision and mission:

- To protect the nation's interest in whatever form these may be threatened;
- To provide adequate protection against any threat, of a military nature;
- To participate in peace support operations;
- To enhance the country's international image and influence;
- To support domestic goal and interest;
- To allow for strategic and operational ethics in the pursuit of national goals and interests.

I. THE AFRICAN SECURITY LANDSCAPE

In the post-colonial, post-Cold War Era Africa has been characterised by the absence of any external military threat, relatively rare instance of inter-state armed conflict, severe socio-economic need, continued vulnerability to political instability, intra-state conflict, non-state or sub-state military and para-military threats and the threat of deprivation resulting from environmental conditions.

Lodge categorised African armed conflict on the basis of the causes or instigators of conflict, as follows:

- Ethnic competition for control of the state.
- Regional or secessionist rebellions.
- Continuation of liberation conflicts.
- Fundamentalist religious opposition to the secular authority.
- Warfare arising from state degeneration or state collapse.
- Border disputes.
- Protracted conflict within politicised militaries.[19]

While some of these causative factors have declined, others appear to be gaining in intensity. The underlying causes of conflict are nevertheless very difficult to eradicate and it is highly likely that for the foreseeable future conflict in Africa will remain predominantly intra- state. This will be accompanied by para-military and non-military threats of criminal or natural origin, which will exacerbate the overall threat to human security on the continent.

II. ASYMMETRY IN THREATS TO AFRICAN SECURITY

Asymmetry is not unique to either Africa or to 21st century conflict. It is a timeless feature of war/conflict but has been given prominence by the nature of security threats in the contemporary world, also in Africa.

Asymmetry has been variously defined or described as "unanticipated or non-traditional approaches to circumvent or undermine an adversary's strengths while exploiting his vulnerabilities through unexpected technologies or innovative means" and "unconventional warfare that seeks to drive the military dimension into the civil dimension to offset Western superiority in high technology". Metz and Johnson describe the concept comprehensively:

> "........asymmetry is acting, organising, and thinking differently than opponents in order to maximise one's own advantages, exploit an opponent's weakness, attain the initiative, or gain greater freedom of action. It can be political-strategic, military-strategic, operational, or a combination of these. It can entail different methods, technologies, values, organisations, time perspectives, or some combination of these. It can be short-term or long-term. It can be deliberate or by default. It can be discrete or pursued in conjunction with symmetric approaches. It can have both psychological and physical dimensions".[20]

Like terrain and weather it is one of the factors to be taken into account in planning and executing military operations. It does not, however, define the role and functions of the military.

III. CONDITIONS PROMOTING ASYMMETRY IN AFRICAN CONFLICT

IV.

V. A number of factors inherent in the security situation in Africa pre-dispose conflict toward asymmetric manifestations. Colonial legacies, ethnic divisions, poor governance and weak state institutions spur challenges to state authority by rebels/warlords/separatists i.e., by non or sub-state entities vying for power and control over resources and territory or fighting for some level of political power and autonomy. There is also the possibility that the War on Terror could increase polarisation and conflict, and precipitate an upsurge in extremism, in areas where there are already significant religious tensions and/or a history of religious conflict.

VI.

VII. Terrain in many conflict areas in Africa provide safe havens for belligerents and funding from illicit minerals gives access to lethal weaponry and enables protracted low-intensity conflict. In addition, large numbers of the population may be displaced by conflict and natural phenomena and may be in need of humanitarian aid to survive, often in large informal settlements and refugee camps. This provides a haven and source of recruitment – sometimes forced – for rebels.

VIII. MANIFESTATIONS OF ASYMMETRY

In these conditions asymmetry may manifests in many forms including:

- Political/military aim. Governments will usually seek to maintain control over and the unity of states within colonial borders. Rebels and/or warlords may seek the autonomy of a part of a country or its resources.
- Method. State militaries may be conventionally organised, trained and equipped. Rebel forces may be highly irregular, using guerrilla doctrine

and tactics, with no clear lines of battle, often intermingling with the local civilian population.

- Technology and Support. State militaries will usually be quantitatively and qualitatively more technologically advanced than rebel forces and conflict may involve disparate forces with distinct technological inequalities. Formal militaries may be highly dependent on external support and logistics, while rebels (and some defence forces) have the ability to live off the land for long periods.

- Will. This involves perceptions of survival or vital interests and will differ significantly between truly democratic governments, power elites monopolising power for personal benefit, rebels motivated by egalitarian ideals, minorities (especially ruling minorities) who feel threatened by majorities and political and/or religious extremists. It also involves the willingness to accept causalities and to die for a cause.

- Normative standards. Parties to a conflict may vary from forces adhering to strict standards of respect for human rights to those who hold scant regard for the rights and/or lives of others. This has resulted in the appalling brutality, even genocide that has characterised conflict in parts of Africa and in a willingness to engage in terrorism that may result in large scale and indiscriminate loss of life.

- Patience. In contrast with the Western (especially US) preference for the quick resolution of conflict, African conflict is usually protracted, sometimes lasting decades without reaching a conclusive resolution.

Such asymmetries must be factored into the planning of military capabilities and execution of operations, but should also be taken into account in the broad context of conflict management and resolution.

IX. NIGERIA'S SECURITY POLICY

One of the central principles of Nigeria's emerging national security policy is that the best way of ensuring one's security is to promote safe environment in region, on continent and globally. The principles of defence is contained in Nigeria's 1999 Constitution and it is reiterated in our posture which states that:

- National security shall be sought primarily through efforts to meet the political, economic, social and cultural rights and needs of the Nigerian people, and through efforts to promote and maintain regional security.

- Nigeria shall pursue peaceful relations with other states. It will seek a high level of political, economic and military cooperation with Southern African states in particular.

Nigeria is, therefore, intensively involved in conflict management and resolution in Africa in collaboration with other African partners, primarily through ECOWAS and the AU. The Nigerian military is intensively involved in several peace missions, including Liberia, Sierra Leone, DRC.... point and it is expected to remain at least at that level.

X. NIGERIA'S DEFENCE STRATEGY

The Defence Policy sets out the principal strategies to be employed in exercising the right and responsibility to ensure the protection of the state and its people against external military threats. These strategies are:

- Political, economic and military cooperation with other states.
- The prevention, management and resolution of conflict through non-violent means.
- The deployment of Defence Force as measure of last resort.

These strategies clearly go beyond the defence of the country and its people against an enemy at the gates and can equally be extended to the West African Sub-region. As Nigeria's commitment to creating a safe environment and the extension of general security by peaceful means.

This intent is reflected in the three military strategic objectives set by the Military Strategy, encapsulating the role and functions of Armed Forces as contained in the Constitution. These are:

- (Self) Defence against aggression.
- Promotion of security (Regional, Continental and Global).
- Supporting the people of Nigeria (in practice, primarily through support to other government departments).

In terms of international law and the UN Charter Nigeria has an inherent right to self-defence against aggression and the self-defence function is undeniably and irrevocably a key component of the Armed Forces mandate. However, the demands of evolving global and continental security landscape and our national security policy have resulted in increased emphasis on promotion of security and the ubiquitous needs of support to the people.

Budgetary constraints and the continued needs of defence transformation have created a certain tension between the requirements to maintain basic (but currently declining) self-defence capabilities while simultaneously satisfying the requirements of the so-called "secondary" functions. In addition, certain emerging security threats lie in a gray area between the military, the police and other departments. The responsibility for the management of such threats is in some cases unclear. There is thus an urgent need to address the balance between the diverse needs and to assign resources accordingly.

ASYMMETRIC CHALLENGES TO AIR POWER

As discussed earlier most of the threats currently dominating the security agenda are by definition asymmetric. This poses particular challenges to air power – challenges that will have to be overcome if air power is to fulfil its potential in countering such threats. Some of the more obvious issues are:

- Careful attention will have to be given to the aim of every operation – to the socio-political end-state that is to be achieved – and to how military means can best be used to achieve or promote that effect, linking the tactical, operational and strategic levels, so that actions at the tactical level do not undermine the strategic aim.
- They require coherence of planning and action can only be achieve if the conflict/threat dynamics are thoroughly understood at every level. The complexity of the situation thus requires the fusion of multi-sensor information into a comprehensive intelligence picture.
- Adjustments may have to be made to force designs/structures and capabilities to accommodate "secondary tasks".
- Adjustments to doctrine may be required to accommodate the requirements of emerging threats
- Airmen and support personnel will have to be trained to cope with the demands of deployment in various roles. The deployment/training cycle will have to be adapted accordingly, cycling between:
  o PSO training
  o Away deployment on PSO's (Promote Security")
  o Conventional training
  o Home deployment ("Support the People")
- Deployment to remote areas means accommodating the high cost of strategic lift within limited budgets and ensuring the integrity of long and vulnerable support/ supply lines.
- Lack of effective air traffic control makes it almost impossible to secure the air space. The detection, identification, tracking and interception of illegal flights imply extensive and expensive air defence systems, again within limited budgets.
- The detection and identification of hostile forces on ground may be problematic due to terrain, vegetation and intermingling with the local population and legitimate traffic.
- The scarcity of high-value targets makes the economics of using expensive, advanced aircraft and weapons questionable. Less advanced but affordable platforms may be preferable.
- Action against air and ground targets will inevitably be limited under restrictive ROE. Planners and aircrew will have to operate within those parameters.
- Terrain, vegetation and concentrations of population may favour asymmetric action by hostile forces.
- Bases and infrastructure may be vulnerable to various forms of asymmetric attack, discussed below.
- The ubiquitous MANPADS make aircraft self-protection essential.
- Support during remote deployments may be hampered by the bureaucracy of procurement processes and dependence on external contractors. Flexible, rapid response systems will have to be devised.
- Compatibility between multi-national forces will be crucial.

VULNERABILITIES OF AIRPOWER TO ASYMMETRY

The use of air power against hostile forces of the kind implied by the emerging threats to security is in itself a manifestation of technological asymmetry. Opposing forces will inevitably employ asymmetric tactics in an attempt to overcome the technological advantage bestowed by air power, or at least to limit its effect.

Tactics that could be used include the following:

Against Aircraft:

- Shoulder launched missiles against aircraft in the landing pattern and in contact areas.
- Mortar/rocket attacks on aircraft flight line, especially at night.
- Infiltration of the local support contingent to sabotage aircraft, aviation fuel, oxygen etc.

Against personnel:

- Infiltration of locally recruited staff to poison water and food of aircrew and support personnel.
- The use of suicide bombers against air and ground crew, living quarters, command centres or other infrastructure.

Against Infrastructure/Support:

- Denial of runways with cheap obstructions.
- Jamming of air traffic control or operational radio frequencies.
- Sabotage of approach and navigation aids.
- Landmines on routes to and from airfields.
- Attacks on overland supply routes, especially aviation fuel deliveries.

XI. AIRPOWER DOCTRINE IN THE CHANGING ENVIRONMENT

The changing nature of the security environment and the threats it entails, characterised by asymmetry and various associated challenges and vulnerabilities, must inevitably impact on the way air power is conceptualised and applied.

If past and present air power thinking has largely been a product of a fascination with technology, then the new security environment is precipitating a revision of thinking that is long overdue. Conflict and war are firstly about the human psyche. More than 2000 years ago the military philosopher Sun Tzu pointed out the central importance of moral influence and the harmony between people and rulers, and of humanity and justice in formulating victorious policies and making their governments invincible. Mao Zedong reflected this when he said, "[w]eapons are an important factor in war, but not the decisive one, it is man and not materials that counts". It is the mind that wields the sword, not the other way around.

Western military thinking has for centuries been pre-occupied with technology. There is, however, an awakening to the critical importance of the human factor, as evidenced by a recent article in the Air Force Times: "If you don't understand the cultures you are involved in; who makes decisions in these societies; how their infrastructure is designed; the uniqueness in their values and in their taboos-you aren't going to be successful."

This realisation has found expression in the concept of Effects Based Operations, which is currently enjoying considerable prominence in Western defence thinking. EBO are defined by the US Joint Forces Command as "[o]perations that are planned, executed, assessed, and adapted based on a holistic understanding of the operational environment in order to influence or change a system behaviour or capabilities using the integrated application of selected instruments of power to achieve directed policy aims." The desired effects often lie in the cognitive and socio-political domains and unless military force is used in ways that effect changes at that level, it may exacerbate the complex security issues of the 21st Century.

This must inevitably influence our view of air power. Some of the changes or required changes in air power thinking are listed in Table 1.

TABLE 1: AIR POWER: TRADITIONAL AND CHANGING VIEWS

Traditional View of Air Power	Air Power in the Changing Environment
Force-on-force combat operations	Avoidance/absence of force-on-force combat
Clearly defined adversary	Adversaries evasive, difficult to identify
Aim: Destruction/defeat of enemy forces classical OODA cycle	Aim: Socio-political effect-importance of UNDERSTANDING before Deciding, Acting
Air superiority role primary	Air superiority uncontested or irrelevant
Air power in autonomous or semi-autonomous role	Air power adjunct/support to ground forces or operations
Technology driven	Technology supported
Intelligence: ORBATS and technology	Intelligence: Politics and culture
Clinical, staff-off	Up close and personal
Predominantly a military matter	Close involvement with local population, civilian agencies, NGO's etc
Flexibility/versatility of Air Power	Mental/psychological flexibility of airmen
Training as AIRMEN	Training as Airmen AND soldier-peacekeepers

REQUIRED CORE COMPETENCES OF THE NIGERIAN AIR FORCE (NAF)

From the evolving security environment, it is fairly obvious that Nigeria is unlikely to face a direct threat from a modern, high-tech advisory in the next twenty yeas. One could not however rule out the possibility of facing a regional opponent that has a defence agreement with an extra-African actor. So the threat Nigeria may likely face is a combination of sophisticated and less mature allies and terrorists. Nigeria must therefore reorganise its air force to enhance its core competencies.

In an effort to guide the overall reorganisation of the air force, capabilities and support structures should be reviewed and upgraded. The NAF should have a new vision to provide a conceptual template of how its constitutional role could be effectively performed, coupled with the leverage of technological opportunities to achieve new levels of effectiveness. Information superiority is the enabler of the Revolution in Military Affairs (RMA), and aliens four new operational concepts needed to significantly enhance joint operations; dominant manoeuvre, precious engagement, full dimensional protection and focused logistics.[21] Characteristics of the information superiority, the operational concepts and resulting strategy follow:

INFORMATION SUPERIORITY

To respond rapidly to any conflict, dominate any situation, and optimise day-to-day operation, accurate, timely and secure information must be available to the NAF. The NAF should have information superiority. The ability to collect, process and disseminate an uninterrupted flow of information while exploiting or denying an adversary's ability to do the same.[22]

DOMINANT MANOEUVER

Dominant manoeuvre is the "multi-dimensional application of information, engagement and mobility capabilities to position and employ widely dispersed airpower to accomplish assigned operational tasks.[23] By moving faster and more numbly than an adversary, dominant manoeuvre will allow a reorganised NAF to control the breath, depth and height of the battle space, and forces an adversary to react from a disadvantaged position or quit.

PRECIOUS ENGAGEMENT

Precious engagement is a "system of systems and would enable the NAF to locate the objective or target, provide responsive command and control, generate desired effect, assess the level of success and retain the flexibility to re-engage with precision when required. Requiring intelligence on enemy forces and expert judgement to match force to the desired effect, the characteristics of precision engagement are precise stand-off capabilities, more capable attack platform and weapons that will inflict minimal collateral damage.[24]

FULL-DIMENSIONAL PROTECTION

From the evolving security environment, it is fairly obvious that Nigeria is unlikely to face a direct threat from a modern, high-tech military opponent in the next twenty years. One could not however rule out the possibility of facing a regional opponent that has a defence agreement with an extra-African actor. So, the threat Nigeria may likely to face a combination of sophisticated and less mature allies and terrorists. Nigeria must therefore develop its air force with certain characteristics.

CHARACTERISTICS REQUIRED FOR THE NAF OF THE 21ST CENTURY

The main characteristics that the NAF must acquire, and to which special attention is to be devoted are as follows:

- **Quality of Human Resources:** This is the most important characteristic that any air force must possess. Special attention needs to be paid to training of personnel, to ensure that qualities of leadership, decision-making skills, motivation and dedication to work and engrained into the system. Professionalising the NAF will allow increasingly complex resources to be managed with maximum effectiveness.

- **Availability:** This consists of ensuring that the NAF are ready to call-up as a prior prerequisite for generating deterrence, coping with a crisis or responding to an aggression. Expertise of personnel and equipment holding will be determinant factors in this connection.

- **Flexibility:** The NAF must be flexible in terms of procedure and organisation of forces. This is a key factor in responding appropriately to the changing circumstances that characterise today's broad spectrum of conflicts.

- **Strategic Mobility:** This is the ability of the NAF to have means of moving necessary combat and support capabilities to the areas of operations.

- **War Fighting Capability or Combat Power:** This is based on effective manoeuvre and fire support capabilities.

- **Survivability:** This is the ability of the NAF units to protect themselves so as to operate in the characteristics environments of modern-day conflicts, where speed of operations, precision and firepower, the need to remain for long periods of time and, on occasions, in environments with a nuclear biological or chemical risk, are key factors.

- **Sustained Action Capability:** This enables NAF to engage effectively in operations for as long as necessary by subsequently relieving the units deployed and providing suitable logistic support.

- **Mobilisation Capability:** The Nigerian Air force must be capable of mobilising its personnel and material resources in order to maintain and, if necessary, restore units' combat power in the shortest possible time.

These characteristics of the NAF are enhanced by the following factors which boost their effectiveness:

- **Joint or Combined Operation:** This will enable efforts of NAF, from when the operations are first addressed, with specific or differentiated characteristics to be combined in a single battle environment. The mode of modern war-fighting is joint operation. No single service fights alone; therefore, enhanced understanding amongst the three services would improve operational efficiency and levels of success.

- **Interoperability:** This is essential in order for the NAF ground, naval and air forces to engage in action with other service and international allies forces. Establishing common standard equipment, doctrine and procedure facilitates easier implementation of operations and logistic support.

- **Advanced Technology:** This is a determining factor as it provides one of the most important advantages today in any situation. Adopting such technology is of particular importance, both as a characteristic of the NAF and for the necessary interoperability with other Allies.

In order to reorganise the NAF, there is the need for intensifying training in the NAF to enable it to easily adopt to joint operation standards, upgrading of equipment, increase in funding levels and enhancement of manpower holdings.

INTENSIFICATION OF TRAINING

The integration of men and equipment is achieved through training. In the NAF as in the other services, raining remains the cornerstone of building a strong and viable air force. This dictum that a weapon is only as good as the man behind it makes this assertion very relevant. Training gives the personnel the required skills and knowledge in modern aeronautic and technology to successfully executive assigned task efficiently. It also enables formation and unit to achieve professional and administrative effectiveness in any operations. Sullivan asserts that the overall objective of training is to achieve tactical superiority over the adversary through adequate knowledge of weapons, effective coordination of their use and the ability to appreciate terrain.[25]

The NAF needs to realise that jointness is the way forward in the post-modern warfare. The fact is that existing joint doctrine and strategy are landpower-centric (grand forces in supported role) and means are not adequately available to assess a crisis and make recommendation for the air force only or anything else only. The basis for change lies in having less concern over which branch is decisive and more concern that the right tools are employed to be decisive. Senator Joseph Liberman of the United States Senate Armed Services Committee noted that:

> the eye-popping advances in technology we are engineering today are paving a path not just to a revolution in military affairs, but to a complete paradigm shift in warfare.[26]

He went on to add that "successfully transforming our military requires that we move to the next level of jointness." By now, virtually every expert believes that future operations will be increasingly inter-agency and combined, and that while competition among the services can assist in determining how best to exploit new capabilities or solve emerging challenges, there should be a much greater emphasis on collaboration.

EQUIPMENT

Currently in terms of number and types, the NAF inventories are not enough for air dominance even in the sub-region. In most cases, their operational status is zero. The only antidote is immediate refurbishing and major modification. The Mig-21 aircraft are for fighter/interceptor and reconnaissance roles. Similarly, the Alpha jets has been tested for close air support and interdiction, the MB-335 may also perform the same role. The superpuma can be re-noted for close support/tactical operation. On the other hand, the F-27 and Do-128-6 and for patrol. The available F-27 troopship can be re-modified for airborne early warning. Finally, the P-12 and the P-35 short and medium range surveillance radar can be re-modified to three-dimensional long-range role. Last but not the least are equipment and communication standardisation and the command and control, since the NAF must operate with the other services.

STRATEGIES FOR REVITALISATION
THE MIG-21

The aircraft has not flown for many years because of lack of spare parts. The condition has so deteriorated that before it can be made air worthy, an extensive refurbishing must be carried out and the aeronautics re-modified to meet the modern standard in communications and navigational systems. The re-modification either be done locally by a friendly African country like Egypt or India. These nations use the same aircraft type and have acquired the technology. This option would be cheaper than employing the manufacturers in Russia or buying new aircrafts. In addition, the pilots and technicians can be retrained and adapted for operational as it obtains in Egypt and India.

ALPHA-JET

In the case of Alpha-Jet, pilots and technicians could manage the aircraft. Although, the aircraft were acquired purely for weapons training until the ECOMOG operation started. The Cameroon have an improved combat version (Impala) acquired from South Africa though France. It is advocated that a few of the aircraft be traded in, to acquire the Lancier Version for day and night attacks, anti-shipping, strinke, maritime air defence and anti-helicopter micro capabilities. Added capabilities include forward-looking infra-red (FLIR) system, variety of weapon capability, all weather missiles, laser guided bombs and missiles and passive and active electronic counter-measures. Air Commodore Okoiye, however, maintained that the Alpha-Jet re-roled missions far beyond its capabilities. The same mistakes should not be repeated with the NAF.

HELICOPTER

The superpuma helicopters should be refurbished and modified locally or an outright trade-in to acquire a few more modern close support helicopters from the manufacturers in Germany or an outright purchase of attack helicopters from Russia.

SURVEILLANCE RADARS

The following radars are in the inventory o the NAF and are located at various stations in the country:

(a) P-12 short range
(b) P-35 medium range
(c) PRV-II Height Finder

Unfortunately, all the equipment are unserviceable due to spares. The Russian manufacturers have stopped production of the series. However, when they were operational, the P-12 and P-35 were instrumented to 360 KM and 370 KM range respectively. A low level, they both have 90 KM effective range. In addition, the P-35 has IFF that is only marked to Russian type of transponder.

Furthermore, when co-located with PRV-II, it is capable of three-dimensional reception. It can also be used for electronic warfare (EW) jamming, but will have to be manually operated in that mode. The P-35 can transmit video pictures to command post within 30 KM.

INCREASED FINDING LEVEL FOR THE NAF

Achieving better funding of the NAF is one of the means to reorganise it since the NAF could be part of a peacekeeping. The end of the Cold War has provided opportunity to expand the utility of air force in multinational peacekeeping. In order to succeed at the type of intrusive activities proposed by Boutros-Ghali's Agenda for Peace, Air Forces are now an integral part of peacekeeping. The preparation and deployment of the NAF for international military engagements require a lot of fund. The NAF on the whole is ill-funded, yet expected to play a crucial role in the changing security environment. This should be reversed.

IMPROVING MANPOWER HOLDINGS

The manpower requirement of the NAF should be increased and training enhanced. With the concept of jointness and the engagement of the NAF in national defence, sub-regional activities and internal security duties, the current level will overstretch the present manpower holding. There would be the need for the Federal Government to increase Ministry of Defence allocation for the NAF to redress these shortcomings. The redressing of these issue would place a reorganised NAF to effectively and efficiently perform is responding constitutional roles.

Finally, the strategic imperative for the airman has always been present. It has, however, been masked by a land power-centric approach to war, the overwhelming firepower approach of previous conventional wars that has prevailed through the various forms of warfare, due to in some cases, the inattention of the airman. Desert storm changed the airman's outlook and supplied confidence in his abilities and capabilities. The stage is set for a newbreed of airmen for the NAF, to change the land-centric conception of war and attain their rightful place.

CONCLUSIONS

Changes in the security landscape over the last decade or two have given increasing prominence to intra and sub-state threats and conflict and to non-military threats to security, at the expense of traditional views of conventional inter-state warfare. In addition, there is an increasing awareness that the resolution of complex security issues requires a thorough understanding of the dynamics of conflict and the achievement of socio-political change. This has led to a re-evaluation of the role, functions and utility of military power.

While air power theory was in the past dominated by a technological perspective, the challenges of the emerging security environment, with all its potential for asymmetry, require a change in the way we view air power. It is no longer not primarily about air superiority and the destruction of enemy forces, but about the subtleties of creating security, of influencing the way people perceive the world and think and act. And it requires a new kind of airman-soldier-not just a techno-warrior, but a soldier who understands that his role is ultimately to help create security.

Air power truly is versatile and multi-faceted instrument and it can find many applications in defence against aggression, promoting security and supporting the people. However, if we are to use it to full effect in the complex security environment of the 21st Century, we must learn to use it with sill and innovation, looking beyond its technology to the way that technology can best be applied to alleviate or address the causes of conflict and insecurity. This means accommodating both the technological and the human dimensions in air power theory and doctrine.

REFERENCES

1.   P. E. Tyler, "U.S Says Early Air Attack Caught Iraq Offguard", *New York Times*, January 18, 1991.
2.   E. Cohen, "The Mystique of U.S Air Power", Foreign Affairs, January/February 1994.
3.   V. Alan, & David, T.O. *et al* "Preparing the U.S Air Force for Military Operations other than War", Santa Monica, California, RAND MR-842RF, 1997, p.128.
4.   T. Mason, "The Future of Air Power". Address to the Royal Netherlands Air Force, Netherlands Defence College, April 19, 1996, p.4.
5.   Ibid., p.6.
6.   J. Collin, "Desert Storm and the Lessons of Learning", Parameters, Autumn 1992, pp.87-88.
7.   Lt.-General George K. Mueliner, USAF "Technologies for Air Power in the 21st Century". Paper presented at a Conference on Air Power and Space-Future Perspectives", Sponsored by the Royal Air Force, London, England, September 12-13, 1996, p.11.
8.   J. S. Peters, The State and the Nigerian Military, Zanus Publishers, 2001, p.138.
9.   M. Yahaya, "The NAF and the Development of Air Power in Imobighe. T. (ed) Nigerian Defence and Security. Issues and option for Policy (Ibadan Macmillan 1987. P. 84).
10. Ibid, p.97.

11. S. R. Looten, Space Force 2020: A Force for the Future (Maxwell Air Force Base, Alabama 1998), p.32.

12. Ibid, p.40.

13. A. H. Cordesman, "The Lessons and Non Lesson of the Air and Missiles War in Kosovo" (Center for Strategic and International Studies, Washington DC., September 1999), p.231.

14. J. Macgregor, The Crisis in African Agriculture, *Africa Insight,* Vol.20, No.1, p.15.

15. N. Omoigu. The place of Armed Forces in the Emerging Regional Scene, Lecture delivered at the NWC, January 19, 2005. p.6.

16. C. Dokubo, "The Niger-Delta and the Crisis of the Nigerian State", *African Journal of Conflict Resolution,* Vol.2, No.1, 2000, p.85.

17. Dokubo. C. Democracy and the Emergence of Ethnic Military. The Case of Nigeria. *Nigerian Forum* 2000.

18. J. M. Jager Air Power in 21st Century Africa Address to the South African Air Force at Sui Pierra van Rynereldt Air Power Centre 20th September 2004. p. 2.

19. T. Lodge, Towards an Understanding of Contemporary Armed Conflicts in Africa, in Malan, M. (ed) ISS Monograph, Peacekeeping in Africa, April 1999, p.18.

20. S. Metz and Douglas V Argentina and US Military Strategy: Definition, Bagmen and Strategy, Strategic Studies Institution. January 2001.

21. R. Owen, Deliberate Force: A Case Study in Effective Air Campaigning (Maxwell AFB Alabama, Air University Press 2000), p.97.

22. K. Hutchinson, Air Mobility: The Evolution of Global Reach (Vienna: Point One VII, September 1999), p.28.

23. R. A. Pape., Bombing to Win: Air Power and Coercion in War (Ithaca, New York: Cornell University Press 1996), p.22.

24. C. J. Bowie, *et al* The New Calculus: Analysing Airpowers Changing Role in Joint Theatre Campaign (Santa Monica, CA RAND 1993), p.84.

25. R.G. Sullivan, "Flexibility Set the Pace at Combat Training" in Army, Vol.43, No.7 (July 1993), p.121.

26. J. L. Liberman, "Transforming National Defence for the 21st Century", (Washington: DC 1999), p.97.

CHAPTER 25

NIGERIAN AIRFORCE-
CHALLENGES AND RESPONSE

PAUL DIKE

INTRODUCTION

The raison d'etre for the Armed Forces of any nation is to ensure the security and protect the perceived interests of the citizens of that state may not necessarily be coterminous with, may in fact contradict, that of another state or non-state actor. If the will of the state must prevail then it must have recourse to force or some means of persuasion. Although diplomacy and dialogue ensure and enhance peaceful coexistence among nations, it is generally accepted that robust military power is a strong source of bargaining power within the international political arena. A point emphasized by Robert J. Art when he noted that:

> Military power plays a crucial role in international politics because states coexist in a condition of anarchy. If a state is attacked, it has to defend itself with whatever means it can muster. Because no authoritative agency can be called on to resolve disputes among states, leaders find it convenient, and often times necessary to threaten the use of force or actually employ it. Though its importance varies from era to era, military power brings some order to international politics and helps make and enforce the rules of the game.[1]

I should add that nations often leverage their military power even in peace time in furtherance of their national interests as noted by John Shalikashvili when he observed that: "the challenge of the new strategic era is to selectively use the vast and unique capabilities of the Armed Forces to advance national interests in peacetime while maintaining readiness to fight and win when called upon"[2].

Before the invention of the aircraft in 1903 by the Wright Brothers, land and sea power were the only coercive instruments available to nations; consequently military engagements were confined to these environments. The introduction of the bomber aircraft into warfare during the Italian-Turkish war of 1911-1916 changed the nature of warfare forever. A third dimension was added to the battle space and a new form of combat power – air power – became cognizable. Since then, the character of warfare has been undergoing radical and continuous change. Air power- the ability to use platforms operating in or passing through the air for military purposes – is quite different from other forms of military power in that it confers the ability to protect force at short notice, over long distances, and in great concentration. Of the three forms of combat power, land, sea and air, none is as versatile as air power – a fact that led Churchill to assert, as far back as 1933, that "not to have an adequate air force in the present world is to compromise the foundations of national freedom and independence".[3] It is not surprising, therefore, that today, air power is not only dominant in warfare, it has also become a versatile instrument for the attainment of state policy in peacetime. In our environment, the purveyor of air power is the Nigeria Air Force.

This chapter will like to start by highlighting the statutory responsibilities of the NAF because in so doing, some of the challenges and contingencies for our air power would become manifest in large measure. I believe also that in a discourse of this nature, a little exposition on the extant and likely threats, from the air perspective that is, would also be helpful. This should lead me to a discussion of how we are organized and equipped to meet the threats and contingencies. Thereafter I will highlight some of the constraints to the Service and how we have responded to them. I will conclude the discourse with my vision of what the NAF should look like in the near future.

ROLE ANALYSIS

The Nigeria Air Force was established by an Act of Parliament in 1964. The same Act specified the mission and roles of the Nigerian Air-force in the national defence and security matric. These have been broadly re-enacted in section 217(2) of the Constitution of the Federal Republic of Nigeria 1999, and Section 1 of the Armed Forces Act (AFA) No. 105 of 1993. However, an important provision of the National Defence Policy (NDP) I should emphasize here is Chapter 5-17 which provides that "the primary responsibility of the Nigeria Air Force is the defence of the Nation and the protection of vital economic interests by air". The NDP stipulates further that:

> The NAF shall be employed, either singly or jointly with other Services in regional and sub-regional operations. Such response capability shall be enhanced for force projection within the region. As a critical element of the interdependent land-naval-air force synergy, air power is a decisive force in warfare. Therefore, in the event of hostilities, the NAF shall deny control of the air to enemy air force and provide the land and naval forces the assistance necessary for them to control their environment. The primary mission of the NAF is the attainment of air superiority....[4],

The implication of this provision is that in the event of any hostility, the air campaign has primacy. Experiences from modern wars like the Arab-Israeli Wars, Falkland and the Gulf Wars, have also confirmed that winning the air war is a condition precedent to the success of other operations – be they on land, sea or even in the air.

The totality of the statutory and Defence Policy provisions translates to a mission for the NAF, which we have summed up in military strategic and operational context as:

> To ensure the integrity of the airspace by gaining and maintaining control of the air while retaining a credible capacity to fulfill

other air power tasks demanded by National defence and security imperatives.

Note that we used the phrase "the airspace" instead of "our airspace". This is in recognition of the fact, the National Defence Policy has done, that 'the Nigerian Air Force may be required to project air power in environments external to ours as in fact it did during the liberation wars in Southern Africa and the ECOMOG operations in Liberia and Sierra Leone.

This unique mission of the NAF demands that it should have capabilities to conduct operations in three broad domains as follows:

a.   Independent operations: these are missions aimed at achieving the operational goals of the NAF (e.g. training and air superiority operations during war);

b.   Joint operations: these are missions in support of the operations of the other services (that is, Army, the Navy and the Police in internal security situations); and

c.   Other missions at the behest of the Government and other civil authorities; for example, in the past we conducted missions for the National Emergency Management Agency, the CBN, INEC and the National Population Commission.

In these three domains, the NAF should be able to generate highly trained and combat ready forces to undertake a number of air power tasks in three clearly distinguishable situations, namely, in peacetime, during crisis, and in war. I will now give some indicative scenarios.

a.   ***Sustenance of Peace through Deterrence:*** The Air Force exists for the purposes of war but the preparation for this role confers on it indirectly a major peacetime role, of deterrence. A well-balanced air force with a credible operational capability to exact rapid retribution constitutes an effective deterrence to potential aggressors. The Air Force can also be used to help avert threats to peace by exploiting the third dimension for surveillance purposes. The fact that any threatening move by a potential antagonist could be detected and met with appropriate responses helps to keep adventurous opponents in check.

b.   **Disaster/Relief Operations:** When disaster strikes in any form, speedy response is vital. Air power can play a key part in alleviating suffering by providing search and rescue services, medical evacuation of the sick and injured as well as delivering food, medicines and other supplies in the shortest possible time, if rendered to foreign countries, as we did to Guinea Conakry in 1983 and to Mozambique during the floods of 2000, such assistance go a long way in enhancing national prestige and fostering good bilateral relations.

c.   **Air Transport Operations:** Air transport operations constitute the most visible peacetime activity for most air forces in the world. The NAF is no exception. The Air Force flies a variety of missions lifting troops, government functionaries and goods locally and to all parts of the World.

d. Maritime and Border Patrol: The surveillance of our territorial waters and Exclusive Economic Zone (EEZ) and our entire borders is an importance peace time function of the Air Force. Such operations ensure that illegal activities like smuggling, piracy, pollution and fish poaching to mention a few criminal activities, are curtailed thus leading to a corresponding boost in the gross domestic product. Let us now consider the utility of the Air Force in crisis situations.

AIR POWER IN CRISIS MANAGEMENT

The unique ability of air power to deploy rapidly and project power over long distances unimpeded by surface features makes it a useful instrument for the management of crises. In this regard, air power offers a wide range of response options. They include:

a. Deterrence: The proven ability of air power to exact rapid retribution, strike deep into hostile territory and deny a potential aggressor the assurance that his homeland is immune from attack, makes air power a strong and explicit deterrence. Thus in some circumstances, the timely and rapid deployment of a credible force could help defuse a potential crisis.

b. **Political Signaling:** Air power can be used to send clear political signals and thus help remove uncertainty and reduce the possibility of miscalculation by an adversary. This can be achieved through overt measures such as increase in alert states or operational deployment of air power assets. Deployment of surveillance assets to monitor enemy activity also sends clear signals as regards ones own intention. The usefulness of political signaling is that it forces the adversary to rethink his course of action and thus reduces the chances of escalation of any crisis.

c. **Punitive Air Strikes:** In crisis situation, air power can be used for punitive strikes short of full-fledged war. This can be as a response to attack by state-sponsored guerrilla or terrorist groups. A good example of a punitive strike is Operation Eldorado Canyon carried out by the United States against Libya in 1986. Also, without going into the right or wrong of the action, the Israeli air strikes against Hezbollah strongholds in Southern Lebanon in 2006 are also illustrative of how air power can exact punishment without resorting to full-scale war.

d. *Support for Friendly Governments:* The deployment of air assets to a friendly government under internal or external threat can help tilt the balance of power in favour of such government. This is a useful crisis management strategy as it provides timely psychological and political support to the friendly government and helps strengthen its resolve in times of tension. In 2002, some NAF Alpha Jets were deployed to Abidjan at the start of the crisis in Cote d'Ivoire. This action served as a useful psychological prop to the government of President Gbagbo at the time.

e. **Evacuation Operations:** Air Power provides the speediest means of evacuating own and foreign nationals from crisis zones. Such operations could be done non-combat or under combat situations. The evacuation of Nigerian nationals from Malabo in the early 1980s by the NAF is a good example. More recently, the NAF had to evacuate some stranded Nigerian citizens from Accra in Ghana when the Togolese border was closed due to the succession crisis that attended the death of President Eyadema.

Thus, if crisis management measures fail and war becomes inevitable, air power can make decisive contributions to the successful prosecution of the war. So let us briefly consider the roles of air power in war.

WAR TIME ROLES

In war, air power offers commanders a wide range of options across the operational spectrum. The unique ability of air power to concentrate military power when and where it is needed has become the dominant feature of modern warfare. The Air Force can conduct independent operations aimed at achieving the immediate operational aims of the air campaign as I stressed earlier, or missions in support of the operational aims of surface forces. It can also conduct both independent and support missions simultaneously depending on the availability of assets. These missions could take one of many forms ranging from surveillance and reconnaissance, to air defence, ground attack, interdiction (deep and battlefield), close air support, to transportation and re-supply.

A prime mission for the Air Force today is the concept of "battle space shaping", whereby air power is used to wear down, demoralize and generally diminish the enemy's ability to fight before their engagement by friendly surface forces. This was what the air campaign in Iraq, "Operation Shock and Awe", was all about. Having enumerated in general terms, some of the tasks which the Air Force can perform in peace time, during crisis and in war time, let us now appraise the threat situation so that we can better grasp the challenge deriving there from.

THREATS AND CONTINGENCIES

Threat as you are all aware is anything, situation or development that can harm the State or hinder it from achieving its interests or meeting the aspirations of the citizens. A broad assessment of the threats to the Nigerian State has been made in Chapter 3 of the NDP. However, it should be noted, as Moskos observed that threats "change in time and character, as well as in specifics"[5] As the perceived threat changes so does the response in terms of force structure and capability.

It is customary to assess threats from two perspective – the domestic and the external; however, it is a nation's evaluation of the total threat that normally shapes its force structure. It is also very helpful to factor in contingencies, which do not constitute "clear and present dangers" in the sense that threats do, but for which it makes military sense to be prepared. Such contingencies fall within the category of what is generally referred to as "military operations other than war" (MOOTW). MOOTW may take the form of peace support operations as we are currently involved in Darfur, Sudan or humanitarian operations – like we saw during the *Tsunami* tragedy in South East Asia, in Hurricane Katrina, and the 2005 earthquake in Pakistan manifest as apparent threats, they nevertheless, demand special capabilities which the military must generate if they are to effectively undertake such missions when the occasion demands. Therefore, the terms "threat" and "contingency" are used interchangeably in some instances even though they do not necessarily mean the same thing. Now to the external threats.

EXTERNAL THREATS

It has often been said that "Nigeria is fortunate in that there are no large, conventional military threats facing its immediate borders.…..[6] While this view' may be correct on the surface, such assumptions should not fundamentally shape our defence planning. Fortunately, the NDP has made a departure from this view. While recognizing that "Nigeria's policy of good neighbourliness has contributed to the relative peace between her and most of her neighbours", the NDP notes that "potential threats still exist, arising primarily from unresolved geo-political issues "[7]. One of such "unresolved issues" is her extensive and largely un-demarcated borders with the four contiguous countries of Benin Republic, Niger, Chad Republic and Cameroon which collectively total about 49000Km. it is reasonable to infer, as has been done in the NDP, that until these borders are properly defined, demarcated and protected, Nigeria will continue to experience border violations and the spill-over effects of conflicts in the neighbouring countries from time to time.

Another source of threat, which is tied to the issue of sub-regional stability, is that of the proliferation of small arms in the sub-region. This in turn has led to the mushrooming of militia groups and increase in banditry. It is not inconceivable that some of the arms being used by the militia groups in the Niger Delta and other parts of the country originate from the various conflict zones in the sub-region. Also, the rise in cross-border banditry, particularly in the North-Eastern Zone of the country, is a direct fallout of the perennial conflicts in Chad Republic. Cross-border economic crimes such as smuggling and piracy in our territorial waters are other challenges demanding military response in one way or the other.

The activities of international terrorist groups are other sources of threat which should be factored into our contingency planning. A worrying trend in this regard is the threat to civil air transportation through hijacking etc or what I will call "air borne terrorism". This dimension of terrorism, though not rampant in the Nigerian airspace at the moment, is a distinct possibility since historical experience has shown that terrorism by its nature is no respecter of "borders or regions". Therefore, the NAF needs to brace up for this type of air threat. Cross – border economic crimes such as smuggling and piracy in our territorial waters are other challenges demanding military response in one way of the other.

The Gulf of Guinea has become very important in the strategic calculations of the world powers in view of the rich oil and gas reserves in the area. This has led to scramble by the world powers for a stake in the area. This development has implications for our defence architecture. The possibility of open confrontation in future, between Nigerian and some powerful nations desperate for access to the vast resources of the region, cannot be ruled out. Air power being the first line of defence and often the first line of attack will bear the initial burden of such a confrontation should it arise. Consequently, the security of the Gulf of Guinea is a major challenge for our air power.

Lastly, as we all know, the character of warfare and thus, the related threats, follow the trends of technology. Globally, ICT-based threats to national assets, particularly economic and military ones, are becoming more rampant. While our defence infrastructure are still primitive in the sense that computerization and automation are still at redimentary levels, it is helpful to remember that cyber crime poses as much threat to military command and control networks as it does to the financial or other sectors of our national life. In addition, we must also begin to contemplate novel kinds of threats like cyber warfare. Therefore, as ICT systems make gradual but sure inroads into our defence infra-structure, we must constantly keep in mind the ever present threats in the cyberspace.

INTERNAL THREATS

There is a consensus amongst analysts that the most potent threats to the Nigerian state are the domestic ones and that the most serious of them is the situation in the Niger Delta. This is in view of the fact that about 80% of Nigeria's foreign exchange earnings come from the arena. The emergence of ethnic and militant groups has also heightened the internal security problems. Other problem areas include the state of the economy, political indiscipline, corruption, religious intolerance and fundamentalism, and ethnic chauvinism. Also worthy of mention are social problems like unemployment, armed robbery and banditry, and the growing cases of economic crimes like crude oil theft and oil bunkering, the vandalisation of oil pipe lines and electricity transmission facilities, and piracy within our territorial waters.

While some of these threats can be reduced or contained through proactive political and social actions, many of them would not have arisen at all if the armed forces were placed in a proper position to perform their duties. If we take the issue of crude oil theft for example, it would be highly impossible for this crime to be perpetrated if the Nigerian Navy and the NAF had effective presence in the maritime environment. The same argument can be advanced in the case of vandalization of oil pipelines and electricity infrastructure. What the nation loses annually (variously, estimated as averaging about 100,000 barrels per day[8]) is considerably more than what is required by the NAF, for instance, to carry out a round the clock surveillance of these facilities.

Other contingencies for which the armed forces must be prepared include Search and Rescue (SAR), man-made and natural disasters, and other forms of humanitarian operations in aid of the civil authorities. I will now shift focus to how the NAF is organized and equipped to meet these threats and challenges, First, the organization.

ORGANIZATION

Let me note here that in 2005, we worked on a new Establishment which was intended to replace the current one that should have expired in 2006. we have suspended the full implementation of the proposed establishment in view of the fact that so far, we have been unable to procure the necessary platforms and equipment required for its wholesale implementation. However, we are implementing some aspects of the proposed establishment which we believe are critical to the actualization of the regenerative mission we have set for ourselves. At present therefore, the NAF is organized into a headquarters and three field commands which are equivalent to divisions of the Army.

HEADQUARTERS NIGERIAN AIR FORCE

HQ NAF is currently made of up of the Office of the Chief of the Air Staff and 4 Staff Branches; in addition there is the Office of the Air Secretary. The CAS Office comprises of the Directorate of Plans, that of Finance and Accounts, the Pay and Accounting Group, the NAF Foundation, the Projects Implementation and Monitoring Team, the Secretariat of the Resident Due Process Team and a Headquarters Camp Organization.

The Operational Branch: As its name implies, the Operations Branch is the nerve centre of NAF operations. It is responsible for the formulation, coordination and monitoring of NAF operational policies and plans. It is also responsible for the formulation of training policy for aircrew. The Branch has five directorates namely, the Directorates of Operations, Training, Air Intelligence, Air Traffic Management and Services and that Regiment. Also, the Presidential Air Fleet (PAF) is administratively under the Branch.

The Inspections Branch: The Inspections Branch is responsible for the formulation of policies for the maintenance of standards and safety in the NAF. It is also responsible for monitoring and ensuring conformity with the stipulated standards for all NAF projects. The Directorates of the Branch include those of Evaluation, Safety, Manuals and that of Research and Development.

The Logistics Branch: The Logistics Branch is responsible for the formulation of policies, planning and monitoring of all logistic functions that support NAF operations. The Branch has five Directorates: Air Engineering, Electrical/Electronics Engineering, Armament, Supply and that of works.

The Administration Branch: The Administration Branch is responsible for the formulation of policies on discipline, service tradition, welfare and morale. It comprises of the Directorates of Administration, Air, Provost, Legal Services, Medical

Services, Education and the Directorate of Public Relations and Information. Now a brief look at the Commands.

THE COMMANDS

Tactical Air Command: The Tactical Air Command (TAC) is the teeth arm of the service under which all the fighting formations or units are grouped. It is tasked with the training and provision of all the operational elements/resources required for the attainment of the NAF Mission. The Command comprises 10 groups reporting directly to the Air Officer Commanding (AOC). All dedicated combat aircraft and most of the airlift assets of the NAF are operated by TAC. The headquarters of TAC is located at Makurdi.

Training Command: The Training Command (TC) is responsible for the implementation of NAF local training policies and programmes. Its headquarters is at Kaduna and is headed by an AOC. TC comprises of 12 groups. Each group has one or more specialized schools for the various manpower needs of the NAF

Logistics Command: The Logistics Command (LC) is responsible for the implementation of the logistics of the NAF. It is also responsible for the procurement, distribution, maintenance and sustenance of all systems and equipment in the service. The Command has 3 Maintenance Depots and a Base Services Group. Its heaquarters is at Ikeja and it is commanded by an AOC. I will now move on to our Force Structure.

FORCE STRUCTURE OR ORDER OF BATTLE (ORBAT)

The issue of force structure is closely interwoven with doctrine; indeed it is not too clear, which of the two concepts drives the other. Whatever the case, it is necessary to heed Valances advice that "the potential air power contribution to security and defence cannot be fully realized without a clear employment doctrine"[9]. Based on our experience, therefore, and in line with the principles of war and those for the employment of air power, the NAF articulated a basic doctrine based on the following operational tenets:

a. Air capability can best be developed and employed in accordance with the principle of unity of command – that is centralized control but decentralized execution.
b. The best employment of the NAF shall be in the offensive.
c. Air superiority is a prerequisite for the successful conduct of combat operations.
d. Air power could be effectively employed singly or in conjunction with surface forces depending on the political objective and the prevailing circumstances.

The NAF doctrine is embodied in the operational concept of "ACTIVE DEFENCE, FORWARD ENGAGEMENT". By this concept, the NAF is strategically defensive, but tactically offensive in posture. This concept is in tandem with Nigeria's non-expansionist policy which is the fulcrum of the overall objectives of our national defence strategy. It should be obvious from the various roles enumerated earlier, that to adequately perform its constitutional responsibilities, the Air Force would need to achieve a high degree of balance in terms of platform mix, equipment, systems and training. This is what is referred to in operational parlance as a "balanced force". The force structure of the NAF was carefully tailored with the foregoing considerations in mind. Thus essentially it is a tactical air force but with inherent capability to meet the strategic objectives of the Government. Let me add here that achieving and sustaining a balanced force has been one of the greatest challenges facing our air force today. It is within this context that I will now discuss our present capabilities.

PRESENT CAPABILITIES

A balanced air force should have the capability to perform all of the four typical functions of tactical air power, namely:

a. Reconnaissance;
b. Counter Air Operations
c. Interdiction, and
d. Combat Air Support Operations

At the height of its glory between 1975 and 1988, the NAF had full capability to conduct operations in all of these four areas. Then it had about 17 difference aircraft types in inventory with an average serviceability rate of over 75% across the fleet.

Between 1990 and 1999, the service suffered a progressive decline due to poor funding. As at 1999, serviceability in most of the fleets was zero, while the few active fleets averaged 25-30%. In addition, flying training had become very erratic. In order to revamp the service and put it on a sustainable operational footing, a fleet rationalization exercise was carried out between 1999 and 2000. This had to be done because it was glaring that we could not effectively sustain a force with 17 different aircraft type especially where there were cases of duplication of aircraft for some of the roles.

The exercise resulted in the decommissioning of the F-27s (The Troopship and MPA); the Jaguar deep attack; the Bolkow BO-105; the Hughes Helicopter trainer; and the Bulldog 123 primary trainer. Also, in 2006 I recommended to the Government that the MiG 21 Interceptor should be phased our considering the huge sum required to modernize them and in view of our planned acquisition of the Chinese F-7NI. We also advised that the DO 128-6 light transport aircraft should be decommissioned and that the C 130 fleet should be pruned down from the current fleet of 8 to a more manageable size of five aircraft. The government accepted these recommendations.

Effectively, therefore, our current ORBAT is as follows:

a. Fighter Fleet The Alpha Jet ground attack located at Kainji is the only fixed wing combat type currently in inventory.

b. Transport Fleet: For airlift, we have the C-130H based in Lagos, for heavy lift; G-222 in Ilorin for medium lift; and the Dornier 228 based in Kaduna and Benin, for light transport/liason.

c. Helicopters: The helicopter fleet is comprised of the Super Puma medium lift helicopter based in Lagos; and the Mi-35P attack helicopter based in Port Harcourt.

d. Trainer Fleet: For training, we have the ABT-18 Air Beetle primary trainer located in Kaduna; the L-39ZA basic trainer based in Kano; the MB-339 Aemacchi advanced also located in Kano; and the Mi-34 trainer helicopter based in Enugu. We have decided to phase out the Mi-34s because its maintenance has been very problematic.

A good number of these aircraft are currently unserviceable. However, various reactivation/upgrade programmes are in progress in most of the fleets. For example, the G222s and the MB-339s have been taken to Italy for overhaul and upgrade. One C-130 has returned from Peridic Depot Maintenance in France and we are preparing to send another shortly. In addition, a contract for the reactivation of 2 Super Puma and the acquisition of an additional one has been awarded to Messrs Eurocoper of France.

NEW ACQUISITIONS

Emerging challenges from our external and internal environments have necessitated the acquisition of some new platforms to replace decommissioned assets or upgrade our capabilities in some vital areas. In this regard, I am happy to inform you that a contract for the supply of a muti-role combat aircraft, the F-1NI, has been signed with the Chinese. As I indicated earlier, the F-7 NI will replace the MiG 21. Payments have also been made for the supply of 6 x Agusta-109 Light Utility Helicopters which will be deployed in the search and rescue, light transport, and light attack roles in addition to other internal security tasks.

With the decommissioning of the F-27 Maritime Patrol Aircraft, the presence of the NAF in the maritime environment is currently highly limited. Given the vast expanse – of our territorial waters and EEZ, it is virtually impossible for the Nigerian Navy alone to effectively police and protect our maritime interests. To address this problem, the NAF last year signed a contract for the delivery of 2 x ATR 42 MPA. Payments have been made and the aircraft should enter service by mid-2009. What then are the major constraints?

CONSTRAINTS

The Nigerian Air Force's main challenge centres on how to enhance and revamp its force structure to be able to respond more effectively to the dictates of joint operations, contemporary and future threats and contingencies. In this regard, the major constraints to the complete regeneration of the service are in 3 broad areas: funding, operations and logistics. It goes without saying that the later two constraints depend substantially on the first.

INADEQUATE FUNDING

It is stating the obvious to say that the economic downturn that the country went through as from the late 1980s took its toll on the Nigerian Air Force. Perhaps venture especially where the underlying technology base is next to zero. Unfortunately, capital allocation to the Nigerian Air Force since 1999 to 2007 has consistently fallen short of actual requirements to fund ongoing projects. In view of the various aircraft rehabilitation/upgrade programmes to which we have been committed and the need to reactivate our infrastructural and support facilities, we estimate that about N25b would be required annually for the next three years to reposition the service to meet its statutory responsibilities.

OPERATIONAL CHALLENGES

The most pressing operational challenges for the NAF for the NAF at the moment are mainly in the areas of fleet reactivation or replacement and aircrew shortage. The problem of fleet reactivation/replacement is tied clearly to the availability of funds as I have just mentioned. However, we have been able to address substantially the issue of aircrew shortage. One of the things we have done is to source for flying training slots overseas to augment local training efforts in our flying schools even though this was a very expensive option. So far, we have trained a total of 24 pilots in South Africa, USA and the UK; a batch of 10 Students pilots are currently undergoing fighter pilots course in the Ukraine. We are sending another batch of 12 students pilots to the United States this quarter for helicopter and transport training. We are also devoting' Resources to the Training of support personnel. The overall philosophy is to ensure that we have the right calibre of manpower in place to man our new acquisitions and the current fleets when they are rehabilitated.

LOGISTICS CONSTRAINTS

Of course the problem of death of fund has also taken its toll on our logistics capacity and infrastructure. Firstly, since everything in the Air Force revolves around air operations, there has also been a noticeable decline in our pool of skilled technical manpower. As I indicated earlier. We have started addressing this problem. Our runways and logistics facilities like hangers, workshops and test benches etc have also deteriorated; some of them would need to be upgraded and modernized.

Finally, there is the problem of lack of military radar coverage. At the moment, the NAF has no capability for identifying aerial intruders since none of the radar stations acquired in the early 1970s is currently functional. As I mentioned earlier, air defence is the primary task of the NAF; this mission cannot be effectively performed without and efficient detection, control and reporting system which the military radar coverage affords. This was to have been achieved through the implementation of the Total Radar Coverage of Nigeria (TRACON) project. Unfortunately, while work has started on the civil aspect, the military component seems to have stalled. In brief, these are some of the more pressing challenge of the NAF. It is obvious that the problems are enormous, but they are not insurmountable if there is the political will. That said, I believe that this chapter will be incomplete without indicating my views on the likely state of the NAF in future and in this regard I am looking at a time-frame of 5 years hence.

FUTURE

Let me start by saying that in an era of dwindling resources and the ever-increasing demand from the social sectors on scarce revenue, the NAF recognizes the need for a holistic long-range plan that would enable the Government spread funding for the Service over a period of time. Ironically, even as funding is on the decline, the operational tasking of the service appears to be increasing. Cognizant of this fact, the Nigerian Air Force submitted a perspective plan titled "THE NIGERIAN AIR FORCE STRATEGIC DEVELOPMENT PLAN (SDP) 2007-2015" to the Government. Our vision for the NAF in the next 5 years is therefore situated within the context of this Strategic Plan.

The NAF SDP contains a comprehensive list of necessary capabilities and major capital projects, with preliminary timings and priorities. The resultant capability requirements are built around four key goals of the National Defence Policy namely, the protection of Nigeria's sovereignty, interests, and territory against external threats; providing support to the civil authorities and civil power in meeting internal security challenges; supporting the Government's wider international interests; and helping to counter the risks from emerging global security problems. A central objective of the Plan, therefore, is to shift the basis of defence planning from the "threat-based" model that has dominated past military thinking to "capabilities-based" model. This "capabilities-based" model focuses more on how an adversary might act rather than who the adversary might be or where a war might occur.

The degree of success we are able to record with the implementation of the Plan would ultimately determine where we stand in five years time. Other variables that will be critical include our internal security situation which has grave implications for the economy; the degree of stability in the West African sub-region and indeed the African continent as a whole. These issues will be important because they will not only determine the availability of resources but will also continue to generate the challenges and contingencies for which the NAF must be prepared.

Thus as we shift focus increasingly from preparation for war against states to "non-traditional functions"[10] or Military Operations Than War, I foresee the NAF enhancing its capability to more effectively meet challenges in the areas of:

a. Peace Support Operations
b. Countering internal threats to the constitutional order;
c. Border patrol;
d. Maritime protection;
e. Search and Rescue operations
f. Disaster relief and humanitarian assistance; and

g. Supporting the Nigeria Police Force (and the Army) in the maintenance of law and order.

h. Supporting the foreign policy initiatives of government.

These missions will call for the induction of new platforms especially helicopters, maritime patrol aircraft and medium lift transport aircraft. How far we are able to achieve this will clearly depend on the health of the economy. Of course, I expect enhanced capability also in our traditional domains of air space defence, ground attack and operational support to the other 2 sister services. To this end, I expect that all our grounded fleets would have been fully rehabilitated and upgraded by 2013. Also, I expect that most of our newly acquired assets namely, the F-7 NI combat aircraft, the Agusta 109 LUH and the ATR 42 MPA would have been fully operational. Finally, I foresee the Alpha-Jet being phased out in the next 5 years as it becomes technologically obsolete and increasingly less cost-effective to operate. The up-graded MB-339 should serve as gap-filler until our economic situation allow for the induction of a suitable light attack type to replace the Alpha-Jet.

Whatever we do in terms of induction of new systems and platforms, not much will be achieved if we neglect the men and women who will operate them. So I foresee a better trained and highly motivated human capital as the foundation on which our air force of the future will be anchored. This is why we have embarked on a massive manpower development progrmamme in all specialties of the service locally and abroad. In 2007 alone, we sponsored over 200 personnel abroad for various course, seminars and conferences. This number is unprecedented when compared to any other period in the past 2 decades.

Meanwhile, 320 TTG has been accredited by the National Board on Technical Education to run ND and HND programmes in various courses for our airmen. Also, earlier this month, the School was re-designated as the Air Force Institute of Technology (AFIT) and affiliated to Cranfield University in the United Kingdom for the award of Masters degrees in aerospace engineering and related discipline. All these developments should impact positively on the human capital in the next 5 years, I foresee a Nigerian Air Force that is well trained, better equipped, and strategically positioned to better respond to the policy dictates of the Government.

CONCLUSION

I have attempted to give you a candid perspective on the role of the Nigerian Air Force in the national security matrix, its challenges and how we are responding to them. Let me conclude by reiterating that as historical experiences have shown, the leadership position that nature has bestowed on Nigeria in the West African sub-region, and indeed Africa as a whole, has annexed to it, responsibilities for the maintenance of peace, security and stability in the region which we cannot ignore or wish away. Therefore, we need a strong military, and in particular a virile air force, to meet our internal and external security challenges and contingencies. As the saying goes, you prepare for war if you want peace.

So, no matter how remote the prospect of conflict may be today, our strategic position in the African region demands that we should always be prepared for the worse case scenario. I believe that no price should be too great to pay to achieve this for, in the final analysis, the alternative may be more costly. We must heed the wise counsel of Frederick the Great that "in the profession of war the rules of the art are never violated without drawing punishment from the enemy...."[11] And the most important of these rules is: be prepared always. Are we prepared?

In today's turbulent world, air power's attributes of rapid response, versatility, flexibility, mobility, firepower, precision and timeliness offer nations the most effective security instrument for achieving their foreign and domestic policy objectives. Be that as it may, without a significant and conscious effort to replace and reactivate platforms and weapons systems, our force structure would not only continue to age but would also continue to lag operationally behind in terms of what is needed to contain extant threats and future contingencies. Most importantly, the potentials of the NAF to contribute to the goals of national security and development would continue to be stunted until the needed investments are made.

ENDNOTES

1. R. J. Art, "Strategies for the Use of Force", in *R. J. Art and K. N. Waltz. (eds). The Use of Force: Military Power and International Politics:* (Lanham: Rowman & Littlefield Publishers, 1999), p. 1.
2. Gen. J. M. Shalikashvilli, in Preface to National Security Strategy of the United States of America http://www.fas.oro./man/docs/nms_feb95.htc.
3. Sir Winston Churchill, speech in House of Commons, 14 March 1933, internet document "Great Aviation Quotes", p. 2.
4. The Nigerian National Defence Policy, Chapters 17.
5. C. C. Moskos, "Armed Forces After the Cold War" in C. C. Moskos, J.A. Williams, and Dr. Segal (eds.) *The Post Modern Military* Oxford: Oxford University Press), p. 16.
6. A Mohammed, "Nigeria's Security Policy Policy", Lecture delivered to course 9, National War College, Nigeria 2000.
7. National Defence Policy, Op. cit, Chapter 3.6.
8. Business Day, (Lagos), Monday, September 15, 2003, front page, Thisday (Lagos) November 29, 2004 and Vanguard (Lagos) January 4, 2005, p. 17.
9. AGB Vail a nee, *The Air Weapon, Doctrines of Air Power Strategy and Operational Art, (London: Macmillan Press Ltd, 1996),* p. 24.
10. Theo Neethling, "Non-Traditional Military Tasks: The Defence Force in Policing and Peacekeeping", Internet Document.
11. Frederick the Great, quoted in Charles M. Westenhoff, *Military Air Power. The Cadre of Military Air Power Opinion and Thoughts* (Maxwell: Air University Press 1990) p. 4

CHAPTER 26

DEFENCE HEADQUARTER CRISIS MANAGEMENT PROCEDURE

I. D. PENAP

INTRODUCTION

Crisis management is about national security, and is dealt with at the highest political level. It involves the coordinated effort of various agencies and ministries of a country. This chapter focuses first on the general framework of the discourse: *Defence Headquarters, Crisis Management and Crisis Management*. Second, is the *principles of crisis management and phases of crisis*. The principle provide a guide for organizing crisis management hierarchy and methodology. The Constitution of the Federal Republic of Nigeria 1999 has already provided the framework. Third is how *Political directives are translated into strategic direction*. I will also look at *Contingency and Crisis Action Planning*. Finally, some *case studies in crisis management and problems associated with crises management*.

CONCEPTUAL CLARIFICATION
DEFENCE HEADQUARTERS

The DHQ is the military component of the MOD. The role of the MOD is a crisis situation is to provide the Government and Ministers with advice on the policy and military – strategic aspects of a crisis. The MOD interprets political decisions and provides policy direction to the DHQ. The head of the DHQ is the CDS. The defence policy has specified the mandate of the DHQ and the role of the CDS. According to the policy, the DHQ is responsible for the *Deployment, employment, sustenance and recovery of forces* deployed externally or within the country. The CDS is the principal military adviser to the government and the professional head of the Armed Forces.

The *Chain of Command* for the planning and conduct of military operations flows from the National Defence Council (NDC) to the Honourable Minister of Defence (HMOD) to the CDS and from him to either the Service Chiefs or the Commander of a Joint Task Force (Comd JEF). Rest with the CDS, who shall also coordinate the three Services.

CHAIN OF COMMAND FOR MILITARY OPERATIONS

According to the defence policy document, the office of the CDS shall be the focal point of military decision – making process in order to achieve the following objectives:

a. Clear hierarchy in the *decision-making process of the Armed Forces*.
b. Optimum utilization of strategic intelligence.

c.   Speed in the *mobilization, deployment and sustenance of forces.*
d.   *Domination of the combat environment.*
e.   *Synergy in the employment of forces through joint capability and training.*
f.   *Acquisition and prompt dissemination of information to the Services during crisis.*
g.   *Coordination of the Armed Forces budget and acquisition process.*

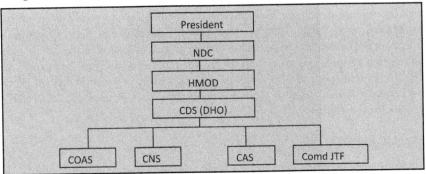

The defence policy goes further to state that the CDS, on behalf of the NDC shall determine and work out the choices and force structure needed to achieve the nation's defence needs. The imperative is to have priorities and military doctrines that will form the basis for the provision of defence assets that meet the most important needs. For the purpose of joint operations and exercise, the DHQ shall have control of the facilities of the forces deployed internally or externally.

CRISIS

According to Wilkenfied, crisis is a perception of a threat to one or more basic values, along with an awareness of the limitation of time for response to the threat, and a high probability of military intervention. It could be perceptions of both an objective threat and a more or less subjective set of national and personal values and goals. A crisis may be local, regional, national or international. It could be a threat to business, social service, industry or a socio-economic or political system.[2] A crisis could be an incident or situation involving a threat to a country, its citizens, military forces, or vital interests that develops rapidly and creates a condition of such diplomatic, economic, political, or military importance that commitment of national military forces and resources has to be contemplated in order to achieve national objectives. In Nigeria, we have experienced different types of crisis, including civil war, border conflicts ethno-religious crises, flood disaster etc. The management of natural and some man-made disasters that the humanitarian in nature is generally referred to as disaster management, ass opposed to crisis management, which this lecture is, primarily, addressing. However, crisis, no matter the type, poses a serious challenge to both the political and military leadership of any country. For leaders who lack judgement, vision and nerve, ordinary problems could easily give rise to crises.

A nation confronted with a crisis has three options to choose from. These are capitulation, war, or crisis management. As this lecture is on crisis management, it is therefore safely assumed that the crisis management option is the best of the three options for any nation, including Nigeria.

The view that crises are undesirable sometimes negates their positive aspects. Crises present opportunities not available in routine policy making. They provide the chance to motivate and mobilize citizens and the bureaucracy to action, to unify, to organize interest group, and to move forward in areas where such programmes might not be possible otherwise. As is often recognized, even severe crises can provide an impetus to improved relations between the states involved. But crisis can also afford manifold opportunities to skilled political leaders to strengthen alliances, to bolster the legitimacy of their regimes, and in other ways to advance their nation's international interests.

MANAGEMENT

The concept of management had broadened in scope with the introduction of new perspective by different fields of study. Horbison and Myers have offered a classic three-fold concept for emphasizing a broader scope for the view of management. They observe management as (1) an economic resource as an economist would regard management as factor of production, (2) a system of authority whereby a specialist in administration and organization would regard management as a system of authority and (3) a class of elite arrangement when a sociologist would regard management as class and status system.

No matter how management is viewed, there are certain agreed functions which management or mangers carry out. These functions include:

a. Decision-making
b. Organizing
c. Staffing
d. Planning
e. Controlling
f. Communication
g. Directing (Leadership).

CRISIS MANAGEMENT

Crisis management refers to measures to identify, acquire and plan and use of resources needed to anticipate, prevent, and/or resolve a crisis or the threat of a crisis. North Atlantic Treaty Organization (NATO) defines crisis management as the coordinated actions taken to defuse crises, prevent their escalation into an armed conflict and contain hostilities if they should result.[4] Two primary elements are the key to defining crisis management. First is the application of control through strategic decisions by the national leadership to prevent war. Second, to advance the national strategy, protecting interests and settling the crisis so that it does not lead to a further crisis. However, the key to both elements is recognizing a crisis at hand. If you do not see the crisis coming, control and strategy are difficult to establish. The central issue is balance between our national strategy, interests and objectives, and actions taken to prevent war[5].

Although the Defence Headquarters is concerned with the role of the Armed Forces in crisis management, crisis Management is actually not a terminology in common usage in the Nigerian Armed Forces, and the reason may not be far fetched. Crisis management or conflict resolution is a strategic function, which is handled by the military top brass before it is translated to a possible campaign at the operational or tactical level.

PRINCIPLES OF CRISES MANAGEMENT

To fully appreciate the mechanics of crisis management, it would be appropriate to first consider the principles. The principles are supposed to be applicable before a crisis and they provided a simple guide for organizing the crisis management machinery, from presidency and below, to deal with national and international situations. The principles represent an institutionalized approach for facing the varied demands of a crisis. The principles are vigilance, education and crisis training, communications, reduced bureaucracy, efficiency, national assembly awareness and knowledge.[7]

Vigilance entails the readiness and promptness to capture opportunities and defeat danger. Vigilance corrects perceptions, and provides for early detection, and recognition of crisis before it happens. In building an efficient and balanced decision-making group, and important step is to institute education and training for those that would be concerned with crisis management. Such training should develop the interagency skills of the career professionals. Education and training ensure that the leadership knows how to control, and what to use in confronting the crisis. The National defence College (NDC) Abuja and National Institute for Policy and Strategic Studies (NIPSS) Kuru, Jos and intended to prepare senior military and government leaders with the tools to deal with all elements of national power. These two prestigious institutions are expected to provide the level playing field for dissemination lessons learnt, and new ideas for crisis detection and management. You should, therefore, regard yourselves as potential crisis managers.

The issue of communication in crisis is vital in order to avoid a shutdown. Also there is the need for educated and experienced staff to maintain communications within and outside the government. In order to react quickly and thereby focus the resources of the government, there should be a single crisis control centre. The Centre should be capable of removing bureaucratic bottlenecks while dealing with a looming crisis. With representatives from the Executive arm, the Ministry of Foreign Affairs (MFA) and Defence (MOD) personnel, based on the National Security Council (NSC) membership, the crisis control centre would monitor possible crisis situation develops. Note that members of the crisis control centre (CCC) are to be selected from the membership of the NSC. Prior to crisis, the centre should exchange information with various government and international agencies, conduct problem-solving exercise and educate and train its personnel. During crisis, the CCC would focus on the implementation of actions directed by the President through the NSC, thus cutting the bureaucratic "red tape".

Efficiency is a conduct of a well though out established crisis procedure resulting from training and education. Explicit, agreed upon ground rules for crisis behaviour, can eliminate some of the uncertainty found in any crisis. Keeping the National Assembly informed of a crisis, and pre-planned response, is critical to bringing the crisis to successful conclusion. This is important because they are the people's representatives and are likely to react.

Knowledge is an understanding gained by actual experience. The principles, as outlined, provide the Presidency and aides the capability of obtaining experience without the potential of war and loss of life. Crisis management training and education serve to gain actual experience for the political leadership and aids before being faced with dealing with actual crisis activities. Note that the consequences of an ill-timed, poorly trained, and mismanaged crisis response mechanism would embarrass a nation. However, a well-trained, robust crisis response team demonstrates a government in control.

PHASE OF CRISIS

There are four phases associated with crisis management. These are the pre-crisis situation development, crisis response and recovery, and finally post-crisis phases [8] as shown:

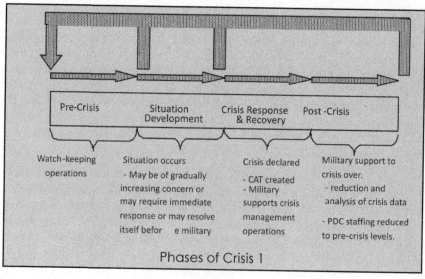

Phases of Crisis 1

The pre-crisis phase is the warning stage, if any. In many instances it is a turning point. If the turning point is entirely missed, then crisis management becomes an "after the fact" exercise or damage control. Early warning or recognition is important at this stage. Early warning could be achieved through good intelligence and secure communications.⁹ Pre-crisis operations include analysis of information received and preparation of situation reports. Pre-crisis operations are characterized by constant situation monitoring, situation assessment and status reporting as highlighted:

a. **Situation Monitoring:** This is maintenance of up-to-date situation monitoring using public information sources, the military, national, and international agency sources. This information will applicable, (examples include, political, social and/or economic activities/problems/trends), situation reports/updates from military or civilian agencies and organizations, joint contingency plans, mapping data such as updated political boundaries, evacuation routes, communications and transportation infrastructures, population densities, police units, etc. Information will be received by radio, email, telephone and audio-visual sources.

b. **Situation Assessment:** Situation assessment requires the assessment of the available situation reports to determine the possibility of potential crises. This may entail the use of Geographic Information System (GIS) capabilities to view situational data with associated maps.

c. **Status Reporting:** Status reporting entails the consolidation of critical crises information into situation reports and disseminating same to appropriate authorities. In the situation or crisis centre, critical information could be displayed on maps, models or as computer graphics.

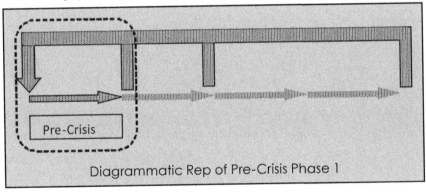

Diagrammatic Rep of Pre-Crisis Phase 1

SITUATION DEVELOPMENT PHASE

Situation development are performed when the potential for a crisis or an actual crisis has been identified. Situation development operations include the following activities: *analysis of information received, preparation of situation reports and conducting preliminary planning* for both military and non-military crisis response operations. Situation development operations also involve *situation monitoring, assessment, coordination, notification, and status reporting.*

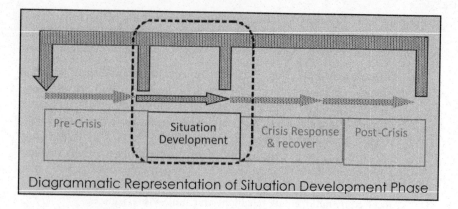

Diagrammatic Representation of Situation Development Phase

CRISIS RESPONSE AND RECOVERY PHASE

Crisis response commences when the crisis is irreversible, and some damage had already been done. Crisis operations, which include crisis response and recovery, are performed once a crisis has been officially declared and until support to the specific crisis has ended. The first step in this period, ideally, it the creation of a Crisis Action Team (CAT). Crisis operations include the following activities: analysis of information received, preparation of situation reports and conducting preliminary planning for both military and non-military crisis response operations. The following functional capabilities are supported at this phase during crisis *operations-crisis monitoring, crisis assessment, planning, coordination, and status reporting.*

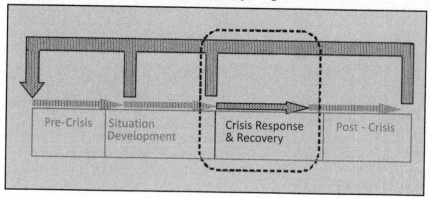

POST-CRISIS PHASE

The post-crisis phase could be likened to the clean-up phase or post mortem. Tier a period of second guessing, self-analysis and recovery.[10] Post-crisis operations are performed once support to a specific crisis has ceased and include analysis of information collected during the previous phases, preparation of after-action reports and creating or modifying plans and Courses of Action (COAs). The following functional capabilities are

a. **After-action Reporting/Analysis.** After-Action Reporting entails reducing the complied data and analysis operations conducted to identify lessons learnt for future plans and operations.

b. **Stand-down**: Stand down amounts to the cessation of military and non-military activities.

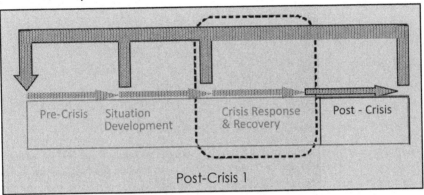

Pre-Crisis Situation Development Crisis Response & Recovery Post - Crisis

Post-Crisis 1

DEFENCE HEADQUARTERS CRISIS MANAGEMENT HIERARCHY AND METHODOLOGY

Crisis management is not entirely a defence affair, it is rather a national issue, which impacts on national security. The management of crisis therefore should be initiated from the political leadership, following a top-down approach. That is why the Constitution of the Federal Republic of Nigeria 1999 recognizes the need for various organs that would tackle issues hat border on national security. At the apex, or Tier 1, are the NSC and the national Defence Council (NDC). The NSC is empowered to advise the President, Commander-In-Chief (C-in-C), on matters relating to public security, including matters relating to any organization or agency established by law for ensuring the security of the Federation. The composition of the NSC is as follows:[11].

a. President, C-in-C - Chairman
b. Vice President - Deputy Chairman
c. Honourable Minister of Defence (HMOD).
d. Honourable Minister of Internal Affairs (HMIA).
e. Chief of Defence Staff (CDS).
f. Honourable Minister of Foreign Affairs (HMFA).
g. National Security Adviser (NSA)
h. Inspector General of Police (IGP)
i. Such other persons as the President may in his discretion approve.

From the composition of the NSC, one can see that it is dominated by the political leadership, except for the CDS, representing the top military echelon, the rest represent the political decision making process or the Executive Arm. It is at this level that the crisis is weighed against national interests; national policies, aims and objectives, that eventually lead to national directives.

The NDC, also in accordance with the Nigerian Constitution, is empowered to advise the President on matters relating to the defence of national sovereignty and territorial integrity. Its composition is as shown:[13]

a. The President, C-in-C   -   Chairman
b. Vice President   -   Deputy Chairman
c. HMOD.   -   Member
d. CDS.   -   "
e. Chief of Army Staff (COAS),   -   "
f. Chief of Naval Staff (CNS)   -   "
g. Chief of Air Staff (CAS)   -   "
h. Any other members that the President may approve.

It could be seen that neither the IGP nor the NSA is a member of the NDC, because the issues for the NDC may have been resolved or decided by the NSC, where both are members. It is at the NDC level that military options are perfected and put into effect, even though, in accordance with the Armed Forces Act No 105 1993 As Amended, the NDC's responsibility "shall not extend to the operational use of the Armed Forces".[14]

Below the NSC and the NDC is the Tier 2, which is the MOD level. At the MOD level, the HMOD implements the directives of the NSC through the DHQ. The HMOD is the Chairman of the Army Council, the Navy Board and the Air Force Council. The statutory compositions are as follows:

a. **Army Council.**[15]
1. HMOD   -   Chairman
2. CDS   -   Member
3. COAS   -   Member
4. Permanent Secretary MOD   -   Secretary.

a. **Navy Board.**[16]
1. HMOD   -   Chairman
2. CDS   -   Member
3. CNS   -   Member
4. Permanent Secretary MOD   -   Secretary.

a. **Air Force Council.**[17]
1. HMOD   -   Chairman
2. CDS   -   Member
3. CAS   -   Member
4. Permanent Secretary MOD   -   Secretary.

CRISIS MANAGEMENT METHODOLOGY

Notwithstanding the gaps in the Nigerian Higher Defence Organization (HDO), at present, the procedure for crisis management for both internal and external crises at the DHQ level may be kick – started from any of the following sources.

a. Directives of the NSC or NDC
b. Office of the NSA
c. Office of the Chief of Staff to the President, C-in-C
d. Office of the HMOD.

Usually, the NSA issues Security Directives, which are converted to Operation Directives by the DHQ and disseminated to the Services accordingly. The Services in turn will issue Operation Orders (OPO) down the line. The Operations Directives issued by the DHQ could be guided by an existing Joint Contingency Plan (JCP) as it pertains to the nature and type of operation or crisis; for example, non-combatant evacuation operation, civil unrest, defence of the Federal Capital Territory (FCT) or Vulnerable Points (VPs), protection of oil installations, border security, external aggression or peace support operations (PSO).

Central to the crisis management procedure is the establishment of a crisis management or operations centre at the DHQ and manned by staff from Policy, Operations, Intelligence and Logistics Departments from the three Services. The Operations Centre should have communications links to the Joint Task Force (JTF) Headquarters set up in the wake of the crisis, in addition to access to both local and foreign news sources, large screen displays, a briefing room and a Local Area Network (LAN). The establishment or activation of the operations centre presupposes that the Armed Forces posses the requisite capabilities to deal the crisis, and the security or operation directives or JCP have spelt out clearly, aspects of command and control, and guidelines for the introduction of troops for external / internal operations. These will be briefly highlighted.

MILITARY CAPABILITIES FOR CRISIS MANAGEMENT.

Crisis response is premised on the ability of the Armed Forces to be military self-sustaining with the necessary command, control and intelligence capabilities, logistics, other combat support services and additionally, as appropriate, air and naval elements. The expected tasks or missions which the Armed Forces could undertake would require their capability for *airborne and air transportable operations, anti- and counter terrorism, amphibious operations, sealift, airlift, humanitarian operations, Search and Rescue (SAR), Close Air Support (CAS), Combat Air Patrol, strategic reconnaissance, coastal defence, special operations, unconventional warfare, Command, Control, Communications, Computers and Intelligence (C^4I), Information Warfare (IW) and Electronic Warfare (EW) etc.* As effective force management is dependent on the military system and force posture, we are also expected to practice the doctrine for joint operations. The operation directive usually spells out who exercises operational command and control and overall command. However, this is dependent on the type and scope of operation.

GUIDELINES FOR PARTICIPATION IN EXTERNAL/INTERNAL OPERATIONS.

The participation in external operations like peacekeeping operations is usually an executive decision, based on either bilateral or multi-national agreements or mandates. The influenced of the world body like the United Nations (UN) and regional organizations like the African Union (AU) and the Economic Community of West African States (ECOWAS) plays a vital role in those decisions, because of the current global emphasis on collective security mechanism. Before accepting to serve in an international peacekeeping operation, Nigeria must obtain in advance the following:

    a.   Mandate, objectives, and concept of operations
    b.   Command and control arrangement
    c.   Civil-military contributions to the operation.
    d.   Rules of Engagement
    e.   The required resource contributions.

Internal Security: In the case of Internal Security (IS) operations like Ops FLUSHOUT II, (now MESA) III, OP RESTORE HOPE, the directives for military involvement were issued by the Presidency to the DHQ after weighing the national security implications, and the need to support the Nigeria Police, in order to safeguard the lives, property and economic assets of the country. Being joint operations, they come under the overall control of the DHQ.

OPERATIONAL DIRECTION

Being able to translate national strategic objectives set by the Presidency into operation directives and plans that will support and achieve those objectives is one of the primary missions of the Services, on the orders of the DHQ. Strategy requires that the joint operation planning does not only involve military plans, but also political-military plans. Thus, the political consequences of a military action must be well thought out. The levels of political-military plans should be well understood, as follows:

    a.   An environment wherein the political concerns may well override military concerns.
    b.   An environment wherein the military and political maneuvering is robust.
    c.   An environment where the military concern is paramount.
    d.   The situation where other elements of national power like the economy is paramount and that military plans need to be crafted so as to support other efforts.

The military planners who is involved in crisis management must master how to translate political ends into military ways and means while at the same time incorporating the correct balance of the political-military level of concerns.[18]. In order to manage a crisis, there should be a national political-military strategy comprising of the core strategy which strengthens the Government's position on its terms with respect to the crisis; in other words, *the crisis prevention strategy that seeks to avert the crisis; the coercive strategy that outlines both military and non-military coercive measures to be taken in harmony against key actors and adversaries; the escalation control strategy that seeks to contain the spread and escalation of hostilities, and finally, the hedging strategies for major geo-strategic discontinuities that would require a full reassessment of the Government's approach to managing the crisis.[19]* All these are derivatives of the political directives for a crisis that would be translated to military directives, where applicable.

Planning in general is a flexible tool. There cannot be one plan that covers all contingencies. Each plan will change and adapt depending on the crisis. In this Chapter, a generic contingency plan will be discussed in order to provide you with a flexible template and guide to structure a contingency plan. The contents of a contingency plan may include an overview and background of the crisis; situation assessment; national interests, strategic purpose and mission; concept of operations; preparatory tasks including force levels, funding and equipment requirements; mission area tasks as distinct from normal, long-term development tasks; specific operation plans for, say, maritime border operations, electioneering violence, refuge evacuation or external aggression.

The format for operation plans should, ideally, follow a standard pattern. A possible format is as follows:

a. Purpose of the plan.
b. Background on how the plan supports the overall operation.
c. Planning assumptions
d. Current situation
e. Mission, strategic and operational objectives.
f. Desired endstate and measures of success.
g. Concept of operations. How the operations will unfold and Milestones.
h. Organizational framework for operations and chain of command.
i. Roles / Responsibilities
j. Specific operational and logistics coordinating instructions.

In crisis planning for an operation that is neither covered by joint planning guidelines nor contingency plans or where there is the need for updating and existing plan, it is usually expected that operational liaison and reconnaissance are undertaken, thus leading to what is referred to as Crisis Action Planning (CAP). CAP process is similar to the joint estimate process of a campaign plan. In the United States (US) and NATO concepts, there are six phases of CAP. These are *Situation Development or Review of the Situation or Geo-strategic Analysis phase; Crisis Assessment or Mission Analysis Phase; COA Development Phase; COA Selection Phase; Execution Planning Phase;* finally, *Execution Phase.* Each phase is further broken down into three stages – *Event, Action* to the taken, and *Outcome.* Please note that the phases may vary from a few hours to months or may be conducted sequentially, concurrently or skipped altogether.[20]

PHASE I – SITUATION DEVELOPMENT

   a. *Event:* An event occurs with possible national security implications

   b. *Action:* DHQ along with other security agencies including the Defence Intelligence Agency (DIA), monitor the situation, and prepare an assessment.

   c. *Outcome:* The event is reported to the Presidency through the HMOD and CDS. A JTF is established.

PHASE II: - CRISIS ASSESSMENT

   a. *Event:* JTF commander's (JTFC's) assessment is received.

   b. *Action:* Increase monitoring and reporting; DHQ Chief of Training and Operations (CTOP) and his joint staff advise on possible military action; this is evaluated by the CDS, HMOD and the Presidency.

   c. *Outcome:* It is decided that military COA be developed.

PHASE III- COURSE OF ACTION DEVELOPMENT.

   a *Event:* CDS issues Warning Order

   d. *Action:* COAs are developed

   e. *Outcome:* TFC sends estimate of COAs with recommendation.

PHASE IV- COURSE OF ACTION SELECTED.

   a *Event:* CDS presents prioritized COAs to the HMOD and the Presidency.

   c. *Action:* CDS advises the HMOD/President, who now selects a COA.

   d. *Outcome:* CDS disseminates COA selection.

PHASE V-EXECUTION.

   a *Event:* CDS issues Operation Directive

   b. *Action:* JTFC develops Operation Order (OpO) and prepares his force.

   c. *Outcome:* JTFC issues his OpO.

PHASE VI-EXECUTION

JTFC executes the order; crisis is resolved and forces are eventually re-deployed. With the execution of the OpO on course, progress is reported through proper channels, which will lead to continuation of the operations, altering them based on changing events, or brings them to cessation. Once the operation reaches a stage where a reasonable conclusion of the crisis is attained, the execution of the military COA terminates. Thus, the last phase of the CAP comes to an end, as does the entire crisis action process.

CASE STUDIES

Case studies in crisis management are intended to evaluate the success or failure of the application of crisis management procedures and organization for different scenarios, thus bringing out the lessons. The DHQ crisis management organization and procedure have been highlighted in this lecture, in the context of the overall national crisis management strategy, vis-à-vis the principles of crisis management, contingency planning and CAP. As course participants, you are in a better position to judge if it is efficient, satisfactory or otherwise. However, suffice it to say that crisis management procedure continues to be developed and perfected with every emerging crisis situation.

Coincidentally, most crisis situations in Nigeria are internal, therefore, not rigidly a military responsibility. The involvement of the military in the resolution of internal crises, therefore, cannot be said to be a proper yardstick for assessing the success or failure of such mechanism. We have in place some contingency plans, both at the joint service and single service levels, while some others are being developed to cater for external aggression, protection of national economic assets and several other threats. Even in the area of disaster management, there is a National Disaster Response Plan (NDRP), for which the Armed Forces had 25 Disaster Reaction Units (DRUs). In terms of external operations or border security, we should be looking at Op Harmony and the Multi-National Joint Force (MNJTF) or Op Flushout I. For is operations are on going and they will be briefly examined. Op Harmony was launched in 1993 in order to protect the territorial integrity of Nigeria over Bakassi Peninsula, which is of vital national interest, against the threat posed by Cameroon. The intervention of the military after the pre-crisis period also helped to restore the confidence of the local population who felt their interests were not being protected. One of the lessons learnt from this was that a potential crises was identified and since the issue in contention was territory, holding the ground at that point in time was the best option. Being an international crisis, and Cameroon choosing to take the matter for arbitration at the International Court of Justice (ICJ) at The Hague was quite in order. OP Flushout I that is MNJTF is a combined operation involving troops from Chad, Niger and Nigeria. The operation was launched in July 1999, on the basis of a tri-partite agreement reached by the Heads of State of the 3 countries. The mission of Op Flushout I was to flush out undersirable elements in order to guarantee the security of the border areas, which at the time were under siege by cross border bandits. This response approach is a success example of crisis management, having eliminated elements of international suspicion, which could lead to limited war amongst any of the neighbours.

Op Restore Hope was launched on 18 August 2003, based on the directive of the Presidency, with the task of containing acts of lawlessness and insecurity in the Niger Delta. It was initially expected to last for 90 days, but this was extended because of the persistent problem in the Niger Delta. Although adequately contained by the troops' presence, the restive militant youths devised other means to perpetrate their onslaught on rival ethnic communities and oil installations. The need to secure the oil installations against sabotage and nefarious activities cannot be over-emphasized. The success of Op Restore Hope does not lie squarely on a military solution, and so the JTF was established to provide a conducive environment for a political settlement, which otherwise could lead to complex emergencies like terrorism and extreme insurgency. It is the political strategy that would lead the military's exit strategy in the Niger Delta. The recent pronouncement by the President for a holistic approach to the problem of the area involving all stakeholders may well be the turning point/end to the crisis and may also mark the exit of the military participation in the area.

The Operation *Flushout III* came into existence as a result of *Problems of Crisis Management.* The predominant problems affecting crisis management have involved difficulties in crisis prediction and timing. General problems in crises handling include initiation of timely, appropriate and adequate response, systematic and procedural constraints on proposed actions; and delays in decision-making because of requirements for intergovernmental coordination. In a study sponsored by the US Defence Advanced Research Project Agency (DAPPA), crisis problems were identified in 18 categories as follow:[21]

a. Problems in crisis timing,
b. System / procedural constraints on action
c. Problems of crisis handling
d. System related delays in decision-making/action
e. Constraints on operations
f. Problems in operating environment
g. Problems in crisis planning
h. Emotional/ideological issues involved, eg, regular crises.
i. Interpersonal factors in decision-making, example, personalities.
j. Force status problems
k. Intelligence failures at decision-making level.
l. Failure in taking appropriate/timely action.
m. Problems in selecting action personnel.
n. Legal issues involved.
o. Resources inadequate for decision-making/action.
p. Information failures by operating forces.
q. Prolonged crisis problems
r. Physiological problems for operating forces.

In a time-dependent and uncertain environment, coupled with rapid growth of information on world events, crisis handling, of necessity, must rely on technological aids. The study further concludes that the frequent occurrence of time-sensitive crisis management problems necessitates rapid development of advanced Command, Control and Communications (C^3) aid to support future crisis management.

CONCLUSION

A crisis usually leaves a nation with three options – capitulation, war or crisis Management. The ability of a country to manage crisis, be it internal or external, is a measure of good leadership and political stability. The inability to manage a crisis or mismanage the crisis response could be embarrassing to a state, and could even lead to a state being branded a 'failed state'. The Chapter has given a holistic view of the subject of crisis management. The principles have been stated as a prelude to understanding the mechanics of crisis management. Various crisis situations and phases of crisis were identified, although there could be other models, but in all cases, the activities in the various phases must encompass the crisis indicators in the pre-crisis leading to stand down along with lessons learnt at the post-crisis phase.

The DHQ crisis management hierarchy cannot be divorced from the overall national crisis management machinery which is, basically, in two major tiers – the NSC and NDC at Tier 1, each under the chairmanship of the President, C-in-C. Below the NSC and NDC level, is Tier 2, under the Chairmanship of the HMOD. The DHQ on the directive of the President or the HMOD, deals with aspects of military capabilities and force level. By this argument, political directives are translated to strategic military directives, which in turn generates activities like contingency planning and CAP. These are vital if military intervention is to be successful. In order to asses the usefulness or otherwise of crisis management, case studies of *Op Harmony*, *Op Flushout 1 and Op Restore Hope and Flushout III* were briefly examined.

END NOTES

1. Brecher M, Wilkenfield J, *A study of Crisis*, University of Michigan Press, 1997, Pages 2-3.
2. http:/www.lions.odu.edu/dnethert/courses/oted795/crisis-mansim_r/tsld006.
3. US National Military Command Centre, *Concept of Operations (CONOPS), Working Document*, 18 August 2000
4. http://www.dtic.mil/doctrine/jel/doddict/natoterm/c/00345.html.
5. Bouchard J. F, Command in Crisis, Colombia University Press, New York, 1991, Page 19.
6. Head RG et al, Crisis Resolution: *Presidential Decision-Making in the "Mayagues" and Korean Confrontation*, Westview, 1978, Pages 2 – 3.
7. Verbeck TJ, *Crisis Management*. Who is in Charge? http:/www.ndu.edu/library/ic6/93F21.pdf.
8. ECOWAS, *C4 Assessment / Crisis Information Management System Architecture*, 12 March 2002, Pages 11 – 18.
9. Fink S, *Crisis Management*, AMACON, New York, 1986, Pages 20-25.
10. Ibid, Pages 20-25.
11. *Constitution of the Federal Republic of Nigeria*, 1999, Third Schedule, Part II, Section 25, Pages 354-355.
12. Ibid, Pages 275-276.
13. Ibid, Page 347.
14. Armed Forces Act No. 105 1999 as Amended, Part II, Section 5 (2), Page 16.
15. Ibid, Page 18.
16. Ibid, Page 19.
17. Ibid, Pages 20-21.

18. http:/www.au.af.mil/au/awc/awcgate/ndu/interagency_complexcrisis.doc.
19. http:/www.au/awc/awcgate/ndu/interagency complex crisis. doc .
20. I. William Zartman, Peacekmaking In International Conflict: Methods and Techniques, Washington D. C: USIP, 2009.
21. Austin CL, *National Crisis Management and Technology* http:/www.edu/library/n3/SSP_89_022.pdf.

CHAPTER 27

INTELLIGENCE GATHERING
IN A CRISIS SITUATION

H. D. ABBO

Future conflict will be fought more by networks than by hierarchies. And whoever masters the network form will gain major advantages. John Arquilla and Ronfeldt[1]

PREAMBLE

Intelligence, Security and Crisis Management are interrelated subjects always at the front burner of public discourse. These concepts however remain the least understood despite the avalanche of criticisms and interest. However, this chapter endeavours to situate and spotlight the fundamental causes of avoidable security intelligence failures and what is widely perceived as the failure of security establishment to meet public and national expectations especially during crisis situations.

The word, *"Crisis"* originated from the Greek Noun, 'Krisis' (choice, decision, judgement), which is derived from the Greek verb, 'Krinein' (to decide). From this origin, the word suggests concerns about decision-making; an underlying reference to a turning point, crossroad or dead-end in decision making. As a term, crisis has been used interchangeably with catastrophe, calamity, or disaster with no attempt to define the severity or scope of a problem. Guth thus implies that the concept of "crisis" is an ambiguous "term of art" that differs widely based upon the severity of a problem[2]. However, in an effort to give concrete meaning to the concept as a meaningful unit of analysis, Barton defines a *"Crisis"* as a situation characterized by surprise; a high threat to important values; and a short decision time[3]. Fink sees a *"Crisis"* as an:

> ....unstable time or state of affairs in which decisive change is impending either one with the distinct possibility of a highly undesirable outcome or one with the distinct possibility of a highly desireble and extremely positive outcome[4].

Both definitions consist of highly elastic terms, but the ideas provide a framework for identifying the boundaries of the concept. In this context and for the purpose of this presentation therefore, crisis can be seen as any natural or man-made event, civil disturbance or any other occurrence of an unusual or severe nature that threatens to cause or causes loss of life or injury to citizens, and / or severe damage to property and requires extraordinary measures to protect lives, meet human needs and achieve recovery. It also reflects the attendant confusion over a development that threatens to completely stifle further progress in any activity. Crisis also denotes a state of disequilibrium in which normalcy is disrupted.

Perhaps, for a clearer understanding of the nature of crisis, we need to identify some of its key and common features. The key features include the following:-

- Low
- High impact
- Uncertain/ambiguous causes and effects
- Differential perceptions

On the other hand, the common features manifest as follows:-

- The situation materializes unexpectedly
- Time is short
- Decisions are required urgently
- Specific threats are identified
- Urgent demands for information are received
- There is a sense of loss of control
- Pressures build over time
- Routine operations become increasingly difficult
- Demands are made to identify someone to blame
- Outsiders take an unaccustomed interest
- Reputations suffer
- Communications are increasingly difficult to manage

A crisis can result from various factors. It can be caused by a series of mismanaged disasters as well as accumulated, unattended or unresolved issues. And like all other problems, a crisis situation requires effective management to forestall the worsening of the state of affairs. Such management requires the identification of the crisis; planning a response and resolving the crisis. However, none of these requirements can be actualized without access to the critical information that enhances full understanding of all underlying factors. There lies the focus of any attendant Intelligence gathering activity following a crisis. Therefore, Intelligence gathering invariably represents a critical facet of the activities aimed at managing the crisis. To this end, we can see the inter-relationship between Security Intelligence, Security Management and Crisis Management.

THE NATURE OF INTELLIGENCE

Intelligence has always been a contested concept. Various scholars have approached it from different and varied backgrounds. McGeorge sees intelligence as "foreknowledge or information obtained by a designated body through a process which involves procurement, processing, interpretation and dissemination to designated consumers for policy decision."[5] His approach recognizes the value of credible and processed information being the product of professionals. He stresses the issue of early alert signal and underscores the importance and relevance of early knowledge of threats and pre-emptive action to forestall or contain disruptive effects on the security of a nation. For Shulshy, intelligence is "information relevant to a government in formulating and implementing policy to further national security interests and deal with threats to those interests from actual or potential adversaries." Though Shulsky sees the threat assessment potentials in intelligence, he fails to differentiate between intelligence and raw information. His definition does not bring out the true meaning of intelligence.

Johnson's definition of intelligence appears to be more relevant: According to him:

> .....*intelligence has to do with a cluster of government agencies that conduct secret activities including counter intelligence, covert action and foremost, the collection and analysis of information from a mixture of open and covert sources*[6].

This definition seems comprehensive and all embracing, for in addition to discussing intelligence, how it is produced, and the bodies that produce it, it also highlights counter-intelligence as well as covert action.

Copley notes that, "*intelligence is the first key to a nation's security, because it can foretell factors and trends which may threaten its sovereignty, stability and the well being of its citizens.*" Copley and Johnson's conceptualization of intelligence approaches cover both the product and the organization responsible for producing intelligence. From the internal security point of view, intelligence is seen as processed information. It is the product of due processes of information gathering, collation, analysis, interpretation and dissemination.

Generally speaking, intelligence is an instrument for early crisis resolution. It is about reducing uncertainty in conflict for early crisis. It remains an analytical product that is significant to security planning and operations. It provides insights concerning exploitable opportunities to defeat the adversary and helps commanders/executives clearly define the desired end state and when that end state has been achieved. In the management of crisis, correct and advance knowledge of groups, persons and associations, which hostile intentions can be decisive. Intelligence also helps to identify and eliminate information shortfalls. Although supporting the effort to reduce or eliminate sources of conflict, intelligence constantly prepares for the worst case scenario.

The role of intelligence can be appreciated from the nature of its requirement by the primary customer who is the person who acts on the information - the executive, the decision-maker, the combat commander, or the law enforcement officer. For example, almost all national leaders want current intelligence or indications and warning intelligence that is specific. Such information is referred to as "actionable" information. But not all actionable information is intelligence. A weather report, for example, is actionable, but it is not intelligence. Depending on the nature of the crisis on hand, such intelligence satisfies the respective needs of these stake-holders towards carrying out various roles in mediation, negotiation, evacuation, public enlightenment, law and order, among others. Towards this end, the challenge is to fully comprehend the ideal nature of intelligence gathering that suits the requirements of particular stakeholders.

Intelligence, however, may not be able to play an effective role in crisis management without a defined structure to coordinate its function in this regard. This requirement can be met by having in place a well coordinated multi-agency crisis management team. This should be complemented by crisis response guides that identify potential crisis situations as bomb threats, violence, fires and other disasters. Intelligence Agencies should focus their intelligence collection plan and structure towards the evaluation of contingency plans for the worst case scenarios and where by such plans fail, intelligence gathering should be redirected towards promptly undertaking the following measures:

- Carryout out an objective assessment of the cause(s) of the crisis.
- Determining whether the cause(s) will have along term effect or whether it will be a short term phenomena.
- Projecting the most likely course of events.

The foregoing lays the requisite foundation for designing the focus of intelligence gathering, which we may now appraise.

THE FOCUS OF INTELLIGENCE GATHERING

Intelligence gathering can be defined as the process, technicalities and apparatus employed to identify, procure and develop information in a manner that will facilitate timely and adequate appreciation of an issue towards effective action. This definition aptly captures the fundamental values of intelligence gathering activities, notably – it must be for a purpose; it must provide information that is of critical value to the consumers; the problem should have a character and scope; there should be timely dissemination to those that have need to know; and the security of the information remains vital at all times.

In a crisis situation, effective intelligence gathering revolves around the identification and satisfaction of the intelligence requirements of the critical stakeholders. It suggests that intelligence managers should have a foreknowledge of the responsibilities and challenges of other stakeholders, such that the collection strategy is geared towards responding appropriately in all given circumstances.

Being that intelligence gathering is a part of crisis management, we should gain further insight of its ideal focus by applying certain principles of Crisis Management including: comprehensiveness; being progressive; being risk-driven; being collaborative; being flexible and professional. These principles need to be applied prior to, during and after the outbreak of crisis. The collaborative principle, for instance, remains highly critical in view of the fact that no one Agency can go it alone during a crisis. Mutual stakeholders in a crisis situation need to harmonize their respective areas of strength towards overall security. Also, the importance of professionalism can not be over-emphasized as it somewhat guarantees the emplacement of time tested standards for competence .

Intelligence gathering should monitor the build up of threat and tension in various sectors of national life. The September 2001 Plateau crisis, was for example, preceded by gradual build up of ethno-religious tension. So also was the disruptive and crippling June 2007 fuel price increase crisis in the country, preceded by threats and tension.

Intelligence should be targeted at preventing violent conflict or effectively controlling conflict. Such focus should respect the need for creating a sense of safety and security among groups. At this state, there should be constant exchange of information between Security Agencies on the one hand and between them and action agencies on the other hand in solving potential, emerging or prevailing crisis.

Intelligence gathering should also facilitate the provision of information, identifications, interpretation and policy options, from which appropriate responses might be taken. To this, intelligence should address the likely needs of an Information Management Centre whose responsibility during crisis, is to cushion the effects of negative reporting, which aggravates crisis situation through undue portrayal of certain dimensions of events.

Overall, Intelligence gathering during a crisis situation should be guided by the following principles.

i.   There should be comprehensive understanding of the nature of the threat, crisis and issues at stake;

ii.   The needs of the government and other action Agencies should be clearly understood and satisfied;

iii. The attendant intelligence should be packaged in a form that facilitates secure as well as easy access and dissemination;

iv.   The source of information must be protected to safeguard personal and national security. This is what is often referred to as source protection.

v.   There should be a deliberate aim at arresting unwanted situations as well as preventing recurrence;

vi.   The intelligence collection should be sustained to meet current and changing demands; and

vii. Intelligence collection should as much as possible, be restricted to only useful, relevant and actionable information[7].

LEVELS OF INTELLIGENCE

There is consensus in security intelligence practice that intelligence could be classified. However, it should always be borne in mind that categories of intelligence are as many as their usage. Even with the categorization based on usage, intelligence could further be classified on the basis of value, status or application depending on whether intelligence is for tactical or strategic usage. Other types of intelligence frequently used are:

a.   Political, economic, technical, crime and security intelligence;

b.   Current, estimate and warning intelligence; and

c.   Human and electronic intelligence.

The point to note is that all these forms of types of intelligence are required in most crisis situations.

Since intelligence is about conflict, Clark (2003) posits that against any opponent in a conflict, three successive levels of action can be taken, namely, *Prevention, deterrence or defeat,* as indicated in the operations spectrum below.

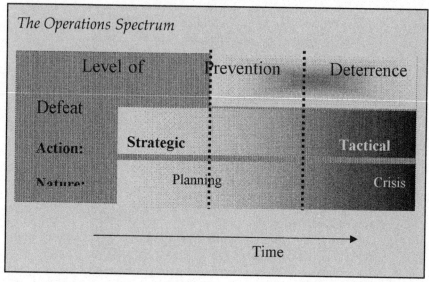

Preventive operations tend to be strategic and to focus on planning while operations intended to deter or defeat are mostly tactical; they transit form planning to managing the developing crisis and executing the plans. The costs of the action tend to increase as one goes from prevention to deterrence to defeat.

Prevention: In prevention, Clark argues that the emphasis is on first trying to prevent a disadvantageous situation (crisis) from developing. Examples include preventing the opponent from acquiring or developing a capability, a strategy, or preventing an unfavorable decision from being made; preventing the opposing negotiations team from taking a certain position; reversing an unfavourable decision that has been made; rolling back a capability; or including the opponent to abandon a development or pull a contested area.

Deterrence: Deterrence, according to Clark, is used when it is too late for prevention. Examples include deterring an attack, deterring the use of a capability or weapons system; deterring the opponent from escalating or aggravating a crisis; or creating uncertainty that induces the opponent to be cautious. Prevention keeps a situation from becoming unfavourable; deterrence focuses on an opponent's potential actions to resolve an already unfavourable situation.

Defeat: Clark asserts that when all else fails, resolve the conflict on favourable terms. In this situation, the opponent should be defeated in armed combat.

Strategic Intelligence: Strategic intelligence deals with long range issues. Monitoring arms limitation treaties, supporting strategic planning in establishments are examples. Strategic Intelligence is perhaps the most critical and important piece of intelligence surrounding a potential or real crisis situation. It implies the particular intelligence that stipulates the specific and potent action that would either forestall the anticipated crisis situation or neutralize one that has already emerged. It provides specific insight into opportunities that can be exploited to prevent, contain or neutralize a crisis.

In most circumstances, it is unwise to abandon strategic intelligence, for without a clear picture of long-term trends, analysts cannot make short-term predictions. The intelligence outfit becomes bankrupt. It not only cannot provide strategic intelligence, it cannot even do decent tactical intelligence, which has been emphasized, it crucial in crisis situations.

Tactical Intelligence: Tactical intelligence deals with issues that require immediate action. Supporting trade negotiations, providing relief to flood or famine victims, enforcing laws, and stopping narcotics or clandestine arms shipments are examples. At the tactical level the intelligence process is very fast. Incoming intelligence is simply added to refine the existing data and an analysis of changes is extracted and reported quickly. The scenario is here and mostly it is known. Now the customer wants details. Intelligence has to be fast and highly reactive. A military commander, for instance, does not care what the tank can do; he already knows that. What he needs to know is where it is and where it is going.

Fast synthesis of data is necessary to support ongoing tactical operations and to allow additional collection to be done intelligently in a short period of time. This short-fuse synthesis is often called fusion and time is of the essence. Fusion is aimed at using all available data sources to develop a more complete picture of a crisis situation, usually with a short deadline. It is also common in intelligence support to law enforcement where time is the critical element[8].

INTELLIGENCE FAILURE

Deficiencies in the management of intelligence at the collection, processing, dissemination and application stages could result in avoidable failures. Lapses, failures and breaches arising from these deficiencies are what are collectively referred to as intelligence failure.

Understanding the reasons for intelligence failure will help mitigate their impact on intelligence support to crisis situations. These reasons revolve around such factors as timeliness, objectivity, usability, readiness, completeness, accuracy and relevance. Intelligence failures manifest in different ways including: over-estimation of events thereby leading to false conclusions; under-estimation that causes intentions and trends to be misread; over-confidence that causes a false sense of security; complacency in the face of clear danger; ignorance that leaves one totally at the mercy of events; poor analytical ability that fails to detect danger even amid huge intelligence information; and apathy of consumers who refuse or fail to act on the intelligence available to them. Three classical cases are considered.

Operation Barbarossa, 1941. Josef stalin acted as his own intelligence analyst, and he proved to be a very poor one. He was unprepared for a war with Nazi Germany, so he ignored the mounting body of incoming intelligence that the Germans were preparing a surprise attack. German deserters who told the Russians about the pending attack were considered provocateurs and shot on Stalin's orders. When the attack nicknamed *Operation Barbarossa,* came on June 22, 1941, Stalin's generals were surprised, their forward divisions trapped and destroyed.

Yom Kippur, 1973. Israel is regarded as having one of the world's best intelligence Services. But in 1973 the intelligence leadership was closely tied to the Israeli cabinet, and often served both as policy advocate and information assessor. Furthermore, Israel's past military successes had led to a certain amount of hubris (arrogance or over-confidence likely to result in ruin or disaster) and belief in inherent Israeli superiority. Israeli leadership considered their overwhelming military advantage a deterrence to attack. Furthermore, the leadership assumed that Egypt needed to rebuild its air force and forge an alliance with Syria before attacking. Israeli intelligence was vulnerable to what became a successful Egyptian deception operation. In this atmosphere, the Israeli officer who correctly predicted the impending attack had his report suppressed by his superior, the Chief Intelligence Officer of the Israeli Southern Command. The Israeli Defense Force therefore was caught by surprise when, without a rebuilt airforce and having kept the agreement with Syria secret, the Egyptians launched an attack on *Yom Kippur,* on October 6, 1973. The attack was ultimately repulsed, but only at a high cost in Israeli casualties[9].

The Panshekara – Kano Incident, 2007: On 17th April, 2007, a Police post in a neighbourhood at Panshekara, Kumbotso Local Government Area of Kano was attacked by persons suspected to be armed bandits. Ten (10) Policemen were killed while rushing to the Police post as reinforcement. The vehicle conveying them was reportedly shot at by persons suspected to be armed bandits. The neighbourhood was under siege by armed bandits whose precise number is not known to date and their identities not conclusively established. The strength and identify of the bandits was the subject of intense speculations as some people were quoted to have said that, they were from Niger Republic while some claimed they were Chadians. The only thing that seems to have been established so far is that most of the assailants spoke Arabic. As for their number, some versions of story claimed that they were less than ten (10) individuals including a woman carrying a baby. Other versions claimed there were about two hundred armed men.

The incident is presented here as classical example of intelligence failure for several reasons. The most important are:

(a)   The incident called to question the capacity, competency and responsiveness of the Nigerian security establishment, especially their intelligence gathering capabilities. Questions have been asked why the NIA, para-military organizations with border security responsibilities, as well as security agencies with internal security responsibilities could not detect a movement of large body of armed men into the country. That is if, they came from any of the neighbouring countries. The fact that they were armed makes it even more intriguing. Why was it also not possible for the civil and local community to detect and report the presence of what undoubtedly was an unusual presence of such large number of foreigners, if at all they were foreigners?

(b) It was very clear from what transpired in the community on 17th April and the days that followed that, the incident brought to the fore the following:

   i.   The country is vulnerable to attack both from within and without;
   ii. The capacity, efficacy and responsiveness of the security agencies in the country are suspect;
   iii. The incident exposed a glaring disconnect between security agencies, their intelligence gathering efforts and community participation;
   iv. Reacting to the incident instead of pre-empting it once more exposed the deficiency of our security posture and strategies;
   v.   Did the time it took to contain the crisis also suggest lack of capacity in any form?.
   vi. Was there any linkage to the so-called earlier "Taliban" attacks sometimes in 2004 in Yobe and Borno States? If there was any, why were the security agencies not able establish this linkage and anticipate the latest attacks?
   vii. There were reports that some of the armed bandits escaped. Why was there no effective mopping up operation? And what post-crisis intelligence do we have?

The Panshekara incident showed there was intelligence failure all through. The Nigerian Security establishment definitely needs to brace up to forestall a re-occurrence.

The nature, character and phase of crisis determine the type of intelligence that is required. This is to say, the intelligence required for a particular phase of crisis could differ from the one required for another phase. The objectives of all intelligence in crisis situations however remains, arresting, resolving or containing of abnormality or disruption. Intelligence in crisis situation could be the type that could facilitate negotiation or dialogue for amicable resolution or the type that would assist security action to arrest a given situation.

Operationally and in most crisis situation, the intelligence that is required is one that will facilitate the interdiction, the prevention and the neutralization of emerging problems and disruption. Intelligence is thus a tool of management of disruption or situations seeking redress. In crisis or threat situations the priority and sequence should be warning intelligence to alert, preemptive intelligence to forestall a crisis and containment intelligence to deal with crisis situations. There are instances when post crisis investigations are launched to acquire intelligence on what went wrong etc. The intelligence focus in such cases is forestalling of re-occurrence. What this means is, the different phases of crisis require different types of intelligence.

There is no shortage of examples of crisis situations. However, this presentation will highlight two incidents that could help graphically illustrate the role of intelligence gathering in crisis situations. The cases are extracts from an unpublished publication by Akoma. These are the September 2001 Jos ethno-religious crisis and the Yobe "Taliban" crisis of December, 2003.

Jos "Ethno-Religious" Crisis: On 7th September, 2001, a misunderstanding started near the Juma' at mosque in Jos metropolis. The immediate cause cited as having triggered the problem was the action of a lady who attempted to cross the mosque during Jumaat prayers. This was apparently a smokescreen and a factor too trivial to have caused the explosion of the tense acrimony and the large-scale mayhem that followed. The main and covert reason for the crisis was the appointment of an ethnic Hausa Muslim, as the Co-oordinator of the National Poverty Eradication Program (NAPEP) for Jos North Local Government, which did not go down well with the indigenes. The crisis thereafter acquired religious characteristics and spread quickly. It elicited very strong opposition, retaliation and response from the Hausa-Fulani community who alleged marginalization, injustice, unfair treatment and discrimination. The entire city was soon engulfed in violence. At the end of it all, 68 bodies were recovered from the streets, 71 houses were burnt, 113 shops vandalized, 5 churches and 7 mosques destroyed.

During studies conducted sequel to the crisis, principal officers of Plateau State Command of the SSS stated that they picked early "signals" and information which indicted that there would be crisis should a non-indigence of Jos be given any political appointment whose functions would impact on the lives of the indigenes. From the other side of the divide were grievances being publicly expressed by the Hausa-Fulani over the refusal of Jos North Local Government Council to issue them certificates of LG origin. Issues were interpreted along ethnic and religious lines between so-called settlers and indigenes. The information and signals were analyzed and intelligence made available to the state government and the police by the SSS. In particular, the indigenes were still nursing grievances over the earlier election of a Hausa-Fulani as Jos LG Chairman during the zero-party election experiment of then President Babangida. For those who regarded themselves as being of Jos indigenous ethnic stock, the Hausa-Fulani has always made efforts to wrestle political power from them. This was the mood until the appointment of the co-coordinator and the mood of the Beroms were again brought to the attention of the Governor by the SSS and deliberated upon at the State Security Council meeting of 23rd August, 2001. The SSS advised that some identified indigenous leaders and Hausa-Fulani personalities should have a round-table dialogue as well as consult widely on how best to resolve their grievances. The Deputy Governor was also advised by the State Director of Security to meet the two parties separately over their grievances.

As tension continued to mount, the SSS advised the Acting Governor, Michael Botmang, to meet them again and discuss the fears, threats and anxieties that were mounting. Intelligence reports on an imminent show down between the two parties were also sent to the Commissioner of Police. With the display of posters and leaflets threatening violence, the SSS in Jos met the co-coordinator and the Chief Imam of the Jos Central Mosque as well as a few Berom leaders and advised them on the need to exercise restraint and caution in view of the state government's determination to resolve the issue amicably.

In his testimony before the Justice Tobi Commission which was set up after the crisis, the then Commissioner Police stated that his office was inundated with reports and copies of leaflets with the inscriptions, 'rise and fight and spill blood for blood'. He observed that the state government was informed of the imminent danger and the Governor advised to meet with religious leaders.

It was clear, therefore, that the Jos crisis of 2001 did not take the state government, the Police and the SSS by surprise. The already existing tension only needed a spark to explode. The encounter between a lady and Muslims during the Jumaat prayers at the mosque provided that spark. This could have been avoided if the earlier intelligence given on the deteriorating relationship between the indigenes and non-indigenes had been attended to. It took the intervention of the Army to restore normalcy in Jos town. The Secretary to the Plateau State Government (SSG) testifying before the Jos Judicial Commission of Inquiry, stated that intelligence was received from the SSS to the effect that a demonstration was planned for 31st August 2001 and that the CP was immediately tasked by the Government to confirm and take appropriate action. He went further to confirm that the reaction and "security reports" from the Police Command gave the "Government the false impression that all was well and that there was no cause for alarm". The then Commissioner of Police in his testimony also acknowledged early receipt of intelligence when he stated as follows: "As Commissioner of Police and jointly with other security agents, we conducted discreet investigations about the happenings and we took certain security measures.... We brought this to the notice of the Government of the State Security Council meeting." The crisis that followed overwhelmed the Police.

The Yobe "Taliban" Crisis of 2003: On 22nd December, 2003 a group of Islamic fanatics called Ahlulsunna Wal-Jama'a alias "Taliban", and led by Usman Ibn Abduljkadir and Abu Umar, attacked the Kanamma Divisional Police Headquarters, Yunusari LGA, Yobe State. They killed PC Mohammed Yakubu and removed arms and ammunition from the armoury. Reacting to the development, the Police mobilized a half unit of the Police Mobile Force (PMF) and some regular policemen and confronted the fanatics on 23rd December, 2003. After about two hours of unsuccessful encounter, the Police retreated. The fanatics re-mobilized and set on fire the residences of the LG Chairman, the PDO, the Police Station, and Government Lodge. Also burnt were the LG Secretariat, residence of the District Head, a Police ALGON Jeep and "Operation Fire for Fire" Isuzu Pick-Up van.

On 28 December 2003, they attacked the Divisional Police Headquarters Geidam, Geidam LGA, and removed unspecified arms and ammunition, N160,000 cash meant for payment of salaries, 2 Police Toyota Hilux Jeeps and Police Communication equipment. They also set on fire the Divisional Police Headquarters, Dapchi Bursari LGA and a Police Hilux Jeep with about 10 rifles in it, the Divisional Police Station, Babangida Tarmuwa LGA, Residence of DPO Tarmuwa and Tarmuwa was also attacked and Aliyo Muhammed (Insp) killed while Ayuba Ali (Sgt) was wounded.

With the military coming in to assist the Police on 31st December, 2003, the extremists fled the area to their camp. During the military operation of 1st and 2nd January 2004, about 9 extremists including 2 women and one child were killed with 5 sustaining injuries; 13 others were arrested at the camp and later 4 others in Borno State. Various arms and ammunition were recovered from the camp.

A post crisis study established that the Yobe Command of the SSS had as early as August 2003 provided intelligence on the presence and build-up of this group. The Command continued to monitor the group and briefed the Governor and the CP as its activities and strength increased with the enlistment of people aged between 20 and 35. The SSS advised the Governor to use the Emirate Council and religious leaders to intervene as the religious activity was likely to provoke crisis.

There was detailed follow up intelligence to the Police on the group's leadership structure, location, strength, ideologies and vulnerabilities. On 6th September, 2003, the then DPO for Yunusari LGA invited the identities leaders for discussion. They ignored the invitation. Given the nature of the group's provocative preaching, the Yobe Command of the SSS engaged the leaders of the group through the traditional council in an interactive session. The group was advised to desist from provocative preaching, anti-government messages and to honour the police invitation. In reaction, the group called on Muslims to disengage their children and wards from Western education.

Intelligence from the SSS to the State Government and Police revealed that in the month of October 2003, the group's preaching sessions had extended to various villages and hamlets. This was followed with the distribution of pamphlets and leaflets which attacked modernity and democracy. The report this time around advised the State Government to use all within its persuasive arsenals to send this group out of the area. The State Government reacted by tasking the State Religious Committee to handle the development.

Covering the activities in November 2003, the SSS reported the group's harassment of women at the streams for un-Islamic dressing and men listening to radio for exposing themselves to Western corruption. The development was deliberated upon during the November 2003 Security Council meeting and the Police was tasked to take appropriate action. Reacting to the pressure mounted by the Police and the State Religious Committee, the group relocated to the border with Niger Republic and from there launched attacks on the Police Stations. It is clear therefore that intelligence was disseminated to the relevant authorities prior to the breakdown of law and order.

On the part of the Yobe State Government, early intelligence was received and deliberated upon during the State Security Council meeting but the Government never believed that the situation was that serious. It therefore delegated responsibilities to the State Religious Committee and relied on its sense of judgement.

It is evidence from this study that intelligence was provided and received by the State and Local Governments as well as the Police but it was not given the desired attention. Even where the Police and State Government appreciated the relevance of the intelligence in early management of the crisis, there was the feeling that the emerging crisis would fizzle out with time. There was also the impression of "doubt" as to the reliability of intelligence from the SSS.

Every kind of Crisis management is usually faced with certain constraints, which if unattended to, undermines the capacity for resolving a disturbing situation. We may simply highlight these constraints as follows;

    i.   Unavailability of, or inadequacy of requisite equipment like operational vehicles, communications, etc.

    ii.   Poor access to modern technology, advanced equipment and other devices.

    iii. Poor crisis management skills such as negotiation skills, which are very rare in the country today.

    iv. Inadequate manpower

    v.   Poor inter-Agency relationship and collaboration

    vi. Poor handling of intelligence reports by action consumers,

While acknowledge the above constraints, it needs to be stressed that the problem is usually not the non-availability of accurate and reliable intelligence. Reflecting the views of others, an intelligence practionner stated that "there is quantum of intelligence in almost all security crises that have so far occurred, but the problem lies in the utility of the intelligence so provided by the action agents". As a another professional colleague stated, after an incident about which he had earlier alerted the State Governor for pre-emptive action, the Governor confided in him after it had happened that "Director, I am sorry, you advised me but I never thought it could be true"[10]

CONCLUSION

The greatest counter measures against crisis situations are embedded in proactive mechanisms that keep the security apparatus adequately prepared for any eventualities in whatever circumstances. As long as error remains in an inevitable human element, failures will remain inevitable. However, the capacity to expect and confront the consequences of such failures ensures that adverse effects are minimal and tolerable for the society.

There is an on-going argument that it may no longer be enough for the Security Agencies to merely provide intelligence, but that they must go the extra mile to justify their existence by ensuring that intelligence products are utilized by the action consumers for the purpose for which they are intended. For intelligence to play its role in pre-empting crises before their manifestation, the Agencies should put in place strategies that would ensure that Governments at various levels as well as other primary consumers all responded promptly and appropriately to the intelligence product. The Agencies themselves need to shape up to constantly collect timely, reliable and well articulated intelligence. As key stakeholders they have move up from their postdictive analysis of events to predictive analysis. They just have to overcome their operational handicaps in the areas of training, funding and equipment and also improve on the public understanding of their functions. In the latter instance, it has been noted that if a climate of trust exists between the public and an establishment, a crisis is easier to redirect than if the public has been concerned about the establishment and if the crisis adds to the apprehension.

REFERENCES

1. John Arquilla and David Ronfeldt, "Cyberwar Is Coming," in Athena's Camp: Preparing for conflict in the Information Age, ed. John Arquilla and David Ronfeldt, (Washington, D. C., RAND Corporation, 1997).

2. David W. Guth, "Organizational Crisis Experience and Public Relations Roles," Public Relations Review 21 (1995): 125.

3. Barton, Laurence Crisis in Organizations (Cincinnati: South-Western Publishing Company 1993) 50.

4. Steven Fink, Crisis Management: Planning for the Inevitable (New York: AMACOM, 1986).

6. Bibliography; Wikipedia. Org. – Crisis – Modern Concepts of Crisis Contemporary Definition and Usage.

5 Incident Reports – Crisis Response Journal http:#www.crisisresponsejournal.com/ DisplayContent.aspx?type=2&id=382

8. Richard L. Russell Intelligence Failures

7. Intelligence Support to operations: Joint Force Employment Briefings; 1.7 Operational Plans and Interoperability Directorate: DOD.

9. Bruce Hugman, Crisis Management, September 2004, Pretoria

10. U Akoma, - The State Security Service and Management of Internal Security in Nigeria, an unpublished Research Project submitted to the National War College, Abuja, 2004.

CHAPTER 28

NATIONAL CRISIS MANAGEMENT PROCEDURE

B. U. MAITAMBARI

PREAMBLE

The subject of this chapter is national crisis management procedure. This should not be a surprise considering the permanent or potential presence of crises in all societies at all times. As a consequence for societies to thrive, they must constantly adopt, review and improve their crises management capabilities. The more societies change, the more they need to modify their crisis management techniques. We are all witnesses to history and the contant evolution and transformation of our world. The post-Cold War era, globalization, democratization and other global socio-political and economic phenomena have thrown up numerous challenges that require new crises management approaches to deal with. Wars have become more lethal and contagious as the world becomes a global village. Therefore, the need for a more articulate, more responsive crisis management techniques have become more relevant now than at any other times[1].

Crisis occur because there is no perfection in the conduct of human affairs. Human systems oftentimes prove inadequate and or sometimes fail without remedy. The interests of nation states will almost always clash over the increasingly dwindling resources available to mankind. This will consequently lead to disputes, which will require a high level of diplomacy to resolve, failing which crisis ensues and results in armed conflict between families, communities, or nations. Conflicts between and within nations occasionally result from the desire of people of a nation or parts thereof, to correct perceived or actual wrongs. Not all conflicts are, however, undesirable, some conflicts lead to the resolution of long-standing grievances and the consequent improvement of relations between the protagonists[2]. This is particularly so if the conflicts are skillfully managed without degenerating into anarchy or total war. Furthermore, no nation can accurately predict all that the future holds. Consequently, situations will arise that nations did not contemplate. It is as a result of these facts, that most nations have developed standard procedures for the management of crises. It is for the same reason, that United Nations (UN) and sub-regional bodies have developed mechanisms for the management of crises. Efficient and effective crisis management procedures are therefore mandatory for all nations, if anarchy and armed conflicts are to be avoided or reduced to the barest minimum[3].

Nigeria has had her fair share of internal crises. Indeed, in one instance, the situation degenerated into an unfortunate full-scale civil war. Similarly, Nigeria has had to contend with crisis and were managed with admirable competence, some could have been better handled. Consequent upon the experiences of the past, various administrations, (civil or military), have over the years, developed a crisis management procedure, which is designed to contain, control and resolve all crises situations with which the Nation has been confronted with from time to time. The procedure has proved very effective in certain circumstances and not so effective others. Lessons have been learnt from situations in which the procedure has not proved very effective and those aspects, which have proved effective over time, have been strengthened. Resolving the crisis in the Niger Delta region is one of the priorities of the President and Commander-in-Chief, Alhaji Umar Musa Yar Adua. To underscore its importance the President in his inaugural address to the nation on 29th May 2007, pledged to resolve the crisis through dialogue, devolution of responsibility, adequate representation and the implementation of the Nigeria Delta master plan[3].

CONCEPTUAL ANALYSIS

Like other concepts and phenomena in the social sciences, there are many variations to the definition of crisis. However for the purpose of this paper, crisis can be defined "as a situation where there is a perception of threat, heightened anxiety, expectation of possible violence and the belief that any action will have far-reaching consequences"[5]. It is also defined as "a time to danger or suspense in politics". Phil Williams, writing about crisis of international proportions, has averred that "...Crises lie at the crucial juncture between peace and war". Continuing, he deposes that "Crisis interactions can result either in the outbreak of war between the protagonists or in the peaceful resolution of the crisis on terms that are at least sufficiently satisfactory to the participants as to make the option of resorting to force seem unattractive"[6]. Most definitions of crisis have elements of uncertainty, fear, tension and danger. All of these elements are usually present in crises situations.

According to Wilkenfield, "crisis is a perception of a threat to one or more basic values, along with an awareness of the limitation of time for response to the threat, and high probability of military intervention"[7]. Crisis could be the perceptions of both an objective threat and a more or less subjective set of national and personal values and goals. It could be an incident or situation involving a threat to a country, it's citizens, military forces or vital interest that develops rapidly and creates condition of such diplomatic, economic, political or military importance that commitment of national military forces or resources has to be contemplated in order to achieve national objective. Phil further deposed that "... crises offer insights into patterns of interaction between states but also into the decision making processes with the governments involved"[8]. Therefore, in a crisis situation, "...the whole of evaluating an initiative of the opponent, deciding on an appropriate response and implementing that response can be seen very clearly"[9]. It is hoped that this presentation will achieve the purpose of revealing the decision making process in crises situations in Nigeria, with due emphasis on crises of international dimensions.

Crisis Management refers to measures to identify, acquire and plan the use of resources needed to anticipate, prevent and/or solve a crisis or threat of a crisis. According to Evan and Newman, Crisis Management connotes "the attempt to control events during a crisis to prevent significant and systematic violence form occurring."[10] North Atlantic Treaty Organization (NATO) defined crisis management "as the coordinate activities taken to defuse crisis, prevent their escalation into an armed conflict and contain hostilities if they should result"[11]. Two primary elements are key to defining Crisis Management –i) the application of control through strategic decisions by the national leadership to prevent war; and ii) to advance the national strategy, protecting interests and setting the crisis so that it does not lead to further crisis. However, the key to both elements is recognizing a crisis at hand. If you do not recognize the crisis coming, control and strategy are difficult to establish. Crisis management is not simply a matter of technical competence. It can not be divorced from policy planning or strategic thinking. At the same-time, it is heavily pressure imposed during a crisis not only increases the tempo of decision-making but also changes its character.

Crisis Management is concerned on one hand, with the procedure for controlling and regulating a crisis, so that it does not get out of hand (either through miscalculations and mistakes by the participants, or because events take on a logic or momentum of their own) and lead to war. On the other hand, it ensures that the crisis is resolved on a satisfactory basis in which the vital interests of the State are secured and protected.

TYPOLOGY

For the purpose of this presentation, crisis can be grouped into external and internal. The two types have different characteristics and management approaches.

EXTERNAL CRISIS

The world has witnessed several crises in the international arena. It will therefore be appropriate to highlight some crises amongst other nations before discussing crises involving Nigeria. This I believe will provide an appropriate background for the examination of the Nigerian response to crisis management.

In 1956, a major conflagration in the form of an all out war involving many nations was averted in the Suez. A crisis of truly international proportions had developed over the interests of many nations in the Canal. What precipitated the crisis was "the attempted tripartite invasion of Egypt by Britain, France and Israel consequent to President Nasser's nationalization of the Suel Canal Company on July, 26th 1956"[12]. The series of events leading to the nationalization were indeed rapid. "The immediate cause of the crisis was Nasser's bid to build a dam across the Nile at Aswan with the initial support of the United States (US)". The US had pledged to provide a larger percentage of the funds required; this was in reaction to a similar offer by the Soviet Union, as it was then called. However, Egypt then recognized the People's Republic of China in 1956. The Americans responded by pulling out of the deal because of Egypt's new level of diplomatic relationship with communist China. It was at this point that Nasser nationalized the Suez Canal Company, "claiming that he needed the income from the Canal to finance the new dam and other development projects".

Britain, France and Israel launched an attack against Egypt. The UN responded by sending a UN Emergency Force (UNEF) which was "dispatched to Egypt to secure and supervise cessation of hostilities and withdrawal of foreign troops, (i.e British, French, and Israel Forces) from the Suez". This UN action was the catalyst to the resolution of the crisis[13].

No discussion on crisis management will be complete, without references to the Cuban Missile Crisis which came about six years after the Suez Canal Crisis. In outline, the CIA had discovered the location of nuclear missiles in Cuba owned by the Soviet Union. The United States, under the leadership of President John F. Kennedy, demanded the removal of the missiles but the USSR under Nikita Khrushchev, was unwilling to do so. A nuclear confrontation starred mankind in the face. The rest of the world watched with bated breath as the two super powers put their crisis management machinery into full operation. The USSR then blinked and agreed to remove the missiles giving impression that the US had won an outright victory. However, there were two important facts, which are not common knowledge. The first is that the US agreed to remove its missiles located in Turkey in return for the Soviet removal of the ones in Cuba. Second, the final decision, which led to the resolution of the crisis, was taken outside official channels. The decision was nevertheless valid and it saved mankind from what was certain to be a tragedy of monumental proportions. These facts should constitute food for thought for all students of crisis management.

Back home in Nigeria, the Bakassi Peninsula Crisis which has just been resolved following Nigeria's demonstration of extreme restraint by accepting the International Court of Justice ruling that ceded the Peninsula to Cameroon is fresh in our memories. The main contention over the oil-rich Peninsula arises from historical and technical claims between Nigeria and Cameroon, as to in whose territory the Peninsula falls. You are all well aware that the crisis developed into an armed conflict, with both Nations sustaining losses in men and material. Happily, the intervention of the UN and the verdict of the World Court laid the foundation for the resolution of the crisis. This is a good example of how to manage an inherited crisis, without losing out by making unacceptable compromises or incurring the wrath of the international community by behaving in a manner capable of being classified as the conduct of a rogue nation. The recent Senate resolution on the matter did not declare the ceding of Bakassi a nullity contrary to Press reports, but merely pointed to the need to ratify the Green Tree Agreement in line with Constitutional provisions.

A further example is the crisis that rocked Nigeria's neighbor to the South, Sao Tome and Principle. Here again, the facts are fresh and available in the public domain. A group of military officers had overthrown the President of the Nation, when he was the guest of the Federal Government of Nigeria in Abuja. The Federal Government of Nigeria, alongside several other Governments all over the world, declared the coup illegal and unacceptable. Nigeria chose to go beyond mere declaration and chose to go beyond mere declaration and was prepared to take action to demonstrate her rejection of the coup. A high-powered delegation led by former President Obasanjo, paid a visit to the country along with the ousted President. The composition of the Nigerian delegation is very instructive for the purposes of this presentation. The former President of Nigeria was accompanied by the National Security Adviser (NSA), the Chief of Defence Staff (CDS), officials of the Ministry of Foreign Affairs, and Representatives of the National Assembly. This was the Nation's crisis management team. Every arm of Government, which has a key role to play, was represented on the team. Happily, the President and his team were able to resolve the crisis and got the President of Sao Tome and Principle restored to power.

Another case was Nigeria's intervention to avert a monumental crisis in Togo, when a section of the Togolese military hastily decided to unconstitutionally install Faure Eyadema, son of late President Gnassingbe Eyadema, as the new President. Conscious of the danger which such unconstitutional action posed to Togo and to the entire sub-region, former President Obansajo, took a firm decision to oppose this unconstitutional act and refused to recognize Faure as the legitimate leader of Togo. He, however, agreed to dialogue with the Togolese leadership, including the opposition, which eventually led to the peaceful resolution of the crisis through elections. It is true that there are still manifestations of discontent in certain quarters, but these can be considered insignificant compared to the fall out that would have taken place if the initial decision had been allowed to stand.

INTERNAL CRISIS

Internal crises often occur within national boundaries occasionally threatening peace and security and even degenerating into anarchy. In order to put good crises management practices in place, it is essential that the nature of some of these crises are examined.

a. Religious Crisis: Nigeria is a multi-religious Nation. The Constitution clearly forbids the adoption of any religion by the State. Section 10 of the 1999 Constitution is unambiguous on this point. The Constitution also guarantees the freedom of religion as a fundamental and inalienable right of the citizen. Consequently, there are occasional clashes between members of the various religions in the Nation. Plateau, Kaduna and Kano States have experienced such crises in recent past. Without doubt, religious crises are the most difficult to manage because of the passion with which the protagonists pursue their objectives. This makes the containment of such uprising an extremely dangerous undertaking. The Maitatsine and Bulumkutu riots are examples, which stretched the resources of Government and the capacity of its officials to the fullest, before being brought under control.

b. Micro-Nationalism: Micro-nationalism ranks next to religious uprisings in the extent to which it directly threatens national security because of its propensity to generate crisis. This phenomenon manifests itself in the emergence of groups of people, usually from the same ethnic stock, who pleading marginalization, threaten and attempt to actualize separation from the Nation. One such group is the Movement for the Actualization of the

Sovereign State of Biafra (MASSOB). It has been observed that, "the fact that these groups come out boldly to assert that they are out to protect their tribal/ethnic interests, is in itself a threat to national integration". Micronationalism, especially when accompanied by violence or the threat of the use of violence, is a criminal offence. It threatens the survival of the nation and unless carefully managed, can rapidly escalate into war. An example of a well managed situation can be found in the flexibility with which the threat of violence in the Niger Delta is being handled in the last few years. Whereas a school of thought advocates dealing with the militia groups with forces, President Yar'Adua has insisted on dialogue and persuasion. The end result is that the rapidly deteriorating security situation in the Niger Delta is being reversed.

c. Communal Clashes: Communal clashes occur in Nigeria frequently because of its heterogeneous composition. It has been observed that, "the heterogeneous characteristic of Nigeria is perhaps the greatest threat to national integration". This is debatable, because heterogeneity could also be a source strength, usually described in the expression, "Unity diversity". Without doubt however, is the fact that such clashes usually occur along ethnic lines, over cultural, economic, boundary or political disputes. This is true of the crises in Plateau State, which was alluded to previously. Some of these problems in the past, have been traced to this disregard of the cultural sensibilities of one ethnic group by another. At times, trouble erupts over Government's demarcation of areas into political units, such as wards of local governments. Whatever the remote and immediate cause, communal clashes undermine national security and usually test the crisis management ability of Government.

d. Labour Unrest: Labour protests are totally legal in all democratic societies. This is particularly so when such protests are carried out in accordance with the laws of the land. However, the experience with Nigeria is that criminals, social miscreants and sundry saboteurs, usually ride on the back of labor protects, to wreak havoc on the Nation. It has been stated that "… the hijacking of labor protests by hoodlums and the subsequent breakdown of law and order…", is one of the major constraints to the management of labor-related protests. Therefore, labor protests which are otherwise legal, occasionally degenerate into crisis situations because of the activities of persons external to the labor movement. The crises such situations generate are injurious to national interests[14].

CAUSES OF CRISIS

Nigeria's internal crises stem primarily from defective political system hitherto enforced through acts of omission or commission by the political class. A political system engenders crisis when it.

a. Allows for inequitable distribution of wealth and positions;

b. Makes little or no effort to curb mass illiteracy, mass poverty, mass deprivation, denial of constitutional rights and miscarriage of justice through a questionable criminal justice system;

c. Thrives on injustice and divide-and-rule tactics; and polarizes the populace along ethnic, religious and economic lines;

d. Fails to tap the country's vast agricultural and mineral resources to diversify the economy;

e. Manipulates the cheap sensibilities of influential but sycophantic opinion leaders in the society;

f. Makes deliberate use of misinformation and communication gap for selfish advantages;

g. Deprives the citizenry access to economic empowerment;

h. Makes no effort to balance the existing disequilibria, mutual distrust and suspicion among the different geo-political units;

i. Enthrones mediocrity in place of merit, excellence and hard work;

j. Discourages the patriotic instincts of Nigerians to contribute to national developments;

k. Imparts a culture of "who-you-know" as license for getting what you want;

l. Sits by and watches, without batting an eyelid, the erosion of prized moral values.

m. Permits the evolution of a new breed of Nigerian youths who have shunned education for quick wealth, irrespective of the sources.

n. Fails to harness the ethnic, socio-cultural, linguistic and religious diversities of the Nigerian nationalities to forge national unity and strength, thus allowing them to constitute the flash-points of division, mutual suspicion, etc;

o. Cares less about the social, economic, political and religious emancipation of its peoples let alone leading the country to take its rightful place among the comity of democratic and industrialized nations of the world.

p. Fails to ensure an effective law enforcement system, especially the Police, which is essential for the maintenance of law and order and the prevention of crises in place[15].

CRISIS MANAGEMENT PROCEDURE

The procedure for the management of crisis in Nigeria can be conveniently divided into 3 inter-locking phases. These are the Pre-Crisis Phase, the Crisis Phase and the Post-Crisis Phase. It is important to remark that the various elements of the phases vary according to the circumstances. In other words, although there are fairly standard procedure, there are slight variations in the steps taken by Government as well as the measures adopted, depending on the nature of the particular crisis.

What is not generally known to the public, is that the machinery of Government for the management of crisis, is always functioning. At no point is the system shut down. During the periods of relative peace and order, the President of the Federal Republic, pursuant to the responsibilities imposed on him by the Constitution, keeps a tab on the security situation through the instrumentality of the security agencies. As a result, Government successfully anticipates and neutralizes several situations, which would otherwise have degenerated into crisis. Government does not usually broadcast these successful anticipation and neutralization of potential descent into anarchy.

During the Pre-Crisis Phase, the office of the National Security Adviser (NSA) closely monitors developments of security interest throughout the nation and in the international community. This is what NSA does through the Joint Intelligence Board (JIB), which meets regularly under his Chairmanship to carry out continuous assessments of the security situation in the Nation and around the world. The State Security Service (SSS) anchors the collation, processing and dissemination of internal intelligence, whilst the National Intelligence Agency (NIA) does the same with respect to the external environment. Other security agencies and Para-military organizations makes their inputs into the system with intelligence and information peculiar to their statutory responsibilities. For instance, the Defence Intelligence Agency (DIA) makes inputs of a military nature into the system, whilst the Nigeria Police (NPF) contributes with respect to criminal Intelligence. The Special Services Office (SSO) provides the secretariat and administrative support for all these intelligence and security activities. Based on the products of the JIB, the NSA routinely briefs the President, Commander-In-Chief of the Armed Forces. Consequently, the President is almost always fully briefed on all developments, local and international which may affect the Nation. This explains why in many instances, Government is able to anticipate rather than manage crisis. Many potentially volatile situations are resolved through the actions of Government based on timely intelligence from the Intelligence Community.

The resolution of some potential crises is achieved through extensive consultations and negotiations between Government agents and the leaders of thought in the locale of the potential crisis. These negotiations and consultations occasionally involve Government Ministers and in some circumstances even the President or his personal representative. It is when all these formal and informal efforts have failed that the situation escalates into a crisis. Once this stage is reached Government mobilizes all its agencies, which may be directly involved in the crisis phase. Up to this point it is the responsibility of the Nigerian Police to maintain law and order. However, since the possibility of the involvement of the Armed Forces is very high during the crisis phase, the Minister of Defence, who would have been involved in the process all along, would be directed to put the Chief of Defence Staff on notice, of the possibility of deployment of troops by the President.

In spite of the fact that the Intelligence Community is always working full steam, now and again, incidents occur and situations develop which degenerate into crisis. This situation may at times be as a result of intelligence failure" or lack of intelligence analysis. In may earlier presentation on this topic, I deposed that the 2001 terrorist attacks in the US were probably due to "intelligence failure". My argument then was that the intelligence agencies in the US had pieces of information, which if professionally analyzed could have saved the US and mankind the tragedy of those attacks. However, revelations from Congressional investigations into the tragedy tend to justify the view that it was probably due more to executive tardiness than intelligence failure. The security agencies and advisers to the Government of the US are trying to impress on the people that the US Government and specially President George Bush had adequate intelligence, to take steps to prevent the attacks. Predictably, the President and his team in the executive are fighting back action to prevent the attacks. The truth must lie somewhere in between. It is very instructive to note that even the most advanced nation on the planet is torn right through the middle over an issue that regularly plagues Third World governments. Back to the crisis phase now, it must be noted that once crisis anticipation fails, Government resorts to crisis management. Upon briefing by the NSA, the President summons and chairs a meeting of the National Security Council (NSC). Thereafter, the National Defence and Security Council (NDSC), meets as the President deems fit. Following from that point, the President acting on the decisions of either or both the NSC and the NDSC puts the primary agency responsible on alert. In most situations of an external nature, it is the Armed Forces that are put on alert. If it is a situation that is strictly internal, it is the Nigerian Police that takes primacy. In either case, almost simultaneously, the Intelligence Community continues its operations and the NSA continues to update the President accordingly.

Other agencies and bodies available to the President are the Federal Executive Council (FEC), the National Council of States (NCS), and the National Emergency Management Agency (NEMA), the National Refugees Commission and the Nigeria Security and Civil Defence Corps (NSCDC). The President is at liberty to consult with one or all of the Senate and House of Representatives. Unless the National Assembly is carried along, the procedure may get stuck, when some legislation is required to give legality to whatever action Government needs to take but which is not provided for in the statute books. Both chambers of the National Assembly already have standing committee with responsibilities for security and related mattes. Meanwhile, as the Police are trying to contain the situation, the Intelligence Community is obtaining, collating, assessing and disseminating intelligence relevant to the crisis. If the situation escalates beyond the capacity of the Police, in an internal situation, the President, who is also the Commander-In-Chief of the Armed Forces, orders the deployment of the military. However, this can be done only subject to some or all of the following conditions:

a. The situation has gone beyond the capacity of the Police;
b. The civil authorities in the locale of the crisis are convinced of the seriousness of the occurrence and request for military intervention;
c. There are real chances that the situation could spread and threaten national integration, and
d. External support is suspected or could be encouraged by the prolongation of the crisis.

There is a critical point during the Crisis Phase, which needs special elaboration. This is the point at which the Police hands over to the Armed Forces. The procedure for handling over to the Armed Forces by the Police has been carefully codified and streamlined. There are standard forms to be completed by the Police officer handing over and the military officer taking over. Everything is carefully documented to ensure a smooth transfer of authority for the operations. This is for both operational and administrative reasons. This procedure has not always been very clear. During the Maitatsine operations in Kano, there was confusion over this procedure.

Indeed, experience has shown that anytime the Police is overwhelmed by a conflict situation, it has been reluctant to hand over to the military for the obvious reason, that doing so, would tantamount to admitting defeat or failure. A recent example is in Kogi State where the Governor asked for military assistance to cub armed robbery and the Commissioner of Police vehemently insisted that the Police was fully capable. This often caused avoidable escalation of conflicts. To overcome this situation, the Internal Security (IS) Procedure has been reviewed to allow for smooth conduct of joint operations and clearly defined points of conflict, at which one service has dominance over the others. The new Standard Operating Procedure (SOP) also emphasizes local containment of crisis through the involvement of security committees from the ward level through to the Local, States and Federal levels.

The post-crisis phase commences with the withdrawal of the Armed Forces and the restoration of local authority to the Police in the crisis area. It should be noted that at this stage, the Intelligence Community is still operating full steam. Therefore, the President is still being given full, up to date and accurate intelligence on the situation. It should be remembered that all the bodies available to the President, namely NSC, FEC, NCS and NEMA are still in regular consultation with the primacy of the role in NEMA, particularly if the crisis was generated by a disaster or if the containment of the crisis, by the security agencies, generated displaced persons and refugees or disrupted social services, such as electricity, water, medical services. As normalcy is restored, the local authority in the crisis area resume normal duties and the security agencies return to routine security functions. It is usual for Government to do a post-mortem of the situation, with a view to taking measures to discover the causes of the problem and preventing a repeat in the future. Post-mortem exercises also help Government decide, where compensatory measures should be taken

GOVERNMENTAL FUNCTIONARIES AND CIVIL SOCIETY

In addition to those already discussed, some other groups within the society have significant roles to play in the management of crisis. Some of the roles are duties imposed by law, others are functions, which derive briefly examined in the succeeding paragraphs:

a. *The Executive:* The role of the Executive, at the top of which is the President, has already been extensively dealt with and will therefore not be discussed any further. It is, however, important to add that the personality of the

President and his strength of character, will seriously affect the resolution of any crisis situation.

b. ***The Legislature:*** The Legislature is the second arm of Government in the Presidential System. The Legislature, which has the constitutional responsibility for making laws for the good governance of the nation, may be called up with urgent legislation to address a crisis. Should the President find it necessary to declare a state of emergency like it was done during the past administration in Plateau and Ekiti States or deploy troops, the Legislature certainly has a role to play. The speed, efficiency and patriotism with which it performs this duty will significantly affect the resolution of the crisis. This point has already been alluded to in the discussion on the Sao Tome Crisis. Members of the National Assembly were included in the Presidents' team to Sao Tome and Principle.

c. ***The Judiciary:*** Quite a number of crises, particularly of a political nature, may require the recourse to the Judiciary for resolution. This is where the dispute revolves around the interpretation of a constitutional provision. Disputes often arise within nations, when key provisions in the constitution are given different interpretations by different groups within the polity. Disputes arising from the interpretation of constitutional provisions, may arise from the nature of legalese adopted in the drafting of most constitutions. Often, the letter and the spirit of the provision may be at variance with each other. In such cases, judicial interpretation may resolve the crisis.

d. ***State Governor:*** The constitution of the Federal Republic of Nigeria 1999, confers on State Governors the responsibility for good governance and maintenance of public order and safety in the states. The primary instrument available to the Governor is the Nigeria Police whose Commissioner in the State may give lawful direction for public safety and public order within the state. There is however a provision that in carrying out such directions, the Commissioner of Police may request that the matter be referred to the President or such Minister authorized for that purpose by the President. There is no provision in the constitution that precludes that Governor from directly contacting the President or such Minister authorized for the purpose by the President in the first instance. It is trite that, what is not expressly forbidden is allowed. The Governor may, therefore, directly seek the intervention of the President if in his judgment, the crisis situation is beyond the capacity of the State Command of the Police to handle. In arriving at such a decision, he should be guided by the advice of the State Security Council, comprising elected executives and professional heads of the security agencies. Indeed, the Constitution empowers the Governor of a State, supported by 2/3 of the elected representatives, to request the President IN WRITING, to declare a state of emergency in the state or part thereof.

e. **Local Government Chief Executive:** At the local government level, responsibility for good governance and maintenance of public safety and order rests on the Chairman who relies on the Divisional Police Officer (DPO). The relationship between both is guided more by convention rather than legal provisions. There is also no legal link created with other security agencies in the form of a Local Government Peace and Security Committee. The Committees may continue to subsist by administrative fiat since the locale of crisis could be far removed from the prying eyes of State Governors. In any case, the Governors require local briefings which the Chairman of the Local Government Councils and the Security agencies particularly the Police and the SSS, are in a better position to offer.

f. *The Media:* The extent to which the media, both electronic and print can impact on the resolution of any crisis can never be over estimated. Indeed, some media reports have been known to create crises through sensational and mendacious reporting. On the positive side, the media are capable of soothing frayed nerves with objective and responsible reporting. For instance, in the wake of the post-election violence in Kenya, all the newspapers came together and had the same headline appealing for peace. This helped to bring about a reduction in the level of violence. Provision of facts about any situation has been shown to make a lot of difference. Conversely, the non-availability of facts on important issues has been known to create gaps, which are filled by the rumour mill, to the detriment of peace in the society. Most governments, therefore, usually ensure that they make maximum use of the media as integral part of their action plan. The constant briefing of the media by both Coalition Forces and Iraqi authorities during Gulf War II is an example of how to cultivate the media in crisis situation.

g. *Traditional Rulers and Religious Leaders:* Traditional leaders sometimes hold the key to the resolution of crisis, particularly internal crisis. This is more so, when the traditional rulers are also religious leaders, as is the case in some parts of Nigeria. Traditional leaders and their religious counterparts usually wield a lot of influence and command enormous credibility. In such circumstances, a credible traditional or religious leaders may be more effective than a body of troops in restoring law and order to a community. Government is keenly aware of this fact and usually solicits the support of these leaders where and when appropriate to prevent or resolve a crisis. This explains the involvement of key traditional rulers in efforts to resolve the current crisis.

h. *Non Governmental Organizations (NGOs):* In most parts of the world, NGOs are regarded as charitable, and neutral and therefore credible. In crisis, as in war, the first casualty is the truth. This is where NGOs are useful as agents of truth. Having the facts about a crisis situation, is often helpful in neutralizing the falsehood peddled by mischief-makers intent on making political capital out of the crisis. NGOs are of course useful in their traditional roles of providing medical and other humanitarian support, particularly when the crisis is in the form of a disaster. Examples are the International Red Cross Society and Doctors without borders.

i. **Professional Bodies:** Professionals can be especially useful in crisis situations. Besides, if a professional group generates a crisis, then members of that group as individuals or as members of the professional organizations, may hold the key to the resolution of the crisis. Furthermore, some professionals are always in sympathy with others or in conflict with others. A good example is the relationship between the Academic Staff Union of Nigerian Universities (ASUU) and the Non-Academic Staff Union of Universities (NASU). Both bodies are always watching the fortunes of each other and reacting accordingly. Therefore, one will always be in a position to provide information on the other or offer advice on how disputes affecting them may be resolved.

J. **Civil Society:** Crises do not occur in a vacuum. It is the civil society, which is usually at the receiving end of the pains and traumas of crises. Therefore, the level of enlightenment, patriotism and general awareness will very significantly influence their attitude to crisis. That attitude will in turn deeply influenced how much understanding and cooperation they give to Government as it battles the crisis. An unenlightened civil society will be difficult to mobilize and manage at any time but more so in a crisis situation. Indeed, the poor reaction of civil society may itself be unwilling to make those sacrifices that they need to make in times of crises. On the contrary, an enlightened and patriotic society, which puts the interest of the nation above its insular interest, will be very cooperative with Government and make the resolution of any crisis less tedious.

Crisis Management is a national issue which impact on national security. The management of crisis therefore, should be initiated from the political leadership (the Executive). The 1999 Constitution of the Federal Republic of Nigeria, recognizes the need for various organs that would tackle issues that border on national security. At the apex are the National Security Council (NSC) and the National Defence Council (NDC). As mentioned earlier on in this presentation, the NSC is empowered to advise the President Commander-in-Chief of the Armed Force, on matters relating to public security. It is at this level that the crisis is weighed against national interest, national directive. It is the decision of the NSC that might activate the NDC, if the matter requires military intervention or support. It is at NDC that military options are perfected and put into effect.

Below the NSC and NDC is the Military of Defence (MOD), which implements the directives of the NSC/NDC through the Defence Headquarters (DHQ). The procedure for crisis management for both internal and external crises at the DHQ level may be kick-started from any of the following sources – Office of the National Security Adviser (ONSA), Office of the Chief of Staff to President, or

Office of the Honourable Minister of Defence (HMOD). Usually, the NSA issues Security Directives, which are converted to Operational Directives by the DHQ and disseminated to the Services (Army, Air force and Navy). The Services in turn issue Operational Orders shown the line. The operational directives usually spell out who exercise operational command and control and overall command. This is dependent on the type and scope of the operation.

Participation in external operations like Peacekeeping Operations is usually an executive decision, based on either bilateral or multi-lateral agreements and mandates. The influence of world bodies like the United Nations (UN) and regional organization like the African Union (AU), and the Economic Community of West African States (ECOWAS), play a vital role in those decisions, as a result of the current global emphasis on collective security mechanism. In the case of internal security, operations like OP FLUSHOUT II, OP RESTORE HOPE, the directives for military involvement are issued by the Presidency to the DHQ after weighing the national security implications, and the need to support the Nigerian Police. Being Joint Operations, they come under the overall control of the DHQ.

CHALLENGES

During periods of national crises, when uniformed analysts make comments about Governments handling of crises, one thing is often clear; they lack understanding of the complex nature of crisis. The complexity of the issues in a crisis, particularly of an internal nature, do not lend themselves to easy and straightforward resolutions. Usually, the issues involved are numerous and complex. Consequently, no one possible solution can be considered and adopted without giving a thought to the ramifications of that solution to other matters and how that solution may impact on other parts of the Nation or what impression it may leave on the minds of the people. For example, the restiveness in the Niger-Delta region is as a result of a complex interplay of economic, social, cultural and political issues. Any solution to the crisis in that region that does not address the various aspects of the crisis is doomed to fail. The complexity of the issues involved in crisis situations is, therefore, a major challenge to the system.

Another major challenge to the system derives directly from the first challenge: the political undertones and implications of the crisis. Virtually every crisis which may be confronted with has political undertones and implications. Even the handling of such apparently straightforward crisis a those resulting from natural disasters, cannot be handled without due sensitivity. This is because whatever action Government takes in one instance immediately sets a precedence. Therefore, Government reaction is constrained and……..by a consideration of future manifestations. Therefore what may appear as simply supply of relief materials in adequate quantities and varieties, become a complex balancing act.

The Constitution of the Federal Republic of Nigeria provide, for several rights, some of them fundamental, for the citizen. International law and conventions also provide for the protection of people everywhere in the world. In the light of these provisions and the absolute need to comply with them, which is most desirable, taking action against individuals and groups in crisis situations, can be very slow and cumbersome. This is one of the major challenges to the system. Even the Americans had difficulties arresting and detaining persons suspected to have participated in or collaborated with the terrorists who smashed airplanes into the Twin Towers of the World Trade Centre in September, 2001. In other words, the need to comply with the provisions of the law, whether international or municipal, slows down the pace of action in the process of managing crisis. This is where the legislature may be constrained to come up with emergency legislations, which may abridge the rights and privileges of people in emergency situations.

Other challenges to the system range from inadequate resources through inter-agency rivalry to inadequate manpower. These are:-

a. **Inadequate Resources:** Crisis management is very expensive. In the first place, no nation has enough resources for all its needs. Nigeria is no exception. The management of crisis requires a lot funds, which are unfortunately in short supply.

b. **Inter-Agency Rivalry:** Undesirable as it is, sustained rivalry between the various agencies of government responsible for crisis management, continues. This leads to duplication of efforts and loss of critical man-hour. In worst cases, it leads to intelligence and / or operational failure.

c. **Citizens' Apathy:** The general lack of security awareness by the citizenry is a major challenge to the system. This lack of security awareness causes some citizens to withhold support from security agents or in worst cases, actually collaborate with those generating the crisis.

d. **Inadequate Manpower:** In spite of the spectacular advances in technology, men and women are still in high demand in crisis situations. The physical manning of entire communities makes a lot of demand on the number of security personnel who need to be deployed. Such numbers of personnel are usually not available. This becomes a drag on the operations.

PROGNOSIS

The success of crisis management mechanism in Nigeria will depend largely on the political will of the Government, as even the most modern and effective crisis management mechanism could be rendered ineffective where political will is lacking. It, therefore, behoves Government to do the following:

a. Ensure perfect harmony and communication flow between the various organs of Government to avoid over-heating the system.

b. Ensure adequate enlightenment of the citizenry to enable them to know their duties and obligations as provided for in Section 24 of the Constitution.

c. Enlightened the citizenry on the simple rules to observe during various types of disasters or crises.

d. Establish a social welfare scheme for unemployment Nigerians to provide them minimum succour until they are employed.

e. Enforce the Anti-Corruption law to the letter in order to stem greed and corrupt enrichment.

f. Re-train, motivate and revitalize the Police to reposition it to effectively play its traditional role of maintaining law and order.

g. Re-energize the intelligence outfits and revitalize the Police operational departments to enhance their efficiency .

h. Encourage and re-engineer the National Boundary Commission and its state counterparts to allow for effective prevention of border crises and timely demarcation of all the internal and international boundaries.

i. Curb the excesses of the Nigerian media, which are noted for sensationalism, negative reporting and deliberate falsehood.

j. Address the culture of violence among Nigerians using the National Rebirth Programme of the National Orientation Agency.

k. Reinvigorate the National Emergency Management Agency's Disaster Reaction Unit to ensure quick response to disasters, and

l. Provide subsidiary training for the Armed Forces and Security agencies in the area of disaster management.

CONCLUISION

In conclusion, I would like to make a few remarks which will capture the main essence of this presentation. First, I wish to re-emphasize that it is impossible for any Government to totally prevent the emergence of crisis situations. Events occur in every nation and assume a momentum of their own, over which Government may have no control whatsoever. Second, the period of relative peace in Nigeria validates the fact that Government successfully anticipates several potential crisis situations and neutralize them before they escalate into full-blown crisis. Third, the crisis management procedure of the Federal Republic of Nigeria is alive, and well, efficient and effective. Fourth, the procedure for crisis management is undergoing modification and it has the flexibility and adaptability to embrace situations and circumstances of rapidly changing developments in our modern world. The sustained peace and order of Nigeria is engineered by the frenzied round-the-clock activities of the Intelligence Community working under the Chairmanship of the NSA and providing accurate, up-to-date intelligence, that enable the President to anticipate and resolve potential crisis before they lead to disorder. These operations of the Intelligence Community are not done in public view. The same procedure assists in the containment of any crises, which have already escalated, and the restoration of law and order after the resolution of any crisis.

This paper has made a case for the strengthening of the national crisis management mechanism which it strongly believes could help salvage the country from the myriads of intractable internal crises. I also believe that only a demonstration of Government political will can ensure the realization of this goal. It is, therefore, my hope that the sustenance of political will by this administration would ensure the emergence of a virile national crisis management system.

REFERENCES

1. J. Muhammad – The Role of Nigeria in Peace Building, Conflict Resolution, and Peacekeeping since 1960

2. P. Akpa – Defence Headquarters Crisis Management Procedures. (MOD, Abuja)

3. T. Akindele – Theory and Practice of Crisis Management. (NDC Lecture, Abuja).

4. D. Enahoro – Crisis Response Procedure and African Military Perspective, 1998.

5. G. Evans, and J. Newman (1992 – The Dictionary of World Politics), 1992.

6. Phill Williams, Contemporary Strategy: Theories and Policies, Crown Helm, 1975.

7. Olusegun Obasanjo, Aid to Civil Authority.

8. Constitution of the Federal Republic of Nigeria, 1999, Government Printer, Lagos.

9. TA Imobighe and IS Zabadi, African Crisis Response Initiative.

10. See B. Job ed. The Insecurity Dilemma: National Security of Third World States: Boulder: Lynne Rienner, 1992.

11. Ken Booth ed. New Thinking about strategy and International Security. London: Harper Collins, 1991.

12. M. Karns and K. Mingst, International Organisations. Boulder: Lynne Reinner, 2004.

13. R. Thakur and A. Schnabel eds. United Nations Peacekeeping Operations. Tokyo: United Nations University Press, 2001.

14. O. Nnoli, National Security in Africa. Enugu: SNAAP Press, 2006.

15. E. Osaghae, The Management of the National Question in Nigeria. Ibadan, PEFS, 2001.

PART FOUR

STRATEGIC RESPONSE

CHAPTER 29

RESTRAINT FACTOR IN NIGERIA'S MILITARY STATECRAFT

C. O. BASSEY

The generation and use of military power as an instrument of prevalence in the global arena constitutes the "Core-complex" of military statecraft. While the use and usability of the Nigerian military as an instrument of statecraft (in pursuit of security and crisis management goals) can be established in the past, the frequency and effectiveness of its role in future contingencies remains a subject of policy debated[1].

This chapter examines a question of central theoretical and empirical import in Nigeria's military statecraft: why Nigerian policy-makers resorted to the military instrument at sometimes and places but not others? It will be contended that a possible explanation of the seeming contradiction between Nigeria's declared and actual military policy resides in the profound restraints on its policy-makers which have combined to inhibit resort to Nigeria's military power in a number of circumstances in which national sentiments, policy objectives and principles dictated such a response.

Generally considered, military statecraft refers to the "production, maintenance, and employment of armed strength in support of government's foreign policy"[2]. It is, thus, concerned with the generation and use of military power as an instrument of prevalence in the international arena. However, in specific historical circumstances in which the military instrument depends on a multitude of factors including ideological and normative convictions, expectations concerning the psychological and political developments in the camp of the opponent, socio-economic factors and inclinations of individual policy-makers.

Seen in this context, a survey of Nigeria's defence planning and foreign policy posture since 1970 suggest a fundamental acceptance and commitment to a realist philosophy which views "military power as but one of the many techniques of statecraft, taking its place alongside diplomacy, economic sanctions, propaganda and so on"[3]. However, while the use and usability of the Nigerian military as an instrument of statecraft (in terms of security and crisis management) can be reasonably established in the past, the frequency and effectiveness of their role in future contingencies remain a subject of speculation.

This chapter represents an attempt to analyse and comprehend a question of central theoretical and empirical importance in Nigeria's military statecraft: why have Nigerian policy-makers resorted to the military instrument at sometimes and places but not in others? In other words, why did the Nigerian government, for example, resort to military force against Habre's forces in the   Lake Chad Basin (April-

May, 1983), intervene in the Liberian and Sierra Leone Civil war (ECOMOG), unilaterally annexed the Bakassi Peninsula, and not against Equatorial Guinea in the 1970s (under Marcias Nquema), or for that matter, in support of the MPLA in Angola or the Patriotic Front in Zimbabwe, despite public pressure in favour of such intervention. Is there a pattern in Nigeria's appeal to military power such that a general proposition can explain both the use and the more frequent non-use of the military instruments?

This question is no doubt of major importance to any endeavour to understand or anticipate the future responses of Nigerian decision-makers in crisis situations. It will be argued that a possible explanation of this seeming contradiction between Nigeria's declared and actual military policy frequently highlighted in extant literature on Nigerian foreign and security policy resides in the profound restraints on its policy-makers (assuming their will to act in support of policy objectives). The general hypothesis in this context, therefore, is that several restraints have combined to inhibit resort to Nigeria's military power in a number of circumstances (Equatorial Guinea, 1974-75; Angola, 1975-76; Zambia-"Rhodesian" frontier, 1979-1980) in which national sentiments, policy objective and principles dictated such a response[4].

For reasons of analytical clarity, the disquisition below proceeds within two broad sub-sections; (i) thematic overview of the restraint factor in military statecraft; (ii) internal and external restraint factors as they impact on Nigeria's military statecraft. The focus will be on two basic issue areas: military-institutional factors, and socio-economic and political factors. The former involves the capability factor of the Nigerian military as it relates to its strategic environment. The latter includes a range of domestic and systemic constraints – political, economic, social and psychological – which may not inhibit resort to coercive measures, depending on the vitality of the issues and the climate of public opinion. It will be argued that these restraints on the instrumental use do not determine governmental behaviour. Actual or manifest behaviour is always conditioned by a host of particular circumstances, and the use of military force does not, of course, vary greatly in this respect.

RESTRAINT FACTOR IN MILITARY STATECRAFT

In analytical terms, consideration of the internal and external restraints on a state's use of military force is part of a broader systematic inquiry into the sources of foreign and defence policy. As a consequence, these restraints are more often than not treated as the "unwanted step-children of political systems", assumed by both foreign and defence policy studies and neither properly or adequately analysed by either[5].

Furthermore, such an inquiry is also inescapably subject to the same gamut of strictures and problems that have so far bedeviled endeavours to develop universal theory of foreign policy behaviour[6]. This caveat, notwithstanding, the use of military power as an instrument of statecraft is seldom a haphazard phenomenon. It may be influenced by certain domestic and external factors/determinants which, although analytically distinct, cannot be completely understood in isolation from the other.

Nigeria is not an exception in this regard. As understood here, the term "restraint" implies a set of factors which converged to hinder a state's use of force. What follows, therefore, is a general consideration of these factors in the light of Nigeria's experience.

National military power can generally be used externally for threatening, deterring, war-fighting, or peace-keeping. It can be employed coercively in order to either influence the behaviour of opponents or alter or preserve the *status quo*. Ideally, the frequency and intensity of states' applications of military power in pursuit of the combination of these objectives are functions of their capability and intentions, viewed within the general context of foreign and domestic political objectives and constraints.

However, in specific circumstances, the military response provoked by external stimulus is invariably conditioned by a set of antecedent factors that either predispose or restrain a society or regime towards a military reaction. In contemporary parlance of strategy, it is these factors that constitute the socio-economic and political component of the military potential of states. Six of these restraint factors on the use of military force as an instrument of statecraft in the contemporary international system have been generally high-lighted in the literature in terms of their sources as internal or systemic[7]. They have also been classified according to the way in which they are generated as either direct or indirect. Furthermore, they have been conceptualized according to the way they inhibit the use of national military power as anticipatory or reactive: long-term. These include the impact of the constantly changing dynamics of modern military technology (particularly nuclear weapons), complex interdependence (the growth of transnational forces and interdependence), the normative devaluation of force as a means of settling conflict, military institutional factor, the productive base of society as well as the nature and character of the political system and process as they operate to retrain or expedite the use of military power as instrument of policy.

It will be argued below that normative restraints as controlling factor in Nigeria's defence and foreign policy behaviour has been considerably diluted since the 1970s. This is the unmistakable conclusion to be drawn from any review of the perceptions and attitudes of Nigerian policy-makers towards the use and usability of national military power as an instrument of policy in Africa[8]. The prime example of this departure from the position of excessive commitment for the normative stipulations in the OAU Charter about the use of military violence was the forceful responses of the Shagari administration to the border crises involving Cameroun and Chad in May, 1981 and April-June 1983, respectively.

In this regard, Nigeria's drive since the early 1970s in support of *bona fide* indigenous governments in Angola, Zimbabwe, Namibia and South Africa short of military action is to be ascribed less to normative considerations than to military impotence. Indeed, with the possible exception of the Balewa era, Nigeria's position on the role of military force in the decolonization of Southern Africa has been remarkably consistent. On this view, General Murtala Muhammed's declaration that "there was no reason why Nigerian soldiers should not go and fight in South Africa alongside the liberation forces, whatever the obstacles" was, and still is, revealing of the prevailing mindset of the officer corps of the Nigerian military[9].

Thus, in principle, Nigeria's commitment to a military solution the basis of the Gowon and Obasanjo administration's proposal for a Pan-African Task Force – in Southern Africa is unquestionable. However, Nigeria's actions so far reliance on diplomatic pressure, economic sanctions (e.g. against Britain over Zimbabwe), logistical and financial support for liberation Movements – falls short of a full scale Cuban style defensive and Offensive military action and is primarily a consequence of certain domestic and systemic restraints in Nigeria's operational environment[10]. These restraints, as already noted, are partly military, and partly socio-economic and political. A detailed examination of these factors constitutes the subject-matter of the two sections below. For analytic reasons (albeit critically cognizant of their contextual convergence of linkage) these restraints on the use of Nigerian military power are classified according to source – internal and systemic – while their influence dynamic – direct and indirect; long-term or short-term; anticipatory or reactive will be highlighted as the examination of the variables proceeds.

INTERNAL FACTORS

Generally considered, the use and usability of national military forces (either for the threatening, deterring or war-fighting) as Klaus Knorr has succinctly noted, is a function (i) of how military capabilities of possible opponents compare quantitatively and qualitatively in military effectiveness; (ii) of the stakes involved in a clash of interests; (iii) of the propensity of governments and generals to accept risks and to behave rationally (iv) of naormative, political and legal restraints[10]. But it is also a function, it may be added, of the "technostructure" (to use Galbraith's terminology) of the state in question since, as O.S. Kamanu has argued, "Ultimately the military capability of any state is a function of its economic and technological level of development"[11]. Critical deficiencies in any one or combination of these factors – especially in the vital economic and technological base – may seriously undermine the use and usability of national military power as an instrument of statecraft.

Nigeria's basic problem it will be argued, resides in or is reflective of its relatively frail underlying socio-economic and technological fabric. It shares with the great majority of the LDCs the constraints of "military policy dynamics in the contemporary context of peripheral capitalism"[12]. In the analysis below, primary consideration will be given to three dominant internal restraint factors – military capability, socio-economic and political – besetting the use and usability of Nigeria's military power as an instrument of policy.

(I) MILITARY-CAPABILITY FACTOR

Since the crux of defence or security policy is the relation of force to national purposes, military capability, by definition, constitutes a fundamental direct restraint on a state's use of force. Thus, from a decision-making standpoint, any consideration of the Nigerian military as an instrument of national policy hinges inescapably on how it qualitatively compares in operational effectiveness with possible opponents. That is, the capacity and the viability of the Nigerian armed forces to function adequately as an instrument of statecraft cannot be computed in isolation; it must need-relate to the strategic environment (both the physical geography and the balance of forces between Nigeria and its potential adversaries), strategy and tactics, and available technology.

However, as historical antecedents have shown, given the variability of factors involved – organization, doctrine, equipment, leadership, training, experience and morale, all in a condition in which contingencies are hard to foresee, such a comparison of national military capabilities is extremely difficult to establish with a high degree of certainty. A more realistic approach to determining or assessing the comparability or readiness of the Nigerian military establishment to meet the challenges of its security role and mission is to integrate both national *capability* and *intentions*, and to do so within a broad picture or framework of its foreign and defence policy objectives and posture.

Viewed in such terms, consideration of Nigeria's military capability assume a further dimension beyond a simplistic and static quantitative comparison between its overall force level and striking power and those of its potential adversaries. It becomes preeminently a situational and doctrinal question; that is, how the perceived threat (from these countries) is manifested and "whether the forces and procedures developed in anticipating them are adequate to deal with the real challenges"[13]. Hence, strictly speaking, Nigeria's military power exists only in relation to particular other nations and regarding particular conflict situations.

For examples, in the 1970s and 1980s given the perceived threat posed by apartheid South Africa to Nigeria's security, the fundamental imperative for its defence planners becomes essentially that of determining, on the one hand, the nature and situational conditions in which this threat might be manifested (direct or indirect), and, on the other hand, the priority structure (offensive or defensive) for dealing with such challenge. Thus, if apartheid South Africa's threat to Nigerian security was rated indirect (such as its support of secessionist forces during the civil war or aiding any of the neighbouring states in a military confrontation, Nigeria would have been adequately prepared to "furnish a mode of action for the circumstance it defines as ordinary"[14].

It was however, in terms of the priority structure for dealing with apartheid South Africa's threat that the enormous restraint imposed by the current level of Nigeria's military capability was readily visible when a shift of focus is made from defensive to offensive strategic option. In the former case, as noted above, the primary "radius of effective military action" is essentially Nigeria's territorial threshold or the "innermost circle" of its security environment. Within this sphere the totality of Nigeria's putative military power (both actual and potential) became the preponderant factor in resisting threats to its national security. In the latter case – offensive strategy – the cost of "transmitting power over space" (the "loss-of-strength gradient", to use

Kenneth Boulding's phrase), the physical geography of Southern Africa, as well as the defensive and offensive capabilities of the South African military necessarily become Cogent factors in any decision by Nigeria to use force. It is on this consideration that one may legitimately argue that the current industrial base and its externally projectable military power is hopelessly inadequate.

However, even within this problematic context of offensive strategic option, a distinction has to be made between *minor* and *major* commitments. The former may involve logistical aid and operational support for the liberation movements. A cardinal example was the Nigerian Air Force logistical operation from Tanzania in support of the Patriotic Front forces based in Zambia and Mozambique, at the height of the war of independence in Zimbabwe (1978-80).

It is, nevertheless, in terms of a major role commitment – either as a part of a Pan-African Task Force or independently in a Cuban style interventionary role in Angola – that the profound restraint imposed on Nigerian decision-makers by current capability of its military forces can readily be appreciated. Since in an offensive role the attacker has to expose himself to damaging counter measures (as the British campaign in the South Atlantic clearly indicated) and, *ceteris peribus*, requires several times as many men and resources, the military strength of Nigeria could hardly be considered adequate for the purpose of establishing a clear military ascendancy over apartheid South Africa.

In quantitative terms this can be seen in the trifleness of the striking power of Nigeria's armed forces vis-à-vis South Africa. In qualitative terms the peripheral designation of Nigerian defence system can be readily seen in the rudimentary or nascent nature of its military industrial complex[15]. This is manifest in the type of weapons produced (assault rifles, armoured cars – and support vehicles, bombs and ammunition), the level of defence industrial production capability, and the age of technology – "Vintage" and Intermediate" military components and systems rather than the "advanced", "lead-edge", or "critical" technologies manufactured in the industrialized countries. Furthermore, since organized R and D (Research and Development) is crucial determinant of national technological capacity, its continued relegation in Nigeria's defence planning in favour of quick-fix solutions can only undermine independent decisions concerning the use and usability of national military power[16].

Nevertheless, just how much and how quickly Nigeria can augment its military capability under the "fog of war" will inevitably depend, among other things, on (a) the strength of its economic base at the given time, (b) its trained reserves, (c) its industrial capacity, political control, technological skill, and (d) its internal communication and pre-planning for mobilization. These variables constitute critical domestic socio-economic and political underpinnings for the production and use of military force. Their under-development in any social system (such as Nigeria) may seriously restrain the use and usability of military force as an instrument of policy. This will be the focus of the next two sub-sections.

(II) SOCIO-ECONOMIC FACTORS

Since the production, maintenance, and use of armed forces requires a variety of goods and services, competing social and economic demands – especially in an under developed polity such as Nigeria – set definite limits to decisions concerning the use of military force as an instrument of policy. The opportunity costs of generating and employing military power, as Knorr has succinctly argued, equal the alternative uses of productive capacity (labour, technology, natural resources, real capital) that has been forgone[17]. His reason is that military policy – the "relation of force to national purposes" – inescapably hinges on structural decisions involving the procurement, allocation, and organization of the men, money, and material which 'go into the strategic units and uses of force'.

In a condition of limited resources-especially in foreign exchange reserves - such an allocation invariably engenders fundamental conflicts between those purposes which relate to the achievements of security objectives and values and those which relates to the achievement of domestic goals – economic development, political stability and social welfare. In this context, if increased effort is made to augment the fighting capability of national armed forces in a stagnating economy – such as Nigeria's since 1982 – then the comprehension of civilian consumption, investment, and non-military public expenditure would tend to be politically harder, especially with a population of over 80 million, and a phenomenal and menacingly high birth rate of approximately 3.7 per cent annually.

In latent terms, however, the Nigerian economic base appears at first glance to be impressive and should be able to support a "well-equipped, mobile and virile defence force" without the concomitant risk of compromising basic development programmes. The country is endowed with a variety of industrial minerals and its agricultural potential is obvious from the number of years Nigeria relied on agriculture both for domestic consumption and export. Its energy base is abundant and potentially supportive of a vibrant industrial economy. Nevertheless, this seemingly encouraging rosy picture by itself is misleading for a number of reasons.

First, the transformation of national economic potential into usable resources is not an automatic process; it depends critically on interlocking administrative, scientific and technological skills, the *sine qua non* of modern industrial states which so far has eluded Nigeria's inept and hedonistic officialdom. Second, Nigeria's low level of industrial capability (especially in the vital areas of machine production and related infrastructure systems) has largely negated the substantive bearing of its economic potential on its capacity to produce and use military force as an instrument of policy.

One of the profound and inescapable consequences for Nigeria's security policy of the above factors – frail socio-economic and technological base – has been a noticeable discrepancy between its foreign policy posture and actual behaviour in crisis situations. For example, when in 1978-79 president Kenneth Kaunda requested the interpositioning of Nigerian military forces between Zambia and "Rhodesia" at the height of the conflict, economic and financial considerations compelled the Nigerian government to respond in the negative. The projected cost of the initial operation (transporting troop and equipment to Zambia) was estimated then at N32 million. The additional cost of approximately N3.5 million a day to maintain the troops in a combat environment exceeded the country's financial capacity, given the budget deficit and contending social and economic demands[18].

The preceding analysis of two of the major sets of restraints – military capability and socio-economic factors on the use of Nigerian military power as an instrument of statecraft is necessarily incomplete without appropriate cognizance of the relevant superstructural variables – in this case the political determinants – whatever the ultimate motivations at work – it is through the political process and through the decisions of government that resort to military force or war comes about. For example, political determination underlies the structural decisions concerning the procurement and allocation of proportion of national manpower and other resources to the military sector "which go into strategic units and uses of force". This determination of the resources available to the government and the "authoritative allocation" of those resources among "military, domestic and foreign purposes is, indeed, the crux of national policy"[19]. It is this political determinant as it operates to restrain the use of military force in the Nigerian context that will be examined in the final section of this categorization of internal restraints below.

(III) POLITICAL FACTOR

The use and usability of national military power as an instrument of policy critically depends not only on the prowess of a country's military establishment, but also, *inter alia*, on the skill of statesmen, the character of domestic base and the shifting dynamics of moral, political and legal restraints. These elements generally constitute the political component of the military potential of states, which may or not influence the use of military force in pursuit of national objectives. The operative conditionals in this political chemistry necessarily resolve around two pivotal factors. One is the nature of the political system: the idea that a state's form of government will influence its propensity to use force. The other is the dynamism of leadership. The latter is considered an elemental requirement for making potent interlocking structural decisions – political, economic, technological and military-strategic – on which the generation and use of military strength vitally depend.

Indeed, since technological advances and economic development (especially in an essentially neo-colonial polity such as Nigeria) critically depend on how motivational resources are structured and managed, government and elite direction in collecting and allocating "social energies" and their choice of priorities remain a key factor.

It is in the context of this first level consideration – rather than the alleged nature of the political system *per se* – that the political factor as a restraint on the development and use of Nigerian military power as an instrument of statecraft is to be constructed. The persistence of what Achebe has termed the 'cult of mediocrity' remains in this regard the fundamental obstacle bedeviling the transformation of Nigeria's economic, social and industrial potentials into suitable military capabilities. As the extensive array of studies in defence management and planning have conclusively shown, the transformation of resources – men, money and material – into actual or ready military power can be effected with more or less skill depending on leadership[20]. The greater the astuteness of the leadership, the more military strength will be derived from allocated resources. Or, to put it differently, the magnitude of inputs required for producing a desired level and type of military strength depends on the efficiency of the transformation. It is a matter of leadership and administrative competence – a component of national military potential which an aspiring regional power such as Nigerian must first cultivate.

The next and final section below dwells on the systemic dimension of the restraints on the use of Nigerian military power as an instrument of policy. The *raison d'etre* of this consideration – as well be argued below – derives from the widespread convention in the analytical literature on the foreign policy of developing countries, that while the external behaviour of states may be explained in terms of their projection of domestic factors and forces into the international political scene (primarily in response to situational stimuli, opportunities and challenges), it is also unalterably conditioned and delimited by countervailing systemic forces. In this respect, therefore, systemic factors constitute an irresistible parameters – in terms of restraints – for Nigeria's military policy.

SYSTEMIC FACTORS

The logical extension of the argument of the preceding paragraph is clearly that, while in terms of source and analytic convenience, restraints on the use and usability of Nigerian military power may be broadly divided into internal and systemic factors, such a division is necessarily obscured by existential and phenomenological convergence of the parameters of its domestic and international behaviour. Because of this demonstrable convergence, the external influences on Nigeria's military policy determinants that derive from the domestic environment.

Thus, as Aluko, Ogunsanwo, Shaw and Stramlau, among others, have incisively argued, the great vulnerability of a post colonial state such as Nigeria to outside influences and pressures has presently conspired to render the conventional distinction between the external and internal dimensions of its foreign and security policy almost meaningless. Within this context, systemic factors become an integral component of resort to coercive power, depending on the force of situational challenges and the stakes involved in a clash of interests. As is to be expected, these systemic factors vary considerably in their intensity or degree of impact on the decision-making process concerning the potency of Nigerian military power as instrument of policy in different circumstances. Three of these systemic variables will be considered in terms of their relative potency in the light of the past and possible crisis situations. These include: (i) the restricted legitimacy of war (normative restraint) both at the global and regional levels, as expressed in what is often nebulously called 'world public opinion' and in Pan-African notions of 'good neighbourliness'; (ii) the possibility of external intervention in support of the opposing actor, as was the case during the civil war; and (iii) the irreducible dilemma and cost of conquest: 'victory is not success'[21].

(I) NORMATIVE RESTRAINT

The variable impact and implications of the normative devaluation of force as a policy alternative in the African subsystem for Nigerian defence policy has been examined above and will not be reiterated here. The global dimension and influence (on the employment of Nigeria's military power) of this growing phenomenon remain to be analysed – 'world public opinion' – which even contemporary dominant powers (such as the U.S) can now ignore only at a price of inevitable isolation.

Defined abstractly, the term 'world public opinion' encompasses opinions that react "to events the world over and are, in part and to a degree, interconnected ... resting on a strong and expanding technological foundation"[22]. The inescapable prerequisite of restraint engendered by the wrath of aroused world opinion is that the state and government in question perceive or anticipate adverse opinion and that they are sensitive to its consequences.

However, in view of developments at both global and regional levels in that last three decade, it is to be expected that the effective weight of the sanction resulting from "world public opinion" varies considerably depending on a host of circumstances and the power status of the state involved. It is this variability which marks it with "vast uncertainty and which lends chance, vagueness and relative weakness to the sanction"[23]. Although this observation holds true in contemporary international crises involving major powers (and their core allies), for a less developed and dependent social formation such as Nigeria, in the event that adverse opinion turns out to be strong – as was the case during the civil war – the reality of its pressure is apt to be appreciated with great immediacy, thus undermining its capacity to sustain effective application of military force in pursuit of national objectives.

Depending on the circumstance, this incapacitation may be consequent upon two systemic backlashes: (a) Embargo on arms, munitions and spare parts, and (b) Political and diplomatic isolation. First, to the extent that Nigeria deploys military systems that are externally acquired and serviced – because the requirements to use them exceed those achieved in the overall level of its civilian economy – then its capacity to utilize military force diminishes if the arms suppliers adjudge such a course of action inimical to their strategic or geo-political interests. This has been one from the experience of the civil war her traditional suppliers of arms – U.S and Britain – in conjunction with their alliers in NATO imposed total embargoes on weapons sales and ammunition for arms purchased before the war[24].

Second, adverse and virulent "world public opinion" may result in the political and diplomatic isolation of Nigeria, thus profoundly undermining its strategic and economic objectives in continental affairs (ECOWAS in particular). This has been the cardinal lesson of Libya in Chad and it is also a specter that would probably have confronted the administration of Shagari if Nigeria had forcefully and unilaterally annexed the disputed territory with Cameroun in May 1981. From this view, if Nigeria flagrantly flouts an internationally sanctioned restraint on military aggression, it may, in the event of success, gain the object of military action but it may also tarnish its mediatory role in intra-African conflicts and provoke attitudes of suspicion and hostility that over the long run may become organized politically, and perhaps militarily as well as the stand-off with Cameroun over the Bakassi suggest.

The implications of the preceding considerations inevitably sensitizes Nigeria's decision-makers to the "costs" imposed by adverse "world public opinion" when considering a military alternative to diplomacy or sanctions. Admittedly, these "cost" are "uncertain to predict", hard to estimate at the moment of decision" and, besides, may only become evident (in political terms) over the longer run. Nevertheless, as a number of commentators have rightly asserted, since any decision to use military force by Nigeria will be most likely directed against a country supported by one (e.g. France and the Francophone West African States) or all of the Western countries, the probability of hostile backlash by these countries becomes an irreducible dilemma which any Nigerian government cannot safely ignore. It is this fact of the probability of an intervention by extra-regional actors in intra-African conflict that constitutes the next set of systemic restraints to the use of Nigerian military power.

(II) EXTERNAL INTERVENTION

From the standpoint of intervening actors, intra-regional conflicts in Africa threatens the *status quo* and as a consequence either generate anxiety among those powers whose economic and strategic interests are mortally at stake or present novel opportunities for new arrivals on the scene. For the former group in particular, since wars on the continental are preeminent catalyst of social change which is fundamentally unpredictable, their concern for the preservation of the *status quo* is generally to be expected, as "no situation is more threatening to nations than one whose outcome has become so uncertain as to have moved beyond their control[25]. The use of military force by Nigeria, whether to punish and subdue irritant neighbours or in pursuit of a wider security objective shares (ECOMOG in Liberia and Sieria and Leone) these uncertain and unpredictable properties and is, therefore, bound to provoke a direct or indirect counteraction from extra-regional powers whose interests will inevitably be affected.

Nigeria's so-called francophone neighbours – Cameroun, Chad, Nigeria, Benin – maintain a variety of defence accords with France, providing for French military advice, training, arms and operational assistance in the event of conflict with a third party. These series of accords are in turn sustained by a specialist *Force d'intervention* available in Southern France to serve at short notice as a mobile reserve[26]. The possible intervention of these forces in any conflict involving Nigeria in the West African sub-zone has become a pivotal factor in Nigeria's strategic policy on Africa has been to stem the spread of Nigeria's influence in West Africa. Consequently, from past records, the French, it is evident, have experimented with various strategies aimed at undermining the emergency of Nigeria as a formidable regional power center "around which indigenous interests can coalesce in relative security and autonomy"[27]. One of these strategies – balkanization – was forcefully dramatized during the civil war, when French assistance sustained the secessionist forces till the end of the war.

At the continental level, external intervention as a restraint on the use of Nigerian military power becomes even more problematic, given the intractable complexity and Byzantine nature of African politics and condition. A condition that sometimes sees such strange-bedfellows as Tanzania, South Africa, Portugal, Rhodesia and Zambia, Senegal, Ivory Coast, and United States sanctioning South Africa's intervention in Angola while at the same time, castigating Soviet-Cuban intervention as a new and potentially unmanageable form of imperialism. It is this shifting pattern of alignment and realignment and the powerful extra-regional involvement they portend that constitute a profound restraint to any decision to project Nigeria's military power beyond its borders.

Finally, the variable and intractable restraint which systemic pressure exercise on both the frequency and intensity of the utility of the Nigerian military as a rational, national and viable instrument of policy does not reside only in normative considerations or the interventionary tendencies of extra-regional powers, but also fundamentally, in the increasing 'cost of conquest'. Figuratively speaking, "victory", as Bernard Brodie reminds us, "is not success"[28].

CONCLUSION

As posited in the preamble, the central concern of this paper revolves around a pivotal set of interrelated factors (domestic and systemic) which impact on Nigeria's military policy: the complex and extensive array of restraints on the use and usability of Nigeria's military power as an instrument of policy. These restraints essentially represent prevalent tendencies which affects, but do *not determine* government behaviour. In the crucial issue of 'war and peace', actual or manifest behaviour of any government is always subject to a host of particular circumstances. Considerations of honour and atavistic forces of nationalism may sometimes override rational 'cost-benefit' calculation (e.g., Tanzania's response to the provocation of Amin Uganda; and the Anglo-Argentine war over the Falklands/Malvinas Islands).

Thus, as Huntington has succinctly argued, military policy (i.e. "the relation of force to national purposes") is not always the result of logic but politics: "more an arena than unity"[29]. Any theory or hypothesis, therefore, that tries to reduce a reality as complex as the range of restraints on the use of Nigeria's military power analysed above to single causative factors may be elegant in its explanatory simplicity, but it is apt to do violence to the known facts of Nigeria's recent history. In other words, considered independently, these restraints factors cannot be said to represent trends that are insurmountably strong and universally coherent in Nigeria's decision-making process concerning the use of force.

Seen in general terms, however, the following conclusion is arguably pertinent. The potency of any one set or combination of these sets of restraints (domestic and systemic) on any Nigerian government's decision to use force depends not only on the vitality of the issue to its security but also on the actor in its strategic environment involved. If the actor involved is any one of Nigeria's midget neighbours, then the decision to use or not to use force will be predicated less upon the factor of military capability than on diplomatic or political ramifications for Nigeria on the continent. Conversely, irrespective of the vitality of issues involved, Nigeria's military response to a powerful regional (e.g. Libya or South Africa) or extra-regional (e.g. France in West-Central Africa) adversary would be subject to a host of internal (e.g. military capability, outlay of international liquidity etc.) or external (e.g. sanctions on weapons and munitions supply) restraints which may paralyze the political will of its decision-makers as was the case with the situation in Zambia in 1979.[30]

Nevertheless, given Nigeria's economic, scientific and technological potentials – assuming the will and competence at the leadership level – these pervasive restraints are not a fixed constant but subject to change over time. In hypothetical terms, for example, if the present commitment of its decision-makers to build a viable military-industrial base by the end of the century yields the expected result, then Nigeria's exercise of independent initiative on matters relating to war and peace will arguably be less subject to adverse systemic forces than is currently the case. However, the persistent crisis of regime legitimacy compounded by structural deformities of the social order has made even the most guarded projection concerning industrialization in Nigeria an extremely fickle (if not fatuous) exercise in futility.

REFERENCES

1. B. Akinterinwa, Nigeria's National Interests in a Globalising World. Ibadan: Bolytag, 2007.
2. K. Knorr, The War Potential of Nations. Connecticut: Greenwood Press, 1972:12.
3. C. Reynolds, Theory and International Politics. London: Martin Robertson, 1973.
4. O. Aluko, Essays on Nigeria's Foreign Policy. London: Allen and Unwin, 1981 and G. Olusanya and R. Akindele eds. The structure and Processes of Foreign Policy Making and Implementation in Nigeria, 1960-1990. Ibadan: Vantage, 1990.
5. C. Bassey, "Nigeria's Defence Policy in Future Continental Order" Nigerian Journal of International Affairs 13: 1987, 83-105.
6. See J. Rosenau, The Scientific Study of Foreign Policy. New York: The Free Press, 1971
7. Northedge, The Use of Force in International Relations. London: Faber and Faber, 1974.
8 Fasehun O. "Nigeria and the Issue of an African High Command" Africa Spectrum, 38/3 (15 Jahrang) 309-315 and J. Garnett "The Role of Military Powers" in John Baylis et. al. Contemporary Strategy N.Y.: Holmes and Meier.,

1980. Also see Hitch, C. (1965) Decision-Making for Defence. Berkeley: University of California Press.

9. Sotunobi A. (1981) Nigeria's Recognition of the MPLA Government of Angola: A Case-Study in Decision Making and Implementation, Lagos: NIIA Monograph Series, No.9 and J. Stremlau. (1977). The International Politics of Nigerian Civil War, 1967-1970. Princeton: Princeton University Press.

10. Ogunsanwo A. (1980) The Nigerian Military and Foreign Policy, 1975 – 1979. Princeton University: Centre of International Studies.

11. O. S. Kamanu, "Nigeria: Reflections on the Defence Posture for the 1980s "Geneve-Afrique Vol. 16, No.1, 1977-78:

12. B. Onimode, A. Political Economy of African Crisis. London: zed, 1988.

13. H. Kissinger, The Troubled Partnership, NY: McGrow Hill, 1965:51.

14. (1992) "Defence Planning and the Nigerian Armed Forces Modernisation Process, 1970-1991: An Institutional 1970-1991: An Institutional Analysis" **Armed Forces and Society** 1992:253 – 277 and C. Bassey, "Nigeria in ECOMOG: The Dilemma of Preventive Diplomacy" in J. Owoeye (eds) Nigeria in International Institutional Institutions. Ibadan: College Press, 1993.

15. J. B. Adekanye "Domestic Production of Arms and the Defence Industries Corporation of Nigeria" *Current Research on Peace and Violence* Vol.4 (1983).

16. C. Bassey, "Nigeria's Quest for a Military – Industrial Complex". Journal of International Studies. Vol. 12. 1988:55. and C. Bassey, "Defence and Strategic Policy in Nigeria's Relations with its Immediate Neighbours" in B. Ate and B. Akinterinwa (eds) *Nigeria and its Immediate Neighbours, Constraints and Prospects of Sub-regional Security in the 1990s,* Lagos, Pumark.

17. K. Knorr. The Power of Nations N.Y.: Basic Books, 1975.

18. O. Aluko, Essays, on Nigeria's Foreign Policy. London: Allen and Unwin, 1981

19. S. Huntngton, The Common Defence N.Y.: Columbia University Press, 1966 see also Huntington, Political Political Order in Changing Societies. N.H.: Yale University Press, 1972.

20. S. Enke Defence Management, Englewood-Cliffs: Frentice – Hall, 1967 and Enthoven, A and Wayne – Smith. K. *How Much Is Enough* N.Y: Harper and Row, 1971.

21. See J. Rosenau, Linkage Politics N.Y.: The Free Press, 1969. Shaw. T. and Aluko. O. Nigeria Foreign Policy. London: Macmillan, 1983.

22. K. Knorr, On the Use of Military Power in the Nuclear Age Princeton: Princeton University Press, 1966:66.

23. K. Knorr, The War Potential of Nations, Connecticut: Greenwood Press, 1972:61.

24. O. Obasanjo My Command London: Heineman, 1981.

25. Rosenau J.N. (1964) International Aspects of Civil Strife Princeton: Princeton University Press.

26. A. Gavshon Crisis in Africa. Harmonswirth: Penguin, 1983.

27. B. E. Ate, "The Presence of France in West Central Africa as a Fundamental Problem to Nigeria" Millenium: Journal of International Studies 12, 2, (Summer, 1983): 21.

28. B. Brodie, War and Politics. London: Colher, 1973.

29. S. Hintington, The Common Defence, op.cit : 3.

30. See E. Koladziej and Harky R. (eds) 1982,Security Policies of Developing Countries, Lexington: Lexinton, 1982 and H. Nelson Nigeria: A Country Study, Washington: American University Press, 1992.

CHAPTER 30

MILITARY STRATEGY AND DOCTRINES

G. O. ENAHORO

PREAMBLE

The term "Military Strategy" presupposes that there is a main stem subject (General Strategy) out of which the military branch grew. Alternatively and considering the accepted norm in the society that is generally viewed with the prism of civil-military affairs, it suggests the existence of a parallel branch or body of knowledge known as "Civil Strategy". These two views are neither completely right nor wrong, as we shall see later on. Just that we should at least, take note of the universal trend whereby the civil society is progressively militarized and the military is being civilianized, each segment seeking to influence decisions in the other.

At some point in time, it has to be somebody's business to do the cost-benefit analysis of military actions, vis-à-vis other options available to states for the conduct of inter-state relations and internal security operations, which is the purview of grand strategy. At the stage, the burden on national resources, both human and materials, becomes clearer and the convenience of selected option is an important as its effectiveness; particularly when the trend is towards holistic conception of security. Grand strategy makes it obvious that it is the political, rather than the military objectives of war that dominates long term and wider scope national planning.

In military strategy, as in grand strategy, clichés and concepts that appear simple are always used but that does not mean that they are easy to understand or even appreciate. As Garnett observed, "when strategists talk of 'taking our' cities, of making 'counterforce' strikes with 'collateral damage' of crossing 'threshold' and of engaging in tactical nuclear 'exchanges' .... It is easy to forget that what is being discussed in such clinical fashion is the extermination of thousands – perhaps millions – of human beings by the most dreaded weapon ever invented"[1]. Understanding military strategy should, therefore, be a conscious effort of national leadership, and we need a clear beginning, such as this paper seeks to present.

This chapter is in two parts. It begins with conceptual discourse, by highlighting the regimes of military strategy, irrespective of any presumption to a given level of knowledge of strategic studies. This part examines the nature and definition of military strategy, its evolution, development, and elements. The import of the segment is to provide a theoretical framework on which military strategy revolves and serve as a prerequisite to analyzing military strategic environment, which is covered in the second part.

THE SPHERE OF MILITARY STRATEGY

Strategy in its early conception has to do with the planning and overall conduct of wars and this view still enjoys popular acceptance. The origin of the word itself, gives it the macho impression. Momah contends that the Greek root, Strategos, translates to "the art of war" or "the art of generalship", which perhaps, influenced the author's definition of strategy as "the management of an army or armies in a campaign, or the art of moving troops and war arsenals, so as to impose on the enemy at preferred place, time and conditions for fighting"[2].

Assuming that the planning and conduct of wars are all that strategy entails, the nature of war would still have influence on the one selected. War should, however, be seen beyond fighting isolated pitched battles, far removed from the centres. It follows that the instruments for setting wars should equally look further a field. It is, perhaps, within this context that Clausewitz defined strategy as "the employment of battle as the means towards the attainment of object of war"[3].

Whereas this definition still emphasized the physical dimension of strategy and the military means employed , it at least, further stimulates thought about "why we fight" or what the author refers to as "the object of war". There is therefore, the need to understand the nature of war. Wright distinguished between war's four manifestations, the military or physical, the psychological, the juridical or legal and the sociological manifestation.[4] Each of these manifestations demands different emphasis in the employment of means. Liddlell Hart explored Helmoth Von Moltke's definition of strategy as the "practical adaptation of the means placed at the General's disposal for the attainment of the object in view". Hart, therefore, sees strategy as "the art of distributing and applying military means to fulfill the end of policy" [5]. Military means is of course the same thing as "the means placed at a General's disposal" that enables him to cope with all dimensions of war. The nature of the "object in view" which Hart refers to as "the end of policy" influences the choice of military force and also determines how best to employ same. It is, therefore, absolutely essential that those who frame strategies should equally understand policy making process.

It is in this regard that one accepts Osgood's suggestion that "military strategy must now be understood as nothing less than the overall plan for utilizing the capacity for armed coercion in conjunction with the economic, diplomatic, and psychological instrument of state power, to support foreign policy most effectively by overt, covert, and tacit means"[6].

In that respect, military strategy should be seen as the optimum utilization of state power in pursuit of national interests. State power is the aggregation of national means in furtherance of war efforts, while national interests relates to the summation of values that are considered vital, major or critical to nation survival. Osgood's definition stretches the realm of military strategy beyond the restricted purview of Generals, perhaps in agreement with current belief that war is too much a pastime to be left to Generals alone.

EVOLUTION OF MILITARY STRATEGY

Before proceeding to highlight some milestones in the evolution of military strategy, it is important to consider the core elements, in Osgood's definitions of strategy, which is "the employment of military means to fulfill ends of policy". This reminder should, at the least, Serve as caution in tracing the origin of military strategy to the Stone Age, when war activities terminated with victory at the battlefields and Generals had, no business, analyzing policies or their political implications.

Stone Age, however, marked the identification of the elements of force in the formulation of strategy. Force, probably still remains, the most important instrument available to all states for the prosecution of conflicts. It can be inferred, for example, that what is today considered as the "strategy of brute force" and to some degree, that of "coercion", were established on the principle of the use of force. According to Beridge "force relates to the seizure or holding of an objective without regard to the wishes of an opponent whereas coercion relate to hurting or threatening an opponent in order to make him or her change his or her mind"[7]. The difference lies in taking what you want and making someone give it to you; between fending off assault and making someone afraid to assault you….". Both brute force and coercion strategies evolved from the study of campaigns from the earliest times and from the compilation on military thoughts that is generally traced to men like Sun Tzu, Thucydides, and Machiavelli.

The Napoleonic era is, nevertheless, generally considered as the appropriate starting point for the study of military strategy. The era witnessed the dawn and practicalization of the traditional strategy that is directed towards the swift and complete destruction of the enemy's fighting force in order to dissuade him from further resistance. Napoleonic strategy, as the traditional strategy of the era is generally called, is really a variant of brute force strategy, and is most suitably employed by a strong state wile confronting a weaker one. The strategy gave vent to "the doctrine of mass armies" through universal conscription that assures a continuous flow of personnel replacement and lowers risks in battle. Another doctrine traceable to this era is "the doctrine of concentrating superior force against the decisive point" or what became known as "hitting the underbelly or the center of gravity of the opposing armies", which itself led to such other doctrines as "offensive operations", "cunning manoeuvre "and" vigorous pursuit. "These were largely continental or more appropriately, land warfare strategies, and doctrines that were designed to cope with problems posed by new technologies beginning from the early nineteenth century. Military theorists like Henri Jomini and Karl Von Clausewitz, who are regarded as "the first modern strategists", are associated with the Napoleonic era.[8].

The industrial revolution, which arose from technological development and capitalism, made land warfare more deadly and (to all appearances), made advanced societies more fragile, principally because they depended on international markets and supplies. This brought into focus the utility of the sea, known to be four times the size of the land, and which served until then, both as facilitator and great barrier to interaction between the segmented landmasses.

Daniel Moran noted, that "Sailing navies were the instruments by which European empires were created...the basic role of navies in war, was to disrupt the sea borne commerce of the other side while protecting their own trade[9]. Alfred T. Mahan thus proposed what he called "sea power" which he considered as the key to world's history, and the central feature of modern war. "The command of the sea strategy", which evolved therein, aimed at defeating the enemy fleet, either by crushing it in battle, which is the "fleet action doctrine" or bottling it up in harbours that is "the doctrine of blockade"[10].

THE IMPACT OF INDUSTRIAL REVOLUTIONS

Over the years, the implementation of the "Napoleonic strategy" in wars has encountered some difficulties that are traceable, first to changes in technology, which confer on nation state, the capacity of bringing apparently infinite supplies of men and materials to the battle areas and secondly, weapons explosion that was a fall-out of technological growth. A major snag of the Napoleonic strategy is that decisions are reached only after prolonged period of mutual attrition out of fall proportion to the issue(s) at stake, at the conclusion of which, both the victor and the vanquished emerge from the conflict, completely exhausted.

A close study of the French revolution, the American Civil War and the First World War, revealed some credibility gaps in the employment of the "Napoleonic Strategy". The strategy is considered not particularly decisive when the war is between wealthy, industrialized and relatively evenly matched powers. Furthermore, throughout the cold war era and even now with the proliferation of nuclear capabilities, the strategy seems a rather suicidal proposition.

It equally proved unhelpful when confronted by unconventional methods of warfare, such as was apparent in Vietnam, Afghanistan, Zimbabwe and Algeria. All these notwithstanding, "Napoleonic Strategy" still has appeal in modern conflicts when the dispute is between a great power or multinational force against a delinquent state such as soviet's invasion of Hungary (1951) and Czechoslovakia (1968); the United State invasion of Grenada (1983), Panama (1989) Iraq (2003); and the ECOMOG intervention in Liberia (1990-1997) and Sierra Leone.

In spite of the flaws in the Napoleonic strategy, states will continue to employ it. Some modern battles in which the strategy was employed include indo-Pakiston conflicts (1947-48, 1965 & 1971); Arab –Israeli wars (1948, 1956, 1967 & 1973); Turkey occupation of modern Cyprus (1974); South African invasion of Angola (1975); Vietnam, occupation of Kampuchea (1978); and British recapture of South Georgia and Falkland Island (1982).

TOTAL WAR STRATEGY

The "Napoleonic Strategy" descended into "Total War Strategy" of the 20th century, which mobilizes a nation's entire military arsenal. It is marked by the induction of aircrafts and missiles. Indeed, the most striking military innovation of the early twentieth century and one whose theoretical implications have proven exceptionally challenging, is war in the air. The Ubiquitousness of air power is self-evident from the fact that the air space covers both the earth's land and water masses. "The command of the air, "which strategy was first made popular by and Italian artillery officer, Giulio Douhet, thus became inseparable from, if not the determining factor in, modern warfare. Arising from the evolution of air power are such doctrines as "strategic bombing" which focuses on the destruction of enemy's war industries and civil infrastructures over an extended period; "pre-emptive strike" which aims at destroying enemy's air assets before they are made operational against own forces; and "air-land battle", which relies on gaining overwhelming air superiority against enemy forces as a prelude to the commitment of ground forces[11].

THE PREVENTIVE WAR STRATEGY

The awesomeness of modern warfare and the quest for the preservation of humanity led to the search for a total solution to conflicts in the form of preventive war strategy. In the words of Bernard Brodie, preventive war is "a premeditated attack by one country against another, which is unprovoked in the sense that it does not wait upon specific aggression or other overt action by the target state, and in which the chief and most immediate objective is the destruction of the latter's over-all military power and especially its strategic air power". In other words, preventive war strategy aims at immobilizing the adversary's war capabilities. The doctrines of "counter-force targeting", "preemptive strikes", "Massive retaliation and a "star war" are all developed to facilitate the preventive war strategy.

INDIRECT APPROACH STRATEGY

The "Indirect Approach" Strategy is yet another variant of the brute force strategy and, has itself, given rise to the strategy of "Protracted" or "Revolutionary War". Berridge asserts that the essence of "Indirect Approach" is "to avoid immediate battle and instead to aim at the dislocation of the enemy's force by movement and surprise" such that at best will make battle unnecessary while at worst it will so weaken the enemy that when battle is finally joined, victory will be more economically purchased". Indirect Approach, which is an alluring strategy for the "weaker power" has Liddell Hart as its more renowned modern advocate.

A classic example of the adoption of the indirect approach strategy in recent times is its employment in the War of Attrition, July 1967- August 1970. That war was principally an artillery battle between Israel and Egypt across the Suez Canal. The Israeli military employed the strategy, using the doctrines of "commando raids" and "deep penetration bombing" to offset the adversary's battlefield superiority when they discovered that the Egyptian artillery outgunned them[12].

The advent of the submarine in sea warfare, which rescued "commerce raiding" from the dustbin of history, and turned it into what appeared for a while to be war-winning strategy, drew inspiration from the indirect approach strategy.

PROTRACTED WAR STRATEGY

The "Protracted" or Revolutionary War" strategy retains the essence of "Indirect Approach" but differs in three aspects. First, it emphasizes more on the use of irregular forces or guerrillas; secondly, high importance is placed on winning over the civil population; and thirdly, efforts are geared towards to demoralization and physical exhaustion of the enemy as a prelude to his defeat. The "Revolutionary War" Strategy is a 20th century phenomenon and its most outstanding exponent is, Mao Zedong. It has found disciples among indigenous movements in African States such as Sudan, Ethiopia, Uganda, Liberia, Democratic Republic of Congo, Rwanda and Burundi, with varying levels of success[13].

The revolutionary war strategy is associated with political movements, rather than states; although a conquered state could employ the strategy against an occupation force such as Ethiopia did against the Fascist Italy during the Second World War. According to Beaufre, the strategy "can only succeed if the issue at stake is of far greater importance to one side than the other as in the wars of colonial Liberation" or if a movement receives assistance from regular armed forces to which it acts as an auxiliary, as the case of the Arab revolt, and in Vietnam.

COERCIVE STRATEGY

The general advance in human knowledge, which is enhanced by technological revolution, shows that it is possible to forestall attack by convincing a potential aggressor that the costs of the action, which he contemplates, will substantially outweigh any possible gain. This is the basis of the "coercive strategy", a form of which is, the "strategy of deterrence ". Although not new, the strategy of deterrence gained currency with the advent of nuclear, biological and chemical warfare and the inter continental ballistic missiles. The horrors of the atomic bombs, which were first dropped in Japan in 1945, and the knowledge that those are child's play, compared with later day invention, appear to strengthen the aura built around the strategy of deterrence[14].

Whether in its early and simple form, or in its present awesomeness with infinitely diverse weapons' delivery system, the strategy of deterrence requires credibility, capacity and communication for effectiveness.

INTRA WAR STRATEGY

With the advancement in information technology, very little is left to conjecture about intentions and capabilities of state and their attitudes to war', hence the need for intra war strategy or coercive bargaining; 'Coercive bargaining' sometimes known as "compellence" or even "coercive diplomacy" entails either the threat of pain or the causing of pain, in the attempt to persuade an enemy to conform to one's will. The strategy offers the possibility of achieving one's objective economically with the little bloodshed. In its offensive mode, coercive bargaining, aims at forcing the enemy to surrender territory, whereas in the defensive, it requires the enemy to suspend an invasion that is already in progress. In conventional warfare, the strategy is particularly associated with pinpoint aerial destruction of key installations as ECOMOG did to the ships at the harbour in Freetown, in furtherance of the enforcement of ECOWAS embargo on Sierra Leone. In total war, the strategy may involve the actual dropping of Atomic bomb on a strategic target as the United States did in Hiroshima and Nagasaki during the Second World War, which could be said to have accelerated the Japanese surrender.

THE COLD WAR AND MILITARY STRATEGY

Some of the strategies and doctrines that took root during the cold war era such as "deterrence" "limited war; and "flexible response" have already been mentioned. Another idea that evolved then is "crisis management", which relates to providing techniques for handling disputes. The context, in which the term "management" is used along side "crisis" connotes control and design of crises, rather than in the true meaning of the word.

The "doctrine of containment" was also given fillip by the cold war as the old battle for the Eurasian Heartland, assumed a new dimension. Over the ages, continental military strategies were weaved around the truism that "who controls the Eurasian Heartland governs the world" and that gravitated to the sea power theory of "who governs the sea governs the world" because he governs the Eurasian Heartland. Of course, it was realized that you have to be a maritime power to rule the sea, which gave vent to "the Rimland theory "and so, denying access to all-season seas, which was what the containment doctrines was about, became the preoccupation of the big powers. The doctrine of containment has since expanded to include limiting adversary's cause of action in pursuit of individual state's or groups interests.

NEW TRENDS IN MILITARY STRATEGY

Strategies that are being employed since the thawing of East/West hostilities are bound to change with changes in the global order. Garuba cautions that as the world move into a new millennium, the concern for international peace and security would continue to grow and incidents of inter-and intra-states conflicts would be unabated. In addition, there would be new pressures on international co-operation, peace and security. The profound structural changes, combined with what appears to be a turbulent crisis in the inter-state system, call for a re-examination of the global mechanisms (strategies) for the management of international security.

Already, new concepts are emerging and these include "multinational intervention", which relates to coordinated military actions against a sovereign state; "peaceful coexistence", which relates to mutual respect for sovereignty and capabilities to a tolerable level to allow for mutual confidence; and "security conference", which relates to adoption of processes where strategic issues are mutually analyzed and consensus arrived at, to lessen international tension. This trend will continue far into the 21st Century[15].

ELEMENTS OF MILITARY STRATEGY

A careful examination of most social phenomena suggests that strategies that are employed would differ to the extent of the differences in some basic elements in the environment and the actors. Some of the most pronounced of these elements are geography, psychology, international politics, technology and military force. A strategy that ignores any of these elements would most certainly be inappropriate and ineffective. We would, therefore, briefly consider how these elements impact on military strategy.

GEOGRAPHY

The element of geography – human and physical – eases, as well as multiplies, the military difficulties of States. A landlocked nation, for example, may not have any need for acquiring naval power nor worry about sea-borne invasion; but she is hamstrung from power projection and would not benefit from massive importation that only sea passage assures. A maritime nation, on the other hand, could aspire to "rule the world" through power projection by its acquisition of sea power; but she will remain susceptible to sea-born threats and challenges to her national shipping.

A nation that is surrounded by potential enemies faces a situation in which the outcome of war would most likely be decided by the opening moves. Such a state could be said to live a psychological cocoon and has no option than to adopt the doctrine of "flexible response", which relates to the military preparedness to react to adversary moves. The state may also have to adopt pre-emptive strategy, as has become the pattern in Arab-Israeli relations.

PSYCHOLOGY

Man dominates strategic thinking because only he has the ability to formulate and execute policies and plans and feel the brunt of these. His interests are, therefore, crucial to military strategy. National character and political / military leadership thus become crucial factors in the formulation of military strategy. Of more significance, however, is the mind and behaviour of man as he kills, maims and destroys or get killed, maimed and destroyed. Thus, at the level of implementation of strategy, there is usually a distinction between the actions of the "rational" from the "irrational" man. It is important to take note that the element of psychology permeates all the processes of strategy formulation.

It is safe, perhaps, to take for granted, the general knowledge that military strategy is all about inter-states relations, which makes gaining knowledge of International politics a fait accompli. International politics relates to the activities of classes of states (great powers, regional powers socialist states, liberal democracies, and so on) and other non-states actors such as the United Nations and multinational corporations; the means that these bodies commonly employ in pursuit of their policies, such as propaganda; and the rules and institutions of the "state system" within which these states and other organs more or less willingly operate[15]. When people advocate the doctrine of self-sufficiency or looking inward, for example, they must do so by first considering the effect on outward events, which could propel counter-actions.

TECHNOLOGY

The knowledge of international politics is made more complex by technological revolution that has turned the world into a global village. Globalization implies introducing fluidity into human endeavours while remaining conscious of events that occur, elsewhere. This development calls for the creation of effective Command, Control, Communication, Computer, Intelligence, and Information (C^4I^2) system. Technological revolution is indeed, seen as the main driving force behind modern strategy. The sheer pace of armament development is awesome enough, for strategists who must, hereafter, battle hard to match doctrines with available weapons and their delivery systems.

The strategy of deterrence, for example, is predicated on the military capabilities of states, which are enhanced by technology. The credibility of forces available, and the understanding that an adversary is well aware of the repercussion of ignoring threats that, are inherent. The strategies of "disarmament" and "arms control" on the other hand, seek to assure a safer world, in spite of technological evolution. The strategy of limited war is largely predicated on the impact of technology on human existence[16].

MILITARY FORCE

In the formulation of military strategies, it is necessary to take into account both ones own and the adversary's military capabilities, which are built around the military force or indeed, military power of the state. Although military preponderance cannot always be translated into battlefield victory, the element of force is known to be at the background of most political actions. This explains why the level of force adopted by states, differs with the strategies adopted. The "Napoleonic Strategy' acknowledges the need for restraint of the force employed; while the strategy of 'coercion' recognizes the possibility of attaining the objectives, with force at the background.

FRAMEWORK FOR MILITARY STRATEGIC POSTURING

Before focusing on the application of military strategy in a given environment, we can now summarize the framework. It has been averred that military strategy, since it first evolved, has undergone some metamorphosis; just like the means (military power) and the ends (policy objectives) it seeks to relate. At all material times, military strategy remains the purview of conceptual minds, and must go beyond the technical details of military problems. Military strategists must, therefore, strive to keep pace with the increasing wealth and organizational power of states and apparently bottomless cornucopia of technological innovation that was first opened up by the industrial revolution and is now made more awesome by the Computer Age. As military power almost equates state power, military strategy now plays a vital role in national survival.

The means or military power that the military strategists employ, should therefore, be seen beyond the physical capabilities to cope with wars, since wars equally manifest in the sociological, juridical, and psychological dimensions. Military strategy is never employed in isolation. In fact, it is only one, of the mechanism available to states for the conduct of international politics. Somehow, the thought of war, the threat of it, the need to prevent it, and the desire for victory seem to underpin other instruments of inter states relations, which is why the theories of peace and security, realism, moral neutrality and rationality underpins strategic assumptions. In any case, military strategy should be planned in peacetime, as well as in wartime, giving consideration always to the various manifestations of war.

Military strategy concerns the interaction of the military with democracy or form of government, as it grapples with international politics and systemic and non-systemic and non-state actors in the international system. Strategies must reflect national power rating, largely modulated by the level of technology of the era.

APPLICATION OF MILITARY STRATEGY

NIGERIA AND THE INTERNATIONAL COMMUNITY

When one sets out to examine an instrument of state power, it is considered reasonable to begin from the time the state itself evolved, even if that instrument predates the state. Talking of the military in Nigeria, for example, will only make sense if it is limited to independent Nigeria. There is perhaps the need to re-emphasize the fact that independent Nigeria evolved into a world that was divided by ideology: and found itself in the Western orbit, by default of colonial heritage. As a western nation, she was not considered hostile to the Soviet cause because of the disposition of a visible segment of its political class. On the other hand, the nation's commitment to the liberation struggles in Africa and freedom from apartheid rule in South Africa was such that made whatever pretensions to capitalism as of official ideology, tolerable to the hard-core communists. Conversely, the initial prevarication on non-violent struggle was also acceptable to the West.

Moreover, Nigeria's membership of the Non-Align Movement made her a theoretical bystander in the cold war. The nation's power potentials, based on the analysis of such elements as (geography including size of landmass and population) national character, natural resources and military force, ensure that both superpowers consulted with her on most issues relating to Africa. African states, observably, acquiesced to the country's continental leadership. The regional leadership claim was facilitated by the fact that Egypt was pre-occupied with Arab-Israeli conflicts and South Africa's apartheid policy made her a pariah in international politics; thus side-tracking two viable contenders.

The position has since altered although Egypt continues to have dual component to Africa and Arab causes with more emphasis on the latter, while the rainbow power coloration in South Africa, remains a distraction in that country's relationship with other African States. Just as the situation in Africa has altered, the world now appears to have put bipolarity behind her and is heading towards multi-centrism with several power nodules although many will argue that there is unipolarity in place. The International system is learning to cope with the sole surviving superpower, whose political leadership vow to keep the United States in global leadership for the interests and the "values of civilization" which she vows to preserve by force, if necessary, happens to include good government, human right and access to strategic resources such as oil. The United States national interests would, to that extent, often be in conflict with those of Nigeria.

The reality of the time is that the world offers very limited options to nations outside the United State orbit. The so-called G-7 is in league with the European Union, which many analysts consider as an extension of the United State cartel. France occasionally mutters dissent. Japan once unsuccessfully tried a stand off but could not go far because she sources all her industrial input externally, which makes her very susceptible to the hegemony's dictates.

The ASEAN countries are still brooding over what they consider the United States tingling of their economy towards the close of the last century for reason, which could be no more, than showing off, who the actual "boss" is. Those newly industrialized states need market for their products far in excess of the 1% that all of Africa, shares in world trade. China enjoys the United States' and European's most-favoured-nation status, in return for 'opening up' and no one knows how much she can afford to toy with that arrangement. The Russian Federation has virtually lost its allies in the Commonwealth of independent Soviet States to the United States led North Atlantic Treaty Organization. She had to make a face saving acceptance speech of the trend, as she grapples with internal contradictions. Non-state actors including the U.N. and A. U. are assuming greater roles in international politics but are not themselves free from the machination of the big powers. This is the world in which Nigeria and other African States must chart their strategic course; and this is the reality of the International environment so critical to military strategy that some commentators always choose to ignore[17].

NIGERIA'S MILITARY CHALLENGES

Nigeria shares land borders with countries whose military forces, individually or collectively, should not, on their own, pose credible military threat. There is, however, the fact that all these neighbours have military pact with France, which analysts claim has economic interests in Nigeria in excess of her entire investments' in all Francophone African countries combined. For that reason, it is often argued that France cannot risk a war with Nigeria, simply to satisfy expressed intention in a treaty. It is, however, a know fact that economic consideration is not the sole criterion for going to war. The chances of multinational military intervention led by the United States and France, appear quite frightening although there are analysts who will write that suggestion off, for its improbability. One shares that view, but for a different reason from what most critics contend. Some people argue that because the United States failed in Vietnam, she will also fail in Nigeria and one considers such reasoning preposterous, porous and illogical. The Vietnam experience is several years behind and the Vietnamese nationalism is legendary and the lessons are not lost to military strategy.

The improbability of United States' led multinational military intervention stems from the same reason why France will not intervene on the side of her Francophone allies. The world is better off without another 'Zone of Turmoil" which could continue to drain the resources of developed and developing nations. Any planned invasion of Nigeria will amount to creating a 'Zone of Turmoil'. If any of her neighbours succeeds because Nigeria has failed to harness her resources, it is only a matter of time before a rematch. The only condition, under which any developed nation will choose to intervene on behalf of the neighbouring countries, is on the understanding that such move would lead to the permanent break-up of Nigeria.

There are those who imagine that breaking up Nigeria is to the advantage of some great powers that find in her, a contender. That could have been true before the Bosnia debacle. As it is, anyone will shudder to propose a strategy that could lead to countless republics without discernible boundaries, which would thereby encourage internecine conflicts in the region. Above all Nigeria's contributions to international peace and security, at least, in filling the gap for the great powers, could be lost to world.

The chances of any other African State invading Nigeria is even less probable. African countries with military forces that could pose credible threat do not share land frontiers, with Nigeria. Egypt, Morocco, Libya and South Africa that have worthwhile naval power, appear to equip their Navies solely for coastal defence. Furthermore, none of the African States has the capacity to support Nigeria's neighbours in a protracted war, which is bound to erupt from supported invasion. The neighbouring countries are themselves, not immune to reprisal actions if they allow other states the use of their territories for the invasion of Nigeria.

Military challenges to Nigeria, therefore , appear mainly limited to those that the nation chooses to get involved in, sequel to its multilateral and bilateral diplomacy. This was the basis of Nigeria's involvement in the various United Nations and African Union peacekeeping missions, and the intervention role she played in Liberia and Sierra Leone. There are of course, operations against internal dissenter. These might grow in the years to come, unless solutions are found to internal contradictions. The dimension and scope those challenges will assume in the years ahead, will remain a function of the nation's foreign and defence policies and the mechanisms emplaced for their implementation.

PAST PERFORMANCE ASSESSMENT: THE NIGERIA MILITARY

In furthermore of her defence policy, Nigeria has employed her military forces, applying diverse military strategies in the last 50 years or so. Forces were equally deployed for internal security operations as well as to the borders in a bid to check incursions over the years. The Nigeria military fought a Civil War, participated in nation building, and provided assistance to civil population in times of emergency.

The country sent military missions to Chad, Somalia, Tanzania, Burundi, Gambia, Sudan etc, and other parts of the world, sometimes under the aegis of the United Nations. Those nations typify the usage to which, the Nigeria Military could be put in support of the nation's political objectives.

What one is not too sure about is how well the forces really performed in these past missions as against the general encomium that is diplomatically paid to all those who risk their lives in the defence of others. In other words, how articulate has the nation's military power been projected: We need to know this in order to appreciate the adequacy of the foreign and defence policy and strategies that were employed.

From vantage observatory position of some three decades, one can, however, provide a few posers, which should guide a realistic assessment of the employment of military efforts in furtherance of national interests. First, in prosecuting the Nigerian Military's aid to civil authority and in giving assistance to the civil population in times of emergency of nation building, what has been the response rate? How much satisfaction has such participation given to the civil population? What professional satisfaction did the military men themselves derive from participation?

Secondly, the defence policy seeks to deter aggression against Nigeria and when deterrence fails, to prosecute the war to her advantage. How far has aggression along the international borders been deterred? How effectively did the military deal with Chad (1983) and Cameroon (1981-2004)?

Thirdly, the Nation took on itself, the functions of a regional hegemon. How smooth did her troops perform in Liberia and Sierra Leone? How many of the numerous problems were foreseen? Why were troops almost bugged down to the extent that a past field commander openly acknowledged that without external support, the last phase (disarmament phase) in Liberia would have ended in fiasco? There are too many more issues agitating the mind. One cannot be too critical in answering some of these because there are operational experiences that are removed from a detached analyst. Even those who would accept this as sufficient excuse or proposed same in defence of noticeable flaws, should at least, admit the fact that some military actions that were taken, might not have been in cognizance of the capabilities of the forces, the level of national integration, and the state of technological evolution. I guess that is the same thing as saying that military actions did not always seem to match the military strategy dictated by the events.

MILITARY STRATEGIC PLANNING AWARENESS

In retrospect, one can assert that Nigeria, like most other states, waits to react to events, which calls to question its strategic planning awareness. The proverbial notion that 'Nigerians are expert in crisis management, adapting the "fire brigade approach" is not helping issues. Fire Brigades can only help to ameliorate and not remove effects.

May be with such attitude, there is no need for strategic planning and there is no basis for awareness; but what is wrong in preventing fire out-breaks? Whose interests are served by preventable colossal losses? But that is what it seems when strategists are ignored, and processes are abandoned. In spite of this limitation, there are many reasons why the Nigerian planner, not just the military planner, is proving to be a strategic enigma. The planning and conduct of military missions' to–date support this notion. First, he knows he hails from a nation reputed to posses abundant resources that could be translated to power potentials and he goes ahead to behave as such, believing that potentialities equal power.

Secondly, the Nigerian planner, through acts of commission or omission, emits strategic messages that keep watchers wondering if political irrationality is not a deliberate policy or whether the country had actually enhanced messages communicated the signals are not taken seriously, and sometimes are ignored, or misunderstood. The actions, which follow, may, in deed, re-convey the massage that is not backed by actual power rating.

Fourthly, lack of internal cohesion, and indeed Nigeria's national contradictions paradoxically convey mixed signals to the international community, which gets restrained from taking counter-action to Nigeria's strategic moves. Unfortunately the pattern seems to encourage the Nigerian planner to continue with his abandonment of vital considerations. Fifthly, and perhaps more critical, is that strategic moves are made or contemplated that do not appear to take international politics into consideration or that ignore it for not too obvious reasons.

Some lessons that can be drawn from these brief highlights on observed lapses are:

a. Like in all decision-making processes, the formulation of military strategies should take full cognizance of the selection of goals, identification of means and recognition of capacity. Only then will there by a synergy between defence policy and its implementation strategies.

b. Potentialities are vital in formulation of strategies but the enhancement process should also be considered since potentials merely form inputs into strategic planning.

c. Basic theories and assumption cannot be ignored in formulating strategy and that, at all times.

d. Mechanism for monitoring the environment for strategic development is desirable at every stage.

e. Domestic cohesion is required to provide firm base for inputting strategies.

f. Adequate attention to international politics is desirable to avoid misperception.

g. Sentiment does not equate patriotism and indeed hampers the strategic formulation process.

CONCLUSION

How best does one conclude a lecture on "Military Strategy"? Efforts were made to show how military power, in its many facets, is employed for the attainment of defence policy objectives. Military Strategy has a language of its own, which always seems so simple yet it requires some conceptualization to appreciate and understand. The formulation of strategy should entail consideration of elements such as geography, international politics, level of technology, psychology and available military force.

The application of strategy is no less daunting and has proved rather challenging in multinational states like Nigeria which has slow pace of national integration, technological growth and economic development. The good thing is that the Nation has men and materials that are crucial to strategy, but there is clearly need for some strategic re-orientation because strategy cannot flow from a strategic vacuum.

REFERENCES

1. J. Garnett, Theories of Peace and Security London: Macmillan, 1970.
2. B. Liddell-Hart, Strategy – the Indirect Approach. London; Gaber and Faber, 1967.
3. Carl Von Clausewitz, On War, edited and translated by Michael Howard and Peter Paret, Princeton: Princeton University Press; a: 1976.
4. Quincy Wright, A Study of War. Chicago: Chicago University Press, 1964.
5. Liddell – Hart Op. Cit:10.
6. R. Osgood, "The Uses of Military Power in the Cold War" in Robert Godwin ed. America Armed, Chicago: Rand McNally, 1969.
7. See J. Keegan, A History of Warfare-London: PRIMLICO, 1994.
8. M. Howard War in European History. Oxford: Oxford University Press, 1976.
9. See P. Paret, Understanding War. NewJersy: Princeton University Press, 1992.
10. P. Paret ed. Makers of Modern Strategy New Jersy: Princeton University Press, 1986.
11. L. M. Paschall, Airforce Command and Control Systems, United States Air Force Magazine, SIGNAL, June 1973.
12. L. Williams, Israel Defence Force. Tel AVIN: Ministry of Defence, 1989.
13. See C. Legum et. Al. Africa in the 1980s: A continent in Crisis. NY: McGraw-Hill, 1979.
14. T. Schelling, Arms and Influence, New Haven: Yale University Press, 1966 and L. Freedman "Military Power and Political Influence "International Affairs, 74, 4 (1998) 762-779.
15. See W. Kaufmann and J. Steinbruner, Decisions for Defence: Prospects For a New Order: Washington D. C: The Brookings Institution, 1991 and R. Paarlberg, "Knowledge as Power" International Security Vol. 29, No. 1 (Summer 2004): 122-151.
16. L. Freedman, The Revolution in Strategic Affairs. Adelphi Paper 318, 1998.
17. See J. Stevenson, "Africa's Growing Strategic Resonance" Survival 45, 4, Winter 2003-2004: 153-172.

CHAPTER 31

CONTINENTAL STRATEGY AND ITS APPLICATION TO NIGERIA

M. S. SALEH

PREAMBLE

In the last two decades or thereabout, the global security environment has experienced relative peace most especially with the end of the Cold War. The peace that was long desired for was short-lived and laced with intra-State conflicts in most countries around the globe. Evidently, controversies and contests over essential resources continue to influence global issues, where state, sectional and group interests have remained central to the factors that drive the world. Thus, the use of war as an instrument of policy to resolve conflicts is bound to remain as part of human existence.

Nations today have diverse means of protecting and promoting their national interests. This is largely due to the New World Order brought about by a vastly changing socio-political and economic environments, revolution in military affairs (RMA) and revolution in Information and Communication Technology (ICT).

These trends continue to promote clashes of interest between and within nations. Throughout human history, intra and inter state conflicts have been on the increase. The decision on whether or not to use military force, especially land power by state leaders and strategists depends on a very careful analysis of their national interests, the costs and the risks associated with the domestic political climate. Against this backdrop, the formulation of national security strategy is, no doubt, vital to any country.

Today most countries around the world have experienced or are facing proliferation of conflicts, particularly on the continent of Africa. National security requires the coordinated interaction of all the elements of national power; political, economic, military, societal and environmental. In the fragile relationship between nations, even the most powerful nations are mindful of how power is employed to attain their political and economic objectives. Thus, while power is the means that is required to achieve an end, strategy attempts to specify how this power will be best employed to achieve the desired end. On the one hand, it is of direction of money, ideas and movement across borders has its bearing on general military activities.

The security interest of people within a country has become an issue of concern to sub-regional, regional and international bodies. With such an environment the plan of action of the Armed Forces for internal and external engagement needs to be reviewed and viewed in its realistic context. According to the Nigeria National Defence Policy, "this assessment is necessary since the environment is both the source of opportunities the state may pursue as well as the threat to its security". It is on the basis of this that the nation would identify its areas of need, and know what is possible and how best to accomplish them.

As a nation, Nigeria has three levels of interests which the Armed Forces have to safeguard. They are the vital, strategic and peripheral interests. In order of importance the vital interest which covers territorial integrity, sovereignty, democracy, economic resources, her citizens and culture is uppermost and cannot be compromised. It is the furtherance of this interest that Defence Policy objectives and task are outlined. When tasks are outlined for the various Services, many options are available. The option best suited, be it preventive, protective, deterrence or force projection would be applied. Continental strategy is a school of military thought that concentrates on land power and its relevance to geopolitics. The aim of this chapter is to discuss continental strategy and its application to Nigeria.

CONCEPTUAL DISCOURSE
STRATEGY

The concept of strategy does not enjoy universal definition. The important point to note about all definitions as they relate to strategy is that strategy is concerned with the relationship between ends and means. Strategy is regarded as the bridge between military means and political ends. It is considered as the ways through which a country gains a competitive edge over another country. Strategy was regarded as purely military term but has now been given liberal interpretation. In his definition, Moltke portends that strategy is "the practical adaptation of the means placed at a general's disposal to the attainment of the object in view" while Liddel Hart refers to it as "the art of distributing and applying military means to fulfill the ends of policy". These definitions although having military terms, release strategy from its traditional straight jacket-war; since it acknowledges that military power can be purposeful in peace time.

National strategy is the art and science of development vis-à-vis political, economic, and informational power of a nation, together with its armed forces, during peace and war, to secure national objectives. While, military strategy is the art and science of employing the armed forces of a nation to secure the objectives of national policy by the application of force or the threat of force. Military strategy must be subordinate to national strategy and must be coordinated with the use of non-military instruments of national power. This is also known as National Grand Strategy. Historically, we have found it difficult to maintain those relationships correctly and we have sometimes fought in the absence of a clear national or military strategy. Strategy is therefore fundamentally about means rather than ends, and in the context of this discourse, will relate to the means of utilizing land power to achieve national objectives.

LAND POWER

Of all types of military power, land power remains the most credible, relevant and sustainable. It is the only form of power that can hold ground and has a flexibility that makes its utility value transcend all forms of conflict and crisis. However, land power is a largely misunderstood term and derives its potency from a combination of other forms of power i.e. sea, air and space. While other forms of power can affect and in fact impact positively on land power, the effect of land power on other forms makes it usually complementary. Thus, there is a need to fully explain land power as well as its elements.

It is generally assumed that everyone knows what the term "land power" means and that everyone also knows the elements of land power. This assumption is largely misplaced as many readers outside the military may be surprised that a universal or working definition (of land power) does not exist. To many military practioners especially soldiers, the concept of land power is so engrained that it is largely apparent. However, the concept of land power in spite of these erroneous assumption is not as apparent as it appears to be.

Conventionally, it was considered safe to equate land power with military power – this was before the invention of the ship and the aircraft. With technological advancement and with nations struggling to have competitive edge, military power now has different but complementary components. It is, therefore, now difficult to perceive military power in one dimension – land. Even with this realization of the advent of sea and air power we are still left with the burden of defining land power.

Traditionally, it is convenient to perceive land power in the context of the ability to utilize land forces to attain military or other objectives on land. This rather narrow context assumed that land power is limited to and restricted by forces and equipment operating on land only. From a historical perspective as asserted earlier, this perception of land power should be the natural expectation as it stems from the land medium on which land operations are conducted. Using these standards, land forces equate to land power, air forces to air power and sea forces to sea power. On the surface, this conclusion appears indisputable and even immutable.

Developments in warfare, however, created a flux in which weapon systems may be based on one medium but their effects felt in another. For example, surface to Air Missiles (SAM) may be based on land but their effects felt in the air; in addition, air force or marine aircraft perform interdiction or close air support missions to influence ground operations. Similarly, a land attack missile is launched from a naval surface or sub-surface but its effects are brought to bear on land. Thus it is believed and rightly too that focusing on where effects occur increase the scope for examining and even evaluating land power. While it may not be out of place to perceive land power in terms of the medium of operation, Johnsen has proposed a more inclusive definition of "LAND POWER" as follows:

> *the ability in peace, crisis and war to exert prompt and sustained influence on or from land"*

This definition reinforces the perception that land power means much more than land forces. It is a broader term that "synergistically subsumes a wide array of forces, organizations and capabilities as well as the mobilization of industrial, technological and sustainment base that support them". Land forces also have tremendous utility value beyond their ultimate responsibility of fighting and winning wars; this implies great versatility.

Land forces are employed, therefore, over a broad spectrum and in a variety of roles consistent with the requirements of internal peace, deterrence, coercion, armed conflict and peace support. Land power consists of all asserts and personnel of a nation organized, structured and equipped including the ability to exert sustained influence on or form land, promptly and decisively. Herein lies the main crux of our discussion – the continental strategy. It is in this latter context that we shall continue our discourse on land power starting with its elements. Element of land power consist of national and military components. This course lends credence to the fact that military power remains part of the means to attain ends. By extension, land power must have a military and national bearing for it to have the bit and where-withal to operate effectively.

NATIONAL ELEMENTS

The national elements of land power include geo-strategic conditions, economic power, population, form of government and national will. Discussion on these can take a whole chapter. For the purpose of keeping within the space line, I will proceed to discussion on military elements of land power. But please remember the crucial importance of this element to the military element.

Military Elements: The military elements of land power include ground forces, instruments that generate and sustain land forces and the human elements.

a. **Ground Forces:** Land power stems from the ground forces which is its major military elements. However, it would be erroneous to think of land power or land warfare without a consideration of joint operations with other elements of power; the armed forces, allied partners, government agencies and international organizations. Thus, the full spectrum and potentials of land power must be perceived in the context of all other sectorial contributions and potentials. Unless these potentials are properly addressed, the ground forces may be unable to function at optimum potential.

b. **Instruments that Generate and Sustain these Factors:** There are some instruments that generate and sustain the factors as mentioned earlier. These are: recruitment, training, equipping and maintaining including sustaining functions that generate and underpin the capabilities of the fighting force, which are essential for creating and sustaining land power. In addition, the doctrinal procedures and systems that guide the functions of the land power are vitally important. Other aspects of optimum importance are the leadership, discipline and morale that bind the force together. Collectively all these factors combined with the assets in the inventory to include the ability to project forces to the point of crisis in sufficient time to act effectively which is of utmost significance to land power.

c. **The Human Elements:** The human dimension of military power has become one of the most significant elements of land power. It is not enough to satisfy the quantitative requirements of manpower. Qualitative considerations such as level of education, computer literacy, adaptive capability, ability to survive as individuals and create synergistic fallouts in a team are vital to land forces. Without a reservoir of talented individuals, power can seldom prevail. Particularly, while sea and air forces are built around weapons systems or support platforms, land forces tend to recruit personnel and then equip them. This philosophical approach stems from the condition that land power essentially, is concerned with changing or controlling human will. It is this human dimension, which gives land forces tremendous versatility.

EVOLUTION OF STRATEGY

War take place in four dimensions – on land, sea, air and in space. Airpower is fundamental to the success of all land operations mainly because of the security and protection it provides. Maritime operations are crucial to operations in or close to a sea environment. A key characteristic of maritime forces is the ability to maintain a presence without occupation and to achieve deterrence without commitment.

The positional advantages gained by ground manoeuvre forces are unique and irreplaceable by other means. The art of seizing, holding and defending ground, blocking and penetrating enemy forces all contribute directly to success in battle. With the mentioned strategies, the effects of ground manoeuvre can be sustained and a long-term presence can be established in a given area. The predominance of land warfare over others types of wars has its antecedents in technological development. The limitations imposed by means of locomotion have been the major determinants of the scope and dimension of wars. As men overcame the constraints imposed by the ability to move, wars began to assume new scope and dimension. Besides, it is only through land warfare that ground can be held-the ultimate aim of any war.

The continental strategy is a product of the Continental school of thought which sees modern land power within the context of a tri-service setting and that it operates in two dimensions. They are intrinsic dimension of military theory and the extrinsic dimension of geographical thought. Strategy is an intellectual discipline. In his book, Military strategy, Rear Admiral J. C. Wylie observed thus:

> "It (Strategy) can and should be an intellectual discipline of the higher order and the strategist should prepare himself to manage ideas with precision and clarity and imagination in order that his manipulation of physical realities, the tools of war, may rise above the pedestrian place of mediocrity. Strategy itself may not be a science (but) strategic judgement can be scientific to the extent that it is orderly, rational, objective, inclusive, discriminatory and perspective".

He further asserted that the study of strategy should not be in a narrow technical analysis, should not be in a conceptual breadth that considers not only military factors. It should be seen as an interaction of political, social and cultural realities, embracing what he described as dichotomous thinking.

According to John M. Collins, at the beginning of the 20th Century, there were six identifiable schools of strategic thought. Three of these schools of thought are the traditional ones of the sea (or naval power school dominated by the teachings of Alfred Thayer Mahan and the astronautically corcil power school founded by the Italian theorist Giulio Douhet. The other 3 schools are more recent, they are the strong nautical (deals with embryonic space strategy), the special operations (or clandestine warfare schools) and the unifying beyond joint or integrated military power. Collins linked the continental school of strategy with the 19th Century Prussian military philosopher, Carl Von Clausewitz.

The concept of continental strategy considers land as the main medium of conflict as against the sea or air. The ultimate aim is the defeat of enemy armed forces by land forces supported by navies and air force. There is a scholarly consensus that sees continental strategy as synonymous with the theory and practice of land warfare. This consensus is summarized in the definition by Roger W. Barnelt:

> *The continental school (of strategy) argues that control over land is the organizing principle of nation states and politics. Man lives on the land, not on the sea (or air) and control of the land for supersedes the importance of control over maritime areas of lines of communication. In historical perspective, conflict far taken place almost exclusively with control over territory as the stake in the context.*

Geography has a significant role in the understanding of the continental system. This is seen in the form of terrain used for maneuver during battle, its physical occupation and content with the army. This assists the soldiers in appreciation and assessing the ground. In many wars of the past and now, the annexation of control of a terrain by land troops has always been viewed as the sign of victory.

As earlier discussed, in continental strategy, there are the intrinsic and extrinsic dimensions. The intrinsic dimension refers to the professional knowledge of the military techniques of land power of an art of war whereas extrinsic dimension refers to the understanding of the geographical role of land power as a factor in ground strategy.

In the extrinsic dimension of continental strategy land power is not considered an autonomous element of war, but as a component of geopolitics in a ground, national or security strategy. The ultimate aim is to integrate land power with all the instruments of state power (diplomatic, military, financial and economic) in order to meet policy objectives. How best these instruments are used is determined by the geopolitical configuration or land frontiers in strategy using the various conflicts between the European powers in the 17th – 19th centuries and the type of questions stale will consider:

> "Was a particularly (European) nation able to calculate its energies upon her front, or did it have to fight on several? Did it share common borders with weak states or powerful ones, or a hybrid – and what advantages and disadvantages did it bring? Could it

easily pull out of a great war in central Europe if it wished to? Could it secure additional resources from overseas?

As Svrehin stated in the 1920s, the geopolitical dimension of modern war requires a dialogue between soldiers and statesmen. For success to be achieved there must be a common understanding of the complex relationship between war, economy and politics.

Many seasoned military scholars have drawn the attention of field commanders to the nature of theory that would operate. American military theorist Robert Leonard posited that they should not only master tactics and operations, but also the intricacies of Grand Strategy because, in the 21st century conditions they will have to operate simultaneously in both worlds.

Chinese analysts view warfare as a grand strategy of supradomain; a combination of politics, economic, culture and religion. They opined that the formation of high strategy requires diverse elements because, in the age of globalization, warfare is in the process of transcending the domain of soldiers, military units and military affairs, and is increasingly becoming a matter of politicians, scientist and even bankers.

A debatable issue is the parameters between war and other socio-political elements, both are facts which cannot be mistaken, that they have a convergent point. Military commanders that will operate in the 21st century will almost certainly require better knowledge of the connections between purely military strategy and the world of grand strategy or national security policy. Hence the need to pay attention seriously to the study of the extrinsic dimension of the continental school of strategy; in order words, the geopolitical role of land power.

In the glare of an era of information technology, no commander will take cover under the old adage of simple soldiering as such a transition especially in developing armies will not be easy. According to Evans, "The history soldier from Helmut von moltke the elder to Douglas Mac Arthur, have drawn their inspiration from the nation that the uniformed professional is above all, a technician of violence, a lancet in the hands of the diplomatic surgeon". For him the act of battle in war suspends politics. This view was summarized by Mac Arthur when he briefed the US Congress in 1951:

> I do unquestionably state that when men become locked in battle that there should be no artifice under the name of politics"

INFLUENCE OF TECHNOLOGY

Technology is said to be scientific knowledge used in practical ways. The revolutionary changes that took place in science and technology over the years have had their impact on warfare. Small arms used in warfare started canon and was used first in 1346 in the battle of Cressey (Jessie Whitefield). Within 300 years, it has metamorphosed into the gun which revolutionized Europe and later global warfare. Similar changes have occurred in geopolitics/military strategy. As at 1901, the strategy propagated by Mahan and Mackinder were two dimensional i.e. Land and Sea. By 2008 the strategic world is five-dimensional, the air, space, electromagnetic spectrum land and sea. In the 1990s due to the expansion of media strategy, there was the belief that continental strategy of land warfare was becoming irrelevant. The agents propagating media strategy were information technology (revolution) and globalization.

In a world of satellites, cell phones, 24 hours television, digital photography and the internet, war is now global. According to Evans "The rise of information technology and the growth of global political economy are seen by social theorist and strategic thinkers as creating a system of global networking that links national, regional and international politics. These linkages tend to erase classic geopolitical formulations". Robert Leonard posited that *"in globalize political conditions, the battle space becomes a singularity both geopolitically and with regard to the elements of geopolitical power namely economics, information, diplomacy and military power"*.

Global telecommunication, many believe would eradicate the continent warfare due to the special nature of modern society. Recently , terms such as "instant wars" "the death of distance", "the end of geography", "the coming of byte city" and "the empire of speed" has been used by many scholars to suggest a drastic change in international politics. The adherents of the end of geography believe that technological innovation in transportation, communication and military weaponry has the potential to overcome the constraints of physical terrain and territorial power and by so doing change the relationship between distance, space and force.

From the military angle, right from the 1990s, advocates of information warfare have been considering the beginning of the end of geography in warfare. They believe that the rise of trinity of sensors, low-observable platforms (or stealth technologies) and precision guided missiles have began to change the entire calculus of conventional conflict. They see information warfare as the potency of the desire of geopolitics and continental strategy.

Over the years many military scholars inclined towards information warfare such as Admiral William Owen and Richard Szatransla have concluded that information revolution and the rise of global networks have altered the whole of time, space and distance in modern warfare. Admiral Owen visualize the battle space as the size of Iraq and North Korea in which there is unprecedented fidelity, comprehension and timelines, by night or day in may kind of weather all the time. Others such as one time US Air Force Chief of Staff Gen Ronald Fogelman believe that in the first quarter of the 21st century you will be able to find, fix or trace and target anything of consequence that moves upon or is located on the face of the each. For Matin Linki, precision guided munitions will separate information from force while cyberspace will tend to eliminate geopolitics, through its influence on military security rather than its influenced on international politics. To them, geopolitics – in the tradition of Mahan, Mackinder, Nicholas Spykman, Henry Kissinger and Zbiyniew Brzenski – has become obsolete.

However, many scholars like Evan still believe that the emergence and dominance of information technology is exaggerated. It is universally argued that time-space relations are being reconfigured, by information networks, but the role of territory as an organizing principle continues to define human social relations. David Lonsedale has added his weight to this by warning that the fifth dimension or the information sphere does not have its environment and cannot apply unilateral forces. Rather, information acts as a medium for more efficient and faster physical expression of strategic power.

It summary, it can be said that information revolution has not so much rendered physical geography and physical military forms of power irrelevant; rather it acts as an enabler to both. Improvement in technology may reduce the timeless challenge of mastering the tactical topography and battling the elements, but will not instantly liberate the heart of warfare from the geographical and realities of the physical world.

Collectively, many scholars have rejected the idea that knowledge from information networks will become more important than knowledge of terrain. Though information technology will not eliminate territorial state and warfare, it will definitely affect the practice of war and strategies. Cyber power will reshape the way kinetic force is applied on physical space using Land, Sea, Air and outer space capabilities. The political context in which geopolitics will operate in the 21st Century will be different from the pas. Nye posited that:

> *Cyberspace will not replace geographical space and will not abolish state sovereignty, but like the town markets in feudal times, it will coexist with theory and greatly complicate what it means to be a sovereign state or a powerful country.*

NIGERIAN CONTEXT

As earlier mentioned, Nigeria has three levels of interest which the Armed Forces have to safeguard. In order of importance, Nigeria's vital interests include territorial integrity, sovereignty, democracy, economy, her citizens and culture. Many factors bear heavily in the selection and evolution of a suitable security strategy for the country. It is very important here to note Nigeria's disposition towards here neighbours and the continent of Africa at large. The country, unlike some advanced countries, does not seek to project military power and influence beyond Africa. Neither does she harbour any expansionist ambitions. Rather, Nigeria is committed to peaceful co-existence with her immediate neighbours and all countries in the West African Sub-Region, Africa and the rest of the World. Consistently, Nigeria has reiterated her commitment to the maintenance of peace in her foreign policy.

Certain other important factors have conspired to foster on the country the continental strategy i.e. Land power in the pursuit and protection of her national interest. The most important of these are geography, population and economy.

With a land mass of 923,768km Nigeria is bounded to the East, West and North by land and to the South by 853km of coastline. It therefore follow that Nigeria has a very long land boarder, more than three time its coastline. It stands to reason that the threat of an invasion over land is greater than via water. To counter this threat the country must develop strong credible Land Force.

The population and demography of the country is a very important factor which impacts significantly on security strategy. Nigeria has a population of over 130 million people. Considering the multi-ethnic and multi-religious nature of this population, it at once becomes a source of strategy in the sense that it provides internal market and human resources for the growth and development of the Nigerian economy. It also represents a secure and abundant source of men for military service. Since continental strategy is hinged on Land Forces, this important resource of the country readily lends itself.

Conversely, the heterogeneous and multi-religious nature of this population poses a huge threat to one of the country's vital interest-the unity or continued existence of Nigeria as one country. The country has experienced much ethnic and religious crises and tensions in all parts of the country and has even survived a civil war from 1967-1970. These tensions and crises still prevail and in some cases are even escalating. These factors more than any other, supports the maintenance of strong, balanced and properly deployed land forces appropriately supported by Naval and Air-force. It is not far fetched to state that Nigeria would have been past tense now if in 1966/67 when the Eastern Region rebelled the Federal Government did not have an Armed Forces to respond with, or that even today without the Armed Forces, particularly the Land Forces, the Nigerian economy would not be critically jeopardized or the country simply disintegrating.

Nigeria is a country blessed with abundant mineral resources. Although more than 70% of the population consist of subsistence farmers the country is richly endowed with the land. There are crude oil and natural gas which are sold abroad for foreign exchange and used locally to power the economy in the form of electric energy, petrol, oil and lubricants. Rivers Niger and Benue with their numerous tributaries provide water for agriculture, fishing and hydroelectricity. The arid north produce cattle, goats, fish grains and all sorts of vegetables. The strategic importance of this becomes apparent only when compared with the economies of Nigeria's immediate and strategic neighbourhood. When it is realized that access to water, rich agricultural land and strategic mineral resources have been the main reasons for interstate and intrastate conflict, the need to properly and adequately secure what we have with appropriately developed and deployed Land Forces becomes even more apparent.

It could be argued that strategic national interests and assets could be protected or defended by Naval or Air power also. That is true, but it is also true that marine and air operations must be conducted from secure bases and ports and fed by an economy operating within an enabling environment provided by a credible Land Force.

CONCLUSION

From a historical perspective, nations employ national power in addition to other means, to achieve their national objectives. Central to national power is military force being its decisive component. The use of military power, however, must always be taken within a wider political context.

The objective of every war must be peace. Therefore, the strategy employed must be such that after victory in war, the peace must be achieved. History is replete with cases of wars that were won but the peace lost. Korea, Vietnam, Afghanistan and Iraq are a few examples. If one of the arms of war remains to impose ones will on another, then every war leaves in its wake ingredients of conflict because none, even in defeat accepts to do the will of the conqueror without some form of resistance.

It, therefore, follows that Land Forces will forever be required to ensure the peace that is to follow any war. Today, for many years the American Land Forces are still in Europe, Japan, Korea, Afghanistan, Philippines and Iraq searching for the peace which ought to have followed the end of their numerous wars.

Finally, I conclude by reiterating that Land power remains the most credible, relevant and sustainable. It is the only form of power that can hold ground and has a flexibility that makes its utility value transcend all forms of conflict and crises. It is the power that can ensure that the will of the victorious and the peace that should follow a war prevail.

REFERENCES

1. CO Onugha, Air Power and Strategy paper delivered to NWC on 25 Oct 04.
2. AC Akoji, Land Power and Strategy Paper delivered to NWC on 21 Oc 04
3. ML Agwai, The Nigerian Army in National Defence Paper deliver to NWC on 7 Jan 04
4. Cal Von Clausewitz, On War ed and trans. Michael Howard and Peter Paret (Princeton, NJ: Princeton Univ Presss, 1976).
5. Warner R. Schitling, et al Strategy, Politics and Defence Budget (New York: Columba Univ Press. 1962).
6. Paul Van Riper and Robert H. Scales Jr, Preparing for War in the 21st century in Parameters, US Army War College Quaterly, Autumn, 1997.
7. Nigerian Armed Forces Joint Vision 2020 (Draft) as of 23 September 2002.
8. Compaigning, US Marine Corps MCDPI – 2
9. AO Ogomudia, "The Evolution of Land Manoeuvre Warfare" Paper delivered to NWC on 30 Oct OI.
10. Chris Pomelly "Reshaping European Armed Forces for 21st Century" NATO Publication Think Piece, October 2000.
11. WT Jansen, Redefining Land Power for the 21st Century, Strategic Studies Institute.
12. Zabadi IS, "Fundamentals of Strategy' Lecture delivered to NWC in Oct 03.
13. DO Enahoro, "Path to Understanding Military Strategy" Paper delivered to NWC on 20 Oct 04
14. O Ogundana, Military Strategy and Doctrine Paper delivered to NWC Oct 01.

15. HOU Adoga, "Compiled Precis on Evolution and Application of Military Strategy" NWC 2001/2002.
16. HOU Adoga, "Compiled Precis on Concept of Strategy" NWC 2001/2002.
17. Nigerian National Defence Policy
18. Evans M (2004) "Continental School of Strategy: The Past, Present and Future of Land Power (National Library of Australia cataloging-in-publication Entry).
19. Clausewitz quoted in Enahoro, "Foundations of Military Strategy", Lecture delivered to the Participants of NWC Course 14, on 19 Oct 05.
20. Paper Titled "Land Warfarer Strategy" presented by the Comd HQ ICCS at the NASME, May 08.

CHAPTER 32

MARITIME STRATEGY AND THE NIGERIAN NAVY

O. S. IBRAHIM

INTRODUCTION

For the past two centuries, the study and concept of maritime strategy has enjoyed prominent and deliberate intellectual introspection. This development is borne out of the ever-increasing dependence on the seas by mankind for political survival and economic prosperity. It must be acknowledged that much of the classical development on the subject within the stated period owed to intellectual efforts that emerged from the environment of past and present major maritime powers[1]. However, the post-Second World War era that precipitated proliferation of sovereign coastal states along with institution of international maritime legal regimes has facilitated contemporary views from other diverse interest groups.

The effects of globalization, trans-national and localized threats, and resource constraints are other factors that have necessitated customized approaches to maritime and naval strategies by many littoral states. It is in the light of this observation that I agree with the necessity of the intellectual discourse today as encapsulated in the topic of my discussion which is *Maritime Strategy and the Nigerian Navy.*

Nigeria's position as the leading maritime state in the Gulf of Guinea further justifies the need for sustained proactive strategic approach to security challenges and threats within the area where substantial part of her revenue is derived. Although the concepts on maritime strategy recognize multi-faceted roles of other military arms as well as political and economic stakeholders, the central role of navies has been acknowledged both in historical and contemporary strategic thoughts.

It is perhaps apt at this point to differentiate between the diffused use of the terms Maritime Strategy and Naval Strategy. To do this I shall rely on Julian Corbett's explanation that "By maritime strategy we mean the principles which govern a war in which the sea is a substantial factor. Naval strategy is but that part of it which determined what part the fleet must play in relation to the action of land forces[2].

For the purpose of this chapter, permit me to differ from the war component of the Corbett explanation by emphasising maritime security in terms of sovereign, exploitation and transit right and interests. In another supportive preceding thought, Alfred Thayer Mahan had asserted that naval strategy has for its end found support, and increase in peace as well as in war, the sea power of a country[3]. Within this understanding, maritime strategy could be interpreted as the driver of national sea power aspirations while naval strategy, being a component of maritime strategy, is employed for use of naval power.

EPISTEMIC CONTEXT

An appraisal of intellectual works on maritime and naval strategies readily reveals that both classical and contemporary thinkers differ in varying proportions on conceptual framework and elemental objectives. This observation notwithstanding, there is a concord on the ultimate aim of maritime strategy and naval strategy which is the development of sea power either individually or collectively by maritime states.

This premise shall form the basis of the ensuring analysis of thoughts on maritime strategy. It must be further admitted that a discourse on maritime strategy cannot be complete without appropriate reference to past erudite conceptual thoughts that still find sustainable relevance in many contemporary navies including the Nigeria Navy.

Prominent among these is Alfred Thayer Mahan's compellation on the necessity of maritime states to develop navies with power projection and commerce protection capabilities[4]. In perhaps a direct advice to Nigeria, Mahan examined the rise of British Seapower over France and warned that coastal states with both continental and maritime interests must favour maritime strategy if they wish to develop their sea power[5]. On naval capability, he argued along with Julian Corbett that, balanced fleet with effective and defensive capabilities are required to achieve sea control[16]. Corbett went further to identify technological currency and identified maritime interests as core foundation elements of maritime strategy[7].

Although Mahan favoured the concept of absolute sea control as an object of maritime and naval strategies, Corbett and indeed, many recent thinkers advocated local sea control characterized by limited objectives in terms of political and military values, time and geography. Contemporarily, cost-effectiveness, technological advances and resource constraints have compelled the wide acceptance of local sea control concept.

From the Soviet era perspective, Gorshkov asserted that a navy is a graphic indicator of the level of development of a country's economy. Along the Admirals Zumwalt and Stanfied Turner, Gorshkov acknowledged the pre-eminence of technology in maritime and naval strategy[8]. He ably practicalised this strategic view in his remarkable modernisation of the Soviet Navy with a focus on enhancement of its political value through power projection capability for deterrence and diplomatic roles[9].

In more recent thought, Eric Grove and Etzold contended that a country's naval capability should be a direct reflection of its economic power. Similarly, in difference to Mahan's thoughts on navalism and colonial outposts, Gough and Bateman advised that contemporary seapower calculations should reflect alliance relationship, access rights to ports and cooperative approach to regional security[10]. Gough went further to predict the strategic orientation of navies by asserting that 'constabulary and regulatory naval roles will grow steadily as states become aware of their rights and duties[11], and that 'a new attitude to sea power may eventually be born; one that emphasizes international duties to safeguard an international maritime community'[12].

The Chief of the Naval Staff, V.Adm GTA Adekeye ably captured the emerging cooperative approach in the African setting by emphasising its cost effectiveness and effort multiplier advantages for African navies and coastguards in view of their limited capabilities[13].

Summarily, maritime strategy operates at the national level where political, economic, military and diplomatic strengths are combined for the promotion and protection of national maritime interests, and ultimately the development of sea power. This view has apparently found a worthy relevance in the emerging US Cooperative Strategy which stresses a unified maritime strategy that 'integrates seapower with other elements of national power, as well as those of friends and allies'[14].

The navy specifies that orientation of naval strategy guides operational and logistics deployment concepts of naval forces in aid of the national maritime strategy. In this context, deterrence, sea control, and power projection capabilities characterized by a balanced fleet backed by robust logistics constitute valued tools for maritime security objectives. Similarly, cooperative strategy at local and multi-national levels has emerged as acceptable components of maritime and naval strategies.

NIGERIAN NAVAL STRATEGY

As embodied in the 1999 Constitution and specifically in Act 20 of the National Assembly, the NN is charged with the undermentioned statutory roles[15]:

a. Defence of Nigeria by Sea
b. Enforcing and assisting in coordinating the enforcement of all customs laws including anti-piracy illegal bunkering, fishery and immigration laws of Nigeria at sea.
c. Enforcing and assisting in coordinating the enforcement of national and international maritime laws ascribed to or acceded to by Nigeria.
d. Promoting, coordinating and enforcing safety regulations in the territorial waters and EEZ.
e. Making of charts and coordinating of all national hydrographic surveys.

When viewed within Ken Booth's perspective on the traditional military, policing and diplomatic roles of navies, it is apparent that NN's statutory responsibilities are predominantly policing. However, within the context of past experiences during the Civil War and Liberia/Sierra Leone crises, it becomes expedient for the NN to emphasize development of sea lift capability. The fact that successive national foreign policies were consistently afro-centric with demonstrative commitment to regional peace further justifies the need for the NN to develop limited power projection capability.

In the earlier wisdom of NN leadership, the Trident Strategy was formulated in 1988 to provide the conceptual and planning framework for its operations. The primary objectives of the strategy include coastal defence, sea control and support to NA through sealift and naval fire[16]. However, with recent threat developments within the internal waters, EEZ and the Gulf of Guinea, there is the requirement for further dynamic interpretation of the Trident Strategy particularly in the light of its policing roles within the coastal defence and sea control arms. Against this background, I shall proceed to take a closer look at the threat scenario within Nigeria's maritime environment.

Currently, over 80 per cent Nigeria revenue is sourced from hydrocarbon exploitation, most of which the extracted within the onshore and offshore area of the coastal belt[17]. Similarly, the bulk of import and export activities are transited through the nation's seaports and approaches. This situation along with expanding deep sea oil exploitation presents credible real and potential threats and vulnerabilities.

First is the rising wave of militant attacks on oil installations within the Niger Delta with attendant hostage taking of foreign nationals and kidnappings. Crude oil and petroleum products theft, and illegal bunkering are other contending and undesirable consequences of the militant activities. The oil theft is estimated to be costing the nation an annual $1.2billion loss of revenue[18]. It is worrisome that the militancy is gradually manifesting export potentials to neighboring states as recently exposed in Equatorial Guinea. Piracy and Armed Robbery at Sea constitute serious threat to Nigeria's maritime interest in view of its increasing occurrence with attendant current rating of Nigerian waters as the most dangerous in Africa next to Somalia[19].

Other threats include poaching of fishery resources by vessels from Asia, Europe and other parts of Africa which costs Nigeria and other Gulf of Guinea states an annual estimated loss of about $370million[20]. Additional indirect effects include environmental degradation, loss of income and livelihood in fishing communities. Trans-shipment of narcotics constitute another threat scenario as the nation begins to emerge as a key transit route in the 'Cape Verde – Canary Islands – Madeira' drug triangle through the use of ships transiting Nigeria.

Although Nigeria has successfully consummated many conflict resolution treaties with her maritime neighbours, there is indeed a subsisting challenge to remain committed particularly with Cameroon in the Bakassi, and Sao Tome and Principle, and Equatorial Guinea under the Joint Development Zone (JDZ) arrangement. Other critical inadequacies include lack of effective maritime domain awareness (MDA) capability and inadequate presence at sea.

Apparently, these vulnerabilities arise substantially from deficiencies of existing NN fleet and operational capabilities. This situation could be attributed to absence of effective national maritime strategy that should prioritise equipping and sustenance of NN operations, in proportion to the economic value and related threats in the maritime environment.

One of the obvious manifestations in contemporary seapower calculations is the diminishing priority of the concept of decisive battle, otherwise known as *"Der tag"* as predominantly obtainable before the end of the Second World War. This development owes partly to the expensive lessons of the Second World War and the wide acceptance of international regimes on maritime sovereignty and exploitation. The increasing mutually beneficial economic and transit relationship among littoral and non-littoral states in the emerging globalized international economy further justified the need for promotion of collective security mechanism in the maritime environment.

Apart from the older North Atlantic Treaty Organization (NATO), the concept of collective maritime security is gaining wide acceptance in Asia, Mediterranean and South American maritime environments. The Gulf of Guinea which constitutes Nigeria's primary domain should not be an exception. Permit me, therefore, to proceed further by highlighting how some of these trends manifest in the Gulf of Guinea with relevant observations on our maritime and naval strategies.

Currently, the Third United Nations Convention on the Law of the Sea (UNCLOS III) constitutes the primary international basis for delineation of sovereign, jurisdiction and exploitation rights for littoral and land-locked states in the maritime environment. The convention is premised on the principles of peaceful and secured use of the seas[21]. Essentially, maritime states derive the extent and level of their maritime security interests based on the convention segregation of internal waters, high seas including attendant rights and privileges. Of particular importance are the provisions for joint rights and development between coastal states in overlapping maritime areas as typified in the Gulf of Guinea.

It is noteworthy that all the maritime states in the Gulf of Guinea have ratified the convention. It is further gladdening to note that the maritime sub-region posses an enviable record of maritime conflict resolution based on the UNCLOS spirit. The implications for maritime states in the developing world such as Nigeria include strategic imperative of promoting the peaceful exploitation spirit of the convention. Consequently, Nigeria's strategic concepts for the defence and security of maritime environment should recognize the sanctity of territorial waters sovereignty, sovereign and jurisdiction rights in the EEZ as well as the principles of transit rights, joint development and protective exploitations.

The Gulf of Guinea Energy Security Strategy (GGESS) is an ongoing initiative between Nigeria, UK, USA, Netherlands and multi-national oil companies operating within the Niger Delta and with representation from neighbouring coastal states bordering the area. It is a collaborative arrangement aimed at addressing the increasing insecurity in the Niger Delta area arising from oil theft, kidnappings, attack on oil installations and foreign workers, arms smuggling, money laundering and illegal oil bunkering[22]. Thus far, the strategic initiative has involved development of Maritime Domain Awareness (MDA) capability, manpower development and deployment of US naval training ships within the Gulf of Guinea.

Significant achievements under the strategy include conduct of maritime policing exercises and ongoing installation of coastal radar, Automated Identification System (AIS) and infrared/optical cameras along the nation's coastline. The installation programme is being implemented under the Regional Maritime Awareness Capability (RMAC). The aim of the installation programme is to facilitate effective monitoring activities within the Niger Delta including adjacent Gulf of Guinea waters. It would also avail an information sharing network among the navies and coastguards in the area. It is worthy to mention that these facilities are already in operation in Cameroon, and Sao Tome and Principle under the GGESS sponsorship.

The GGESS is considered a welcome initiative that would require political will among stakeholders for sustenance through adequate finding, training and an effective information sharing mechanism. On the part of the NN, we recognize our responsibilities under the initiative in the operational maintenance of the sensor facilities, development of competent manpower and collaboration with other navies / coastguards and local maritime security agencies. I am glad to inform you that necessary implementation plans are ongoing.

In the aftermath of the September 11, 2001 terrorist attack on United States of America, one of the attendant collateral revelations is the potential vulnerability of the maritime environment and activities to the new wave of borderless terrorism, particularly the ship-port interface and adjacent coastal waters. This realization gave birth to the new security measures for ships and ports encapsulated in the International Ship and Port Security Code (ISPS Code) under the Safety of Life at Sea (SOLAS)[23]. As posited by V Adm John Morgan and R Adm Charles Martgolio, both of USN, policing the maritime domain will require substantially more capability than United States or any other individual nation can deliver[24]. This observation encapsulated the premises for conceptual thoughts on a 1000 ships by navies and coastguards worldwide in which the ships would routinely operate with one another on a voluntary and elective basis and without any one state being in charge. The explicit goals of the concept include:

a. Expansion of maritime security by increasing MDA for knowledge and understanding of activities at sea.
b. Facilitation of readily available assets for response to crises and emergency at sea or in the littorals.
c. Capacity building for reinforcement of safety of trade and commerce.

Although the specifics of the concept are still in the developmental stage, the appealing feature of the 1000-ship concept lies in its cooperative and voluntary model based on shared maritime security interests. It is posited that the concept would present a cost effective strategy to the Gulf of Guinea maritime security challenges. Considering the low capacity of most of the navies within the Gulf, it is apparent that concerted efforts must be initiated towards platform acquisition, development of MDA capabilities and an effective information sharing network. As the dominant local state, Nigeria and indeed the NN have a leading role to play in this direction. There is a danger of a delayed response in the likely dominance of maritime security in the Gulf of Guinea by foreign navies where nations have significant economic interest therein.

In an explicit demonstration of the US growing interest in Africa and related security concern, a separate unified command, known as African Command (AFRICOM) was recently established. Its stated mission is to promote a stable and secure African environment in support of US foreign policy through military activities, partnerships and assistance programmes with African Military forces[25]. The command is scheduled to become fully independent by 30 Sep 08. The relevance of this highlight on AFRICOM derives from three reasons. First is the recent change in the Federal Government's Position on AFRICOM which currently supports the initiative. According to the Honourable Minister of Foreign Affairs, Chief Ojo Maduekwe; AFRICOM is one that will continue to exist for US cooperation with African militaries in the area of training, logistics and equipment support[26]. He further identified the common objective of capacity building and fight against terrorism.

The second reason emanates from the substantial American interest in the Gulf of Guinea crude oil exploitation which accounts for about 15 percent of US import. This factor will inevitably necessitate increased US naval presence and partnership programmes with Gulf of Guinea states and armed forces, some of which have already been initiated. Against this development, it is expedient for the Federal Government and the Armed Forces to develop appropriate strategic response to the AFRICOM initiative with a view to achieving beneficial partnership. In the context of maritime security, Nigeria must register the imperatives of preserving her maritime sovereign and jurisdiction rights and her recognition terms for AFRICOM while exploiting possible human and logistic capacity building offered on maritime security. Joint exercises, platform acquisition, MDA capacity development and training are suggested partnership options.

The third reason relates to the implied pressure on Nigeria to develop its naval capability in order to sustain a dominant local sea power status in the Gulf of Guinea. Doing otherwise is to defer our sovereign maritime interests and security to uncontrollable foreign influence. This calls for appropriate maritime strategy for equipping the NN and an effective deployment (naval) strategy.

WAY FORWARD

From the foregoing, it is apparent that contemporary views on maritime strategy recognize the imperatives of effective naval capability, cooperative security mechanisms at local and multi-national levels, with the ultimate objectives of peaceful and secured use of the seas. For Nigeria, development within the internal waters and the Gulf of Guinea which constitute her primary area of maritime interest calls for a coherent strategic approach that would guarantee peaceful exploitation and unhindered access in this area. It is against this background that the following remedial strategic approaches are proffered:

a. As a beneficiary of the post-UNCLOS regime, Nigeria is under obligation to abide by the spirit of the terms while promoting same with other users particularly in the Gulf of Guinea. This is a maritime strategy for peaceful exploitation and cost-effective security.

b. Nigeria should prioritise maritime strategy in relations to continental strategy. This calls for development of a robust maritime strategy to protect her exploitation and transit activities in the maritime environment where much of her wealth is derived.

c. Nigeria must sustain a central role in the collective maritime security system in the Gulf of Guinea. Nigeria's core interest in the strategic approach should emphasise protection of sovereign, jurisdictional and exploitation rights. Other beneficial interests include assisted acquisitions, training and MDA capacity building.

d. Development of a viable maritime strategy that must emphasize credible naval power. Inclusive in this, should be a maritime industrial base and manpower, effective maritime domain awareness capability and collective maritime security mechanism in the Gulf of Guinea.

e. The NN should be re-capitalized for internal waters and coastal defence, sea control, power projection and sea lift capability.

In relation to the NN and the Trident Strategy, there is the urgent need to expand the coastal defence objective towards development of reverine operations capability, acquisition of robust MDA facilities and institution of effective manpower development programmes. OPVs, sealift ships, inshore patrol crafts and corvettes are imperatives for the strengthening of the sea control and sea lift responsibilities of the NN as recognized in the Trident Strategy. Similarly, the proposed NAF acquisition of MPA when tallied with increased NN Air helicopter fleet would provide an effective surveillance capability.

CONCLUSION

In conclusion, attempt has been made in this discussion to highlight relevant rudimentary views on maritime and naval strategies, particularly as they relate to Nigeria's maritime environment and interest. For Nigeria, adjacent waters within the Gulf of Guineas stretching from the coastal inland waters to the limits our EEZ represent the legal strategic are of interest where effective maritime and naval strategies must address. Our continuous reliance on the Gulf of Guinea for economic and political survival dictates the imperative of developing appropriate capability for maritime security.

From the maritime strategy perspective, it was posited that Nigeria is under obligation to embrace cooperation maritime security strategy under favourable terms that would protect her core sovereign, jurisdictional and exploitation interests in the Gulf of Guineas. Other strategic approaches proffered include promotion of UNCLOS objectives and acquisition of MDA capability. For the NN to fulfil its statutory roles, there is a compelling need for fleet-recapitalisation with acquisition of OPVs, sealift vessels, IPCs, logistics vessels and helicopters. The necessity of re-articulating the coastal defence objective to emphasise enhanced capability for MDA and riverine operations was also stressed.

REFERENCES

1. Osinowo AA, Royal Navy in the Twenty-First Century-Strategic Thoughts in Kerr G (Ed) Peter Mitehall Essays 2003 Austtralian Navy pp 17-26.
2. Corbett J, Some Principles of Maritime Strategy, USNI Press 1988.

3. Mahan AT, The Influence of Sea Power upon History 1660-1783, in Jablonsky D (Ed) Roots of Strategy Book 4, Stackpole Books, Racknishburg.
4. Ibid
5. Ibid
6. Ibid
7. Corbettt J, Some Principles of Maritime Strategy, USNI Press 1988.
8. Osinowo AA, Opcit.
9. Ibid
10. Gough BM, Maritime Strategy: The Legacies of Mahan and Corbett as Philosophers of Sea Power, Royal United Services Institute for Defence Studies, Winter. 1988, p56.
11. Ibid
12. Ibid
13. Adekeye GTA VAdm, Welcome Address to Seapower for Africa Symposium 29-31 May 06 Abuja.
14. Roughead G. Adm (USA) at al, A. Cooperative Strategy for 21ˢᵗ Century: Seapower Presents an Historical First. http:// www.navy.mil accessed 27 May. 2008.
15. Armed Forces Act No 20 of National Assembly.
16. Koshoni PS (Adm), Sea Power and National Objectives' in Oladimeji OA (Ed) Sea Power: Agenda for National Survival NN, 1989, pp 19-20.
17. Gilpin, R, Enhancing Maritime Security in the Gulf of Guinea, Strategic Insights. Vol. IV Jan 07. http://www.ccc.nps.navy.mil/si/2007/Jan/gilpin accessed 28 May 08.
18. Ibid
19. Ibid
20. Ibid
21. UN, UNCLOS UN Press 1983.
22. Golawyn DL and Morrison JL, A Strategic Approach to Governance and Security in the Gulf of Guinea, Centre of Strategic and International Studies, Washington Jul 05 pp 5-16.
23. IMO, ISPS Code, p6.
24. Ullman H, the 1000-ship Navy-Turning A Slogan into a Strategy, Proceedings USNI Oct 06.p10.
25. US African Command, Fact Sheet, May 2008.
26. Josiah O, Nigeria Backpedals from AFRICOM, The Punch Newspaper 28 May 08 p11.

CHAPTER 33

AIR STRATEGY AND THE NIGERIAN AIRFORCE

B. G. DANBABA

PREAMBLE

The strategic planning process, as it relates to the military could simply be broken down into six steps. The first step spells out the National interests, which is translated from the National purpose by government. Simply put, it is the general and continuing end for which a state acts. For Nigeria, these interests include the safeguard of our territorial integrity and the prosperity and well being of the Nigerian people. The second step is appraisal of the threat upon which the third step-identification of politico-military objects – will be based. In Step 4, strategies are formulated in concert with policy guidelines. I must emphasize, however, that the thought process involved in doing so is carried out within the framework of the prevailing strategic environment. In other words, strategies cannot be transferred from one time period to another without a proper appreciation of changes that might have occurred.

In step 5, which is resource allocation, present and projected capabilities are compared with the required resources to assess the feasibility of plans. Resources are allocated without incurring intolerable risks. If a mismatch exist between our desires and assets – the ends and the means – then step reconciles the mismatch and offers alternative.

When the environment within which a particular military strategy involves the employment of platform operating in the air, the air strategy forms an elements of military strategy. In some conflicts, it may indeed constitute the military strategy. At this juncture it is necessary to understand the term "Dominant Strategy", which you will come across in contemporary strategic thought regarding the most effective strategy for conventional warfare. While a compromise is often achieved between the three main types, that is Land, Maritime and Air, it is that predominating or leading strategy that is referred to as the Dominant Strategy. The choice will very much depend on geographical considerations, power potential, national psyche, the nature of conflict and threat, and the desired result.

Warfare has come a long way from when the potentials of airpower were limited to softening the ground for ground invasion, to contemporary times when the total number of targets hit in the first day of the Gulf War was equal to the number of targets hit in two years (1942 & 1943) by the 8th US Air Force during the Second World War. What changes have brought airpower to such limelight and precipitated its employment in contemporary warfare.

To achieve this, I shall first run through the background and evolution of airpower. Thereafter, I will discuss the application of air power in recent conflicts and highlight future trends in the employment of air power. Lastly, I will briefly look at the relevance of Nigeria's airpower to national security and highlight the role of the NAF in Nigeria's Defence Strategy. While I will not specifically dwell on the role of technology in air power, I will from time to time identify its influence in the course of my presentation.

EVOLUTION OF AIRPOWER

Contrary to the often held believe that the history of airpower dates back to the Italo – Turkish war of 1911, its application as a concept was first prophesied by the Jesuit priest Francesco de Lana – Terzi in 1670 when he stated that "flying crafts could one day be manoeuvred over buildings and ships at sea to drop artificial fireworks and fire-balls". Nevertheless, the official birthday of airpower, according to Tony Mason, is put at 1893 when a Major Fullerton of the British Army prophesied at a Army Engineers Conference in Chicago that "*future wars may well start with a great air battle*", that "*the arrival over the enemy capital will probably conclude the campaign*" and that "*Command of the air would be an essential prerequisite for all and air warfare*". However, the expression 'airpower' defined as "*the ability to use platforms operating in or passing through the air for military purposes*" was first recorded in HG Wells, 'The War in the Air' in 1908.[1]

The first step to fulfilling the visualization of airpower came in 1903 with the successful flight of the Wright brothers in the United States. By 1909, aircraft had been inducted into military service and was used for the first time in combat by the Italians in their war with Turkey in 1911. By the beginning of World War One, Germany, France and the USA had developed air corps as part of their land forces. Britian, on the other hand, formed two separate air corps as part of its military and naval forces. The outbreak of World War One saw the involvement of light wooden bi/tri planes with maximum speeds of 100 mph and very limited load carrying capacity in such roles as reconnaissance the artillery observations, and eventually the bombing of population centres. The aerial conflict inevitably developed into direct engagement between opposing aircraft to prevent the adversary from gaining military advantage from the air. Thus, establishing the first doctrine of airpower, which is to gain control of the air. The July 1917 bombing raid of London by German Gotha bombers and the establishment of a British bombing unit in France, known as the independent force to conduct reprisal raids against Germany gave birth to the concept of strategic bombing, independent of missions in support of surface forces. Although the damage caused as a result of bombing was insignificant, its psychological effect was profound. By the end of the war, all subsequent roles of airpower had either been established or attempted. In the case of surface forces, roles such as close air support, reconnaissance, anti-submarine warfare, convoy escort and maritime strike had become essential considerations in existing land and maritime strategies.[2]

The inter war period witnessed a rise in the public profile of aviation and improvement in the effectiveness of war planes. It also witnessed the articulation of thoughts on airpower doctrine and strategy. Of the various advocates that contributed to the early development of airpower, none were more influential than Giulio Douhet, Air Marshal Trenchard and General Billy Mitchel.

Douhet, an Italian military officer, regarded as the father of air power argued in his book, 'Command of the Air', that command of the enemy's airspace should be the first objective during war and having achieved it, subsequent bombing of industrial and population centres would be so disruptive and destructive that the enemy would be compelled to use for peace, even before their "army and navy had time to mobilize at all". He maintained that airpower could win a war independent of land and sea power. Although Douhet has been influential in the development of airpower, especially in the US and Britain, he has been criticized for over stating the impact of airpower, especially with respect to the morale of the people.

Marshal of the Air Force, Lord Trenchard, like Douhet, believed that air superiority was the first step towards overall military success. As the RAF's first Chief of the Air Staff, his primary interest and focus was in the offensive nature of airpower and its application in strategic bombing. Unlike Douhet, however, he rejected the notion of bombing population centres as indiscriminate. He advocated that the destruction of the enemy's industrial infrastructure and its attendant effect on the lives of its people would like Douhet compel them to sue for peace. Yet like Douhet, Trenchard over estimated the effects of bombing on morale and national will. Its is evident from the Second World War that developed industrial nations have a degree of resilience which can permit them to continue to fight and maintain a will to win not withstanding the diminished capacity.

Billy Mitchell, the earliest American air power theorist, advocated the use of air power to destroy the enemy's field forces, on land and at sea. He noted that "neither armies nor navies can exist unless the air is controlled over them". Influenced by Douhet, he believed that strategic bombing cold paralyse a nation's vital centres and break the will of the people. However, like Trenchard, he did not advocate the bombing of population centres. In addition, he firmly believed in and called for the independence of an air force.[3]

World War Two was the next major landmark in the evolution of air power. It provided a unique opportunity to test and refine existing doctrine. Importantly, it was the development of tactical air power and the evolution of air-land battle concepts. The German Blitzkrieg was a classical example of swift combined arms manoeuvre style warfare supported by tactical airpower and directed by effective command control. It ensured the defeat and occupation of Poland in 3 weeks and the subsequent occupation of Western Europe. At sea in the pacific theatre, we witnessed carrier based airpower usurp Mahan's big battle doctrine for command of the sea at the Battles of Coral Sea and Midway. For the first time in naval history, naval battles were fought by ships beyond visual range and without traditional naval gunfire exchange. The Battle of Midway, in particular, marked the turning point of the war in the Pacific and established the decisive nature of airpower in warfare.

Unlike the successes recorded with tactical airpower on land and at sea, the result of strategic bombing was mixed. The disappointment experienced in the early period of the war were mainly due to shortcomings associated with the aircraft e.g. aircraft size, limited payload and poor navigation equipment, which prevented the accurate delivery of the requisite level of explosives on targets. On the other hand, the high losses suffered, especially by the Allied forces, were due to the undue confidence in the bomber's invulnerability and their consequent failure to deploy long range fighter escorts until the latter period of the war. In the case of the Germans, it may appear from the Luftwaffe's Regulation 16 (the Conduct of the Aerial War") that because the primary mission of the Luftwaffe was to be within the framework of combined operations in priority. Indeed, General Walter Weaver, the Luftwaffe first Chief of Staff who directed the publication of Regulation 16 recognized the need for long range bombers and planned for their production accordingly. However, after his death the Luftwaffe focused on producing dive bombers to the detriment of long range bombers. Lack of long – range heavy bombers for sustained strategic bombing against the UK and USSR was a serious shortcoming that cost Germany dearly.

World War Two served in identifying two key lessons in the employment of airpower. Firstly, all air assets must be unified under one air commander. Secondly, winning the control of air is an essential prerequisite to any modern land/sea offensive. While the war disproved Douhet and Mitchell's assertion that strategic bombing of population centres would lead to capitulation, it also questioned the morality of such an act, particularly with regards to Hiroshima and Nagasaki where both theories seem to have been vindicated by the atomic bomb. The influence of air power in World War Two can best be summed up in the words of Winston Churchill. According to him, "*for good or ill air mastery is today the supreme expression of military power*. And fleets and armies, however necessary and important, must accept subordinate rank. This is a memorable milestone in the march of man".[4]

The development of nuclear weapons in the Post – World War Two period and the influence of nuclear deterrence detracted from the development of air power doctrine. Thus, the lack of preparedness by the West in particular, for low intensity conflicts that ensured in both Korea and Vietnam. From Korea to Operation Iraqi Freedom, we have learnt that political imperatives at the strategic level may restrict the effective employment of air power. We have equally learnt that technology provides an edge in aerial warfare and indeed governs the growth of air power. Aspects of air power have gradually been transformed by technological advances, like precision guided munitions and stealth, and new theories of application.

Modern day advocates of these new theories are the 2 Johns-Boyd and Warden, both Colonels and fighter pilots in the United States Air Force.[5] Boyd's Theory of Conflict and Warden's Theory of Strategic Attack dwell on the goal of defeating the enemy through strategic paralysis. The theory of strategic paralysis is not exactly new-both JC Fuller and Liddell Hart envisioned a decisive role for air power in inducing strategic paralysis. Indeed, paralysis of the enemy underpinned the strategic bombing concepts of early air power theorist. However, unlike these early theorists whose emphasis was on economic warfare, Boyd and Warden theorized paralyzing the enemy command.[6] The roots of their approach can be traced to Sun Tzu who wrote that:

> *"the general rule of the use of the military is that it is better to keep a nation intact than to destroy it, it is better to keep an army intact than to destroy it. Therefore, those who win every battle are not really skilful; those who render other's armies helpless without fighting are the best of all".[7]*

According to Boyd, "Machines don't fight wars. Terrain doesn't fight wars, Humans fights war. You must get into the mind of humans. That's where the battles are won". Stating that rational human behaviour is processed through the OODA loop – a cycle of 4 distinct tasks; observation, orientation, decision and action – Boyd insists that a winner will be he who can process the cycle faster and more accurately than the enemy until a point that the enemy's action become totally inappropriate to the prevailing situation. It other words, render the enemy powerless by denying him the time to mentally cope with the rapidly unfolding war situation. Boyd believed that the inherent characteristics of air power lend itself to the tempo and multiple tasking necessary to disorient and confuse the enemy and thus render him powerless.

Warden on the other hand stated that "real exploitation of airpower's potential can only come through making assumptions that it can do something we thought it couldn't do… we must start our thinking by assuming we can do everything with air power, not by assuming that it can only do what it did in the past". Given airpower's inherent characteristics and the current capabilities of the aircraft, Warden insists that *"we can now wage in parallel as opposed to the serial operations that constrained us in the past"*. Viewing the enemy as a system of 5 strategic rings, he identified the innermost ring as the leadership and the most crucial component of the system. Following the leadership were organic essentials, infrastructure, population and fielded forces in that descending order of importance to the overall functioning of the system. According to Warden, targeting the command element through decapitation was an effective and efficient means of incapacitating the system. If not feasible, perhaps due to political reasons, then strategic paralysis could be induced through attacks on the outer rings. The air campaign should, thus, be designed to selectively or simultaneously incapacitate the 5 rings in order to achieve system paralysis.[8]

To sum up the evolution of airpower, let me outline its very essence in warfare through Philip Meilinger's Ten Propositions on the employment of air power:

a. Whoever controls the air generally controls the surface.
b. Air power is an inherently strategic force.
c. Air power is primarily an offensive weapon.
d. Air power is targeting, targeting is intelligence and intelligence is analyzing the effects of air operations.
e. Air power produces physical and psychological shock by dominating fourth dimension-time.

f. Air power can simultaneously conduct parallel operations at all levels of war.

g. Precision air weapons have redefined the meaning of mass.

h. Air power's unique characteristics require centralized control by airmen.

i. Technology and air power are integrally and synergistically related.

j. Air power includes not only military assets but aerospace industry and commercial aviation.

Having done that, let us now take a look at the application of air power in recent conflicts. In doing so, I would take 1 example – the Gulf War of 1991. I have chosen this particular war because, of all recent conflicts, it exemplifies:

a. The technological edge in air war.

b. The decisive nature of air power and its significance in recent military strategies.

I have also chosen this example to ease our understanding when I discuss the implications of contemporary and future trends of airpower strategy on small nations. Another recent conflict that you may find interesting is the Israeli-Hezbollah conflict, which presents us with an understanding of the limitations posed by politics and other issues to the employment of air power. Rather than dwell on this during my presentation, I would rather discuss it during the Q & A session if you so wish. Now to OP DESERT STORM.

OPERATION DESERT STORM

OPERATION DESERT STORM commenced on the night of 16/17 January 1991. In the first 24 hours, 152 discrete targets in addition to other Iraqi forces and SAM sites were targeted. Never before in the history of warfare had so many separate air attacks been executed in a single day. In a week, the Allied Coalition had achieved Air Supremacy. What was different about the concept of the air campaign from previous air campaigns? The air campaign took advantage of capabilities offered by technology to paralyse Saddam's Command and Control, neutralize his capacity to fight, reduce his military production base and create the conditions to control its capacity to build weapons of mass destruction. The air war plan was drawn by Col Warden based on his Theory of Strategic Paralysis and the Conduct of Parallel Warfare. The term 'parallel' is derived from basic electrical circuitry, whose design you may recall is either serial or parallel. In a serial design, electricity flows from one light bulb before another can be lit in sequence. In a parallel circuit, the current reaches and lights up all the bulbs simultaneously. Applied to war and the application of force, it provides us the terms serial and parallel warfare.

Prior to OPERATION DESERT STORM, airpower had been applied serially to take out enemy defences before attacking high value targets. The huge effort required to suppress enemy air defences and the time required to accomplish these tasks limited the number of high value targets that could be attached. Furthermore, it tended to prolong the air campaign as a whole. A simultaneous attack, on the other hand, on a range of high value targets requires little or no suppression of enemy air defences, ensures surprise with the attendant paralyzing effect within a short time. Simultaneous attack in war has always been desirable, especially to achieve surprise as was the case during the Arab-Israeli Six-day War. However, such attacks were never planned to the degree of parallel war witnessed in DESERT STORM for three main reasons. Firstly, there was the requirement for mass to compensate for lack of precision weapons. Secondly, the number of air assets required for force packages were high. Lastly, an operational doctrine designed to achieve control over an adversary rather than his destruction to achieve military objective was absent. Stealth and precision technology resolved the first two problems and enabled the resolution of the third concept as put forward by Boyd and Warden, armed at achieving control over an adversary.

The air campaign plan for DESERT STORM consisted of four phases:

a. Phase One – The suppression and destruction of Iraqi Air Defence.
b. Phase Two – The destruction of strategic targets, telecommunications networks, military industrial complexes, railroads and bridges.
c. Phase Three – The destruction of the Iraqi Army's physical capacity to fight and psychological will to resist.
d. Phase Four – The provision of close support to ground units.

Although the quest for control of the air was paramount, most phases were executed concurrently. After the first 3 days, Iraqi air operations had virtually ceased. In a total of 43 days of air operations, the coalition flew over a hundred thousand sorties and dropped some 88,500 tons of bombs, 6,500 of which were PGMs. The effectiveness of the air campaign was central to the decisive victory of the Coalition.[9] It is instructive that the total weight of effort of the Coalition was just slightly lower than that of the Allied Forces during their Strategic Air Offensive against Germany between 1939 and 1942.[10]

Will we continue to see airpower applied in its current form? What future lies ahead in terms of its capabilities and application? Alvin and Heidi Toffler have suggested that there is an immutable relationship between the manner in which societies create wealth and the way in which they fight wars. Since we are now at the fringe of the information age, it follows, therefore, that the future employment of airpower will be intimately linked to information.[11] Indeed the foundation has already been laid with an aspect of OPERATION DESERT STORM – the strategic and operational pursuit of information dominance.

Arquilla and Ronfeldt of the Rand Corporation referred to these future battles for information dominance as 'cyber wars'. According to them, *"Cyber war refers to conducting, and preparing to conduct, military operations according to information-related principles". It means disrupting if not destroying the information and communications systems, broadly defined to include even military culture, on which an adversary relies in order to 'know' itself: who it is, where it is, what it can do when, why it is fighting, which threats to counter first, etc. It means trying to know all about an adversary while keeping it from knowing much about oneself. It means turning the 'balance of information and knowledge' in one's favour, especially if the balance of forces is not. It means using knowledge so that less capital and labour may have to be expended".[12]*

Closely scrutinized, Arquilla and Ronfeldt are advocating strategic paralysis through attacks on key information –related centres of gravity. This may represent a shift from the command-targeted approach strategic paralysis put forward by Boyd and Warden to an information-targeted approach. Airpower integrated with space power does provide the requisite leverage for controlling both the third and fourth dimensions and for achieving rapid dominance in war. More or less in the same lines are those who advocate the use of non-lethal weapons in combination with cyber war technology as a more effective means of parallel warfare. Focusing on effects, this school of thought uphold that Effects Based Operations would be less destructive and would be a preferable option for parallel warfare than is currently practiced.

While the future employment of airpower may well be determined by the pace of technology. Its employment in the pursuit of other traditional national security interests may not be very different than currently obtains. Coercion and humanitarian activities will continue to serve as veritable instruments in international relations, and only air power can provide the timely response so required. We may now ask that given the current and future trend in the employment of air power, what implications are there for small air forces, especially those of the Third World? Do small air forces have the resources to conduct parallel warfare? Would they have the resources required for cyber war? These are questions, which are debatable. While small but technologically advanced air forces many be able to do so within the framework of coalition warfare, technologically dependent air forces may not. It follows, therefore, that while technology continue to drive airpower development and doctrine, small air forces, especially those of the Third World must strictly tailor their air power according to their respective national interests and not, as is often suspected, by the dictates of contemporary doctrine.

They must develop doctrine, which will not only ensure continuity in the traditional pursuit of national interests but also ensure their relevance and effectiveness in asymmetric conflicts with technologically advanced air forces. The cost of technology and its application in air power development is astronomical and will certainly be beyond the reach of poorer nations. For example, it costs about $32m for one Tornado F3, while the F-22, a new generation multi-role combat aircraft is projected to cost $143.5m. Small third world air forces have no recourse but to develop relevant air power doctrine and I urge you all contribute to this debate. Now let us look at Nigeria's air power and its relevance to national security.

NIGERIA'S AIR POWER AND ITS RELEVANCE TO NATIONAL SECURITY.

The Nigerian Air Force, the military force component of Nigeria's airpower, was duly established and specifically tasked by Federal Republic of Nigeria 1999, and Section 1 of the Armed Forces Act (AFA) No. 105 of 1993. Broadly these tasks are:-

a. Defence of the territorial integrity of Nigeria by air
b. Provision of assistance in aid to civil authority
c. Performing such other functions as may be prescribed by an Act of the National Assembly.

In addition to the requirement of defending the nation by air, the National Defence Policy also stipulates the protection of vital economic interests by air. Pursuant to this, the Nigerian Air Force is trained and equipped to be deployed for a multitude of tasks ranging from preserving the peace and disaster relief of political signaling and supporting friendly foreign governments in times of crises. If and when war becomes inevitable, the Nigerian Air Force can decisively contribute to its successful outcome. In this regard, therefore, let's look at the NAF in Nigeria's Defence Strategy.[13]

Global uncertainties and the rapidly changing faces of threat determine the level and shape of a nation's air power, bearing the state of economy. NAF ORBAT and the operational doctrine portray the defensive role dictated by Nigeria's defence policy. NAF concepts is defensive in the sense that our air power platforms are not too large to convey an aggressive posture to our neightbours. Nevertheless, it possesses the complements of air defence, offensive air support, maritime air operation, light and medium transport, sufficient to deter any aggressor within our sub-region.

The status of NAF inventory and ORBAT is presently being modified with the on-going fleet rationalization policy, essentially to reflect our operational concept of "ACTIVE DEFENCE...FORWARD ENGAGEMENT".[14] However, it can be concluded that although the number of platforms in our inventory is small, the NAF has a fair mix of aircraft that should provide a balanced tactical air force to meet the objectives of our national defence strategy.

Nigeria is a littoral nation with over 800nm of rich coastline and a maritime area of 84,000 sq nm. The nation is abundantly blessed with vast landmass, large manpower potential and good geography. Apart from oil that accounts for over 80% of our Gross Nationally Product (GNP), there are large deposits of untapped mineral, which should be protected. We have key vulnerable points (VPs) of strategic importance, such as oil refineries and installations, electric power generation stations, and other vital industrial facilities that require effective and continuous protection against air and surface attacks. Considering the vastness of the country, it is unlikely that our surface forces would be able to provide timely and adequate surveillance, early warning and security essential for the protection of vital economic assets. This situation underscores the urgent need to accord air power development top priority in the nation's defence strategy.

Areas where the NAF would play vital roles include the protection of our maritime assets in conjunction with the NN, especially with the discovery of large reserve of petroleum in our deep waters. It is noteworthy that our hydrocabon rich Gulf of Guinea is attracting global focus and interest of powerful nations like the United States and China. The role of NAF will be shaped by variables such as this in the near future. The volatility of the West African sub-region; the continuing war on terrorism, disaster preparedness and indeed the proliferation of small arms, and its impact on growing insurrection will continue to influence our geo-strategic interests. Thus, at every level from humanitarian aid to the greater role to play in meeting these future challenges.

This enhanced role for the Nigerian Air Force from internal security challenges and of course, challenges arising from government's foreign policy commitments is growing by the day, yet resource allocation to the defence sector is dwindling. Understandably, the government has embarked on building a more compact but well-equipped defence force that should be able to respond speedily to the challenges of national and sub-regional security. Notwithstanding, pragmatic budgetary releases and appropriate funding is expected.

Our success during Ops Liberty in Liberia and Op Sandstorm in Sierra Leone viewed from the perspective of our role as a sub regional leader, reinforces the need for our Armed Forces to function as an integrated team backed by an air force that retain the capacity to support government's robust foreign policy. Moreover, it is gratifying to note that, the reactivation of the G-222 medium transport aircraft and Super Puma helicopter, and planned induction of modern platforms like the F-7NI fighter aircraft, the Agusta 109 helicopter and the ATR 42 Maritime Patrol Aircraft should enhance the NAF's ability to project power within the sub-region and Africa.[15]

CONCLUSION

In conclusion I have situated airpower strategy within the framework of military strategy explaining the meaning of the term 'Dominant Strategy'. Thereafter, I took you through the evolution of air power and its employment from the First World War to OPERATION IRAQI FREEDOM highlighting the various strategic thoughts in the process.

I also discussed the role of technology in air power and noted its influence in shaping current strategic thought on strategic paralysis and the conduct of parallel war as put forward by Warden and employed in the Gulf Wars. Having explained the concept of parallel warfare designed to control the enemy towards a particular end state, I looked into the future employment of air power. I stated that based on the Tofflers' theory on the relationship between society and war, the future employment of air power will be information related. While the theory of strategic paralysis will continue to be relevant it would focus on information targeting with both the third and fourth dimensions playing crucial roles. I then went on to question the ability of small air forces, especially those of Third World nations to conduct same. I advised that small third world air forces must develop doctrine compatible with their circumstances and avoid the doctrinal band-wagon effect, especially as the cost of contemporary air power is prohibitive.[16]

Therefore, I looked at the relevance of the Nigerian Air Force to Nigeria's national security highlighting the role of the Service during peace-time and in crisis situation. Finally, I briefly examined the NAF in Nigeria's Defence Strategy and informed you that the on-going aircraft reactivation effort and the planned induction of new combat and maritime patrol platforms would go a long way in enhancing our ability to project power on the sub-Continent.

REFERENCES

1. James Corum, The Luftwaffe: Creating the Operational Air War 1918 – 1940.
2. Shaun Clarke Strategy, Air Strike and Small Nations.
3. Collins, Military Strategy: Principles, Practices and Historical Perspective.
4. Alvin and Heidi Toffler, War, Wealth and a New Era in History.
5. Fadok, Boyd and Warden: Air Power's Quest for Strategic Paralysis.
6. Warden, John A. III. The Air Campaign.
7. Sun Tzu. The Arts of War.
8. David Deptula, Effects Based Operations: Change in the Nature of Warfare.
9. H. G. Wells, The War in the Air.
10. Saboor and Idowu, Allied Strategic Air Offensive Against Germany.
11. Alvin and Heidi Toffler op. Cit.
12. Tony Mason, Air Power, A Centennial Appraisal.
13. NAF Fleet Policy October 2001.
14. Nigerian Air Force – Basic Air Power Doctrine 2000
15. NAF Aircraft Restoration Plan 2000.
16. Bishop, The Encyclopedia of 20th Century Air Warfare.

CHAPTER 34

NIGERIAN MILITARY CAPACITY FOR GLOBAL AND REGIONAL PEACE SUPPORT OPERATIONS

I. D. PENAP

PREAMBLE

The history of mankind is replete with conflicts and the attendant quest for security. As societies developed and communities emerged, conflict took various forms of dimensions. It arises as a result of clashes of interest and other forms of disagreements between individual, groups or organization as well as within and between sovereign states. In that wise, most conflicts are associated to resources utilization, political power tussles and quest for social supremacy. Where such disagreements occur on vital interest of such individuals, groups or states, they may led to clashes, contention, confrontation, or ultimately violent conflicts involving the use of arms.

Contrary to expectations, violent conflicts did not subside at the end of the Cold War in the 1990s. Many countries thereafter witnessed the proliferation of internal conflicts. In some cases, these crises were limited to constitutional disputes between the government in power and various opposition groups. In other instances, territorial disputes, armed ethnic conflict, civil wars and the collapse of governmental authority pose the principal threat. Africa, for instance, is the continent that suffers most from intra-state conflicts. These conflicts have resulted in loss of human lives, wanton destruction of property and untold suffering of innocent citizens. During the 1980s, for example, Africa was ravaged by nine wars, of which that of Sudan, Ethiopia, Angola, Mozambique and Uganda were major ones.[1] Death tolls recorded in these wars ranged from 60,000 in Angola to about three million in the Sudan. A survey of armed conflicts in Africa from 1990-2006 is widely reflected in the literature[2]. The continued wars in Africa and other countries of the world make it imperative to respond to potentially explosive situations at their earliest manifestations in order to prevent escalation. Response to crises and conflict could be in different form, which includes political mediation, economic dimensions and military intervention.

The United Nations (UN) is the organization charged with maintaining world peace and security. Despite the end of the Cold War, the demands on UN in the area of keeping peace and security had considerably increased. Thus, the UN has had cause to intervene in several crises in various parts of the world within the last 4 decades. However, the frequent outbreak of hostilities, especially in Africa and a few other parts of the world has overstretched UN resources. This necessitated the endorsement of regional and sub-regional groupings such as North Atlantic Treaty Organization (NATO), African Union (AU), Economic Community of West African States (ECOWAS) and Southern African Development Commission (SADC), among others, in the settlement of such crises. Chapter VIII of the UN Charter empowers the United Nations Security Council (UNSC) to encourage the settlement of local disputes through regional arrangements. Thus, the need for peaceful co-existence and resolution of conflicts necessitated a third party approach to the settlement of conflicts through the instrument of peace support operations (PDO).

PSO was a term first used by the military to cover Peacekeeping (PK) and Peace Enforcement (PE) operations. PSO is now widely used by many civilian agencies to describe their activities in complex humanitarian emergencies. PSOs are multifunctional operations in which impartial military activities are designed to create a secure environment and to facilitate the efforts of the civilian elements of the mission to create a self sustaining peace[3] They may include PK and PE, as well as conflict prevention, peacemaking, peace building and humanitarian operations. There are three ways in which member states of the UN and regional organizations contribute towards achieving the set goals of a PSO. These are in the contribution of PK force, logistics contingents and the provision of military observers (MILOBS).

Nigeria has been actively involved in the management of international peace and security since the attainment of independence on 1 Oct 1960. In 48 years of her existence as a nation, Nigeria's political leaders have continually designed and fashioned her foreign policies using her armed forces to achieve international, continental and sub-regional peace and security through PSO. Within the period, the Nigerian military has participated in various peace missions under the UN, AU and ECOWAS arrangements. Nigerian troops are currently on PSO in the Sudan and Liberia.

It is against this background that this chapter examines Nigerian military capacity to participate in PSO both at global, regional and sub-regional levels. The topic is, therefore, very apt as it will afford us the opportunity to appraise the situation in the past with a view to proffering solutions for enhancing Nigeria military capacity in present and future PSOs. The chapter will start with conceptual discourse, before assessing the Nigerian military capacity for regional and global PSO as a basis for highlighting the various challenges and prospects of future PSO at regional and global levels.

CONCEPTUAL DISCOURSE

In order to adequately address the topic of this chapter some key variables need to be defined for better understanding. The key variable identified in this topic are military capacity and PSO.

MILITARY CAPACITY

According to Concise Oxford English Dictionary 2003, the word 'military' relates to, or characteristics of soldiers or the armed forces of a country.[7] It includes all organized groups, regular and irregular, national and tribal, uses violence for political and social ends.[8] The Nigerian military, in consonance with the Constitution, consists of the Army, Navy and the Air Force.

The other word 'capacity' means the ability or power to do something.[9] 'Military capacity', therefore, implies the ability or the power of the military to perform or achieve a specified mission. For a successful accomplishment of task or mission, the military would need to assess its capacity holistically to avoid failure or being bogged down in any mission. In that wise, consideration will be given to force structure, equipment, doctrine, personnel and sustainability among others. This applies to all spectra of operations be it conventional, asymmetric or PSO.

In the context of military capacity for PSO, the various tasks which the peacekeepers would undertake will dictate the preparations to be carried out by the military. The tasks could include forced entry and separation of warring parties, conducting patrols and escort duties, disarmament and demobilization. Other non conducting patrols and escort duties, disarmament and demobilization. Other non-combat tasks take the forms of reconstruction and reintegration of warring groups as well as conducting inspections and verification exercises. Liaison and coordination with Civilian Police and other civilian actors in the operations areas is also important for the achievement of a military mission. In addition, the influence of the media in the shaping of public opinion, which is likely to affect military operations, needs to enhance their capacity before induction and deployment.

PEACE SUPPORT OPERATIONS

PSO is a generic term for peacemaking; peacekeeping, peace building and peace enforcement operations. It also includes political, diplomatic, military and humanitarian efforts to control conflict and to promote reconciliation being used to respond to complex intra-state conflicts involving widespread human right violations as opposed to more traditional peace keeping. Thus, PSO are critical all activities which involve peace related containment and resolution. They cover all activities which involve peace related operations. PSO are usually organized by the UN, multi-national, regional or sub-regional organizations but could also be based on bilateral agreements between countries. It may be co-ordinated at the global, regional or sub-regional levels under the auspices of various organizations. Some of these organizations include the UN, AU, ECOWAS, SADC, Organization for Security and Co-operation in Europe (OSCE), and NATO. The UN employs PSO as one of the means to advance world peace and security. Other means include diplomacy, negotiation and mediation.

PSO evolved out of the UN" resolve to keep international peace and security and to promote understanding among people and between communities. The UN Charter itself does not specifically address the issue of PSO, however, Chapter VI of Charter provides for the pacific settlement of disputes, which forms the legal framework for PSO.

Peacekeeping: PK is a PSO conducted following an agreement or ceasefire that has established a permissive environment where the level of consent and compliance is high and the threat of disruption is low.[14] These operations are conducted to monitor and facilitate the implementation of an existing truce agreement and support diplomatic efforts to reach a long term political settlement. PK is based, therefore, on those techniques, such as negotiation and mediation, which promote consent and the active cooperation of all parties to the peace process. In principle and practice, force can only be used in self defence, but this need not preclude the robust use of means, which includes the use of force to gain the initiative and achieve the overall mission.

Peace Building: Peace building is a PSO employing complementary diplomatic, civil, and when necessary, military means to address the underlying causes of conflict and the long-term needs of the people.[15]. It requires a commitment to a long term process and may run concurrently with other types of PSO. In this type of operation, military as well as civilian involvement is normally required. Peace building activities include restoring civil authority, rebuilding physical infrastructures and re-establishing commerce, schools and medical facilities among others. An example of a peace building operation was the US and its allies assistance to Europe and Asia otherwise referred to as the Marshall Plain in the Post World War 11 era.

Peacemaking: Peacemaking is a PSO conducted after the initiation of a conflict to secure a ceasefire or peaceful settlement that involves primarily assets.[16] Military activities that support peacemaking include infrastructure for civil military relations and security assistance operations.

Humanitarian Assistance: Often, the military institution is assigned tasks of assisting aid agencies in providing security while the impact on the well being of an affected environment. There are times when such security assistance has to be forced through against armed opposition. Such assistances are always provided at a cost to the primary task of PSOs, which may be perceived as impartiality. It is therefore imperative that additional tasks are supported by adequate strength and tensparency. Humanitarian assistance is therefore a relief action founded on human right of every individual to request and receive aid necessary to sustain life and dignity from competent authorities or local, national, government and non-government authorities.[17]

Peace Enforcement: PE operations are coercive operations required in the absence of consent, or at least in the expectation of one, or all, of the parties failing to comply with agreed conditions.[18] The peace support force must be capable of applying credible coercive force and must apply the provisions of the peace agreement impartially. To be credible, a PE must be perceived as being willing and capable of over-matching whatever opposition it might be offered. Furthermore, a commander needs the operational flexibility to be able to enforce compliance in the face of opposition, to promote consent where there is indifference and to maintain and reward consent where it exists.

NIGERIAN MILITARY CAPACITY FOR REGIONAL AND GLOBAL PEACE SUPPORT OPERATIONS.

The requirements for the conduct of PSO under either regional or global organizations are quite demanding. Troops Contributing Countries (TCC) are expected to be self sustaining depending on the type of arrangement they have with the sponsor organization, they must, therefore, prepare adequately before deploying for any PK operations. Otherwise, the effect on the troops in particular and the nation in general could be counter-productive. It is based on this premise that it becomes imperative to carry out an assessment of the Nigerian military capacity for regional and global PSOs. The assessment will, however, be limited to training, equipment and funding.

Training: Inadequate training for PSO is one of the deficiencies associated with the Nigerian Military preparations. The training hitherto provided to units was inadequate like guard duties and other ceremonial parades along side preparations for operation thereby spending less time on training. Things have, however, improved with the establishment of the PK Wing by the NA in ICCS, Jaji. The centre conducts induction training for units earmarked for PSO and also runs Military Observers Course for officers.

Not long ago, the US Army was involved in preparing NA troops for UN operations. The training was conducted under Operation FOCUS RELIEF. Many units benefited from the training and it actually enhanced the NA capacity for PSO. Other infrastructure available to Nigerian military personnel for PSO training includes among others, the Pearson's International Peacekeeping Institute in Canada and Kofi Annan Peacekeeping Institute in Ghana. In exploring the experiences of others, there is need to solicit for support from other countries and the international community to enhance Nigeria's capacity.

EQUIPMENT:

The provision of adequate equipment for the Nigerian military to prosecute PSOs has always been a recurring problem. The Nigerian military currently goes to PSO with less equipment when compared with UN Table of Organization and Equipment (TOE). The UN stipulates what a unit TOE for an operation, and subsequently reimburses the country of such units based on its TOE standard. Nigeria's participation in UN operations over the years provided an opportunity for equipping her forces. However, some challenges still exist, which the Nigerian military is making frantic efforts at resolving. Arrangements are going for direct funding of units earmarked for PSO by commercial banks. They are to be refunded by the FG on agreed terms. In the field, the Nigerian government still uses the wet lease system in all UN operations. This implies providing all the required equipment while the UN reimburses accordingly. In most cases, it has not been easy for Nigeria to meet the UN requirements equipment wise.

FUNDING:

Funds required for PSOs need to be budgeted for and readily mobilized for use when the need arises. The initial funding of a nation's contingent rests with the government for the first 60 pending reimbursement by the UN. This is not, however, the case at the regional and sub-regional levels where the capacity of members states to fund PSO is very low. Based on other competing demands, it is unlikely that Nigeria would be able to sustain PSO for a protracted period without the support of sponsoring organization or body. To enhance its capacity for PSO, the NA recently had a parley with consortium of banks to sensitize the banks on the opportunities inherent in the funding of PSOs by corporate bodies. When the agreement is finally sealed, it is envisaged that the military capacity in PSO would be enhanced.

IMPACT ANALYSIS

The promotion of international peace and security is one of the cardinal foreign policy objective of Nigeria. She, therefore, values and respects the principle of peaceful settlement of disputes as enshrined in the charters of the UN, AU and ECOWAS. In pursuance of this foreign policy objective, Nigeria made enormous sacrifices in terms of human and material support for peace and security in the world. She has earned the respect of her African neighbours and friends in the international community. Most of Nigeria's PK activities have been conducted in Africa under the auspices of the UN, AU and ECOWAS and some by bilateral agreement. In about four decades, Nigeria has participated in not less than 20 PSO's and related missions globally.

Thus, Nigeria has been a regular participant in both global and regional PSOs and has therefore made valuable contribution to peace and security in Africa and around the globe. The facts available also indicate that Nigeria is still a willing contributor to all types of PSOs that are not at variant with her foreign policy objectives. The Nigerian military has abundant human resources capable of being employed both at global, regional and sub-regional peace initiatives. However, her dwindling economy since the early 1980s has raised many questions as to whether she could continue to sustain her roles and functions in PSOs in the nearest future. Notwithstanding the economic problems, it is in Nigeria's strategic interest to continue to bid for more UN sponsored PSOs with a view to deriving maximum economic and political benefits therein.

The Nigerian military has impacted positively in various PSOs she has participated increasingly too, the employment of the Nigerian military in these operations is a significant measure for achieving and maintaining international peace and security. The impacts of the Nigerian military on regional and global PSOs is examined under the UN, AU and ECOWAS.

PSO has been used more often by the UN as a tool for conflict management. The first UN PKO in which Nigeria participated was the UN Operation in the Congo (ONUC). Nigeria's participation in that operation was from November 1960 – June 1964.[21] The contingent was made up of two battalions with supporting troops totaling

1,400 soldiers and members of the Nigerian Police. [22] Thus, Nigeria's contributions became the third largest national force in the ONUC.

Nigerian troops and the Nigerian Police in the Congo operation gave good account of themselves as they performed very well with many winning medals and special commendations. The troops served in 4 of the 6 provinces of the Congo, (Kivi, Katanga, Kansai and Leopoldville), while the Nigerian police served only in Leopoldville. The Nigerian Contingent demonstrated high discipline, good humour and valour in the Congo.

Nigeria's participation in the ONUC remains one of her first major efforts at playing a role in an African conflict. The overall achievement of this operation was the compete restoration of law and order in the Congo which helped to enhance the maintenance of internal peace and security. It also brought out the need for better training and coordination of UN operation from planning and deployment, through logistics and communication. Nigeria's perception reinforced by the political will and determination has always upheld the UN ideals and international peace and security around the globe with special attention to Africa which forms the centre-piece of her foreign policy.

The first attempt by the then OAU (now AU) to intervene militarily in the internal affairs of a member state was in Chad between 1981 and 1982. The organization had in the past played some contributing role towards the resolution of boundary disputes and other crisis within the African continent. Nigeria has to intervene in Chad following pressure for the OAU to step into the matter. Consequently , the organization therefore dispatched a force consisting mainly of Nigerian troops.

The first and only OAU peacekeeping mission in Chad was to be composed of 5,000 men under the command of Nigeria's Maj Gen. Ejiga. The OAU was unable to meet the force level due to the failure of some countries to meet their pledges. In the course of the operation only 3,000 troops were mustered to conduct the entire operations. The troops were from Nigeria, Senegal and Zaire (now RC). Added to the limitation in manpower, resources were also slim due to the poor financial states of most member countries and the failure of the OAU to secure contributions from some advanced countries. Thus, unable to sustain the operations, OAU's Chad Operations moved from one uncertainty to the other with Nigeria contributing the highest cost. Consequently, the OAU lost authority necessary for a multinational peacekeeping force as the TCCs assumed direct control over the conduct of their respective troops.

Starting from 1990, another dimension was added to Nigeria's participation in international PK. Nigeria played a paramount role in the formation and deployment of the ECOMOG to Liberia in August of the year. The Nigerian Contingent (NIGCON) of ECOMOG was formed in response to the decision by ECOWAS to intervene in the Liberian conflict, and the request for member countries to contribute troops for the formation of a PK force.

Beyond contributing troops, Nigeria also bore the major burden in supporting contingents from other countries during ECOMOG Operations in Liberia and Sierra Leone. Contrary to the initial agreement that each country would be self-sufficient for the first 30 days only, ECOWAS was unable to fulfill its commitment. Consequently, other countries relied heavily on Nigeria especially for logistical support. In 1998, it was reported that after 7 years in Liberia, "Nigeria spent three billion dollars on the operations". In fact, by the end of the operation in 1998, Nigeria had spend at least \$4.5 billion not only in providing for her national contingent, but to sustain the entire operation in Liberia.[28]

There is no doubt that the formation, deployment and operations of ECOMOG in Liberia and Sierra-Leone contributed immensely to the stabilization of government and political economy of the countries. ECOMOG which was championed, financed (and with more troops contribution by Nigeria) has achieved a lot for West Africa, and indeed the African continent. The nation has set a record in conflict management, especially in the calculus of the interplay of PK, PE, peacemaking and peace building. The Nigerian led ECOMOG has no doubt served as a model for conflict management, and this model has interested many regions of the World. The nation has further shown clearly that regional PK can function among poor and weak nations despite logistic limitations associated with them.

The major impacts of the Nigerian military in regional and global PSO could be grouped under promotion of peace and stability in the world, promotion of democracy and good governance, lead nation role and offering of military assistance to African countries.

PROMOTION OF PEACE AND STABILITY:

In her bid to promote peace and stability in the world, the Nigerian military has contributed to the restoration and sustenance of sub-regional, regional and global peace. In the sub-region, the activities of ECOMOG in Liberia and Sierra Leone with the performance of the Nigerian troops stabilized the countries, which eventually brought peace and stability to them. This in turn prevented the domino effect that would have engulfed the West African sub-region.

Promotion of Democracy and Good Governance: The Nigerian military has contributed to the sustenance of democracy and good governance worldwide. The institution of a legitimate government through elections in Liberia and the restoration of an overthrown government in Sieria Leone and recent deployment in support of the democratic government in Cote d'Voire are good pointers to the commitment to the rule of law and democratic governance.

LEAD NATION ROLE

Nigerian military has been assuming leadership role responsibilities in PSOs. She has demonstrated this through the protection of her force in various PSOs at global, regional and sub-regional levels. The Nigerian military is always ready to lead, coordinate and build consensus among her allies in execution of PSOs. Nigeria unilaterally initiated PSO in Chad in 1979 and also spearheaded troop development in AU PK mission in the Sudan among others. In the same vein, the Nigerian military provided a model PSO for other regional bodies like SADC.

OFFERING OF MILITARY ASSISTANCE

The Nigerian military has been in the fore front of rendering military assistance to African countries in training and equipment for better participation in PSO. The AFCSC, NDC and other Nigerian military institutions offered various courses to our African brothers. The PK Wing in ICCS is being developed to accommodate foreign students in tactical PK training.

CHALLENGES AND PROSPECTS.

The Nigerian military has faced the challenges of PK missions despite the enormous cost of her participation. This can be regarded as a clear demonstration of her commitment to peace and security in Africa and the world, without hinderance to the challenges and demands posed by resource limitations. It is anticipated that the Nigerian military will continue to play a major role in the achievement of the national defence and foreign policy objectives related to sustenance and restoration of peace. Apart from being the most populous and leading black nation in the world, Nigeria is blessed with great human and natural resources that assists in that direction. However, Nigeria's participation in international PSO has not been without problems. For better future performance in PSO these problems need to be addressed.

CHALLENGES

The involvement of Nigerian military in international PK operations particularly ECOMOG brought out same lapses and challenges. Notably, among them are obtaining political consensus prior to intervention, complexity of mission and mandate, balance and command structure in a multinational force, and transitional arrangements from military to civilian authority. Humanitarian and human rights issues and financing the entire operations have also been some outstanding problems. There were also problems associated with political directions, force command structure and balance arising from the dominance of one country over other TCC.

Nigeria suffered greatly during the first intervention in Liberia in 1990 in providing financial supports for other ECOWAS members. Endowment fund was established with initial amount of 50 million dollar being proposed. This fund received no contribution. Generally, assistances from other sources were slow and members states that contributed troops threatened to withdraw from the force, unless there was substantial financial support for ECOMOG operations.

Logistics problems are another set of hindrances in impeding peacekeeping operations. The immediate past UN Secretary General, Kofi Annan was quoted as saying that "the security council was unlikely to commit the necessary funds to the ventures". [30] Therefore, in the face of non-availability of centralized logistics, participating countries suffered in lift and other logistics capabilities. Consequently, most TCC relied on Nigeria for logistical support. There is the need to obtain adequate logistics support before embarking on such operations in the future. Perhaps, the establishment of logistic bases in each sub-region would alleviate related problems in future PSO.

Another challenge is that Nigeria has not received any commensurate diplomatic, economic or strategic benefits for its enormous human and financial commitment to peacekeeping missions. Instead, Nigeria continues to be the target of unprovoked attacks in some African Countries. Moreso, even the governments of countries that benefited from peacekeeping efforts of Nigeria have paid back very badly as evident in the action of former Liberian President, Charles Taylor who brutally authorized the killing two Nigerian Journalists.

PROSPECTS

Despite the problems confronting Nigeria's peacekeeping efforts, she continue to send troops on PSO with recorded successes. It is worthwhile venture as troops undergo profitable exposure to foreign troops and services. The various PSOs have served as eye opener to the essential need of working together. PK has become one of the most, missions with multiple functions. It is now viewed as a continuous on-the –field training experience for the Nigerian military.

Nigeria has actually been using the mechanism of PSO to translate her inspiration and quest for African leadership into reality. Its contributions to PSO have contributed to boosting the country's military and diplomatic status within the international system. Arising from peacekeeping, therefore, more African countries and indeed the outside world have come to appreciate the centrality of Nigeria to African affairs.

With specific reference to UN operations, the participation of Nigerian military in PK has been a source of revenue for the nation. This is so because, TCCs to UN PSO are entitled to various claims. These claims range from reimbursements on contingent own equipment taken to mission areas, items of food from home countries, clothing and gear, troops monthly allowance, specialist and fatality allowances. For instance, reimbursement on major equipment and provision for self-sustainment for the initial two battalions in UNAMSIL from 27 December 1999 to 26 January 2000 amounted to US $798,063." Thus, contrary to the popular impression that Nigerian military participation in PK operations is always a drain on the economy, the reality is that such participation, especially in UN operations and missions constitutes a source of foreign exchange earnings for the country.

CONCLUSION

PSO is an instrument for the maintenance of international peace, security and stability although it is not a substitute for a permanent solution to international conflict. As part of her contribution to global peace, Nigeria has participated in

PSO both at sub regional, regional and global levels under the ECOWAS, AU and UN respectively. The nations decision to participate in PSO aptly described her zeal to fulfill her foreign policy objectives and contribute to international peace and security.

Participation in international PSO has had some positive effects on the Nigeria foreign policy, defence policy and socio-economic interests. For the country as a whole, PK has been more beneficial when undertaken under the auspices of the UN. It has contributed immensely to the exposure of Nigerian military in joint training along side other contingents and creates awareness in modern military hardware. It has also helped Nigeria to translate her inspirational quest for African leadership into centrality of Nigeria to African affairs.

In examining Nigerian military impact at regional and global PSO an attempt was made to look briefly at selected PSOs where Nigerian military has participated. The PSO in Congo, Chad, Liberia and Sierra Leone were mentioned. The problems of finance, logistics and command and control are always recurring. Other problem areas include communication, training and political will. These problems are being addressed locally and regionally. The Nigerian military has impacted positively through her contribution to international peace and stability, promotion of democracy and good governance, her lead role function and offering of military assistance to regional African countries. The challenges of PSO globally are complex and require concerted efforts to resolve. The Nigerian military alone may not overcome them without government and foreign assistance. Increased collaboration by the West and regional bodies in training and assistance are, therefore, commendable and need to be sustained for enhancing our capacity in regional and global PSOs. This would further assist the Nigerian military to explore fully the benefits accruing from participating in PSO.

ENDNOTES

1. Dokubo, C. "The African Union and the Mechanism for Conflict Resolution: Prospects and Challenges. P.3
2. Ibid
3. Peace Support Operations Joint Warfare Publication 3-50 p 1-1
4. The Nigerian Army Diary 2000
5. CIA World Fact Book 2007.
6. Oni, SK (eds) *The Nigerian Army in ECOMOG Operations: Liberia and Sierra Leone, (Ibadan: Sam Bookman Publishers, 2002).*
7. The Concise Oxford Dictionary (COD) Tenth Edition, 2003.
8. Ibid
9. AG Adewuyi, Majo Gen, Nigeria's Military Capacity for Regional and Global Peace Support Operations. A Lecture Delivered to the Participants of National War College Course 13 on 9 Mar 2005.
10. Op. cit COD
11. Op cit Adewuyi

12. Ibid
13. Op cit JWP.
14. Peace Support Operations for the NA, 2005, p.1-2.
15. Ibid p 1-2
16. Ibid p 1.2.
17. White ND, The United Nations and the Maintenance of International Peace and Security. (Manchester, UK: Manchester University Press, 1990).
18. Op cit PSO Doctrine
19. Op cit
20. Ibid
21. Nigeria 35 Years in Global Peacekeeping. Published by Office of Defence Adviser Permanent Mission of Nigeria to the UN, New York USA. 1995 p 20.
22. Ibid
23. Op cit, Oni SK
24. Ibid
25. Ibid.
26. Col. MB Marwa "Preparing NA Troops for UN Operations: A better Option" Chief of Army Staff Conference 1996.
27. Ibid
28. Ibid
29. Ayissi and Robin-Edward Poulton (ed), *Bound to Cooperate: Conflict, Peace and People of Sierra Leon,* (Geneva UNIDIR, 200) p. 113.
30. Annan K, *The Causes of Conflict and Promotion of Durable Peace and Sustainable Development in Africa.* (New York 1998).
31. Op cit Oni SK.

CHAPTER 35

STRATEGIC RESPONSE: PEACE SUPPORT OPERATIONS

OGABA OCHE

INTRODUCTION

The desire to bring an end to warfare and replace it with functional forms of interaction has been a major pursuit of nation-states. Indeed, it was with the aim of bringing about an end to the scourge of war and converting "swords into plowshares" that the United Nations (UN) was established in 1945. Although the reason behind its formation was the elimination of war, the UN was not initially equipped with adequate institutional mechanisms to achieve this monumental task. However, the turbulence of the international environment compelled the evolution of Peace Support Operations (PSO) as an instrumental imperative for managing and resolving conflicts as well as for maintaining international security. This paper will look at UN peace support operations which entails an initial focus on the background to UN peacekeeping and the reasons behind its transformation to PSO's.

THE UN AND PEACEKEEPING

One of the primary purposes for which the UN was established, which is stated in Article I of its Charter, is to "..maintain international peace and security" and to take "..effective collective measures for the prevention and removal of threats to the peace." It is in view of this fundamental role of the UN, and against the background of the failure of the League of Nations to maintain peace, that the involvement of the UN in peacekeeping as a method of conflict management can best be understood and appreciated.

The international community, in its efforts to make the UN more effective, gave the latter the authority, through the Charter, to identify parties that are guilty of aggression and to take effective steps to bring such conflicts to an end and to punish guilty parties to such conflicts. Under Article 24 of the Charter, the Security Council has the primary responsibility of maintaining international peace and security. In order to help it attain this objective, it is empowered by Article 29 to establish such subsidiary organs as it may find necessary for the performance of its functions. Nowhere in the Charter, however, is there provision for the establishment of a permanent peacekeeping force for the UN. Instead, peacekeeping operations have been handled on ad hoc bases with the Security Council or General Assembly passing enabling resolutions which determine the purposes for establishing such peacekeeping forces, as well as general guidelines for their operations.

The importance and significance of the involvement of the UN in peacekeeping operations cannot be over-emphasized. This was lucidly communicated by the former Secretary General of the UN, Boutros Boutros-Ghali, when he stated that, between 1990 and 1994,

> ... the United Nations has been called to more peacekeeping operations than in the previous 45 years... This year (1994) the UN spent $3.3 billion on peacekeeping – more than double the amount just two years ago. The demand for operation, the number of personnel, the size of the budget involved are all of vastly greater magnitude.

The above quotation gives an idea of the scope of demand for the intervention of the UN in conflict situations around the world. Most of these peacekeeping operations were of the "Traditional or Cold War" types which were basically military operations that were established by the UN to help control conflicts that had been identified by the Security Council as constituting a threat to international peace and security. Such operations served as interim measures that helped to create and maintain ceasefire as well as buffer zones between belligerent states or groups thereby facilitating the search for a lasting peace agreement through diplomatic channels. A prime example of UN traditional peacekeeping is the United Nations Operation in the Congo (ONUC) which was established in July 1960, following a breakdown of law and order immediately after the attainment of independence by the Congo.

Cold War or traditional peacekeeping can broadly be divided into two sub-types. These include the unarmed military observer missions such as the United Nations Observer Mission in Liberia (UNOMIL), which was established to monitor a ceasefire and elections in Liberia. The second sub-type is the armed infantry-based force which is used when there is the need to control disputed territory in the form of a buffer zone from which forces of the belligerent sides have agreed to withdraw. An example of this is the United Nations Emergency Force (UNEF) that was established in July 1956 to monitor the withdrawal of English, French and Israeli forces from Egyptian territory. Another example is the United Nations Aouzou Strip Observer Group, which was established in May 1994 to monitor the withdrawal of Libyan forces from the disputed Aouzou Strip in Northern Chad.

Until the end of the Cold War such traditional peacekeeping operations mostly had traditional ceasefire monitoring mandates and no direct peace-building responsibilities. The "entry strategy" or sequence of events and decisions that led to UN deployment was generally straightforward. It usually involves the existence of a war in which a ceasefire is brokered, there is an invitation to monitor ceasefire compliance and deployment of military observers or units to do so, while efforts continue for a political settlement. Traditional peacekeeping, which treats the symptoms rather than sources of conflict, has no built-in exit strategy and associated peacemaking was often slow to make progress. As a result, traditional peacekeepers have remained in place for 10, 20, 30 or even 50 years (as in Cyprus, the Middle East and India/Pakistan). By the standards of more complex operations, they are relatively low cost and politically easier to maintain than to remove. However, they are also difficult to justify unless accompanied by serious and sustained peacemaking efforts that seek to transform a ceasefire accord into a durable and lasting peace settlement.

Since the end of the cold war, United Nations peacekeeping has often combined with peace-building in complex peace operations deployed into settings of intra-State conflict. Those conflict settings, however, both affect and are affected by outside actors: political patrons; arms vendors; buyers of illicit commodity exports; regional powers that send their own forces into the conflict; and neighbouring states that host refugees who are sometimes systematically forced to flee their homes. With such significant cross-border effects by state and non-state actors alike, these conflicts are often decidedly "transnational" in character.

The risks and costs for operations that must function in such circumstances are much greater than for traditional peacekeeping. Moreover, the complexity of the tasks assigned to these missions and the volatility of the situation on the ground tend to increase together. Since the end of the cold war, such complex and risky mandates have been the rule rather than the exception: United Nations operations have been given relief-escort duties where the security situation was so dangerous that humanitarian operations could not continue without high risk for humanitarian personnel; they have been given mandates to protect civilian victims of conflict where potential victims were at greatest risk, and mandates to control heavy weapons in the possession of local parties when those weapons were being used to threaten the mission and the local population alike. In some extreme situations, United Nations operations were given executive law enforcement and administrative authority where local authority did not exist or was not able to function.

SECURITY ENVIRONMENT OF THE 1990'S

Throughout the 1990's a number of developments occurred that necessitated reexamination of UN peacekeeping globally. As indicated earlier, there was an explosion in demands for peacekeepers during the 1990s which tested both the capabilities and resources of the United Nations throughout the decade. The unprecedented need for peacekeepers was complicated by the changing role they would play. More and more frequently peacekeeping forces were called upon to intervene in hostile (that is, non-consensual) and dangerous situations to protect besieged populations. Unfortunately, in many cases the UN failed to meet these daunting challenges and UN military failures seemed to become commonplace.

This was reflected in the United Nations' inability to bring more men, money, as well as new ideas to the enterprise of peacekeeping. The UN Secretariat was grossly under-staffed and under-funded. As at the beginning of 2000 the Department of Peacekeeping Operations had only 32 military officers to plan, recruit, equip, deploy, support, and direct some 27,000 soldiers that comprised the 15 missions that were underway at the time. UN police forces faced a similar situation: a staff of only nine police officers working out of UN headquarters was called upon to support

8,000 UN police in the field. The Department of Peacekeeping Operations (DPKO) administrative budget (which was equal to 1/50th of the field teams' budget) was utterly insufficient to support the teams in the field.

The United Nations therefore clearly lacked the resources to effectively fulfill its peacekeeping mission. This point brought into sharp focus the UN's lack of independence and inability to assume a leadership role in international crisis situations given the fact that, at the time, the UN hardly enjoyed the support of the United States for its international engagements. Indeed, towards the end of the century the United Nations was arguably a body that was in constant search of material and financial support and coherent political backing from member states.

Another significant factor had to with the security situation in Africa. Nowhere was the scope and intensity of violence during the 1990s as great as in Africa. While the general trend of armed conflict in Europe, Asia, the Americas, and the Middle East fell during the 1989-99 period, the 1990s witnessed an increase in the number of conflicts on the African continent. During this period, 16 UN peacekeeping missions were sent to Africa. (Three countries-Somalia, Sierra Leone, and Angola-were visited by multiple missions during this time.) Furthermore, this period saw internal and interstate violence in numerous sub-Saharan states.

In 1999 alone, the continent was plagued by 16 armed conflicts, seven of which were wars with more than 1,000 battle-related deaths (Journal of Peace Research, 37:5, 2000, p. 638). In 2000, the situation continued to deteriorate. Renewed heavy fighting between Eritrea and Ethiopia claimed tens of thousands of lives in the lead-up to a June ceasefire and ultimately the signing of a peace accord in December; continued violence in the Democratic Republic of Congo (DRC), Sierra Leone, Burundi, Angola, Sudan, Uganda, and even Nigeria as well as the outbreak of new violence between Guinea and Liberia, in Zimbabwe, and in the Ivory Coast brought new hardship and bloodshed to the continent. Indeed, there was a consensus among many observers that the level of violence in Africa had reached an all time low point. This is in addition to the fact that the potential exists for more civil wars.

Other variables that affect the difficulty of the quest for peace include the sources of the conflict. These could range from economics (e.g., issues of poverty, distribution, discrimination or corruption), politics (an unalloyed contest for power) and resource and other environmental issues (such as competition for scarce water) to issues of ethnicity, religion or gross violations of human rights. Political and economic objectives may be more fluid and open to compromise than objectives related to resource needs, ethnicity or religion. Second, the complexity of negotiating and implementing peace will tend to rise with the number of local parties and the divergence of their goals (e.g., some may seek unity while others may seek separation). Third, the level of casualties, population displacement and infrastructure damage affect the level of war-generated grievances, and thus the difficulty of reconciliation, which requires that past human rights violations be addressed, as well as the cost and complexity of reconstruction. At the turn of the century therefore the challenges for the United Nations and the West vis-à-vis Africa were tremendous.

"AN AGENDA FOR PEACE" AND THE PANEL ON UNITED NATIONS PEACE OPERATIONS

In a farsighted attempt to come to grips with the growing forms of insecurity the then UN Secretary General, Boutros Boutros-Ghali, in January 1992, presented a report entitled An Agenda For Peace to the UN Security Council. In the report he argued that the aims of the UN in managing conflict and new forms of insecurity must be:-

To seek to identify at the earliest possible stage situations that could produce conflict, and to try through diplomacy to remove the sources of danger before violence results;

- Where conflict erupts, to engage in peacemaking aimed at resolving the issues that have led to conflict;

- Through peace-keeping, to work to preserve peace, however fragile, where fighting has been halted and to assist in implementing agreements achieved by the peacemakers;

- To stand ready to assist in peace-building in its differing contexts: rebuilding the institutions and infrastructures of nations torn by civil war and strife; and building bonds of peaceful mutual benefit among nations formerly at war;

- And in the largest sense, to address the deepest causes of conflict: economic despair, social injustice and political oppression.

The means through which these could be achieved was basically four-fold. These include preventive diplomacy which is action to prevent disputes from arising between parties, to prevent existing disputes from escalating into conflicts and to limit the spread of conflicts when they occur. Secondly there is peacemaking which is action to bring hostile parties to agreement, essentially through peaceful means. Thirdly the report identified peace-keeping which is the deployment of a United Nations presence in the field, hitherto with the consent of all the parties concerned, normally involving United Nations military and/or police personnel and frequently civilians as well. Quite significantly, peace-keeping is a technique that expands the possibilities for both the prevention of conflict and the making of peace.

The remaining means is that of post-conflict peace-building which refers to action to identify and support structures which will tend to strengthen and solidify peace in order to avoid a relapse into conflict. Therefore, while preventive diplomacy seeks to resolve disputes before violence breaks out; peacemaking and peace-keeping are required to halt conflicts and preserve peace once it is attained. If successful, they strengthen the opportunity for post-conflict peace-building, which can prevent the recurrence of violence among nations and peoples.

Carrying the process a step further the current UN Secretary General, Kofi Annan, convened a High Level Panel on United Nations Peace Operations,

in March 2000, to make a thorough examination of UN peacekeeping and security activities while being guided by a number of considerations. These considerations included

i.   Emphasis upon the importance of clear, credible and adequately resourced Security Council mandates;

ii. The importance of focus on conflict prevention and its early engagement, wherever possible;

iii. The need to have more effective collection and assessment of information at United Nations Headquarters, including an enhanced conflict early warning system that can detect and recognize the threat or risk of conflict or genocide;

iv. The essential importance of the United Nations system adhering to and promoting international human rights instruments and standards and international humanitarian law in all aspects of its peace and security activities;

v.   The need to build the United Nations capacity to contribute to peace-building, both preventive and post-conflict, in a genuinely integrated manner;

vi. The critical need to improve Headquarters planning (including contingency planning) for peace operations;

vii. The recognition that while the United Nations has acquired considerable expertise in planning, mounting and executing traditional peacekeeping operations, it had yet to acquire the capacity needed to deploy more complex operations rapidly and to sustain them effectively;

viii. The necessity to provide field missions with high-quality leaders and managers who are granted greater flexibility and autonomy by Headquarters, within clear mandate parameters and with clear standards of accountability for both spending and results;

ix. The imperative to set and adhere to a high standard of competence and integrity for both Headquarters and field personnel, who must be provided the training and support necessary to do their jobs and to progress in their careers, guided by modern management practices that reward meritorious performance and weed out incompetence;

x.   The importance of holding individual officials at Headquarters and in the field accountable for their performance, recognizing that they need to be given commensurate responsibility, authority and resources to fulfill their assigned tasks.

After a period of five months the High Level Panel on United Nations Peace Operations submitted a report to the UN Secretary General which is now commonly referred to as the Brahimi Report after the Chairman of the Panel, Mr Lakhdar Brahimi. Having made a comprehensive study of, and recommendations for the reform of UN peacekeeping, it can be safely said that this report is central to the development of UN Peace Support Operations. The Report made far reaching recommendations which, in highly abridged form, included the following:

i. The need for the United Nations and its members to establish more effective strategies for conflict prevention, in both the long and short terms, in addition to the frequent use of fact-finding missions to areas of tension in order to support short-term crisis-preventive action.

ii. The need for robust peace support doctrines and realistic mandates. This means that United Nations military units must be capable of defending themselves, other mission components and the mission's mandate. Rules of engagement should be sufficiently robust and not force United Nations contingents to cede the initiative to their attackers. It means that mandates should specify an operation's authority to use force. It also means bigger forces, better equipped and more costly but able to be a credible deterrent. Security Council mandates should also reflect the clarity that peacekeeping operations require for unity of effort when they deploy into potentially dangerous situations.

iii. The need for new headquarters capacity for information management and strategic analysis. This implied that a new information-gathering and analysis entity be created to support the informational and analytical needs of the Secretary-General and the members of the Executive Committee on Peace and Security (ECPS). Without such capacity, the Secretariat will remain a reactive institution, unable to get ahead of daily events, and the Committee will not be able to fulfill the role for which it was created.

iv. The Report emphasized the need to assemble the leadership of a new mission as early as possible at United Nations Headquarters, to participate in shaping a mission's concept of operations, support plan, budget, staffing and Headquarters mission guidance. To that end, it recommended the systematic compilation of a comprehensive list of potential special representatives of the Secretary-General (SRSGs), force commanders, civilian police commissioners, their potential deputies and potential heads of other components of a mission, representing a broad geographic and equitable gender distribution.

v. The Report noted that the first 6 to 12 weeks following a ceasefire or peace accord are often the most critical ones for establishing both a stable peace and the credibility of a new operation. Opportunities lost during that period are hard to regain. It therefore recommended that the United Nations define "rapid and effective deployment capacity" as the ability to fully deploy traditional peacekeeping operations within 30 days of the adoption of a Security Council resolution establishing such an operation, and within 90 days in the case of complex peacekeeping operations.

vi. The Report recommended that Headquarters support for peacekeeping should be treated as a core activity of the United Nations, and as such the majority of its resource requirements should be funded through the regular budget of the Organization. It also recommended management review of DPKO because staff shortages were plainly obvious. For example, it was clearly not enough at the beginning of 2000 to have 32 officers providing military planning and guidance to 27,000 troops in the field, nine civilian police staff to identify, vet and provide guidance for up to 8,600 police, and 15 political desk officers for 14 current operations and two new ones, or to allocate just 1.25 per cent of the total costs of peacekeeping to Headquarters administrative and logistics support.

vii. The need to establish Integrated Mission Task Forces (IMTFs) with staff from all over the United Nations system seconded to them, to plan new missions and help them reach full deployment. Such personnel would include those responsible for political analysis, military operations, civilian police, electoral assistance, human rights, development, humanitarian assistance, refugees and displaced persons, public information, logistics, finance and recruitment. Indeed, the involvement of such diverse components and units would be at the heart of a PSO.

viii. The Report stressed the imperative of the UN Headquarters and the field missions alike to establish a substantive, global, Peace Operations Extranet (POE) communications network, through which missions would have access to, among other things, databases and analyses as well as lessons learned from previous missions.

THE STRUCTURE OF PEACE SUPPORT OPERATIONS

Peace Support Operation (PSO) was a term first used by the military to cover both peacekeeping and peace enforcement operations, but is now used more widely to embrace other peace-related operations which include conflict prevention, peacemaking, peace building and humanitarian assistance.

In a war fighting operation the military campaign plan is the major functional activity. This makes the military force commander the principal actor and the general focus is upon the war effort. In this scenario political issues are dealt with at the strategic level. However, in a Peace Support Operation (PSO) a wide range of political, diplomatic, economic, humanitarian and other considerations are drawn down to the operational level and need to be coordinated and harmonized at that level into some form of strategic framework or mission plan. In such circumstances military activities will be but one functional line among several areas of operations. It would, therefore, be inappropriate for the Military Force Commander to be the in-theatre Head of Mission. In such a complex PSO the Head of Mission is usually a political representative of the authorizing political body. He has to manage the interactions between external political activities and the in-theatre actions of all military and civilian agencies. The Head of Mission will also have to manage the reality that just as political decisions may impact directly at the tactical level, so also may tactical actions directly influence political policy decisions.

PSOs encompass a wide range of tasks that include elements of traditional peacekeeping as well as new tasks. PSO's may involve both coercion and the application of military force, or the means of diplomatic persuasion and inducement. Military tasks should be seen as either supporting or assisting civilian agencies or the local authorities, or as trying to create security conditions in which these agencies can more effectively address the underlying causes of the complex emergency. The delineation between military tasks and activities and those of civilian agencies may not always be clear; however, military tasks involved in PSO's may include the following:

- The control and verification of compliance with peace agreements or ceasefire agreements which may require combat actions.
- Negotiation and mediation efforts to augment diplomatic initiatives and to persuade conflicting parties to fulfill agreements on the peaceful settlement of a conflict.
- Contributing to diplomatic conflict prevention strategies through security sector reform programs or the deployment of military assets, generally air and maritime, as a form of political signaling.
- The guarantee, or denial of, freedom of movement (FOM) to specific groups or parties. Such actions at the operational level may involve the engagement of military assets in sanctions and embargo operations, and at the tactical level may involve operations to ensure the delivery of aid.
- The conduct, supervision or support for mine-clearing and Explosive Ordnance Disposal (EOD). It is necessary to emphasize, however, that the legal responsibility to clear mines and other ordnance rests with those who lay them. In the first instance military mine-clearing assets will concentrate on clearing locations and lines of communications to support military operations. Subsequently the military may be tasked with operations in support of the wider PSO.
- Demilitarization or demobilization operations, including those involving foreign military personnel. While the PSO force may focus on disarmament, the control of weapons and the training of the rump of the indigenous forces, demilitarization and demobilization will only be effective and durable if it is part of a wider peace building strategy, that is, if there is an infrastructure to sustain those who are demobilized.
- Supporting humanitarian relief and assistance operations to civilian populations, including refugees. In this case the military becomes directly involved in the provision of major humanitarian relief operations when there are no civilian agencies available or when conditions make their employment impractical and as a last resort. Military activities in this area

should focus on providing support and assistance to those civilian agencies for which humanitarian activities are their main and principal function.

- Providing support to human rights agencies and organizations such as Amnesty International in order to eliminate human rights abuses.
- Assisting in planning and monitoring elections.
- The military may be tasked with supporting the restoration of civil order and the rule of law, including the apprehension of war criminals and the provision of evidence to the International Criminal Court if necessary. Not all military forces, however, are trained directly for such roles and may only be able to provide a support function to other law enforcement agencies.
- Lastly, the military can be involved in assisting in the coordination of activities supporting economic rehabilitation and reconstruction.[20]

Examples of PSO's include the United Nations Mission in Sierra Leone (UNAMSIL); the United Nations Organization Mission in the Democratic Republic of Congo (MONUC); and United Nations Mission in Ethiopia and Eritrea (UNMEE).

PEACE SUPPORT OPEARATIONS: A STRATEGIC RESPONSE TO CONFLICTS

Through its extensive analysis of peace operations and its recommendations the UN Reports effectively elevated the concept of traditional peacekeeping to that of Peace Support Operations. Essentially United Nations Peace Support Operations entail three principal activities: conflict prevention and peacemaking; peacekeeping; and peace-building. Long-term conflict prevention addresses the structural sources of conflict in order to build a solid foundation for peace. Such structural sources of conflict may include issues pertaining to the allocation of values, identity crises and perceived relative deprivation among others. Where those foundations are crumbling, conflict prevention attempts to reinforce them, usually in the form of a diplomatic initiative. Such preventive action is, by definition, a low-profile activity; when successful, it may even go unnoticed altogether.

Peacemaking addresses conflicts in progress, attempting to bring them to a halt, using the tools of diplomacy and mediation. Peacemakers may be envoys of Governments, groups of states, regional organizations or the United Nations, or they may be unofficial and non-governmental groups, as was the case, for example, in the negotiations leading up to a peace accord for Mozambique. Peacemaking may even be the work of a prominent personality, working independently.

Peacekeeping is an old enterprise that has evolved rapidly in the past decade from a traditional, primarily military model of observing ceasefires and force separations after inter-state wars, to incorporate a complex model of many elements, military and civilian, working together to build peace in the dangerous aftermath of civil wars.

Peace-building is a term of more recent origin that defines activities undertaken on the far side of conflict to reassemble the foundations of peace and provide the tools for building on those foundations something that is more than just the absence of war. Thus, peace-building includes but is not limited to reintegrating former combatants into civilian society, strengthening the rule of law (for example, through training and restructuring of local police, and judicial and penal reform); improving respect for human rights through the monitoring, education and investigation of past and existing abuses; providing technical assistance for democratic development (including electoral assistance and support for free media); and promoting conflict resolution and reconciliation techniques.

CONCLUSION

Although the recommendations of the respective Reports were accepted in their entirety the one area that was left untouched and constitutes an impediment to the enterprise of PSO's has to do with the political will to establish Peace Support Operations in the first place. It has been argued that for any PSO to be successful, it requires the support of the five permanent members of the Security Council. Although the processes of drafting the mandate of the force, allocating troops and providing support are carried out at the level of the Secretariat, the fact that the permanent five provide the bulk of the funds and military equipment, in addition to their institutional position at the apex of the UN system, means that their support is vital for the success of any PSO.

REFERENCES

1. Osita Eze, "Legal Aspects of Peacekeeping" in M.A. Vogt and A.E. Ekoko (eds) Nigeria in International Peacekeeping Lagos: Malthouse Publishers, 1993.

2. Report of the Panel on United Nations Peace Operations available on the Internet at http://www.un.org/peace/reports/peace_operations/

3. Patrick J. Garrity "The United Nations and Peacekeeping" in Burton Yale Pines (ed) A World Without a UN: What Would Happen if the UN Shut Down?, Washington DC: The Heritage Foundation, 1984.

4. Boutros Boutros-Ghali, "Peacekeeping Hazards" in World Focus, Vol.15, No.10, October 1994.

5. UN Peacekeeping Operations (Background Notes), New York: United Nations Department of Public Information, 2001.

6. The Year in Review-UN Peace Operations in 2001, New York: United Nations Department of Public Information, December 2001.

7. Trevor Findlay "Multilateral Conflict Prevention, Management, and Resolution" in Stockholm International Peace Research Institute Yearbook, 1994, New York. Oxford University Press, 1994.

8. Basic Facts About the United Nations, New York: United Nations Department of Public information, 1992.

9. Marrack Goulding "Current Rapid Expansion Unsustainable Without Major Changes" in John Roper, Masashi Nishihara, Olara A. Otunnu and Enid C.B. Schoettle (eds) Keeping the Peace in the Post-Cold War Era: Strengthening Multilateral Peacekeeping, New York: The Trilateral Commission, 1993.

10. Boutros Boutros-Ghali, "An Agenda for Peace: Preventive Diplomacy, Peace-Making and Peacekeeping" in Stockholm International Peace Research Institute Yearbook 1993, New York: Oxford University Press.

11. Philip Wilkinson, "Sharpening the Weapons of Peace:Peace Support Missions and Complex Emergencies" in International Peacekeeping, Vol.1 No.1, 2000.

12. The Blue Helmets: A Review of United Nations Peacekeeping (2nd ed.), New York: United Nations Publication, 1990.

13. A.E. Ekoko "Nigerian United Nations Peacekeeping to the Congo 1960-1964: A Historical and Political Analysis" in M.A. Vogt and A.E. Ekoko (eds) Nigeria in International Peacekeeping 1960-1992, Lagos: Malthouse Press, 1993, pp.45-67.

14. 50 Years of UN Peacekeeping, New York: United Nations Department of Public Information, 1998, pp.20-22.

15. Paul Clayson and Trevor Findlay "Case Studies on Peacekeeping: UNOSOM II, UNTAC and UNPROFOR" in Stockholm International Peace Research Institute Yearbook 1994, op. cit., p.63.

16. Duane Bratt, "Explaining Peacekeeping Performance: The UN in Internal Conflicts" in International Peacekeeping, Vol.4, No.3, 1997.

SHORT BIOGRAPHICAL STATEMENT

The lecturer, Dr Ogaba Oche, holds a doctorate degree in Political Science, which he obtained from Ahmadu Bello University, Zaria. He lectured in the Department of Political Science, University of Jos, from 1989 to 1994 where he taught several undergraduate and post graduate courses. He moved to the Research and Studies Department of the Nigerian Institute of International Affairs in 1994 where he is presently a Senior Research Fellow in the Division of International Organizations. Dr Oche has a number of publications in his primary area of academic interest, which are international relations and conflict studies.

CHAPTER 36

THE NIGERIAN NAVY AND SECURITY CHALLENGES IN THE GULF OF GUINEA

CHARLES QUAKER-DOKUBO

INTRODUCTION

The Gulf of Guinea has not always ranked high in global energy calculations or in the foreign policy agenda of Western countries.[1] However, the situation is fast changing as more oil and gas reserves are being discovered in the region. The region has witnessed the most active exploration and production for oil and gas in the African continent and one of the most active in the world.[2] The Gulf of Guinea has been compared to the Gulf of Mexico, with potential reserves equal to those of Kuwait.[3] Also, the region is reported to be rich in fisheries and manganese noodles. In addition, the American National Intelligence Council forecast indicates that sub-Saharan Africa will account for 25% of all US crude oil imports by 2015, compared with 16% at present.[4] It is for these reasons that the Gulf of Guinea has become a strategic supplier to the US and global oil markets.[5]

The politics of crude oil has always been an area of strategic interest to both producers and consumers. Some major countries that are dependent on crude oil and natural gas have become wary of the reliability and security of their traditional supply sources as a result of political insecurity, especially in the Middle East. Competition for influence in the Gulf is fierce. European interests remain fully engaged. China, India and other Asian countries have greatly enlarged their engagement along multiple lines with both positive and negative results.[6] The presence of these external interests within the Gulf of Guinea has generated security issues which must be addressed to safeguard the interests of Nigeria and other states of the sub-region.

Nigeria's defence policy objectives seek to ensure stability within the West African sub-region.[7] Ogohi, a former commandant of the National War College, posits that, "our goal is crystal clear, to make Nigerian Armed Forces the most capable and efficient in the continent, a full partner in the United Nations (UN) or African Union operations, a valued member of the Commonwealth, and an effective partner in ECOWAS, the Gulf of Guinea inclusive. The Nigerian Navy, as a member of the Nigerian Armed Forces, shares in this goal." The Nigerian navy, like other navies, has three functions: policing, diplomatic and military. In peacetime, policing function is predominant and concerns the maintenance of national maritime laws over Nigeria's sea frontiers. The Nigerian navy provides coastal defence, including the protection of Nigeria's maritime assets both onshore and offshore. Additionally, operating jointly with the Nigerian army and/or the air force, provides sub-regional sea policing in defence of Nigeria's maritime objectives.[8]

The security challenge of the Nigerian navy in the Gulf of Guinea stems from the requirement to police Nigeria's Exclusive Economic Zone (EEZ) of 84,000 sq. nms. The challenges also arise from the leadership posture that Nigeria has assumed in the sub-region.

In this chapter, an attempt will be made to critically assess the importance of the Gulf of Guinea and its emerging security challenges, bearing in mind the projection of foreign forces and the role the navy can play in the circumstances. The vast sea area presents challenges to the Nigerian navy in its capability to project, maintain and sustain its presence within the sub-region in view of renewed external interests. However, the poor state of the navy's platforms, among others, has, in recent times, limited its effectiveness in meeting these commitments and obligations.

The above constraints are exacerbated by the relatively low capacity of the navies of other member states. Their inability to police beyond their national borders has exposed the region's vulnerability to exploitation by unauthorized trawlers and fishing vessels, and others with criminal intentions. These challenges to the Nigerian navy necessitated this research project.

CONCEPTUALIZATION OF TERMS: SECURITY, SEA-POWER AND NAVIES

In its fundamental form, to be secure is "to feel free from threats, anxiety, or danger".[9] Thus, security is a function of how we feel, not whether we are justified in feeling so.

Security cannot be described in black and white terms. Buzan, who labelled security as an "essentially contested concept",[10] argues that it generates unresolved debates about meaning and application because its ideological content distorts empirical factors.[11] Ole Weaver argues along similar lines. He views security as a socially constructed concept with a specific meaning within a specific context.[12] An examination of the academic debate will help us understand current concerns about security. Traditionally, security refers to the realist theory that dominated international relations until the end of the Cold War. According to this, security was inseparable from an environment in which no single government had the power to enforce laws or resolve conflicts outside its own immediate jurisdiction.

The will to security is born out of a primal fear. States must rely on their own efforts in order to be secure, defined by realists as the self-help system. In this context, each state struggles against others for power and their survival is therefore closely bound up with its ability to enforce its will. The traditional definition of security is: "to secure the state against those objective threats that could undermine its stability and threaten its survival."[13] According to this definition, security policy is based on rational assessment by knowledgeable analysts in which clearly defined threats are identified and appropriate strategies to counter them are developed.

A state's military power is measured against the power of other states. In order to achieve minimum security, the state must possess sufficient military power to deter a hostile attack, or at least be able to defend itself. This led to a preoccupation with the balance of military power and the attainment of such power. Factors such as force, cohesive power and inter-state conflict dominated superpower rivalry during the Cold War. The nuclear balance between the Soviet Union and the US is often cited as a prime example. According to Zielonka, Cold War security was about the relationship between states. The focus was on sovereignty, alliances, inter-state negotiations, strategic deterrence and other nuclear-related issues. Domestic stability, legitimacy of political institutions, law enforcement and economic welfare were secondary.[14] John Herz[15] coined the term "security dilemma" for what he saw as an anarchic environment in which groups of individuals were left to fend for themselves. In order to do so, they had to strive for more power, which, in turn, rendered other states insecure and therefore also strive for more power. This created a never-ending process whereby one's security led to another's insecurity. In 1988, Joseph S. Nye and Sean Lynn-Jones concluded that the most commonly used conceptualization of security included key words like 'threat', 'control' and 'military force'. This corresponded to Stephen Walt's definition of security studies as "the study of the threat, use and control of military force."[16]

The concept of security adopted in this chapter is a broad one, what Buzan sees as the "pursuit of freedom from threat. Its bottom line is about survival, but it also reasonably includes a substantial range of concerns about the conditions of existence."[17] In this regard, the most important analytical task of African and Third World countries in the post-Cold War world is to locate the complex causal relationships among these threat dimensions.

Thus, African security in this study will be defined as the ability of African nations to prevent all forms of threat to their survival, ranging from external aggression to economic, political, social and cultural insecurities, whilst also grappling with the challenges of nation-building and good governance.[18]

SEA POWER

Sea power entails at least three elements – the control of international maritime trade, the operation of navies in war, and the use of navies to achieve political influence in peacetime.[19] Mahan identified six principal conditions affecting the sea power of nations: geographical position, natural resources and climate, extent of territory, population, character of the people, and government policy.[20] However, Corbett updated these to include economic strength, technological development, dependency on maritime trade, sea resources, and government policy.[21] Similarly, Roskill defined sea power as consisting of strength, bases and transport (which include men, merchant fleets, and the dockyards where ships are built and repaired).[22] Richmond viewed sea power as:

> *That which enables a nation to send its armies and commerce across those stretches of sea and ocean which lie between its country and countries of its allies and those territories to which access to war is needed and to prevent its enemies from doing same.*[23]

Another unique feature of sea power is that modern navies not only operate on the surface of the ocean but in the depths below and the air space above. Thus, sea power is inseparable from air power.[24]

> *The combination of a nation's capacity for international maritime commerce and utilization of ocean resources, with its ability to project military power in the seas, for the purpose of sea and area control and from the sea, in order to influence events on land by means of naval forces.*[25]

The concept of sea power is applicable to the security concerns of a globalizing world economy.[26] The ultimate goal is unrestricted access to the world's common transportation routes, as well as markets and materials. A strong naval presence encourages stability and security which, in turn, ensures globalization.[27]

NAVIES

Navies are one of the policy instruments of the state and the maritime component of a nation's defence force.[28] Adekeye stated that, "navies are of critical importance to maritime states."[29] He further asserts that strategists are unanimous in the belief that the reason for establishing a navy is to protect commerce.[30] Morris, in his hierarchy of naval expansion, used four criteria: initial weaponry, modernity and weapon equipment, supplementary naval power, and corroborating national power base.[31] Consequently, he classified navies of the world into nine: major global force projection (complete), major global force projection (partial), medium global force projection, medium regional force projection, adjacent force projection, offshore territorial defence, inshore territorial defence, constabulary, and token.[32] Morris ranked the US navy as the only complete major force projection, the former USSR as partial, and Britain and France as medium. The Nigerian navy was placed in the sixth category. The other navies of member states of the Gulf of Guinea were considered as either constabulary or token. Conversely, Booth based his classification on perceived roles and geographical range: global, ocean going, contiguous seas, and coastal seas. The Nigerian navy was classified as coastal seas.

THE STRATEGIC IMPORTANCE OF THE GULF OF GUINEA

There is growing awareness that the vast resources in the Gulf of Guinea are being undermined by multifaceted domestic, regional and international threats and vulnerabilities. Rather than contributing to political stability and economic prosperity, pervasive insecurity has resulted in more than $2 billion in annual financial losses, significantly constrained investment, and a growing crime rate. Historically, the concept of security in many African countries has been associated with the perpetuation of a regime (and not necessarily the welfare of its inhabitants). It has also been primarily land-centric. Consequently, maritime security arrangements in the Gulf of Guinea have received scant policy attention.

A number of recent national and regional initiatives suggest a paradigm shift as commercial entities, non-governmental organizations and other stakeholders increasingly recognize the wide-ranging benefits of enhanced maritime security. This study provides an overview of the maritime resources in the Gulf of Guinea. For the purpose of this study, the Gulf of Guinea is defined as the eleven coastal countries between Ghana and Angola. This sub-region has a coastline of some 5,500 kilometres, or roughly the size of the Gulf of Mexico. The maritime domain may be described as "all areas and things on, under, relating to, adjacent to or bordering on a sea, ocean, or other navigable waterways, including all maritime related activities, infrastructure, people, cargo and vessels and other conveyances".[33] In terms of geographical scope, the maritime domain could be defined as (a) territorial waters twelve nautical miles from the coast; (b) contiguous zone or coastal waters twenty-four nautical miles from the coast; and (c) the EEZ 200 nautical miles from the coast. Exerting effective governance over this vast area is daunting.

EXTERNAL INTERESTS IN THE GULF OF GUINEA

Since the late 1990s, and particularly after the tragic September 11, 2001 hijacking in the United States, there has been a resurgence of global strategic interest in the Gulf of Guinea. Central to this the rising profile is the West's energy security calculations both as a source of increased, steady supply of oil and of profit for the Western oil majors.[34] A great deal of excitement has been generated by some think-tanks in the West, as well as among leading American policymakers and oil company executives, as to the prospects of maximizing their gains (in competition against Britain, France and China) in the new scramble for oil.[35] They point to the fact that the region currently provides 15% of US oil imports, rising to 25% by 2020.[36] Since, as has been observed, the US will be more dependent on foreign oil, it needs to increase its supplies from sources that may not be entirely "friendly" as a matter of "US national strategic interest."[37] This strongly implies the linking of energy to national security and the projection of US military might on a global scale. Proactive policies are consequently high on the agenda. For example, the former US president, George Bush, has a background in the oil industry; his vice-president, Dick Cheney, was the chief executive of Halliburton (a US oil services and engineering/construction multinational); and Condoleeza Rice, the former national security adviser and now the secretary of state, was on the board of Chevron between 1991 and 2001. The oil lobby's clout is reflected in the support provided to the political campaigns, the profits from oil investments overseas, and the jobs generated back home.

The race for oil is also impelled by American concerns about rapidly expanding Chinese and Indian imports, with the former offering attractive deals to Third World producers competing with American companies.[38] Some US strategists are already linking incursions by Chinese companies into African oil producing states and what it portends for the country's security within a global context.[39] A critical spin-off is the rapid securitization of the Gulf of Guinea's development (protecting the market by military means) in the contexts of the U.S energy security interests and the incorporation of the Gulf of Guinea in the global war on terror.

As a pointer to this new interest, the United States navy has of recent deployed her vessels in the sub-region, one in Accra, Ghana and the other in the Congo, in order to:

> "... enhance our operations in the ungoverned regions in Africa", and that the "Gulf of Guineas for example is an area where a navy presence would send a strong message; for security, stability and reconstruction operations are needed in this important region, and the U.S along with our NATO allies, will be there to help.[41]

To underline its seriousness, the US also established a separate unified command for Africa that because fully operational by 30 September 2008. According to the Pentagon, its permanent headquarters will be somewhere, as yet undisclosed, on the continent itself. Nigeria's oil and military power make it the most important country in the region politically, but a strong US presence there could antagonize the Niger Delta militants, as well as the country's Muslim population. Ghana may prove more suitable.[42]

US INTERESTS

This new attention to Africa is far from altruistic. It has a hardcore strategic interest in protecting access to oil and gas reserves (mainly in the Gulf of Guinea) as part of the drive to reduce dependence on unstable Middle East supplies. The US consumes about a quarter of the world's oil and imports nearly half of what it consumes. Sub-Saharan Africa presently accounts for about 15% of oil imports. By 2010, oil production from Angola, Equatorial Guinea, Chad and South Africa could double to over ten million barrels per day; Africa's share of US oil imports could rise to 20%. Furthermore, sub-Saharan Africa has entered the early stages of the geopolitical contest for hydrocarbons between the US and China. China's primary interest in Africa is strategic rather than ideological, namely, to establish resource security, trade and investment opportunities, and diplomatic legitimacy. In the increasing thirst for oil (28% of its imported oil comes from Africa), China has established strong ties with regimes out of favour with the West, such as Sudan and Zimbabwe.

Washington's second strategic interest is to prevent the spread of Islamic extremism among the roughly 400 million Muslims in Africa. While the vast majority of these Muslims have not demonstrated any marked inclination towards terrorism, and recruitment in regions of concern such as East Africa has not shown signs of an exceptional rise, radicalism has increased in Nigeria and Somalia. Sudan's government remains staunchly Islamic and of significant counter-terrorism concern. Should peace agreements unravel, the country runs the risk of becoming a failed state. A broad US strategic imperative is to prevent jihadist infiltration of weak or failed states like Somalia.

There are more weak and failed states in sub-Saharan Africa than in any other region in the world. Moreover, they afford relative freedom of action to illicit actors because of communications and transport difficulties exacerbated by corrupt officials and are therefore highly susceptible to becoming terrorist havens. In fact, the US and its allies have provided considerable help in training and financial support to cooperative governments in East Africa and the Horn, and in north-central Africa to Chad, Mali, Mauritania and Niger.

The two US interests in maintaining access to hydrocarbons and countering trans-national Islamic terrorism coalesce in Nigeria, where stability is threatened by an inequitable political and economic balance between politically dominant Christians, restive Muslims and disadvantaged Niger Delta militants. Nigeria has the largest general population (about 130 million) in sub-Saharan Africa, including the largest Muslim population (roughly sixty-five million). While inter-religious tensions have not threatened outright civil war, Christian-Muslim violence has produced thousands of fatalities since 1999. Furthermore, Western oil interests provide targets of relatively high political and economic value.

US VALUES

The US has played a role in countering Africa's many chronic problems. For example, it was party to the 2005 G8 Gleneagles agreement on channelling aid and debt relief to Africa. It has also played a role in helping to resolve the civil war in Sudan, and has declared the Khartoum-backed ethnic cleansing of non-Arabs in Darfur to be 'genocide'. Beyond these, however, American efforts in addressing regional problems have been limited. The establishment of AFRICOM may help to reverse the trend by lending greater focus to relief and peacekeeping contingencies. At the press conference announcing the creation of a regional command, a Pentagon spokesman indicated that many of its missions would be 'non-kinetic', i.e., humanitarian assistance and disaster relief, and that the command would generally be geared towards establishing stability. Indeed, combatant commanders have increasingly assumed lead diplomatic roles in the implementation of US foreign policy. For example, it was neither the office of the secretary of defence nor the state department but rather the commander of US naval forces in Europe which hosted the inaugural Gulf of Guinea Maritime Security Conference in October, 2004. The intelligence collection and operational preparation for the command will place the US in a better position to act. Should a future US administration take a more proactive approach in Africa, the command would be play a central role and the paralysis that occurred over the genocide in Rwanda in 1994-95, for instance, would be far less likely.

The command will also be able to play a peacekeeping role, although this is unlikely to be carried out by American troops. Like other major powers, the US would prefer that African forces be used on African territory as in Darfur and, more recently, Somalia. But the reality is that, in future, they may not always be available and, even then, may not be up to the job. Somalia will present the next test. The European Union is the third largest destination of the Gulf of Guinea oil exports after North America and Asia. There is as yet no outstanding dependency as European member countries are free to buy oil wherever they want. In November 2000, the European

Commission published a green paper on the security of energy supply. Its central findings were as follows:

> *The European Union is consuming more and more energy and consuming more and more energy products. Community production is insufficient for the Union's energy requirements. As a result, external dependency from energy is constantly increasing.[44]*

However, energy dependency in selected member countries like France, Portugal, Spain and Germany is high and rising at a time when supplies from the North Sea are declining. At current levels, imports will rise from 50% to 70% over the next twenty years.

ENERGY SECURITY, THE WAR ON TERROR AND DEVELOPMENT

The United States has recognized that a trade-off must occur in Africa, as exemplified by Congressman William Jefferson's statement:

> *So Africa provides the oil, helps us with human intelligence, helps us with our access to the Middle East so we can have a forward presence. Our trade-off has to be to help develop Africa with what makes our country work: transportation and information technology.[50]*

At a meeting of members of Congress and representatives of the business community in 2002, many speakers spoke highly of the African Growth and Opportunity Act (AGOA) when concerns of a prolonged 'resource curse' in Africa were raised. Developed in 2000, AGOA is available to qualified African countries and provides the most liberal access to American markets available to any region that does not have a free trade agreement with the United States. Eligibility for AGOA is based upon:

> *Have(ing) established, or (are) making continual progress toward establishing the following: market-based economies; the rule of law and political pluralism; elimination of barriers to U.S trade and investment; protection of intellectual property; efforts to combat corruption; policies to reduce poverty, increasing availability of healthcare and educational opportunities; protection of human rights and worker rights; and elimination of certain child labour practices. These criteria have been embraced overwhelmingly by the vast majority of African nations, which are striving to achieve the objectives although none is expected to have fully implemented the entire list.*

However, there are several problems apparent in the capacity of AGOA to generate visible development. Firstly, AGOA encourages African countries to remove trade barriers to American products in the hope of producing long-term African-American free trade agreements. Despite what the US considers to be unacceptable barriers to trade, the country increased exports to Africa by 40% between 2003 and 2005; Africa doubled exports to the US in the same period. However, over 90% of the growth in trade from Africa to the US can be attributed to Chad, Angola, Equatorial Guinea and Nigeria, where growth was based almost solely on increases in oil exports. Therefore, AGOA's impact on African development has been negligible. Secondly, AGOA is not an outreach programme; therefore, there is little support for those people in Africa who desire to develop an export company. Finally, certain countries with a high GDP per capita, most notably Equatorial Guinea, have been denied access to AGOA despite the economic realities that indicate that the majority of the population is living in abject poverty. While AGOA is a good start to fairer trade for African nations, it will have limited impact on African development, and will contribute little to preventing the 'resource curse' associated with resource-dependent economies.

AGOA is only one development mechanism created by the US to promote overall development. The Millennium Challenge Account (MCA) is another trade-based initiative whereby the US will distribute ODA to countries which demonstrate good governance, respect for health and education, and sound economic policies that foster enterprise and entrepreneurship. President Bush has committed $5 billion over five years to this fund. However, like AGOA, MCA targets only a subset of actors, primarily those which have already achieved minimum levels of development, including Uganda, Botswana and China. In other words, MCA and AGOA tend to by-pass both oil-exporting countries, and failing and failed states, which remain the focus of other American foreign policies driven by energy security concerns and the War on Terror. A third development commitment followed pressure from the American evangelical movement, which pushed the Bush administration to propose a $15 billion emergency relief fund for HIV/AIDS based on the abstinence-before-contraception approach. The US Institute for Peace suggests that there is a strong positive correlation between population health and state capacity. The HIV/AIDS prevention fund will both increase the prospects for development in West Africa and fulfil the other goals pursued by the current America foreign policy strategy.

ENERGY SECURITY AND AMERICAN FOREIGN POLICY

Africa's position in the world changed dramatically after September 11, 2001. Never before had the world been so compelled to secure oil resources outside the Persian Gulf. When Africa was declared a national strategic interest of the United States, the continent was unprepared for the onslaught of corporate, military and international attention. Driving America's foreign policy in Africa is the fear that, in the words of President Bush, "America is addicted to oil". In the 2001 *National Energy Strategy Report*, his vice-president, Dick Cheney, grumbled about America's "dependency on foreign powers that do not have America's interests at heart". The Gulf of Guinea provided an alternative source of oil which was, for the most part, not only outside the scope of OPEC but in a region more open to Westernization. According to one congressman:

> *There is a chance for us to overcome some of the issues of bad governance through democratic influences. These things are not foreseeable in the*

Middle East. There is a greater prospect for good governance, for the
flourishing of democracy, for our supporting democratic institutions,
in Africa, and therefore, for having democratic partners in Africa
than there is in the Middle East.[51]

Additionally, there are four practical reasons why West African crude is highly attractive to the United States. Firstly, West Africa has greater market openness to foreign companies than other established oil-producing regions and US energy imports are more secure when American companies supply the oil. Moreover, according to industry sources, companies are able to make greater profits per barrel in West Africa's offshore oilfields than any other region in the world. Secondly, transportation between the Gulf of Guinea and the US is shorter and therefore accrues fewer costs. Thirdly, most African crude is located offshore, which isolates the oil from political upheavals and theft. Lastly, African oil is low in sulphur, which provides the high gasoline yield preferred by American refineries. Despite the overwhelming benefits of West African crude, there are also drawbacks. Most importantly, the US faces political and economic risks when investing in a region with rampant bureaucratic and political corruption, which also entails having to partner with governments that have incurred a legacy of human rights abuses. Additionally, should West African development continue to decline, America risks situations similar to that of the Middle East where investments and oil supplies cannot be easily guaranteed.

CHINA

China has an indirect and increasingly important influence on both the formulation and effects of US foreign policy in West Africa. As late as 1993, China was self-sufficient in oil; since then, its demand has more than doubled, creating greater competition in global energy markets.[52] In early November 2006, forty-eight African countries were invited to China for a summit to discuss the country's 'mutually beneficial' interests in Africa. In the same summit, China promised to double its aid to Africa in the coming years.[53] Currently, China receives significant and growing oil imports from Sudan, Angola, Chad, Congo and Equatorial Guinea. China's insatiable appetite for oil has led it directly to West Africa, whose markets are not dominated by state-owned companies, OPEC has so far failed to establish a strong footing, and new oil reserves are being discovered at an unprecedented rate.[54] China has a long history in Africa. Since the late 1950s, China has provided weapons to African groups pursuing independence, given university scholarships to many African students and provided aid in emergencies.[55] In addition, China maintains a 'hands-off' policy in which aid comes free of economic and political constraints.

China has a two-pronged approach to Africa: to generate new markets for manufactured goods and; more importantly, to secure oil supplies, which quadrupled between 2000 and 2005 to $40 billion. The US Department of Energy estimates that, between 2002 and 2025, China's total energy consumption will rise by 153%. China already has a significant presence in Sudan, and recently closed a $2.3 billion deal to acquire a 45% stake in off-shore Nigerian oilfields.[56] While China's presence in West Africa does not present a threat to the US, the country's investment strategies and diplomatic tactics are troubling for several reasons. Firstly, China's 'aid for oil' strategy has undermined international efforts to bring about transparency and political reform. For example, when the international community held back loans and aid to pressure Angola to create greater transparency in the oil sector, China stepped in with a $2 billion package (most notably for infrastructure) in return for remaining a key oil supplier. In addition, all infrastructure projects must be contracted to Chinese firms, who will often import Chinese workers. In other words, the recipient country benefits from the completed infrastructure but rarely profits from the construction.

The second problem lies in China's capacity to undermine US aid polices. The much-touted AGOA has been put at risk for two reasons: China is flooding African markets with low-cost textiles, thereby reducing the ability of African manufacturers to compete in domestic markets; and there is evidence that China is moving manufacturing facilities to Africa in order to profit from preferential access to European and American markets. The challenges that China poses to the US in West Africa has increased American concerns that China will "undo much of the progress that has been made on democracy and governance in the last 15 years in African nations". However, there are concerns that as the US buckles to corporate interests and energy security they will themselves undo much of the progress in the region.

Thus far, China's presence in the African oil industry has had limited influence on American foreign policy. However, the country's capacity to undermine US development efforts has generated increasing fears that competition for resources between the two nations will lead to a race for the bottom.

SECURITY CHALLENGES AND VULNERABILITIES

Although the force projection by the United States and others might lead to a new arms race, the main challenges are poaching piracy, national and trans-national crimes, disputed boundaries, and environmental degradation.

Poaching: An inability to exercise control over its maritime domain has made it difficult for states in the Gulf of Guinea to enjoy the full benefits of their significant fisheries. Recent studies suggest that poaching by vessels from Asia, Europe and other parts of Africa costs the sub-region some $370 million annually. Additionally, poaching also has human security costs. Households and individuals are affected directly via reduced availability of seafood in local markets. Data from the Food and Agricultural Organization indicates that fish accounts for most of the protein intake in the sub-region: 63% in Ghana, 62% in Equatorial Guinea and 52% in Sao Tome and Principe.

Piracy: The International Maritime Bureau ranks the Gulf of Guinea as one of the most troubled global waterways. Since the late 1990s, this sub-region consistently ranked among the top piracy hot spots worldwide. Between 2002 and 2004, piracy attacks exceeded recorded incidents in the rest of the continent. While there is some debate about definitional issues (including certain categories of petty theft) and data reliability, there is broad consensus that criminal activity in the Gulf of Guinea is worrisome.

National and trans-national crime: Growing crime complicates the tenuous security climate. Poor maritime governance significantly facilitates oil theft (also referred to as "illegal bunkering") in the Niger Delta region, with dire regional ramifications. This highly organized activity costs the sub-region about $1.2 billion annually in lost revenue.[58] Additionally the criminal gangs have contributed to the proliferation of small arms and light weapons in the region. Recent evidence suggests that the weaponry is becoming more sophisticated as the criminals seek to evade national law enforcement personnel.[59] Another criminal trend worth noting is the trans-shipment of narcotics. The Gulf of Guinea is becoming a major narco-trafficking hub. A significant amount of high-grade cocaine seized in what Spanish authorities have dubbed "the new drug triangle between Cape Verde, the Canary Islands and Madeira"[60] was routed via the Gulf of Guinea in vessels manned by crews from the sub-region.

Disputed Boundaries: Enduring disagreements over maritime boundaries could precipitate armed conflict, particularly when the disputed areas possess significant economic potential or are strategic transportation hubs. These disputes also make it difficult for countries in the sub-region to address shared security challenges in a collaborative manner. Examples of maritime disputes in the Gulf of Guinea include those between Nigeria and Cameroon over the Bakassi Peninsula (which has been recently settled), Equatorial Guinea and Cameroon over an island at the mouth of the Ntem River, and Gabon and Equatorial Guinea over the Mbane Island and Corisco Bay boundaries.

Environmental degradation: Pollution and environmental degradation are relatively unchecked in the Gulf of Guinea. The 2005 Abuja Declaration[61] reiterates issues highlighted in analyses by the Food and Agricultural Organization[62] which indicate that mismanagement of fisheries resources in the sub-region has led to stock depletion, ecological imbalance and environmental degradation. Less than 25% of the countries in this sub-region have ratified the 1990 Convention on Oil Pollution Preparedness, Response and Cooperation.[63] The Conservation Association – the oil industry's focal point for communication – is working with African governments to encourage the ratification and implementation of relevant conventions. Their objectives in the Gulf of Guinea are articulated in the Convention for Cooperation in the Protection and Development of the Marine and Coastal Environment of the West and Central African region.[64] Although the petroleum industry has been singled out as a major polluter improper domestic and industrial waste disposal also poses a significant threat.

VULNERABILITIES

Maritime domain awareness: As mentioned earlier, the traditional land-centric approach to security in the sub-region contributed to a systemic neglect of maritime forces in both absolute and relative terms. It is, therefore, not surprising that countries in the sub-region are unaware of most of the traffic in their territorial waters. Basic equipment (such as functioning surveillance systems), material (including patrol craft) and trained personnel are in short supply. According to data published by the International Institute for Strategic Studies, patrol boats are deficient in the sub-region, with most listed assets categorized as "unseaworthy" in Angola, Benin, Congo and the Democratic Republic of Congo[65]. Poor maritime domain awareness undermines security by making it possible for criminals to operate with impunity – thereby jeopardizing safety.

Legislative and judicial arrangements: While countries in the sub-region are signatories to most relevant international conventions,[66] only a few have taken concrete measures to ratify and institutionalize these protocols domestically.[67] Creating and enforcing the provisions would require sustained political will, enacting enabling legislation, strengthening relevant institutions and enforcing mechanisms, and devoting adequate financial and human resources to maritime security. This vulnerability is highlighted in local media reports about poachers apprehended in the sub-region who often have to be released after paying only minimal fines because the country in question lacked the right laws in their statutes. However, even when appropriate laws exist (as they do in most countries) the ability to effectively prosecute depends on the strength and independence of the judiciary.[68]

Weak infrastructure: Most port and surveillance infrastructure is in need of repair, upgrading or replacement. Failure to pay sufficient attention to this crucial aspect of maritime security over the years is partly responsible for the current state of affairs. According to the International Maritime Organization, countries in this sub-region are yet to fully comply with standards for port safety and security outlined in the International Ship and Port Facility Security Code, to which all countries are signatories. In addition, an estimated 85% of the vessels registered are more than twenty years old, rendering them susceptible to accidents.[69]

SOME HUMAN SECURITY IMPLICATIONS

The security challenges outlined above have had wide-ranging effects on human security in the Gulf of Guinea, some of which have already been discussed. Together, they undermine economic activity, hinder the movement of goods and services, and make it difficult for these countries to attain their development goals. By affecting these areas, maritime security problems compound the sub-region's human security challenges. Therefore, understanding the implications of continued maritime insecurity (in all its forms) makes a strong case for urgent, comprehensive and collaborative reform.

Economic Loses: Poaching undermines the local fishing industry, crime acts as a disincentive to commerce because it increases the cost of doing business, and pollution undermines tourism by degrading the beach and marine environments. The fiscal impact of these losses is felt via lost landing fees, licensing fees, taxes and levies, as well as via the onerous spending required to respond to security incidents.

The quantum of annual losses exceeds debt service requirements on multilateral loans in the sub-region. This suggests that efforts to reduce these losses could enhance government revenue, thereby facilitating more investment in health, education and poverty reduction. Potential additional revenue could also be used to fund maritime security initiatives.

At a micro level, constrained economic activity limits the employment opportunities of coastal populations. Unemployment and low wages exacerbate human security concerns in the sub-region. Perhaps the most significant losses results from lost investment. Although some researchers estimate some $10 billion worth of investment in the Gulf of Guinea's petroleum sector from 2005-2015, continued instability in the Niger Delta could force investors to reconsider their decisions.[70] Maritime instability is one reason why many investors have shown relatively little interest in the sub-region's potentially lucrative fishing and tourism industries.

Trade and Shipping: The safety/security of shipping routes and facilities is also important because an overwhelming proportion of trade in the sub-region traverses the maritime domain. Insecure and inadequate facilities constrain activity and raise both transportation costs and insurance premiums. For example, the failure of most cocoa exporting countries in the Gulf of Guinea to comply with the European Cocoa Association's June, 2004 directive on port security resulted in higher insurance costs for operators in those countries. However, some countries are already taking steps to address this issue.

ROLE OF THE NIGERIAN NAVY IN THE GULF OF GUINEA

Nigeria, by virtue of her geographical size, large population, economic potential and military capability, is perceived as a hegemon by countries that make up the Gulf of Guinea Commission. Similarly, her huge investment in oil and gas demands that she provides the desired leadership role in defence of the Gulf of Guinea. The ability of the navy to credibly perform its role will ensure peace and security, as well as sustained economic growth and development, within the sub-region.

ASSESSMENT OF THE CAPABILITY OF THE NIGERIAN NAVY

Fleet: The fleet is structured into classes and types of ships as shown in Annex A. While attempts have been made to ensure that its operational commands possess a good mix of ships, the fleet are allocated equally to both commands. The breakdown shows the following: one frigate, two corvettes, six fast attack craft, two mine-counter measures vessels, three patrol craft, four buoy tenders, eight inshore patrol craft, two landing ship tanks, one survey ship and four helicopters.

However, only nine out of forty-four platforms, representing about 20% of its assets, are operationally available. This has adversely affected its capability to effectively perform its role. Similarly, the present policy of equal allocation of ships to both operational commands does not meet the operational requirements for the defence of Gulf of Guinea maritime environment. Furthermore, sustained presence at sea and strategic deterrence would require dedicated platforms such as submarines, offshore patrol vessels, additional frigates, underway replenishment ships, adequate logistics support and well-trained manpower, all of which are presently lacking.

OPERATIONAL CONSTRAINTS OF THE NIGERIAN NAVY

From the foregoing, it is evident that attaining optimal naval capability requires adequate funding and technical expertise, both of which are presently lacking. Also, the current Nigerian Navy ORBIT lacks most of the dedicated platforms required to achieve sustained presence at sea. Similarly, about 80% of its present assets are not operational as most of its platforms are presently undergoing docking and repairs.

The Navy has not been able to effectively perform some of its assigned roles due to the following main reasons:

a.   Inadequate funding for capital expenditure meant for the purchase of spare parts.

b.   Lack of desired maritime culture.

c.   Lack of appropriate technical expertise to enhance shipbuilding and integrated maintenance.

d.   Lack of dedicated platforms and an ageing fleet.

The assessment of the armed forces of the Gulf of Guinea member states showed that none was in a position to defend their maritime environment. The suggestion that member nations come together for the defence of their common maritime domain became imperative. However, lack of political will, mistrust among member states, inadequate funding and the fact that most members belong to multiple economic communities means that this will not be easy.

Consequently, it is desirable that member states of the Gulf of Guinea and selected external interests like the US evolve a collective security arrangement for regional peace and security. In the same vein, the Navy's policy thrust, categorized as short-, medium- and long-term plans aimed at rejuvenating the fleet to meet present and future challenges, needs to be vigorously pursued. Furthermore, the dockyard could enter into a joint venture partnership with a reputable shipbuilder to facilitate technological transfer and enhance integrated ship maintenance and the acquisition of skilled manpower. Also, the proposed bill on the Nigerian Navy funding by government and stakeholders in oil and gas industries presently before the National Assembly for legislation could be passed into law.

CONCLUSION

The Gulf of Guinea is undoubtedly emerging as an important element of the global economy. Equatorial Guinea is a rising economic force in the region. Other countries, such as Sao Tome and Principe, are expected to evolve in the future. National resources and changes in geopolitical parameters remain the main advantage of the region. However, its enormous potential can be challenged by the ongoing demographic changes, unreasonable policy choices, weak institution as well as persistent exposure to adverse factors (war, national disasters, commodity price and exchange rate volatility). The regions policy-makers should start these countries economies to face the challenges ahead so as to exploit the economic to the fullest.

The Gulf of guinea must be a haven of stability for it to become a development zone. To this end, countries of the region need to establish increased regional arrangements to safeguard peace, and internal and cross-border conflicts should be promptly resolved in line with what is instituted at the African Union level. On the security front most countries of the Gulf of Guinea lacks a functioning Navy, Coast Guard or sophisticated custom service. Riverine transportation routes and land based pipeline systems are extensive and not well policed, and offshore oil and gas installation are largely unprotected. Lack of surveillance permit piracy and crude product theft. There is no capacity for intelligence sharing that would be necessary to track illegal activity across borders. This implies that any strategy will have to be built from bottom-up, incrementally through a long-term effort.

Finally, the asymmetry of power between Nigeria and other states in the region makes it imperative, for her to be the hub in establishing an effective maritime strategy. The Nigerian Navy should be provided the necessary assets for it to fulfil its constitutional role. Navies are there to fight. They are designed to fight at sea and to project power when required to promote national interest and the international aims and objectives of their government. The Nigerian Navy is facing structural obsolescence and need to replace its aging fleet and platform to perform a creditable job in the Gulf of Guinea.

ENDNOTES

1. A Strategic U.S. Approach to Governance and Security in the Gulf of Guinea: A report of the CSIS Task Force on the Gulf of Guinea Security, July 2005. http/www.csis.org
2. Ibid
3. Ibid
4. Ibid
5. Ibid
6. M. Kupolokun, "Petroleum and Security in Africa." Paper presented to the National Security Council, September 2003, p. 4
7. R. Oritsejafor, "National Defence Policy Objective." Lecture delivered to participants of the National War College, October 2006, p. 24
8. Ibid
9. S. Lindstrom, "The Changing Nature of Security." Workshop report on the status of international mediation studies, 6 October 2005, p. 18.
10. B. Buzan: *The European Security Order Recast* (London: Harvester, 1990), p. 18
11. L. Richard: "Ideology and Change," in Buzan, B., & Barg, J. (eds): *Change and the Study of International Relations* (London: Pluto Press, 1981), p. 83

12. R. Lipschutz: "On Security," Lipschutz (ed.): (New York: Columbia University Press, 1999), pp. 1-23
13. C. Zoppo E.: "The Issues of Nordic Security: The Dynamics of East-West Politics in Emerging Technologies and the Definition of National Defence," in Caro, E.Z. (ed.): *Nordic Security at the Turn of the Twenty-First Century* (New York: Greenwood Press 1992), p. 29
14. J. Zielonka: "The Decaying Pillars of the Westphalian Temple: Implications for International Order and Governance," in James, F. Rosen & Ernest Czempedi (eds.): *Government without Government* (Cambridge: Cambridge University Press, 1992), p. 139
15. J. Herz: "Idealist Internationalism and the Security Dilemma", in *World Politics*, January 1950, pp. 157-9
16. Ibid, p. 58
17. J. Nye & Lynn-Jones, S.: "International Security Studies," in *A Report of a Conference on the State of the Field International Security*, Vol.12, 1988, p. 27
18. B. Buzan: "The Case for a Comprehensive Definition of Security and the Institutional Consequences of accepting it," Working Papers, Centre for Peace and Conflict Research, Copenhagen, 1990, p. 2
19. Ibid, p. 7
20. Dokubo, C.: "African Security in the 21st Century," in Akindele, R., & Ate, B. (eds.) *Beyond Conflict Resolution* (Vantage Publishers 2000), p. 184
21. E. Groove: *The Future of Sea Power* (Annapolis: Naval Institute Press 1990), pp. 229-32
22. B. Wirtz: *et al: Strategy in the Contemporary World* (New York: Oxford University Press, 2003), p. 119
23. M. McGwire: *Maritime Strategy and the Sea Powers*, Adelphi Papers (London IISS, 1976), p. 15
24. O. Biobaku: "Maritime Strategy and Strategy," lecture delivered at the National War College, October, 2005, p. 18
25. Writz, B., & Cohen *et al*. op. cit., p. 114
26. Ibid, p. 120
27. Ibid, p. 127
28. Ibid, pp. 132-133
29. Biobaku, O.O., op. cit., p. 11
30. Ibid, p. 16
31. G. Adekeye: "The Nigerian Navy in National Defence," lecture delivered at the National War College to participants of course 14 January, 2006, p. 18
32. Ibid, p. 21
33. A. Morris: *Expansion of Third World Navies* (London: Macmillan 1989), p. 25
34. Ibid, p. 30
35. "The National Strategy for Maritime Security" (Washington DC, The White House, September, 2005), p. 1
36. C. Obi "Conflict and Peace in West Africa", in *News from the Nordic Africa Institute*, No. 1, January, 2005
37. Global Security Organization, (undated)

38. M. Peal: "Oil on Troubled Waters", in *Financial Times*, March 22, 2005
39. V. Vale: "US Policy towards the Gulf of Guinea," in Tub Marz and Yales, D. (eds.): *Oil Policy in the Gulf of Guinea*, Friedrich Ebert Stiftung, 2004, p. 18
40. C. Obi "The Oil Paradise: Reflection on Violent Dynamics and (Mis) Governance in Nigeria's Niger Delta," African Institute, Occasional Paper 2004, p. 23
41. Ibid. p. 26
42. C. Obi ibid, p. 28
43. *The Guardian*, March 21, 2006
44. IISS Strategic Comments: www.IISS.org/stratcom
43. Ibid
45. *Oil and Gas Journal*, 2005, Vol. 2, Issue 7
46. C. Obi, op. cit., 2005
47. C. Dokubo: "The Unending Conflict in the Mano River Basin," *Nigerian Journal of International Affairs*, 2006, p. 81
48. C. Obi, op. cit., p. 18
49. *Africa Confidential* (2006)
50. C. Obi, op. cit., p. 18
51. Congressman William Jefferson was recently implicated in a scandal involving igate (a two-way broadband technology), where he was paid to bribe officials in Nigeria, Ghana and Cameroon to buy the technology, while convincing the US military to test it. Jefferson was caught with $90,000 in his freezer.
52. Oil can be stolen from offshore platforms; however, with adequate security it is reasonably easy to protect.
53. Yorgin (2006)
54. Stanway (2006)
55. US Corporate Council on Africa, 2003
56. M. Klare, "America, China and the Scramble for Africa's Oil," *Review of African Political Economy*, Vol. 33, No. 108, June 2006
57. Ibid, p. 305
58. M. Klare, ibid. p. 304
59. Estimates based on calculations by the Africa Center for Strategic Studies
60. Africa Center for Strategic Studies, *Topical Seminar on Energy and Security in Africa: Programme Highlights* (Washington DC Africa Center 2005), p. 23
61. E. Pape "West Africa: The New Drug Triangle," *Newsweek*, August 29, 2005
62. The Abuja Declaration on Sustainable Fisheries and Agriculture in Africa, adopted by heads of state at the NEPAD "Fish For All Summit" in Abuja, Nigeria August, 25, 2005
63. Food and Agricultural Organization, "Implementation of the International Plan of Action to Prevent, Deter and Eliminate Illegal and Unregulated Fishing", *FAO Technical Guidelines for Responsible Fisheries No. 9* (Rome FAO Press, 2000)
64. IMP/IPIECA, *Report on the Launch of the Global Initiative Programme on Oil Pollution Preparedness, Response and Cooperation* (London: UK, FAO Press, 2002)

65. IMO/IPIECA: *Report on IMO/IPIECA Global Initiative on Oil Spill Preparedness, Response and Cooperation for West and Central Africa* (Libreville, Gabon, IMO August, 2006)

66. International Institute for Strategic Studies: *The Military Balance* (Oxford: Oxford University Press, 2006)

67. Notably the International Maritime Organization's International Ship and Port Facility Security

68. A. Kamal-Deen "Legal and Policy Dimension of Coastal Dimensions of Coastal Zone Monitoring and Control: The Case in Ghana," *Ocean Development and Internal Law* (2004), pp. 179-194

69. United Nations Conference on Trade and Development: "Review of Regional Developments: Sub-Saharan Africa," in *Review of Maritime Transport* (Geneva, UNCTAD, 2003)

70. O. Marie: "Emergence of the Gulf of Guinea in the Global Economy: Prospects and Challenges," in IMF Working Paper WP/05/235 (Washington, DC International Monetary Fund, 2005)

CHAPTER 37

MILITARY OPERATIONS OTHER THAN WAR

L. O. JOKOTOLA.

PREAMBLE

The totality of human experience over time has shown in practical reality that conflict is a natural consequence of human interaction. Thus, in its simplest form, conflict could be seen as an unending cycle of human activities bringing about differences in opinions, views and interests between individuals, groups or states. This term conflict has also been aptly described by Dougherty and Pfaltgraf as:

> *A condition in which one identified group of human beings is engaged in conscious opposition to one or more other identifiable groups pursuing what are or appear to be incompatible goals[1].*

It is in an attempt to go further in the discourse on conflict that Lewis Coser identified it as: "As a struggle over and claims to scarce resources in which aims of opponents are the neutralize, injure or eliminate these rivals". However, when conflict becomes rather violent, it is simply known as war which Clansewitz describes as: "A duel on an extensive scale ...An act of violence pushed to its utmost bounds".

The First and Second World Wars, Arab Israeli wars as well as Operation Desert Storm are contemporary examples of wars at international levels. It is also pertinent to state that the theory and practice of waging war had continually been influenced by military thinkers of various era. One school of thought proposes moderation in the prosecution of war (Sun Tzu), while another school of thought emphasizes the logical ideal and "the absolute' (Clausewitz) which eventually came to be translated into wagging 'total war' beyond all bounds of restraint. The essence of this, in the opinion of Clausewitz, was stated in the dictum that: "To introduce into the philosophy of war a principle of moderation would be an absurdity – war is an act of violence pushed to its utmost bounds".

Contributing to the evolution of the art of warfare were theoritists like JTC Fuller and Liddel Hart who postulated the importance of manoeuvre in the conduct of war. This thinking formed the basis for the development of the maneouvrist approach concept of warfare, which has since the 1980s been adopted by the British Army, the US Army and some NATO members. The Nigerian Armed Forces have also embraced the new concept by introducing it into the curriculum. Basically, the concept entails the blending of the two elements of freedom of movement and psychological paralysis, to enable the attacker inflict maximum damage and dislocation on the enemy with least cost to himself. This would result in economy of force which is considered as the central features in waging modern war.

An appraisal of the current security environment obtainable in the world today would place all countries somewhere in the spectrum of conflict. Many countries would be in situations of conflict other than war while others would be at war itself. In realization of the need to maintain international peace and security after the Second World War, the United Nations (UN) was formed with one of its objectives being the prevention of conflicts wherever they may arise. So central was the issue of peace and security to the UN that the very first article of the UN Charter states that the main objective of the UN is "to maintain international peace and security". In carrying out this task, Charter VI of the Charter provides for the pacific settlement of disputes by a variety of peaceful measures including negotiation, enquiry, mediation, conciliation, arbitration and judicial settlement. On the other hand, Charter VII of the same chapter permits the use of political and economic pressure as well as armed force to coerce sovereign states.

Presently, we have come across varying classifications like preventive diplomacy, (peacekeeping), peace building and of most recently, the vexed issue of peace enforcement in addition to peacekeeping. It is in attempt to further illuminate these ever-evolving concepts that we shall attempt to focus on another concept in this regard. This brings me to the subject matter of our discussion, which is "Military Operations Other Than War", (MOOTW). It is a topic that has in recent years gained prominence over and above earlier operational phrases such as Internal Security and Low Intensity Conflicts, which are themselves variants of MOOTW. The distinguishing characteristics of MOOTW is that subordinated to the political imperatives throughout. They will be designed to prevent conflict, restore peace by resolving or terminating conflict before escalation to war, or assist with the rebuilding of peace after conflict[2].

It is in this regard that this chapter which seeks to throw more light on the concept of MOOTW is very appropriate so that all of us as stakeholders of the business of military may understand it sufficiently enough to keep pace with the international environment. In order to achieve this, it is my desire this morning to have an examination of MOOTW covering epistemic and operational issues such as:

    a.   Conceptual Clarification
    b.   Origin of MOOTW
    c.   Employment and Types of MOOTW.
    d.   Principles and Planning Considerations.
    e.   Factors affecting MOOTW.
    f.   Nigerian Armed Forces and MOOTW

CONCEPTUAL CLARIFICATION

The term 'Military Operations Other Than War' (MOOTW) is formulated by the rule of contraries, stressing their specifics as opposed to conventional military operations. However, to fully understand the concept there is the need to first understand war and its twin component of military operation. While writing the forward to the book "Psychology of Military Incompetence ", Brigadier Sheford Bidwell defined such as survival, or the acquisition of desirable territory ". This sociological definition of war perhaps mainly focuses on "Victory" as the object. Victory in this context could be seen as a net gain of benefits over cost which is meant to achieve some form of glory. The implication of this definition is that war has to be conducted in line with certain rules. For example, it has to be fought between two parties using certain weapons. Ths definition however does not capture the legal implications of war which has been further defined as "Contention by force; or the art of paralyzing the forces of an enemy… War is not only an act, but a state or condition, for nations are said be at war not only when their armies are engaged, so as to be in the very act of contention, but also when they have any matter of controversy or dispute subsisting between them which they are determined to decide by the use of force, and have declared publicly, or by their acts, their determination so as to decide it[3]". The additional value added by this definition is the requirement for use of force to assert our will over the enemy and the need for war to be declared by either of the two parties.

Despite the seemingly all embracing outlook of this second definition, John A Vasque in his book, this war puzzle believes that no single definition can probably offer all the true definition of the concept of war[4]. He therefore adopted a working definition as offered by Hedley Bull, which states that "war is organized violence carried out by political units against each other". By this definition, war is not seen simply as conflict, but a deteriorating extension of it. Furthermore, war is seen not just as a random violence, rather it has patterns that are laden with activities and rules just as it has focus and direction. This working definition is certainly deep enough to capture the real big wars such as 2nd World War that lasted for so long and very distinctive in terms of human causalities. This concept would probably not include the type of armed conflicts which are commonly described as war. For the purpose of this discussion, wars would be seen as an agglomerate of series of large scale military operations.

According to Frank J. Kendrick, MOOTW is "an umbrella term encompassing a variety of military operations conducted…, to deter war, resolve conflict, promote peace, or support civil authorities… with the overall goals of pursuing national initiatives and counter potential threats to a nation's security interest". It is quite different from war in that war unlike MOOTW comes in the form of large scale sustained combat operations usually declared when instruments of national power are unable to achieve national objectives[5].

It is however important to note that MOOTW that involves combat such as peace enforcement may have many of the same characteristics of war which include active combat operations and employment of most combat capabilities. Despite this, MOOTW has its peculiar characteristics. First, MOOTW could hardly be exclusively military, secondly MOOTW are more sensitive to political considerations than actual war, as political consideration permeate all levels and influence operations and tactics. The relevance of the high accord given to the primacy of political objectives was underscored during Kosovo crisis where list of targets had to be approved by all participating countries according toWesley Clark in his book Waging

Modern War. To this end, it behooves on all military personnel to understand the political objective and the dangers posed by inappropriate actions and also remain aware of changes to operational situations as well as to political objective that may warrant to change in military operations. As a result of this, they have more restrictive rules of Engagement (ROE). Additionally differences between MOOTW and war could be identified in their purpose and range.

a. The purpose of MOOTW is more multiple and cold keep changing, that is from deterrence of potential aggressors to providing humanitarian assistance, or actually engaging in combat. The strategic importance of MOOTW contributes to attainment of nation security objectives by supporting deterre3nce, forward presence and crisis response options. Deterrence is achieved from the belief that a credible threat of retaliation exist, and also due to the existence of various MOOTW combat options, like peace enforcement, strikes and raids. Forward presence is achieved by foreign military training, Naval port visits and military to military contact while crisis response may include for example, employment of overwhelming force in peace enforcement, a single precision strike or emergency support to civil authorities.

b. The range and duration of MOOTW will give further insight into the concept of MOOTW that provides a wide range of options, which involves the use or threat of force when other instruments of national power have failed to arrest a potentially hostile situation and not involving use or threat of force, which includes disaster relief, peacekeeping, and humanitarian assistance. MOOTW also involves simultaneously with combat MOOTW i.e. humanitarian assistance in conjunction with peace enforcement operations. MOOTW may be conducted on a relatively short period of time, i.e. strike and raids or an extended period to achieve the desired end state. What ever it is has been chosen for its conduct, MOOTW evolved over the years through a lengthy but winding loops of operational realities.

ORIGIN OF MOOTW

The concept of MOOTW first surfaced in the US military after the demise of the cold war. It was this occurrence (i.e. end of cold war) that brought about a drastic change in the sphere of international security. Consequently, the United States and its allies as well as Russia implemented large scale reductions of conventional and strategic weapons, downsizing their armed forces as a whole, and going ahead with conversion of defence industry. Nonetheless, the military in virtually all the countries of the world remains the largest and the most organized institution with defence expenditure as a rule exceeding those of any other ministry or private corporation. Furthermore, in response to the growing number of unconventional crises around the globe brought about by changes in threats to security such as famine, natural disasters, and political disintegration, it became obvious that there is need for armed forces to intervene. These interventions in what haws been termed the "New World Order" have manifested in the form of disaster and humanitarian assistance, friendly coalition building, non-combatant emergency evacuations, counter drug operations and support for civil authority.

Although the tendency is to ascribe the emergence of MOOTW to US and other Western Nations, evidence, however, exist to show otherwise. For example, Nigerian Armed Forces and indeed Armed Forces of various African countries have at one time or the other conducted several Internal Security Operations in aid of Civil Authority and participated in United Nations, Regional and Sub-regional Peace Support Operations (PSO). These forms of operations and many others that are short of war are generally classified as Military Operations Other Than War (MOOTW), which is still lacking in our case. The current emphasis of developed armies, allied forces and military alliances such as NATO is the formal training and preparations for the conduct to MOOTW. This is understandably due to the changes taking place in the global strategic environment. For example, MOOTW offers a myriad of options that can be used to complement a good number of other instruments of national power by developed Armed Forces to combat modern threats, conflicts and force projection. The situation is not, however, completely restricted to developed Armed Forces. Those Armed Forces from developing countries such as Nigeria have also had the privilege to do the same even if it is not as perfect. At least our outstanding record in Liberia, Sierra Leone and lately Darfur are there for the world to see.

EMPLOYMENT AND TYPES OF MOOTW

Available literatures classify MOOTW into two major categories. These are the MOOTW operation conducted in peace and war time. Let us now take a closer look at these categories beginning with MOOTW in peace time.

MOOTW IN PEACE TIME

MOOTW in peace time operation that are conducted in situation devoid of military hostilities. Although these operations are embarked upon by members of the armed forces, they are usually either conducted in arid or civilian, or as a default preventive measure before the out break of hostilities. Such category of MOOTW could also be conducted as a precursor operation before the out break of full scale military engagement. These type of operation will normally include but not limited to such operations as Military Assistance, Nation Assistance, Search and Rescue, Noncombatant Evacuations, Slow of Force, Counter Drug Operation/Anty-Banditry Operations, Humanitarian Assistance and Disaster Relief.

    a.   Military Assistance: National Armies conduct Military Assistance operations to provide military articles, training and defence related services authorized by the home government. Such operations/assistance is permissible so long as it does not jeopardize the military security of the state providing it. Military Assistance is a key instrument of foreign policy projection. In the United State of America such operation are strictly controlled by the

Foreign Assistance Act of 1961 which deals with Interrelated Military Education and Training (IMET). In Nigeria, it is controlled by the Ministry of Defence through Defence Headquarters. Examples of such operation include Nigerian Military Training Aid to Sierra Leone and Liberia and the US Military Training Aid to Nigeria during the early years of the Obasanjo Administration.

b. **Nation Assistance:** Nation Assistance programs promote stability and orderly progress, thus contributing to the prevention of conflicts. When internal conflicts exist, nation assistance is aimed at removing it's root causes. It is used as a primary source of the successful resolution of the conflict in line with the National Defence and Development Strategy of the nation. Nation assistance includes general missions such as assisting the country with infrastructural projects, training health care workers, and training of military forces. Nigeria has carried out nation assistance on many occasions in the past most especially in Africa countries such as Liberia, Sierra Leone, Guinea and Cote d'voire.

c. *Search and Rescue:* Search and rescue operation are sophisticated actions requiring precise execution. They may be clandestine or overt. This operation may include the rescue of Nigerian or foreign nationals. Search and Rescue operation requires timely intelligence and detailed planning. Such operations may be required in peace time as well as in conflict or war. Though Nigeria has statutory institutions saddled with search and rescue operations, the assistance derived from the military is unquantifiable. The Disaster Response Units that are located across the country are designated by Armed Forces locations.

d. *Non-Combatant Evacuation:* Non Combatant Evaluation (NCE) is normally conducted to evacuate civilians and non-essentially military personnel from conflict location to a safe haven. This operation is conducted to evacuate citizens whose lives are unsafe from hostility or natural disasters. It could also include the discerning evacuation of citizens of the host nation and other country's nationals. When military forces are employed in NCE, a Force Commander is appointed to coordinate the operation. NCE operation differs from other military operations since the direction of the operation would remain with the Ambassador of the host nation at the time of the evacuation. Furthermore, the order to evacuate is a diplomatic rather than a military decision. An example of NCE is the 1991 operations to evacuate nationals of US and other countries from Somalia and Republic of Congo. Nigeria carried out NCE in Liberia at the outset of the Liberian Civil War. The recent xenophobic attacks in South Africa also made the National Assembly to commence preparations for the evacuation of Nigerian nationals from South Africa.

e. *Peace Support Operation:* Peace Support Operation (PSO) is carried out to support diplomatic efforts at maintaining peace in conflict areas. Such operation require the consent of the belligerents to the presence of peace keeping forces, as well as nonse of force. Such consent represent an

539

DEFENCE POLICY OF NIGERIA: CAPABILITY AND CONTEXT

explicit agreement, permitting the introduction of a neutral third part. PSO involves ambiguous situations that require the force to deal with extreme tension and violence without becoming a participant. Examples of PSOs include UN operation in Cyprus since 1964 and Cambodia (1991 - 1992). There are of course examples of enforcement operation that do not comply with aforementioned limitations. Examples include NATO operation in Bosnia since 1995 and Kosovo since 1999. Other examples at both regional and sub-regional levels are currently on-going and need no emphasis.

    f.   ***Humanitarian Operations:*** These types of operations which are conducted in crisis zones for their part include the following: assistance in natural disasters and other emergencies; assistance to refugees and displaced persons; ensuring the security of humanitarian operations .e.g. by facilitating access for international humanitarian organization and service officers to disaster areas. Its also includes protection of humanitarian aid convoys and depots as well as seaports and airports used to deliver humanitarian aids. When properly executed military participation in humanitarian assistance and disaster relief operation has long term positive effects. Such participation demonstrate good will and engenders mutual respect. At home, it provides soldiers the opportunity to demonstrate their skills while helping their fellow citizens. The Nigerian Armed Forces have been involved in humanitarian operations in Chad and Niger, during the drought periods in these countries and on several occasions within Nigeria most especially during disaster such as floods, plane crashes and riots leading to internal displacement.

Operations conducted in peace time are designed to preclude the onset of conflict. Conflict may arise due to uncontrollable factors. Since conflict may arise gradually or abruptly, commanders must be prepared for this eventuality by continuous operational assessment and re-evaluation. This would aid the identification of needed military capabilities in the even of conflict. Such identification assists national level decision makers to determine mobilization requirements. Some of such operations that would be considered in this paper includes: Terrorism, Insurgency/Counter Insurgency Operations and Support for Insurgency.

    a.   *Terrorism:* Terrorism is carried out to counter or intimidate government or societies pursuing goals that are generally diplomatic, religious or ideological. Combating terrorism involves defensive (antiterrorism) and offensive (counter terrorism) actions.

Anti-terrorism: Antiterrorism includes all measures that installations, units and individuals take to reduce the probability of their falling victim to a terrorist act. It includes those defensive measures that reduce the vulnerability of individual and property. The extent of these defensive measures varies, based on assessment of the local threat. These measures include:

    a.   Being personally aware and knowledgeable of personal protection techniques.
    b.   Implementing crime and physical security programs to harden the target.
    c.   Making installations and personnel less appealing as terrorist targets.

Counter-terrorism: Counter-terrorism includes the full range of offensive measures to prevent, deter and respond to terrorism. Local measures include only those actions taken to terminate an incident or apprehend individuals responsible for terrorist acts.

Insurgency and Counter Insurgency Operations: Insurgency and counter insurgency are two aspects of the same process. However, they differ in execution. Insurgents assume that appropriate change within the existing system is not possible or likely. Insurgency therefore focuses on radical change in diplomatic control and requires extensive use of covert instrument and methods. Counter Insurgency uses principally overt methods and assumes appropriate change within the existing system. C Insurg Operations are military, para-military, political, economic, psychological and sociological activities undertaken by the government, independently or with the support of friendly nations, to defeat insurgency. The support could include training, arming, provision of technical and information support, humanitarian and non emergency assistance. C Insurg operations were very common during the Cold War, when the contending super powers of the USA and the USSR were fueling insurgency in pursuit of their ideological interests.

Supporting for Insurgency: Contrary to C Insurg. MOOTW can also be conducted in the form of providing support for insurgency (guerrilla) movements in other countries. Examples of this abound at both local and international levels. While the US provided support for the Mujahedin in Afghanistan in 1979-1989, the intrigues of ECOMOG in Liberia in Sierra Leone are still fresh in our memories.

Others: The other forms of MOOTW operations are so numerous to serialize in this paper. These include sanction enforcement (e.g. the) 1993 operation along Haitan coast and no-fly zone enforcement in Iraq since 1992 and Bosnia since 1993 show of force as in US patrolling of insurgency bases after a coup attempt in Phillippines in 1989[6].

Principles and Planning Considerations of MOOTW principles: The principles of war though principally associated with large-scale combat operations generally apply to MOOTW, though sometime in different ways. However, political considerations and the nature of many MOOTW require an underpinning of additional principles. Thus 6 MOOTW principles are established. These are: Objective, Unity of effort, security, restraint, perseverance and Legitimacy. While the first three of these principles are derived from the principles of war the remaining three are MOOTW specific and would be the focus in this paragraph.

a.   *Restraint:* This entails applying appropriate military capability prudently and judicious use of force. It requires the careful balancing of the need for security, the conduct of operations and the political objectives. Commanders must take proactive steps to ensure their personnel understand the ROE, which is more restrictive and sensitive to political concern to MOOTW. Also, ROE should be consistently reviewed and revised as necessary,.

b. *Perseverance.* This emphasis the preparation for measured, protracted application of military capability in support of strategic aim. Some MOOTW may require years to achieve the desired result and will often involve political, diplomatic, economic and informational measures to achieve result. Thus, there is need for patient resolute and persistent pursuit of national goals in other to achieve success.

c. *Legitimacy:* In MOOTW, legitimacy is frequently a decisive element and is based on the perception by a specific audience of the legality, morality or rightness of a set of actions. The right use of psyops, humanitarian and civil organizations assists in developing a sense of legitimacy. Legitimacy may depend on adherence to objectives agreed to by the international community, ensuring that action is appropriate to the situation and fairness is the rule in dealing with various factions.

Planning Consideration: Plans for MOOTW are prepared in similar manner as plans for war. The developments of a clear definition, understanding, and appreciation of all potential threats is to particular importance. The following should be borne in mind.

a. *Unit Integrity.* Attempts should be made no maintain unit integrity, as units are best able to accomplish a mission when deployed intact. When existing units are deployed, they operate under existing procedure and easily adapt to the mission situation as against an ad hoc force, which is less effective and takes time to adjust to requirement of the mission. Thus, it is important to deploy troops that have trained and operated together and when possible with appropriate joint force capability.

b. *Intelligence and Information.* MOOTW requires a multidiscipline, all-source coordinated intelligence. In this regard, Human Intelligence (HUMINT) is important as it can provide the most useful source of information; supplements signal intelligence and overhead imagery. Of note is that intelligence collection in MOOTW focuses on understanding the political and economic factors that affects the situation. Also important is the transportation infrastructure in AOR. Counter Intelligence (CI) should be pursued, as protection of the force requires that essential elements of friendly information be safeguarded.

c. *Command and Control:* Commanders should be flexible in modifying standard arrangement to meet specific requirement of each situation and promote unity of effort. However, interoperability of communication system is critical especially when civil authorities are involved in the operation. If in a multinational operation, command and control can be based on the lead nation option in which a particular nation takes effective charge, parallel option which allows multinational partners to retain greater operational control of their force or the regional alliance hinged on the influence exerted by a nation in a regional leadership position. This was the case with Nigeria in ECOMOG now UNMIL.

d. *Coordination:* Coordination is important to critically determine the basis for the operation being conducted. The Armed Forces must cooperate with other agencies to deal effectively with the diplomatically sensitive situation present in conflict.

e. *Balance:* Commanders must balance the combat readiness of the troops against the volatile environment in which they function in MOOTW. A balance must also be reached between diplomatic goals, scales, intensity and nature of military operations supporting those goals.

f. *Planning for Uncertainty:* Commanders must build flexibility into their plans and operations. Conflict situations are full of uncertainty as presented by both the threat and the diplomatic conditions that limit Army options.

g. *Identification of Risks:* Military commanders must identify ways and means of increasing their options while limiting the enemy's options. Successful military commanders do not run out of options. Risk taking is considered as part of options decision. Risks are weighed against the probability of success, available intelligence and other factors available to the commander in his decision cycle.

h. *Public Affairs:* Planning for public affairs is very crucial especially where there can be significant political impact. Media reporting influences public option, which may affect the perceived legitimacy of an operation and ultimately influences the success or failure of the operation. Thus, a well-defined and concise public affairs plan, which should provide open and independent reporting and answers to media queries, is essential. It should also anticipate response to inaccurate media analysis.

i. *Psychological Operations and Coordination with NGOs:* Military Psyops, which constitute a planned, process of conveying messages to and influencing selected target groups, is desirable. Success may depend on direct control or influence over the operational area mediums of mass communication (Radio, TV, Newspaper). Coordination with NGOs through the establishment of Civil Military Operation Cell (CMOC) should be provided.

j. *Logistics and Medical Support:* Logistics support for operation and employment of logistics unit and elements must be worked out if on a foreign land, the status of forces agreement must be adhered to while effort must be made to limit the adverse effect on host nation economy. Availability of logistics infrastructure like airport, seaports etc should be considered. Medical support to troops taking part especially preventive medicines to reduce the threat of uncontrolled problems is important.

k. *Termination of Operation:* The planning should include actions to be taken as soon as operation is complete. The redeployment of specific units as soon as their part in the operation is completed should be scheduled. This will ensure that troops are ready for future deployments.

l. *Multinational Operations:* Planning should take into account the following – political climates, language barrier, cultural background, military capabilities and training, equipment interoperability and logistic support system coordination[7].

FACTORS AFFECTING MOOTW

Before I take a specific look at Nigeria as a way of rounding up this discussion on MOOTW, I want to quickly highlight some areas of obvious difficulties in the conduct of the operation and likely benefits that may accrue to nations involved in MOOTW if these are overcome.

Planning: Planning especially at the operational level is a continuous process. Rapidly changing diplomatic conditions may change the desired objective, composition and sequencing of conflict operation. Planners may prepare multiple branches and sequels to enhance their ability to provide timely support. Senior army commanders require a flexible force structure to enable their organization to achieve the desired strategic end. Planning for MOOTW could be very strenuous and time consuming if the operation is to be successfully executed. The environment (theatre of operation) where the troops will operate be well known to them. Most often than not planning for MOOTW has continued to be a problem to nations involved with these operations most especially developing countries. Planning does not just involve the logistic requirements for the operation there is also the need to cater for adequate knowledge of the mannerisms of the troops, their customs, cultures and traditions. For peace keeping operations in Africa and sub region, there is usually difficult in assembling troops because of varying degrees of national commitments couple with the ever dwindling resources. There should be devotion to make adequate arrangements for logistics, rotation of troops, welfare visits, exchange and collection of mails. It is necessary to employ well trained officers in planning as they would usually posses the knowledge and skills for quick and long appreciations of the problems to be encountered by the peace keepers.

Finance: A major thorny issue in declining or accepting any form of MOOTW operation is finance. This, to a large extent has prevented some countries from contributing materials or troops for MOOTW. Peacekeeping for example is an expensive venture depending on whether the operation is UN sponsored or a regional initiative like ECOMOG, the participating country is expected to mobilize its troops and provide the logistics necessary for such mission.

Structure: Military leaders conduct MOOTW without a declaration of war. The absence of this declaration restricts the structure of the theater of operation. In MOOTW, the commander does not establish a theater of war or operation unless it is a major conflict. Diplomatic consideration predominates over purely military requirements and constraints C^2. The commander has a greater level of freedom than in peace time but must coordinate closely with non military agencies. Whatever the terrain, the command must establish C^2 structures for conduct of the operation. The non recognition of the structure of MOOTW operations in the formation or design of the developing countries Armed Forces training has been very detrimental to the performance and the overall efficiency of our forces. The type of training which we had was conventional enemy but the types of crisis envisaged by MOOTW are far away from this[8].

Administration: To deploy a body of troops for MOOTW operation requires that the right administrative and logistic support which can have a profound effect on the mission be put in place. The concept of jointness as it is expected to be practiced within the Armed Forces can probably not be better demonstrated by any other operation than MOOTW. Many nationals of developing countries their immediate evacuation in the past. Poor administrative coordinate and lack of appropriate networking have delayed moves that would have saved lives.

Knowledge of other Language: Most MOOTW operations especially those relating to peace keeping operations are always multinational assignment. Knowledge of more than one language particularly that of the country of operation is of immense advantage to participating troops. In the case of disasters, the level of interaction is usually up to the lowest level of the masses within affected country who probably speak only dialects. The recent earthquake in China and flooding / hurricane disaster in Myanmar are glaring examples. To that end, nations should deliberately encourage the study of languages as a subject of priority among their troops. Every additional language should be considered a planning imperative for MOOTW.

Other Factors. Apart from the above listed problems, others include:

    a.   Responsibility to protect
    b.   Sovereignty of states
    c.   Consensus building
    d.   Political interference
    e.   Interagency coordination.

MOOTW holds plenty of promise in this era of globalization with many observers as political scientists believing that interstate war has become obsolete. According to Michael O. Hanion, certain assumptions are behind this thinking and these include the nuclear revolution, destructive effects of industrial age vis-à-vis evolution of conventional weapons, interdependent alliance systems, the spread of democratic governments and the realities of modern economics deemphasizing territorial acquisition. He also believes that this thinking could be a major intellectual error and tragic mistake, because the international system is not static, so there is always the remote possibility that states, democratic or not could very well go to war. In essence, we should not lull ourselves to sleep, thinking that the smaller military missions useful as they are would forever be the only pre-occupation of nation's armed forces. But for now as far as we are concerned, that is what we have and they are useful. As further evidence of the emerging security environment, these less than war missions of the military hold the promise for the successful conduct of collective global security, because of their physical capabilities. These include transportation, command and control hardware, self-sufficiency, and the unity of goals.

NIGERIAN ARMED FORCES AND MOOTW

Despite Nigeria's very high reputation in the sphere of PSOs, the country is still at its infancy in the conduct of *MOOTW in its larger* dimensions. For example area like forward presence and of force projection at least, within the West African sub-region are still lacking. The level of Nigeria's participation in multinational training exercises especially, those conducted in the sub-region especially the one codenamed RECAMP is not encouraging. The inability of Nigeria to effectively participate in this exercise robs her Armed Forces of the opportunity of force projection. Nigeria would therefore, need to avail her Armed Forces the opportunity to partake in such exercises in future.

As long as the world is beset with conflicts, Nigeria cannot isolate herself from participating in the resolution of these conflicts. Nigeria therefore would continue to provide assistance and contribute troops to *MOOTW* operations. Nigeria's strength and recognition globally be taken positively to increase these roles.

The Way Forward: In order to improve the local security situation and enhance Nigeria's international presence, influence and regional power status, the need to utilize and array of operations provided by *MOOTW* cannot be over emphasized. To achieve this, the following areas need to be addressed.

    a.   *Training:* The need to continue with the training and retraining of our force is an imperative. The aim should be to ensure that officers and their soldiers understand the objectives, principles and characteristics of *MOOTW.* Furthermore, additional effort should be made to ensure that individuals and units have the skills for a given *MOOTW* and that the staff can plan, control and support the operation. This can easily be realized if essential individual and unit training, field and situational exercise and range classification are implemented as a routine.

    b.   *Multinational Exercise:* There is the need to step up our involvement in multinational exercises especially those within the sub-region. This would enhance interoperability and commonality with allied forces which we could certainly have to do business with in operation.

    c.   *Logistics Support:* The need for adequate equipping and kitting of our troops to enable them conduct *MOOTW* in both internal and external environment is very important. The Armed Forces need to have the capability to launch and sustain itself in *MOOTW* operations.

    d.   *Forward Presence and Show of Force:* This can be provided through multinational exercise, Navy port visit, foreign military training assistance and high level military to military contacts. The essence of forward presence among others is that in the event of plans to conduct *MOOTW* outside Nigeria, forward presence forces are usually deployed first considering their location and knowledge of the region. This was the situation with the initial deployment of NA troops in Sierra Leone in 1997 and in Liberia in 2003 just by lifting forward presence troops that were already in Liberia and Sierra Leone respectively.

    e.   *Political Will:* Irrespective of the strategies that may be propounded, the government in place must have the political will to commit and sustain troops for *MOOTW* operation both internally and externally and externally.

This is very crucial as political objectives drive *MOOTW* at every level from strategic to tactical. Moreso, in *MOOTW* operations like humanitarian assistance, the DHQ would often be in a support role to Ministry of Foreign Affairs for outside operation and agency like National Emergency Management Authority (NEMA) and state governments for the execution of those operations that are internal to us.

CONCLUSION

There is no doubt that *MOOTW* poses challenges for which our Armed Forces need to be prepared. This operation is in addition providing a real stiff test to our commanders and their personnel who have always set their goals on the execution of conventional military operations. The only way out is to ascribe high priority to *MOOTW* when training and equipping the Armed Forces. Another issue that must be addressed is that of a *MOOTW* doctrine for the Armed Forces that is presently begging for attention. It is expected that more opportunities will be extended to the Armed Forces to participate in the conduct of *MOOTW* considering the internal situations in the country and the unending crisis in Africa.

Irrespective of the situation and whenever we choose to intervene, the pertinent questions that should be uppermost in the minds of our planners include: Are we guided by certain principles? Have we established the parameters for participation? and, Are we really prepared to adhere strictly to what is acceptable standard applicable within the international environment. The subject of Military Operations Other Than War is now a popular concept that is gaining prominence in the global-geo-strategic security environment.

REFERENCES

1. J. E. Dougherty and R. Pfaltzgraf, Contending Theories of International Relations N. Y: Harper and Row, 1981.
2. E. Stepanova, Military Operations Other Than War: The US View, internet source, www, findarticle com/e/articles/mi-mo JAP.
3. David Crist, Military Operations Other Than War. Internet source.
4. Vasque John A, The War Puzzle (Cambridge, Cambridge University Press 1993)
5. O. Azazi, Lecture on *MOOTW* delivered to participants of NWC Course III.
6. US Department of Defence, Joint Doctrine for Military Operations other Than War. (Joint Pub 3 - 07).
7. US Joint Doctrine, Joint Force Employment briefing modules *httpllen.wikipedic/ military operations other than war.*
8. Brian Holder Reid, Military Power Land Warfare in Theory and Practice (Frank CASS, London 1997).

CHAPTER 38

THE MILITARY IN PEACE SUPPORT OPERATION

F. O. OKONKWO

PREAMBLE

Peace Support Operation (PSO) is a third party approach to conflict resolution covering all aspects of peace efforts. Depending on political, geographical, economic or religious circumstances and considerations, PSO could be enunciated at bilateral, sub-regional, regional/continental and global levels. In the conduct of PSO, there are no enemies. All troops within the mission area are to be regarded as friendly troops. Such troops must be conversant with the principles guiding the conduct of this type of operation which include: firmness, impartiality, clarity of intention, anticipation, avoidance of the use of force and integration;

Peace support operation was a term first used in the military to cover peacekeeping and peacekeeping and peace enforcement but also those other peace related operations. Since peacekeeping by the United Nation standard is the most acceptable means of conflict management and resolution strategy, the United Nation (UN) defines peacekeeping operation as "An operation involving military personnel but without enforcement powers established by the UN to help maintain or restore peace in areas of conflict"[1].

The chapter covers both conceptual and operational issues in peace support operations:

- a. Concept of PSO and the place of peacekeeping.
- b. Objectives and impact of the military in PSOs.
- c. The limitations and challenges of military power in PSOs.
- d. The future of traditional military PSOs
- e. Paying for peace and dictating the political outcome.

CONCEPTUAL CLARIFICATION

As already mentioned, peace support operation is a third party approach to conflict resolution. It covers for example, conflict prevention, peace making, peace building, peacekeeping, peace enforcement and humanitarian operations. Without active and willing involvement of the host nation in PSO there can be no self sustained peace. In the conduct of complex PSO, military activities should be viewed as only one of several lines of operation which will be conducted with either a peacekeeping or peace enforcement profile. The complete range of PSOs as defined by NATO are as follows:

- a. Peace Support Operation PSO: PSO are multifunctional operation involving military force and diplomatic and humanitarian agencies. They are designed to achieve humanitarian goals on a long term political settlement, and are conducted impartially in support of a UN or sub-regional mandate. These include peacekeeping, peace enforcement, conflict prevention, peace making, peace building and humanitarian operations.

b.   Peacekeeping: Peacekeeping operations are generally undertaken under chapter VI of the UN charter with the consent of implementation of a peace agreement.

c.   Peace Enforcement: Peace enforcement operations are coercive in nature and undertaken under chapter VII of UN charter when the consent of any of the major parties to the conflict is uncertain. They are designed to maintain and re-establish peace or enforce the term specified in the mandate.

d.   Conflict Prevention : Conflict prevention activities are normally conducted initiative to preventive deployment of forces intended to prevent dispute from escalating into armed conflict or from spreading. Conflict prevention can also include fact finding mission, consultations, warnings, inspections and monitoring. Prevention deployment within the framework of conflict prevention is the deployment of operational forces possessing sufficient deterrent capabilities to avoid a conflict.

e.   Peacemaking: peacemaking covers the diplomatic activities conducted after the commencement of a conflict aimed at establishing a ceasefire or a rapid peaceful settlement. They can include the provision of good offices, mediation, conciliation, diplomatic pressure, isolation and sanctions.

f.   Peace Building: Peace building covers actions which support political, economic, social, and military measures and structures, aiming to strengthen and solidify political settlements in order to redress the causes of conflict: this includes mechanisms to identify and support structures which tends to consolidate peace, advance a sense of confidence and well being, and support economic reconstruction.

h.   Humanitarian Operations: Humanitarian operations are conducted to relieve human suffering. Military humanitarian activities may accompany, or be in support of, humanitarian operations conducted by specialized civilian organizations.

The United Nation concept known as "peacekeeping" came into being through the Canadian sponsored General Assembly" as it was not in the original charter. There are basically two types of peacekeeping operations. The first form being the observer mission which is usually made up of a group of unarmed military officers, mandated to carryout specific assignments after a ceasefire between two adversaries who have consented to the mission. Examples UNMOGIP (Afghanistan and Pakistan), UNIMOG (Iran and Iraq), UNAVEM (Angola) UNMEE (Ethiopia and Eritrea). The second type is the peacekeeping force which is usually larger, lightly officers and soldiers who are moderately equipped when necessary and armed with a mandate. Examples are many, UNTAG, UNIFIL, ECOMOG, ECOMIL etc.

In certain cases however, the intransigence of some belligerent could lead to the peace-enforcement to enable it contain the immediate security challenges on the ground as was the case in Liberia and Congo. The introduction of peace enforcement to the mandate of peacekeeping has had a multiplying effect on the danger potentials which made Celestine Bassey to state that "peacekeeping forces may encounter a variety of coercive tasks as there can be no guarantee that they will be able to function entirely without gunfire and blood shed[2]". The introduction of peace-enforcement makes bloodshed inevitable and may either prolong or shorten the duration of the mission and equally make such peacekeeping costly in terms of lives and material.

The ECOMOG experience is a graphic example of peace-enforcement operations. The peace support operations in Liberia were unique in many ways. It was an att4empt by Africans, especially the West Africans to resolve a conflict within their own community without the usual international support, pressure and encouragement from their former colonial masters. It was a sub-regional initiative by a sub-regional organization without political, military and logistic support from the regional organization. As the civil war continued, ECOWAS decided at its summit in Banjul, Gambia in July 1990 to establish a mediation committee to develop a peace plan which called for a ceasefire, the introduction of a military presence called ECOWAS Monitoring Group (ECOMOG), a ceasefire to establish an interim government, the return of refugees and for a free and fair election.

The initial attempt by ECOWAS mediation committee failed as warring factions refused to heed the plea of Heads of State of ECOWAS. Charles Taylor on various occasions rebuffed attempts to resolve the conflict by ECOWAS Standing Monitoring Committee (SMC). The uncompromising attitude of some of these factions particularly the NPFL led to the establishment of ECOMOG on 7 August 1990 for the purpose of keeping the peace, restoring law and order and ensuring that the ceasefire was respected. Some of the Liberian factions, especially Taylors NPFL, saw ECOMOG as an effort by the sub-region to deny them the fruit of victory. On 9 September 1990, President Doe visited the ECOMOG Headquarters to see the Force Commander, General Quino without invitation and was abducted and later murdered by Prince Johnson, the breakaway leader of Independent National Patriotic Front of Liberia (INPFL). The murder of President Doe did not speak well of ECOMOG which immediately secured approval to change its mandate from peacekeeping to peace-enforcement.

Soon after ECOMOG changed its mandate to peace-enforcement, it began employing offensive weapons including aerial bombardment to bring NPFL which was increasingly becoming ruthless in its attack on peacekeepers into submission. The conflict continued virtually unabated for the next six years, a period during which series of agreement were signed and rapidly broken by factions in their unbridled quest for power. The situation in Liberia remained fluid.

The use of peace-enforcement option by ECOMOG provided the opportunity for ECOMOG to deploy in virtually all parts of Liberia which was significant. It also curtailed the excesses of stubborn warring factions and brought international recognition and support to ECOMOG. If AU had the resources to do the same in Rwanda, the genocide of April 1994 would have been averted. The peace-enforcement initiative was again repeated in Sierra-Leone and NATO adopted a similar stance in Bosnia crisis and in Kosovo. We shall discuss further on peace enforcement later in the presentation[3].

THE MILITARY IN PSO: OPERATIONAL ANALYSIS.

The objective and impact of the military in PSO is to stabilize the situation and return the destabilized country to peace or at least relative peace. How the peacekeeping force achieve this, is another question. Let us give a break to ECOMOG operation in Liberia and use ECOWAS Mission in Liberia (ECOMIL) operation to explain further. The hostilities in Liberia after the 1997 elections caused grave humanitarian consequences and posed great threat to the sub-regional peace and security. This situation remained unchanged despite ECOWAS concerted efforts to restore peace and promote democracy in Liberia. Several other initiatives were taken particularly by Liberians in Diaspora. All these initiatives gave birth to the International Contact Group on Liberia (ICGL) whose mandate was to facilitate, coordinate and complement existing peace efforts towards resolving the Liberian crisis.

ECOWAS in coordination with the ICGL, UN and AU made various contacts the warring parties, Government of Liberia, Liberian United for Reconciliation and Democracy (LURD) and the Movement for Democracy in Liberia (MODEL) in order to resolve the dispute through dialogue. General Abdulsalmi Abubakar, our former Head of State was nominated to serve as ECOWAS Mediator/Facilitator for the Liberian Peace Talk which commenced on 4th June 2003 in Accra, Ghana. The discussions for the ceasefire led to the signing of an agreement on 17th June 2003 by three belligerent parties namely Government of Liberia, LURD and MODEL. This agreement was not fully respected as fighting resumed the following day 18th June 2003, hence calling for urgent deployment of ECOWAS troops on the ground.

ECOMIL was, therefore, formed on the authority of ECOWAS Heads of State as a result of the Ceasefire Agreement between the GOL, LURD and MODEL in Accra on 17th June 2003. By this agreement, ECOWAS was to establish a force to be deployed as an Interpositional Force (IPF) between the warring factions. The force was to secure a ceasefire, stabilize the security situation in Liberia and create a favourable condition for the establishment of an International Stabilization Force (ISF). The force therefore commenced its deployment on 4th August 2003 to execute its mandate after the pre-deployment reconnaissance to Liberia[4].

ECOMIL operation is one operation that created a nightmare for both the operators and those that ordered the operations. This operation before it commenced, received varied opinions and expectation from people. The operation was seen by many as an impossible operation particularly those who participated or have good knowledge of

ECOMOG operation in Liberia. The initial deployment of ECOMIL was compared with a childless man whose wife is about to deliver and the man is left guessing whether or not she would deliver peacefully. The question in the minds of many was whether or not the initial troops would land peacefully at Robert International Airport. A former ECOMOG Force Commander described the initial troops as a sacrifice by Nigerian Government. Then came the day which was 4th August 2003, the first batch of troops landed in a professional manner ready for action and were besieged by journalist of different nationalities and Liberians. The world was grateful to ECOWAS for such a bold step to land troops in Liberia at such a difficult period.

The deployment of ECOMIL to Liberia steadily changed the situation and succeeded in negotiating the withdrawal of the LURD combatants from Bushrod Island which culminated in the handover of the Freeport to ECOMIL. The deployment to Bushrod Island did not only save many Monrovians from starving to death, but created the enabling environment for the smooth distribution of humanitarian aid to other parts of Liberia. Although ECOMIL Force was small, its success in Liberia was wonderful.

ECOMIL was proactive and focused. Quite unlike ECOMOG operation in Liberia which used enforcement to achieve its objective, there was less emphasis in the use of force throughout ECOMIL operation. ECOMIL extensively employed military diplomacy to achieve its objective of stabilizing the situation in Liberia. The problem of Liberia was the seat of power in Monrovia and ECOMIL wasted no time focusing on the stabilization of Monrovia and its immediate environs. The quick success achieved by ECOMIL was because of the strong team spirit of every group that had a hand in the operation. From the Heads of State and Government of ECOWAS through the ECOWAS Defence and Security Commission to ECOMIL Force and its collaborators, it was a team work at its best. The success of ECOMIL began with the decision of Heads of State and Government, spearheaded by the President of Nigeria for ECOMIL to deploy on the 4th of August 2003 and not 15 August as contained in the deployment plan. If ECOMIL had failed to deploy on this date, the mandate would have been unachievable because the Government of Liberia would have taken delivery of the imported arms and ammunition seized by ECOMIL on 7th August 2003.

ECOMIL operation was the first time that member states made pledges and honoured such pledges without waiting for reminders. This was because the ECOWAS Defence and Security Commission (DSC) was involved from the onset at the highest level of the sub-regional military. It was equally the first time that the usual conflicting interests between Anglophone and Francophone countries were non-existent in the mission. As at October 2003, ECOMIL was able to stabilize the situation in Liberia, insert an interpositional force between GOL and MODEL on Buchanan-Harbel highway, between GOL and LURD along Gbanga and Moronvia highway and between GOL and LURD along Monrovia Tubmanburg highway, thus accomplishing its mandate within the approved timeline without firing a shot. ECOMIL was equally able to build confidence between the GOL and LURD, GOL and MODEL and between LURD combatants and GOL police. The ability of ECOMIL force to seize arms and ammunition imported by the government and to move out thousands of government militia out of Monrovia confirmed ECOMIL neutrality and secured the needed acceptance of the force by the rebels. Hence neutralizing the usual hostile postures of Liberian rebels.

CHALLENGES

Coming back to ECOMOG experience, the establishment of ECOMOG during the Liberian armed conflict situation suggest the increasing incapacity of the affected regime in containing the crisis initiated by insurgent groups. A more credible legal basis for ECOWAS intervention in Liberia is the huge humanitarian disaster steering at the face of the entire ECOWAS sub-region; this situation created sufficient ground for ECOWAS to mount military action aimed at containing the crisis. Peace is a precondition to development, consolidation of democracy and creation of a conducive environment within which people and states can realize their full potential. It has however been accepted since after ECOMOG operation that sub-regional efforts backed by adequate support seems to be the best situation in the use of military power in conflict resolution. However, for the effectiveness of a sub-regional effort, there is the necessity to have a lead nation to spearhead such intervention as was the case in ECOMOG in which Nigeria performed this role. Spearheading the intervention by ECOWAS in Liberia and Sierra-Leone, the Nigeria led sub-regional ECOWAS force, was able to restore Liberia and Sierra-Leone to some normalcy[5].

Military power is meant for the achievement of specific objectives and therefore should not be misdirected or misused. ECOMOG intervention in Liberia was principally to save the regime of Samuel Doe and prevent NPFL led by Charles Taylor from taking over power. In the long run Charles Taylor became the President of Liberia while Samuel Doe lost his life in a miserable circumstance. Again in Sierra Leone, Nigeria led ECOMOG force battled Paul Koromah's forces to return President Tijan Kabah to power. These developments were not pleasing to the International Community and General Abacha's opposition members who charged that "Nigeria exports what it doss not have, (democracy) and imports what it produces in abundance, petrol". This was particularly so because of the huge expenditure on regional conflict resolution while Nigerians are dying in poverty. The government of Ghana and Liberia were quite unhappy with the unilateral decision by Nigeria to remove by force Maj Koromah's AFRC government without consultation. A number of Francophone member States of ECOWAS specially Burkina Faso and Cote d'Ivoire were also not happy with Nigeria. These challenges must have accounted for the failure of ECOWAS to implement the decision sponsored by Nigeria in 1998 to transform ECOMOG into the organ of sub-regional security even though Nigeria maintained the largest contribution in terms of men, money and material.

Limitations and challenges that confront a military power in PSO can be extremely painful. Apart from the problems among members states, they still have operational challenges which included inadequate logistics, lack of equipment, troops allowances etc. It is very obvious that without political will and cooperation from all participants in a Peace Support Operation, there may be unnecessary delays and difficulties in meeting the agreed timelines which characterized ECOMOG operations. There were deep divisions among the members state of ECOWAS contrary to ECOMIL experience. Ironically, it was the non-troops contributing countries that made the greatest noise and forced a formidable opposition against the countries that contributed troops to actualize ECOMOG. ECOMOG operation took a large part of the resources of Nigeria, Ghana and some other countries to achieve stability in the West Africa sub-region. Some member states were critical of the dominance of ECOMOG by Nigeria. To allay such fears, the Yamoussoukro decision of 3 March 1998 was specially formulated to contain cautionary provisions to ensure that the existing ECOMOG force structure was broadened and made more representative. It also called for the periodic rotation of the post of force commander. The question here is which country within the sub-region has the enabling resources to provide a better leadership role[6]?

Limitations and challenges as negative as they were in ECOMOG peacekeeping efforts, the initiative was successful. It should be stressed here that it is only the regional determination, the strengthening of the peacekeeping force, the support of the UN and the International Community that is capable of making compliance of a mandate possible. ECOMOG in Liberia was a test case in regional peacekeeping effort. It proved that because of the close proximity of nations within a region, they tend to persist in their effort at finding solutions to the regional problem than nations outside the region. This was the situation in ECOWAS. Despite many mistakes, internal wrangling, excessive casualities in the field and the economic burden of keeping troops in Liberia for a long period, ECOWAS remained resolute until its efforts received international acceptance. The operation also proved that when regional stability is at stake, member states could endure the long period of hardship associated with it than would nations from outside the region.

As we have positive factors in regional PSO efforts so also do we have negative factors. Close affinity and proximity which was a positive factor in ECOWAS deployment equally became a negative factor when some nations within the region tend to provide support to some factions to subvert the peace effort because of their close affinity and proximity. Such development could be problematic as witnessed in the Liberian crisis. Neutrality by member states must be total and should not be taken for granted. From ECOWAS experience, regional peacekeeping force with International support is capable of achieving better result than the traditional UN peacekeeping operation. The greatest challenges to regional peacekeeping effort in Africa is poverty and limited resources of most African States. At the beginning of ECOWAS peacekeeping effort, only Nigeria, Ghana and Guinea were saddled with the heaviest burden while the other troops contributing member states played some appreciable roles.

ECOMOG Operation as unique as it was experienced great limitations and challenges being the first of its kind in the region. ECOMIL Operation which came after it witnessed lesser limitations and challenges except in the areas of language, staff duties and the usual logistics. The multinational procedures of troops deployed in regional operations. ECOMIL was made up of troops from English, French and Portuguese speaking countries with different operational procedures. In this regard, it would be instructive to encourage more interaction in terms of training exercises and courses among nations of the region. The total dependence on a donor partner for logistic support was a near disaster. This was particularly so because of the initial difficulties countered by the Pacific Architectural Engineers (PAE) in shipping items to Monrovia. No contingency plan was put in place in case the pledges made were not honoured. As it turned out, the donor communities pledged more than they were ready to deliver. The lesson learnt from this development was that missions should not depend solely on the goodwill of donors for the support of major operations. This again touches on the issue of poverty and limited resources by most African states. Here again the issue of peace fund for our continental conflict mechanism is questioned. As Brownson Dede lamented "never can the OAU mount civilian or military observer missions, let alone peacekeeping operations with a peace fund that has no funds".

FUTURE OF THE MILITARY IN PSOS

Presently, the study of conflict has preoccupied the social scientists and professional soldiers because of the sophistication of modern weapons technology and means of delivery, the robust techniques of warfare and the overall capacities in arsenals of major powers. The high stake inherent in and attached to the issue of war and peace explains why the search for peace through prevention, management and resolution of conflicts has become the most important preoccupation of the United Nations and other regional organizations established for the maintenance of internal peace and security since the Second World War. While the classic notion of peacekeeping may have served the purpose of cold war period, it has tuned out in recent times to be inadequate for the challenges of emergent post cold war era. The notion of peacekeeping presently has undergone tremendous transformation. Specifically, it has integrated political, military and humanitarian considerations transcending tradition UN peacekeeping roles such as the monitoring of ceasefire, separating of hostile forces and maintaining of buffer zones[7].

After the UN tragedy in Somalia, and Angola, and the ECOMOG success in Liberia, there has been African-wide consensus on the collective use of force for peacekeeping operation whose perspective needed to be harmonized. In this regard the traditional UN instrument on collective security need to reflect the new issues and expand the scope of peacekeeping to include the African perspective for better handling of peace support operation particularly at the regional level. The UN Security Council tends to reflect the strategic priorities of its permanent members, a situation that calls for urgent restructuring of the UN Security Council to positively reflect Africa's consensus and efforts[8].

The UN basically cannot do much beyond chapter VI peacekeeping in the realm of military intervention. Africa coalitions, on the other hand, have proven themselves capable of conducting fairly sustained multinational operations that have involved some heavy combat engagements which leaned toward peace-enforcement rather than regional peacekeeping. Rather than distinguishing between different kinds of peace support operation by categorizing them as conflict prevention, peacemaking, peacekeeping, post-conflict peace-building or peace-enforcement, factors should be identified that would characterize different operation and have different implications for the assessment of whether or not they should be attempted. For the purposes of analysis, three major factors are suggested: legitimacy, level of force used, and type and stage of the conflict that is to be managed[9].

Legitimacy of an operation, which in turn is a function of consent, impartially, credibility and effectiveness. Legitimacy refers to the acceptance of the peacekeeping force by the international community and by the parties to the conflict, its mandate and the way it relates to the conflict. The degree of legitimacy also affects security and stability in the conflict area. Many see peacekeeping as " an operation that enjoys the consent of parties" whereas peace enforcement is one that does not. Although impartibility is perhaps considered the most fundamental of traditional concept of peacekeeping, it is extremely difficult to maintain in practice. As Kofi Annan puts it, "impartiality does not-and not-mean neutrality in the face of evil". The Dayton agreement which gave birth to the implementation force (IFOR) led by the North Atlantic Treaty Organization (NATO) embarked on peace-enforcement mission in Bosnia without UN willingness to exercise the mandate. They form a mutually destructive or mutually reinforcing cycle with legitimacy. An increase in the peacekeeper credibility will render them more effective and will strengthen their legitimacy. In contrast, should the peace keepers prove to be ineffective, their credibility will be seriously undermined and their legitimacy damaged[9].

The level of force used affects legitimacy and all its constituent elements such as the corresponding question of consent. Through the years, the concept of the use of force only in self defence has been steadily extended in the course of several missions especially after the end of the cold war when the concept was extended to include the defence of UN equipment and defence of the mission. This reflects the evolved notion of impartially, where loyalty to the mission and its goals has precedence over all other parties and concerns. Although the use of force is perceived by some as an attractive tool, force without its political counterpart diplomacy can only have a limited effect. Use of force and diplomacy pursue same overall goal.

The type of conflict in which the peace support force intervenes is a pivotal factor in the context of deployment. Still most conflicts evade classification into civil wars, interstate, or international conflicts and Smith suggested that the existing terminology is simply inadequate. In order to avoid the pitfall of these classifications, Sabin prefers the general features of future conflicts as follows:

    a.   There will be significant diversity in the types of war,

b.   Future conflicts will be complex or multidimensional. The move increasingly away from "a clear front line, to one in which antagonists have a growing range of coercive options, almost independent of distance and in which multiple actors with multiple interests interact in ways very different from the classic bipolar duel".

c.   Conflict will be marked by asymmetry with regard to differences in military skill and technological capability, but also to respective levels of commitment and ruthlessness.

d.   Increasingly, conflicts are politicized, involving a struggle for hearts and minds, particularly in the case of civil war or external intervention. They also become a contest of image due to role of the media.

All Sabin's characteristics point to the fact that peace support operation will be launched in increasingly difficult conditions. It is therefore absolutely essential for the interventionists to understand the dynamics of the conflict, in order to operate effectively and to be perceived as legitimate. The nature of future conflicts also suggests that a wide range of tools will have to be used in order for an operation to be successful. In practice, the forces have to relate to the conflict before relating to the parties. In addition to the type of conflict, the mission will face very difficult circumstances due to the stage in which the conflict is at time of intervention. Thus pre-conflict deployment is usually impossible and highly unlikely without the explicit consent of a given local authority or authorities. Whereas peacekeeping in a post-settlement context is the most straightforward, intervention in ongoing conflict is excessively difficult. Thus, different issues will be at the fore front, depending on whether the force is being deployed preventively in an ongoing conflict or in an operation in the wake of ceasefire or a peace agreement. Ironically, as Woodward points out, "Intervention is usually late when significance level of violence has become undeniable, but also when situation has become far more complex and more difficult to manage for outside actors".

NEW THINKING

International law is a seductive determinant for a decision to intervene, due to its supposed neutrality and legitimacy. A legal approach strengthens the legitimacy of an operation in that it ensures that at least a minimum of consent is given at the onset. These determine not only when action is allowed or called for but also what type of action may be taken in the course of the mission. However, when being asked to decide on instruments to implement international norms in Kosovo or Rwanda, the UN system failed. A major problem in the UN system is the fact that judicial and executive power lie in the same hands, namely those of the Security Council. As a result, there is no division of power and the act of deciding on action and legalizing it is one and the same.

The notion that there is responsibilities to assist others in terms of crisis, especially innocent civilians, is one of the founding principles of the UN. This is also reflected in early statement by Hammarskjold who explained that the "prohibition against intervention in internal conflicts cannot be considered to apply to senseless slaughter of civilians or fighting arising from tribal hostilities"[10]. Speaking almost forty years after Hammarskjold, Kofi Annan essentially represents the same point of view when he states that "the need for timely intervention by international community when death and suffering are inflicted on large numbers of people, and when the state nominally in charge is seen unable or unwilling to stop it". This development is seen "high politics" by countries such as Canada. To an increasing degree also, public option is an important determinant of a state's decision whether or not to act and what action to take if any.

Since the publication of Boutros-Ghali's paper: "An agenda for peace" calls for regional organization to bear a greater share of responsibility for regional security have been growing louder. The official argument for regional action points to the proximity of regional neighbours to a given conflict which implies a more immediate interest in its solution as well as to the fact that such states are an immediate subject of a conflict's regional implications such as refugees and arm flow. Despite the lack of impartiality example in Liberia and East Timor, these will quite often be the only ones willing to taken action and incur the cost of action. An argument in favour of regional intervention is also that the success of a peace support operation hinges on it not being opposed by neighbouring countries. Although positive influence is not as easy to pinpoint, it is clear that when the regional context is hostile to the process, peace effort is doomed. Therefore the direct involvement of regional countries in peace support effort is desirable as most of them have the required capability. All these developments suggest a critical review of the traditional UN peace support operation to meet the present day situation.

The new thinking after the ECOMOG success in Liberia is to have a new conceptual model which permits changing of mandate from peacekeeping to peace-enforcement. This framework or conceptual model is shown at figure 1 emphasizes concept as a critical divide between peacekeeping and peace-enforcement. However, what differentiates the peace-enforcement from peacekeeping is rather the necessity to use force in order to ensure compliance. Impartially, both as a principle and as a definitive boundary between peace and war remains intact. The importance of consent in so far as it may promote compliance is recognized not as a principle but as something which though desirable, declines with increasing coercion. The awareness contributions to the judicious use of force. The relationship between peacekeeping, peace-enforcement and war is illustrated clearly in figure 1. in fact, compliance is presently at the heart of both the evolving US and British doctrines on peace-enforcement[11]. The new framework or conceptual model has already been published in the UK joint warfare publication for the Armed Forces. It is believed that the UN charter will in future be undated to include peace enforcement mandate in both inter and intra-state conflict for regional bodies which guarantees safety of lives and effectiveness of their mechanism for conflict management. This will surely come through going by Kofi Annan's declaration that "For the United Nations, there is no higher goal, no deeper commitments, and no greater ambition than preventing armed conflict".

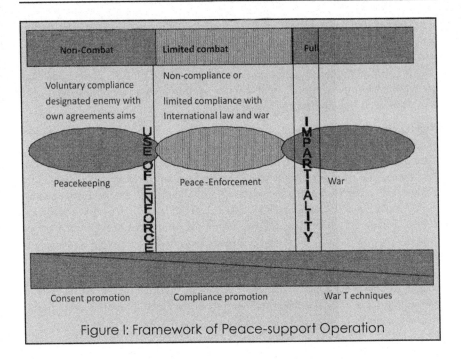

Figure I: Framework of Peace-support Operation

FRAMEWORK OF PEACE-SUPPORT OPERATION 1

During the PSO in Somalia, the US was specifically criticized for operating under a separate military command and for launching raids inconsistent with the basic tenets of UN peacekeeping operation. The US decision to order raids on Serbia air fields demonstrated how "unilateral action by one member of the coalition can damage the legitimacy of the entire force and cause quick splits among its members". General Ratko Mladic was blunt on this development when he remarked that: "I see no reason (UN) personnel should still be deployed in Bosnia, nor do I know how to protect you after the brutal attack against the Serb people. You have turned the peace forces into occupiers". The sudden unilateral action by the US was probably because the situation was not developing in line with the expected outcome. Nigeria took a similar unilateral action in Sierra Leone to remove major Koromah[12].

The financial burden of PSO depends on the scale of the crises and the nature of the mission. In ECOMOG operation in Liberia, the main burden was on few member states of ECOWAS. Nigeria shouldered greater burden than any other member state with about 80 percent of the force. With such expenditure and force strength, Nigeria tends to dictate the shape of the mission and the possible political outcome.

Peace-enforcement operations require extra finances, equipments and logistics to accomplish. The large number of troops and the enormous logistics required particularly without Mutual Assistance on Defence (MAD) certainly leaves open the issue of hegemony by a strong regional power in peace-enforcement operation as was the case in Liberia. As Olu Adeniji puts it: "the absence of the MAD structure appropriate for the situation (in Liberia) imposed on Nigeria the burden of leadership translated into the overwhelming preponderance of Nigerian troops in ECOMOG and therefore its veto-power type of role in the direction of the operations, including the almost total monopoly of the appointment of the ECOMOG command. That predominance implies also the risk that the operation could be totally derailed if some upheavals were to occur in Nigeria itself"

Nigeria's intervention in Chad in 1978 was a purely bilateral effort. The operation paved the way for the AU sponsored peacekeeping operation in Chad in 1982. Although US, Britain and France offered some logistics support to start off the mission they failed to sustain the peacekeeping force to the end. The question now is why? It was understood that out of the 12million dollars (U$ 12m) earmarked by the US, only U$6.6m was actually used to support the AU force. Unfortunately for the AU, it realized too late that the sole aim of the funding from the three western powers was to see Libya's withdrawal. This again confirms that paying for the peace by a power is to afford such power the right of dictating the political outcome of the funded peace support operation. Experience has shown that the interest of major powers in any peace support operation is also in the final determination of the political outcome of such conflict and not only in the humanitarian situation in the area of conflict[13].

CONCLUSION

The chapter has dwelt extensively on military in peace support operation. Peace support operations are multifunctional operations involving military forces, diplomatic and humanitarian agencies. PSO include peacekeeping, peace-enforcement, conflict prevention, peacemaking, peace building, and humanitarian operations. We have been able to discuss the concepts of PSO and the place of peacekeeping, objectives and impact of the military in PSOs, the limitations and challenges of military power in PSO, the future of traditional military PSOs and paying for the peace and dictating the political outcome.

In discussing these points, we were able to use our experiences in International, regional and sub-regional PSOs to buttress our points: UN in Bosnia and Somalia, OAU in Chad and ECOWAS in Liberia. We have equally able to discuss ECOMIL operation in Liberia focusing on its unique mission, challenges and accomplishments, as a basic for future peace-support operations by ECOWAS or AU.

REFERENCES

1. United Nation   The Blue Helmets: A Review of United Nations Peacekeeping" (New York, 1991).

2. C. O. Bassey   "The Peacekeeping Approach to Management: A Conceptual Overview", MA Vogt and A. E. Ekoko (Eds) Nigeria in International Peacekeeping 1960-1992 (Lagos: Malthouse Press).

3	A. I. Olurin	"Peacekeeping as a Military Operation" (Presentation at NWC Nigeria 2002).
4	F. O. Okonkwo	"Organization of African Unity/African Union Mechanism for Conflict Management: An Evaluation" (NWC Research Paper 2002)
5	Mark Malan	"Boundaries of Peace Support Operation: The African Dimension" (ISS Monograph) Series No.44) 2000
6.	R. A. Akindele	Conflict and Conflict Management in Africa: The Role of the OAU (African Union and Economic Community of West African States (ECOWAS) (Presentation at NWC Nigeria 2002).
7	I. Williams	"Strategic Planning of Peacekeeping Operations" MA Vogt and AE Ekoko (Eds) Nigeria in International Peacekeeping 1960-1992. (Lagos: Mathouse Press Ltd 1993)
8.	R. Thakur	"From Peacekeeping to Peace Enforcement: The UN Operation in Somalia" The Journal of Modern African Studies 32, 3 (1994)
9.	T. Thomas	"The Crisis Management in Bosnia: Problems and Recommendations" The Journal of Slavic Military Studies 8, 3, (1995)
10.	Kofi Annan	"Causes of Conflict and the Promotion of Duration Peace". Secretary General's Report to the Security Council (1998).
11	British Defence Doctrine	Peace Support Operations: Joint Warfare Publication 3 – 50
12	Commander TRAOCD NA	"Tactics B: Lecture Notes on Senior Senior Staff College Exam". (Military Publication) 2006
13	C. Garuba (ed)	"International Peace and Security: The Nigerian Contribution". (Gabumo Publishing Limited) 1997

CHAPTER 39

AMPHIBIOUS OPERATIONS

W. G. YANGA

PREAMBLE

Amphibious warfare or operations which involve the use of marine vessels to invade the territory of other people for whatever reasons are not new. History tells us that perhaps the first known amphibious assault was at the battle of Marathon in 490 BC where the Persians (now Iraq) established beachheads in their attempt to invade Greece. Julius Caesar also used merchant vessels to carry infantry and cavalry expeditions against the British Isles in 55BC. Christopher Columbus' landings in the Caribbean initiated Spanish and subsequently European colonization of the Americas.

Contemporary historians however usually begin amphibious warfare discussions with the failure of the Gallipoli campaign in the First World War. Allied forces attempt to make headway through Turkey by landing troops ended in a disaster at Gallipoli beaches. It became clear that the conflict would not be ended by costly frontal assaults or in the words of Winston Churchill, "Sending our Armies to chew barbed wire"

Amphibious warfare became relegated as a World War I niche and no serious thought was given to its utility after that period. But World War II saw tremendous development and refinement in the art of amphibious warfare that its operations constituted perhaps the greatest tactical innovations of the war. In the Pacific as well as the European theatres, allied amphibious capabilities proved the means for regarding strategic initiatives.

At the home front, British troops onboard HMS ST GEORGE raided Akassa in an amphibious assault in 1896. They suffered heavy casualties from the people of Brass who countered the invasion with cannons fired from ashore. The relics of that invasion are still intact in Brass and Akassa in Bayelsa State. In the Nigerian civil war, it would have been difficult for Federal troops to capture Bonny and Calabar without amphibious landings.

From the foregoing, amphibious warfare is very familiar and common to us all. However, for the purpose of this chapter let me restate the basic definition by most authors. Amphibious operations is best described at *that aspect of warfare that integrates virtually all types of water and air craft, weapons of naval and landing forces in a concerted military effort against a hostile or potentially hostile shores.* Nigeria today is faced with numerous strategic military challenges from the global environmental as well as the domestic front. Therefore, in line with the objectives of this book, I

562

would discuss the subject from a strategic perspective but without proffering specific strategic solutions to where there are problems.

Amphibious operations is one of the most complex of all military operations and thus the most demanding in its planning and execution. It normally requires extensive air participation and its characterized by closely integrated efforts of forces trained, organized and quipped for different combatant functions. Amphibious operations may be conducted in order to:

(a) Prosecute further combat operations.
(b) Obtain a site for an advance naval of air base
(c) Deny the use of an area of facility to the enemy.
(d) Show presence
(e) Capture important installations located to the coastline such as a major harbour, point facilities and communication of strategic value.

The salient requirement of an amphibious operations is the necessity for swift uninterrupted building of sufficient combat power ashore from an initial zero capacity to full coordinated striking power as the attack progresses towards the amphibious task force final objectives. Special measures are introduced to meet the requirements from the basis of the organizational and technical differences between the amphibious and land warfare.

The amphibious assault must be conducted in the face of certain additional and distinguishing difficulties. Natural forces, unfavourable weather, seas, surf and features of hydrograph – represent hazards not normally encountered in land warfare. Technical problems of logistics presented by loading thousand of troops and large quantities of materials into ships as widely separated embarkation points, moving them to the objective, then landing them in exactly the proper sequence, usually on open beaches or landing zones and under initial fire, all require extraordinary attention *in form of detailed planning. During the movement from ship-to-shore, troops are especially vulnerable.* Possible employment of nuclear, biological and chemical (NBC) weapons by the enemy is a threat to the amphibious task forces, as to any other offensive action, and require the exercise of effective counter measures, both active and passive, during all stages of the operation.

The closest cooperation and most detailed coordination among all participating forces in an amphibious operation are essential to success. The must be a clear understanding of mutual obligations and of the special capabilities and problems of each component. These factors tend to create problems in the preparation for amphibious operations that are more extensive than for other types of military operations. As Maj Gen Sir Charles Callwell observed (1905), *"Soldiers and sailors in the past, knowing little of each other's duties and objects often failed to appreciate them in times of crisis. There are huge and persisting differences between land warfare and sea warfare; yet of necessity amphibious operations comprise warfare where land and sea meet".*

The amphibious operation is a complete operation within itself and includes planning, embarkation of troops and equipments, rehearsals, movement to the objective area, final preparation of the objectives, assault landing of troops and accompanying supplies and equipments in support of the landing force until termination of the amphibious operation. Traditionally, there are five types of operations. They are:

a. **Amphibious Assault:** The principal type of amphibious operation is the amphibious assault, which involves the process of landing a credible forces to secure an area against opposition by sea craft and or helicopters in furtherance of subsequent operations. It also involves the seizure and temporary occupation of territory belonging to an active or potential enemy.

b. **Amphibious Withdrawal:** Amphibious withdrawal is an amphibious operation involving the extraction of forces by sea in naval ships, craft or helicopter from a hostile or potentially hostile shore. Withdrawal from a hostile shore can be made as a result of a termination of an operation, the redeployment of units to different areas, under enemy pressure or voluntarily. This is inherently different from withdrawal planned as part of a raid. A raid withdrawal is predetermined, but the amphibious withdrawal is based on the prevailing situation as well as on strategic and tactical considerations.

c. **Amphibious Demonstration.** Amphibious Demonst is used to deceive the enemy through a show of forces causing the enemy to adopt a course favourable to the opponent. Steps are taken to make the enemy believe that a landing is actually taking place and is intended to confuse the enemy as to actual time, location, or strength of the main operation.

d. Amphibious Raid. An raid is an amphibious operation involving swift incursion into or temporary occupation of an objective followed by a planned withdrawal. Raids are conducted for the purpose of inflicting loss or damage, creating a diversion, executing deliberate deception operations, destroying enemy information gathering systems to maintain operational security and capturing/evacuating individuals and /or material.

e. **Non-conventional Amphibious operation:** Not all amphibious operations conducted can be included in the four types discussed above. Forces may be called upon to conduct non-conventional operations that may closely parallel one of the four types for example non combatant evaluation operations may closely parallel amphibious raid.

PLANNING IMPERATIVES OF AMPHIBIOUS OPERATIONS

Planning for amphibious operation is a continuous process from the receipt of the initiating directive to the termination of the operation. It requires concurrent, parallel and detail planning by all participating forces. The planning imperatives must necessary include the following:

a. Flexibility and jointness
b. Intelligence

c. Maritime and air supporting units
d. Relative rates of build up.
e. State of training
f. Availability of assault shipping
g. Location and timing of landings.
h. Logistics and maintenance.

A) FLEXIBILITY AND JOINTNESS

The fact that opposing forces are not initially in physical contact significantly increases the likelihood of unforeseen contingencies which may confront the amphibious task force. No preconceived directives, however detailed and carefully prepared, would provide for every eventually. Consequently, the plans must be flexible so that these contingencies would be handled with the most effective and economical use made of assigned forces.

B) INTELLIGENCE ON ADVERSARY

Accurate and adequate intelligence provides fundamental information about the adversary and the operation environment. It is a prerequisite for sound amphibious operations planning. Assessment of the adversary's capabilities, intentions and decision making means that, they can be considered in the planning process. Thus, factors such as the adversary's centre of gravity, objectives and end sate would be properly assessed. This would facilitate successful landing and build up, particularly that of the beach area, sea approaches, beach exits and suitability of lines of communications hinterland for rapid development and to sustain the operation.

Reconnaissance of the AOA will be necessary to obtain information that would assist in detailed and accurate planning. It is pertinent that all items of intelligence are jointly assessed and priorities for reconnaissance agreed upon. Further to normal tactical intelligence, there will be need for information on roads and tracks, bridges, airfields, topography, local population and resources. However; care must be taken so as not to allow reconnaissance activities prejudice surprise.

C) MARITIME AND AIR SUPPORTING UNITS

Once the Landing force scheme of manoeuver ashore is formulated, detailed planning of other plans for maritime and air support units are developed. Plans for naval forces and participating air forces, as appropriate, provide for transporting, protecting landing and supporting the land force. The adequacy of forces for the operation must be constantly re-examined. The main supporting tasks for the maritime and air support effort are as follows:

Navy:

1. Escort and defence of amphibious shipping against air, surface and subsurface attacks. Additionally, counter-mining threats during the movement to and within the amphibious objective area.

2. Maintenance of the landing forces during the assault and build up phases.

3. Provision of air and naval fire support.

Air Force

    (1) Reconnaissance.

    (2) Interdiction.

    (3) Close Air Support

    (4) Destruction or neutralization of specific fortifications and concentrations.

    (5) Mining

    (6) Air supply.

D) RELATIVE RATES OF BUILD-UP

Relative rates of build-up are fundament to amphibious operations. The enemy may have balance forces in the areas, which could be quickly concentrated against the landing or he may have advantage of relatively short lines of communication for quick reinforcements and supplies. The Landing force will be limited in its initial strength and rate of build-up by the availability of ships and aircraft. The choice of landing areas and the kind of operations that could be conducted at any stage of the landing would be greatly influenced by the relative rates of build-up. however, everything possible must be done to delay the enemy's reinforcements.

C) STATE OF TRAINING

Operations from amphibious ships require specialized knowledge and techniques. The availability of specially trained troops may be a limiting factor. One technique would be to spearhead the assault with amphibious trained troops and reinforce them with normal units.

e). Selection of initial land objectives in some cases would be determined by the size of the force that can be landed and maintained ashore with the landing ship and craft available for operation. Planning may be complicated by the amount of supplies required by the landing force in the initial mounting, the shortage of ships, their different speeds and distances from the mounting base where an amphibious operations is being planned. A particularly notable feature of the Anglo-American conduct of amphibious assault in World War II was the invention of well armed amphibious tractors for the transport of troops from offshore line of departure of point inland, the development of amphibious tanks and shipping on all scale[5].

F) LOCATION AND TIMINGS OF LANDINGS

The location and timings of the landings are factors of predominant importance and are primarily determined by the overall objectives of the operation and the operational plan of the landing force. However, it may not be practicable or feasible to effect successful landings at times and places based on these requirements alone, as natural factors such as unfavourable weather, sea, surf and features of hydrography may be impediments. To select beaches and landing site to take advantage of or overcome the *limitations placed by other consideration*, D Day and H Hour could also be a compromise to take advantage of natural and operational considerations.

G) LOGISTICS AND MAINTENANCE

Logistics is a fundamental and critical part of the conduct of an amphibious operation and must be planned accordingly. However, maritime units deployed as self contained units, do require regular supply of fuel and few weeks of provisions and consumables. Ships fuelled and stored to the maximum practical levels would maintain flexibility for tasking.

The units to be deployed would require resupplies from an afloat supply base. Generally, the smaller and less sophisticated the ship, the greater reliance on external support. Some small vessels like landing craft and mine warfare units may require their own dedicated support ships. In sustained amphibious operations, the *Landing ship Equipment (LSE) will be vital, particularly as a maintenance unit for repairing equipment which will inevitably become defective with continuous use over time.*

BASIC COMMAND RELATIONSHIPS

Generally, the Joint Force Commander (JFC) establishes command relationships and assigns authority to subordinates based on the operational situation, the complexity of the mission, and the degree of control needed to ensure that the strategic intent to satisfied. The CATF exercise authority through their respective chains of command. Within the Amphibious Operation Area (AOA), CAFT is given specific authority, as prescribed by the *commander having overall authority for the operation.* The CATF will exercise the degree of control prescribed in the initiating directive over forces not a part of the ATF when such forces are operating within the AOA after the arrival of the advance force or the ATF. When such forces are merely passing through the AOA, control will be exercised only to the extent of preventing or minimizing mutual interference.

Subject of the overall authority of CATF, responsibility for conduct of operations ashore and for security of all personnel and installations located within the area of operations ashore is vested in Commander Land Force (CLF). CLF's authority includes operational control of all forces, including airborne and/or air assault forces, operating ashore within the landing area, or as directed by the commander who issued the initiating directive. Though, upon termination of the amphibious operation, command relationships will be as directed in the initiating directive.

The relationship during operational planning for an amphibious operation is unique with respect to command relationships in that operational control (OPCON) of forces is normally not passed to CATF until the amphibious operation plan is approved by the commander who issued the initiating directive. Regardless of the status of forces, when the initiating directive is received, special, planning relationships are observed during the planning phase. These planning relationships designed to ensure that both naval and LF considerations are adequately factored into decisions made concerning the conduct of the amphibious operation. CATF, CLF, and other commanders so designated in the initiating directive are coequals in planning matters and decisions. All decisions must be reached on a basis of common understanding of the mission, objectives, and procedure and on a free exchange of information. Any differences between commanders that cannot be resolved are referred to their common superior in the operational chain of command. Once the LF is embarked on amphibious shipping, CATF assumes full responsibility for the ATF and for the operation. If a change in the mission occurs after commencement of operations or if an amphibious operation is initiated from an afloat posture, coequal planning relationships, either as described above or as specified in the initiating directive, will apply to any subsequent planning.

CATF is normally the only Navy Commander that exercises authority over or assumes responsibility for the operation of land and air force units. An exception exists when a CATF has designated a Navy commander below the ATF level as commander of a subordinate task organization composed of Navy and land/air force units. The decision to delegate authority over land/air elements below the level of the ATF is by CATF during the planning phase, after consultation with CLF/CAF. When CAFT issues an order to such subordinate commander that affect the corresponding land/air elements, CLF will be informed and consulted before the order is issued. When authority over LF elements is delegated below the level of CATF, relationships between such a commander and a related LF/AF Commander are substantially the same as those between CATF, CLE and CAF. The direct chain of command of Navy and LF/AF component commanders of the ATF is restablished upon dissolution of the subordinate task force(s) or group(s) or upon the release there from of the portion of the commander assigned to it.

In the course of planning and executing amphibious operations, CATF obtains and considers the opinions and professional judgement of appropriate commanders. This requirement, however, in no way limits CATF's authority. Parallel chains of command between the naval force, LF and in some cases, Air force elements of an ATF create special requirements for consultation. No significant decision contemplated by a commander in one chain of command that affects the plans, disposition, or intentions of corresponding commander in another chain of command will be made without consultation with the commander concerned.

All necessary orders from one commander affecting personnel under command of corresponding commander at a parallel of command are, insolar as possible, issued through the appropriate counterpart commander. The foregoing will not affect the paramount authority of a commander of a ship or aircraft over persons embarked therein concerning matters affecting safety and good order of his ship or air craft or authority of senior officer present to act in an emergency.

CONDUCT OF AMPHIBIOUS OPERATIONS

The phases of an amphibious operations follow a well-defined pattern or sequence of events or activities which are planning, embarkation, rehearsal, movement to the objective area, and assault and capture of the objective area. Some of these phases overlap. Planning, as a separate phase of an amphibious operations, is the period between the issuance of the initiating directive to embarkation. It is a continuous process that extends from the time the initiating directive is issued to the end of the operation.

During the planning phase, training shortfalls may be discovered. They may require extensive individual training as well as training with other elements of the amphibious task force. As plans are developed, appropriate personnel must be adequately briefed on the overall plans and their individual and collective responsibilities.

During the embarkation phase, the landing forces assigned to the amphibious task force, with their equipment and supplies, are assembled and loaded in assigned shipping sequence. This sequence is designed to support the landing plan and the scheme of manoeuver ashore. Supplies and equipment must be prepared for loading before the assault shipping arrives in the embarkation area. Lighters should be completely serviced, fuel and water cans filled, accessories placed, and radio and navigation equipment waterproofed. A final inspection ensures all craft and equipment is in proper condition, securely lashed, adequately protected, and ready for the operation.

If ships are to be loaded offshore, the embarkation area should be organized so that amphibians use different beach areas. Lighters to be embarked aboard the same ship are marshaled together and escorted by naval guide boats to their assigned craft. Craft are loaded aboard assault shipping so that debarkation in the amphibious objectives area is in the proper order.

The rehearsal phase of an amphibious operation is the period where elements of the taskforce, or the task force in its entirely, conduct one or more exercise under conditions similar to those expected at the beachhead. The purpose of the rehearsal is to test the adequacy of plans and communications, the timing of detailed operations, and the combat readiness of participating forces. It ensures all echelons are familiar with the plan. The three types of exercise are:

A. SEPARATE FORCE REHEARSALS.

Element whose tasks are not closely associated with those of the main body of the amphibious task force normally conduct separate rehearsals. The advance force and the demonstration force are examples of elements that conduct separate rehearsals.

B. STAFF REHEARSALS

All staffs scheduled to participate in the operation conduct staff rehearsals. Conducted before integrated" rehearsals, they usually take the form of command post or game board exercises. If possible, these exercises test communications facilities.

C. INTEGRATED REHEARSALS

The rehearsals phase should include at least two integrated rehearsals for the assault phase. The first rehearsal omits actual bombardment and unloading supplies but stresses communications and control in executing ship-to-shore movement. The final rehearsal uses the actual operations plans. It includes token naval gunfire, air support with live ammunition, extensive troop participation and sufficient unloading to adequately test tactical and logistical plans, operation of ship-to-shore movement control organization, and the functioning of the shore party.

The fourth phase of an amphibious operation is the movement of the takes force to the amphibious area. This includes the departure of ships from loading points, the passage at sea, and the approach to and arrival in assigned positions in the objectives area. The task force is divided into movement groups which proceed on prescribed routes. Alternate routes are designated for emergency use. Movement groups are organized based on the speed of the ships involved and the time they are needed in the objective area. Some movement groups are scheduled to arrive in the objective area before D-day; some, on D-day; and others, after D-day.

Movement groups that arrive before D-day are the advance force. If surprise is essential, such a force may not be used. The advance force prepares the objective are for assault. It conducts reconnaissance, minesweeping, preliminary bombardment, underwater demolitions, and air operations. Movement groups arriving on D-day are the main body of the task force. They consist of one or more transport groups, landing ship groups, support groups, or carrier groups. Movements groups that arrive after Day-day provide resupply after the initial assault.

The assault phase of amphibious operations begins when the assault elements of the main body arrive at their assigned position in the objective area. This phase includes a sequence of six activities which are:

a. The assault area is subjected to naval gunfire, missile fire, and air bombardment.
b. Helicopters, landing ships and crafts, and amphibians move the landing force.
c. Assault elements of the landing force land in drop and landing zones and on the beaches.
d. Waterborne, helicopter-borne, air-dropped, and air-landed forces unite and seize the beachhead.
e. Naval forces provide logistic, air, and naval gunfire support throughout the assault.
f. Remaining landing force elements go ashore to conduct any operations required to support the mission.

AMPHIBIOUS OPERATIONS

It would not be out of place to first look at a few historical developments of some *amphibious power* that might offer us an insight into developing ours. According to Geoffrey Till *"The chief utility in history for the analysis of present and future lies in its ability, not to point out lessons, but to isolate things that need looking at....history provides insights and questions, not answers".* The employment of amphibious forces today and the methods they use have their roots in the ideas evolved since Gallipoli and the experiences of a wide range of operations. A look at the British, American and former Soviet Union will help in this regard.

BRITISH PERSPECTIVE

In the days when the Royal Navy commanded the seas, continental commitments were met by the judicious financial and material support of alliances, together with use of economic blockades and not by sending armies across the channel. At that time, Britain was able to launch imperial expeditions at sea unhindered and untroubled by the need to obey the most basic operational procedures. However, the growing prospects of war in Europe brought out the importance of harmonizing land and sea warfare, thus bringing the influence of maritime power to bear on military operations. It was noted then that the best naval supremacy could achieve in a continantal war was a limited intervention I an unlimited war. Some abortive expeditions of the royal Navy at Copenhagen (1897), Dardanelles (1807) and Walcheren (1809), proved the strategic value of an amphibious capability, which could threaten a wide area of the littoral state and commit disproportional large enemy forces to coastal defence.

When the need to land a British expeditionary force at the flanks or rear of the advancing German Army in 1914 arose, Gallipoli was chosen after several considerations. It was however discovered that the means to embark on an amphibious operation were lacking. The Army and the Royal Naval very rarely exercised together, and no combined plan of operation for any given contingency had ever been worked out. Invariably, little consideration had been given to the application of technological advances to combined operations against the shore, especially in naval gunnery. Although amphibious warfare was not the only neglected sphere of operation in 1914, the resulting debacle at Gallipoli in 1915 had a long lasting repercussion.

After Gallipoli, it was a widely held conviction in British doctrine that such amphibious operations were no longer feasible. It was opined that technology favoured the defender, who could respond quickly by redeploying troops by train and armoured forces by road. Even the Air Force opposed the concept on the grounds that, with the advent of the airplane, open craft could not reach the shore, and the power projection was best achieved by bombing. The Royal Navy (RN) itself did not object to this line of thinking, since mines and submarines were seen as added hazards facing amphibious landings. Instead, the RN stated that it was *'contemplating war as an affair on the high sea'.* The Government, already beset with serious economic problems, espoused the British Way in Warfare as the most cost effective option. From 1935 to 1939 therefore, the government pursued a strategy of 'limited liability to avoid allocating strong forces to the continent. It concentrated instead on Home and Imperial Defence, albeit with significant reservations, and adopted the trusted concept of strangulating its European enemies by economic blockades.

On the positive side, there were a few brigade landing exercises and some of the basic groundwork for amphibious operations were carried out. Consequently, the "Manual of Combined", which laid down a sound doctrine for amphibious operations, was promulgated as a result of Staff College exercises and a study of the lessons of Gallioli. These efforts were however small and poorly funded undertakings, lacking both institutional bedrock of officer training and influence from government circles. There was therefore no widespread knowledge of the art of amphibious warfare; sparse equipment, trained and experienced officers and men were also lacking. The resentment to the development of amphibious capability in Britain continued till events of WWII and more recently the Falklands landings in 1982 proved otherwise.

THE AMERICAN PERSPECTIVE

The United States Marine Corps (USMC) took a more positive view of the outcome of the Gallipoli Campaign, possibly because they, unlike the British Armed Forces, were not scarred by the disaster. They therefore used the lessons as part of a platform for establishing a new primary role as amphibious forces, after being employed as colonial infantry, line infantry, ships' guard and base defenders throughout their history. They however went through a period of uncertainty after Vietnam, which period was looked upon as the obituary for amphibious warfare. During this period, the USMC saw the amphibious fleet reduced from 162 ships in 1969 to 65 in 1079, and many of the remainder growing towards obsolescence without any plans for replacement. The reasons for this phasing out were that:

a.   The maritime strategy at the time offer little opportunity for amphibious forces in a general war.

b.   The Central front was viewed as th main and, only area of strategic priority. Any forces therefore not designed for the main battle were regarded as of secondary importance and investment in amphibious shipping was of little value.

c.   The role for which the amphibious forces were ideally equipped, that is global power projection, was of a minor concern in the aftermath of Vietnam.

Just like in United Kingdom, amphibious operations in US nearly faced extinction in spite of operational successes recorded during the World War II in the Pacific and Korean War in the 60s. In fact, the Secretary of Defence at that time, James Schlesinger exerted great pressure on the USMC to re-specialize towards a conventional role on the central front. This though again was to be negated when a major amphibious demonstration was conducted in the Persian Gulf in 1991. American marine forces stationed off Kuwaiti shores forced Saddan Hassain to deploy massively, Republican Guards along the Southern Iraqi boarder thus diverting attention from the main thrust of the allied forces.

THE SOVIET UNION PERSPECTIVE

The moribund Soviet Union conducted one of the few successful amphibious operations in the First World war, when the Army and Black Sea Fleet combined in 1916 to attack Trebizond in Turkish Anatolia. After the Russian Revolution, however, they 'considered as unrealistic the use of naval forces in a struggle against a shore defended by a strong enemy, so the fleet was not trained for it'. They were more concerned with the defence of the homeland against amphibious forces, a bitter lesson of their struggle against the white Russian and their allies in 1919.

The credit for the re-establishment of the Soviet naval infantry in 1963 was accorded to Admiral Gorshkov who was the architect of the ambitious maritime strategy and had distinguished himself in amphibious operations near Odessa in 1941. however, despite the substantial build up of the Soviet Navy in the 60s and 70s, the amphibious forces did not expand significantly, although they were used regularly on exercise and foreign deployment. The Soviets had expressed, more openly than the Western powers, their concern about the survivability of the amphibious force in a nuclear war. Gorshkov himself expressed this doubt when he commented that; *This experience is not fully applicable to the waging of armed combat at sea with use of neclear weapons for encounter between naval forces"*. He was however to quell this doubt later in his conclusion that the ancient task of sea landing retains its importance even in present day conditions.

THE PLACE OF AMPHIBIOUS OPERATIONS IN NIGERIA'S MILITARY STRATEGY.

We have discussed the concept and conduct of amphibious operation with some historical strategic thoughts. Let us now use the *expose to examine what place amphibious operations should have in Nigeria's military strategy but first let us recall some of our own experiences.*

The Nigerian Armed Forces has so far embarked on 3 amphibious operations and 2 large scale amphibious exercises; OPERATION SEADOG in 1985 and TAKUTE EKPE in 2003. while 2 of the operations were conducted to land Nigerian troops ashore in Bonny and Calabar during the Nigerian Civil War, the third was in Operation Liberty during ECOMOG operations in Liberia. The first amphibious operations embarked upon during the civil war by the Nigerian Armed Forces in 1968 was the Bonny landing. Under command of Rear Admiral (then Captain) NB Soroh as ATFC, Brig Gen Adekunle of the 3rd Marine Commando operating with the Nigerian Navy made a successful landing at Bonny town. NNS OBUMA (NIGERIA), NNS PENELOPE, NNS LOKOJA, NNS OGOJA, NNS ENUGU, M.V Bode Thomas and M.V King Jaja were ships used for sealift operation and Naval Gunfire Support.

After the successful liberation of Bonny town, 3rd Maritime Commando embarked on NNS NIGERIA and NNS OGOJA sailed to Calabar entrance for a similar amphibious operation. At Parrot Island, NNS OBUMA provided intensive gunfire support targeted at Oron and Calabar, which led to the final landing and subsequent capture of the 2 towns in 1968.

Following the experience of the Nigerian Civil War, the first ever planned joint military exercise by members of the Nigerian Armed forces was Operation SEADOG in 1985, an amphibious operations exercise designed primarily as a show of force around Calabar in response to the killing of some Nigerian soldiers by Cameroun Gendarmes along Aquayefe River in 1981. Operation SEADOB, exercise though well conceived and properly planned for the first time exposed the Nigerian military to the peculiarities and complexities of jointness which is one of the most essential parameters of amphibious operations. The exercise was a success from the planning phase through embarking, rehearsal and movement phase but had to be aborted before the assault phase towards Calabar approaches due to difficulties experienced by the component elements of the participating services in the area of harmony of communications, and effective command and control functions. Then in 2003, another attempt was made in Ekpe area of Lagos State code-named- TAKUTE EKPE. That again was a virtual failure for reasons of technical complexities, lack of joint training and communications. Troops could not land is planned from the designated naval platforms.

ECOMOG EXPERIENCE

Again, in 1990 when it became necessary for Nigerian government to evacuate Nigerian citizens being held hostage in Liberia during the Liberian civil war, NNS AMBE, NNS DAMISA and Tug Dolphin Mira were tasked to proceed to Liberia to conduct a non-combatant evacuation of Nigerians stranded in that country. The 3 ships were refused entry in Port of Monrovia on arrival by the offensive action of the warring factions. These ships later sailed to Free Town, Sierra Leone. While in Free Town, West African Heads of State met in Yamoussoukro, Ivory coast under the auspices of ECOWAS and deliberated on the protocol of defence. The communique issued at this meeting often referred to as the Yamoussoukro Accord" created the legal framework for the formation of ECOWAS Monitoring Group (ECOMOG). Consequently, a taskforce consisting of the Nigerian Army embarked on naval ships eventually sailed from Free Town, Sierra Leone to Liberia and made a forced landing in the port of Morovia. The Air Force later joined the operations. This operation provided the eventual staging post (Beach head) for ECOMOG operations in Monrovia.

Lessons learnt from these experiences and the new thinking globally may have led to the decision by Defence Headquarters (DHQ) to evolve the idea of harmonization of Armed Services aimed at achieving the concept of jointness thus improving our fighting efficiency as a combat force. What then is the Nigerian Military Strategy?.

OVERVIEW OF NIGERIA'S MILITARY STRATEGY

Nigeria's military strategy derives from analysis of the Defence Policy. The policy itself analysis the global, regional and domestic environments which you are quite familiar with. The military deduction is that:

   a.   The security environment is unpredictable and fraught with dangers and uncertainties. That until all the challenges are completely and satisfactorily resolved, the possibility of external military threat against the country exists.

b. For some time to come, there will exist at both continental and regional levels, zones or pockets of conflicts Nigeria will commit her troops to resolve them.

c. The domestic security environment is still fragile and delicate.

The import of the above deductions is that the Nigerian military strategy should be to develop armed forces that are cohesive with a credible fighting force that is integrated, interoperable and capable of quick reaction as well as knowledge driven. The bottom line however, is that threat to Nigeria or the need to deploy Nigerian troops is not absent. We cannot therefore limit the ways and means, otherwise the strategies for countering the threats or resolving crisis. We might have reason to land troops internally or within the sub region at least. If we have cause to embark again on any type of amphibious operation, how prepared are we? To the best of my knowledge, there exists neither a Nigerian joint amphibious warfare nor planned routine exercise among other constraints.

CONCLUSION

In concluding this lecture, it is noteworthy to emphasize that amphibious operations is one of the most complex of all military operations. A major requirement of an amphibious operation is the necessary for swift uninterrupted accumulation of sufficient combat power ashore from an initial zero capacity to full coordinated striking power. This means detailed planning that goes beyond the initial stage. Indeed, it is a continuous process from the receipt of the initiating directive to the termination of the operation.

Furthermore, the complex nature of amphibious operations demands that command relationship between commanders have to be clearly delineated. To this end, the Joint Force Commander establishes command relationships and assigns authority to subordinates.

It is pertinent to also state that the conduct of amphibious operations follows phases that are well defined and may overlap. The various phases are: planning, embarkation, rehearsal, movement to the objective area and lastly assault and capture of the objective area.

In trying to determine the relevance of amphibious operations in Nigeria's military strategy, I examined amphibious warfare perceptions by 3 major powers and the Nigerian military's historical involvement in amphibious operations. A summary of the analysis of the National Defence Policy shows that threats to Nigeria still exist both from the international and domestic environments. Thus, the Nigerian military will continue to be involved in crisis management from time to time. The pertinent questions therefore, are; should we limit our strategies to resolving crisis by neglecting some aspects of warfare? Should the need arise, is the Nigerian military ready to embark on an amphibious operation? What should we do now?

Distinguished participants, I think that I have agitated your minds sufficiently to generate fruitful discussions. I thank you so much for listening and God bless.

REFERENCES

1. http:wwwsparacus shoolnet.co.uk2wwamphibious.him
2. US Joint Publication 3-02 Joint Doctrine for Amphibious Operations.
3. Australian Army Operations in the south-West Pacific: 1942-45 John Grey.
4. http:wwwanswers.com/topic/amphibious-operation-military.
5. DMW Presentation on amphibious Operations.
6. Michae Evans Amphibious Operation-The Projection of Sea Power Ashore. IV Bassey's (UK) Ltd Sea Power series (c) 1990.
7. Indian Army Manual on Amphibious Warfare 1986 Part II Operations.
8. FAS Military Analysis Network US Navy Ship Amphibious Forces. Internet http//www.fas.org.man.dod101/sys/ship/amphibious.m
9 The New Webster Dictionary of English Language, International Edition (Lexicon Publications 1993).
10. Microsoft Encarta Encyclopedia, 2004 Edition.
11. The New Webster Dictionary of the English Language, International Edition (Lexicon Publications 1993).
12. Amphibious Operations quoted on website htt.//www.answers.com/topic/amphibious operations-military.
13. Corbett-Some principles of maritime strategy.
14. Internet http//www.fas.org.man.dod101/sys/ship/amphibious.htmning force supplies.
15. Bob-Manual Al, Amphibious Operation-A lecturer delivered to participants the National War College Course II on Monday 3 March 2003.
16. http:www.globalsecurity/org/military/library/policy army/fm55-50htm.
17. Nigeria's Defence Policy, 2006.
18. Soroh NB, Asailor's Dream; Auto-biography; Crucible; Publishers Ltd, Lagos, 2001.
19. Nigerian Navy, the making of the Nigerian Navy in the Gulf of Guinea.

CHAPTER 40

THE NIGERIAN NAVY AND MARITIME SECURITY

MICHAEL BONCHUK

PREAMBLE

The decline of military confrontation between the western powers and the former Soviet bloc and the increased rights and obligations of the coastal states in the wake of 1982 Convention of the Law of the Sea (UNCLOS), have necessitated the extension of maritime defense perimeters of the Coastal States sea words. This has brought about a major challenge in the maritime security environment.

On the world's oceans and in the regional seas, the use of Military Power at sea in support of foreign policy objectives and maritime interests is becoming available to an increasing number of coastal and maritime states. As competition for the use of the sea increases so will the potential for maritime conflicts. The legitimate use of military power as an instrument of foreign policy, must be tempered by a recognition of the rights of other actors in the maritime environment.

Donaldson has recognized three categories of naval power that can be deployed at sea. The first is the attempt to influence the outcome of foreign policy; the second is to protect those interests which are perceived to be strategically vital; the third is to enforce policy or legislation within an area of national jurisdiction[3].

Within each category a range of force is available. An objective of the use of force at sea is to influence foreign policy. The application of force may vary from the destruction of some, or all of the enemy's resources (i.e. war), through the threat of their destruction, (deterrence capability), to a demonstration of limited force at sea short of war, to coerce an adversary or support a friendly state (naval diplomacy). The types of force which may be employed by the navy include strategic nuclear or conventional strike forces, power projection through aircraft carrier battle groups and amphibious capacity, the control of an area of sea for a limited period of time or the denial of its use to an adversary; the protection of friendly and neutral shipping and the establishment of a maritime presence to reinforce foreign policy objectives.

When exercising power to protect vital interests, Maritime states attempt to influence the outcome of events in their favour, or at least, to minimize undesirable outcomes through the use threat of force. The enforcement of national policy and legislation within areas of national jurisdiction has traditionally been a paramilitary function, normally carried out by agencies other than navies. In the wake of the Third United Nations Conference on Law of the Sea (UNCIOS III), however, the increased areas of responsibility, both geographic and functional accorded to maritime nations have led many analysts to seek a greater range of maritime strategies to bear on the problem.

The successful execution of maritime strategy requires a maritime capability to protect the area in question. With the extension of the Exclusive Economic Zone (EEZ) of most maritime states to 200 miles, the ability to locate and identify illegal or unauthorized activity, and a flexible means of conducting maritime enforcement which can be tailored to the means of each case have become an onerous task. The tools or strategies employed are satellites, maritime patrol aircraft, fixed and mobile sensors such as radar or sonar, lightly armed ships and a maintenance of maritime presence in waters of national jurisdiction.

The end of the eighties was marked by a sea of change in the global strategic context brought about by what has been widely labelled the end of the cold war between the western powers and the Soviet bloc. Defence communities through out the world are therefore compelled to re-appraise strategies of quantifying the scale and nature of the threat to individual nations and their allies in the post cold war security environment.

This has ushered in a realignment of power structure in the international system. The determining factors for alliance formation and behaviour of states are now economic and military – perhaps mainly economic. Komar has indicated that the post-cold war international system is dominated by emerging powers that compete for poles of influence, each having its resource base. The western pole (W.P.) consists of the U.S.A. at the center and Canada, and its resource base is South America. The European Pole (E.P.) has Germany at the center, European Union Countries, and Africa serves as the resource base. The East Asian Pole (E.A.P.) has China and Japan at the center and this includes countries of South East Asia serving as the resource base. These poles compete for scarce resources and shipping routes using oceans all over the world[2]

For instance, Soviet collapse brought dramatic changes that influenced the maritime security environment. First, the superpowers have undertaken a major re-evaluation of their maritime strategies in light of their improved relations. Due to higher costs and budgetary pressures, together with limited success in confidence building measures, the governments of Russia and USA have been able to consider reducing their naval forces and some procurement programmes.

The new co-operation within the U.N. Security Council resulted in decisive collective peace enforcement action in the Persian (Arabian) Gulf after the occupation of Kuwait by Iraq on August 12, 1990, etc. The third change in the maritime strategic environment brought about by the easing of East-West tensions has been the redirection of maritime forces, hitherto committed to major global conflicts, to lower level of violence and lower order threats such as regional conflicts, pollution and drug running, etc.

The lessened threat of superpower aggression may reduce the risk of military intervention in the calculations of some states. Generally, there is a movement towards defence co-operation in maritime surveillance which could save efforts in policing by an individual state. The potential for local conflict to develop a maritime component is accordingly greater and is affecting the security calculations of many maritime states[3].

Another new feature on the maritime scene is the trend to address military issues in the context of wider security concerns on a regional basis. Progress seems to have been made in dialogue towards a common understanding of co-operative security measures in the Antarctic, the Mediterranean, the Baltic and the South Atlantic. Much still have to be done in the South Atlantic and the Gulf of Guinea. This chapter is an analysis of some of the challenges brought about by the end of the cold war and its implication for Nigeria's maritime security.

GEOPOLITICAL CONTEXT

As mentioned above, the current American view of maritime security is no longer the containment of Soviet military power, but to promote and protect U.S. vital interests. Regional conflicts could, therefore, either "push or pull" the US to protect her vital interests particularly in maritime states. The emphasis is on a forwarding presence, crisis response and power projection. As US access to bases on foreign soil remain dominant in her maritime strategy, the importance of both the air craft carrier battle group and an amphibious capability would be reinforced in the minds of US policy makers. The United States is showing a rare, but understandable interest in quarring oil from Africa. This is informed by the crisis in the Middle East, its reliable source of energy supply. Since the event of September 11, 2001 – the bombing of the World Trade Centre in New York, it has dawned on Washington that it has to source its strategic oil from else where. This assumes a realization by Washington that the Middle East oil supply may prove less reliable in the years ahead amid its captaincy of the global war on terrorism and the crisis in Iraq.

The Bush Administration has, thus, since 2002, declared Africa's oil as one of strategic importance to Washington. Most of Washington's oil needs coming from Africa's Gulf of Guinea, the South Atlantic, would by 2022, account for a quarter of its strategic reserve. Almost half of the projected $50 billion from the Gulf of Guinea oil would flow into Nigeria's foreign reserves. Other countries – Sao Tome, Equatorial Guinea, Cameroon, Gabon and Angola would scramble for remnants.

Beyond oil, observers of developments in civil society expected that Washington might flex its brawn to the effect that all members of Gulf of Guinea Commission shorn corruption, embrace democracy, free enterprise, respect for human rights and the environment, press freedom, protection of the ethnic minorities from political eclipse and as may be necessary, equitable distribution towards the eradication of poverty.

It is believed by US policy makers that these practices could help the cause of durable peace in the Gulf of Guinea and the Niger Delta in particular for oil exploration and production to take place. Thus, the ultimate aim of the US presence in the South Atlantic is the building of a new regional security pact involving all countries within the Senegal – South Africa axis – to ward off drug peddlers, gun-runners, human traffickers, oil bunkerers or stealing of other people's crude oil, fish poachers, among others. This scenario including Washington's desire to have its military stationed in the Niger Delta has serious security implication in the South Atlantic, the Gulf of Guinea and the Niger-Delta in particular. It is, therefore, imperative for the Nigerian Navy to be operationally ready to contain extra-ordinary powers in its duty of defending Nigeria's maritime resources and the territorial integrity of the country.

On the other hand, Russia, faced with the escalating cost of remaining militarily competitive with NATO forces, the question of whether an improved internal economic situation will translate into increase defence expenditure has become argumentative. On the strength of evidence, Russian maritime strategic doctrine remains for the main time defensive, with an emphasis on sea control and sea denial in the ocean approaches to the North-East Atlantic, the North-West Pacific, the Arctic and continued access to ice-free ports.

The Third United Nations Conference on the Law of the Sea did not include the military uses of the sea explicitly in its deliberations. With the decline of super power military hegemony on the world's seas, the "paradigm shift", already under way, from a regime entirely dominated by traditional maritime powers to one in which all coastal states demand a say in oceans affairs will accelerate. Regional disputes over maritime boundaries, resources, sea use, maritime sovereignty, freedom of navigation and the role of navies to counter external and internal threats will increase as the "in-filling" of ocean space takes on new psycho-legal meaning. An important new development is that many regional disputes are becoming increasingly more lethal with the proliferation of advanced technology now available to internal militia groups, thus, compounding the policing role of navies. The military implications of these developments have profound influence on the way nations perceive the post cold war global geo-strategic maritime environment. The coincidence of the emergence of a "new world order" has security implications for Africa, the West African sub-region and Nigeria in particular.

History has taught many that the neglect of maritime power can culminate in a cession of sovereignty and secondly, that it takes decades to revert to being a considerable maritime power after a period of neglect and decline. The implications of the end of the cold war are now apparent. The situation at the global level is moving towards reconciliation. At the regional and sub-regional levels ethnic strife, conflict and tensions have escalated. Low intensity conflicts and crises are adversely affecting developments in many states. Threats to internal security and sub-nationalism have preoccupied most of the governments in Africa and Asia.

Alongside the end of the cold war, the historic Treaty on Laws of the Sea has also revived latent maritime disputes and confrontation. While some states have adopted a confrontational attitude over maritime zone delimitation, there is enough scope within the United Nations Convention on the Law of Sea (UNCLOS), to settle disputes amicably through negotiation and arbitration. Besides disputes over delimitation, clashes of interests in exploitation of maritime resources and freedom of navigation are also likely to escalate.

An evaluation of the interest of developed countries reveals that Africa with its oceans will remain an area of interest to extra regional powers. The region holds about fifty-four off shore oil reserves; sixty-three percent of strategic raw materials, thirty percent of gas which comprises thirty percent of the total worlds production and is a potentially large consumer market.

The extra-regional interest goes beyond access to resources or potential markets. The control of strategic maritime ports from the South Atlantic to the Gulf of Guinea is strategically vital to these powers. The vacuum created by the inadequate naval presence in the region also provides ample scope for extra-regional powers to operate with unrestricted flexibility. It is believed that strong regional navies would put great economic strain on the extra-regional powers to maintain their naval superiority. In the event, these powers would find it necessary to either accommodate regional powers or maintain their naval superiority[4].

The adoption of a Common Defence and Security Policy for Africa is premised on a Common African perception of what is required to be done collectively by African states to ensure that Africa's common defence and security interests and goals, especially as set out in Article 3 and 4 of the Constitutive Act of the African Union, are safeguarded in the face of common threats to the continent as a whole.

The Common Africa defence and security policy focuses on terrestrial forces for the conduct of peace support operations in support of conflict prevention, management and resolution. The maritime aspect of this policy include, Africa's maritime interest, maritime threats to African peace and security, Africa's maritime assets and capabilities, principle of common defence and security and ways of enhancing common defence and security[5].

At the sub-regional level (and the West African sub-region in particular), Nigeria is a maritime power in the Gulf of Guinea which is estimated to contain up to ten percent of the world's oil and gas reserves as well as being a rich fishing ground. With the risk of oil production and transportation in the Middle East, the Gulf of Guinea has become an attractive option for the U.S.A. for the procurement of its oil requirements. The quality of the crude petroleum deposits in the region is said to be higher to that obtained in the Middle East. The geo-strategic Niger-Delta maritime environment and the multitude of oil platforms, prospecting and productive activities constitute very attractive targets for foreign interests and oil prospecting companies from the West. The Economic Community of West African States (ECOWAS) could play a vital role in the defence of the Gulf of Guinea. Since Nigeria is an influential member of ECOWAS, the mutual defence pact between members' states could be expanded to cover the Gulf of Guinea in a defence and security arrangement.

Arising from the above therefore, Nigeria has enormous challenges facing her as a maritime nation. Nigeria shares maritime boundaries with Benin Republic, Cameroon and Equatorial Guinea along and astride – the Atlantic Ocean, and land boundaries with Chad and Niger Republics. The challenges posed to her include protecting the Nigerian coast-line from internal and external intrusions, protecting the coastline against violation, protecting and securing the three different zones: (1), In-shore coastline (2) the shore line shelf (3) blue/deep waters and (4) developing coastal surveillance strategies and capabilities. Nigeria's maritime interest could be broadly classified into three categories: Strategic interests are primarily oriented towards safe-guarding the security of the state. It would have different connotations in peacetime than during war. The role of the navy is also likewise, oriented towards either war or in peace[6.]

The maritime interest implies freedom of navigation for shipping, the enforcement of laws of the sea and more importantly protecting trade and shipping routes. In Nigeria, merchant ships carry over ninety five percent of the country's sea borne trade. It is, therefore, important that these interests are protected. Subsequent to the UNCLOS treaty, resource based interests have escalated sharply. Exploitation of oil and gas and offshore minerals, fishing, harnessing of internal wave and tidal energy creation of artificial space in off-shore areas are some spheres where interest would grow. Resources in the Exclusive Economic Zone (EEZ) can be considered as an extension of those on land and therefore need be viewed with some security concerns. It can be said that the maritime interests of Nigeria primarily concern security and economy and have a natural tendency to expand with time.

The 1964 Navy Act assigned to the navy the tasks of defending territorial waters; of training in naval duties, of conducting hydrographic surveys, of assisting in the enforcement of customs laws, and of undertaking other missions assigned by the government. Its specific tasks in the 1980s included defence against sea borne attack and protection of international shipping and of offshore oil and sea resources particularly preventing or prosecution of illegal bunkering and lifting of petroleum.

Two official acts set forth Nigeria's maritime interest and policy. Decree number 10 of April 1987 promulgated a National Shipping Policy, and the Navy Board's approval of a maritime defence strategy announced in April 1988, shifted Nigeria's strategic focus toward the South Atlantic because of external threats to its economic interest to the southeast. Nigerian naval strategist conceptualized the navy's maritime mission as defence in-depth within the three overlapping parameters. Level one, the highest priority, was coastal defence and inshore operations involving surveillance, early warning, anti-smuggling and anti-piracy operations; protecting offshore oil installations, search and rescue; and policing out to 100 nautical miles. Level two encompassed the maintenance of a naval presence in the Exclusive Economic Zone (EEZ) for monitoring, policing, preventing dumping of hazardous materials or toxic waste and marine research. Level three the outer ring, involved surveillance, intelligence gathering, training and flag showing; independent and joint exercises; and allied operations[7.]

The Navy's maritime defence roles, officially known as the Trident Maritime Strategy, comprised three elements contributing toward national military strategy. The first element was sub-regional sea control to defend Nigeria's national and maritime interests and to execute the national shipping policy by protecting sea-lanes. The second element, coastal defence, included protection of the coastal zones approaches, territorial waters, and the EEZ. In the third element, the navy was to provide adequate sealift and gunfire support to the army in amphibious operations. This ambitious strategy requires a force structure or "force in being" for power projection beyond our coastal waters. It requires strong, navy or coastal surveillance capabilities to combat maritime security threats and to realize tremendous economic gains by defending vital maritime and fisheries interest against unauthorized foreign exploitation.

A maritime defence strategy that favours regional or sub-regional responsibilities will, no doubt lead to bigger roles for the Nigerian navy and force expansion in all dimensions far in excess of what is needed for coastal defence and surveillance of the EEZ. The trident maritime strategy has been criticized on various grounds because it is too ambitious and lacks the transport and strength elements to operate it. For example, it was conceptualized using the concentric circle theory to priorities areas of vital interest to meet Nigeria's strategic objectives but without adequate operational or naval capabilities.

Contemporary maritime security challenges of the Nigerian navy resulted from the dynamics of the socio-political and security changes within the African, West African sub-region and Nigeria. The ensuring global and universal liberal democracy that accompanied the collapse of the Soviet Union has compounded the security challenges of the Nigerian navy. Some individuals and groups are exploiting the recent democratization of Nigeria to ferment violent clashes and illegalities in the country. They perpetuate these acts under the cover of group self-determination, grievances arising from perceived political and economic marginalization particularly in the Niger-Delta region.

Illegal bunkering of petroleum products and crude oil, poaching of valuable aquatic resources; illegal trafficking in drugs and small arms through the countries sea lanes and dumping of toxic waste etc, constitute some of the maritime threats to the nation's internal security. The increased violent acts of armed youths of the Niger delta who disrupt activities in the oil and gas industry and the hijacking of foreign nationals may "pull or push" western and American forces to intervene in order to protect their investments and economic interest in the Niger Delta region[8].

The geo-strategic Niger Delta maritime environment and the multitude of oil platforms, prospecting and productive activities constitute very attractive targets for terrorist acts especially now that transnational terrorism is on the increase. These poses serious threats to the security, stability and socio-economic development and growth of the region.

The instability in the maritime environment is frequently compounded by skirmishes along the Nigeria-Cameroon borders due to the dispute over the Bakassi Peninsula. Cross border incursion by fish poachers, petroleum products smugglers, armed gangs and other criminal elements is another source of threat to the Nigerian nation. It is against this background that the Nigerian Navy should evolve a credible maritime defence strategy to protect the oil platforms in the Niger Delta region against external and internal threats. In pursuant of the above, Edward Luttwark has queried; what is a "Navy in the absence of a maritime strategy?"[9]. It is worth stating that the concept of maritime strategy is not synonymous with naval strategy. Maritime strategy should not be considered exclusively naval, because it necessarily include naval, air, and ground combat and support forces in a maritime context with the intention to bring these forces to bear on the enemy at the decisive point.

MARITIME DEFENCE STRATEGY

In evolving a maritime defence strategy capable of protecting the oil platforms in the Niger Delta from external and internal threats, such a strategy derives from a comprehensive well articulated national strategy for the attainment of economic, political and military objectives. Nigeria could evolve a national strategy to include regional or sub-regional strategy from top down approach. The maritime environment could also be isolated, analyse the national dependence on the sea and propose a maritime strategy as a component of the overall national policy in a bottom up approach[10].

The National Shipping Policy set up a National Maritime Authority. The policy recognizes the need of maritime defence in making provision in section 591 (1) and (ii) for the bulk cargo carrying for Nigeria in its national defence or other national requirements.

Maritime defence forces are closely associated with a nations sea-borne trade and other components of sea power that an analysis of maritime defence strategy ought to begin with the importance of their contributions to sea power and the multiplier effects of "Ships Taken Up From Trade" (STUFT) to the navy in war. The phrase maritime defence forces relates to the recognition of the roles of air power, for instance, in a maritime operation when such air power may not be an integral part of the navy or naval forces.

A maritime defence strategy ought to recognize the systematic nature of sea power with diverse components linked together to make an effective whole both at the high level of military activities and at the level of maritime policy and maritime surveillance. Sea power of the state is a system characterized not only by the presence of links between its component parts but also by the inseparable union with the environment – the ocean in mutual relation with the system expressed in its wholeness. Sea power is therefore integrative composite concept and maritime defence its component part. Sea power is that strength in naval ships, associated aircraft, weapons and support services which enables a country to promote the political and economic interest of itself and its allies in peace time and supremacy over enemies at war.

For sea power to be effective in meeting all manner of maritime threats, it must derive its stamina and strength from its individual component parts. This ensures that sea power consists of a wide range of capabilities to meet a variety of maritime threats. Many of these threats may not be purely military but their effect could be very devastating to the economic and social well-being of the country.

For example, and as indicated earlier, in the Niger Delta region of Nigeria, the activities of ethnic militia, protest by environmental right groups, the activities of sea pirates, oil bunkerers, smugglers, fish poachers, etc could compromise the security of the region and the destruction of oil platforms. The region houses the strategic industries in the oil and gas sectors, petro-chemical and liquefied natural gas pipelines. The Calabar channel is located in the region and ocean going trade could be jeopardized. The regions contribution to the national economy cannot be underestimated as petroleum products alone contribute over eighty percent to the national economy. The maritime defence strategy of Nigeria ought to be determined or conditioned by the interplay of the factors mentioned above.

The emerging shift in the strategic focus of national defence since 1987 presumes a strong navy in its military and policing roles. Systematic conception and designing of maritime defence forces should consider configuration for peace and military application for war. The salutary effect of intensified policing of offshore assets since 1984 on the oil sector shows benefits of a strong navy in peace, in war there will be no other protection at sea but the navy[11].

For Nigeria to evolve a maritime defence strategy and secure her maritime assets, it must link the diverse components of sea power to its strategy given the inadequacies of the trident strategy. For example, the trident strategy lacks the strength and transport elements, it has no maritime guard system; there is no operational link between the Nigerian airforce and the merchant fleet. The absence of a ship building repair industry results in lack of amphibious vessels and landing platform docks.

A maritime defence strategy must be erected on the doctrine of joint operations between the component parts of sea power in a maritime context. The army should provide amphibious cover, while the Nigerian Navy could complement the army with sea lift, surface action and mine counter and underwater warfare, the Nigerian air force with air lift elements and fire power to cover other components of sea power.

To be incorporated into the strategy are maritime fleet, maritime guard system, the police, customs, immigration, marine police, air surveillance, intelligence gathering and control and the incorporation of a deterrence capability through the introduction of a merchant fleet or a fourth arm of defence, a unified command for effective joint operations in the Gulf of Guinea or collective security in the sub-region. The strategy in the final analysis should reflect changes in the international, sub-regional systems and to boost Nigeria's capabilities to police and defend the oil platforms in the Niger Delta region. Since the country strives to gain economically through ECOWAS trade liberalization, her maritime interest will become prominent in the sub-region. It would therefore be logical to co-operate with other ECOWAS members to ensure stability within the sub-region by establishing a mutual defence for collective security arrangement. ECOWAS protocol on defence currently lacks a maritime component, its expansion and incooporation of naval – maritime forces of member states would increase capability for maritime defence.

In order to have a "force in being" for power projection, the development of an amphibious projection platform capability cannot be overemphasized. This force projection beyond local or regional seas can be met by the acquisition of large ocean going, diesel-electric submarines, such as type 209 or an Agosta at 1200 tons or Walvus TR 1700 or type 2400 to extend patrol over 5000kms. This would give Nigeria prestige (naval diplomacy, and deterrent capacity to control events in the sub-region[12].

Operationally, these platforms are meant for offensive and defensive mining operations, intelligence gathering and beach inspections. The incorporation of a sub-marine arm into a maritime strategy, reinforces capabilities to block the enemy sea approaches and harbour and reinforce key points.

Another deficiency noted in the trident strategy is that both the Nigerian Army and Airforce in their current formations are not properly suited for enhancing mobilization and deployment of an intervention force during a rapidly developing crises in the sub-region or in any internal policing threat. The third arm of the trident strategy can only be effective within the context of a tri-service combination with para-military organizations.

Finally, one of the greatest problems facing developing countries is military dependence. This has affected the evolution of concepts and doctrines of defence. A major weakness noticed in the trident strategy is that its doctrines and concepts lack indigenous conceptualizations and environmental parameters. The instruments, equipment and platforms for enforcing the trident strategy are dependent on foreign acquisitions. This explains why there is no clear cut doctrine of maritime defence strategy.

Perhaps Michael Howards observation explains why:

> *Small states trying to develop their own political-military doctrines have few options and less freedom to formulate their own doctrines. A great power can first design its desired doctrine and then build and acquire the weapons best suited for the implementation of that doctrines, a small weak, state has to obtain the weapons that are available to it and only then formulate its doctrine accordingly[13]*

For Nigeria, the weapons suggested in the trident strategy cannot be acquired without injury to other sectors of the economy. This has been one of the problems facing Nigerian defence analysts. In discussing options and prospects for the future, a coherent strategy is essential for a nation or an armed force. In the case of the Navy and as Luttwark observed, "… only in strategy may rational ideas be found to inform the choice of sea and air platforms, to provide meaningful guidelines for sub-system designed priorities, and to define the pattern of requisite developments[14]. In this context, for a nation for a nation to evolve a credible defence policy it must first of all understand the nature and character of internal threats to its corporate existence. Some defence analysts believe that the greatest enemy to the Nigerian state is its internal threats arising from its ethnic composition, religions cleavages, poverty, hunger and the crisis in the Niger Delta, etc.

In contrast to the maximalist who exposes the "top down approach", the minimalist advocates a "bottom up" approach in the defence of the country against internal and external threats. They hold the view that Nigeria should concentrate on defending her contiguous borders and internal threats since the state of the economy and our equipment inventory or level of technological development cannot allow her to project power at the continental level.

Though both the maximalist and minimalist differ on approach to national defence, they seem to agree that the survival of any nation as a viable and dynamic entity depends to a large extent on the evolution of a grand strategy that would effectively integrate and direct the main elements of the nation's power towards the attainment of set political goals. Essentially, grand strategy is a states plan for obtaining security in the competitive and changing global environment whether viewed from the maximalist or minimalist perspective[15]

It involves the integration of military, economic, social, political and diplomatic factors that contribute towards a successful long-term policy. Contemporary events reveal that security has become both military and economic and the integration of the two factors within the framework of a grand strategy has become imperative. Any grand strategy for the attainment of political objectives would therefore take into consideration the aggregation of the security interest of all individuals, communities, ethnic groups, political entities and institutions that inhabit the Nigerian territory. The primary objective of any national security policy should aim at the presentation of the safety of the country, i.e. the protection of the sovereignty and her assets.

It must also strengthen the country to advance her interest and objective to contain instability, control crime, eliminate corruption, enhance genuine development, progress, growth and to improve the welfare, well being and quality of life of its citizens. Consequently, Nigeria's defence policy for the future must be capable of responding effectively to both global technological challenges and the peculiar circumstances of her domestic and regional environment. This assumes greater significance when one realizes that modern technology has transformed the pattern of conflicts and warfare to the extent that no single service can prosecute a war on its own. Currently, trends in the defence policy should focus on the need to facilitate the join deployment of our armed forces and other security establishments to meet the country's security needs.

The necessity of a vibrant defence organization is further attested to by Huntington when he stated that, "a state can achieve little by diplomacy alone unless it has the military strength and the political will to back up its demands[16]. This assertion is gaining more currency in the activities of the USA and Britain who has been resorting to military power to back their diplomatic initiatives against Iraq in 1991 and 1992 are instructive in this regard.

Though Nigeria is dedicated to the principles of peaceful coexistence and pacific settlement of international disputes, the reality is that the security challenges are on the increase. The need therefore arises now, more than ever for Nigeria to continue to maintain a credible defence structure that is capable of supporting the nations aspiration to the status of an economically viable, stable and effective player in the international system.

The armed forces must therefore plan to meet the new security challenges posed to it. Strategic planning is a complex and ongoing process of change. A comprehensive strategic planning process should be oriented towards the future. It is based on a thorough analysis of foreseen or predicted trends and scenarios of the possible alternative futures, as well as the analysis of internal and external data. It creates a framework for achieving competitive advantage by thoroughly analyzing the state, its internal and external environment and its potential.

Planning is a formalized procedure to produce an articulated result, in the form of an integrated system of decisions. Thinking about and attempting to control the future are important components of planning. This enables states to respond to the emerging trends, events, challenges and opportunities within the framework of national purpose and interest.

The country's defence policy must therefore reflect these emerging and futuristic trends. Defence policy has to do with the provision, deployment and use of military resources to promote the nations security as well as to facilitate not only the protection but the pursuit of the perceived national interest of the state within the international system. By its natures, defence policy exists in two worlds, the domestic and external environments. It is not only concerned about protecting the state against aggression from outside, but also concerned with protecting the state from internal threats, violations and disruptions.[17]

This brings into focus the situation in the Niger Delta, our maritime environment. It is true that the Nigerian navy is primarily charged with the defence of the nation's maritime interest. It is also the only service that is charged with diplomatic roles. In carrying out these tasks resulting from these responsibilities the Nigerian navy must be able to meet with the changing pattern of threats in the maritime environment.

The Niger Delta houses oil platforms that are not protected against attacks by either militants or external threats through espionage or surveillance. The British, American, Indian, Norwegian, etc, navies have put in place "force structures," in terms of operational equipments, doctrines of maritime defence, information gathering systems to warn in advance attempts by such groups to destroy such technological complex installations.

The Nigeria navy as currently constituted does not have such a "force structure," operational doctrine, a maritime defence strategy and information gathering systems to monitor, detect the movement of militia groups or those on espionage mission. This has resulted in militia groups seizing oil platforms and flow stations. These platforms are complex technologically and once they are sunk or destroyed, the Nigerian economy could collapse since oil production and the revenue accruing to the state is the main stay of the nation's economy.

However, years of military rule has compromised the operational readiness of the armed forces to carry out its primary role. Besides that, the trident maritime defence strategy has to be revised to meet the new challenges posed by the post cold war security environment.

About 100,000 barrels of crude oil stolen from Nigeria daily is sold to dealers waiting at the country's shores as well as to a number of petroleum refineries along the west coast. At an average cost of about $25 per barrel, at that time the country was losing a colossal sum of about $2.5bn daily from crude oil theft. Apart from the initial capital investment in platforms, only a small fraction of this amount is required to ensure effective air and naval presence in the area, a fact that would definitely deter the adventures. Constant air border patrol between the army air force and the presence of amphibious or composite maritime brigade of airborne support along side other state agencies would provide a "maximum force" that the country needs to protect and go beyond its shores. This would also provide vital intelligence to the police and the army and serve as deterrence to the bandits[18].

An integrated composite maritime defence strategy must be oriented towards technology and technological changes and acquisition of platforms. A warship can be a symbol of goodwill or threat. It is a versatile platform, which is almost self-contained and can be deployed quickly at the scene of action and as easily disengaged. This versatility in managing a crisis or threat through graduated response is only peculiar to a war ship. It can send out signals ranging from friendship to menacing threats[19].

These features are integral part of sea power and maritime defence strategy. Sea power can be used very effectively to support political, policing roles of navies and diplomatic objectives. This has been seen first in the days of "gunboat diplomacy" and is equally prevalent today as evidenced in US deployments in Grenada and Haiti, etc. With changes in the political and geo-strategic environment, some of these roles have become predominant. The end of the cold war and the consequent mitigation of threats of general and limited wars have shifted focus of the navies away from military role, but political situations can change rapidly faster than the rate at which a navy can therefore not pretend to side-track the military role.

The new geo-strategic environment poses new challenges to naval planners because they have implications for Africa, the sub-region and Nigeria in particular. From these fall outs, which impinge on Nigeria's policies, national interests and threat perception, a maritime defence strategy must propose new directions to the year 2015. Emanating from the defence policy will therefore be the strategic objectives of the maritime strategy.

The Nigerian navy should be able to design a maritime defence strategy that would be able to, project power and conduct surgical maritime operations in defence of the territorial integrity of Nigeria, control and protect the vast living and non-living resources in Nigeria's littorals, provide efficient maritime mobility, i.e. transport strength element in pursuance of the projection of the nation's military and diplomatic objectives. It must also ensure safe maritime environment for economic activities sea borne trade, etc.[20].

The navy must therefore erect a "force in being" in a maritime context to meet the contemporary maritime security challenges. The country's maritime strategy, must be oriented towards safeguarding the security of the state, to ensure her freedom of navigation for shipping and enforcement of laws of the sea and protection of her resources, gas, oil offshore-inshore platforms. This requires strong naval or coastal surveillance capabilities to combat maritime security threats and to realize tremendous indirect economic gains by defending vital maritime and fisheries interest against unauthorized foreign exploitation.

The Nigerian navy must be operationally ready to perform the difficult task of policing the open seas and at times will also be expected to provide assistance in humanitarian missions, since the deployment of navies in U.N. peacekeeping missions is likely to escalate. Current changes and challenges in the maritime security environment following the UNCLOS III, world navies can no longer act in isolation. The Nigerian navy must have to co-operate and co-ordinate with other elements of sea power particularly in the South Atlantic and Gulf of Guinea. Calls on foreign ports and interaction with regional navies at sea will provide an impetus to fostering of friendly relations.

Thus, against the backdrop of prevailing geo-political and socio-economic development of the world especially Africa the West African Sub-region and Nigerian in particular, the resulting national security needs should influence the maritime strategy of Nigeria. The strategy must therefore capture the requirements for an effective navy that is versatile, proactive, resilient and adaptive to an ever changing socio-political landscape.

Consequently, the development of the Nigerian navy should be geared towards the establishment of a balanced navy. The trident maritime strategy lacked the strength element to operate it. However, whatever the political and economic philosophies that motivates a nation, military power and national security which are fundamental to all other problems of government, cannot be imagined.

Alexander Hamilton underscored the critical nature of these two factors when he stated that safety from external and internal dangers is "the most powerful director of national conduct". He went further to state that, even liberty must, if necessary give way to the dictates of security because for more safety nations are willing "to run the risk of being less free". Adam Smith, believed that the secret of material prosperity of a nation lies in minimum governmental interference with freedom of the individual. He was willing to conceive that this general principle must be compromised when national security is involved for "defence is much more important than opulence".

Fredrick List sums the above when he submitted that:

> *Power is of more importance than wealth ... because the reverse of power – namely feebleness leads to the loss of all that we possess, not of acquired wealth alone, but of our powers of production, of our civilization, of our freedom, even of our freedom, even of our national independence, into the hands of those who surpass us in might ...[21]"*

The above sums up the need for a strong navy in the pursuit of our national defence and the securing of the country's maritime interest. The size of the navy and its operational readiness would be a decisive factor in protection of our vast maritime interest. The navy must be properly trained, equipped, highly motivated, operationally combat ready to contribute to the security of Nigeria and policing the platforms in the Niger Delta.

It must also participate in the national defence, diplomacy initiatives through building international trust with adequate sea lift for the Nigerian army. Also, the Nigerian navy should be able to provide forces needed to respond to any sub-regional and regional conflicts as may be required under the ECOWAS and A.U. Charters for peace support and humanitarian operations. At the same time it should support Nigeria's maritime interest and must possess the strength and transport capabilities to respond to any conflict that could adversely affect Nigeria's interests.

Current operational readiness of the Nigerian navy to meet the above strategy leaves much to be desired. The navy would have to purchase new platforms to meet the challenges of the maritime defence strategy.

Clausewitz in his treatise On War said, "Every age has its own kind of war, its own limiting conditions and its own preconceptions. Technology has changed the way wars are fought. Modern technology has led to greater lethality and mobility which call for new methods of organization, training, mobilization and projection of forces. Modern technology hinges on information.

The U.S.A. military has laid the key parameters that will dominate warfare in the 21st century via the Joint Vision (JV) 2020, with its four essential ingredients. These include the strategic context based on USA interests globally, availability of modern technology and the more likelihood of a symmetric warfare. The others include the acronym DOTMLPF, which are doctrine, organization, joint training, material, high quality people and requisite facilities. The last of the ingredients is the enabling concepts of decision superiority (information) and innovation.

The Nigerian navy has to modernize and transform for future battle space and internal policing. It must strive to attain superiority in command, control, communication concepts, intelligence, surveillance and reconnaissance. Existing equipment should be modernized while ensuring that new platforms are acquired and personnel trained to handle these equipments. Modernization, retraining and procurement of modern equipments to ensure greater professionalism are central to the evolution of a maritime defence strategy.

The major constraint against the above is directly attributable to issue of funding for the purchase of platforms and programmes. In most developed countries a significant part of the national budget goes to defence as security and stability are considered to be major contributors to a healthy economy. A nation that is free from external and internal threats has greater opportunity to expand its economic base through the attraction of foreign investments, proper planning and controlling of its activities. The defence budget should not compromise the security of the nation. There is need to review the defence budget from 0.5% to at least 3% of the annual total budget to defence in the next 10 to 15 years. This would enable the army to purchase new platforms, to be more compact, modern, balanced, well-trained better equipped and technologically advanced with a much more motivated manpower.

In order to erect a credible maritime defence strategy the defence headquarters must remove operational bottlenecks in inter-service combat functions, by giving firm policy guidelines on command, control, communications and intelligence. The Defence Industries (Corporation (DICON) is expected to meet the requirement of the services, in terms of arms and ammunition, including weapon systems[22].

It is also intended to provide the base for Nigeria's Defence Industrial Complex. All these structures should ideally accommodate any threat to Nigeria's national interests and objectives, through a proper decision-making mechanism.

With the democratization of the country and changes in the global security environment, new challenges arising from the security needs of the increased oil and gas prospecting and production offshore have significantly increased the need for a new maritime strategy and for naval presence offshore.

Furthermore, the instability in Niger Delta with the rising incidents of illegal bunkering of crude and other petroleum products, pipeline vandalization and threat to oil production platforms, the navy now requires appropriate strength and transport assets to combat the threats.

The joint concept of maritime operations which is the thrust of modern military doctrine should be entrenched in the training programme. Naval personnel, army, airforce, customs, immigration, coastal guard, etc. should be instructed particularly in areas where there is commonality in the skills and competence required in maritime strategy.

In terms of assets to combat these threats, in shore and off shore patrol vessels, high speed flat bottom boats and maritime aerial surveillance air craft should be "in being" for surgical maritime operations[23]

The Niger Delta maritime environment provides cover for the militants and other groups that perpetuate crimes in the region. Provision of superior weapons surveillance and intelligence would expose these militants before they perpetuate their nefarious acts. For example, acquisition of anti-submarine war-fare (ASW) platforms could execute anti-submarines, anti-air anti-surface, mine laying and other operators depending on the threat. A series of maritime operators from searching to sinking submarine (ASW) is called anti-submarine warfare. The modern submarines have improved capabilities in performances, quietness, offensiveness and can bring safety of maritime traffic[24].

The airforce should acquire platforms that would assist the navy in joint operations in a maritime context. For instance, the object of Anti-Air Warfare is defending surface groups and ships against an attack from the air. Flight performances and offensive capability of aircraft would improve the capability of the navy. Most surface ships and submarines mount anti-surface missiles to protect any threat from the air against surface ships. Accordingly, the maritime defence strategy should form multilayered air defensive system composed of the guns and missiles and the introduction of escort platforms to safeguard merchant shipping during war and to detect movements of militia groups.

Recently, maritime strategies have introduced surface ships that mount long range surface to surface missiles, and its tactics is shifting from exchanging fire by guns to launching surface to surface missiles from a distance. Offensive capabilities against the surface forces are vital to attack hostile ships intend to assault the country, to defend our users from attack of energy ships mounted surface to surface missiles and secure the safety of maritime traffic and platforms.

On the other hand, mine warfare is divided into nine countermeasure operation which aims at removing mines laid by enemies, and mining operation which aims at laying mines to protect from enemies landing invasion and coastal defence. In order to deter landing in road and passing the channel by enemy, the mining operation is also conducted on the occasion of making minefields on the shore or channel where enemy landing invasion will be expected.

In a maritime context, electronic warfare is defined as operations to detect and make reverse use of the enemy's magnetic waves while detecting the enemy and security effective use of magnetic waves. In electronic warfare there are three measures that are useful in the maritime environment. First is Electronic Support Measure (ESM) equipped with an electronic detection and missile alarm system, second, is the Electronic Counter Measure (ECM) equipped with electronic jamming and chaff rocked launcher and third, is Electronic Counter-Counter Measure (ECCM) with various radas capable of avoiding enemy's electronic counter measure[25].

For a defensive oriented maritime strategy it is important for the navy, airforce, army, customs, immigration and coast guard to carry out constant warning and surveillance operations over vessels moving in the waters through patrol air craft and vessels and engage in collecting information on movements and equipment of both foreign and local vessels (Ekerua)[4].

Transporting personnel, equipment, material to the shore in the operational areas outlying waters is one of the important missions of a maritime strategy. Landing ships should contribute to the stability of national life through rescuing and ferrying goods to the sites in case of emergency and disaster. They could also support the army and participate in U. N. peacekeeping operations.

In case of emergency, it is important to search and rescue personnel. Rescue amphibious operations, rescue helos (for aerial rescue) in the Vicinity of the air-base and submarine rescue vessel for rescuing submarines are vital transport elements required in a maritime strategy.

Thus, a united command comprising the army, providing a composite brigade of amphibious, mechanized groups with supporting arms, the Nigerian navy providing logistic, sealift, surface action and marine counter, undersurface group, submarines, and merchant ships, and the airforce, to provide airlift element maritime patrol element and other strike element, immigration, customs, coastal guard with support vehicles, communication gadgets, surveillance and information gathering on movements of groups, etc are vital ingredients that contribute to a maritime strategy[25].

The above would enable the navy to have a "force in being" in a maritime context that is rational and sustainable through a planning function that is holistic in approach. A navy that will be well equipped, well trained, well led and well motivated to achieve success in the tasks it undertakes, respond to tasks that might rise and build its capacity to respond to long term maritime defence and national security challenges would be best suited to execute a maritime strategy and protect our vital maritime resources and oil platforms in the Niger Delta.

CONCLUSION

Since maritime defence is not synonymous with naval defence, it is envisaged that maritime defence forces should reflect the composite nature of sea power to include, the army in amphibious operation, air force to assist the navy in a maritime context, naval forces to protect police sea lanes, a maritime or coastal guard, marine police, customs, immigration, police, officials of the federal environmental protection agency and those from the federal ministry of transport, Ports Authority, etc. The above para-military forces would bring their specialized services to bear in a maritime context in evolving a maritime defence and security regime.

The Third United Nations Convention on the Law of the Sea (UNCL&SM) has also changed the nature and character of maritime defence forces. The UNCLOS updated and codified existing law in a progressive process. More importantly, it contains constitutive features that embody some new concepts, create new laws and establish new institutions that mankind has to grapple with. Some of these changes brought new implications and institutional policy changes that have transformed the management of maritime conflicts, maritime security, defence and ocean regime governance.

In order to defend the oil platforms the maritime defence strategy should aim at achieving the following objectives:

    (a)   to erect and train a specialized and permanent "force structure" whose main aim would be to police and protect the oil platforms in the Niger Delta, as opposed to the current practices of appointing task forces on an adhoc basis;

(b) to equip the maritime defence forces with modern weapons such as: escort patrol boats to intercept and repel attacks on oil platforms;

(c) to provide naval craft for a wide range of maritime defence and law enforcement;

(d) to provide communication gadgets for air surveillance and movement, detection of militants;

(e) to provide specialized training in view of the composite nature of sea power for intelligence gathering;

(f) to provide search and rescue equipments to improve performance and to safeguard maritime traffic.

(g) to provide electronic support measures equipped with detective alarm systems around approaches to the oil platforms in order to prevent their being sunk;

(h) to provide offshore patrol boats, patrol crafts to combat smuggling, fish poaching, oil bunkering, dumping of hazardous toxic waste, etc;

(i) to provide small and medium sized equipments for specialized functions for personnel as logistic support to enhance the strength and transport element of forces;

(j) to protect the vast living and non-living resources in Nigeria's territorial waters;

(k) to adopt a common doctrine/common training standards;

(l) to allow greater interoperability equipment, effective communication and communal control arrangements; and

(m) efficient medical services.

From the foregoing analysis the Niger Delta region is not only the soft underbelly of the Nigerian economy, it is also of strategic importance to the nation. The need to protect the oil platforms and other strategic industries cannot be underrated.

Currently, the maritime strategy in theory has been articulated superficially to adapt to changes in the national and international political, military and economic environment. It focuses more on coastal defence than internal policing. However, in practice, it is a strategy whose goals far exceed the resources available for their implementation and therefore fraught with dangers if not properly addressed.

The strategy lacks the appropriate strength and transport elements – sea lifts, both naval and maritime ships, as well as developed ship building and repair infrastructure to replace losses in peace and war as well as a well developed industrial base, research and development to sustain and nourish the strategy. By not incorporating the air element as part of the means to the end-aircraft are essential component of maritime forces necessary for the prosecution of war at sea and land forces, the strategy lacks merit.

In order to accomplish the fundamental and complimentary aims of the trident maritime strategy both the short and long term measures need to be put in place bearing in mind the country's economic predicaments.

It is hoped that the establishment of maritime headquarters at Port Harcourt whose scope would be expanded to cover the sub-region through a collective defence strategy involving ECOWAS countries, a naval control of shipping (NCS) centers at Lagos, Port Harcourt, Warri, Sapele and Calabar to ensure operational control, equip sail and ship routes for safety; establishment of a Central Maritime Guard System (CMGS) at Port Harcourt to complement the policing roles of the nation's maritime forces in terms of surveillance, intelligence gathering and maintaining vessels, crafts and aircraft within loom from the coast; acquisition of operational submarines as a "lead force" for conventional deterrence and to enhance a force projection capability to enhance the strength element, particularly anti-air warfare in defending surface; encouraging ship owners to increase their merchant fleet and increasing the shape and size of the National Shipping line to meet the provisions of UNTAD: 40 . 40 . 20. This would enhance the nation's sea borne trade, and strategic sealift during emergencies, etc. These steps if appropriately adopted would strengthen the navy to undertake its role of defending our maritime waters from internal and external threats.

REFERENCES

1. B. Donaldson, "The Ocean and Strategic Interests" in Maritime Affairs: A World Handbook, A Reference Guide for Modern Ocean Policy and Management. (Longman, Current Affairs, UK, 1991,p.12)

2. R. W. Komer, "Military and Political Policy: Maritime Strategy and Coalition Defence, Foreign Affairs, Vol. 3, Summer, USA, 1982.

3. J. Singh and C. Bernauer, Security of the Third World Countries, United Nations Institute for Disarmament Research, Dartmouth, Brookfield, 1993.

4. A. Adetomiwa, "Challenges Facing Nigeria as a Maritime Nation" The South African National War College, 16H15, Nigeria, Lagos, 1982.

5. A. Oladimeji, "Maritime Defence Strategy: An Overview of its Evolution, Concepts" in Ekoko, A. E. and Vogt. M. A. (ed). Nigerian Defence Policy: Issues and Problems, Malhouse Press Limited, Oxford, UK, 1990.

6. S. O. Afolayan, "The Nigerian Navy in National Defence "Lecture Delivered to Participants of Course 12, National War College Review, (US) February, 1976, 1976, p. 28.

7. E. N. Luttwark, "War, Strategy and Maritime Power" in Naval War, College Review, (U.S) February, 1976, p. 28.

8   E. I. Okpo, "Nigeria's Maritime Strategy in a Changing International Security Arrangement" Essay submitted in partial fulfillment for the Award of the Fellowship of the National War College, Lagos, January, 1993, p .41.

9   K. W. Sharon & P. J. Garrity, US Defence Strategy After Cold War". The Washington Quarterly, Vol. 15, No. 2, Spring 1992, p. 12; also Rothkopt, "Living between the Wards" CEO International Strategies, Vol. 111, No. 11, October – November, 1990, p. 26.

10. E. I. Okpo, "Nigerria's Maritime Strategy in a Changing International Security Arrangement", 1976, p. 26.

11. E. N. Luttwark, "War, Strategy and Maritime Power" in Naval War College Review, (U.S) February, 1979, p. 26.

12 T. A. Imobigbe, "The Organizational Structure of Nigeria's Defence Establishment" in Nigeria Defence and Security Issues and Options for Policy (ed) by T. A. Imobighe, Kuru N. I. S. S, 1987.

13. M. Howard, "Isreal's Political and Military Doctrine" International Affairs Review, No. 3, 2, July 1973.

14. E. N. "Luttwark, War, Strategy and Maritime Power" 30.

15. C. O.Bassey, Nigeria's Quest for a Military – Industrial Complex," Nigerian Journal of International Studies, 1987, p. 24.

16. S. Huntington, Cited in Lt. Gen. M. L. Agwai (rtd), "The Nigerian Army in National Defence" Being delivered to the participants of National War College Course 12, 2004, p. 16.

17. D. A. Briggs, "The Challenges fo External Threats to Nigerian Sovereignty", Nigerian Journal of International Studies, Lagos, Nigeria, 1986, p. 25.

18. J. J. Wuyep, "The Nigerian Airforce in National Defence", a lecture delivered to participants to Course 12, National War College, Abuja, D/H January, 2003, p. 24.

19. R. W. Komer, "Military and Political Policy: Maritime Strategy and Coaliton Defence, Foreign Affairs, Vol. 3, Summer, USA., 1982, p. 20.

20. S. Koshoni, Securing the South Atlantic: Options in Policy and Strategy", Nigerian Institute for Strategic Studies, NIPPS, Kuru, Jos, 1987, p. 10.

21. F. List, cited in Agwai, "The Nigerian Army in National Defence". A paper delivered to course 12 participants, National Defence College, Abuja, 2004.

22. C. O. Bassey, "Nigeria's Quest for a Military Industrial Complex" Nigerian Journal of International Studies, 1987, p. 30.

23. O. Clarkson, Former Instructor Air Training School Markudi, Interview held at Calabar, 18th August, 2006.

24. V. E. Clark, Maritime Defence Joint Doctrine Operatons, Joint Doctrine Publications, Hierarchy, Vol. 2, 2003, p. 44.

25. I. Motosho, Former Signal Officer, Signal Army Headquarters, Lagos, 13 September, 2006.

26. O. Ekerua, Manager, Technical, Nigerian Maritime Authority, Lagos, 12 May 2006.

27. A. Omolode, Retired Controller of Customs, Lagos Interveiw held at Yaba, Lagos. 10th August, 2006.

CHAPTER 41

CONCLUSION:
FUTURE CHALLENGES AND PROSPECTS

CELESTINE BASSEY

Foreign Policy objectives must be brought into balance with the resource capabilities of Nigeria. To set objectives or to assume certain foreign policy first and then strain resources and distort domestic priorities in order to meet their concomitants in terms of militry capability is to set the cart before the horse.

O. S. KAMANU (1)

Defence policy discourse will be incomplete and inconclusive without an attempt at conjecture about future direction from past and current trends. This is particularly so in a condition of changing dynamics of Nigeria's operational environment (both domestic and systemic) which may either provoke activist and forceful response to regional challenges (as was the case in the 1990s) or compel more introspective postures and muted policy behaviour.

Either trend in governmental perceptions and definitions of Nigeria's defence policy response is bound to have implications for the role-orientation of the national armed forces and defence planning. However, unhappily, despite the researches, projections or forcecasts of new futurologists[2], neither subsequent developments in internal environment (capabilities factors relating to the industrial and economic infrastructures and military strength) nor concomitant policy response can be predicted with much certainty. So this chapter in essence dwells on specific salient issue-areas in Nigeria's military statecraft, within the context of probable regional and global environments of the 21st century. The first section, below establishes the contextual framework (possible changes and directions in relevant global and continental parameters) of Nigeria's future defence policy options and planning. This is followed by a reasoned evaluation (to the extent that this is possible) of Nigeria's status within the regional subsystem which may or may not affect decision-makers' perception of what role it should play in future crises. The third section examine policy choices concerning the structural transformation challenges operational capabilty of Nigeria's armed forces. The two final sections consider respectively, current debates, proposals and probable policy directions concerning (i) the 'nuclear option' and (ii) security or stabilisation force under ECOWAS or African Union.

A). THE FUTURE OF MILITARY POWER: GLOBAL AND CONTINENTAL DIMENSIONS.

As the extensive modernist versus realist debate of the 1980s and early 1990s corroborates, academic projections about future directions, role, and usability of national military power as an instrument in the contemporary international system can, in the words of Immanuel Kant, "become a trap for the unwary and the overbold". The manifold difficulties of forecasting future roles for national military instrument of statecraft are fairly obvious.

Given the overall complex of reality involved, and the formidable problems of computing global and regional distribution of the relevant changes in parameters, such a futuristic exercise is at best analytically tentative, prescriptively quixotic, and, in certain cases, a dangerous misdirection of effort. Since national military systems and their employment are intended to achieve national policy objectives in the international arena, their usability and effectiveness is always conditional on particular circumstances. In order words, whether national military forces and their operational doctrines contribute to the achievement of national security policy goals, and the extent of any contribution, depend upon the nature of defence policy objectives as well as on the properties of the international arena and the suitability of military systems and their use. In short, the continued utility of national military power is a function of their suitability to both policy and international evironments, since successful strategic policy and performance – whether in the role of deterring, threatening, peace support operations or war making --- demands that capabilities, objectives, and environments are properly reconciled. The complex inter-relatedness of these variable, and ther inescapable impact on national policy concerning the use of military force, can be more than illustrated; it can also be explained (see chapter one).

However, the question of paramount importance to this chapter is whether the contemporary international system dominated as it is by considerations of security that makes national militaries an indispensable instrument of policy will contine indefinitely? Or is the system of nation-states (and nascent international regimes) in a 'revolutionary process fo change' that is making war, national military power, and security concerns obsolete? While recent events in human history – engendered by the inexorable and constant dynamics of social and technological parameters – have profoundly undermined convenient assumptions that 'things will be as they are in the present', recent research on projection and forecasting has failed to reduce the essential unpredictability of future trends and events. Arguably, the introduction of such imaginative techniques and instruments as the Delphi Technique Gamina, simulation and increasingly sophisticated computer system in policy planning have constituted a major departure from past practice of reliance on sheer judgment, yet their usefulness can be exaggerated[3]. Projection from recent trends – on which these techniques operate—is at best an indication of what is possible. It would be problematic enough to identify all the variables (political, miliary, economic, social, ideological, cultural, demographic, technological, etc). that have affected systemic transformation in the past, and might conceivably do so in the future. It is almost impossible to measure properly these dynamic factors[4].

Although the 'behavoural revolution' in the social sciences since the late-1950s has considerably sharpened the methodological basis of observation relating to relevant future trends, and sometimes even allows us to 'measure' (attach weight to) them in a rough fashion, trends are affected by other forces in ways and with strengths that are impossible to predict. These difficulties are inherent in any desire to predict events that are essentially unique.

A glaring example, at the regional level, of this 'hopelessness of prediction' or conjecture about the future was the sudden collapse of the portuguese empire in Africa in the mid-1970s (and the tremendous and step-level impetus it gave to decolonization in Southern Africa) and the Soviet Union at the global level of strategic interaction. The dramatic nature of the former development (engendered by the coup in Portugal in 1974 which followed a series of costly military setbacks for the Portuguese military command in Mozambique, Angola and Guinea-Bissau) became only too obvious from the pessimistic (in some cases derisive) writings and projections in the early 1970s about the prospect of liberation in Southern Africa by the 2,000[5]. These writings (some of which specifically disputed the possibility of independence in Angola, Mozambique, and Zimbabwe by the end of century) now stand as monuments to academic orthodoxy and misperception constituting in the words of Mazrui, "an onlooker's separation from the demands and processes of active revolutionary struggle[6]"

Despite these demonstrable difficulties in forecasting future developments both at the global and regional levels, it remains the indispensible and indeed urgent – task of national defence planning which guides a state's strategic policy, to anticipate expected politico-military environment five, ten or fifteen years hence, within which resort to military force might occur. This process involves, interalia, making informed conjectures and assumptions about future contingencies: the probable nature and properties of the international system and configuration of itnernational power, future opponents and capabilties, and the future possible impingement of dominant military forces on extra-regional conflicts; estimates of such variables as the effectiveness and impact of new battlefield technologies, the probable duration of a future conflict, the direction of probable enemy strategy, doctrine and planning, and manner in which threats to national security are likely to develop[7]. Taken together these variables constitute the strategic environment of national defence policy, which inescapably affects the relation of military power to national purposes. This assessments (erroneous or correct) in turn form the bases or assumptions underlying national defence policy postures. Such assessments aslo proved the 'scientific data' for doctrinal developments which provide 'the goal-oriented guidance' for military procurement, organization, and operation.

The tentative assumption and analytical position regarding in the future of the military as an instrument of policy, both at the global and regional levels, offered in this chapter are preeminently minimalist. While not altogether disputing the 'modernist' / 'idealist' argument about the profound and emerging transformation in the mode of relations between states which, according to analysts of this school of thought, make military force 'less and less relevant to human aspirations' it is to be contended here that those developments stressed by modernists are secondary perturbations (dependent rather than independent or controlling variable) in the rise of what John Herz has aptly described as the 'new territoriality'[8]. In other words, barring a major catastrophe such as a cataclysmic confrontation between the major powers, the international system will remain in the foreseeable future essentially state-centric. So too will the security imperatives which presently frame and inform international transactions, although, as argued in chapter one, they must now be understood in wider and subtler terms than the crude employment of military force. The international system will thus 'divided against itself'. As Kenneth Waltz reminds us, it remain, and will still be, a 'self-help system'.[9]

The logical derivative from the foregoing is that as long as automomous states are militarily sovereign, force will remain the ultimate arbiter in the settlement of interstate conflict. Since this is the inherent dynamic of contemporary international system, resort to force by governments in situations unyielding to pacific strategies becomes a 'systemic necessity' and, hence, inescapable, unless the system itself is essentially transformed. It is in this context that the conceptualisation of 'war and peace' as opposite sides of the same coin, whose casual foundation rests on competing nation-state units, by such eminent theorists as Raymond Aron and Hans Morgenthau is to be understood[10]. For example Aron's postulate of relations among states as consisting of the 'alternatives of war and peace', is invariably based on his assumption that a 'political unit claims the right to take justice into its own hands and to be the sole arbiter of the decision to fight or not to fight[11]".

His supporting argument (as Morgenthau's) is equally obvious from his massive treatise: that since statemen, acting in pursuit of their national interests, operate in an anarchical international environment (distinguishable from a national environment by the absence of authoritative political institutions, legal systems, and commonly accepted standards of conduct) war is almost inevitable. Put differently, war is the natural, logical and perhaps almost inevitable relationship among 'communities' who, in the absence of supranational governmental entity, reduce their political relations to a competition (as well as cooperation or indifference) for prevalence with an 'admixture of firepower'.

From this perspective, two hypotheses concerning the future of the military instrument in statecraft at both global and regional levels may be established. First, a system of competing national units carries the risk of military force. And second, military force, as manifested in war, is a means not an end in itself, however, justified in the name of the beliefs and values of nation-states. In this regard, it is not surprising that the use of military force or the threat of its use is often fired by the 'false and malificient religion' the ideology of nationalism. Nationalism, as Toynbee rightly notes, 'provides the symbols, values and beliefs in devotion to which modern people everywhere, cling to unlimited and restricted sovereignty and thereby make it impossible, thus far, to make even a modest beginning in the direction of limited world government which could put an end to power politics and international anarchy'[12].

The policy corollary of Toynbee's observation is of course that to ensure their survival as sovereign units, states must make the preservation or improvement of their 'power of resistance' a principal objective of their foreign policy. This transformation into policy consideration of what is in itself a mere consequence of the international system as a 'threat system' follows less from an abstract conception of praxis as critics of realism are often quick to assert. On the contrary, such a behavioural tendency on the part of governments, irrespective of status, ideological persuasion or political system, attests to the profound secuirty concerns which continue to remain rooted in the very nature of the international system. Traditionally, this goal has been pursued through 'balance of power' policies and collective security measures (military alliance) which, inter alia, sought to preserve the status quo by preventing (or neutralising) the rise of hegemonic powers. The dynamic of action in this respect remains the consideration that because of the difficulty of achieving peace through international law and organization, or even by means of world government, it is necessary to devise other arrangements for the management of power.

Thus, both the balance of power and collective defence systems approaches are to furnish important regulatory devices to prevent any one nation or group of nations from achieving hegemony[13]. This policy trend was as much a feature of pre-1945 Europe as it now is of contemporary internatioal system dominated by formindable military powers. It is also arguably an emerging tendency in a regional subsystem such as Africa, given the explosive combination of such unsettling factors as: (i) The intrusion of external powers in regional conflicts, (ii)Rising defence expenditures, (iii)Regional revalries, (iv)Economic collapse (v)Political instability (iv)Civil strife (vii)Moribund dictatorships, and (viii)Syndrome of failed and collapsed states. These seem to mark an irreversible trend towards regional vigilantism and realpolitik rather than the primacy of 'intra-system solutions' based on normative considerations. As John Burton aptly concludes: "there is probably no greater common factor than the assumption that states depend for their existence upon power, and achieve their objectives by power, thus making the management the power the main problem to be solved"[14].

Seen within this analytical framework, it may thus be speculated that, both at global and continental levels, military power will in future, as at present, continue to be a crucial factor in structuring international relationships. The high aggregate level of world expenditures on military forces supports this assumption. For example, by 2008 world military spending was running at about $410 billion yearly or nearly, '$1 million a minute-about 500 percent more than the 1980-1990 average'[15]. In regional terms, Africa's rate of militarisation outstripped that of every other region outside the Middle East in the 1990s. By 2008 continental tensions and rivalries had pushed annual weapon costs up to $20 billion. Such a high rate of defence spending among African countries is indicative of the inexorable tendencies on the part of an increasing number of governments to achieve a significant level of miliary strength from a relatively meagre foundation, to advance their interests and objectives against real or potential adversaries.

Given this unabated and combative trend toward "militarism" (an extension of military influence to civilian spheres, including economy and socio-political life) and "militarisation" (the rush to armaments, the growing role of defence establishments in national and international affairs, the use of force as an instrument of political power etc.) at both regional and global levels, the paramount challenge for Nigeria (as a political entity with definite foreign and secuirty policy objectives) remains to argument its military option while exercising circumspection in use. As the 2008 Report of Armed forces Transformation Committee notes:

> *Global events in recent years have profound implications on the strategic environment of Nigeria. This has reinforced the need for military to support foreign policy objectives, for as much as Nigeria will continue to play a vital role in the global response to these emerging security challenges.… The increased international interest in the crude oil deposit in the Gulf of Guinea and the use of neighbouring countries as staging posts for subversive activities or prosecution of proxy wars cannot be discounted[15]*

The Report, therefore, concluded that the Nigerian Military "must be ready to actively participate in the protection of the Gulf of Guinea in concert with allies and to face series of low intensity conflicts such as proxy wars, insurgencies aided and abetted by foreign interest". Perhaps the greatest difficulty facing any systematic discussion of the future of Nigeria's defence policy is: (i) how to draw the necessary distinction between what is desirable and what is possible, and (ii) the possibility of confident prediction about the anticipated strategic environment (the three 'concentric circles' of Nigeria's foreign and security policy environment five, ten, or fifteen years hence) within which Nigeria's military power might be activated in crises.

The first of these two considerations necessarily involves accurate balancing of objectives and commitments (such as preventing a deterioration in the geographic and military status quo in the neighbouring states) within the overall context of its current and projected capabilities. Policy objectives may be desirable but unrealistic in terms of given national capabilities and hence court failure. They may be unrealistic because the military and non-miliary means of international prevalence available to the Nigerian government are insufficient to produce desired policy results such as the expensive peace support operations in Liberia and Sierra Leone; because employing Nigerian armed forces in certain ways is inappropriate in certain conditions to a particular policy goal, such as restoring normalcy to Chad through peacekeeping. However, for a number of reasons it is far from easy to calculate the relevance of military means to the achievement of certain policy objectives. It is far from easy to foresee precisely because the 'relevant realities and their interaction are complex', because the total problem must for purposes of decision-making, 'be decomposed into manageable parts', and because 'the results of these analysis must be brought together and sensibly intergrating for proper decision-making'[16].

Part of the reason for the trauma of the two Nigerian peacekeeping operations in Chad (independently in 1979 and as part of the OAU Force in Chad in 1982) and peace-enforcement operations in Liberia and Sierra Leone was due to over estimating the receptivity of the various domestic factions, or, more appropriately, understimating the delimitations imposed by the 'farrago of confusing and confounding contradictions' in the Chadian, Liberian and Sierra Leonian polities about such operations.

The second consideraton concerns future developments in Nigeria's primary strategic environment: the African subsystem which impact on its security interests and, as a consequence, may necessitate the employment of national armed forces either coercively in order to influence the behaviour of opponents or in order to alter or preserve the status quo by sheer military feat; or, furthermore, providing the mechanism for interventionary or 'preventive diplomacy' (Peacekeeping) for intra or interstate conflict, where such an endeavour may be considered appropriate. This environment necessarily encompasses three basic properties: (i) situational conditions which may provoke a military reaction; (ii) probable opponents ; and (iii) probable allies.

Regarding the first category, two probable seenarios, involving the West Africa subzone may be posited. In the West African subzone it may be speculated that a deterioration in the geographic, military and political status quo in any neighbouring country with inevitable spillover effect for Nigeria, in terms of refugees and armed incursions into border towns etc. may in future prompt an interventionary military response on the part of Nigeria. It, therefore, makes a considerable difference whether or not those countries on the immediate strategic horizon of Nigeria enfeebled as they are by increasing poverty will be wrenched by civil strife and so susceptible to direct and indirect aggression such as French interventionism or mercenary adventurism which in the past has affected such West African countries as Benin, Chad, Guinea, Togo and Nigeria.

The latter development - mercenary adventurism – has been of cardinal concern to successive Nigerian governments, as the Nigerian - Benin defence accord in 1979, following the abortive attempt by a company of mercenaries of French and American origin to overthrow the socialist government of Kerekou, attests. However strenuously denied by the countries involved, a survey of the pattern and mode of operation of the numerous instances of mercenary involvement in Africa is revealing in one vital respect: that mercenarism has become an adjunct of the 'Third Option' force (covert operation) at the disposal of extra-continental powers seeking to ensure favourable outcomes in areas of vital economic and strategic importance to them [17]. As Jonathan Bloch has rightly noted, 'if one reason has to be sought for the increase in their use it lies in the changed balance of power in the post-colonial World: today unofficial means have to be used to change the situation in former dependencies"[18]. This observation points to the geopolitical underpinning of an increasing mercenary menace in contemporary Africa, as recent by the recent attempts to overthrow the government to Equitorial Guinea and Madagaslar suggest.

Nigeria's doctrinal response articulated by the Obasanjo government following the Benin episode was to declare mercenarism, as well as other forms of external acts of subversion, as "grave threat" to be met by superior counterforce. In this respect, article 16 of the ECOWAS Defence protocol may be seen as providing the legal and normative basis for Nigeria's military response to such contingencies should its assistance be requested by a fellow member state[19]. Collateral concerns include: Cross border banditry, violent crimes, natural /man made disasters, small arms trafficking, and internal convultions..[20]

Regarding the second category of variables in Nigeria's strategic environment, it obviously makes a difference whether the power considered the most threatening to the cohesiveness and survival of Nigeria as a political unit (France) will engage in indirect as well as direct aggression. Alternatively, whether the present trend towards reciprocal accommodation and mutually beneficial economic relationship between Nigeria and France may become paramount. The pervasive and tenacious involvement of France in West-Central Africa has been widey seen by Nigerian defence planners as constituting a direct affront to its national security and also impeding 'the growth of the country's political, economic and cultural interests in the region, as France's support for the Cameroun over the Bakassi Peninsula suggests.

Furious French resistance and economic blackmail of 'francophone' West African countries in the 1970s nearly aborted Nigeria's effort to create the politico-economic and military institutionals base (ECOWAS) for the transformation of prevailing regional neo-colonial structures and power relations. As Paris rightly perceives, the emergence of Nigeria as the regional power centre around which indigenous interests can coalesce in relative security inevitably expedites the retrenchment of the neo-colonial structures of the French 'commonweath' and the progressive development of autonomous systems of power in the 'new sovereign region'. Since French economic interests entail its strategic presence in West-Central Africa involving, as in the past, blatant military intervention and undisguised manipulation of midget states the antagonistic relationship between Nigeria and France is arguably bound to continue in the foreseeable future.

Regarding the final category of factors in Nigeria's strategic environment, it certainly makes a difference in the future to Nigeria's defence planners whether ECOWAS and the AU crumble or retain a degree of consensus on crucial regional issues. For example, the unqualified support given to the Nigerian position at OAU Summit on Angola in 1976 by the majority of African states (despite the determined effort to the contrary by the American government under President Ford), provided the normative basis for Nigeria's diplomatic offensive to legitimise Cuban involvement and defeat South Africa. As one analyst argued in the stormy period of decolonisation in the 1980s:

The proposal for closer inter-African diplomacy is more than a sentimental contribution to the quest for the elusive goal of African unity... An integrated and co-ordinated approach to African diplomacy, involving joint action by a combination of regional or sub-regional states would, on the other hand, be more likely to generate greater diplomatic impact. It is therefore significant, in this respect, that West Africa's Nigeria participates jointly with Southern Africa's front-line states in the search for a diplomatic solution to the Namibia problem. Such common action enhances African credibility, stengthens the African position and puts maximum pressure on South Africa and the Western Contact Group engaged in the drawn-out Namibian negotiations[20].

Judging from the current inertia within the AU, it may be speculated that this institutional mechanism binding Nigeria's potential allies in any intra-regional conflict is weak as grave economic condition, political imbroglios and extra-regional pressures deepen. Indeed, as the fairly high level agreement exhibited in the Literatures suggests, the combination of extra continental forces and intracontinental developments does not bode well for a significantly improved African future.

Analytical support for such an unpromising appraisal derives from two sources. The first is essentially extrapolative: the conventional wisdom regarding the ineluctable Linkage of the past, present, and future, concerns developments in five major areas of intra-and inter-state relations, at least on direction, if not on the degree, of trends: national integration, state action, elite control, Pan-African cooperation, and the frequency and intensity in recent years of conflict spiral and external linkages. While the aggregate effect of these multiple centrifugal pressures on the functioning of the AU cannot be lightly discounted, it is equally true that history is full of surprises. As Sammy Buo has rightly noted: 'Although the African group of states is also rife with contradictions of one sort or the other, what binds the group together is stronger than what divides it and this is an adequately valid reason for African states to place the highest diplomatic priority on cooperation between and among themselves in crisis conditions[21]. Such cooperation and opposition by a group of African States (Nigeria, Tanzania, and Kenya) dissuaded France and its Western allies from sponsoring the so-called Pan-African force of regional proxies in the wake of the Sheba episode of May 1978 and subsequent American and French sponsored schemes such as RECAMP and ACRI.

It is in the above context that the future utilization of the military option by Nigeria in regional conflict has to be predicated upon the overt or tacit diplomatic support of probable allies in the continent, as was the case during the civil war of 1966-1970 and Peace Support Operations in Liberia and Sierra Leone. The emerging consensus between Nigeria and Libya over Chad in the early 1980s imposed serious operational constraints on French military forces there, as its casualties mount in the face of attrition[22]. Should such cooperation develop and mature in future, especially within the institutional context of an ECOWAS defence force (ECOBRIG) or a broadly based continental defence system, then the feasibility, frequency and utility of the military option in Nigerian foreign policy may increase proportionately, assuming the political will, heightened offensive capability of the Nigerian armed forces, and sound economic base.

However, since any future military response by Nigeria to systematic challenges cannot be isolated from the prevailing climate of opinion at the global level (especially the attitudes and perceptions of weapons-supplier states), the political direction and strategic configuration at the international level including the kinds of intervention from outside that may be launched in support of regional clients become part of the contextual calculus determining resort to military force. As Timothy Shaw explains:

> *Conflict resolution and political Liberation in the African continent, and regional integration and political cooperation in West Africa, bring Nigeria up against a variety of extra-African interests and institutions: super and great powers and a range of international and transnational organizations are also involved in such issues. East-West conflicts and intra-western tensions as well as corporate and religious concerns are all reflected in such ostensibly 'African' issues. The interrelatedness of global and regional factors can be seen in Nigeria's several African roles: In continental. Southern African and West African Issues[23].*

Nevertheless, it has been the primary contention and argument of this study that in crisis situations involving vital national interests and concerns, the decision to use or not to use force by the Nigerian government is less subject to adverse systemic normative influences and pressures than to considerations of national capabilities and costs. In this regard, it may be hypothesized that the primary determinants of Nigeria defence policy reside preeminently in domestic capability factors. In other words, the utility and usability of military power as an instrument of Nigerian statecraft will depend on the difference between aggregate national values (as expressed in policy goals and objectives) and aggregate national capabilities. This is turn presupposes the emergence of Nigeria as a de facto regional power with a viable socio-economic base and local "military industrial" complex, both of which, constitute the primary foundation of military statecraft. The rest of this chapter will, therefore, be devoted to an examination of these salient issue areas in Nigeria's defence policy and planning within the speculative context of her regional power position ten, fifteen or twenty years hence.

B. NIGERIA AS A REGIONAL POWER

The regional-cum-middle power model, with which Nigeria has been identified in the literature on Africa's international relations, subsumes a wide variety of variables, the totality of which constitutes the 'essence of national power' and influence. These include, in quantitative demographic, material and geographic terms, such static and dynamic factors as population; economic endowment strategic location;

territorial expanse; military capability; and institutional organization and leadership. In behavioural terms, the distinguishing characteristics of a regional/middle power include broad but often geographically – delimited interests and commitments; mediation in intra-regional conflicts; assertiveness in world politics through multilateral and regional organizations; economic and diplomatic influence; non-alignment; and degree of freedom of political manoeuring in the global arena[25].

Based on these variegated indices (substructural and superstructural as well as behavioural) it would be apposite to contend in the African regional context, as Timothy Shaw observes, that "there has been emerging, since 1975, a certain hierarchy and inequality of power attributes among African States'[26]. Nigeria arguably belongs to that group of evolving 'middle powers' in the international/regional system which, as Shaw puts it, 'possess a range of national attributes which distinguish them from the majority of states'[27]. A cursory comparison of the total population, total armed forces, the estimated GNP and infrastructural base of Sub-Sahara African states (with the exception of apartheid South Africa) clearly substantiates this fact. With a gross national product greater than that of all other Black African countries combined, coupled with its significant human resources (qualitative and quantitative), territorial expanse of 356, 669 square miles and military strength, Nigeria may rightly be considered primus inter pares in black Africa.

However, despite this incontrovertible and potentially formidable convergence of capability properties and infrastructural base of Nigeria vis-à-vis other states in the subsystem, the extent to which these constitute or portend significantly increased power and influence (as opposed to mere status and stature) in the continent is highly debatable. The phenomena of coercive and non-coercive power and influence cannot be merely equated with the domestic attributes of states in the global system.

In the context presently discussed (the military as an instrument of prevalence in interstate relations) because coercive power limits the conduct of a actor subjected to it, influence – adaptation of one actor's behaviour in compliance with, or in anticipation of, another actors' demands can be seen to reside in the capabilities that permit the power wielder to exercise effective pressures of threats. But power can also be construed as synonymous with, and limited to, the influence/prevalence over the behaviour of the target actor that is actually achieved. On the first view, 'power' and 'influence' are something that powerful states have and can accumulate. On the Second view, power and influence are effect, that is, the leverage actually enjoyed in an interaction[28].

While there has been a tendency among orthodox writers to visualize power and influence in the former terms, most theorists today especially of the revisionist persuasion conceive of them as prevalence actually achieved. Thus Charles Reynolds has argued that the 'power' of the United States at any given moment is not 'a quality, or state, but is evaluated in terms of the achievement of specific aims'. Hence an inability to secure policy objectives in Indo-China over the late-1960s is 'a better indication of its power than a hypothetical capacity to destroy the world or its opponents. In short, power is as power does[30]". Viewed within this analytical context, to take or to posit as axiomatic that Nigeria is 'powerful' and 'influential' in regional affairs because of certain objectives factors of the Nigerian state-population, location, territory, resources and military capability is logically unsound and politically untenable. Such a commonly held assumption by Nigerian and non-Nigerian scholars and decision-makers alike is undoubtedly a reflection of widespread misperceptions and intellectual pitfalls rooted in three principal 'errors of evaluation' identified by Morgenthau.

The first of these errors discounts the relativity of power 'by erecting the power of one particular nation into an absolute'. The second takes 'for granted the permanency of a certain factor that has in the past played a decisive role', thus overlooking the dynamic change to which most power factors are subject. And the third imputes to one key factor a decisive importance to the neglect of all the others. Put differently, as Morgenthau explains:

> The first error consists in not correlating the power of one nation to the power of other nations, the second consists in not correlating actual power at one time to possible power at some future time, and third consists in not correlating one power factor to others of the same nation.

Thus, although Nigeria's relative strength and singular role in continental affairs over a variety of issues (such as Chad and ECOWAS regionally and Angola, Zimbabwe, Namibia, South Africa, and Western Sahara continently) in the last couple decades have enhance the country's status and stature considerably, it is nevertheless neither empirically proven nor behaviourally foreordained that this new activism necessarily elevates it to the 'immortal rank' of power and influence of dominant regional actors such as Brazil and India.

Two major reasons may be adduced for this skepticism about Nigeria's middle power position. This first follows from a balance sheet of its experience in conflict diplomacy since independence in 1960. The second is rooted in internal capability factors (structural as well as super structural) in the short and long term futures. This is because Nigeria's fragile and depression prone socio-economic and industrial base profoundly impacts on policy considerations concerning the use of military power in crisis circumstance. This in turn is exacerbated by institutional disarray and turmoil following each successive regime, a symptom of the persistent praetorian condition which possibly might be aggravated in the short-term by a variety of significant structural conditions that cannot be readily incrementally alleviated[33].

Regarding the first observation the score board of success in conflict diplomacy as an index of Nigeria's power and influence the record has been undeniably mixed. On the surface and measured against the scale of effort and investment from the 1970s to 2008, it seemed Nigeria has registered more frustration than success in regional conflict diplomacy and management. Instances of apparently successful exertion such as those in support of MPLA in Angola in 1975, the patriotic Front in Zimbabwe in 1978-80 and Peace Support Operations in Liberia and Sierra Leone have been over shadowed by the failure of peace-mission in (a) East Africa in 1979 (Tanzanian invasion of Uganda), (b) Horn of Africa (Ethiopia and Somalia over the Oganden), (c) Chad (between Habre and Weddeye forces), (d) Western Sahara (between Morocco and Mauritania on the one hand, and Polisario and Algeria, on the other), and (e) the border dispute between Angola and Zaire following the Shaba crisis of 1978.

One explanatory hypothesis for this apparent asymmetry of success and failure is that in the former cases Angola, Zimbabwe and Liberia/Sierra Leone 'success' was due considerably to the fortuitous combination of favourable regional and external conditions. In the former cases, the involvement of the hated regional parish apartheid South Africa and the clandestine activities of Western powers (particularly the U.S. and Britain) in a manner considered inimical to African interests generated unprecedented consensus on the part of several African and non-African states which eventually ensured a positive outcome. In the latter case, polarization within the OAU coupled with unremitting external involvements precluded any possibility of successful Nigerian initiatives. Together, these instances perhaps constitute a cautionary signal to its decision-makers that Nigeria's power, like that of all other actors, is limited. This is all the more so for a developing polity, one whose 'international actions and internal formations are significantly constrained by its place in the world system'.

Regarding the second observation, if as argued above 'power' and 'influence' as relational properties, it is, nevertheless, and inescapable fact of the contemporary international system that a state's capacity of coercive or non-coercive action depends on its particular power base. This is so because power generated in an interaction between unequal actors resides in the relation. In other words, it results from asymmetries in the capabilities and needs of the actors involved. The essential inequality lies in the "superior actor both being able to resort to positive or negative sanctions" while at the same time being in a position to neutralize whatever damage might result from the weak actor's countervailing strategies. Knorr has noted in this respect that "an actor with ample resources, able to satisfy the urgent inequality and acquire power over the needy actor"[36]

Thus, as a major industrial power, France, unlike Nigeria, has exerted considerable influence in west-Central Africa through hegemonial domination of its former colonial dependencies. The basis of this power and influence over 'francophone Africa' is rooted in the integration of these client states into a network of neo-colonial dependencies sustained by French economic and military power. One evidence of this domination and prevalence is monetary[37]. Another prominent indicator of French power and influence is military. This involves the large presence of French military personnel on French controlled military bases, and the deployment of these forces for interventionist purposes in the region[38]. As one analyst has aptly noted, "That France can make and unmake regimes from Libreville to Nouakchott without suffering serious prohibitive costs exposes its actual political, economic and military power and influence in the region[39].

Conversely, Nigeria, although indisputably primus inter pares in black Africa because of its material and human endowment, is hardly yet in a position to replicate even a semblance of French political clout in the sub-continent due to its essentially underdeveloped and dependent economy. Since the conversion of putative or basic capabilities in forms (e.g., military forces and developmental aids) that make them directly usable for the exercise of power is highly contingent on a number of intervening factors (domestic and systemic), Nigeria's endowment with the elements of strength that constitute national putative power and influence is obviously important, but not a sufficient, leverage for regional prevalence.

The transformation of its relatively immense resources into usable bases of influence will inescapably depend on its emergence as the de facto regional power centre around which indigenous (African) interests and actor can coalesce in relative security and autonomy. This necessarily involves developing the technological, economic and military capacity to satisfy the urgent needs of other states in the region through complex horizontal and vertical links: financial, technical, trade, investment, developmental aid, military cooperation, etc.

Only such a complex penetration through exchange transaction asymmetries capable of manipulation (denying valuable markets, preempting sources of supply, disinvestment, or reduction of developmental aid) can generate for Nigeria the basis of coercive and non-coercive power and influence in black Africa. Arguably, the absence of this irreducible minimum (at least until the ideals of both ECOWAS and the vision 2020 become a reality) for a systemic power play underscore, for example, the singularly unsuccessful attempts by Nigeria to halt the outrageous killings of former national leaders in the wake of the Rawling and Doe coups in Ghana and Liberia, respectively, and influence a range of current developments in the continent. In former cases, Nigeria's imposition of an embargo on petroleum products was bound to have limited coercive or deterrent value because of the availability of alternative sources of supplies.

Similarly, Habre's volte face on the Nigerian sponsored Kano and the OAU peace accords for Chad may have been less likely if his estimate of net costs of resistance favoured compliance. In the event, the Shagari's administration's refusal to consider peace enforcement/suppression action (the Libyan approach) as a logical alternative to inaction (as suggested by the generals) had the inevitable consequences of lowering the stake threshold for Habre in terms of making the response of the OAU Force in Chad predictable[40]. In the immediate term, Nigeria's aspiration to become, as Olatunde Ojo put it, 'the industrial heart of West Africa with all the political power that it may bring, not only, within Africa but also in the world at large', is patently bleak. As Peter Evans aptly observes, the structure of the Nigerian economy is:

> *In many ways more suggestive of the period in classic dependence than of the current period of dependent development in Brazil and Mexico....Except for the oil industry, which is a classic enclave, Nigeria is primarily an agricultural country. The manufacturing investment it contains is a fraction of that which international capital*

> *has chosen to locate in Brazil and Mexico. Yet, the international*
> *business community is beginning to discuss Nigeria the way they*
> *discussed Brazil at the beginning of the Seventies as a potential*
> *members of the 'semi-periphery'[41].*

Nigeria's evolution into a de facto regional power will unalterably depend on the rapidity of the transformation of its national economy from what Shaw has characteristically described as an "oil-extraction and commodity production base' into a 'self-reliant' and productive industrial economy. This will in turn depend on fundamental reorientation in structural and value parameters through comprehensive corrective strategies such as those currently being attempted by the new government.

However, despite the widespread pessimism and projections of some dependency scholars[42], to admit the existence of multiple dysfunctions in the socio-economic order of Nigeria is not to foreclose the possibility of evolutionary change. As Biersteker and Schatz, among others, have acknowledge, Nigeria's potential for generating an indigenous economic and industrial base through structural reforms and intermediate technology is considerable. The former, for example, has reasoned that:

> *The presence of necessary conditions for feasible indigenous production*
> *in Nigeria and the demonstration of local capabilities during the*
> *civil war suggest …that feasible alternatives to the Mult-National*
> *corporation exist in Nigeria. These alternatives would not necessarily*
> *provide a superior product of a greater output than the multinationals,*
> *at least at the outset. But the example suggests that whatever losses*
> *might initially take place in economic terms would probably be smaller*
> *and short-term than predicted by neoconventional writers and would*
> *be compensated for by immediate gains in terms of technological*
> *innovations and employment effects[43].*

Indeed, an interim report issued by the OECD Development Centre on the development of low-cost or intermediate technology is largely supportive of Biersteker's conclusion. The ingenious technical designs and managerial competence in the former Eastern Region ('Biafra') of Nigeria during the civil war was cited as a case suggesting 'that isolation can have positive effects on the development of technology, and notably on a society's ability to rely on its own inventive force'.

First, several industrial units were kept operational after the mass departure of their expatriate staff. Spare and replacement parts were 'machine-tooled locally, as ingenious cannibalization and mechanical miracles" substituted for the dearth of imported parts. Second, new intermediate production technologies were 'developed and employed in indigenously organized firms even as the war progressed'.

Third, an extensive experiment in weapons research and production programme was initiated, also utilizing 'intermediate technologies based on local innovative capabilities'. These include the construction of armoured vehicles along with a variety of guns, ammunition, land mines, rockets, grenades, stand-cannon, and even aerial bombs[45]. Finally, and most significant perhaps (since petroleum refining is generally considered among the 'highest' technology industries) was the demonstrable capability to refine petroleum and related products by Biafran scientists and engineers, 'on a large scale, in numerous and widely distributed locations, and without the assistance of expatriate technicians or direct supervision[46]'. As the sea, air and land blockade of the federal forces tightened around 'Biafra' these petroleum products from locally designed plants kept essential transport and military machines moving throughout 'Biafra' until its final collapse in 1970. As one observer described it:

> *The Biafran refiners, many of them trained in the Port Harcourt plant, effectively set up refineries under war time conditions. They undertook research to improve quality and extend the range of products. These efforts went some way towards dispelling the myth that refining technology was beyond the immediate capacity of Nigerian.*

Although these unprecedented achievement in black Africa in a short period of three years (1967-1970) were largely ignored by the comprader bureaucratic and self-aggrandizing elite (fuelled as it was by ethnic jealousies) which dominating critical federal policy planning agencies in the 1970s, and 1980s comprehensive measure designed to utilize and expand indigenous technological and innovative capabilities now constitute the centerpiece of the new Nigerian strategy on industrialization based on the policy of public – private partnership [48]. The magnitude of the current effort (succinctly described by Adedeji as 'increasing substitution of factor inputs derived from within the system for those derived from outside') is evident in the proliferation of scientific and technological planning and policy-making bodies. These include the various R & D establishments under the Ministry of Science and Technology.

However, while these endeavours may be considered an impressive beginning in the African context, the actual spin-off for the Nigerian economy – both in terms of the translation of research into practical application and the necessary multiplier effect- will depend on the extent to which extant organizational and attitudinal problems are confronted and resolved. Apart from critical factors influencing the output of R & D units (co-ordination, finance, underutilization and misuse of science and technology manpower for activities not relevant to S & T development), incisively analysed in the Nigerian context by Babatunde Thomas, Obande, O. Teriba and M. Kayode, among others, fundamental social and psychological problems remain[40].

To the extent that these can be overcome and the present concentration on the development of indigenous capabilities supplemented by vertical technological transfer generate a viable socio-economic and industrial base, the ineluctable growth of Nigeria into a de facto regional power (invariably assumed by its dominant scholars in the field of foreign policy) may readily translate into reality. Otherwise, Nigeria's sobriquet as a problematic power' may outlive even the most pessimistic of projections in the current literature. The next section examines one of the most widely debated and salient issues in Nigeria's defence policy and military statecraft: the debate about the nuclearisation of its defence system in response to adverse systemic developments.

C. THE NUCLEAR OPTION

The nuclear option controversy which surfaced in Nigeria policy, media and academic circles since the late-seventies, was again a clear indication of the importance increasingly accorded the military underpinning in Nigeria foreign policy planning[50]. This is all the more so in the orbit of nuclear diplomacy, given Nigeria's earlier commitment in the nineteen sixties and early seventies to the declaration of Africa a 'nuclear-weapon-free zone' (no nuclear tests, bases, storage or transport) by the United Nations General Assembly (1965 and 1974)[51]. The complex socio-economic, bureaucratic and intellectual constituencies which underscore the current *volte face* (in terms of changing perceptions and outlook for nuclear policy decision-making since late 1980s) has been highlighted in the literature[52]. In line with the stipulated parameters of this chapter, the brief critique below focuses on the politico-strategic context of Nigeria's decision concerning the acquisition of a viable retaliatory nuclear capability: political/military incentives, and infrastructural feasibility and prospects.

INCENTIVES FOR ACQUISITION:

Advocates of the nuclear option for Nigeria have invariably advanced two fundamental reasons: status and security. In the first category-status-perhaps the most forceful argument has been advanced by Ali Mazrui in his 1979 BBC Reith lectures. Possession of nuclear arsenals, he contended, invests states in contemporary international system not only with supreme military force, but also with international status and political power. In this context, the existential question which arises is whether the Non-Proliferation Treaty, 'designed to minimize the number of countries that have a nuclear capacity, and ultimately intended especially to discourage Third World countries from going nuclear', could not conceivably be regarded as an extension of the 'old philosophy of imperialism as a monopoly state of warfare'[51] Mazrui answered in the affirmative: 'those who insists on monopolizing nuclear know-how themselves, he contends, are heirs to Pax Britannica, seeking to end tribal wars in distant lands while arming to initiate world wars from their own heartland[52]. Africa, he urges, should 'give up the idea of promoting itself as a nuclear – free zone... and estimate the chances of at least a continental consortium within Africa of nuclear energy, linked to a strategy of developing a small nuclear section in the military establishment of Nigeria for the time being, and in Zaire and black-ruled South Africa later'[53].

For Mazrui as well as other exponents of this view[54], nuclear proliferation constitutes a 'process of military democratization":

> *It seeks to break monopolies in weaponry in the hands of the northern warlords. Nuclear proliferation also seeks to break secret societies based on forbidden nuclear knowledge under the control of the West and the Soviet bloc[55].*

Thus for Nigeria in particular, and for black Africa in general, joining the 'nuclear club' should be seen not as dangerous misdirection of effort from the current imperative of economic development, but as per force a 'new initiation, an important rite de passage, a recovery of adulthood' in a world preeminently framed and informed by security relations. As Mazrui unreserved put it:

> For the 1980s and 1990s, Nigeria should move toward making itself a nuclear power unless steps are taken before then by the world as a whole to put an end to nuclear weapons universally. The development of a nuclear capacity by Africa's largest country is probably a necessary precondition if Africa's diplomatic marginality is to ended. Nigeria should follow the example of its fellow giants – Brazil in Latin America and China and India in Asia and pursue the goal of a modest nuclear capability. My own reasons for urging such a capability have nothing to do with making Nigeria militarily stronger. My ultimate desire is that the world as a whole should be militarily safer. Only when the Western nations and the Soviet bloc discover that they cannot keep the rest of the world from engaging in the nuclear "dream" unless they themselves give up nuclear weapons will the world at least address itself to the fundamentals of human survival[56].

As earlier suggested, this status-cum-diplomatic consideration advanced by Mazrui is only part of the overall complex of reasons proffered by proponents of the nuclearization of Nigeria. In the 1980s, security consideration constituted the other imperative: the nuclear option for Nigeria is a necessary counter to the developing threat of a "nuclear blackmail from the South African albinocracy"[57]. In his overview of 'Africa and the Bomb', Sammy Kum Buo alluded to this growing concern among policy planners as well as informed public in Africa:

> Just as French nuclear tests in the Sahara in the 1960s may have provoked Africa's anti-nuclear diplomatic efforts, South Africa's frenzied pursuit, in the 1970s, of a nuclear – weapon capability may now be responsible for Black Africa's seemingly more favourable attitude towards the acquisition of nuclear weapons by Black African countries…Proposals have therefore been made for Nigeria, in particular, and Black Africa, as a whole, to achieve nuclear weapons not only to face what is seen as a racist South Africa's nuclear threat to the rest of Africa but also to enhance Africa's diplomatic clout[58].

On this view apartheid South Africa's intensive nuclear programme over the past couple of decades, combined with its avowed strategy for survival, posed a mortal threat to Black Africa. In this regard, Nigeria's nuclear option was viewed in terms of its assumption of leadership in a common front ("continental African security Community" (CASC) against the perceived peril from the white laager of South Africa.

As then a parish state which combined the 'disadvantages of pygmies and paranoids along with more visceral and unremitting opposition by its regional enemies and isolation from most of the rest of the world' apartheid South Africa arguably had the clearest incentives to increase its military power, 'the shortest technical distance (in the African context) to go to build a bomb, and the least to lose in doing so'. Under the pretext of the 'Atoms for Peace' South Africa received extensive inputs in terms of the technology, facilities (reactors) and expertise, from Western countries notably the U. S., U. K., France and FRG for its nuclear development schemes[59]. As a consequence, it was generally assumed that South Africa has the capacity (especially with its Israeli connection) to produce nuclear explosive devices, however primitive, and it did in actual fact produce and stored atomic bombs before the end of the Laager.

Although its limited capacity in delivery technology puts Nigeria outside the direct orbit of apartheid South Africa's nuclear blackmail', the latter's interest in battlefield or theatre nuclear delivery systems such a nuclear artillery (e.g., the American 155 MGS Howitzer assembled in South Africa), battle-field missiles (e.g. Cactus), aerial bombs and air-to-ground missiles (for its Canberras, Buccanners, and Mirage) brought neighbouring African states into striking distance. Among other things, the apartheid regime (as part of its forward defence' strategy) apparently hoped either to forestall any eventuality of these territories becoming bases for future Pan-African Task Force or to frighten these governments into desisting from supporting the liberation movements (PAC and ANC).

It is on this ground, above all else, that advocates of a nuclear option for Nigeria conceive its utility: a nuclear balance of power between Nigeria and Boer South Africa'. Former Nigerian President, Shagari expressed this position in his address to the Foreign Policy Association in New York: "Nigeria will not allow Africa to be subjected to nuclear blackmail by South Africa... it reserved the right to do whatever she could to protect herself if racist South Africa persisted in acquiring nuclear weapons to threaten the continent[60].

It cannot be doubted that the underlying concern i.e., contemporary developments both in the global and regional arenas expressed by proponents for the nuclearisation of Nigeria is growing. This is especially so, as Frank Barnaby the director of SIPRI has noted, because the present countries in possession of nuclear arsenals have repeatedly rejected the call 'to assure the non-nuclear-weapon parties of the NPT that the weapons they have renounced would not be used against them[61]. However, it is logically unsound to equate the mere fact of existence of nuclear weapons in a given country with claims to relative status and security. For Nigeria in particular, and other LDCs aspirants in general, the problem is essentially one of credibility. That is, even if Nigeria successfully develops its nuclear option either through expensive independent exertions or the 'shop around' approach, the likelihood of its employment is minimal.

In the first place, the target of Nigeria's nuclear defence option (apartheid South Africa) is over 80 percent African and it is ulikely that any Nigerian government would willingly imperil the lives of the great majority of South Africans even in the face of extreme provocation from the Afrikaner regime. Such a consideration alone deprives Nigeria of one of the cardinal elements in deterrence relationship:

intention. Credible deterrence is primarily a function not only of capability but also of the estimated intentions of a nation's leadership to use the military potential at its deposal. In other words, while South Africa's tactic of cultivating irrationality through nuclear weapons acquisition may have the intended psychological effect on neighbouring states, similar effort on the part of Nigeria to create a condition of 'mutual alarm' or mutually assured retaliation cannot but have a 'hollow ring'.

And in the second place, given the present and foreseeable level of technology in Nigeria, the problem of the gap between test detonation of a bomb and the 'weaponisation' and delivery system costs of meaningful nuclear weapon status would remain. In India, these costs provoked resistance to a full-fledged bomb programme inside the military establishment, which feared a drain on funds for conventional weapons. Several domestic opponents of any weapons related nuclear programme in Nigeria had this factor in mind when they counseled that 'we should handle this growing nuclear obsession with care.

> *The apparent strength of our economy is illusory; the kind of confrontation we envisage with any outside power (in the light of our present foreign policy) is not likely to be settled by resort to nuclear weapons but conventional (army, air-force and naval facilities and weaponry); the technology for production of nuclear weapons is very expensive and complicated and depends on a developed educational and technical base. For the rest of this century we may not be able to master it and produce an effective weapon. To direct several billions of naira as India is dong leaving 90 percent of the population in deprivation is unjustified and indeed socially criminal[62].*

It may, therefore, be concluded on the basis of the above observation that the incentives argument-security and status-in the Nigerian context constitutes at best a misguided preoccupation of the 'new bureaucratic and intellectual constituencies-research scientists, the diplomatic service, political and military elite-which as Robert D'A Henderson has pointed out, have 'emerged in favour of a stronger emphasis on the nuclear factor' in Nigerian decision making[63].

However, in the final analysis policy decisions in this, as in other areas of the national defence planning, may not be entirely governed by the 'limits of rational action'. The central problem is that in Nigeria, as no doubt in other countries as well, governmental organizations have their own competing interests. In their desire to protect or increase their influence, size, and budget, they are likely to oppose policy choices that reduce or jeopardize their missions and instead lobby for courses of action apt to promote 'organizational prosperity'. It is in this context that a number of domestic detractors in Nigeria have viewed with increasing alarm the undisguised attempts of the nuclear scientific community (associated with the Nuclear Regulatory commission) to combine with military bureaucratic and industrial interests to push the frontiers of their research into the military realm[64]. Since Nigeria, as Moyibi Amoda has noted, 'fits into the category of those who have nominal programmes but with the future potential to expand them, it is, therefore, appropriate to assess the future possibilities and prospects for Nigeria in this nuclear domain[65].

PROSPECT

Despite countervailing efforts to control proliferation by international regimes, such as the International Atomic Energy Agency (IAEA), the technical information required to design and manufacture a nuclear explosive device is now quite readily available, as is the necessary expertise[66]. This trend has been considerably heightened in recent times by the increasing commercialization of nuclear technology and research/production facilities under the so-called 'Atoms for Peace' clause of the Non-Proliferation Treaty which explicitly commits (Articles IV) the nuclear powers to aid the non-nuclear weapons states in 'development of peaceful nuclear energy capabilities, including the fullest possible exchange of equipment'.[67]. As a consequence (as the cases of France, India, Iran, Pakistan and North Korea clearly demonstrate), acquisition of nuclear weaponry has now become a by-product of a 'peaceful' nuclear programmes and delivery systems the by products of 'peaceful' space programmes. In terms of both money and manpower, a national nuclear force can now be acquired at relatively low cost, as technological advances (especially in laser enrichment) and the burgeoning market for nuclear materials and technology outside the framework of any NPT regime render existing international safeguards largely ineffective. The Indian nuclear explosion, for example, cost about \$500,000, including the cost of the plutonium and the preparation of the test site[68].

For a relative newcomer to the field such as Nigeria, such a 'civilian route' to weapons acquisition might prove to be particularly attractive. First, experience from civilian utilizations may facilitate the construction and operation of clandestine facilities for bomb production (e.g., Israel and South Africa). Second, the establishment of a nuclear fuel cycle for peaceful programme create a permanent weapons base or option for chaining regimes in Nigeria, thus enhancing policy calculations and planning for future contingencies. And third, proceeding via the 'civilian route' or under 'civilian flag' may reduce the political costs that might be incurred by the acquisition of a nuclear fuel cycle reactor (reprocessing plant) designed specifically for military purposes. Since the development of nuclear explosives or nuclear weapons hinges ultimately on political considerations (e.g., backlash from the international community, which may not be easy to predict and could potentially be severe), the use of civilian fuel cycles elements as intermediary steps in the development of bombs offers the best possible route.

Although at present Nigeria is unlikely to have an operational nuclear reactor prior to the year 2020, it can readily purchase components for a small national uranium reactor producing about 20kg of plutonium 239 a year (more than enough for two atomic bombs) secretly on the open market for a cost of less than \$20 million.69. As the Taiwan and South African examples show, the same can be done in the field of reprocessing technology: a small chemical reprocessing unit could be clandestinely acquired and run by the military. Since considerable deposits of uranium are already known to exist in Nigeria (in Benue, Niger, Sokoto, Cross River, and Bauchi States), it would not be too difficult to obtain fuel for a reactor.

Beyond these fortuitous circumstances, however, formidable problems remain to be overcome if the present or future government of Nigeria decides to press on with a nuclear programme. First, given the paucity of national technological and related skills in this field, considerable sums of money maybe needed to recruit foreign expertise (possibly from India, Pakistan, Brazil or Egypt) to Staff available facilities and support infrastructures. Even though Nigeria's human resources in this area has been growing steadily in the last decade (with many trained scientists opting for the bigger 'pies' of Europe and North America), as Henderson has noted, 'for the near future, Nigeria will lack enough highly-trained nuclear scientists, engineers, and technicians to support a modest nuclear research programme'[70].

Second, given the current paranoia in the industrial West about an 'Islamic' or 'Black' bomb, even as these states demonstrate a remarkable tolerance of a 'Jewish' or 'Boer' bomb, it is to be expected that Nigeria's attempt in the future to secure the essential prerequisite (access to commercial reprocessing plant or a Uranium-enrichment plant) for the production of nuclear weapons will be an uphill task. Already her negotiations with the West German Kraftwekunion (KWU) and the Canadian government for the 450 megawatt medium – sized and 600 megawatt Candu reactors, respectively, have been linked to strict IAEA safeguards (including supervision, inspection, and return of spent fuel rods) over all of Nigeria's nuclear installations.

However, these domestic and systemic hurdles, notwithstanding, the future possibilities and potentials for Nigeria in the field of nuclear energy and weapons acquisition are considerable. If unforeseen adverse regional developments compel a major national nuclear programme, Nigeria can pursue a 'shop around' approach for production collaboration with current LDCs which are not parties to the NPT. Future non-NPT suppliers (such as India and Brazil) with compelling reasons (the need to become more competitive or to counteract great powers) could be possible candidates.

Nevertheless, the current emphasis placed upon the development of the country's conventional military power as well as its domestic military industrial complex' reduces the probability that available resources will be channeled into such a costly venture. The preoccupation of successive Nigerian government and regimes since the mid-1970s with improving the armed forces' efficiency, modernizing its conventional firepower and creating a regional mobility for its forces supports this order of priorities.

Thus given its dubious strategic values to Nigeria in existing and likely future, condition, the pressing problems of the armed forces modernization programme commanding immediate attention, and the nascent technological base and political inertia, it is to be expected that the nuclearisation of Nigeria's defence system will continue to receive low priority in national planning. In the late 1970s and 1980s even if apartheid South Africa successfully tested and deployed nuclear arsenal, it would still be far from certain that Nigeria could respond in a similar fashion. Rhetoric notwithstanding, any policy response by Nigeria to nuclear threat from apartheid South Africa, had to be predicated upon the calculations and perceptions of the Front Line States' governments. The reasons were fairly obvious.

First, as suggested above, these States were the most likely to be affected by South Africa's nuclear blackmail, since its existing capability in delivery systems (bomber command) necessarily delimits the penetration and striking distance of its forces beyond their immediate strategic environment. And, second, should Nigeria eventually development atomic or nuclear device, operational imperatives concerning its 'radius of effective military action-that is, the capacity of its military services to 'transmit power over space' necessitated forward positioning in Southern Africa. It is not altogether certain that any one of the FLS governments would have found such an offer inviting enough to risk the possibility of a preemptive strike by a fiendish regime whose domestic and international policies had been anything but rational. In the final analysis, there is a fairly good degree of consensus in the informed public that, as the Punch Editorial of 1st July, 2009 put it, "because of our low level of technological development and notoriously deficient maintenance culture and enforcement of industry regulations", it would be suicidal for this country to embark on the costly venture of nuclear power technology and infrastructure. Investing in modest nuclear technology programme in the Universities by way of training indigenous manpower (regulators and promoters) may be more defensible. In the final section of this chapter, a review of one of the most immediate and salient, if problematic, issues in Nigerian defence policy and planning, will be made within the context of the changing dynamics of its operational environment.

E. NIGERIA AND REGIONAL STABILIZATION FORCE

Both the rationale and the changing attitudes of successive Nigerian governments (from Balewa to Yar'Adua), as well as the substantive propositions so far put forward concerning a collective defence system for Africa, have been extensively discussed in the literature. What, therefore, remains is to appraise Nigeria's role in any such regional arrangement to deal with security crises within or around African States.

As is evident from the extensive debate within and outside the AU on this topic[71], proposals in the seventies for a regional defence system invariably envisage a synthesis between Nkrumah's old idea of an African High Command designed 'to keep imperialist invaders at bay' (the concept of selective security) and the Morocco-Seegalese sponsored continental peace-enforcement/peacekeeping mechanism (the concept of 'preventive diplomacy') designed to 'put the African house in order'. The objectives of this proposed Pan-African Task Forces, as Ofoegbu succinctly explained was: i) to assist in restoring intraregional peace; ii) to keep extra-continental powers and foreign adventurers out of purely African affairs; and iii) to generate first an African response to African problems and establish the urgent institutional mechanism to counter the increasingly ominous apartheid South African military pressure on 'Front Line States[72]'

However, owing to the continued and paralyzing 'foot dragging by the AU on the formation of a continent-wide African defence force' there was a significant reorientation in both thinking and planning from continental to sub-regional levels, with the expressed hope that such an approach would eventually 'spill over into other regions of Africa, constituting both core and example for a continental security system[73]'. Tenous arrangements now exist in the African Union (AU) in terms of a new security regime "predicated on collective security to be operationalized by an African standby Force (ASF), early warning system (EWS), a panel of the wise (PW) and a peace fund (PF). The African Standby Force provides the Operational arm to be Peace and Security Council, a "rapid reaction capacity to be fully developed by 2010[74]". It has a scalar rather than a coordinative design, a "standby system that will build on the military capabilities of African regional organizations"[75]. Accordingly, the African Standby Force is expected to comprise a "system of five regionally 3000-4000 troops and between 300 and 500 military observers, police units, and civilians specialists on standby in their countries of origin"[76]. In strategic terms, the sub-regional standby a brigade is, as specified in the protocol, expected to:

> *Engage in observation and monitoring of cease fires, peace support missions; the intervention of member states to restore Peace and Security; preventive deployment to prevent conflict from spreading or escalating or to prevent the resurgence of violence after parties to a conflict have reached an agreements; Peace-building, especially disarmament and demobilization, and the provision of humanitarian assistance.[77]*

Nigeria's role in ECOBRIG is presently considered a sine qua non for its viability and credibility and it is, therefore, in the institutional context of ECOWAS that Nigeria's role in a multi-lateral defence structure can be meaningfully considered in the immediate term, especially in the light of ECOMOG Peace Support Operations in Liberia and Sierra Leone.

At least in theory, if not in reality so far, the inauguration of the 'protocol relating to mutual assistance on defence' at the May 1981 summit of ECOWAS in Freetown, Sierra Leone, establishes both the organizational parameter and political momentum toward the integration of ECOWAS armed forces into a collective force[78]. As envisaged by the treaty, military contingents from the armies of the Members States will constitute the Allied Force of the Community (AAFC) under a Force Commander. The AAFC are, inter alia expected to conduct joint military exercises designed to enhance their organizational effectiveness and response in crisis situations.

The operational and political direction of the Forces is to be overseen by a supreme organ (the Defence Council of ECOWAS), comprising the Ministers of Defence and Foreign Affairs of member states, through a subordinate apparatus the Defence Commission consisting of Chiefs of defence staff. In addition a Deputy Executive Secretary for Military Affairs is to be attached to the ECOWAS Secretariat in Lagos. His functions are to include 'updating plans for the movement of troops and logistics and initiating joint exercises, preparing and managing the military budget of the

Secretariat, and studying and making proposals to the Secretariat, in respect of matters relating to personnel and equipment within his jurisdiction[80]'

In terms of institutional task and role, three types of major crisis-area have been identified in the protocol: i) aggression from a non-member state (Articles 6 and 10; ii)conflict between member states (Article 17) and (iii) internal conflict in a member state (Article 19). In the first case, military action is anticipated if judged expedient by the Defence Council. In the second case, interventionary diplomacy and peace-keeping are envisaged. And in the third case, a necessary distinction has been made between external involvement (such as mercenary adventurism) and domestic insurrection. While a collective response is judged appropriate in the first context, the treaty rules out military intervention in the latter.

Viewed within the existing parameters, AAFC must necessarily be considered significant and unprecedented achievement in regional experimentation in Black Africa. Indeed, extant frontier and political disputes in West Africa (e.g. between Mali and Upper Volta, Ghana and Togo, Senegal and Guinea-Bissau, Nigeria and Cameroun) and the increasing incidence of mercenary adventurism and failed/collapsed states in Africa have made a collective approach to crisis-management in the region imperative in the face of AU paralysis. As one analyst has noted: In historical terms the memories of the 1970 Portuguese aggression against Guinea and the mercenary invasion of Benin, the overall need to enhance stability in ECOWAS member states incessantly beset by military coups and civil strife contributed to the high priority which West African leaders apparently accorded to the establishment of a defence pact"[81]

As the dominant economic and military power within the West African sub-zone, Nigeria's commitment and role in the development of the defence institution of ECOWAS is undisputably paramount. Apart from being the single largest donor to community finances, only its forces presently have the combination of mobility, equipment and operational experience required by contingencies stipulated in articles 6 and 10 of the protocol. Conversely, both the national security and geo-strategic interests of Nigeria, would be advanced if such a collaborative trend was sustained. As Aluko rightly observed:

> For security reasons Nigeria does not want to be surrounded by small countries that are heavily dependent on extra-African powers, especially France, for their military, political and economic survival. It is firmly believed in Nigeria that as long as there are clients West African states closely tied to European powers Nigeria's own security cannot be assured. Such states can be either manipulated against Nigeria or used as a staging ground by foreign powers who wish to cause disaffection and confusion in the country. The experience of the last civil war when Dahomey (now Republic of Benin) was used briefly in 1969 for airlighting arms and relief supplies to Biafra brought home this points to the Nigerian leaders more clearly than ever[82].

Furthermore, as operational imperatives in any collective defence system require a certain degree of standardization, interoperability and rationalization, it is not altogether inconceivable that the nascent 'military-industrial complex' of Nigeria might in future provide a less expensive alternative to extra-regional sources, especially if the current foreign exchange crisis facing these countries continues. Already for reasons of proximity and the relative availability of the Naira (compared) with the dollar or franc, Nigeria is increasingly becoming the source of a range of industrial products (especially cars and trucks assembled in Nigeria, as well as vital raw materials from the iron and steel complex at Ajaokuta).

However, while for both Nigeria and Black Africa, the necessity of creating an irreversible dynamic towards a continental 'security community through instituting regional planning mechanisms technically essential for the politically desirable task of coping with Africa's 'flashpoints' cannot be doubted, fundamental reservations still persist as to the feasibility of such an arrangement either at present or in the future[83]. The major problems (rooted in the multiple disorders and the Byzantine nature of African politics) bedeviling such a collaborative venture can readily be seen in West Africa. Besides the obvious structural problems (economic dependence, technological underdevelopment, organizational incompetence, military weakness), ideological fractions, vertical links with extra-regional forces, powerful inter-personal animosities among leaders raise serious questions about the ECOWAS Defence past ever developing into a genuine multilateral defence force[84]. This skepticism is reinforced by the non-ratification of the Pact by several members since its declaration in 1981. Thus the question remains whether there is sufficient harmony of interests within the community to sustain such an endeavour, despite ECOMOG Operations in Liberia and Sierra Leone and the equal demand for intervention in Corte d' viore at the initial stage of the domestic conflagration.

It is evident from extensive publications on ECOWAS that opinions on this question differ markedly. Nevertheless, the conventional 'problem oriented approach through which the issue of African regional defence has been analysed has to be qualified by recognition of the fact that 'human institutions do sometimes and to some extent evolve in unwilled directions, violating the intentions and confounding the expectations of their founders and operations[85]'. As Iris Claude has noted in relation to international organization in general:

> *The course of its development may be determined less by the consciously adopted plans of governments which participate in its functions, or the officials who serve it, than by the cumulative influence of day-to-day pressures and case-by-case directions[86].*

Viewed in these terms, the question as to whether ECOWAS armed forces would successfully merge into a regional system can best be answered by reference not to ECOWAS's Charter or sociopolitical realities, but to the unpredictable properties (political, ideological, psychological, technological, and economic features) of future regional and global arenas.

In concrete terms, the emergence of a viable African defence system (continental or regional) will depend, among other things, on the extent to which African states can evolve (a) into relatively separate subsystems regionally (b) an independent foreign policies nationally. In other words, African states must eventually demonstrate the capacity to 'enjoy foreign policy autonomy as a group or groups and to accept the disciplines of foreign policy grounded in external realities as individual actors[87]'. In the sphere of defence policy and planning, this consideration will necessarily involve a gradual shift in focus from vertical defence partnerships (e.g., defence treaties with France) with extra-regional powers to horizontal intra-African defence exchange and cooperation. It is not at all certain whether such measures would follow or await solutions being found to the pressing structural problems of economic dependence and technological underdevelopment. It should be noted, however, in sum, that the successful implementation of plans relating to collective economic or strategic self-reliance in isolation from the prevailing conflict environment in Africa is utterly unrealistic. Basic choices of development strategy are always political as well as economic, and they cannot be implemented in isolation from the transnational and political fabric of the given milieu. In other words, functional collaboration of the type envisaged by the Lagos Plan and NEPAD is not viable without a high degree of mutual trust, substantial faith in the permanence of the joint economy and at least a fundamental base of common socio-political aims which regional security mechanisms can arguably generate.

In overall conclusion to this volume, it is to be expected that military power will remain an integral part of the range of instrumentalities of Nigeria's foreign policy. Its use and usability will, however, continue to be subject to a range of domestic and systemic conditions whether industrial, infrastructural or nuclear questions are being treated. This is the subject of the current policy debate on armed forces transformation in Nigeria: "the transformation of military culture, institutional capabilities and the capabilities of individuals".[88] In the Nigerian context, as a recent Report notes, "Military transformation implies reforming all aspects of the military organization in order to ensure combat effectiveness and enhance operational efficiency. Thus, for Nigeria's defence planners, transformation of the Armed Forces of Nigeria connotes "a process of reforming the essential constituents of national defence management system and enhancing the operational efficiency of the AFN in meeting security challenges of the 21st century"[89]. In specific terms, according to the Chief of Defence Staff, General A. O. Azazi, in order for the Nigerian Armed Forces to possess the capabilities to meet the complexities and challenges of the multi-dimensional 21st century battle space, it needs to be transformed into a defence force capable of responding rapidly and decisively across the full spectrum of operations, in order to guarantee national security, or if necessary win wars, or out-rightly influence the global environment to the advantage of our country".[90] In the light of Nigeria's experience in armed forces modernization process since 1970, there is no doubt that such a systemic transformation can only occur in the context of industrial development in Nigeria. As Raymond Aron reminds us, "an army always resembles the country from which it is raised and of which it is the expression"[91]. As concluded in chapter ten of this volume, the tragedy of Nigeria's military development, as could so far be observed, is that productive capacities of the Nigerian State- as reflected in the level of technological advances – have lagged behind organizational and doctrinal innovations.

REFERENCES

1. O. S. Kamanu, "Nigeria: Reflections on the Defence Posture for the 1980" Geneve-Afrique 16, 1, 1977-1978, p. 38.
2. Such Seminal endeavour can be seen, inter alia, in two volumes edited and co-edited by Timothy Shaw: To Shaw ed., _Alternative Future for Africa,_ (Bouder: Westview, 1982); Shaw nd Aluko (eds.), _Nigerian Foreign Policy,_ (London: Macmillan, 1983). See also James Scarrit, _Analysing Political Change in Africa_, (Boulder: Westview, 1980) and Mazrui and Patel, _Africa: The Next thirty Years_ (Brighton: Julian Freedman, 1974).
3. For a critique of these techniques as they relate to military planning, see Oskar Morgenstern _et al., Long Term Projections of Power: Political, economic and military forecasting,_ (Cambridge: Ballinger, 1973); and Yu. V. Chuyev and Yu. B. Mikhaylov; _Forecasting in Military Affairs_: a Soviet view, (Moscow: Military Publishing House of the Ministry of Defence of the USSR, 1975).
4. For an excellent analysis of the problem of measurement in the social sciences, see Ernest Nagel, The Structure of Science, (N. Y.: Harcourt, Bruce and World, 1961); and Adam Przoworski and Henry Teune, The Logic of Comparative Social Inquiry, (N. Y.: John Willey and Son; 1970).
5. See particularly the following publications: J. Bowyer Bell, "The Future of Guerrilla Revolution in Southern Africa", in Africa Today (Denver), 19, Winter 1972, pp. 7-15; Lewis Gann, "No Hope for Violent Liberation: a strategic Assessment" in Africa Report, (Washington), 17, February 1972, pp. 15-19; H. Grundy, Guerrilla Struggle in Africa: an analysis and preview, (N. Y.: Bantam, 1971); and Sheridan Johns, "Obstacles to Guerrilla Warfare a South African Case Study", Journal of Modern African Studies, 11, 2, (June 1973), pp. 267-303.
6. A. Mazrui, "A case for Violence" Adelphi Papers, 156, January 1980, p. 15.
7. For an elaboration on this theme, see Morgenstern _et al., Long Term Projections of Power;_ and Cheyev and Mikhaylov, _Forcasting in Military Affairs: a Soviet view._
8. John Herz, "The Territorial State Revisited, J. Rosenau, (ed.) International Politics and Foreign Policy, (N.Y.Free Press, 1969), p. 82.
9. Kenneth N. Waltz, Theory of International Politics, (N. Y.: Addison-Wesley, 1979), p. 107; see also his revisionist essay, "The Myth of National Interdependence" in Charles Kindleberger (ed.), The International Corporation, (Cambridge: MIT Press, 1970), pp. 203-223.
10. Raymond Aron, Peace and War, (N. Y.: Doubleday, 1966) and Hans Morgenthau, Politics Among Nations, (N. Y.: Knopf, 1978).
11. Ibid., p. 8.

12. Arnold Toynbee, "The International Out look", International Affairs, 23, (October 1974), p. 476.

13. See Inis Claude, Power and International Relations, (N. Y.: Random House, 1962), and Arnold Wolfers, Discord and Collaboration, (Baltimore: The Johns Hopkins press, 1962)

14. J. W. Burton, International Relations: a general theory, (Cambridge University Press, 1967), p.46.

15. Report of Armed Forces Transformation Committee (DHQ, 2008).

16. Knorr and Morgenstern, Political Conjecture in Military Planning, p. 7.

17. As an international pariah, few governments would formally admit to any association with the 'Dogs of War'. Indeed, most countries have in theory enacted laws banning the recruitment of their nationals as mercenaries. See, for example, the United States Neutrality Act and the British Foreign Enlistment Act (1870).

    Also see Ward Chrchill, "US mercenaries in Southern Africa: The Recruiting Network and US Policy", Africa Today, 27, 2, 1980, 21-46; A. Mockler, The Mercenaries, MacMillan, 1970. Jonathan Block, "The Dogs of War Exposed", Africa Now, 13, May 1982, p.39.

18. See John Stockwell, In Search of Enemies, (London: Future, 1979); and also "The CIA and the Violent Option", Africa, 85, September 1978, pp. 52-55.

    It was in response to this instrumental use of mercenaries by extra-continental powers that the OAU's convention on mercenarism declared as 'grave threat' the activities of mercenaries to the 'independence, sovereignty, security, territorial integrity and harmonious development of member states'. The convention further states that the crime of 'mercenarism' is committed by any individual, group or association, representative of the state or the state itself who, with the aim of opposing by armed violence a process of self-determination, stability or territorial integrity of another state, practices any of these acts.

(i). Shelters, organizes, finances, assists, equip, trains, promotes, supports or in any manner employs bands of mercenaries. (ii) Enlists, enrolls or tries to enroll in the said bands; (iii) Allows those activities to be carried out in any territory under its jurisdiction or in any place under its control or offers facilities for transits, transports or other operations of these forces. See Colin Legum (ed.), Africa Contemporary Record, Volume, 9 (London: Collins, 1976), p. A9.

19. See ECOWAS Document A/SP3/5/81, "Protocol Relating to Mutual Assistance on Defence' in Official Journal of the Economic Community of West African States, Vol. 13, (June 1981), pp. 9-13.

20. Bassey Eyo Ate, "The presence of France in West Central Africa as a Fundamental Problem to Nigeria", Millennium 12, 2 (Summer 1983), p. 110.

21. Federal Government of Nigeria, News Review 29 February 1984, p. 11. Issued by the Information Service of Nigeria High Commission, Ottawa, Canada and Sunday Times 5 June 1988, p. 8.

22. Sammy Buo "Priorities for Diplomacy", West Africa, 23 May 1983, p. 1228. See also O. Aluko. "African response to external intervention in Africa Since Angola", African Affairs, 80, 319 (April 1981), pp. 158-179.

23 Ibid, p. 122.

24. Timothy M. Shaw, "Introduction: Nigeria as Africa's Major Power" in Shaw and Aluko (eds.), Nigerian Foreign Policy, p. 4.

25. See B. Akinterinwa (ed), Nigeria and the Development of the African Union: Ibadan: Vantage Publishers, 2005.

26. This definition no doubt conveys the mainstream Liberal assumptions in strategic analysis. See John Garnett, "Strategic Studies and its Assumptions", in John Baylis et al., Contemporary Strategy: Theories and Policies, (London: Croom Helm, 1980), Chapter One; and Ken Booth, "The Strategic Paradigm" in Booth, "Strategy and Ethnocentricism, (N.Y.: Holmes and Meier, 1979), Chapter One. For an alternative conceptualization, definition and projection, see T. Shaw and O. Fasehun, in Shaw and Aluko (eds.) Nigerian Foreign Policy, (London: Macmillan 1983).

27. Timothy M. Shaw, "Inequalities and Interdependence in Africa and Latin America", Cultures et Development 10, 1, (January 1978), p. 29.

28. Ibid., p. 29.

29. For an evaluation of the concepts of power and influence, see, inter alia, Karl Deutsch, "On the concepts of Politics and Power" in James Rosenau (ed.) International Politics and Foreign Policy, (N.Y., Free Press, 1969); M. Sullivan International Relations: Theories and Evidence, (N. J.: Prentice-Hall, 1976); and R. Mansbach and J. Vasquez In Search of Theory: A New Paradigm for Global Politics, (N. Y.: Columbia University Press, 1981).

30. Mansbach and Vasquez, Ibid, Part 1.

31. Charles Reynolds, Theory and Explanation in International Politics, (London: Martin Robertson, 1973), p. 180.

32. This widespread assumption that Nigeria is Africa's great power was one of the foci of a blistering attack by one of Nigeria's leading novelists – Chinua Achebe; see the chapter entitled "False Image of Ourselves" Trouble with Nigeria, Enugu: Fourth Dimension 1985.

33. Morgenthau, Politics among Nations, p. 153.

34. See I. Akintunde Technological Development through self Reliance Ibadan: University Press, 1994.

35. For an in-depth examination of Nigeria's mediation efforts in these crises, see Alaba Ogunsanwo, "The Nigerian Military and Foreign Policy, 1975-1979: processes, principles, performance and contradictions", Princeton University Center for International Relations, 1980, Research Monograph, No. 45. Also see J. Garba, Diplomatic Soldiering (Ibadan: Spectrum, 1987).

36. Shaw and Fasehun, "Nigeria in the World System: alternative approaches, explanations and projections" p. 212.

37. Knorr, The Power of Nation, p. 8.

38. See D. Bon and K. Mingst, "French Intervention in Africa: Dependency or Decolonization" Africa Today 27, 2, 1980, pp. 5-20. see also, Bassey E. Ate African Decolonization and Regional Politics: a conceptual approach, unpublished ms., Lagos, NIIA, 1982.

39. See, among others, James Goldsborough, "Dateline Paris: Africa's Policeman' Foreign Policy 33, Winter 1978-79, pp. 174-90, and P. Lellouche and D. Moist "French Policy in Africa: a lonely battle against destabilization" International Security, 3,4, (Spring 1979), pp. 108-133.

40. In a conference on Chad organized by the Nigerian Institute for International Affairs (NIIA), the Nigerian force commander in Chad, Maj. General Ejiga, argued that Nigeria had enough troops in Chad to impose peace on the warring factions, and that 'recommendations were made to President Shedu Shagari to use the force to effect that purpose, but he refused'. See West Africa, 2 April, 1984. Nigeria unquestionably had sufficient 'fire power' to prevent Habre's Force Armee du Nord (FAN) from recapturing N'Djamena in violation of the OAU resolution, if Shagari had so decided. However, given Chad's political maze and powerful external influences (France and the United States) which sustained Habre's military machine through bases in Sudan, it is doubtful whether such a policy (Pax Nigeriana) was either politically advisable or military sound at the time.

41. Peter Evans, Dependent Development: the alliance of multinational, state and local capital in Brazil, (Preinceton: Princeton University Press, 1979), pp. 308-309.

42. See, for example, Segun Osoba, "The Deepening Crisis of the Nigerian National Bourgeoisie" Review of African Political Economy 13 May-August 1978, pp. 63-77; and Okwudiba Nnoli (ed.), Path to Nigerian Development (London: zed, 1982).

43. Thomas Biersteker, Distortion or Development? Contending Perspectives on the multinational corporation, (Cambridge: The MIT press, 1978), p. 100. although utilizing a different analytical premise, Sayre Schatz appears to be even more optimistic about the development potential of Nigeria. In his treatise on Nigerian Capitalism, Schatz in a characteristically liberal-reformist perspective, sees the Nigerian economy as transitional from 'guided international nature-capitalism with a welfare tendency' to 'a nationalist nature-capitalism tendencies;. See Sayre P. Schatz, Nigerian Capitalism (Berkeley: University of California Press, 1977), p. 7.

44. Nicholas Jequier, Low-Cost Technology-an inquiry into outstanding policy issues, an interim report of the study sessions held in Paris, 17-20 September 1974, (Paris: OECD Development Centre, 1975), p. 17.

45. de St. Jorre, The Nigerian Civil War (London: Hodder and Stoughton, 1978), p. 224. See also Frederick Forsyth, The Biafra Story (Baltimore: Penguin Books, 1969), p. 113.

46. Jequier, Low-Cost Technology, pp. 9-10, and especially p. 101.

47. Terisa Turner, "Two Refineries: a comparative study of technology transfer to the Nigerian refining industry", World Development 5 (1977), p. 242.

48. See the Fourth National Development Plan, Federal Government of Nigeria, Lagos, 1980; see also F. A. Adetula "Technology and Nigeria's National Development", National Institute Library, Kuru, Nigeria, (SEC-4, 05, 1982).

49. See Thomas, "Strengthening of National Technological Capacity for Development – the Nigerian case". Ibrahim James, "Impediments to vertical Transfer of

Technology in Nigeria" <u>Nigerian Forum</u> 2, 5, (May 1983), pp. 1110-1116 and O. Teriband M. Kayode, "Issues in Industrialization" in Teriba & Kayode (eds.) Industrial Development in Nigeria: patterns, problems and prospects (Ibadan: Ibadan University Press, 1977), pp. 3-10.

50. See, <u>inter alia,</u> Uduak Mboho, "Nigeria Needs Atomic Bomb", <u>Chronicle</u> 2 May 1981; S. (Ogunbule "Nigeria and the Nuclear Weapon a technological, economic and political appraisal" <u>Financial Punch,</u> 9 May 1981; Charles Lakin-Smith "should Nigeria join the Nuclear Club" <u>Chronicle</u> 12 May 1981;O. Ejiyere, "Nigeria and the Bomb" <u>Sunday Times</u> 19 April 1980; Joe Okolo, "Nigeria's Hope of Nuclear Weapons", <u>West Africa</u> 19 May 1980; "V=C wants institute for Nuclear Studies", <u>New Nigerian</u> 4 March, 1980 and "The Nuclear option" PUNCH Editorial, 01 July, 2009.

51. Nigeria was one of the key African states who relentlessly canvassed in the United Nations (between 1960-1976) for 'denclearisation of Africa's following a series of French atomic tests in the Sahara Desert in 1960.
For the OAU declarations on the same theme, see OAU; CIAS/Plen. 2/Rev.2, 25 May 1963; CM/Res. 28(2), 29 February 1964; CM/Res. 38 (3), 17 July 1964; and AHG/Res. 11 (1), 21 July 1964; and G. Nweke, "African Perceptions of Global Disarmanent and Prospects for denuclearization of the Continent" <u>Nigerian Journal of International Affairs</u> 8, 1, 8, 1, (Winter 1982), pp. 37-59; and Robert D' A Henderson and Robert D' A. Henderson, "Nigeria Forum, 1, 5, (July 1981), pp. 409-424; Moyibi Amoda, "Is Nigeria Ready for Nuclearized Military Technology" Nigerian Forum, 1, 5, (July 1981), pp. 184-189; O. Ogunbadejo, "Africa's Nuclear Capability", <u>The Journal of Modern Africa Studies,</u> 22, 1 (March 1981), pp. 9-43; and Charles Dokubo, "Nuclear Issues and Nigeria" Africa Journal of International Affairs and Development. Vol. 5, No 1, 2006.

52. Ali Mazrui, <u>The African Condition</u> (London: Heinemann, 1980), p. 122.

53. 100 <u>Ibid.,</u> P. 135

54. For variations on this same view, see Kenneth N. Waltz, <u>The Spread of Nuclear Weapons: more may be better. Adephi Papers No. 171 (London: IISS, 1981);</u> <u>Asok Kapur,</u> "The Nuclear Spread: a Third World view" <u>Third World Quarterly</u> 11, 1 (January 1980), pp. 59-75.

55. Mazrui, <u>The African Condition,</u> p. 136.

56. Mazrui, "The Computer Culture and Nuclear Power: political implications for Africa" in Timothy M. Shaw (ed.) <u>Alternative Futures for Africa</u> (Boulder: Westview, 1982), pp. 251-252.

57. See Okolo's interview with Iya Abubakar, the first Nigerian Minister of Defence in the Shagari administration (1979-1983) in <u>West Africa</u> 19 May 1980, pp. 872-874 and editorials of <u>Daily Sketch</u> (Ibadan) 30 September 1980; <u>Daily Times,</u> 30 September 1980; and <u>National Concorde</u> (Lagos), 30 September 1980, PUNCH Editorial, July 2009.

58. Sammy Kum Buo, "Africa and the Bomb", <u>West Africa</u> 2 January 1984, pp. 21. see also T. Adeniran "Nuclear proliferation and black Africa: the coming crisis of choice" <u>The Third World Quarterly</u> 3, 4 (October 1981), pp. 672-683.

59. For the extensive collaboration between South Africa and NATO Powers in the nuclear field, see U. S. Military <u>Involvement in Southern Africa</u> edited by Massachusetts Association and Concerned Africa Scholars. Chapter Nine; Z. Cervenka and Barbara Rogers, <u>The Nuclear Axis-secret collaboration between West Germany and South Africa:</u> (N. Y.: Freedman, 1978); and J. E. Spence, "South Africa: the Nuclear option" in J. Roherty <u>Defence Policy Formation</u> (Durham: Carolina Academic Press, 1980).

60. This assumption was heightened following a US intelligence report in 1980 of a probable South Africa – Israeli test of a nuclear device in the Southern Oceans (between South Africa and the Anthartica). Although for political reasons, the Carter administration preferred ambiguity to outright confirmation, it was, nevertheless, revealed in a British television programme, "World in Action", that South Africa obtained previous to the incident, 3000,000 shell casings capable of delivering a two-to-three kiloton nuclear device with the connivance of American officials in the Pentagon. See Thomas O' Toole, "New Zealand Confirms Mystery Atom Test" <u>The Gurdian Weekly</u> (Manchester) 25 November 1979, and "SA Ships in zone of suspected N-Blast", <u>The Guardian</u> (London) January 31, 1980, and "Shagari Addresses Foreign Policy Body" <u>Daily Times,</u> 6 October 1980.

61. Frank Barnaby, "Can Nuclear-Weapon Proliferation be Prevented?" <u>Bulletin of Peace Proposals,</u> 1, 1977, p. 12.

62. Editorial, New Nigerian, 24 November, 1980.

63. Henderson, "Nigeria: future nuclear power?", p. 421.

64. This tendency toward elite (bureaucratic, institutional, policy etc.) coalitions, bargaining and competition on issues of national security was clearly apparent in the <u>laisser faire</u> politics in The Second Republic. The issue concerning organizational task expansion and funding for the Atomic Energy Commission was raised by a member of the Finance Committee of the National Assembly at a Conference on Science and Technology (NIPSS, Kuru, 14-17 March 1983) and immediately became a subject of passionate debate.

65. Amoda, "Is Nigeria Ready for Nuclearized Military Technology?", p. 187.

66. See Sverre Lodgaard, "International Nuclear Commerce: structure, trends, and proliferation potentials" <u>Bulletin of</u> Peace proposals, 1, 1977, pp. 15-31.

67. For a critique of NPT resolutions, see Asok Kapur, "Nuclear Proliferation in the 1980s" International Organization 36, 3, (Summer 1981), pp. 535-55. Richard Betts, "Paranoids, Pygmies, Pariahs and Non-proliferation" <u>Foreign policy</u> 59, 4 (Spring 1981), pp. 875-894; and Louise Rene Beres, "The Porcupine Theory of Nuclear Proliferation: shortening the quills", <u>Parameters</u> 9, 3 (September 1979), pp. 31-37.

68. Barnaby, "Can Nuclear-weapon proliferation be Prevented?', p. 9.

69. Lodgaard, International Nuclear Commerce", p. 23.

70. Henderson, "Nigeria: future nuclear power?", p. 412.
See also Celestine Bassey, Collective Amnesia or Perpetual Debate? The African Security Agenda" in David Fashole Luke and Timothy M. Shaw (eds.) <u>Continent in Crisis The Lagos Plan of Action and Africa's Future Development</u>

(Washington: UPA, 1984) pp. 73-103; T. A. Imobighe, "An African High Command: the search for a feasible strategy of continental defence" African Affairs 79, 315 (April 1980), pp. 241-254; O. Fasehun, "Nigeria and the Issue of an African High Command: towards a regional and/or continental defence system?" Africa Spectrum 80, 3, (15 Jahrang), pp. 309-318, and B. Meyers, "An Analysis of OAU's Effectiveness at Regional Collective Defence" in Y. El. Ayouty (ed.) The organization of African Unity After ten years (N. Y.: Praeger, 1975), pp. 118-134.

71. See, for instance, OAU Proceedings and Reports of the Defence Commission – DEF1/COMII/SRI Addis Ababa, January 1964; OAU DEF1/COM11/SRI Cairo, July 1965; OAU, DEF1/COMIV/SRI, Rabat, June 1972; OAU Bulletin 20/79, July-August 1979, Monrovia and A. Seegers, "South African Liberation: touchstone of African solidarity" in B. Arlinghaus (ed.) African Security Issues (Boulder: Westview, 1984), pp. 185-202.

72. Ofoegbu, The Nigerian Foreign Policy, p. 94.

73. Fasehun, "Nigeria and the Issue of an African High Command" p. 315. Also see Brig. H. Hananiya, "Nigeria's defence policy against South Africa"; Brig. B. A. Idiagbon, "Strategies for Liberation of Southern Africa" National Institute Library, Kuru, Nigeria and R. S. Jaster, A Regional Security Role for Africa's Front-Line States, Adelphi Papers No. 180 (London: IISS, 1983); and D. Anglin The Frontline States and the Future of Southern Africa (Presented at conference on Indian Ocean, Dalhousie University, Canada, October, 1982..

74. K. Powell and T. Tieku, "The African Union's new security Agenda" International Journal Autumn 2005: 937-952.

75. R. Jackson, "The dangers of Regionalizing International Conflict Management: The African Experience" Political Science 52, 1, (2000).

76. C. Deconig, "Refining the African Standby Force Concept" ACCORD, Special edition issue 2, 2004.

77. See Article 10 of the Protocol. Also see E. Baimu and K. Sturman, "Amendment to the Africa's Union's Right to intervene: A slight from human security to Regime Security" African Security Review 12, 2, 2003.

78. ECOWAS Document A/SP3.5/81. "Protocol Relating to Mutual Assistance on Defence' in Official journal of the Economic Community of West African States (ECOWAS) Vol. 3, (June 1981), pp. 9-13.

79. Intermitent military exercises between Nigeria and Republique de Benin and between Ghana and Upper Volta have since been conducted on annual basis.

80. Africa Research Bulletin, Vol. 18, 15 July 1981, p. 6072.

81. Julius Okolo, "Securing West Africa: the ECOWAS Defence Pact" The World Today 39, 5, May 1983, p. 179. Also Nigeria" (National Institute Library, Kuru, 1982).

82. Aluko, Essays in Nigerians Foreign Policy, pp. 13-14.

83. Bassey, "Collective Amnesia or Perpetual Debate", pp. 73-103 and Femi Otunanjo. "Ideology and Military Integration in Africa" Current Research on Peace and Violence, 3 (3-4), 1980, pp. 216-228.

84. See Okolo, "Securing West Africa: the ECOWAS Defence Pact"; David Ogunsade, "Stumbling Blocks of ECOWAS Defence Pact" Daily Times (Lagos), 6 December, p. 2; and New Nigerian (Kaduna), 22 October 1979.

85. Inis Claude, Swords into Plowshares (N. Y.: Random House, 1964), p. 10.

86. Ibid. p. 11

87. James Mayall, Africa: the Cold war and after (London: Elex Books, 1971), p. 162.

88. Report of Armed Forces Transformation Committee, April 2008:8

89. "Military Transformation: A. Clear Leadership, Accountability and Management Tools Needed to enhance DOD's efforts to transform military capabilities". Report to congressional committee by the US Government Accountability Office, 2004).

on can be obtained
ₓ.com

'6
)01B/40/P